An Introduction to
WORLD
MYTHOLOGY

SECOND EDITION

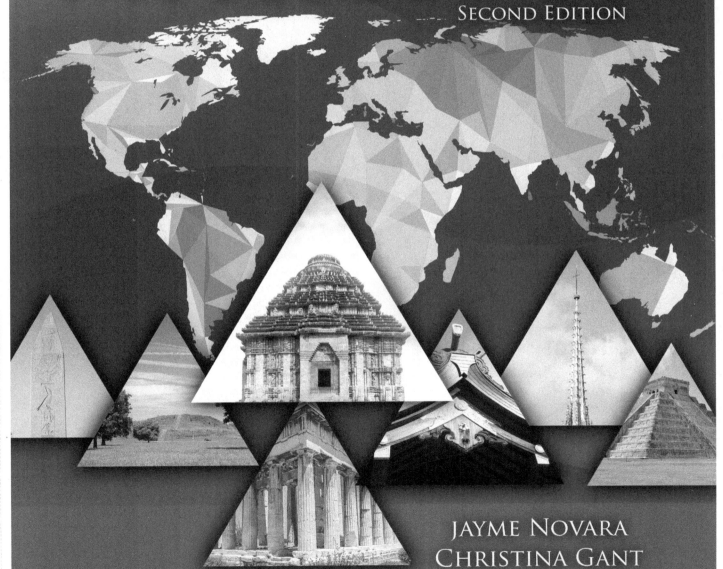

JAYME NOVARA
CHRISTINA GANT

Kendall Hunt
publishing company

Kendall Hunt
p u b l i s h i n g c o m p a n y

www.kendallhunt.com
Send all inquiries to:
4050 Westmark Drive
Dubuque, IA 52004-1840

Contents

THE MYTHS OF SCANDINAVIAN AND SLAVIC COUNTRIES   163

Introduction   164

THE MYTHS OF THE BRITISH ISLES   259

Introduction   260

THE MYTHS OF AFRICA   307

Introduction   308

THE MYTHS OF ASIA   339

Introduction   340

About the Authors

© Hannah Anderson

Jayme Novara

Jayme Novara is Associate Professor of English at St. Charles Community College. She teaches Mythology and has interests in Gender Studies and American Indian Studies. She lives in St. Louis, Missouri.

© Joseph Gant

Christina Gant

Christina Gant is Assistant Professor of English at St. Charles Community College. In addition to Mythology, she teaches Creative Writing and a variety of interdisciplinary seminars in the honors program.

We Wish to Thank

OUR DEPARTMENT
OUR LIBRARIANS
OUR PUBLISHERS AT KENDALL HUNT
OUR STUDENTS
OUR FAMILIES

1

An Introduction to Mythology

Source: Christina Gant

What is Myth?

"Without a knowledge of mythology much of the elegant literature of our own language cannot be understood and appreciated."

—Thomas Bulfinch

"I've come to the conclusion that mythology is really a form of archaeological psychology. Mythology gives you a sense of what a people believes, what they fear."

—George Lucas

1

"Religions, philosophies, arts, the social forms of primitive and historic man, prime discoveries in science and technology, the very dreams that blister sleep, boil up from the basic, magic ring of myth."

—Joseph Campbell

"In imitating the exemplary acts of a god or of a mythic hero, or simply by recounting their adventures, the man of an archaic society detaches himself from profane time and magically re-enters the Great Time, the sacred time."

—Mircea Eliade

To some, mythology means tall tales that are pure fantasy, superstition, or even fairy tales. Others think of legendary heroes or stories of gods, goddesses, and imaginary creatures. And some think of folktales or fables— stories that teach lessons. But myths do not always begin with "Once upon a time." While many of these stories can be classified as myth, a truer understanding of myth is more about the sacred tales of a group of people, often the basis for spiritual belief, that help them understand the world and their place in it. However, no single definition can cover all aspects or truly encompass the totality of what it means to study myths.

These myths do not necessarily need to be considered "true" or "real," as many cultures are not concerned with concrete reality. Karen Armstrong argues in *A Short History of Myth* that,

"A myth, therefore, is true because it is effective, not because it gives us factual information. If, however, it does not give us new insight into the deeper meaning of life, it has failed. If it *works*, that is, if it forces us to change our minds and hearts, gives us new hope, and compels us to live more fully, it is a valid myth."

The point of myth is not to scrutinize it for its glimpses into the truth of a culture or people, but to enrich our lives. As Edith Hamilton writes in her seminal text *Mythology*,

"The tales of Greek mythology do not throw any clear light upon what early mankind was like. They do throw an abundance of light upon what early Greeks were like—a matter, it would seem, of more importance to us."

It is the underlying morals, values, or meanings behind myths that make them true to the group of people who recite, chant, sing, or read them.

It's tempting for people to classify myth as "other people's religion," as Joseph Campbell once pointed out. It's easy to dismiss the beliefs of others, regarding them as "myth," especially if they are antiquated or very different from our own. Understanding this error is crucial to our study of the texts of other cultures. We do not want to fall into the trap of constantly comparing the stories of others with our own; we do not want to make value judgments about which stories are "better," "more sophisticated," or "more believable" based on our personal experience. While it's true that many of the beliefs illustrated in these stories are no longer currently practiced, some are still the living, sacred texts of religious belief systems. We must treat all myths, and the cultures who told them, with respect.

Some scholars, like Carl Jung and Joseph Campbell, consider myths as deeper understandings of shared human experiences or conditions. Jung wrote extensively about the "Collective Unconscious," which is a way to see the connections between so many cultures' myths as representative of universal motifs. Though there are certainly many similarities within and between cultures, we must use caution when applying one culture's theories to another culture's stories. Applying the values of Greek myths to the values of Native American myths, for instance, is not fair or accurate. The value in studying myths from a world perspective, as this text does, is to discover the beliefs and systems of past cultures, to look more clearly at the history of a location and glean more about the identity of its people. We look to art, music, poetry, sculpture, and literature to tell us more about the people who believe in these stories.

Who Studies Myth, and Why

The study of mythology in Western society has evolved significantly over the years. It is now a common practice to teach myths from all over the world—not just "Classical" myths of Greece, Rome, and Mesopotamia. An interest in multicultural approaches to the literature of mythology has given academics several points of entry to discuss these texts. But this is not a new field.

Even the ancient Greeks explored the meaning and function of their stories about the gods, claiming some as true and others as fantasy. Early Christians classified all these stories as false, devaluing them, until interest in them was renewed during the end of the Renaissance and into the Enlightenment period. Early scholars were concerned with comparing myths to discuss what they illustrated about human life in general. While this appears to be a sound pursuit, it leads to the question of what to do with the assumptions the studies reveal, and it can cause one to lose sight of the historical and cultural context of the stories by trying to focus solely on their common elements.

Social anthropologist Sir James Frazer (1854–1941), popularly known for his book *The Golden Bough,* was considered a pioneer in the field and was interested in rituals and how myths explain the natural world. Culturalists, like Emile Durkheim (1858–1917) for example, examined how societies shape myths. The nineteenth century witnessed both the rise and decline of the study of comparative mythology, along with interest in folklore, resulting in the study being divided among various academic disciplines. Anthropology took the lead, with an interest in preserving cultural identities, followed by psychology, geared toward the relationship between myth and the unconscious mind. Carl Jung (1875–1961) and Sigmund Freud (1856–1939) were leaders in this field. In the twentieth century, scholar Joseph Campbell (1904–1987) brought the study of myth into popular consciousness with his literary and spiritual approaches, building on the work of Jung, and others, and developing the theory of the monomyth (see Hero Myths).

Another prominent scholar whose work was influential is anthropologist Claude Levi-Strauss (1908–2009). Unlike the theories of Freud and Jung, who saw the unconscious mind as a key to a culture's myths, Levi-Strauss took a structural approach. He believed a culture's language provided the basis for their formation of myths.

Historian and religious scholar Mircea Eliade (1907–1986) was another leading contributor to the field. He believed myths serve primarily a religious function, and that ancient people were more attuned to the sacred than those of the modern age. By studying myths, he believed modern people could reconnect to the experiences of the ancient past.

Most recently, scholars are advocating for the study of the texts of mythology, not only the stories themselves. For mythology does not only describe the myths, but also the methods by which people approach them. In addition, we also need to consider who told the tale, and why. What sociological function did the myth serve in its civilization? Were the tellers and listeners men or women, rich or poor, old or young? We can't separate the myths from our study of them, just as we can't remove the stories from their cultural context. As we examine myths, our perspectives must always be considered.

Today there are myriad approaches one can take in the study of mythology. While there is no "correct" way to discuss myths, we must be aware that psychological study, while it's undeniably appealing, tends to separate the stories from their cultural and historical context. That doesn't mean we need avoid it—in fact, it's a thought-provoking analysis—just remember that the stories cannot be separated from the people who created them. The same holds true for literary study—the subject of this text. We must keep in mind the origin of the tales.

This is merely a brief summary of a few noted developments in the discipline. The field is complex and nuanced. There is no way to recreate the experience of each story in its proper place in time. However, we can shine a light on moments of truth, of what it means to be human, in the sharing of these stories. We may never know what they "mean" or be able to analyze every symbol or motif, but we must be content with that.

Key Concepts and Definitions

Because myths occur in various forms, promote different modes of worship and belief, and have such a varied history, there is a vocabulary that helps us to fully understand the mythmakers, scholars, and interpretations. Here are several concepts that will aid in your study.

Types of Myth

- ▶ Cosmic Myths: These are the myths that are concerned with creation and destruction. They seek to answer the questions, "Where did we come from? Where am I going after this?"

- ▶ Cosmogony: Stories that explain the origin of the world. David Leemings calls this "The process by which chaos becomes cosmos, no-thing becomes some-thing."

- ▶ Divine Myths: The exploits of supernatural beings (sometimes gods and goddesses), the stories of who and what they influence, and how they came about are referenced in myths of the Divine. These myths occasionally explain creation of the world, humans, animals, or demi-gods.

- ▶ Heroic Myths: Sometimes called "sagas" or "epics," these myths explore the great deeds of heroes or heroines. They are typically told by people who would not have been present to witness the events, thus creating tales of the human past.

- ▶ Etiological Tale: These stories explain why things are the way they are. "How the leopard got his spots" or "How death came into the world" are common tropes in these tales. It is human nature to be interested in our surroundings and the causes of our experiences.

Systems of Belief

- ▶ Polytheism: The belief in many gods, who may or may not interact with the human world.

- ▶ Henotheism: A polytheistic system with one god as a ruler or leader.

- ▶ Pantheon: Meaning "all gods," these are the officially recognized gods of a culture.

- ▶ Pantheism: The belief that all creation is identical to divinity; the universe is god.

- ▶ Monotheism: The belief in one god, who is to be worshipped.

- ▶ Dystheism: The understanding that a god or gods are not wholly good all the time and can decide to become malevolent.

- ▶ Animism: Attributing a soul to inanimate objects, plants, animals, and natural phenomena.

- ▶ Shamanism: A complex practice that generally consists of belief in an unseen spiritual world accessible only to a shaman; the shaman uses altered states of consciousness to interact with this spirit world.

Creation Myths

There are many ways in which the world, the landscape, animals, and people are created. Each myth approaches creation differently, though there are similarities within cultures, locations, and belief systems. Listed here are explanations of the most common forms of creation, though it is not meant to be an exhaustive list of methods.

▶ **Ex Nihilo**. From the Latin "Out of Nothing," this type of myth is surprisingly diverse. There are myths in which the world literally appears from nothing, which are easy to classify as Ex Nihilo. The term "chaos" can be applied to this form of creation as well, though it has multiple definitions. The modern definition of chaos brings to mind imagery of particles colliding, worlds shaking, or general anarchy (as is shown in the Norse myth of Niflheim and Muspelheim colliding, or the Roman creation of the world). Another definition of chaos is, however, a void (which is seen in Greek creation). The idea of nothingness is difficult to imagine, but many myths attempt to quantify the kind of chaos they refer to. Both forms of chaos feature prominently in the creation of the earth.

▶ **Dismemberment of a Primordial Being**. When gods and goddesses are immortal, the question arises, what happens to their bodies after being "killed" or deciding to "die"? If their bodies cannot disappear, they often become a feature of the earth, or a part of human beings. Dismemberment refers to the physical cutting, tearing, ripping, or otherwise dismantling of one's entire body or a body part. A primordial being may become mountains, rocks, the sea or rivers, trees, clouds, stars and the moon, and humans. This is a very common theme among nearly every culture.

Bruce Lincoln, in his book *Myth, Cosmos, and Society: Indo-European Themes of Creation and Destruction*, coined the term "alloforms" (same substance in alternative form) to refer to the way the particular body parts of the dismembered being's body are transformed in a specific way. For example, a being's breath becomes the wind, the bones become rocks, hair becomes grass. Having the cosmos created from the primordial being's body in this manner gives further significance to the substance of the world, as it was the actual body of a divine being and those features sustain life. While Lincoln was referring to Indo-European myths in his book, his term can be applied generally.

► **Emergence**. Several stories from tribes of American Indians show humans emerging from underground. They often start as lesser beings or insects, and evolution of the humans, animals, and the world around them occurs as they ascend into the upper worlds.

► **Earth Diver**. A few forms of this type of creation exist. In one popular form, a god or gods send down from the heavens a person or animal to scope out the earth below. Typically this person or animal will attempt to find earth underneath the water and the creation of the world of humans is formed. In another version, the world exists only as a watery surface, and an animal dives down to search for mud to fashion the earth.

► **Cosmic Egg**. In many Eastern myths, the beginning of the world is seated in an egg. Many myths (like the concept of Yin and Yang) include opposites, or twins in the womb-like egg, waiting to be set free upon the earth. The theme of twins in hero myths often starts with this type of creation story.

Hero Myths

Mythologist Joseph Campbell has perhaps done more than any other scholar to popularize the study of mythology. A prolific author and lecturer, he is best-known for his book *The Hero With a Thousand Faces* and his four-part work *The Masks of God*.

As outlined in *The Hero With a Thousand Faces*, the theory of the monomyth suggests that all mythic epics share a common narrative structure. Referred to as "the hero's journey," the monomyth follows the protagonist on his or her quest—a journey that mirrors human rites of passage, as well as psychological experiences and dreams. Campbell incorporated many psychological concepts, of particular interest is the idea of the archetype. In his book *Man and His Symbols*, Carl Jung describes archetypes as "primordial images," manifestations of "symbolic images," conscious representations of what Freud called "archaic remnants"—mental forms, or character roles, that humans understand and identify, collectively, by their patterns of behavior. In literature, we recognize these archetypes as serving a particular role, such as the Hero, the Guide, or the Temptress (see Types of Myth).

Here is a brief explanation of the hero's journey:

> The journey usually begins by describing the hero's exceptional, even miraculous, birth. This is almost always part of the story. The hero is born special. The child then goes through a coming-of-age period, overcoming a variety of struggles, and is often aided by helpers—it's not unusual for these helpers to provide supernatural assistance. The "call to adventure" comes with the arrival of the herald—another archetypal figure. The herald signals that the adventure is about to begin, and the hero either willingly accepts or at first refuses. Eventually, though, the journey must begin. The hero proceeds through several ordeals, typically including a "road of trials," and other tests that must be passed, before finally experiencing the "supreme ordeal." The hero appears to fail, but finds a way to overcome and gain the prize, whatever that may be.

Not every story includes all parts of Campbell's outline. The journey can be external or internal, and can be applied to great mythic epics as well as contemporary works of fiction. The path of the hero is also the path of the individual, so "the hero's journey" can be useful when applied to life as a tool for self-discovery.

To put it in simplistic terms, this theory claims that since we are all human beings, we must naturally share certain aspects of consciousness—basic emotions and drives, fears, etc. These common experiences and patterns can be found in myths around the world. While this approach does offer excellent points for exploration, it does have its critics—mainly for its risk of oversimplifying the myths. However, for literary purposes, the monomyth gives us a common starting point when discussing hero myths.

Along the Hero's Journey

► Individuation: A psychological term that conveys a quest for identity or personal growth. This stems from the understanding that we can all see our lives as a hero's journey.

► Collective Unconscious: Jung's belief that we have "innate psychological characteristics, common to all human beings." This accounts for our appetite for hero myths, because we see ourselves in the hero.

► Motif: A literary term that helps to classify recurrent images, patterns, or themes in a story.

► Archetype: Jung's concept of universally recurring symbols, patterns, or characters. There are many archetypes in mythology, especially those figures that the Hero encounters on her journey. Not all of these archetypes are encountered in every Hero myth, and one character may appear as several different archetypes during the course of the journey. Following are a few of the most well-known archetypes.

► Hero: The ultimate mark of the Hero is self-sacrifice. Through encountering death (physical or metaphorical), the Hero shows the capacity to give of himself for the benefit of another or an entire community. The Hero must learn something and bring back that knowledge to share with others.

► Herald: The person or event that calls the Hero to the adventure. This can be a circumstance, or a person who appears to inform or challenge the Hero to his quest.

► Mentor: Often an old man or woman, the Mentor guides the Hero, gives her information, and bestows gifts or objects upon the Hero, which will aid in her quest. The Mentor is sometimes a former Hero. They act as motivators and fonts of wisdom. The Mentor can be internal; the Hero may rely on her own values and worldview to guide her through her journey.

► Ally: Throughout the journey, the Hero will encounter people who support him. These can turn into trusty "sidekicks," going along the Hero's journey with him, or the Ally might only be united with the Hero against the same Enemy.

► Enemy: There is typically at least one nemesis whom the hero must overcome. The Enemy may be the keeper of an item the Hero seeks to retrieve, or may be actively trying to kill her. The Hero usually has a final encounter with the Enemy near the conclusion of the journey.

► Threshold Guardian: A villainous character, but not the same as the Enemy. A Threshold Guardian attempts to block the path of progress. Dragons, henchmen, trolls, parents, etc., are examples of these barriers. These characters serve as tests to the hero's abilities and worthiness to continue on the journey.

► Shadow: The Shadow self can be used to express the Hero's inner feelings of unworthiness, insecurity, or doubt. The Shadow self can also serve to humanize the Villain, giving a backstory that allows the audience to sympathize with him. The Shadow may also serve as a Shapeshifter.

► Shapeshifter: In the realm of the supernatural, a Shapeshifter can literally change its shape to confuse, distract, or otherwise throw off the Hero. In a more realistic world, the Shapeshifter may simply be represented by a character who has a change of heart or constantly shifting emotions.

► Trickster: Tricksters can serve as comic relief in an otherwise action-packed drama, or as an ego-checker for the Hero. The Hero herself might act as Trickster in order to overcome obstacles.

► Goddess: A prophetess, an old crone, or a wise old woman may serve in the role of the Hero's meeting with the Goddess. She offers information, insight into the future, or prophecy of what will come. This can help to assuage the doubt the Hero feels midway through her journey. Sometimes a book may serve this purpose, giving aid to the Hero through research or information that she was not previously given.

► Temptress: The Hero may become sidetracked from his mission, usually at the hands of a Temptress. She can be a damsel in distress in need of rescue, a lover who wants him to stay, a femme fatale, or a manifestation of his desire to quit the journey and give in to selfish desire.

Trickster Myths

The trickster archetype is found all over the world, but by far they are most well-known among the North American and African cultures. This character—part hero, part trouble-maker—occupies an essential place in mythology.

In North America, the most well-known tricksters are Raven of the North Pacific region, and Coyote of the Great Plains. In fact, there are more recorded stories about Coyote than all other trickster tales combined. According to Susan Feldmann, "Coyote appears as the personification of unbridled appetite and a conglomeration of all the vices" (17). He represents primal drives of lust, greed, and gluttony, and is often outsmarted by those he intends to trick. His exploits often lead to unintended, but sometimes positive, outcomes. A study in contradictions, he is often portrayed as both cruel and clownish, a combination of selfishness and foolishness. Raven has similar qualities, though often includes more transformative actions, and is more often seen in a heroic light than other tricksters. He has a voracious appetite, cheats and seduces, but also creates. There are several instances of what's called the Raven Cycle, where Raven has a series of adventures that contribute to the creation of the world.

There are many other trickster figures in North America and Africa, and they are nearly always animals. Besides Coyote and Raven, the list includes Hare, Mink, Otter, Blue Jay, Spider, and Fox. Possibly evolved from animal deities from prehistory, the trickster serves a complicated but essential role—sometimes stupid, sometimes clever, and often humorous; some trickster tales are told simply for entertainment.

While they're often animals or shape-shifters in North America and Africa, in other parts of the world they typically take human form, or exist as gods, demi-gods, even giants. Notable tricksters from other cultures include Loki, Maui, Hermes, Krishna, and Prometheus. Like the North American and African tricksters they, too, are often the victims of their own schemes or are driven by selfish desires. Tricksters are typically male; female tricksters are quite rare. Some do seem to have good intentions; most are morally ambiguous. But while they can appear to be blatantly villainous at times, it's important to understand they are not evil.

Tricksters are inventive, enigmatic, and sometimes creators; they almost always act without regard for the consequences of their actions. They challenge authority and the assumptions of a culture and can be agents of transformation. According to Lewis Hyde, in his book *Trickster Makes This World*,

> In short, trickster is a boundary-crosser. Every group has its edge, its sense of in and out, and trickster is always there, at the gates of the city and the gates of life, making sure there is commerce. He also attends the internal boundaries by which groups articulate their social life. We constantly distinguish—right and wrong, sacred and profane, clean and dirty, male and female, young and old, living and dead—and in every case trickster will cross the line and confuse the distinction . . . trickster is the mythic embodiment of ambiguity and ambivalence, doubleness and duplicity, contradiction and paradox.

Sometimes he doesn't merely cross the line, but actually draws it, or he moves it or erases it entirely. The trickster is always part of this threshold, as well as crossroads. He's a traveler, and can also serve as a messenger.

Despite the problems they cause, tricksters are often honored by their respective cultures. This is the paradox that makes the trickster such a fascinating character.

There are lessons to be learned from the trickster. At the very least he teaches rules of behavior, often in a comical way, and reveals the perils of acting solely on instinct. On the other hand, he represents the necessity of releasing inhibitions, testing rules and boundaries, breaking taboos, and laughing at ourselves.

The Great Goddess Hypothesis—The Earth Mother

Myths are often found in cultural artifacts, and it's here where a controversial theory was born—the great goddess hypothesis—with several small figurines found in parts of Europe in the early twentieth century.

These tiny carvings depict the female form with the breasts, hips, and bellies greatly exaggerated, suggesting that they may symbolize fertility. A few of them have markings such as spirals, crescents, or triangles, but there are few other details. The discovery of numerous statues like this, that date from approximately 30,000 to 5,000 BCE, have caused some historians, archaeologists, and anthropologists to believe that perhaps the people of the Paleolithic and Neolithic periods worshipped a great mother goddess. And perhaps this meant that those people had a more equitable social order—possibly even matrifocal or matriarchal.

© frantic00/Shutterstock.com

The problem with this theory is that those figurines were discovered in a wide variety of places—from different time periods and cultures. One might be tempted to say that this, then, proves it was a widespread belief, but there is no context for the statues—that's the issue of concern among scholars. We can't accurately interpret the meanings of these artifacts without more information.

The theory didn't begin with the discovery of the statues, however. In the late nineteenth century there was already a belief that primitive societies were matrifocal. In *The Golden Bough*, Sir James Frazer wrote about fertility rites involving a goddess and her consort-son. Jung and other psychoanalysts expanded on this idea—the Great Mother archetype. It's an interesting debate, with compelling evidence on both sides.

In the mid-1980s, the notion came under scrutiny by archaeologists. Questions have been raised—for example, how can we know that these figures were sacred, or even goddesses? How can we be certain these shapes represented fertility and motherhood? And we don't know for what purpose they were used. Are we projecting our modern ideas onto these objects?

Yet the statues themselves are still considered strong evidence for widespread goddess-centered worship. And many ancient myths tell of great goddess figures playing a role in creation. Traces of the great goddess can be found, if we know where to look. Vegetation and fertility myths offer us one place to see these remnants.

Another strong argument in favor of the Great Goddess is the change in human lifestyles. Mircea Eliade speculated there was a time when humans had little understanding of the reproductive process. The woman may have been seen as solely responsible—giving her a prominent role. But as people learned more about the reproductive process, possibly due to the practice of animal husbandry, the male role in procreation became apparent. This shift in consciousness, some believe, led to the view of the female as a field to be fertilized—as is illustrated in several myths.

Eventually, as farmers became marginalized by more the specialized work of city life, women became relegated to the home. This development was gradual and complex, taking place over thousands of years, but many cite this progression as a reason why the great goddess figure became diminished in favor of a male god as supreme ruler.

Settled communities were also more vulnerable to nomadic peoples, since agriculture didn't develop all at once in all places. Invaders brought different ideas with them and imposed their beliefs on the people they conquered or, at the very least, caused a blending of ideas and practices. It would have been easy for early evidence of goddess worship to be erased, especially since by the time we have myths being recorded in writing, the great goddess may have already been displaced by male gods.

One particularly interesting theory in favor of the goddess is presented by Leonard Shlain in his book *The Alphabet Versus the Goddess*. He focuses on this single question: "How did the invention of the alphabet affect the balance of power between men and women?" (2). While many scholars have explored the connection between language development and myths, this book covers, in detail, how this change could have contributed to the replacement of worship of a Great Goddess. He continues, stating that while there are many factors that influence the changes, "the introduction of the written word, and then the alphabet, into the social intercourse of humans initiated a fundamental change in the way newly literate cultures understood their reality" (6–7). He states:

> The Old Testament was the first alphabetic written work to influence future ages . . . The words on its pages anchor three powerful religions: Judaism, Christianity, and Islam. Each is an exemplar of patriarchy. Each monotheistic religion features an imageless Father deity whose authority shines through His revealed Word, sanctified in its written form. Conceiving of a deity who has no concrete image prepares the way for the kind of abstract thinking that inevitably leads to law codes, dualistic philosophy, and objective science, the signature triad of Western culture.

Shlain proposes that "the profound impact these ancient scriptures had upon the development of the West depended as much on their being written in an alphabet as on the moral lessons they contained" (7). Shlain is not claiming development of language as negative, but points out its changes on the Western spiritual perspective, and positing that it helped lead to the rise of patriarchy.

> Goddess worship, feminine values, and women's power depend on the ubiquity of the image. God worship, masculine values, and men's domination of women are bound to the written word. Word and image, like masculine and feminine, are complementary opposites. Whenever a culture elevates the written word at the expense of the image, patriarchy dominates. (7)

Vegetation and Fertility Myths

This somewhat broad category of myths reflects people's anxieties about survival—in both hunting-gathering societies and settled, agricultural groups. They can also be etiological tales, explaining changing seasons or other cycles. But they seem to share a common thread—they deal with cycles of birth, death, and rebirth. In addition, by studying these myths we can find traces of how the role of the goddess changed over time and became less significant, making way for the eventual authority of the supreme god. Even in early agrarian societies a great mother goddess may still have been present as a supreme deity, but eventually the balance of power that was once equal in the vegetation cycle became male-dominated.

The process of sowing and harvesting has long been seen as parallel to the human reproductive cycle—impregnation, gestation, and birth. Early on, the female role was still strong, as her connection to the earth was essential. This continued in agricultural life. According to Mircea Eliade, "Woman and feminine sacrality [were] raised to the first rank. Since women played a decisive part in the domestication of plants, they become the owners of the cultivated fields, which raises their social position" (Schlain 34).

Prior to an agricultural way of life, we can speculate the goddess figure had more significance. Again, this is just a theory, supported only by a few artifacts such as statues and cave paintings. For hunting societies, we do have evidence that suggests the importance of shamanistic rituals where an earth-goddess (and possibly other deities) may have been invoked for a successful hunt. With the agricultural revolution, the goddess figure gives up some of her power in favor of balanced responsibility. There are many myths that describe rituals that represent a type of "sacred marriage" intended to ensure a successful growing season.

Often in these stories the god and goddess are a couple, sharing the roles in partnership. In many cases, the god figure is also the offspring of the goddess and he eventually matures to become her consort. Then, he dies, and is reborn, the symbolic resurrection representing the rebirth of the land for the next cycle. The motif of the dying god being "cut down" in his prime is symbolic of the harvest—in some myths his body is dismembered and scattered. In some cultures, the dying god figure can also become an underworld king or ruler of the dead, or represent a "scapegoat" or tragic hero who dies for society as a form of sacrifice. There is great variety among these myths.

Some scholars have explored the connection between the ancient shaman and the male vegetation gods, linking them to tricksters, and yet their role has been transformed as well. According to Leeming and Page:

> The wildness, the magic, the promiscuity of God in his mask as old shaman-trickster have been transformed by the Dying God of the Neolithic period into the controlled and relatively orderly practices of domesticated procreation, agriculture, and animal husbandry. As the wild berries and grasses, the wild animals, and the Great Mother herself have been contained in the village walls, so has God. (qtd. in Voth 255)

From the Earth to the Sky: The God as Father

However, the balance in vegetation myths isn't always kept, and doesn't always remain even. As we've discussed, as agrarian societies became more complex, many of these myths were abandoned in favor of a supreme male god, often a sky-god, and the goddess's role was minimized or forgotten. Sky-gods were important in many early myths, but their role expanded and their authority increased over time. Remember, myths weren't stagnant. Cultures changed and adapted their stories. Periods of conflict, societies invading and conquering others, contributed to the changes in how people viewed their deities. Sometimes the old myths were preserved, but usually they were blended with new ideas and sometimes abandoned entirely in favor of the myths of either a conquering culture or new ways of viewing the world. During these times of change and assimilation, many deities became marginalized, absorbed, or were given new roles and titles. In addition, sky-gods were often warriors and leaders, so their position of authority seems inevitable.

Again, we turn to scholar Mircea Eliade's account of this trend. In his book *Patterns in Comparative Religion*, he points out that "many early creator gods are associated with the sky. Ideas of 'height,' 'on high,' and infinite space all have religious value. But the sky is also remote, detached, and inaccessible" (qtd. in Voth 230). Sometimes the role of the sky-god is assumed by other deities, called "fecundators" (fertilizers) who aid with food production and keeping the land fertile, as in vegetation myths during agricultural times.

Some of these changes involve reducing the feminine role of giving "birth" to things, to a male-centered act of "making" things. This changed the relationship not only between deities and the natural world, but also the way humans considered nature and viewed their deities. Often these myths tell the story of a conflict between male and female deities, where the male wins the battle. Sometimes the goddess is even described as a monster. But sometimes she does win, and is able to hold her ground, at least for a time.

In *Myth in Human History*, Grant Voth explains,

> Social and political circumstances also favored the supremacy of male over female deities. Kings now presided over complex societies that featured new male-oriented occupations. As fewer people were needed for agriculture and more for other tasks, the power of the fertility goddess waned, and new pantheons—largely male—emerged. By this time, the sky god was ready to consolidate all other deities into himself and finally to emerge as sole lord and creator, the ultimate Father. (257)

Where do Myths come From?

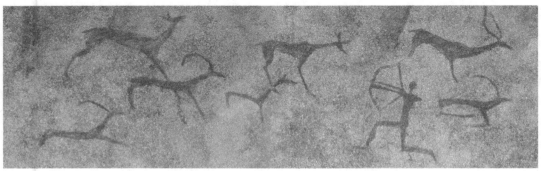

© gerasimov_foto_174/Shutterstock.com

The impulse to ask questions of our existence and experience is not new to the human species. In fact, we have archaeological evidence to show that Neanderthals created systems of spiritual understanding: they buried their dead with objects they thought the dead would need in the afterlife. Armstrong writes,

The Neanderthal graves show that when these early people became conscious of their mortality, they created some sort of counter-narrative that enabled them to come to terms with it. [. . .] From a very early date, therefore, it appears that human beings were distinguished by their ability to have ideas that went beyond their everyday experience.

The Paleolithic Age (20,000–8,000 BCE) of humans did not have forms of writing, but communicated their beliefs in another way: through cave paintings. The caves in Lascaux, France, and Altamira, Spain, are the most well-known of these earliest forms of art. But recent findings on the island of Sulawesi, Indonesia, and the Kimberly area of Australia show that this form of documentation existed across the world. These early paintings show animals and people, hunting and wearing masks, the earliest of shamanic rituals, and hand prints. Though the context of these cave paintings is lost, it is clear that Paleolithic people invested time and effort to create records of their existence.

Aside from art, many early people did not have a form of writing with which to communicate their stories. This means that mythology began in oral tradition, which has both advantages and disadvantages. An oral story requires no ability to read or write; one simply speaks. Oral stories can be equally accessible to the young and old, and many rituals surround these tales. For instance, there are stories that may only be told in winter, or stories that can only be recited to the initiated. These rituals bond a community through their shared experience with the myth. But, like the children's game "Telephone," we know that it does not take long for a message to become changed when retold. When a myth has been told for hundreds of years, we can be sure that the version we read is not exactly the same as when it was first uttered. People embellish to make their version more interesting, people forget parts and improvise, or the story is lost due to the language dying.

Cultures who developed written language face the same double-edged sword. The written word sets down a story in its current form, so there is less of a chance that the person reciting the story will stray from this version. The written form of stories carry through for thousands of years, as evidenced by the Mesopotamian myths of *Gilgamesh* and the *Enuma Elish,* which were etched onto stone tablets in cuneiform over 4,000 years ago. But writing can be lost, burnt, broken, and stolen. There is also the spiritual belief that a story is still alive when told, but the spirit of the story is killed when written down. Written myths are only readable by those who can read, which presents the problem of access, and more specifically, to those who can read the language. Mistranslations abound when stories are transferred from one language to another.

When missionaries from various religious sects began to gather myths, many of them had good intentions. Missionaries often recognized that the indigenous culture was quickly disappearing, and sought to document the myths, customs, and language of the people they encountered. However, missionaries came with ulterior motives of conversion and civilization, which sometimes crept into their translations of an indigenous culture's myths. We have to read carefully, and with a skeptical eye, when we rely on the myths written by colonizers, explorers, and missionaries.

Missionaries and explorers tended to think of the mythology of an indigenous culture as their religion, which is why they wished to convert them to a new set of beliefs. But myth does not have to be one's religion, in the sense of a worldview that praises or worships a kind of deity. Mythology is often the way that people explain their lives, which shares characteristics with religion, but is not necessarily the same concept. If we look at the myths of a culture, we see metaphors for their internal struggles and characters who uphold the agreed upon values of a culture. While many religions have these types of stories, one does not have to think of mythological stories as a religion. To do so promotes a personal viewpoint above that of who the myth belongs.

A form of translation, rationalization can hinder the myths that have come to a modern audience. Rationalization happens when a story changes to better suit the needs of a new audience. For example, the original stories recorded by the Grimm Brothers share common threads with many Disney movies, but they have been sanitized for child viewers; few parents would want their child to see blood spurting from a severed heel, or birds pecking the eyes out of the stepsisters in *Cinderella*. Rationalization is why there is no one "true" version of a myth. Take, for instance, the Indian hero epic *The Ramayana*. A. K. Ramanujan's article "The 300 Ramayanas" posits that there are as many versions of this epic as there are people who have told it. Each story has a different focus, or a small part might be left out, or a different character upheld as the most virtuous. As people change, so do their stories, and multiple retellings of the same basic story can occur within the same culture.

How to use this book

Timelines

You may not be familiar with the kind of timelines we use in this text. Many Americans have grown up with dates signified with "BC" (Before Christ) and "AD" (Annus Domini, The Year of the Lord). Because these dates clearly promote a Western, Christian worldview, but much of this text focuses on myths that do not use the birth of Christ to measure time, we use instead "BCE" (Before the Common Era) and "CE" (The Common Era). On a timeline, they look like this:

3000 BCE   2000 BCE   1000 BCE   0   1000 CE   2000 CE

Discussion Questions

The discussion questions that appear after the chapters are meant to be thought-provoking and to promote your own insights into the text. Use these to determine if you've read carefully, if you're thinking about the myths' connection to other texts, and to see if you want to conduct more research.

More Research

Each myth gives a quick introduction that focuses on the culture, the time it may have been written, what language it may have been written in or spoken by, and a bit of historical context. Use these introductions as a starting point that can aid in your reading, but don't be afraid to conduct more research about a culture or myth that you want to know more about. We've provided a bibliography for each chapter that can get you started in seeking out primary and secondary source material.

The Focus of this Text

While there are a variety of excellent texts on the subject of mythology, we perceived that some parts of the world weren't getting the attention they deserve. The focus of many books and courses has been Western-centric; learning about mythology has come primarily from the Greek and Roman traditions, with Egyptian and Mesopotamian myths playing a supporting role. But an entire world history of stories exists that need not be treated as less important.

For this book, we attempted to give a broad array of myths from every corner of the world, including countries, cultures, tribes, and people you may have never heard of. Rather than focus only on the well-known epics, we sought out some of the lesser-known, and sometimes shorter stories of a culture that convey the values and traits of that society. While no book can feature all myths of the world, we hope this sample will stretch your understanding of mythology to include those cultures outside the realms of standard study.

As this text is intended for a semester-long college class, it is an introduction to the study of the literature that makes up world mythology. From a literary perspective, we can read these myths best by considering their multiple levels of meaning. Look for symbols, metaphors, and clues in each story to see what they reveal about the culture and how their worldview was informed. Undoubtedly some of our understanding will lack the appropriate context due to time and translation, but by examining the myths as pieces of literature, we can find the deeper connections, themes, and beliefs present around the world.

Myths belong to their tellers, but they can also belong to us. We can't deny their original context, nor can we deny our modern perspective. Myths help us ponder the "big" questions about life: who are we? why are we here? where did we come from, and where are we going? what is the meaning of life? Despite advances in technology and science, we still have these basic human questions. Our modern experience may be quite different, but there are some shared experiences: survival, labor, death, societal structure, relationships, pleasure, and our existence with the natural world. But, ultimately, we must let the myths speak for themselves.

The context of the myths is important, and yet we can still attempt to relate to the stories on a personal level. In understanding the past and the perspectives of other cultures we can think more deeply, more clearly examine ourselves, and perhaps find some company as we navigate an increasingly complex world. We still tell stories, and seek explanations. We experience awe. This is the timeless experience of myth.

BIBLIOGRAPHY

Armstrong, Karen. *A Short History of Myth*. Cannongate, 2005.

Campbell, Joseph. *The Hero With a Thousand Faces*. Princeton University Press, 1949.

---. *The Masks of God*. Vol I–IV. Penguin, 1976.

Eliot, Alexander. *The Universal Myths: Heroes, Gods, Tricksters and Others*. Meridian, 1976.

Feldman, Susan. *The Storytelling Stone: Traditional Native American Myths and Tales*. Delta Publishing Co., 1999.

Frazer, James. *The Golden Bough*. Macmillan, 1922.

Hamilton, Edith. *Mythology*. Little Brown, 1942.

Hyde, Lewis. *Trickster Makes This World: Mischief, Myth, and Art*. Farrar, Straus, and Giroux, 1998, 2010. Kindle edition.

Jung, Carl. *Man and His Symbols*. Dell, 1964.

Kane, Sean. *Wisdom of the Mythtellers*. Broadview Press, 1994.

Leeming, David. *Myth, A Biography of Belief*. Oxford University Press, 2002.

---. *Mythology: The Voyage of the Hero*. Oxford University Press, 1998.

Leeming, David, and Margaret Leeming. *A Dictionary of Creation Myths*. Oxford University Press, 1994.

Leonard, Scott, and Michael McClure. *Myth and Knowing.* McGraw Hill, 2004.

Lincoln, Bruce. *Myth, Cosmos, and Society: Indo-European Themes of Creation and Destruction.* Harvard University Press, 1986.

Ramanujan, A. K. "The 300 Ramayanas." *The Collected Essays of A.K. Ramanujan.* Oxford University Press, Jan. 2004, pp. 131–160.

Shlain, Leonard. *The Alphabet Versus the Goddess.* Penguin, 1998.

Voth, Grant L. "Myth in Human History." *The Great Courses.* The Teaching Company, 2010.

Chapter 2

THE MYTHS OF THE MIDDLE EAST

© martrioshka/Shutterstock.com

INTRODUCTION

Part 1: Creation and Destruction

Sumerian Hymn to Ishtar

The Enuma Elish (Babylonian)

Creation in Egypt

The Avesta (Zoroastrian)

The Hebrew Creation Story of Genesis

The Story of Creation in the Qur'an

The Eleventh Tablet of the Epic of Gilgamesh—The Deluge

The Hebrew Story of the Flood (Genesis Chapters 6–9)

The Muslim Story of the Flood (Qur'an, Suras 11 & 71)

Part 2: Tricksters, Lovers, and Other Tales

Isis and Osiris (Egyptian)

Inanna and Dumuzi (Akkadian)

Part 3: Journeys of Heroes and Heroines

The Epic of Gilgamesh (Sumerian/Babylonian)

© martrioshka/Shutterstock.com

The ancient Middle East is often referred to as "the cradle of civilization." Due to its ideal location, agriculture began there on a large scale, leading to further advancements in civilization. The rivers in the area provided rich farmland—the annual flooding cycle of the Nile River in Egypt mirrored the cycle of birth, death, and renewal for the people. In addition, Mesopotamia, which means "the land between two rivers," was also fertile land, yet faced with the unpredictable flooding of the Tigris and Euphrates Rivers, leading to the earliest flood myths originating in this region. These important aspects of geography also played an important role in the culture of the people and in their myths.

To understand the scope of these myths, a brief understanding of the time period is useful. First of all, Mesopotamia was an important location for several reasons. Rapid development of city-states based on wealth from metalworking and agriculture caused great expansion and desire for control. This led to political unrest and conflict. Invasions and blending of languages over time created several phases of Mesopotamian culture.

The earliest period in Mesopotamia is called the Sumerian phase. Around 3000–2000 BCE, invaders came from the north, bringing the Akkadian language. They conquered the Sumerians, and Akkadian became the official language. However, much like Latin is still used for religious purposes, Sumerian was still used in a similar way. The next group to invade, the Amorites from Babylon, also wrote in Akkadian; this is the Babylonian phase. And, finally, people from Assyria came to occupy the area. They also wrote in a form of Akkadian (called Assyrian). The Assyrian capital city was Nineveh, which was destroyed in 612 BCE. The standard text of *Gilgamesh* was preserved there, in a great library that burned. Fortunately, the tablets, being stone, survived.

Not necessarily the oldest myths in the world, but the oldest written versions come from this part of the world. In Mesopotamia, these stories were written in cuneiform ("wedge-shaped") script, which was originally used in recordkeeping, but later became a way to transmit actual narrative. A wooden stylus was used to make impressions in clay, which was then baked. This system was invented by the Sumerians around the fourth millennium BCE and evolved over time to a system with hundreds of symbols—a variety of syllabic signs and some that represent words. Interpretation of this writing is quite difficult, adding even more challenge to translating the stories.

Not long after, around 3100 BCE, Egyptians began writing in the form of hieroglyphic script, a system that began with drawings of objects that represent sounds. These detailed writings often look like works of art themselves. They were first used on pottery and stone, later on the walls of tombs and temples, and eventually papyrus. The word "hieroglyphic" is a Greek word from *hieros*, meaning sacred, and *glypho*, meaning inscription. The Egyptians believed their god Thoth invented writing.

One thing to keep in mind is that Egyptian religious belief is syncretistic, meaning they added new deities and tales but didn't eliminate anything. This caused the body of beliefs to grow and become even more complex. Gods and goddesses would take on new functions and responsibilities, even new names, often resulting in combined deities, such as Amon-Re. There is no standard collection of myths and most exist only in fragmented allusions on the walls of tombs or on coffins. While the beliefs, rituals, and political climate of the region may have changed, it's interesting to note that worship of the goddess Isis persisted throughout almost every period in their history.

It is often difficult to comprehend the history of ancient Egypt, which spanned 3,000 years. This list shows the dates of the basic time periods of ancient Egypt:

- ► Early Dynastic Period, 3100–2686 BCE
- ► Old Kingdom, 2686–2181 BCE (great pyramids were built)
- ► First Intermediate Period, 2181–2040 BCE
- ► Middle Kingdom, 2040–1650 BCE
- ► Second Intermediate Period, 1750–1550 BCE
- ► New Kingdom, c. 1550–1069 BCE
- ► Third Intermediate Period, c. 1069–656 BCE
- ► Late Period, c. 664–343 BCE
- ► Graeco-Roman Period, 332 BCE–642 CE

While Egyptian religion experienced many changes during their long history, they were relatively unaffected by outside beliefs, unlike Mesopotamia, an area constantly at risk of invasion from other groups.

For instance, when the Persians conquered Babylon, they introduced their Zoroastrian faith to the region. This brought a sharp change from the Babylonian's polytheistic worldview, eventually leading to a monotheistic tradition that would soon spread into west Asia, over centuries giving way to Judaism, and Christianity, and Islam.

In addition, when the culture of the Greeks and Romans arrived, gods and goddesses of the Middle East, in turn, were made known in Europe.

Part 1: Creation and Destruction

© Jacqueline Gray

Sumerian Hymn to Ishtar

In a world of patriarchal religious systems, it is sometimes surprising to find that many of the world's first systems of belief worshipped women. The Sumerians, like the early Egyptians and earliest Babylonians, revered and exalted women for their connectedness with the natural world and ability to create life as mothers. In many places in Sumeria and Mesopotamia, women held status in marriage, law, and religion.

Women in ancient religions were priestesses in temples and many hymns were written in respect to women. When reading the texts of ancient Sumerian stories there are two dialects; the hymns which opened longer stories or rites were written in "the women's language." This does not mean it is an entirely different language, but that it is a more emotive, poetic, beautiful, and expressive tone that serves to inspire by way of poetry.

It is interesting to note that the Sumerians typically worship the goddess Inanna, but that this particular hymn is addressed to the Akkadian goddess, Ishtar. The two are mostly interchangeable. This hymn was written in approximately 1600 BCE.

HYMN TO ISHTAR

To thee I cry, O lady of the gods,
Lady of ladies, goddess without peer,
Ishtar who shapes the lives of all mankind,
Thou stately world queen, sovereign of the sky,
And lady ruler of the host of heaven—   5
Illustrious is thy name.... O light divine,
Gleaming in lofty splendour o'er the earth—
Heroic daughter of the moon, oh! hear;
Thou dost control our weapons and award
In battles fierce the victory at will—   10
crown'd majestic Fate. Ishtar most high,
Who art exalted over all the gods,
Thou bringest lamentation; thou dost urge
With hostile hearts our brethren to the fray;
The gift of strength is thine for thou art strong;   15
Thy will is urgent, brooking no delay;
Thy hand is violent, thou queen of war
Girded with battle and enrobed with fear...
Thou sovereign wielder of the wand of Doom,
The heavens and earth are under thy control.   20

Adored art thou in every sacred place,
In temples, holy dwellings, and in shrines,
Where is thy name not lauded? Where thy will
Unheeded, and thine images not made?
Where are thy temples not upreared? O, where   25
Art thou not mighty, peerless, and supreme?

Anu and Bel and Ea have thee raised
To rank supreme, in majesty and pow'r,
They have established thee above the gods
And all the host of heaven... O stately queen,   30
At thought of thee the world is filled with fear,
The gods in heaven quake, and on the earth
All spirits pause, and all mankind bow down
With reverence for thy name.... O Lady Judge,

Thy ways are just and holy; thou dost gaze
On sinners with compassion, and each morn   35
Leadest the wayward to the rightful path.

Now linger not, but come! O goddess fair,
O shepherdess of all, thou drawest nigh
With feet unwearied... Thou dost break the bonds
Of these thy handmaids... When thou stoopest o'er   40
The dying with compassion, lo! they live;
And when the sick behold thee they are healed.

Source: Donald A. Mackenzie, *Myths of Babylonia and Assyria*, 1915.

Hear me, thy servant! hearken to my pray'r,
For I am full of sorrow and I sigh
In sore distress; weeping, on thee I wait.   45
Be merciful, my lady, pity take
And answer, "'Tis enough and be appeased."

How long must my heart sorrow and make moan
And restless be? How long must my dark home
Be filled with mourning and my soul with grief?   50
O lioness of heaven, bring me peace
And rest and comfort. Hearken to my pray'r!
Is anger pity? May thine eyes look down
With tenderness and blessings, and behold
Thy servant. Oh! have mercy; hear my cry   55
And unbewitch me from the evil spells,
That I may see thy glory... Oh! how long
Shall these my foes pursue me, working ill,
And robbing me of joy?... Oh! how long
Shall demons compass me about and cause   60
Affliction without end?... I thee adore—
The gift of strength is thine and thou art strong—
The weakly are made strong, yet I am weak...
O hear me! I am glutted with my grief—
This flood of grief by evil winds distressed;
My heart hath fled me like a bird on wings,   65
And like the dove I moan. Tears from mine eyes
Are falling as the rain from heaven falls,
And I am destitute and full of woe.

What have I done that thou hast turned from me?
Have I neglected homage to my god   70
And thee my goddess? O deliver me
And all my sins forgive, that I may share
Thy love and be watched over in thy fold;
And may thy fold be wide, thy pen secure.

How long wilt thou be angry? Hear my cry,   75
And turn again to prosper all my ways—
O may thy wrath be crumbled and withdrawn
As by a crumbling stream. Then smite my foes,
And take away their power to work me ill,
That I may crush them. Hearken to my pray'r!   80
And bless me so that all who me behold
May laud thee and may magnify thy name,
While I exalt thy power over all—
Ishtar is highest! Ishtar is the queen!
Ishtar the peerless daughter of the moon!   85

DISCUSSION QUESTIONS

1. As a hymn of praise to the goddess Ishtar, there are a surprising amount of mentions of violence. "Thy hand is violent, thou queen of war" and "At thought of thee the world is filled with fear" are examples. Find other examples and explain why the writer chooses to depict Ishtar in this way.

2. There are many contrasting images in this hymn of fear and compassion. Locate the lines that describe Ishtar as compassionate and affectionate and the places she promotes fear. How do we reconcile this opposing imagery?

The Enuma Elish (Babylonian)

Introduction

The Babylonian Epic of Creation is one of the oldest pieces of writing that has been found. Carved into stone tablets by using cuneiform writing, these seven tablets hold perhaps the oldest account of creation, gods and goddesses, and the hero Marduk's role in creating Babylon. It is nearly impossible to date this story, but the tablets seem to have been written during the second millennium BCE. There are clues, like dialect, names, and locations that tell us it was written sometime during the reigns of various rulers near the Tigress and Euphrates Rivers, anywhere from 1936–1104 BCE. It is likely, however, that the story has been told in its oral form for thousands of years before it was set in stone. The tablets were rediscovered in the mid-1800s.

The *Enuma Elish*, named after the first lines of the story, begins with deities who represent different properties of water and air, before engaging in an intergenerational conflict that ends in murder. The widow Tiamat, distraught and angry, creates a team of monsters to visit evil upon the murderers—her own children. What ensues is a battle of supernatural talent between Tiamat and the chosen hero, Marduk. The creation of the earth, human beings, and the beautiful city of Babylon are central events in *The Enuma Elish*, setting the stage for the Mesopotamian worship of Marduk.

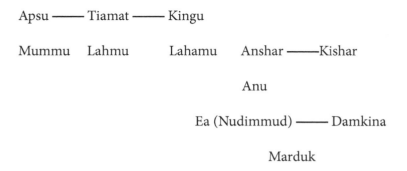

THE ENUMA ELISH

TABLET I
The Creation of the Gods
When the heavens above were yet unnamed,
And the name of the earth beneath had not been recorded,
Apsu, the oldest of beings, their progenitor,
And Tiâmat, who bare each and all of them—
Their waters were merged into a single mass.   5
A field had not been measured, a marsh had not been searched out,
When of the gods none was shining,
A name had not been recorded, a fate had not been fixed,
The gods came into being in the midst of them.
The god Lahmu and the goddess Lahamu were made to shine, they were named.   10
Together they increased in stature, they grew tall.
Anshar and Kishar came into being, and others besides them.
Long were the days, the years increased.
The god Anu, their son, the equal of his fathers, was created.
The god Anshar made his eldest son Anu in his own image.   15
And the god Anu begat Nudimmud the image of himself.
The god Nudimmud was the first among his fathers,
Endowed with understanding, wisdom, and speech,
Exceedingly mighty in strength above his father Anshar who begat him.
Unrivalled amongst the gods his brothers …   20
The confraternity of the gods was established.

The Young Gods Enrage the Creator Generation
The gods of that generation would meet together
and disturb Tiâmat, and their clamour reverberated.
Her belly was stirred up to its uttermost depths.
They annoyed her by playing inside Anduruna.   25
She became mute,
Though their ways were not good, she indulged them.
Apsu could not diminish their noise.
At that time Apsu, the progenitor of the great gods,
Shouted out and summoned Mummu, the advisor of his house, saying,   30
    "O Mummu, my steward, who makes me rejoice,
    Come, to Tiâmat we will go."
They went to Tiâmat,
They took counsel together about the gods, their children.
Apsu took up his voice and,   35
To Tiamat he spoke of the matter,
    "Their ways are grievous,
    By day I find no peace, by night I have no rest.
    Verily I will make an end of their ways, I will sweep them away!
    There shall be a sound of lamentation; lo, then we shall rest."   40

Source: E.A. Wallis Budge, *The Enuma Elish,* The Babylonian Epic of Creation, 1921.

Tiâmat on hearing this
Was stirred up to wrath and shrieked to her husband,
Until she was sick. Then she raged all alone,
She uttered a curse, and unto Apsu, spake, saying,
   "How can we destroy what we have made?   45
   Verily their way is grievous, but we shall be peaceful."

Apsu and Mummu Plan to Destroy Young Gods
Mummu disagreed and gave counsel to Apsu,
The counsel of Mummu was dire [in respect of the gods]:
   "Come, destroy their ways.
   Then by day thou shalt find peace, and by night thou shalt have rest."   50
Apsu listened, his face grew bright,
For they were planning evil against the gods, his children.
Mummu embraced his neck ...
He took him on his knee, he kissed him.
They planned the attack in the assembly,   55
But the curses were repeated to the gods, Apsu and Tiamat's eldest sons.
The gods listened;
They began a lamentation...
Endowed with understanding, the prudent god, the exalted one,
Ea, who ponders everything that is, searched out their plan.   60
He brought the plan to stand still.
He recited a cunning incantation, very powerful and holy.

The Young Gods Fight Back
Ea recited a spell that made the waters of Apsu still,
Sleep came to Apsu and he slept soundly
Ea took the crown from atop the head of Apsu,   65
Took the belt from the waist of Apsu,
His mantle of lordship taken and placed upon Ea himself.
Ea slew the crownless Apsu,
And tied Mummu with nose-rope.
He built his house atop Apsu,   70
And grasped Mummu by the rope.
After slaying his enemies,
Ea rested with no noise inside his home
And gave it the name Apsu and made chapels,
His own place to live there,   75
Ea and his lover Damkina lived happily there.

Marduk is Born
In this house was destined
*Bel, sage of the gods, to be born.
Inside Apsu, Marduk was created;
Inside Apsu, Marduk was born.   80
Ea created him,
Damkina bore him.
He was suckled by goddesses
And reared by nurses who filled him with awesomeness

*The term Bel is a title, similar to "Lord."

Anu gave birth to four winds   85
The whirlwind and the dust storm
The calm wind and the flood-wave
And put them into the hand of Marduk to let him play.

Tiamat Plans Revenge for the Death of Apsu
The winds stirred Tiamat again and she was unable to rest.
The gods saw and they formed a band, and went forth to battle to help Tiâmat.   90
They were exceedingly wroth, they made plots by day and by night without ceasing.
        "They killed Apsu, your husband and you were mute.
        They have created the four winds and stir up your belly again.
        We cannot rest!
        Do you care nothing for your husband?   95
        Are you not a mother?
        We are tired and cannot rest. Do you not love us?
        Will you remove them so we can sleep?
        Go to battle and avenge your husband!"
Tiamat became convinced. She spoke,   100
        "Let us do as you have advised.
        Those inside Apsu will be destroyed.
        They have become evil and disobeyed those who have created them."

Tiamat Creates an Army of Monsters
They offered battle, fuming and raging.
They set the battle in array, they uttered cries of hostility,   105
Mother Khubur, who fashioned all things,
Set up the unrivalled weapon: she spawned huge serpents,
Sharp of tooth, merciless in attack
She filled their bodies with venom instead of blood,
Grim, monstrous serpents, arrayed in terror,   110
She decked them with brightness, she fashioned them in exalted forms,
So that fright and horror might overcome him that looked upon them,
So that their bodies might rear up, and no man resist their attack,
She set up the Viper, and the Snake, and the god Lahamu,
The Whirlwind, the ravening Dog, the Scorpion-man,   115
The mighty Storm-wind, the Fish-man, the horned Beast
They carried the Weapon which spared not, nor flinched from the battle.
Most mighty were Tiâmat's decrees, they could not be resisted,
Thus she caused eleven monsters of this kind to come into being,
Among the gods, her first-born son who had collected her company,   120
That is to say, Kingu, she set on high, she made him the great one amongst them,
Leader of the hosts in battle, disposer of the troops,
Bearer of the firmly grasped weapon, attacker in the fight,
He who in the battle is the master of the weapon,
She appointed, she made him to sit down in goodly apparel,   125
        "I have uttered the incantation for thee.
        I have magnified thee in the assembly of the gods.
        I have filled his hand with the sovereignty of the whole company of the gods.
        Mayest thou be magnified, thou who art my only spouse,
        May the Anunnaki make great thy renown over all of them."   130

She gave him the Tablet of Destinies, she fastened it on his breast, saying,
"As for thee, thy command shall not fall empty,
whatsoever goeth forth from thy mouth shall be established."
When Kingu was raised on high and had taken the heavens
He fixed the destinies for the gods his sons,   135
"Open your mouths, let the Fire-god be quenched,
He who is glorious in battle and is most mighty, shall do great deeds."

TABLET II
Word of Tiamat's Monsters Reaches the Gods
Tiâmat made solid that which she had moulded.
She bound the gods her children with evil bonds.
Tiâmat wrought wickedness to avenge Apsu.
When Ea had harnessed his chariot he went to meet his grandfather Anshar,
Ea hearkened his story,   5
[Ea and Anu have attempted battle with Tiamat, to no avail,
Ea Repeats Lines 105–137 of Tablet I to Anshar]

Marduk is Chosen to Fight Tiamat
The Lord Anshar, the Father of the gods, spoke majestically,
Ea lifted up his heart, he addressed the Anunnaki, and said,
"He whose strength is mighty shall be an avenger for us.
The perfect one of Anshar, father of the gods,
The heir of his father who rushes into battle: Marduk the Hero!"   10
Ea called Marduk to the place where he gave oracles,
Marduk came and Ea addressed him,
"O Marduk, hear the counsel and advice of your father,
You are the son who refreshes his heart,
Draw near and enter the presence of Anshar,   15
Stand there with joy, when he looks upon you and he will be at rest."
The Lord Marduk rejoiced at the word of his father,
He approached and took up his place before Anshar.
Anshar looked upon him and his heart was filled with gladness.
Anshar kissed Marduk's lips, and his fear was removed. Then Marduk said,   20
"My father, let not the opening of thy mouth be closed,
I will go, I will take away the fear in your heart.
Anshar, let not the opening of thy mouth be closed,
I will go, I will take away the fear in your heart."
Anshar said to Marduk, "What man is the cause of the battle which made you go forth?   25
It is Tiâmat, who is a woman, who will pursue you with weapons."
Marduk responded, "Grandfather, Rejoice your hearts and be glad.
You shall soon trample upon the neck of Tiâmat!"
So Anshar replied, "Rejoice our hearts and make us glad.
Go soon and trample upon the neck of Tiâmat.   30
My son, who understands everything,
Cast deep sleep upon Tiâmat with your holy spell.
Go with great speed!"
The Lord Marduk rejoiced at the word of his father,

His heart leaped with joy, to his father he spoke,   35
    "O Lord of the gods, Overlord of the Great Gods,
    Should I as your avenger
    Slay Tiâmat and bestow life upon you,
    Summon a meeting, proclaim and magnify my position,
    Sit down together in friendly fashion in Upshukkinaku.   40
    Let me issue decrees by the opening of my mouth.
    Whatever I create, let it remain unaltered,
    That which my mouth utters shall never fail or be made undone."

TABLET III
The Council of the Gods Convenes
Anshar opened his mouth, and
Unto the god Gaga, his envoy, spoke,
    "O Gaga, my envoy, who makes me glad.
    I will despatch thee unto the gods Lahmu and Lahamu.
    To let them know and understand the intention of my heart   5
    Bring before me
    All the gods.
    Let them make a council, let them sit down to a feast
    Let them eat bread, let them drink sesame wine.
    Tell them this story:"   10
[Anshar Repeats Lines 105–137 of Tablet I to Gaga]
Gaga spreads the word of Anshar:
    "I sent the god Anu, but he could not prevail against her.
    Nudimmud was afraid and turned back,
    Marduk, your son, the envoy of the gods, hath set out.
    His heart is stirred up to oppose Tiâmat.   15
    Hasten ye therefore, issue your decrees speedily
    That he may go to meet your mighty enemy."
Gaga departed and hastened upon his way
To the god Lahmu and the goddess Lahamu, the gods his fathers, reverently
Reverently he did homage, and he kissed the ground at their feet.   20
And he told them the story of Anshar:
    [Gaga repeats lines 105-137 of Tablet I to Lahmu and Lahamu]
The gods Lahmu and Lahamu heard, they wailed loudly,
All the Igigi gods wept bitterly:
    "Who were our enemies until the gods were sent to tell us?
    We cannot comprehend the work of Tiâmat."   25
They gathered themselves together and they went,
All the great gods, who issue decrees.
They entered in, they filled the court before Anshar.
Brother god kissed brother god in the divine assembly,
They held a meeting, they sat down to a feast,   30
They ate bread, they drank the sesame wine,
The taste of the sweet drink confused their senses
They drank themselves drunk, their bodies were filled to overflowing,
They were overcome by heaviness of drink, their spirits were exalted.
They issued the decree for Marduk as their avenger.   35

Tablet IV

They founded for him a majestic canopy,
Marduk seated himself in the seat of kingship
in the presence of his fathers, who said unto him:

    "You are honourable and great among the gods.
    Your position is unrivalled, the words you utter become as fixed as the sky.   5
    From this day onward your command shall not be altered.
    The power to exalt to heaven and to cast down to the earth
    Both shall be in your hand,
    That which comes from your mouth shall be established,
    Against your utterance shall be no appeal.   10
    No one among the gods shall overstep your boundary,
    Worship, which is the object of the sanctuary of the gods,
    Whensoever they lack it shall be forthcoming in your sanctuary,
    O god Marduk, you are our avenger.
    We have given you sovereignty over the whole creation,   15
    In the council Your word shall be exalted,
    Your weapon shall never fall from your hands,
    It shall break the head of your foe.
    Lord, whosoever puts his trust in you, spare his life,
    And the god who devises evil, pour out his soul."   20
[Marduk shows his power by making a cloak disappear and reappear]
They rejoiced and adored him, saying, "Marduk is King."
They conferred upon him the sceptre, the throne, and the symbols of royalty
They gave him the unrivalled weapon, the destroyer of the enemy, saying:

    "Go, cut off the life of Tiâmat."
    "Let the wind carry her blood into the depth under the earth."   25
The gods, his fathers, issued the decree for the god Bel.
They set him on the road which leads to peace and adoration.

Marduk Prepares for Battle

He strung his bow, he set ready his weapon,
He slung his spear, he attached it to his body,
He raised the club, he grasped it in his right hand.   30
The bow and the quiver he hung at his side.
He set the lightning in front of him.
His body was filled with a glancing flame of fire.
He made a net wherewith to enclose Tiâmat.
He made the four winds to take up their position so that no part of her might escape,   35
The South wind, the North wind, the East wind, the West wind.
He held the net close to his side, the gift of his father Anu,
He created the "foul" wind, the storm, the parching blast,
The wind of "four," the wind of "seven," the typhoon, the wind incomparable
He despatched the seven winds which he had made,   40
To make turbid the inward parts of Tiâmat; they followed in his train.
The Lord raised up the wind-storm, his mighty weapon.
He went up into his chariot, the unequalled and terrible tempest.
He equipped it, he yoked thereto a team of four horses,
Pawing the ground, champing, eager to fly,   45
the odour of their teeth bore fetidness.

They were skilled and they were trained to trample under foot.
His brightness streamed forth, his head was crowned.
He took a direct path, he hastened on his journey.
He set his face towards the place of Tiâmat, who was enraged   50
On his lips his spell he restrained,
An antidote to her magic his hand grasped.
At that moment the gods were gazing upon him with fixed intensity,
The gods, his fathers, gazed upon him, they gazed upon him.

Marduk and Tiamat Battle

The Lord approached, he looked upon the middle of Tiâmat,   55
He searched out the plan of Kingu, her husband.
Marduk looked, Kingu staggered in his gait,
His will was destroyed, his motion was paralysed.
And the gods his helpers who were marching by his side
Saw the collapse of their chief and their sight was troubled.   60
Tiâmat shrieked but did not turn her head.
With lips full of rebellious words she maintained her stubbornness
    "... thou hast come as the Lord of the gods, ha!,
    They have appointed you in the place which should be theirs."
The Lord raised up the wind-storm, his mighty weapon,   65
Against Tiâmat, who was furious he sent it, saying:
    "You have made yourself mighty, you are puffed upon high,
    Your heart was stirred to battle
    After you watched your husband die.
    Meanwhile you have exalted Kingu to be your husband,   70
    And made him to usurp the attributes of Anu.
    You have planned evil.
    Against the gods, my fathers, you have wrought evil.
    Let your troops gird themselves, let them rely on their weapons.
    Stand up! You and I, let us fight!"   75
On hearing these words Tiâmat
Became like a mad thing, her senses became distraught,
Tiâmat uttered shrill cries again and again.
That on which she stood split in half at her own words.
She recited an incantation, she pronounced her spell.   80
The gods of battle demanded their weapons.
Tiâmat and Marduk, the envoy of the gods, roused themselves,
They advanced to fight each other, they drew nigh in battle.
The Lord cast his net and made it to enclose her,
The evil wind that had its place behind him he let out in her face.   85
Tiâmat opened her mouth to its greatest extent,
Marduk made the evil wind to enter it whilst her lips were open.
The raging winds filled out her belly,
Her heart was gripped, she opened wide her mouth panting.
Marduk grasped the arrow, which pierced her belly,   90
He clave open her bowels, he slit her heart,
He brought her to nought, he destroyed her life.
He cast down her carcass, he took up his stand upon it,

Marduk Punishes His Enemies
After Marduk had slain Tiâmat the chief,
Her host was scattered, her levies became fugitive,   95
And the gods, her allies, who had marched at her side,
Quaked with terror, and broke and ran
And betook themselves to flight to save their lives.
But they found themselves hemmed in, they could not escape,
Marduk tied them up, he smashed their weapons.   100
They were cast into the net, and they were caught in the snare,
The creatures of the world they filled with their cries of grief.
They received Marduk's chastisement, they were confined in restraint,
And the Eleven Creatures which Tiâmat had filled with awfulness,
The company of the devils that marched with her   105
He threw fetters, he tied them with nose-ropes,
They and their resistance he trod under his feet.
The god Kingu who had been magnified over them
He crushed, he esteemed him as having as little worth as a dead god.
Marduk took from him the Tablet of Destinies, which should never have been his,
He sealed it with seal of his making and fastened it on his breast.   110
After he had crushed and overthrown his enemies,
He made the haughty enemy to be like the dust underfoot.
He established completely Anshar's victory over the enemy,
The valiant Marduk achieved the object of Nudimmud Ea,
He imposed strict restraint on the gods whom he had made captive.   115

Marduk Makes the Heavens from Tiamat
He turned back to Tiâmat whom he had defeated,
The Lord Marduk trampled on the rump of Tiâmat,
With his unsparing club he smashed her skull.
He slit open the arteries of her blood.
He caused the North Wind to carry it away underground.   120
His fathers, the gods, looked on, they rejoiced, they were glad.
They brought unto him offerings of triumph and peace,
The Lord Marduk paused, he examined Tiâmat's carcass.
He created marvels from her monstrous corpse.
He separated flesh from hair, he worked cunningly.   125
He slit Tiâmat open like a flat fish cut into two pieces,
The one half he raised up and shaded the heavens therewith,
He pulled the bolt across, he posted a guard,
He ordered them not to let her water escape.
He crossed heaven, he contemplated the regions thereof.   130
He took for himself the house Nudimmud made
The Lord Marduk measured the dimensions of the Apsu,
He founded Esharra, a place like unto it,
The temple Esharra, which he made to be heaven.
He made the gods Anu, Enlil and Ea to inhabit their own cities.   135

TABLET V

Marduk Creates the Sun and Moon

He appointed the Stations for the great gods,
He set in heaven the Stars of the Zodiac which are their likenesses.
He fixed the year, he appointed the limits thereof.
He set up for the twelve months three stars apiece.
According to the day of the year he made figures.   5
He founded the Station of Jupiter to settle their boundaries,
That none might exceed or fall short.
He set the Station of Bel and Ea thereby.
He opened great gates under shelter on both sides.
He made a strong corridor on the left and on the right.   10
He fixed the zenith in the heavenly vault
He gave the god Nannar his brightness and committed the night to his care.
He set him for the government of the night, to determine the day
To Nannar he said,
    "At the beginning of the month when you rise over the land,   15
    Make your horns to project to mark six days of the month
    On the seventh day make like a half-crown.
    The fourteenth day will be the mid-point
    When Shamash looks at you from the horizon.
    And your horns will begin to lose their points   20
    Always bring the day of disappearance close to the path of Shamash."

Marduk Creates the Rest of the Earth from Tiamat

Marduk made the clouds to scatter.
He raised the wind, making rain,
The fog rolled, by collecting her poison,
He allowed for himself to let his hand control it.   25
He took her head and heaped it up as mountains,
Opened up her springs; let the water gush out.
From her eyes ran the Euphrates and the Tigris,
Closed up her nostrils.
He made clear-cut mountains from her udder.   30
Bored waterholes to drain off the catchwater.
He laid her tail across it, tied like a dam,
He set her thighs to hold up the sky,
And with half of her he made a roof to fix up the earth
He made the insides of Tiamat surge,   35
Spreading his net, to make it fully extend,
He made heaven and earth to touch.
He established the bounds of the earth.

The Bowstar

When he was finished, he threw down his reins and gave them to Ea.
The Tablet of Destinies, once in possession of Kingu,   40
He took and read to Anu.
The gods, his fathers, looked on the earth which he had made,
They observed how craftily the bow had been constructed,
They extolled the work which he had done.

Then the god Anu lifted up [the bow] in the company of the gods.   45
He kissed the bow, saying,
   "May she go far!"
He proclaimed the names of the bow to be as follows:
   "Verily, the first is 'Long Wood,'
   The second is Victory   50
   Its third name is 'Bow Star in Heaven'"
He fixed a station for it among the constellations
And decreed the destiny of the bow.

TABLET VI
Marduk and Ea Create Mankind
On hearing the words of the gods,
The heart of Marduk moved him to carry out miracles.
He opened his mouth, he spoke to Ea that which he had planned in his heart,
He gave counsel, saying:
   "I will solidify blood, I will form bone.   5
   I will set up man. 'Man' shall be his name.
   I will create the man 'Man.'
   The service of the gods shall be established,
And I will set them the gods free.
   I will make twofold the ways of the gods, and I will beautify them.   10
   They are now grouped together in one place, but they shall be partitioned in two."
Ea answered and spoke a word unto him,
For the consolation of the gods he repeated unto him a word of counsel,
   "Let one brother be given,
   Let him suffer destruction that men may be fashioned.   15
   Let the great gods be assembled,
   Let this chosen one be given in order that they may be established."
Marduk assembled the great gods, and issued a decree,
He opened his mouth, he addressed the gods;
the King spake a word unto the Anunnaki saying,   20
   "That which I stated before was true.
   This time also I speak truth. There are those who opposed me.
   Who was it that created the strife,
   Who caused Tiâmat to revolt, to join battle with me?
   Let him who created the strife be given as sacrifice,   25
   I will cause the axe in the act of sinking to do away his crime."
The great gods, the Igigi, answered him,
Unto the King of the gods of heaven and of earth,
The Prince of the gods, their lord they said:
   "It was Kingu who created the strife,   30
   Who made Tiâmat to revolt, to join battle with you."
They bound him in fetters and brought him before Ea,
They inflicted punishment on him, they let his blood,
From the blood of Kingu Ea fashioned mankind for the service of the gods,
And he set the gods free.   35

The Construction of Babylon
After Ea had fashioned man he laid the service of the gods upon him.
For that work, which pleased him not, man was chosen.
Marduk, the King of the gods, divided the gods,
He set the Anunnaki up on high.
He laid down for Anu a decree to serve as protector and guard.   40
He made twofold the ways on the earth and in the heavens.
The Anunnaki of the heaven,
The Anunnaki of the earth.
They spoke unto Marduk, their lord,
    "Now that we are free,   45
    What benefit have we conferred upon you?
    Come, let us make a shrine, whose name shall be renowned;
    Come at night, our time of festival, let us take our ease therein,
    On the day that we reach it we will take our ease therein."
On hearing this Marduk lit up   50
The features of his face shone like the day exceedingly.
    "Create Babylon, this construction you desire,
    Let it be a city, fashion a splendid shrine."
The Anunnaki began to work the mould for making bricks,
In the second year the shrine was as high as a hill,   55
And the summit of Esagila reached the celestial Ocean.
They made the temple tower to reach the celestial Ocean;
Unto Marduk, Enlil, Ea shrines they appointed,
It stood before them majestically:
At the bottom and at the top they observed its two horns as the moon.   60
After the Anunnaki had finished the construction of Esagila,
And had completed the making of their shrines,
They gathered together for a feast.
In Bab-ili, the abode which they had made,
Marduk made the gods his fathers to take their seats   65
    "This Babylon shall be your abode.
    "No mighty one [shall destroy] his house,
    the great gods shall dwell therein."

[The gods feast and consecrate the shrine of Esagila, and then issue decrees. Next Marduk assigns seats to the Seven Gods of Fate and to Enlil and Anu, and then he displays the famous BowStar. When the text again becomes connected the gods sing a hymn of praise to Marduk. Lahmu, Lahamu, and Anshar all proclaimed the names of Marduk. Marduk has just been addressing the gods.]

In Up-shukkinaku he appointed their council for them. They said,
    "Of our son, the Hero, our Avenger,   70
    We will exalt the name by our speech."
They sat down and in their assembly they proclaimed his rank.
Every one of them pronounced his name in the sanctuary.

TABLET VII
One of the 50 Epithets to Marduk
Verily, he holdeth the beginning and the end of them, verily ...
    "He who entered into the middle of Tiâmat resteth not;
    His name shall be 'Nibiru' the seizer of the middle.

He shall set the courses of the stars of the heavens,
He shall herd together the whole company of the gods like sheep.   5
He shall ever take Tiâmat captive, he shall slit up her treasure,
   he shall disembowel her."
Among the men who are to come after a lapse of time,
Let these words be heard without ceasing, may they reign to all eternity,
Because he made the heavenly places and moulded the stable earth.   10
Father Bel proclaimed his name, "Lord of the Lands."
All the Igigi repeated the title.
Ea heard and his liver rejoiced, Saying,
   "He whose title hath rejoiced his fathers
   Shall be even as I am; his name shall be Ea.   15
   He shall dispose of all the magical benefits of my rites,
   He shall make to have effect my instructions."
By the title of "Fifty times" the great gods
Proclaimed his names fifty times, they magnified his going.

DISCUSSION QUESTIONS

1. What do you think the "noise" of the younger generation represents?

2. Look at the places that Nudimmud's name changes back and forth to Ea. When do those changes occur? What is significant about a person's name changing?

3. There are many ways to look at the battle between Marduk and Tiamat—age, sex, and the physical elements of the earth. Explore each of these and think about the ways in which Marduk and Tiamat were matched and the significance of the outcome. Do we see remnants of this outcome today?

4. When Marduk creates the world from Tiamat's body, it's a very violent scene. Likewise, human beings are made from the king of the monsters, Kingu. What does this say about us humans, from the perspective of the gods?

Creation in Egypt

There are several competing creation stories from Egypt, but there's no evidence that this was a concern for the ancient Egyptians. Over the 3,500 years of their history, many profound changes took place—it's not surprising that there are multiple stories and that this presents challenges for modern readers. The following are excerpts from the Heliopolis Creation Story, the Memphis Creation Story, Stories of the Afterlife, and the Hermopolis Creation Story.

Heliopolis was an important religious center in ancient times. This myth dates from around 2300 BCE and has been compiled mainly from the *Pyramid Texts*.

Egyptian myth often had political significance—stories were used to support the divinity of the pharaoh and his right to rule. In this case, around 700 BCE, a pharaoh named Shabaka is said to have discovered an old papyrus that contained an account of creation. He had this engraved on a stone—we now refer to this as the Shabaka Stone. Since 1805 it has been in the British Museum. It was long thought to be simply a millstone. Scholars studied this stone and discovered that the inscriptions date to 1300–1075 BCE, hundreds of years before Shabaka ruled. The text refers to a god of Memphis named P'tah, the supreme god.

There are several stories on the stone, but only three can be read. One of them contains the text of a creation story. Referred to as the "Memphite Theology," this version claimed the story from Heliopolis was actually part of a creation by Ptah, a supreme deity and creative force in the universe. In this way, the previous story was not false, but merely part of P'tah's design.

In this version, Ptah existed before the Ennead (the original nine deities). Ptah was the primal mound—clump of earth—on which Atum stood. Then Ptah created Atum and the other gods; this method has a single creator god causing the world to begin by the power of this thought and words.

The Hermopolis creation myth is similar to the story from Heliopolis, but a few additions have been made. Another group of deities are introduced here—the Ogdoad (eight)—and this group of four male–female pairs serve the purpose of creating order from chaos. The elements they represent include primordial waters, infinity/formlessness, darkness, and hiddenness. The males had the heads of frogs; the females had heads of snakes. There are a variety of roles for the creator god in this myth—Atum, Amun, Ra, or Thoth. In one version he is born from a lotus blossom, then creates the Ogdoad, followed by the Ennead. Another version has the creator hatching from a cosmic egg. These deities retreat to the underworld after creation but they continued to take part in maintaining order. They are cited as being responsible for the flooding of the Nile, the rising of the sun, and supporting all life in general. The Ogdoad includes: Nun and Naunet (water), Amun and Amaunet (hiddenness), Heh and Hauhet (infinity), and Kek and Kauket (darkness).

HELIOPOLIS CREATION STORY

At the beginning the world was a waste of water called Nu (Nun) and it was the abode of the Great Father. He was Nu, for he was the deep, and he gave being unto the sun god who hath said: "Lo! I am Khepera at dawn, Ra at high noon, and Tum (Atum) at eventide." The god of brightness first appeared as a shining egg which floated upon the water's breast, and the spirits of the deep, who were the Fathers and the Mothers, were with him there, as he was with Nu, for they were the companions of Nu.

Now Ra was greater than Nu from whom he arose. He was the divine father and strong ruler of gods, and those whom he first created, according to his desire, were Shu, the wind god, and his consort Tefnut, who had the head of a lioness and was called "The Spitter" because she sent the rain. In aftertime these two deities shone as stars amidst the constellations of heaven, and they were called "The Twins."

Then came into being Seb (Geb), the earth god, and Nut, the goddess of the firmament, who became the parents of Osiris and his consort Isis and also of Set and his consort Nepthys. Ra spake at the beginning of Creation, and bade the earth and the heavens to rise out of the waste of water. In the brightness of his majesty they appeared, and Shu, the uplifter, raised Nut upon high. She formed the vault, which is arched over Seb, the god of earth, who lies prostrate beneath her from where, at the eastern horizon, she is poised upon her toes to where, at the western horizon, bending down with outstretched arms, she rests upon her finger tips. In the darkness are beheld the stars which sparkle upon her body and over her great unwearied limbs.

When Ra, according to his desire, uttered the deep thoughts of his mind, that which he named had being. When he gazed into space, that which he desired to see appeared before him. He created all

Source: Donald MacKenzie. *Egyptian Myth and Legend,* 1907.

things that move in the waters and upon the dry land. Now, mankind were born from his eye, and Ra, the Creator, who was ruler of the gods, became the first king upon earth. He went about among men; he took form like unto theirs, and to him the centuries were as years.

MEMPHIS CREATION STORY

There took shape in the heart, there took shape on the tongue the form of Atum. For the very great one is Ptah, who gave [life] to all the gods and their kas through this heart and through this tongue, in which Horus had taken shape as Ptah, in which Thoth had taken shape as Ptah.

Thus heart and tongue rule over all the limbs in accordance with the teaching that it (the heart, or: he, Ptah) is in every body and it (the tongue, or: he Ptah) is in every mouth of all gods, all men, all cattle, all creeping things, whatever lives, thinking whatever it (or: he) wishes and commanding whatever it (or: he) wishes.

His (Ptah's) Ennead is before him as teeth and lips. They are the semen and the hands of Atum. For the Ennead of Atum came into being through his semen and his fingers. But the Ennead is the teeth and the lips in this mouth which pronounced the name of every thing, from which Shu and Tefnut came forth, and which gave birth to the Ennead.

Sight, hearing, breathing—they report to the heart, and it makes every understanding come forth. As to the tongue, it repeats what the heart has devised. Thus all the gods were born and his Ennead was completed. For every word of the god came about through what the heart devised and the tongue commanded.

Thus all the faculties were made and all the qualities determined, they that make all foods and all provisions, through this word, to him who does what is loved, to him who does what is hated. Thus life is given to the peaceful and death is given to the criminal. Thus all labor, all crafts are made, the action of the hands, the motion of the legs, the movements of all the limbs, according to this command which is devised by the heart and comes forth on the tongue and creates the performance of everything.

Thus it is said of Ptah: "He who made all and created the gods. And he is Ta-tenen (the risen land), who gave birth to the gods, and from whom everything came forth, foods, provisions, divine offerings, all good things. Thus is recognized and understood that he is the mightiest of the gods. Thus Ptah was satisfied after he had made all things and all divine words."

He gave birth to the gods,
He made the towns,
He established the nomes,
He placed the gods in their shrines,
He settled their offerings,
He established their shrines,
He made their bodies according to their wishes.
Thus the gods entered into their bodies,
Of every wood, every stone, every clay,
Everything that grows upon him
In which they came to be.
Thus were gathered to him all the gods and their kas,
Content, united with the Lord of the Two Lands.

It is believed that the line, "Thus life is given to the peaceful and death is given to the criminal," refers to the Egyptian concept of judgment and the afterlife.

Source: Miriam Lichtheim. *Ancient Egyptian Literature,* 1973.

Egyptian Afterlife

Due to their practice of mummification, it may appear as though the Egyptians had a fascination with death; but more accurately, they loved life and felt despair when contemplating its end. The Egyptians were aware of man's vulnerability in the face of nature—death was beyond their control and they recognized this, so they found comfort in the hope of an afterlife. To ensure safe passage one must be mummified, and also be prepared by following the instructions of the Book of the Dead.

The Book of the Dead is not a single book but refers to scrolls containing spells and rituals for the purpose of guiding a deceased person through the judgment process in the afterlife. These scrolls were buried with the body. Osiris, as lord of the underworld, was also judge of the dead, but there were many trials one faced to ensure successful passage to reach him.

It was believed that the body contains something called *ka*—the life force, or essence, the self, and this must be preserved in the afterlife so it could reunite with the *ba* (often depicted as a bird with a human head) which was what they called the personality or what we might call the soul, to create something called the *akh*—the perfect spirit that could enjoy the afterlife. The process of mummification took seventy days and was a series of seventy-five ritual acts that would transform the corpse into a vessel for the *ka*.

After preparation and burial, the next stage was said to be a dangerous journey for the spirit. The way to the afterlife was believed to be a series of challenges and struggles, a perilous journey for the soul. It mirrored the movement of the sun each day, passing through darkness to emerge once again. They believed that death was not the end, but the beginning of a journey that could end with the soul reaching paradise—or it could end with the equivalent of a second, real death.

This decision was made in a place they called the Hall of Two Truths, or the Hall of Judgment. The hieroglyphic script on the Book of the Dead gave directions and served as protection on this journey. These scrolls contained special incantations and information about the journey to the afterlife.

Anubis, god of the dead, depicted with the head of a jackal, would greet souls as they arrived. He was both the guardian and guide; it was also his job to make sure the person reached the place of judgment. The ultimate goal was to be judged worthy to proceed on to the Field of Reeds—paradise, the place of eternal life.

In addition to the possibility of facing monsters and demons and other trials in the afterlife, the deceased also faced forty-two gods at forty-two separate doors and at each one the person would have to prove his worth and deny having committed sins. It wasn't a process of confession, it was more like a denial of wrongdoing such as not lying, cheating, killing, and so on. This indicates that one must have lived a good, moral life in order to be worthy of the afterlife. It is also sometimes called the "negative confessions." This would give the deceased person a clean slate, a clear conscience.

After those responses were completed successfully, the deceased moved forward, and when the series was complete he would meet the god Horus, the final escort to the Hall of Judgment. This is where Anubis would weigh the heart against the feather of the goddess Ma'at (truth). The heart was the most important organ in the body; it was believed that this is where the soul lived. It was left in the body during mummification; it was the person's essence and total being, the seat of the mind. All one's deeds-both good and bad-were kept there. At this point the person handed over his heart scarab, a type of amulet included with burial.

The heart scarab was usually a stone shaped like a scarab beetle, inscribed with a spell from the Book of the Dead and was intended to prevent the heart from revealing too much—a way to keep secrets. This wasn't a form of cheating but, rather, good preparation—a way to make peace with one's emotions. The spell it contained was supposed to help the person pass that final judgment, allowing for passage into the afterlife.

When the heart was placed on the scales opposite the feather, the heart shouldn't be heavier; yet, it shouldn't be too light, either. Actually, balance was the goal. Hearts that were too heavy were eaten by a creature called Ammit—the Devourer of Souls. She was a monster, a combination of creatures depicted with the head of a crocodile and also part lion and part hippo. She would consume anyone found guilty in the Hall of Judgment. If one's heart were eaten, that was the end of existence. This was the worst possible fate one could imagine.

If a person's heart passed the test, then he or she would be guided by Horus into the presence of Osiris to achieve immortality.

© Jacqueline Gray

The Avesta (Zoroastrian)

The structure of *The Avesta* is a series of conversations between the leader of the religious movement, Zarathustra, and the god of wisdom, Ahura Mazda. Zarathustra, or Zoroaster, as he is more commonly known, can be compared to other prophets, like Buddah or Muhammad, who receive word from a heavenly figure. Zoroastrianism is the name of the religious movement that Zarathustra began, having received instruction from Ahura Mazda.

The Persian belief system of Zoroastrianism relies on Dualism, the idea that there exists a good creative force, and an evil destructive force who continually battle for control of our universe. In Zoroastrianism, these beings are Ahura Mazda (light, wisdom, goodness), and Ahriman (darkness, death, destruction). Zarathustra was interested in the natural world and the elements that we live by. The translator of the text, Darmesteter, writes of Zarathustra's methods, "He sees good and evil, life and death, sickness and health, right and wrong, engaged in almost equal conflict. He sees in the sun the origin of light and heat, the source of comfort and life to man. Thus, he institutes the doctrine of Dualism and the worship of Fire."

The text written after these conversations, *The Avesta,* consists of five parts, full of hymns, devotionals to gods and angels, and "the Vendîdâd," which tells of the creation of the earth, the forces of good and evil, and the first man, Yima. The texts of *The Avesta* that we can read today have been pieced together from the era of Sāsānian kings of the third century CE. Supposedly, when Alexander the Great conquered Persia, the original texts of *The Avesta* were destroyed.

THE CREATION OF THE SIXTEEN GOOD LANDS

Ahura Mazda spoke to Zarathustra, saying:

"I have made every land dear to its people, even though it had no charms whatever in it: had I not made every land dear to its people, even though it had no charms whatever in it, then the whole living world would have invaded the Airyana Vaêgô.

The first of the good lands and countries which I, Ahura Mazda, created, was the Airyana Vaêgô, by the Vanguhi Dâitya. Thereupon came Ahriman, who is all death, and he counter-created the serpent in the river and Winter, a work of the Devas. There are ten winter months there, two summer months; and those are cold for the waters, cold for the earth, cold for the trees. Winters fall there, the worst of all plagues.

The second of the good lands and countries which I, Ahura Mazda, created, was the plain which the Sughdhas inhabit. Thereupon came Ahriman, who is all death, and he counter-created the locust, which brings death unto cattle and plants.

The third of the good lands and countries which I, Ahura Mazda, created, was the strong, holy Môuru. Thereupon came Ahriman, who is all death, and he counter-created plunder and sin.

The fourth of the good lands and countries which I, Ahura Mazda, created, was the beautiful Bâkhdhi with high-lifted banners. Thereupon came Ahriman, who is all death, and he counter-created the ants and the ant-hills.

The fifth of the good lands and countries which I, Ahura Mazda, created, was Nisâya, that lies between Môuru and Bâkhdhi. Thereupon came Ahriman, who is all death, and he counter-created the sin of unbelief.

The sixth of the good lands and countries which I, Ahura Mazda, created, was the house-deserting Harôyu. Thereupon came Ahriman, who is all death, and he counter-created tears and wailing.

The seventh of the good lands and countries which I, Ahura Mazda, created, was Vaêkereta, of the evil shadows. Thereupon came Ahriman, who is all death, and he counter-created the Pairika Knâthaiti, who clave unto Keresâspa.

The eighth of the good lands and countries which I, Ahura Mazda, created, was Urva of the rich pastures. Thereupon came Ahriman, who is all death, and he counter-created the sin of pride.

The ninth of the good lands and countries which I, Ahura Mazda, created, was Khnenta which the Vehrkânas inhabit. Thereupon came Ahriman, who is all death, and he counter-created a sin for which there is no atonement, the unnatural sin.

The tenth of the good lands and countries which I, Ahura Mazda, created, was the beautiful Harahvaiti. Thereupon came Ahriman, who is all death, and he counter-created a sin for which there is no atonement, the burying of the dead.

The eleventh of the good lands and countries which I, Ahura Mazda, created, was the bright, glorious Haêtumant. Thereupon came Ahriman, who is all death, and he counter-created the evil work of witchcraft. And this is the sign by which it is known, this is that by which it is seen at once: wheresoever they may go and raise a cry of sorcery, there the worst works of witchcraft go forth. From there they come to kill and strike at heart, and they bring locusts as many as they want.

Source: James Darmestetter. *The Zend-Avesta in Sacred Books of the East,* 1900.

The twelfth of the good lands and countries which I, Ahura Mazda, created, was Ragha of the three races. Thereupon came Ahriman, who is all death, and he counter-created the sin of utter unbelief.

The thirteenth of the good lands and countries which I, Ahura Mazda, created, was the strong, holy Kakhra. Thereupon came Ahriman, who is all death, and he counter-created a sin for which there is no atonement, the cooking of corpses.

The fourteenth of the good lands and countries which I, Ahura Mazda, created, was the four-cornered Varena, for which was born Thraêtaona, who smote Azi Dahâka. Thereupon came Ahriman, who is all death, and he counter-created abnormal issues in women and barbarian oppression.

The fifteenth of the good lands and countries which I, Ahura Mazda, created, was the Seven Rivers. Thereupon came Ahriman, who is all death, and he counter-created abnormal issues in women and excessive heat.

The sixteenth of the good lands and countries which I, Ahura Mazda, created, was the land by the sources of the Rangha, where people live who have no chiefs. Thereupon came Ahriman, who is all death, and he counter-created Winter, a work of the Devas.

There are still other lands and countries, beautiful and deep, longing and asking for the good, and bright."

The Myth of the First Man Yima

Zarathustra asked Ahura Mazda, "O Ahura Mazda, most beneficent Spirit, Maker of the material world, thou Holy One! Who was the first mortal, before myself, Zarathustra, with whom thou, Ahura Mazda, didst converse, whom thou didst teach the Religion of Ahura, the Religion of Zarathustra?"

Ahura Mazda answered, "The fair Yima, the good shepherd, O holy Zarathustra! He was the first mortal, before thee, Zarathustra, with whom I, Ahura Mazda, did converse, whom I taught the Religion of Ahura, the Religion of Zarathustra.

Unto him, O Zarathustra, I, Ahura Mazda, spake, saying, 'Well, fair Yima, son of Vîvanghat, be thou the preacher and the bearer of my Religion!'

And the fair Yima, O Zarathustra, replied unto me, saying, 'I was not born, I was not taught to be the preacher and the bearer of thy Religion.'

Then I, Ahura Mazda, said thus unto him, O Zarathustra, 'Since thou dost not consent to be the preacher and the bearer of my Religion, then make thou my world increase, make my world grow: consent thou to nourish, to rule, and to watch over my world.'

And the fair Yima replied unto me, O Zarathustra, saying: 'Yes! I will make thy world increase, I will make thy world grow. Yes! I will nourish, and rule, and watch over thy world. There shall be, while I am king, neither cold wind nor hot wind, neither disease nor death.'

Then I, Ahura Mazda, brought two implements unto him: a golden seal and a poniard inlaid with gold. Behold, here Yima bears the royal sway! Thus, under the sway of Yima, three hundred winters passed away, and the earth was replenished with flocks and herds, with men and dogs and birds and with red blazing fires, and there was room no more for flocks, herds, and men.

Then I warned the fair Yima, saying: 'O fair Yima, son of Vîvanghat, the earth has become full of flocks and herds, of men and dogs and birds and of red blazing fires, and there is room no more for flocks, herds, and men.'

Then Yima stepped forward, in light, southwards, on the way of the sun, and afterwards he pressed the earth with the golden seal, and bored it with the poniard, speaking thus: 'O Spenta Ârmaiti, kindly open asunder and stretch thyself afar, to bear flocks and herds and men.'

And Yima made the earth grow larger by one-third than it was before, and there came flocks and herds and men, at their will and wish, as many as he wished. Thus, under the sway of Yima, six hundred winters passed away, and the earth was replenished with flocks and herds, with men and dogs and birds and with red blazing fires, and there was room no more for flocks, herds, and men.

And I warned the fair Yima, saying: 'O fair Yima, son of Vîvanghat, the earth has become full of flocks and herds, of men and dogs and birds and of red blazing fires, and there is room no more for flocks, herds, and men.'

Then Yima stepped forward, in light, southwards, on the way of the sun, and afterwards he pressed the earth with the golden seal, and bored it with the poniard, speaking thus: 'O Spenta Ârmaiti, kindly open asunder and stretch thyself afar, to bear flocks and herds and men.'

And Yima made the earth grow larger by two-thirds than it was before, and there came flocks and herds and men, at their will and wish, as many as he wished. Thus, under the sway of Yima, nine hundred winters passed away, and the earth was replenished with flocks and herds, with men and dogs and birds and with red blazing fires, and there was room no more for flocks, herds, and men.

And I warned the fair Yima, saying: 'O fair Yima, son of Vîvanghat, the earth has become full of flocks and herds, of men and dogs and birds and of red blazing fires, and there is room no more for flocks, herds, and men.'

Then Yima stepped forward, in light, southwards, on the way of the sun, and afterwards he pressed the earth with the golden seal, and bored it with the poniard, speaking thus: 'O Spenta Ârmaiti, kindly open asunder and stretch thyself afar, to bear flocks and herds and men.'

And Yima made the earth grow larger by three-thirds than it was before, and there came flocks and herds and men, at their will and wish, as many as he wished."

DISCUSSION QUESTIONS

1. So much of the focus on the "Creations of the Sixteen Good Lands" is on sin, suffering, and anarchy. Why might Ahura Mazda call these "the good lands" amid such chaos?

2. Is there an order of progression as the Sixteen Lands are created?

3. Why does Yima seem to have been chosen by Ahura Mazda?

4. What is Yima's role in creation?

The Hebrew Creation Story of Genesis

The Old Testament of the King James Version of the Bible

The books Genesis, Exodus, Leviticus, Numbers, and Deuteronomy make up The Pentateuch (a Greek term, meaning "five scrolls"). It is also known as The Torah (which means "the law"). The text of The Pentateuch was written in Hebrew, and called "The Five Books of Moses." Moses is a prophet not unlike the Buddha or Muhammad or Jesus in importance to his faith. It was believed that God spoke directly to him and no one else, and that he was the man to whom the entire Torah was ascribed.

The Pentateuch was created by priestly scholars during the Jewish exile in an effort to keep spirits up and to preserve the beliefs of the people. The stories that were agreed to be told are in narrative form and relate their beliefs about everything from the creation of the universe, to Israel's entrance to the "promised land." Moses' death in Deuteronomy marks the end of the narrative, the purpose of which is to tell the story of the Holy Lord. When the Jews returned from their exile, the Pentateuch was complete and many pieces of writing emerge to allow us to date the written word of these first five books between 1000 BCE–500 BCE.

In the following three chapters, we are shown the creation of the universe and the earth, of the animals that inhabit it, and of man and woman. Pay attention to God's style of creation by Thought and Voice and notice patterns of repetition that are present in these verses.

THE FIRST BOOK OF MOSES: CALLED GENESIS

Chapter 1 (Verses 1-31)

In the beginning God created the heavens and the earth.
And the earth was without form, and void; and darkness was upon the face of the deep.
   And the Spirit of God moved upon the face of the waters.
And God said, Let there be light: and there was light.
And God saw the light, that it was good: and God divided the light from the darkness.
And God called the light Day, and the darkness he called Night. And the evening and the
   morning were the first day.   5
And God said, Let there be a firmament in the midst of the waters, and let it divide the waters
   from the waters.
And God made the firmament, and divided the waters which were under the firmament from
   the waters which were above the firmament: and it was so.
And God called the firmament Heaven. And the evening and the morning were the second day.
And God said, Let the waters under the heaven be gathered together unto one place, and let
   the dry land appear: and it was so.
And God called the dry land Earth; and the gathering together of the waters called the Seas:
   and God saw that it was good.   10
And God said, Let the earth bring forth grass, the herb yielding seed, and the fruit tree yielding
   fruit after his kind, whose seed is in itself, upon the earth: and it was so.
And the earth brought forth grass, and herb yielding seed after his kind, and the tree yielding
   fruit, whose seed was in itself, after his kind: and God saw that it was good.
And the evening and the morning were the third day.

Source: The King James Bible

And God said, Let there be lights in the firmament of the heaven to divide the day from the night; and let them be for signs, and for seasons, and for days, and years:

And let them be for lights in the firmament of the heaven to give light upon the earth: and it was so. 15

And God made two great lights; the greater light to rule the day, and the lesser light to rule the night: he made the stars also.

And God set them in the firmament of the heaven to give light upon the earth,

And to rule over the day and over the night, and to divide the light from the darkness: and God saw that it was good.

And the evening and the morning were the fourth day.

And God said, Let the waters bring forth abundantly the moving creature that hath life, and fowl that may fly above the earth in the open firmament of heaven. 20

And God created great whales, and every living creature that moveth, which the waters brought forth abundantly, after their kind, and every winged fowl after his kind: and God saw that it was good.

And God blessed them, saying, Be fruitful, and multiply, and fill the waters in the seas, and let fowl multiply in the earth.

And the evening and the morning were the fifth day.

And God said, Let the earth bring forth the living creature after his kind, cattle, and creeping thing, and beast of the earth after his kind: and it was so.

And God made the beast of the earth after his kind, and cattle after their kind, and every thing that creepeth upon the earth after his kind: and God saw that it was good. 25

And God said, Let us make man in our image, after our likeness: and let them have dominion over the fish of the sea, and over the fowl of the air, and over the cattle, and over all the earth, and over every creeping thing that creepeth upon the earth.

So God created man in his own image, in the image of God created he him; male and female created he them.

And God blessed them, and God said unto them, Be fruitful, and multiply, and replenish the earth, and subdue it: and have dominion over the fish of the sea, and over the fowl of the air, and over every living thing that moveth upon the earth.

And God said, Behold, I have given you every herb bearing seed, which is upon the face of all the earth, and every tree, in the which is the fruit of a tree yielding seed; to you it shall be for meat.

And to every beast of the earth, and to every fowl of the air, and to every thing that creepeth upon the earth, wherein there is life, I have given every green herb for meat: and it was so. 30

And God saw every thing that he had made, and, behold, it was very good. And the evening and the morning were the sixth day.

Chapter 2 (Verses 1-25)

Thus the heavens and the earth were finished, and all the host of them.

And on the seventh day God ended his work which he had made; and he rested on the seventh day from all his work which he had made.

And God blessed the seventh day, and sanctified it: because that in it he had rested from all his work which God created and made.

These are the generations of the heavens and of the earth when they were created, in the day that the Lord God made the earth and the heavens,

And every plant of the field before it was in the earth, and every herb of the field before it grew: for the Lord God had not caused it to rain upon the earth, and there was not a man to till the ground. 5

But there went up a mist from the earth, and watered the whole face of the ground.

And the Lord God formed man of the dust of the ground, and breathed into his nostrils the breath of life; and man became a living soul.

And the Lord God planted a garden eastward in Eden; and there he put the man whom he had formed.

And out of the ground made the Lord God to grow every tree that is pleasant to the sight, and good for food; the tree of life also in the midst of the garden, and the tree of knowledge of good and evil.

And a river went out of Eden to water the garden; and from thence it was parted, and became into four heads.   10

The name of the first is Pison: that is it which compasseth the whole land of Havilah, where there is gold;

And the gold of that land is good: there is bdellium and the onyx stone.

And the name of the second river is Gihon: the same is it that compasseth the whole land of Ethiopia.

And the name of the third river is Hiddekel: that is it which goeth toward the east of Assyria. And the fourth river is Euphrates.

And the Lord God took the man, and put him into the garden of Eden to dress it and to keep it.   15

And the Lord God commanded the man, saying, Of every tree of the garden thou mayest freely eat:

But of the tree of the knowledge of good and evil, thou shalt not eat of it: for in the day that thou eatest thereof thou shalt surely die.

And the Lord God said, It is not good that the man should be alone; I will make him an help meet for him.

And out of the ground the Lord God formed every beast of the field, and every fowl of the air; and brought them unto Adam to see what he would call them: and whatsoever Adam called every living creature, that was the name thereof.

And Adam gave names to all cattle, and to the fowl of the air, and to every beast of the field; but for Adam there was not found an help meet for him.   20

And the Lord God caused a deep sleep to fall upon Adam, and he slept: and he took one of his ribs, and closed up the flesh instead thereof;

And the rib, which the Lord God had taken from man, made he a woman, and brought her unto the man.

And Adam said, This is now bone of my bones, and flesh of my flesh: she shall be called Woman, because she was taken out of Man.

Therefore shall a man leave his father and his mother, and shall cleave unto his wife: and they shall be one flesh.

And they were both naked, the man and his wife, and were not ashamed.   25

Chapter 3 (Verses 1-24)

Now the serpent was more subtle than any beast of the field which the Lord God had made. And he said unto the woman, Yea, hath God said, Ye shall not eat of every tree of the garden?

And the woman said unto the serpent, We may eat of the fruit of the trees of the garden:

But of the fruit of the tree which is in the midst of the garden, God hath said, Ye shall not eat of it, neither shall ye touch it, lest ye die.

And the serpent said unto the woman, Ye shall not surely die:

For God doth know that in the day ye eat thereof, then your eyes shall be opened, and ye shall be as gods, knowing good and evil.   5

And when the woman saw that the tree was good for food, and that it was pleasant to the eyes, and a tree to be desired to make one wise, she took of the fruit thereof, and did eat, and gave also unto her husband with her; and he did eat.

And the eyes of them both were opened, and they knew that they were naked; and they sewed fig leaves together, and made themselves aprons.

And they heard the voice of the Lord God walking in the garden in the cool of the day: and Adam and his wife hid themselves from the presence of the Lord God amongst the trees of the garden.

And the Lord God called unto Adam, and said unto him, Where art thou?

And he said, I heard thy voice in the garden, and I was afraid, because I was naked; and I hid myself.   10

And he said, Who told thee that thou wast naked? Hast thou eaten of the tree, whereof I commanded thee that thou shouldest not eat?

And the man said, The woman whom thou gavest to be with me, she gave me of the tree, and I did eat.

And the Lord God said unto the woman, What is this that thou hast done? And the woman said, The serpent beguiled me, and I did eat.

And the Lord God said unto the serpent, Because thou hast done this, thou art cursed above all cattle, and above every beast of the field; upon thy belly shalt thou go, and dust shalt thou eat all the days of thy life:

And I will put enmity between thee and the woman, and between thy seed and her seed; it shall bruise thy head, and thou shalt bruise his heel.   15

Unto the woman he said, I will greatly multiply thy sorrow and thy conception; in sorrow thou shalt bring forth children; and thy desire shall be to thy husband, and he shall rule over thee.

And unto Adam he said, Because thou hast hearkened unto the voice of thy wife, and hast eaten of the tree, of which I commanded thee, saying, Thou shalt not eat of it: cursed is the ground for thy sake; in sorrow shalt thou eat of it all the days of thy life;

Thorns also and thistles shall it bring forth to thee; and thou shalt eat the herb of the field;

In the sweat of thy face shalt thou eat bread, till thou return unto the ground; for out of it wast thou taken: for dust thou art, and unto dust shalt thou return.

And Adam called his wife's name Eve; because she was the mother of all living.   20

Unto Adam also and to his wife did the Lord God make coats of skins, and clothed them.

And the Lord God said, Behold, the man is become as one of us, to know good and evil: and now, lest he put forth his hand, and take also of the tree of life, and eat, and live for ever:

Therefore the Lord God sent him forth from the garden of Eden, to till the ground from whence he was taken.

So he drove out the man; and he placed at the east of the garden of Eden Cherubims, and a flaming sword which turned every way, to keep the way of the tree of life.

DISCUSSION QUESTIONS

1. Genesis tells the creation of man three different times (see 1:27, 2:20, and 5:1 "When God created humankind, he made them in the likeness of God. Male and female he created them, and he blessed them and named them 'Humankind' when they were created."). What is different about each of these creations? Why are these differences significant?

2. What does the "tree of knowledge of good and evil" come to symbolize in this story?

3. Is there a sense to the order of the creation of the universe and the beings created?

4. Knowing that this story was told during the exile of the Jewish people, are there traits that seem particularly comforting or useful to those who are wandering, but faithful?

The Story of Creation in the Qur'an

The Qur'an is the holy text of the Muslim world. Sometimes in English we see the title spelled *Koran*, but the more correct pronunciation and Arabic-to-English rendering is indeed Qur'an. The Qur'an is compiled of 114 Suras, each containing many verses. A Sura is much like a chapter, in that it contains material about a story or lesson and verses are often memorized and recited. Islam is the religion and Muslims are the people who practice the religion. It is important to treat all of our texts with respect, and that means knowing and using the correct language when speaking about them.

The Qur'an is looked to as the true word of God, as revealed to the Prophet Muhammad. In 570 CE, Muhammad was born in Mecca. He worked in trade and he married. Muhammad was always a spiritual man who had much knowledge about the current religions of his world (Christianity and Judaism were practiced, as well as many tribal religions) and spent much time meditating. One night in 610 CE while he meditated at Mount Hira, outside of Mecca, the angel Jibreel (or Gabriel) descended and ordered Muhammad to "recite." Muhammad began to speak what he believed were the words of Allah. Jibreel visited him several times throughout Muhammad's life and each time the messages were recorded and became the holy text. Muhammad died in 632 CE.

It is difficult and perhaps not intended for a reader to begin at Sura 1 and finish with Sura 114 in chronological order. There is not an order to the subjects or stories. It is, as one translator stresses "above all a book of guidance, each sura adds to the fuller picture and to the effectiveness of the guidance." Another stylistic point of interest is that God speaks directly and often employs the royal "We" to represent himself (i.e., "We created you" when it was just one person who created).

The word "qur'an" actually means "reading/reciting" and it adds to the experience of the verses to listen to them being read. Muslim schoolchildren participate in recitation contests and the Qur'an is recited many times a day in predominantly Muslim countries.

The portions of the Qur'an that follow are verses that mention the creation of the earth, the creation of men and women, and the story of Adam and his wife being thrown out of the garden.

THE STORY OF CREATION

Sura 7: The Heights (Verses 52-57)

Your Lord is God, who in six days created the Heavens and the Earth, and then mounted the throne: He throws the veil of night over the day: it pursues it swiftly: and he created the sun and the moon and the stars, subjected to laws by His behest: Is not all creation and its empire His? Blessed be God the Lord of the Worlds! Call upon your Lord with lowliness and in secret, for He loves not transgressors. And commit not disorders on the earth after it hath been well ordered; and call on Him with fear and longing desire: Verily the mercy of God is nigh unto the righteous. And He it is who sends forth the winds as the heralds of his compassion, until they bring up the laden clouds, which we drive along to some dead land and send down water thereon, by which we cause an upgrowth of all kinds of fruit.—Thus will we bring forth the dead. Haply you will reflect. In a rich soil, its plants spring forth abundantly by the will of its Lord, and in that which is bad, they spring forth but scantily. Thus do We diversify our signs for those who are thankful.

Source: Rodwell, J.M. (translator). *The Quran,* 1909.

Sura 16: The Bee (Verses 3-16)

He hath created the Heavens and the Earth to set forth his truth; high let Him be exalted above the gods they join with Him! Man hath He created from a moist germ; yet lo! man is an open caviller. And the cattle! for you He created them: in them you have warm garments and gainful uses; and of them you eat: And they beseem you well when you fetch them home and when you drive them forth to pasture: And they carry your burdens to lands which you could not else reach but with travail of soul: truly your Lord is full of goodness, and merciful. And He hath given you horses, mules, and asses, that you may ride them, and for your ornament: and things of which you have no knowledge hath he created.

Of God it is to point out "the Way." Some turn aside from it: but had He pleased, He had guided you all aright. It is He who sendeth down rain out of Heaven: from it is your drink; and from it are the plants by which you pasture. By it He causeth the corn, and the olives, and the palm-trees, and the grapes to spring forth for you, and all kinds of fruits: verily, in this are signs for those who ponder. And He hath subjected to you the night and the day; the sun and the moon and the stars too are subjected to you by his behest; verily, in this are signs for those who understand: And all of varied hues that He hath created for you over the earth: verily, in this are signs for those who remember.

And He it is who hath subjected the sea to you, that ye may eat of its fresh fish, and take forth from it ornaments to wear—thou seest the ships ploughing its billows—and that you may go in quest of his bounties, and that you might give thanks. And He has thrown firm mountains on the earth, lest it move with you; and rivers and paths for your guidance, And way marks. By the stars too are men guided.

Sura 41: Verses Made Plain (Verses 8-11)

Do ye indeed disbelieve in Him who in two days created the earth? and do ye assign Him peers? The Lord of the worlds is He! And he hath placed on the earth the firm mountains which tower above it; and He hath blessed it, and distributed food throughout it, for the cravings of all alike, in four days: Then He applied himself to the Heaven, which then was but smoke: and to it and to the Earth He said, "Come ye, whether in obedience or against your will?" and they both said, "We come obedient." And He made them seven heavens in two days, and in each heaven made known its office: And we furnished the lower heaven with lights and guardian angels. This, the disposition of the Almighty, the All-knowing.

Sura 96: Clots of Blood (Verses 1-5)

Recite, in the name of thy Lord who created;— Created man from Clots of Blood:— Recite thou! For thy Lord is the most Beneficent, Who hath taught the use of the pen;— Hath taught Man that which he knows not.

Sura 78: The News (Verses 8-26)

Have we not made the Earth a couch?
And the mountains its tent-stakes?
We have created you of two sexes,
And ordained your sleep for rest,
And ordained the night as a mantle,
And ordained the day for gaining livelihood,
And built above you seven solid heavens,
And placed therein a burning lamp;
And we send down water in abundance from the rain-clouds,
That we may bring forth by it corn and herbs,

And gardens thick with trees.
Lo! the day of Severance is fixed;
The day when there shall be a blast on the trumpet, and ye shall come in crowds,
And the heaven shall be opened and be full of portals,
And the mountains shall be set in motion, and melt into thin vapour.
Hell truly shall be a place of snares,
The home of transgressors,
To abide therein ages;
No coolness shall they taste therein nor any drink,
Save boiling water and running sores;
Meet recompense!

Sura 6: The Cattle (Verses 2-3)

He it is who created you of clay then decreed the term of your life: and with Him is another prefixed term for the resurrection. Yet have you doubts thereof! And He is God in the Heavens and on the Earth! He knows your secrets and your disclosures! and He knows what you deserve.

Sura 39: The Troops (Verses 6-8)

Had God desired to have had a son, he had surely chosen what he pleased out of his own creation. But praise be to Him! He is God, the One, the Almighty. For truth hath he created the Heavens and the Earth: It is of Him that the night returneth upon the day and that the day returneth upon the night: and He controls the sun and the moon so that each speedes to an appointed goal. Is He not the Mighty, the Gracious? He created you all of one man, from whom He afterwards formed his wife; and of cattle He hath sent down to you four pairs. In the wombs of your mothers did He create you by creation upon creation in triple darkness. It is He who is God your Lord: the kingdom is His: There is no God but He. How then are ye so turned aside from Him?

Sura 7: The Heights (Verses 9-10, 18-24)

And now have we stabilized you on the earth, and given you therein the supports of life. How little do ye give thanks! We created you; then fashioned you[...] "And, O Adam! dwell thou and thy wife in Paradise, and eat ye whence ye will, but to this tree approach not, lest ye become of the unjust doers." Then Satan whispered them to shew them their nakedness, which had been hidden from them both. And he said, "This tree hath your Lord forbidden you, only lest ye should become angels, or lest ye should become immortals." And he swore to them both, "Verily I am giving you good counsel." So he beguiled them by deceits: and when they had tasted of the tree, their nakedness appeared to them, and they began to sew together upon themselves the leaves of the garden. And their Lord called to them, "Did I not forbid you this tree, and did I not say to you, 'Verily, Satan is your declared enemy?'" They said, "O our Lord! With ourselves have we dealt unjustly: if thou forgive us not and have pity on us, we shall surely be of those who perish." He said, "Get ye down, the one of you an enemy to the other; and on earth shall be your dwelling, and your provision for a season." He said, "On it shall ye live, and on it shall ye die, and from it shall ye be taken forth."

1. Examine the various materials used to create humans. What is significant about multiple materials being mentioned in different Suras of the Qur'an?

2. From the sampling of Suras you've been given, what are some of the themes you are able to see in how Allah speaks to his followers (and nonbelievers)?

3. Allah calls the world "into obedience." How does this phrase signify Allah's relationship with his creation?

4. Find the passages that discuss "paradise." In what ways is this story similar to the previous story in "Genesis"?

The Eleventh Tablet of the Epic of Gilgamesh — The Deluge

Introduction

For more on the history of *The Epic of Gilgamesh*, see the Heroes Section.

The flood myth contained in the eleventh tablet of *The Epic of Gilgamesh* is fascinating because of its age, its thoroughness, and its connection to subsequent flood myths. The specific age of the story is difficult to pinpoint, but through archaeological evidence of the stone tablets, and the understanding that stories were told in oral form long before they were written, scholars guess that *Gilgamesh* has been told since 2100 BCE. That an entire section of the *Gilgamesh* story was dedicated to the hero pursuing the immortal survivor of this flood is important. Gilgamesh sought out Utanapishtim after the death of his best friend Enkidu; he sought the secret to immortality for himself. Utanapishtim and his wife, both the only known immortals on earth, told Gilgamesh the story of their survival. Thus, Tablet eleven contains Utanapishtim's story of a god warning him of the impending disaster, counseling him on how to build a ship, and the bestowal of immortality on him and his wife.

THE EPIC OF GILGAMESH—THE DELUGE
Tablet XI

Gilgamesh said unto Utanapishtim, to Utanapishtim the remote: 1

> "I am looking at you, Utanapishtim.
> You are not altered; you look as I look.
> Verily, nothing about you is changed; you are just as I.
> Moved is my heart to do battle,   5
> But you are at leisure and lie upon your back.
> How were you able to enter the company of the gods and see life?"

Source: E. A. Wallis Budge. *The Babylonian Story of the Deluge as Told by Assyrian Tablets from Nineveh*, 1920.

Utanapishtim begins to tell Gilgamesh the Story of the Deluge:

Utanapishtim said to Gilgamesh:
    "I will reveal to you, O Gilgamesh, a hidden mystery,   10
    And a secret matter of the gods I will declare
    Shurippak, a city which you yourself know,
    On the bank of the river Euphrates is situated,
    That city was old and the gods dwelling within it—
    Their hearts induced the great gods to make a wind-storm   15
    Their father Anu,
    Their counsellor, the warrior Enlil,
    Their messenger En-urta and
    Their prince Ennugi.
    Nin-igi-azag, Ea, was with them in council and   20
    Reported their word to the house of reeds."

Ea's Call to Utanapishtim (who is sleeping in a reed hut):

    "O House of reeds, O House of reeds! O Wall, O Wall!
    O House of reeds, hear! O Wall, understand!
    O man of Shurippak, son of Ubara-Tutu.   25
    Throw down the house, build a ship,
    Forsake wealth, seek after life,
    Abandon possessions, save thy life,
    Carry grain of every kind into the ship.
    The ship which thou shalt build,   30
    The dimensions thereof shall be measured,
    The breadth and the length thereof shall be the same.
    Provide it with a roof like Apsu."

Utanapishtim answers Ea:

I understood and I said to Ea, my lord: 35
    "I comprehend my lord, that which you have ordered,
    I will regard it with great reverence, and will perform it.
    But what shall I say to the town, to the multitude, and to the elders?"

Ea's Warning of the Deluge:

Ea opened his mouth and spoke   40
And said to his servant, myself,
    "... This is what you say to them:
    The god Enlil has formed ill-will against me,
    Therefore I can no longer dwell in your city,
    And never more will I turn my countenance upon the soil of Enlil.   45
    I will descend into the ocean to dwell with my lord Ea.
    But upon you he will rain riches:
    A catch of birds, a catch of fish
    An abundant harvest,
    In the morning cakes of darkness,   50
    In the evening, a rain of wheat shall fall upon you."

Building the Ship:

As soon as the dawn broke
The countrymen gathered.
The weak man brought bitumen,   55
The strong man brought what tools were needed.
On the fifth day I decided upon its plan.
According to the plan its walls were 10 *Gar** high,
And the circumference of the roof was equally 10 *Gar.*
I measured out the hull and marked it out   60
I cover the deck six times.
Its exterior I divided into seven,
Its interior I divided into nine,
Water bolts I drove into the middle of it.
I provided a steering pole, and fixed what was needed for it,   65
Three *sar*** of bitumen I poured over the inside wall,
Three *sar* of pitch I poured into the inside.
The men who bear loads brought three *sar* of oil,
Besides a *sar* of oil which the offering consumed,
And two *sar* of oil which the boatman hid.   70
I slaughtered oxen for the work people,
I slew sheep every day.
Beer, sesame wine, oil and wine
I made the people drink as if they were water from the river.
I celebrated a feast-day as if it had been New Year's Day.   75
I opened a box of ointment, I laid my hands in unguent.
Before the sunset the ship was finished.
Since the launching was difficult.
The shipbuilders brought the rollers of the ship, above and below,
Two-thirds of it stood clear of the water-line.   80

Loading the Ship:

With everything that I possessed I loaded it.
With everything that I possessed of silver I loaded it.
With everything that I possessed of gold I loaded it.
With all that I possessed of living grain I loaded it.   85
I made to go up into the ship all my family and kinsfolk,
The cattle of the field, the beasts of the field, all handicraftsmen I made them go up into it.
The god Shamash had appointed me a time, saying:
     "The Power of Darkness will at eventide make a rain-flood to fall;
     Then enter into the ship and shut thy door."   90
The appointed time drew nigh;
The Power of Darkness made a rain-flood to fall at eventide.
I watched the coming of the approaching storm,
When I saw it terror possessed me,
I went into the ship and shut my door.   95
To the pilot of the ship, Puzur-Amurru the boatman
I committed the great house, together with the contents thereof.

*10 Gar = 120 cubits; 1 cubit = 1/2 meter
**1 sar or shar = 8,000 gallons

The Abubu (the Cyclone):

As soon as the gleam of dawn shone in the sky
A black cloud from the foundation of heaven came up.   100
Inside it the god Adad thundered,
The gods Nabû and Marduk went before,
Marching as messengers over high land and plain,
Irragal tore out the post of the ship,
En-urta went on, he made the storm to descend.   105
The Anunnaki brandished their torches,
With their glare they lighted up the land.
The cyclone of Adad swept up to heaven.
Every gleam of light was turned into darkness.
The land looked as if Adad had laid it waste.   110
A whole day long the flood descended.
Swiftly it mounted up and the water reached to the mountains.
The water attacked the people like a battle.
Brother saw not brother.
Men could not be recognized from heaven.   115
Even the gods were terrified at the cyclone.
They betook themselves to flight and went up into the heaven of Anu.
The gods crouched like dogs and cowered by the wall.

Ishtar's Lament:

The goddess Ishtar cried out like a woman in labor.   120
The Lady of the Gods lamented with a loud voice:
    "Verily the former dispensation is turned into mud,
    Because I commanded evil among the company of the gods.
    When I commanded evil among the company of the gods,
    I commanded battle for the destruction of my people.   125
    Did I of myself bring forth my people,
    That they might fill the sea like little fishes?"
The gods of the Anunnaki wailed with her.
The gods bowed themselves, and sat down, and wept.
Their lips were shut tight in distress.   130

The Storm Abates:

For six days and nights
The storm raged, and the cyclone overwhelmed the land.
When the seventh day approached the cyclone and the raging flood ceased:
—now it had fought like an army.   135
The sea became quiet and went down, and the cyclone and the rain-storm ceased.
I looked over the sea and a calm had come,
And all mankind were turned into mud,
The land had been laid flat like a terrace.
I opened the air-hole and the light fell upon my face,   140
I bowed myself, I sat down, I cried,
My tears poured down over my cheeks.
I looked over the quarters of the world—open sea!

After twelve days an island appeared.
The ship took its course to the land of Nimush. 145
The mountain of Nimush held the ship, it let it not move.
The first day, the second day, the mountain of Nimush held the ship and let it not move.
The third day, the fourth day, the mountain of Nimush held the ship and let it not move.
The fifth day, the sixth day, the mountain of Nimush held the ship and let it not move.
When the seventh day had come 150
I brought out a dove and let her go free.
The dove flew away and then came back;
Because she had no place to alight on she came back.
I brought out a swallow and let her go free.
The swallow flew away and then came back; 155
Because she had no place to alight on she came back.
I brought out a raven and let her go free.
The raven flew away, she saw the sinking waters.
She ate, she pecked in the ground, she croaked, she came not back.

Utanapishtim Leaves the Ship: 160

Then I brought out everything to the four winds and offered up a sacrifice;
I poured out a libation on the peak of the mountain.
Seven by seven I set out the vessels,
Under them I piled reeds, cedarwood and myrtle.
The gods smelt the savour, 165
The gods smelt the sweet savour.
The gods gathered together like flies over him that sacrificed.

The Gods Discuss the Deluge:

Now when the Lady of the Gods came nigh,
She lifted up the priceless jewels which Anu had made according to her desire, saying: 170
    "O ye gods here present, as I shall never forget the lapis-lazuli jewels of my neck
    So shall I think about these days, and shall forget them nevermore!
    Let the gods come to the offering,
    But let not Enlil come to the offering,
    Because he would not accept counsel and made the cyclone, 175
    And delivered my people over to destruction."
Now when Enlil came near
He saw the ship; then was Enlil wrathful
And he was filled with anger against the gods, the Igigi saying:
    "What kind of a being has escaped with his life? 180
    He shall not remain alive, a man among the destruction!"
Then En-Urta opened his mouth and spake
And said unto the warrior Enlil:
    "Who besides the god Ea can make a plan?
    The god Ea knoweth everything." 185

Ea Chastises Enlil for Making a Cyclone

Ea opened his mouth and spoke
And said unto the warrior Enlil,
   "O Prince among the gods, thou warrior,
   How could you, not accepting counsel, make a cyclone?   190
   He who is sinful, on him lay his sin,
   He who transgresses, on him lay his transgression.
   But be merciful that not everything be destroyed; be long-suffering that
   Man be not blotted out.
   Instead of making a cyclone,   195
   Would that a lion had come and diminished mankind.
   Instead of you making a cyclone,
   Would that a wolf had come and diminished mankind.
   Instead of you making a cyclone
   Would that a famine had arisen and laid waste to the land.   200
   Instead of you making a cyclone
   Would that Urra had risen up and laid waste to the land.
   As for me I have not revealed the secret of the great gods.
   I made Atra-hasis* to see a vision, and thus he heard the secret of the gods.
   Now therefore allow yourself to be counselled."   205

Ea deifies Utanapishtim and his Wife:

Then the god Ea went up into the ship,
He seized me by the hand and brought me forth.
He brought forth my wife and made her to kneel by my side.
He turned our faces towards each other, he stood between us, he blessed us: 210
   "Formerly Utanapishtim was a man merely,
   But now let Utanapishtim and his wife be like unto the gods, ourselves.
   Utanapishtim shall dwell afar off, at the mouth of the rivers."
And they took me away to a place afar off,
and made me to dwell at the mouth of the rivers.   215

*Atra-hasis is an Akkadian flood hero. The god Enki comes to him in a dream and warns him of the impending deluge. His name means "exceedingly wise."

DISCUSSION QUESTIONS

1.   What is the cause of this flood? How do the gods react before, during, and after the deluge?

2.   Consider the other flood myths in this chapter. How does Ea's instructions to Utanapishtim differ from the other flood stories?

3.   Why is Utanapishtim rewarded with immortality? Why might he have been chosen by Ea to build the ship?

The Hebrew Story of the Flood

That there are many similarities between the Genesis story of the flood and the story of the flood as told in Gilgamesh is no surprise. On the surface, the two stories are the same in essentials: both tell the story of a man who is warned and given the task of building a ship to escape a coming flood and they have to endure the harassment of those who say the task is impossible and unnecessary. Both flood stories build their ships with similar materials and when the rain ends, the hero lets out a raven and a dove and offers a sacrifice.

We are told that ten generations have passed since the creation of Adam and Eve and mankind has continued to fall. What is interesting about the Genesis account of the flood is that choice given between good and evil, and that the flood is brought about because God has judged humankind to have fallen from a state of "good" to "wickedness" and is "corrupt with violence."

For more information about the writing of Genesis, see the introduction to the Hebrew Creation Story. The book of Genesis was written approximately 1000 BCE–500 BCE, but was told orally long before it was written.

In the following four chapters from Genesis, note the role of God, the acts taken by Noah, and the promise (or covenant) that God makes with Noah after his family survives.

THE FIRST BOOK OF MOSES CALLED GENESIS (CHAPTERS 6-9)

Chapter 6 (Verses 1-22)

And it came to pass, when men began to multiply on the face of the earth, and daughters were
    born unto them,

That the sons of God saw the daughters of men that they were fair; and they took them wives
    of all which they chose.

And the Lord said, My spirit shall not always strive with man, for that he also is flesh: yet his
    days shall be an hundred and twenty years.

There were giants in the earth in those days; and also after that, when the sons of God came in
    unto the daughters of men, and they bare children to them, the same became mighty men
    which were of old, men of renown.

And God saw that the wickedness of man was great in the earth, and that every imagination of
    the thoughts of his heart was only evil continually.   5

And it repented the Lord that he had made man on the earth, and it grieved him at his heart.

And the Lord said, I will destroy man whom I have created from the face of the earth; both man,
    and beast, and the creeping thing, and the fowls of the air; for it repenteth me that I have
    made them.

But Noah found grace in the eyes of the Lord.

These are the generations of Noah: Noah was a just man and perfect in his generations, and
    Noah walked with God.

And Noah begat three sons, Shem, Ham, and Japheth.   10

The earth also was corrupt before God, and the earth was filled with violence.

And God looked upon the earth, and, behold, it was corrupt; for all flesh had corrupted his way
    upon the earth.

And God said unto Noah, The end of all flesh is come before me; for the earth is filled with
    violence through them; and, behold, I will destroy them with the earth.

Source: King James Bible

Make thee an ark of gopher wood; rooms shalt thou make in the ark, and shalt pitch it within and without with pitch.

And this is the fashion which thou shalt make it of: The length of the ark shall be three hundred cubits, the breadth of it fifty cubits, and the height of it thirty cubits.   15

A window shalt thou make to the ark, and in a cubit shalt thou finish it above; and the door of the ark shalt thou set in the side thereof; with lower, second, and third stories shalt thou make it.

And, behold, I, even I, do bring a flood of waters upon the earth, to destroy all flesh, wherein is the breath of life, from under heaven; and every thing that is in the earth shall die.

But with thee will I establish my covenant; and thou shalt come into the ark, thou, and thy sons, and thy wife, and thy sons' wives with thee.

And of every living thing of all flesh, two of every sort shalt thou bring into the ark, to keep them alive with thee; they shall be male and female.

Of fowls after their kind, and of cattle after their kind, of every creeping thing of the earth after his kind, two of every sort shall come unto thee, to keep them alive.   20

And take thou unto thee of all food that is eaten, and thou shalt gather it to thee; and it shall be for food for thee, and for them.

Thus did Noah; according to all that God commanded him, so did he.

Chapter 7 (Verses 1-24)

And the Lord said unto Noah, Come thou and all thy house into the ark; for thee have I seen righteous before me in this generation.

Of every clean beast thou shalt take to thee by sevens, the male and his female: and of beasts that are not clean by two, the male and his female.

Of fowls also of the air by sevens, the male and the female; to keep seed alive upon the face of all the earth.

For yet seven days, and I will cause it to rain upon the earth forty days and forty nights; and every living substance that I have made will I destroy from off the face of the earth.

And Noah did according unto all that the Lord commanded him.   5

And Noah was six hundred years old when the flood of waters was upon the earth.

And Noah went in, and his sons, and his wife, and his sons' wives with him, into the ark, because of the waters of the flood.

Of clean beasts, and of beasts that are not clean, and of fowls, and of every thing that creepeth upon the earth,

There went in two and two unto Noah into the ark, the male and the female, as God had commanded Noah.

And it came to pass after seven days, that the waters of the flood were upon the earth.   10

In the six hundredth year of Noah's life, in the second month, the seventeenth day of the month, the same day were all the fountains of the great deep broken up, and the windows of heaven were opened.

And the rain was upon the earth forty days and forty nights.

In the selfsame day entered Noah, and Shem, and Ham, and Japheth, the sons of Noah, and Noah's wife, and the three wives of his sons with them, into the ark;

They, and every beast after his kind, and all the cattle after their kind, and every creeping thing that creepeth upon the earth after his kind, and every fowl after his kind, every bird of every sort.

And they went in unto Noah into the ark, two and two of all flesh, wherein is the breath of life.   15

And they that went in, went in male and female of all flesh, as God had commanded him:
and the Lord shut him in.
And the flood was forty days upon the earth; and the waters increased, and bare up the ark,
and it was lift up above the earth.
And the waters prevailed, and were increased greatly upon the earth; and the ark went upon
the face of the waters.
And the waters prevailed exceedingly upon the earth; and all the high hills, that were under
the whole heaven, were covered.
Fifteen cubits upward did the waters prevail; and the mountains were covered.   20
And all flesh died that moved upon the earth, both of fowl, and of cattle, and of beast, and of
every creeping thing that creepeth upon the earth, and every man:
All in whose nostrils was the breath of life, of all that was in the dry land, died.
And every living substance was destroyed which was upon the face of the ground, both man,
and cattle, and the creeping things, and the fowl of the heaven; and they were destroyed
from the earth: and Noah only remained alive, and they that were with him in the ark.
And the waters prevailed upon the earth an hundred and fifty days.

Chapter 8 (Verses 1-22)
And God remembered Noah, and every living thing, and all the cattle that was with him in the
ark: and God made a wind to pass over the earth, and the waters assuaged;
The fountains also of the deep and the windows of heaven were stopped, and the rain from
heaven was restrained;
And the waters returned from off the earth continually: and after the end of the hundred and
fifty days the waters were abated.
And the ark rested in the seventh month, on the seventeenth day of the month, upon the
mountains of Ararat.
And the waters decreased continually until the tenth month: in the tenth month, on the first
day of the month, were the tops of the mountains seen.   5
And it came to pass at the end of forty days, that Noah opened the window of the ark which he
had made:
And he sent forth a raven, which went forth to and fro, until the waters were dried up from off
the earth.
Also he sent forth a dove from him, to see if the waters were abated from off the face of the
ground;
But the dove found no rest for the sole of her foot, and she returned unto him into the ark, for
the waters were on the face of the whole earth: then he put forth his hand, and took her,
and pulled her in unto him into the ark.
And he stayed yet other seven days; and again he sent forth the dove out of the ark;   10
And the dove came in to him in the evening; and, lo, in her mouth was an olive leaf pluckt off:
so Noah knew that the waters were abated from off the earth.
And he stayed yet other seven days; and sent forth the dove; which returned not again unto
him any more.
And it came to pass in the six hundredth and first year, in the first month, the first day of the
month, the waters were dried up from off the earth: and Noah removed the covering of the
ark, and looked, and, behold, the face of the ground was dry.
And in the second month, on the seven and twentieth day of the month, was the earth dried.
And God spake unto Noah, saying,   15
Go forth of the ark, thou, and thy wife, and thy sons, and thy sons' wives with thee.

Bring forth with thee every living thing that is with thee, of all flesh, both of fowl, and of cattle, and of every creeping thing that creepeth upon the earth; that they may breed abundantly in the earth, and be fruitful, and multiply upon the earth.

And Noah went forth, and his sons, and his wife, and his sons' wives with him:

Every beast, every creeping thing, and every fowl, and whatsoever creepeth upon the earth, after their kinds, went forth out of the ark.

And Noah builded an altar unto the Lord; and took of every clean beast, and of every clean fowl, and offered burnt offerings on the altar.   20

And the Lord smelled a sweet savour; and the Lord said in his heart, I will not again curse the ground any more for man's sake; for the imagination of man's heart is evil from his youth; neither will I again smite any more every thing living, as I have done.

While the earth remaineth, seedtime and harvest, and cold and heat, and summer and winter, and day and night shall not cease.

Chapter 9 (Verses 1-29)

And God blessed Noah and his sons, and said unto them, Be fruitful, and multiply, and replenish the earth.

And the fear of you and the dread of you shall be upon every beast of the earth, and upon every fowl of the air, upon all that moveth upon the earth, and upon all the fishes of the sea; into your hand are they delivered.

Every moving thing that liveth shall be meat for you; even as the green herb have I given you all things.

But flesh with the life thereof, which is the blood thereof, shall ye not eat.

And surely your blood of your lives will I require; at the hand of every beast will I require it, and at the hand of man; at the hand of every man's brother will I require the life of man.   5

Whoso sheddeth man's blood, by man shall his blood be shed: for in the image of God made he man.

And you, be ye fruitful, and multiply; bring forth abundantly in the earth, and multiply therein.

And God spake unto Noah, and to his sons with him, saying,

And I, behold, I establish my covenant with you, and with your seed after you;

And with every living creature that is with you, of the fowl, of the cattle, and of every beast of the earth with you; from all that go out of the ark, to every beast of the earth.   10

And I will establish my covenant with you, neither shall all flesh be cut off any more by the waters of a flood; neither shall there any more be a flood to destroy the earth.

And God said, This is the token of the covenant which I make between me and you and every living creature that is with you, for perpetual generations:

I do set my bow in the cloud, and it shall be for a token of a covenant between me and the earth.

And it shall come to pass, when I bring a cloud over the earth, that the bow shall be seen in the cloud:

And I will remember my covenant, which is between me and you and every living creature of all flesh; and the waters shall no more become a flood to destroy all flesh.   15

And the bow shall be in the cloud; and I will look upon it, that I may remember the everlasting covenant between God and every living creature of all flesh that is upon the earth.

And God said unto Noah, This is the token of the covenant, which I have established between me and all flesh that is upon the earth.

And the sons of Noah, that went forth of the ark, were Shem, and Ham, and Japheth: and Ham is the father of Canaan.

These are the three sons of Noah: and of them was the whole earth overspread.

And Noah began to be an husbandman, and he planted a vineyard: 20

And he drank of the wine, and was drunken; and he was uncovered within his tent.

And Ham, the father of Canaan, saw the nakedness of his father, and told his two brethren
   without.
And Shem and Japheth took a garment, and laid it upon both their shoulders, and went
   backward, and covered the nakedness of their father; and their faces were backward, and
   they saw not their father's nakedness.
And Noah awoke from his wine, and knew what his younger son had done unto him.
And he said, Cursed be Canaan; a servant of servants shall he be unto his brethren.   25
And he said, Blessed be the Lord God of Shem; and Canaan shall be his servant.
God shall enlarge Japheth, and he shall dwell in the tents of Shem; and Canaan shall be his
   servant.
And Noah lived after the flood three hundred and fifty years.
And all the days of Noah were nine hundred and fifty years: and he died.

DISCUSSION QUESTIONS

1. Why did the Hebrew God wish to flood the Earth? Compare and contrast these reasons with the other
    flood myths you have read.

2. What is the response that Noah receives when he tells others that he is building an ark?

3. Which seems to be worse: the 40 days and nights of rain, or the 150 days of waiting for the water to
    abate?

4. What is the promise that God makes with Noah after the flood? Compare and contrast this to the other
    gods in the other flood myths.

The Muslim Story of The Flood as told in the Qur'an

Suras 11 & 71

The Qur'an, dictated by the Prophet Muhammad after his first revelation from the angel Jibreel (Gabriel) in 610
CE, tells the story of the flood with a familiar hero: Noah. For more information about Gabriel and the Qur'an,
see the introduction to the Creation Stories of the Qur'an.

The story of the flood is told twice in the Qur'an. Sura 11 tells the story of Nuh's (Noah's) attempts to warn
others, and finding no believers, he sets about building the ark. When the ark is afloat during the storm, his
own son asks to board the ark. Sura 71 is much more focused on the unbelievers' response to Nuh and the
punishment inflicted upon them for not heeding Nuh's warning that Allah would destroy them if they did not
ask for forgiveness for their sins. In both parts, Noah is the believer among disbelievers, and rewarded for his
unwavering faith.

Allah is the speaker in the Suras, and remember that Allah often uses the "Royal We" to describe himself. So
when he says "We sent Nuh" that means "He sent Nuh."

SURA 11: THE HOLY PROPHET

And certainly We sent Nuh to his people: "Surely I am a plain warner for you: That you shall not serve any but Allah, surely I fear for you the punishment of a painful day."

But the chiefs of those who disbelieved from among his people said: "We do not consider you but a mortal like ourselves, and we do not see any have followed you but those who are the meanest of us at first thought and we do not see in you any excellence over us; nay, we deem you liars."

He said: "O my people! tell me if I have with me clear proof from my Lord, and He has granted me mercy from Himself and it has been made obscure to you; shall we constrain you to (accept) it while you are averse from it? And, O my people! I ask you not for wealth in return for it; my reward is only with Allah and I am not going to drive away those who believe; surely they shall meet their Lord, but I consider you a people who are ignorant: And, O my people! who will help me against Allah if I drive them away? Will you not then mind? And I do not say to you that I have the treasures of Allah and I do not know the unseen, nor do I say that I am an angel, nor do I say about those whom your eyes hold in mean estimation (that) Allah will never grant them (any) good—Allah knows best what is in their souls—for then most surely I should be of the unjust."

They said: "O Nuh! indeed you have disputed with us and lengthened dispute with us, therefore bring to us what you threaten us with, if you are of the truthful ones."

He said: "Allah only will bring it to you if He please, and you will not escape: And if I intend to give you good advice, my advice will not profit you if Allah intended that He should leave you to go astray; He is your Lord, and to Him shall you be returned."

Or do they say: "He has forged it?"

Say: "If I have forged it, on me is my guilt, and I am clear of that of which you are guilty."

And it was revealed to Nuh: "That none of your people will believe except those who have already believed, therefore do not grieve at what they do: And make the ark before Our eyes and (according to) Our revelation, and do not speak to Me in respect of those who are unjust; surely they shall be drowned."

And he began to make the ark; and whenever the chiefs from among his people passed by him they laughed at him.

He said: "If you laugh at us, surely we too laugh at you as you laugh (at us). So shall you know who it is on whom will come a chastisement which will disgrace him, and on whom will lasting chastisement come down. Until when Our command came and water came forth from the valley."

We said: "Carry in it two of all things, a pair, and your own family—except those against whom the word has already gone forth, and those who believe."

And there believed not with him but a few.

And he said: "Embark in it, in the name of Allah be its sailing and its anchoring; most surely my Lord is Forgiving, Merciful."

And it moved on with them amid waves like mountains; and Nuh called out to his son, and he was aloof: "O my son! embark with us and be not with the unbelievers."

Source: E. H. Palmer, The Qur'an. Part 1: I-XVI in Sacred Books of the East Vol 6 & 9, 1880.

He said: "I will betake myself for refuge to a mountain that shall protect me from the water."

Nuh said: "There is no protector today from Allah's punishment but He Who has mercy"; and a wave intervened between them, so he was of the drowned.

And it was said: "O earth, swallow down your water, and O cloud, clear away."

And the water was made to abate and the affair was decided, and the ark rested on the Judi,

And it was said: "Away with the unjust people."

And Nuh cried out to his Lord and said: "My Lord! surely my son is of my family, and Thy promise is surely true, and Thou art the most just of the judges."

He said: "O Nuh! surely he is not of your family; surely he is (the doer of) other than good deeds, therefore ask not of Me that of which you have no knowledge; surely I admonish you lest you may be of the ignorant."

He said: "My Lord! I seek refuge in Thee from asking Thee that of which I have no knowledge; and if Thou shouldst not forgive me and have mercy on me, I should be of the losers."

It was said: "O Nuh! descend with peace from Us and blessings on you and on the people from among those who are with you, and there shall be nations whom We will afford provisions, then a painful punishment from Us shall afflict them. These are announcements relating to the unseen which We reveal to you, you did not know them—(neither) you nor your people—before this; therefore be patient; surely the end is for those who guard (against evil). And to Ad (We sent) their brother Hud.

He said: "O my people! serve Allah, you have no god other than He; you are nothing but forgers (of lies). O my people! I do not ask of you any reward for it; my reward is only with Him Who created me; do you not then understand? And, O my people! ask forgiveness of your Lord, then turn to Him; He will send on you clouds pouring down abundance of rain and add strength to your strength, and do not turn back guilty."

They said: "O Hud! you have not brought to us any clear argument and we are not going to desert our gods for your word, and we are not believers in you: We cannot say aught but that some of our gods have smitten you with evil."

He said: "Surely I call Allah to witness, and do you bear witness too, that I am clear of what you associate (with Allah). Besides Him, therefore scheme against me all together; then give me no respite: Surely I rely on Allah, my Lord and your Lord; there is no living creature but He holds it by its forelock; surely my Lord is on the right path. But if you turn back, then indeed I have delivered to you the message with which I have been sent to you, and my Lord will bring another people in your place, and you cannot do Him any harm; surely my Lord is the Preserver of all things."

And when Our decree came to pass, We delivered Hud and those who believed with him with mercy from Us, and We delivered them from a hard chastisement.

SURA 71 NUH (NOAH)

Surely We sent Nuh to his people, saying: "Warn your people* before there come upon them a painful chastisement."

He said: "O my people! Surely I am a plain warner to you that you should serve Allah and be careful of (your duty to) Him and obey me. He will forgive you some of your faults and grant you a delay to an appointed term; surely the term of Allah when it comes is not postponed; did you but know!"

He said: "O my Lord! surely I have called my people by night and by day! But my call has only made them flee the more, and whenever I have called them that Thou mayest forgive them, they put their fingers in their ears, cover themselves with their garments, and persist and are puffed up with pride. Then surely I called to them aloud, then surely I spoke to them in public and I spoke to them in secret. Then I said, 'Ask forgiveness of your Lord, surely He is the most Forgiving. He will send down upon you the cloud, pouring down abundance of rain, and help you with wealth and sons, and make for you gardens, and make for you rivers. What is the matter with you that you fear not the greatness of Allah? And indeed He has created you through various grades: do you not see how Allah has created the seven heavens - one above another, and made the moon therein a light, and made the sun a lamp? And Allah has made you grow out of the earth as a growth. Then He returns you to it, then will He bring you forth a new bringing forth. And Allah has made for you the earth a wide expanse, that you may go along therein in wide paths.'"

Nuh said: "My Lord! Surely they have disobeyed me and followed him whose wealth and children have added to him nothing but loss. And they have planned a very great plan.

And they say: 'By no means leave your gods, nor leave the gods Wadd, nor Suwa; nor Yaghus, and Yauq and Nasr.'* And indeed they have led astray many, and do not increase the unjust in aught but error."

Because of their wrongs they were drowned, then made to enter fire, so they did not find any helpers besides Allah.

And Nuh said: "My Lord! Leave not upon the land any dweller from among the unbelievers, for surely if Thou leave them they will lead astray Thy servants, and will not beget any but immoral, ungrateful children. My Lord! Forgive me and my parents and him who enters my house believing, and the believing men and the believing women; and do not increase the unjust in aught but destruction!"

*Nuh is to warn his people because they have not been worshipping, pious, or obedient.
*These gods are idols, represented by the following: Wadd is a huge man, Suwa a female, Yaghus is a lion, Yauq a horse, and Nasr a vulture.

DISCUSSION QUESTIONS

1. What are some of the differences between the two suras that you see in the telling of the flood?

2. How does Nuh responsed to his peers?

3. How do you think Nuh felt about his son (in Sura 11)? What does this say about his relationship with God?

4. Compare and contrast this flood myth to the previous flood myths you have read.

Part 2: Tricksters, Lovers, and Other Tales

Isis and Osiris (Egyptian)

Introduction

Isis and Osiris, the children of Geb and Nut, loved each other while still in the womb—they are brother and sister, as well as husband and wife. But more than merely a love story, this is also a heroic tale about a wife's search for her husband. The story is a vegetation myth, but it has political significance as well, establishing the divine kingship of the pharaoh. The living pharaoh is equated with Horus; when he dies, he becomes the king of the underworld—Osiris (god of grain). Isis was considered the epitome of the devoted wife and mother, as well as possessing powerful magic. It is said that the Nile River sprang from her tears. Worship of Isis extended far beyond Egypt, even into the Roman Empire.

The most complete version of the story comes to us from the Roman writer Plutarch. It is believed that because the Isis and Osiris story was so well-known among the Egyptians it didn't need to be recorded—there are hundreds of allusions to it in Egyptian writing, but yet no complete account of the story. The version here comes mainly from the account of Plutarch, from two translations. The portion of the story that concerns the conception of Horus is told in various hieroglyphics and, since this is not explicit in Plutarch, the text has been supplemented as noted.

THE MYTH OF OSIRIS

In course of time the prophecies concerning Osiris were fulfilled, and he became a great and wise king. The land of Egypt flourished under his rule as it had never done heretofore. Like many another 'hero-god,' he set himself the task of civilizing his people, who at his coming were in a very barbarous condition, indulging in cannibalistic and other savage practices. He gave them a code of laws, taught them the arts of husbandry, and showed them the proper rites wherewith to worship the gods. And when he had succeeded in establishing law and order in Egypt he betook himself to distant lands to continue there his work of civilization. So gentle and good was he, and so pleasant were his methods of instilling knowledge into the minds of the barbarians, that they worshipped the very ground whereon he trod.

Set, the Enemy

He had one bitter enemy, however, in his brother, Set. During the absence of Osiris his wife Isis ruled the country so well that the schemes of the wicked Set to take a share in its government were not allowed to mature. But on the king's return Set fixed on a plan whereby to rid himself altogether of the king, his brother. For the accomplishment of his ends he leagued himself with Aso, the queen of Ethiopia, and seventy-two other conspirators. Then, after secretly measuring the king's body, he caused to be made a marvellous chest, richly fashioned and adorned, which would contain exactly the body of Osiris. This done, he invited his fellow-plotters and his brother the king to a great feast. Now Osiris had frequently been warned by the queen to beware of Set, but, having no evil in himself, the king feared it not in others, so he betook himself to the banquet.

Source: Plutarch. *Plutarch's Morals.* Edited by William W. Goodwin, 1874. E.A. Wallis Budge. *Legends of the Gods,* 1912.

When the feast was over Set had the beautiful chest brought into the banqueting-hall, and said, as though in jest, that it should belong to him whom it would fit. One after another the guests lay down in the chest, but it fitted none of them till the turn of Osiris came. Quite unsuspicious of treachery, the king laid himself down in the great receptacle. In a moment the conspirators had nailed down the lid, pouring boiling lead over it lest there should be any aperture. Then they set the coffin adrift on the Nile, at its Tanaitic mouth. These things befell, say some, in the twenty-eighth year of Osiris' life; others say in the twenty-eighth year of his reign.

When the news reached the ears of Isis she was sore stricken, and cut off a lock of her hair and put on mourning apparel. Knowing well that the dead cannot rest till their bodies have been buried with funeral rites, she set out to find the corpse of her husband. For a long time her search went unrewarded, though she asked every man and woman she met whether they had seen the richly decorated chest. At length it occurred to her to inquire of some children who played by the Nile, and, as it chanced, they were able to tell her that the chest had been brought to the Tanaitic mouth of the Nile by Set and his accomplices. From that time children were regarded by the Egyptians as having some special faculty of divination.

The Tamarisk-tree

By and by the queen gained information of a more exact kind through the agency of demons, by whom she was informed that the chest had been cast up on the shore of Byblos, and flung by the waves into a tamarisk-bush, which had shot up miraculously into a magnificent tree, enclosing the coffin of Osiris in its trunk. The king of that country, Melcarthus by name, was astonished at the height and beauty of the tree, and had it cut down and a pillar made from its trunk wherewith to support the roof of his palace. Within this pillar, therefore, was hidden the chest containing the body of Osiris. Isis hastened with all speed to Byblos, where she seated herself by the side of a fountain. To none of those who approached her would she vouchsafe a word, saving only to the queen's maidens, and these she addressed very graciously, braiding their hair and perfuming them with her breath, more fragrant than the odour of flowers. When the maidens returned to the palace the queen inquired how it came that their hair and clothes were so delightfully perfumed, whereupon they related their encounter with the beautiful stranger. Queen Astarte, or Athenais, bade that she be conducted to the palace, welcomed her graciously, and appointed her nurse to one of the young princes.

The Grief of Isis

Isis fed the boy by giving him her finger to suck. Every night, when all had retired to rest, she would pile great logs on the fire and thrust the child among them, and, changing herself into a swallow, would twitter mournful lamentations for her dead husband. Rumours of these strange practices were brought by the queen's maidens to the ears of their mistress, who determined to see for herself whether or not there was any truth in them. So she concealed herself in the great hall, and when night came sure enough Isis barred the doors and piled logs on the fire, thrusting the child among the glowing wood. The queen rushed forward with a loud cry and rescued her boy from the flames. The goddess reproved her sternly, declaring that by her action she had deprived the young prince of immortality. Then Isis revealed her identity to the awe-stricken Athenais and told her story, begging that the pillar which supported the roof might be given to her. When her request had been granted she cut open the tree, took out the coffin containing the body of Osiris, and mourned so loudly over it that one of the young princes died of terror. Then she took the chest by sea to Egypt, being accompanied on the journey by the elder son of King Melcarthus. The child's ultimate fate is variously recounted by several conflicting traditions. The tree which had held the body of the god was long preserved and worshipped at Byblos. Arrived in Egypt, Isis opened the chest and wept long and sorely over the remains of her royal husband.

All legends agree in saying that she took the form of a bird, and that she flew about unceasingly, going hither and thither, and uttering wailing cries of grief. At length she found the body, and with a piercing cry she alighted on the ground. Isis came, Nephthys came, the one on the right side, the other on the left side, one in the form of a *Hat* bird, the other in the form of a *Tchert* bird, and they found Osiris thrown on the ground in Netat by his brother Set. Isis fanned the body with her feathers, and produced air, and at length she caused the inert members of Osiris to move, and drew from him his essence, wherefrom she produced her child Horus.

Meanwhile Set, while hunting by the light of the moon, discovered the richly adorned coffin and in his rage rent the body into fourteen pieces, which he scattered here and there throughout the country. Upon learning of this fresh outrage on the body of the god, Isis took a boat of papyrus-reeds and journeyed forth once more in search of her husband's remains. After this crocodiles would not touch a papyrus boat, probably because they thought it contained the goddess, still pursuing her weary search. Whenever Isis found a portion of the corpse she buried it and built a shrine to mark the spot. It is for this reason that there are so many tombs of Osiris in Egypt.

Of the parts of Osiris's body the only one which Isis did not find was the male member, for the reason that this had been at once tossed into the river, and the lepidotus, the sea-bream, and the pike had fed upon it; and it is from these very fishes the Egyptians are most scrupulous in abstaining. But Isis made a replica of the member to take its place, and consecrated the phallus, in honour of which the Egyptians even at the present day celebrate a festival. Isis and Nephthys reassembled Osiris's body, wrapping it with oils and linens and completing the sacred rites. Isis fanned Osiris with her feathers, and they pronounced words of magic upon him. Osiris became king of the dead.

The Vengeance of Horus

By this time Horus had reached manhood, and Osiris, returning from the Duat, where he reigned as king of the dead, encouraged him to avenge the wrongs of his parents. Horus thereupon did battle with Set, the victory falling now to one, now to the other. At one time Set was taken captive by his enemy and given into the custody of Isis, but the latter, to her son's amazement and indignation, set him at liberty. So angry was Horus that he tore the crown from his mother's head. Thoth, however, gave her a helmet in the shape of a cow's head. Another version states that Horus cut off his mother's head, which Thoth, the maker of magic, stuck on again in the form of a cow's.

Horus and Set, it is said, still do battle with one another, yet victory has fallen to neither. When Horus shall have vanquished his enemy, Osiris will return to earth and reign once more as king in Egypt.

DISCUSSION QUESTIONS

1. Explore the mother-son-consort relationship in this story. Consider the significance of Isis bringing Osiris back to life and the conception of Horus, and the fact that the pharaoh is equated with both Osiris and Horus. In addition, Isis is often personified as the throne of Egypt.

2. Why does Isis free Set, and what are the implications of this gesture? What function does Set serve in this myth and in the larger Egyptian pantheon?

3. Explore the roles of each character as playing a role in the vegetation myth. What function does each of them serve?

4. What insights can be gained about Egyptian culture from this story?

Inanna and Dumuzi (Akkadian)

Ishtar was most likely of Semitic origin; a goddess associated with agriculture and the fertile earth—a "great mother" figure. Ishtar is her Akkadian name; the Sumerians called her Inanna.

Worship of Ishtar spread into western Asia and even Egypt and Greece. Many lesser goddesses may have become merged with her during this progression, furthering her popularity. She is often addressed as "mother of the gods," and "queen of heaven." It seems that among nearly all Semitic-speaking peoples, Ishtar was worshipped. To the people of Canaan and Greece she was known as Ashteroth or Astarte; it's possible that she could even be the origin of the cult of Aphrodite. Sometimes Ishtar was called the daughter of Anu, the sky-god, or the child of Sin, the moon-god. The biggest threat to her name was her association with Ninlil, the consort of Enlil, the Mesopotamian storm-god, and she became known as a goddess of war and battle. This is rare for a goddess, to be both identified with fertility and war. Since Ishtar was also identified with Damkina, wife of Ea, she could be not only Tammuz's consort, but his mother as well. The son-lover is a common motif in agricultural myths, and it may also explain why this type of story exists in so many cultures. The spread of her worship is remarkable.

The myth of Tammuz possibly dates from 4000 BCE, perhaps earlier. It's possible that the name Tammuz comes from the Akkadian name Dumu-zi, which means "son of life," or "only son." Another source is possibly Dumu-zi-apsu, meaning "offspring of the spirit of the deep," which identifies him as son of Ea, god of water. But he is not a simple god. An Akkadian hymn addresses him as "Shepherd and lord, husband of Ishtar the lady of heaven, lord of the underworld, lord of the shepherd's seat." He has been referred to as a shepherd of the sky—his flock being clouds that send rain upon the earth. As a shepherd, too, he can be identified with the community.

Ishtar's devotion and love for Tammuz can be said to symbolize the courtship of the sun-god of spring by the fertility goddess. The god is destroyed by summer's unrelenting heat and must be restored. This is why some versions of the Descent of Ishtar say she goes in search of her husband. He dies at harvest time and the land is barren until he returns. It is also said that Ishtar was associated with the storage of grain and that Tammuz was associated with the grain itself or the power to grow it, meaning that she becomes the vessel to keep the grain. She is also the fertile field—the womb.

The description of the underworld in these myths is quite dreary. This was not a place of judgment or punishment, and certainly not reward, but a place covered in dust—dark and gloomy. Many passages of the myth say the inhabitants are dressed in feathers. Perhaps this relates to Tammuz's association with the sky.

These segments tell the story from Ishtar's decision to marry Tammuz (or Dumuzi—the choice of name depends on the translation used), through their courtship, and the descent to the underworld.

In this Sumerian myth, found on a fragmented tablet, we see a motif that is similar to the biblical story of Cain and Abel. Cain, a farmer, kills his brother Abel, a shepherd. In this case, the conflict concerns Inanna's choice of a consort.

The characters of our poem are four in number: the seemingly ubiquitous Inanna; her brother, the sun-god Utu; the shepherd-god Dumuzi; the farmer-god Enkimdu. The plot is as follows. Inanna is about to choose a spouse. Her brother Utu urges her to marry the shepherd-god Dumuzi, but she prefers the farmer-god Enkimdu. Thereupon Dumuzi steps up and demands to know why she prefers the farmer; he, Dumuzi, the shepherd, has everything that the farmer has and more. Inanna does not answer, but Enkimdu, the farmer, who seems to be a peaceful, cautious type, tries to appease the belligerent Dumuzi. The latter refuses to be appeased, however, until the farmer promises to bring him all kinds of gifts and—here it must be stressed the meaning of the text is not quite certain—even Inanna herself.

The intelligible part of the poem begins with an address by the sun-god Utu to his sister Inanna:

INANNA AND DUMUZI

"O my sister, the much possessing shepherd,	1
O maid Inanna, why dost thou not favor?	
His oil is good, his date-wine is good,	
The shepherd, everything his hand touches is bright,	
O Inanna, the much-possessing Dumuzi . . .,	5
Full of jewels and precious stones, why dost thou not favor?	
His good oil he will eat with thee,	
The *protector* of the king, why dost thou not favor?"	
But Inanna refuses:	
"The much-possessing shepherd I shall not marry,	10
In his new . . . I shall not *walk*,	
In his new . . . I shall *utter no praise*,	
I, the maid, the farmer I shall marry,	
The farmer who makes plants grow abundantly,	
The farmer who makes the grain grow abundantly."	15

A break of about twelve lines follows, in which Inanna continues to give the reasons for her preference. Then the shepherd-god Dumuzi steps up to Inanna, protesting her choice—a passage that is particularly remarkable for its intricately effective phrase-pattern:

"The farmer more than I, the farmer more than I, The farmer what has he more than I?	
If he gives me his black garment, I give him, the farmer, my black ewe,	
If he gives me his white garment, I give him, the farmer, my white ewe,	
If he pours me his first date-wine, I pour him, the farmer, my *yellow* milk,	
If he pours me his good date-wine, I pour him, the farmer, my *kisim*-milk,	20
If he pours me his 'heart-turning' date-wine, I pour him, the farmer, my bubbling milk,	
If he pours me his *water-mixed* date-wine, I pour him, the farmer, my *plant*-milk,	
If he gives me his good portions, I give him, the farmer, my *nitirda*-milk,	
If he gives me his good bread, I give him, the farmer, my *honey*-cheese,	
If he gives me his small beans, I give him my small cheeses;	25
More than he can eat, more than he can drink,	
I pour out for him much oil, I pour out for him much milk;	
More than I, the farmer, what has he more than I?"	

Source: Samuel Noah Kramer. *Sumerian Mythology: A Study of Spiritual and Literary Achievement in the Third Millennium B.C.*, 1944.

Follows four lines whose meaning is not clear; then begins Enkimdu's effort at appeasement:

"Thou, O shepherd, why dost thou start a quarrel?
O shepherd, Dumuzi, why dost thou start a quarrel?   30
Me with thee, O shepherd, me with thee why dost thou compare?
Let thy sheep eat the grass of the earth,
In my meadowland let thy sheep *pasture*,
In the fields of Zabalam let them eat grain,
Let *all* thy *folds* drink the water of my river Unun."   35
But the shepherd remains adamant:
"I, the shepherd, at my marriage do not enter, O farmer, as my friend,
O farmer, Enkimdu, as my friend, O farmer, as my friend, do not enter."
Thereupon the farmer offers to bring him all kinds of gifts:
"Wheat I shall bring thee, beans I shall bring thee,   40
Beans of . . . I shall bring thee,
The maid Inanna (*and*) *whatever is pleasing to thee*,
The maid Inanna . . . I shall bring thee."

And so the poem ends, with the seeming victory of the shepherd-god Dumuzi over the farmer-god Enkimdu.

The Courtship of Inanna and Dumuzi

This myth seems to have been the basis for a "sacred marriage" ritual that took place during the New Year's festival. A temple priest and priestess would enact the roles of Inanna and Dumuzi; their union would ensure the fertility of the land during the next season. It is a Sumerian poem, dated approximately 1700 BCE.

The agricultural deity Tammuz (Hebrew name for Dumuzi) achieved lasting prominence among the Babylonian gods—he died, was mourned, and returned. All the evidence points to his great importance to the people's religious lives.

THE COURTSHIP OF INANNA AND DUMUZI

Inanna, at her mother's command,   1
Bathed and anointed herself with scented oil.
She covered her body with the royal white robe.
She readied her dowry.
She arranged her precious lapis beads around her neck.   5
She took her seal in her hand.
Dumuzi waited expectantly.
Inanna opened the door for him.
Inside the house she shone before him

From *Inanna: Queen of Heaven and Earth* by Diane Wolkstein and Samuel Noah Kramer (Translators). Copyright © 1983 by Diane Wolkstein and Samuel Noah Kramer. Reprinted by permission.

Like the light of the moon.   10
Dumuzi looked at her joyously.
He pressed his neck close against hers.
He kissed her.
Inanna spoke:
"What I tell you   15
Let the singer weave into song.
What I tell you,
Let it flow from ear to mouth,
Let it pass from old to young:
My vulva, the horn,   20
The Boat of Heaven,
Is full of eagerness like the young moon.
My untilled land lies fallow.
As for me, Inanna,
Who will plow my vulva?   25
Who will plow my high field?
Who will plow my wet ground?
As for me, the young woman,
Who will plow my vulva?
Who will station the ox there?   30
Who will plow my vulva?"
Dumuzi replied:
"Great Lady, the king will plow your vulva.
I, Dumuzi the King, will plow your vulva."
Inanna: 35
"Then plow my vulva, man of my heart!
Plow my vulva!"
At the king's lap stood the rising cedar.
Plants grew high by their side.
Grains grew high by their side.   40
Gardens flourished luxuriantly.
Inanna sang:
"He has sprouted; he has burgeoned;
He is lettuce planted by the water.
He is the one my womb loves best.   45
My well-stocked garden of the plain,
My barley growing high in its furrow,
My apple tree which bears fruit up to its crown,
He is lettuce planted by the water.
My honey-man, my honey-man sweetens me always.   50
My lord, the honey-man of the gods,
He is the one my womb loves best.
His hand is honey, his foot is honey,
He sweetens me always.
My eager impetuous caresser of the navel,   55
My caresser of the soft thighs,
He is the one my womb loves best,
He is lettuce planted by the water."
Dumuzi sang:

"O Lady, your breast is your field.   60
Inanna, your breast is your field.
Your broad field pours out plants.
Your broad field pours out grain.
Water flows from on high for your servant.
Bread flows from on high for your servant.   65
Pour it out for me, Inanna.
I will drink all you offer."
Inanna sang:
"Make your milk sweet and thick, my bridegroom.
My shepherd, I will drink your fresh milk.   70
Wild bull, Dumuzi, make your milk sweet and thick.
I will drink your fresh milk.
Let the milk of the goat flow in my sheepfold.
Fill my holy churn with honey cheese.
Lord Dumuzi, I will drink your fresh milk.   75
My husband, I will guard my sheepfold for you.
I will watch over your house of life, the storehouse,
The shining quivering place which delights Sumer
The house which decides the fates of the land,
The house which gives the breath of life to the people.   80
I, the queen of the palace, will watch over your house."
Dumuzi spoke:
"My sister,* I would go with you to my garden.
Inanna, I would go with you to my garden.
I would go with you to my orchard.   85
I would go with you to my apple tree.
There I would plant the sweet, honey-covered seed."
Inanna spoke:
"He brought me into his garden.
My brother, Dumuzi, brought me into his garden.   90
I strolled with him among the standing trees,
I stood with him among the fallen trees,
By an apple tree I knelt as is proper.
Before my brother coming in song,
Who rose to me out of the poplar leaves,   95
Who came to me in the midday heat,
Before my lord Dumuzi,
I poured out plants from my womb.
I placed plants before him,
I poured out plants before him.   100
I placed grain before him,
I poured out grain before him.
I poured out grain from my womb."
Inanna sang:
"Last night as I, the queen, was shining bright,   105
Last night as I, the Queen of Heaven, was shining bright,*

sister: a term of affection
shining bright: Inanna was the morning star

As I was shining bright and dancing,
Singing praises at the coming of the night –
He met me—he met me!
My lord Dumuzi met me.   110
He put his hand into my hand.
He pressed his neck close against mine.
My high priest is ready for the holy loins.
My lord Dumuzi is ready for the holy loins.
The plants and herbs in his field are ripe.   115
O Dumuzi! Your fullness is my delight!"
She called for it, she called for it, she called for the bed!
She called for the bed that rejoices the heart.
She called for the bed that sweetens the loins.
She called for the bed of kingship.   120
She called for the bed of queenship.
Inanna called for the bed:
"Let the bed that rejoices the heart be prepared!
Let the bed that sweetens the loins be prepared!
Let the bed of kingship be prepared!   125
Let the bed of queenship be prepared!
Let the royal bed be prepared!"
Inanna spread the bridal sheet across the bed.
She called to the king:
"The bed is ready!"   130
She called to her bridegroom:
"The bed is waiting!"
He put his hand in her hand.
He put his hand to her heart.
Sweet is the sleep of hand-to-hand.   135
Sweeter still the sleep of heart-to-heart.
Inanna spoke:
"I bathed for the wild bull,
I bathed for the shepherd Dumuzi,
I perfumed my sides with ointment,   140
I coated my mouth with sweet-smelling amber,
I painted my eyes with kohl.*
He shaped my loins with his fair hands,
The shepherd Dumuzi filled my lap with cream and milk,
He stroked my pubic hair,   145
He watered my womb.
He laid his hands on my holy vulva,
He smoothed my black boat with cream,
He quickened my narrow boat with milk,
He caressed me on the bed.   150
Now I will caress my high priest on the bed,
I will caress the faithful shepherd Dumuzi,
I will caress his loins, the shepherdship of the land,
I will decree a sweet fate for him."
The Queen of Heaven,   155

*kohl: cosmetic used on the eyes

The heroic woman, greater than her mother,
Who was presented the me by Enki,
Inanna, the First Daughter of the Moon,*
Decreed the fate of Dumuzi:
"In battle I am your leader,   160
In combat I am your armor-bearer,
In the assembly I am your advocate,
On the campaign I am your inspiration.
You, the chosen shepherd of the holy shrine,
You, the king, the faithful provider of Uruk,   165
You, the light of An's great shrine,
In all ways you are fit:
To hold your head high on the lofty dais,
To sit on the lapis lazuli throne,
To cover your head with the holy crown,   170
To wear long clothes on your body,
To bind yourself with the garments of kingship,
To carry the mace and sword,
To guide straight the long bow and arrow,
To fasten the throw-stick and sling at your side,   175
To race on the road with the holy sceptre in your hand,
And the holy sandals on your feet,
To prance on the holy breast like a lapis lazuli calf.
You, the sprinter, the chosen shepherd,
In all ways you are fit.   180
May your heart enjoy long days.
That which An has determined for you—may it not be altered
That which Enlil has granted—may it not be changed.
You are the favorite of Ningal.
Inanna holds you dear."   185

Ninshubur, the faithful servant of the holy shrine of Uruk,
Led Dumuzi to the sweet thighs of Inanna and spoke:
"My queen, here is the choice of your heart,
The king, your beloved bridegroom.
May he spend long days in the sweetness of your holy loins.   190
Give him a favorable and glorious reign.
Grant him the king's throne, firm in its foundations.
Grant him the shepherd's staff of judgment.
Grant him the enduring crown with the radiant and noble
diadem.   195
From where the sun rises to where the sun sets,
From south to north,
From the Upper Sea to the Lower Sea,
From the land of the huluppu-tree to the land of the cedar,
Let his shepherd's staff protect all of Sumer and Akkad.   200

*the Moon: Nanna

As the farmer, let him make the fields fertile,
As the shepherd, let him make the sheepfolds multiply,
Under his reign let there be vegetation,
Under his reign let there be rich grain.
In the marshland may the fish and birds chatter,   205
In the canebrake may the young and old reeds grow high,
In the steppe may the masbgur-trees grow high,
In the forests may the deer and wild goats multiply,
In the orchards may there be honey and wine,
In the gardens may the lettuce and cress grow high,   210
In the palace may there be long life.
May there be floodwater in the Tigris and Euphrates,
May the plants grow high on their banks and fill the meadows,
May the Lady of Vegetation pile the grain in heaps and mounds.
O my Queen of Heaven and Earth,   215
Queen of all the universe,
May he enjoy long days in the sweetness of your holy loins."
The king went with lifted head to the holy loins.
He went with lifted head to the loins of Inanna.
He went to the queen with lifted head.   220
He opened wide his arms to the holy priestess of heaven.
Inanna spoke:
"My beloved, the delight of my eyes, met me.
We rejoiced together.
He took his pleasure of me.   225
He brought me into his house.
He laid me down on the fragrant honey-bed.
My sweet love, lying by my heart,
Tongue-playing, one by one,
My fair Dumuzi did so fifty times.   230
Now, my sweet love is sated.
Now he says:
'Set me free, my sister, set me free.
You will be a little daughter to my father.
Come, my beloved sister, I would go to the palace.   235
Set me free."
Inanna spoke:
"My blossom-bearer, your allure was sweet.
My blossom-bearer in the apple orchard,
My bearer of fruit in the apple orchard,   240
Dumuzi, your allure was sweet.
My fearless one,
My holy statue,
My statue outfitted with sword and lapis lazuli diadem,
How sweet was your allure. ..."   245

The Descent of Ishtar

The Akkadian myth "Ishtar's Descent to the Nether World" was already known prior to the discovery of the Sumerian (Inanna) text. It is believed that the Akkadian version dates to 1200 BCE, while the Sumerian is older (1900–1600 BCE). Scholars believe the Akkadian version actually dates back to a Sumerian original, replacing Inanna with Ishtar.

The longer Sumerian version of the "Descent of Inanna" consists of 30 tablets and fragments containing over 400 lines that, fortunately, exist in nearly perfect condition. These tablets were carefully pieced together by dozens of scholars, taking more than a century of work. It is believed the tablets date from 1750 BCE. They were discovered in the ruins of Nippur between 1889–1900 by a team from the University of Pennsylvania—the first American excavation in the area. Following the discovery, naturally, came the painstaking process of identification and translation. The pieces were divided between museums with thousands of miles between them, making this process even more difficult. Finally, in 1914, the first five pieces were published. Still, much of the text was unintelligible. In 1937, the first half of "The Descent" was partially reconstructed. Work on the tablets continued for decades. The portions featured here come from two scholars who participated in this process.

No one is certain why Ishtar decides to visit the underworld. Some say Ishtar is seeking to overthrow her sister, Ereshkigal, Queen of the underworld. In the Sumerian version, she attempts to do this and fails. As a result, her corpse is hung from a nail. She was revived after Enki/Ea appealed on her behalf, but was required to find someone to replace her in the underworld. Because her consort, Dumuzi, did not appear to miss her in her absence, as he seemed to be enjoying himself on the throne, she chose him. He tried to escape, but was eventually captured. Eventually, Inanna and Dumuzi's sister, who are both mourning him, make an arrangement that Dumuzi only has to spend half the year in the underworld—his sister takes his place for the other half.

Here, we begin with the Akkadian version of the descent, translated by M. Jastrow, followed by an excerpt from the Sumerian version (translated by Wolkstein and Kramer) which recounts Inanna's return and Dumuzi's banishment in greater detail.

DESCENT OF THE GODDESS ISHTAR INTO THE LOWER WORLD

To the land of no return, the land of darkness,	1
Ishtar, the daughter of Sin* directed her thought,	
Directed her thought, Ishtar, the daughter of Sin,	
To the house of shadows, the dwelling, of Irkalla,*	
To the house without exit for him who enters therein,	5
To the road, whence there is no turning,	
To the house without light for him who enters therein,	
The place where dust is their nourishment, clay their food.	
They have no light, in darkness they dwell.	
Clothed like birds, with wings as garments,	10

*Sin is the moon god
*Irkalla: another name for the underworld

Over door and bolt, dust has gathered.
Ishtar on arriving at the gate of the land of no return,
To the gatekeeper thus addressed herself:

"Gatekeeper, ho, open thy gate!
Open thy gate that I may enter!   15
If thou openest not the gate to let me enter,
I will break the door, I will wrench the lock,
I will smash the door-posts, I will force the doors.
I will bring up the dead to eat the living.
And the dead will outnumber the living."   20

The gatekeeper opened his mouth and spoke,
Spoke to the lady Ishtar:
"Desist, O lady, do not destroy it.
I will go and announce thy name to my queen Ereshkigal."

The gatekeeper entered and spoke to Ereshkigal: 25
"Ho! here is thy sister, Ishtar ...
Hostility of the great powers ...
When Ereshkigal heard this,
As when one hews down a tamarisk she trembled,
As when one cuts a reed, she shook: 30
"What has moved her heart what has stirred her liver*?
Ho there, does this one wish to dwell with me?
To eat clay as food, to drink dust as wine?
I weep for the men who have left their wives.
I weep for the wives torn from the embrace of their husbands;   35
For the little ones cut off before their time.
Go, gatekeeper, open thy gate for her,
Deal with her according to the ancient decree."

The gatekeeper went and opened his gate to her:
"Enter, O lady, let Cuthah* greet thee.   40
Let the palace of the land of no return rejoice at thy presence!"

He bade her enter the first gate, which he opened wide, and took the large crown off her head:
"Why, O gatekeeper, dost thou remove the large crown off my head?"
"Enter, O lady, such are the decrees of Ereshkigal."
The second gate he bade her enter, opening it wide, and removed her earrings: 45
"Why, O gatekeeper, dost thou remove my earrings?"
"Enter, O lady, for such are the decrees of Ereshkigal."
The third gate he bade her enter, opened it wide, and removed her necklace:
"Why, O gatekeeper, dost thou remove my necklace?"
"Enter, O lady, for such are the decrees of Ereshkigal."   50
The fourth gate he bade her enter, opened it wide, and removed the ornaments of her breast:
"Why, O gatekeeper, dost thou remove the ornaments of my breast?"

* The heart was considered to be the seat of intellect and the liver controlled emotions.
* Cuthah: ancient city devoted to the cult of Nergal, god of the underworld. Nergal threatened to
    behead Ereshkigal, but she saved herself by becoming his wife; Nergal then obtained kingship in
    the underworld.

"Enter, O lady, for such are the decrees of Ereshkigal."
The fifth gate he bade her enter, opened it wide, and removed the girdle of her
    body studded with birthstones.*   55
"Why, O gatekeeper, dost thou remove the girdle of my body, studded with birth-stones?"
"Enter, O lady, for such are the decrees of Ereshkigal."
The sixth gate, he bade her enter, opened it wide, and removed the spangles off her hands
    and feet.
"Why, O gatekeeper, dost thou remove the spangles off my hands and feet?"   60
"Enter, O lady, for thus are the decrees of Ereshkigal."
The seventh gate he bade her enter, opened it wide, and removed her loin-cloth.
"Why, O gatekeeper, dost thou remove my loin-cloth?"
"Enter, O lady, for such are the decrees of Ereshkigal."

Now when Ishtar had gone down into the land of no return,   65
Ereshkigal saw her and was angered at her presence.
Ishtar, without reflection, threw herself at her [in a rage].

Ereshkigal opened her mouth and spoke,
To Namtar, her messenger, she addressed herself:
"Go Namtar, imprison her in my palace.   70
Send against her sixty disease, to punish Ishtar.
Eye-disease against her eyes,
Disease of the side against her side,
Foot-disease against her foot,
Heart-disease against her heart,   75
Head-disease against her head,
Against her whole being, against her entire body."

After the lady Ishtar had gone down into the land of no return,
The bull did not mount the cow, the ass approached not the she-ass,
To the maid in the street, no man drew near,   80
The man slept in his apartment,
The maid slept by herself.

[The second half of the poem, the reverse of the tablet, continues as follows:]

The countenance of Papsukal, the messenger of the great gods, fell, his face was troubled.
In mourning garb he was clothed, in soiled garments clad.   85
Shamash* went to Sin, his father, weeping,
In the presence of Ea, the King, he went with flowing tears.
"Ishtar has descended into the earth and has not come up. The bull does not mount the cow,
    the ass does not approach the she-ass.
The man does not approach the maid in the street,   90
The man sleeps in his apartment,
The maid sleeps by herself."

Ea, in the wisdom of his heart, formed a being,
He formed Asu-shu-namir the eunuch.

* girdle of birthstones: Sometimes referred to as a "birth girdle," this garment was sewn with
    stones believed to ensure that pregnant women had an easy delivery.
* Shamash: the sun god

"Go, Asu-shu-namir, to the land of no return direct thy face! 95
The seven gates of the land without return be opened before thee,
May Ereshkigal at sight of thee rejoice!
After her heart has been assuaged, her liver quieted,
Invoke against her the name of the great gods,
Raise thy head direct thy attention to the khalziku skin."* 100

"Come, lady, let them give me the khalziku skin, that I may drink water out of it."
When Ereshkigal heard this, she struck her side, bit her finger,
"Thou hast expressed a wish that can not be granted.
Go, Asu-sbu-namir, I curse thee with a great curse,
The sweepings of the gutters of the city be thy food, 105
The drains of the city be thy drink,
The shadow of the wall be thy abode,
The thresholds be thy dwelling-place;
Drunkard and sot strike thy cheek!"

Ereshkigal opened her mouth and spoke, 110
To Namtar,* her messenger, she addressed herself.
"Go, Namtar, knock at the strong palace,
Strike the threshold of precious stones,
Bring out the Anunnaki,* seat them on golden thrones.
Sprinkle Ishtar with the waters of life and take her out of my presence." 115

Namtar went, knocked at the strong palace,
Tapped on the threshold of precious stones.
He brought out the Anunnaki and placed them on golden thrones,
He sprinkled Ishtar with the waters of life and took hold of her.
Through the first gate he led her out and returned to her her loin-cloth. 120
Through the second gate he led her out and returned to her the spangles of her hands and feet.
Through the third gate he led her out and returned to her the girdle of her body, studded with
    birth-stones.
Through the fourth gate he led her out and returned to her the ornaments of her breast.
Through the fifth gate he led her out and returned to her her necklace. 125
Through the sixth gate he led her out and returned her earrings.
Through the seventh gate he led her out and returned to her the large crown for her head.

[The following lines are in the form of an address—apparently to someone who has sought release for a dear one from the portals of the lower world.]

"If she (Ishtar) will not grant thee her release, 130
To Tammuz, the lover of her youth,
Pour out pure waters, pour out fine oil;
With a festival garment deck him that he may play on the flute of lapis lazuli,
That the votaries may cheer his liver.
Belili* had gathered the treasure, 135
With precious stones filled her bosom.

khalziku skin: a bag that contains the waters of life.
Namtar is the god of pestilence
Annuaki/Anunnaki: "those of royal blood"—upper class gods
Belili is the sister of Tammuz

She scattered the precious stones before her,
When Belili heard the lament of her brother, she dropped her treasure,
"Oh, my only brother, do not let me perish!
On the day when Tammuz plays for me on the flute of lapis lazuli, playing it for me with   140
    the porphyry ring.*
Together with him, play ye for me, ye weepers and lamenting women!
That the dead may rise up and inhale the incense."

It is suggested here that Ishtar's spouse, Tammuz, must take her place in the underworld. However, his sister Belili (in Sumerian, Geshtinanna, goddess of the grape vine) will take his place for half the time. This is similar to the Sumerian version that follows. In the Sumerian, translated by Diane Wolkstein, the removal of Inanna's consort (Dumuzi) to the underworld is more explicit.

THE RETURN

Inanna was about to ascend from the underworld   1
When the Annuna, the judges of the underworld, seized her.
They said:
"No one ascends from the underworld unmarked.
If Inanna wishes to return from the underworld,   5
She must provide someone in her place."

As Inanna ascended from the underworld,
The galla, the demons of the underworld, clung to her side.
The galla were demons who know no food, who know no drink,
Who eat no offerings, who drink no libations,   10
Who accept no gifts.
They enjoy no lovemaking.
They have no sweet children to kiss.
They tear the wife from the husband's arms,
They tear the child from the father's knees,   15
They steal the bride from her marriage home.

The demons clung to Inanna.
The small galla who accompanied Inanna
Were like reeds the size of low picket fences.
The large galla who accompanied Inanna   20
Were like reeds the size of high picket fences.
The one who walked in front of Inanna was not a minister,
Yet he carried a sceptre.
The one who walked behind her was not a warrior,
Yet he carried a mace.   25
Ninshubur, dressed in a soiled sackcloth,
Waited outside the palace gates.
When she saw Inanna

porphyry: a type of fine-grained stone, often containing crystals

Source: Diane Wolkstein and Samuel Noah Kramer. *Inanna: Queen of Heaven and Earth,* 1983.

Surrounded by the galla,
She threw herself in the dust at Inanna's feet.   30

The galla said:
"Walk on, Inanna,
We will take Ninshubur in your place."

Inanna cried:
"No! Ninshubur is my constant support.   35
She is my sukkal* who gives me wise advice.
She is my warrior who fights by my side.
She did not forget my words.
She set up a lament for me by the ruins.
She beat the drum for me at the assembly places.   40
She circled the houses of the gods.
She tore at her eyes, at her mouth, at her thighs.
She dressed herself in a single garment like a beggar.
Alone, she set out for Nippur and the temple of Enlil.
She went to Ur and the temple of Nanna.   45
She went to Eridu and the temple of Enki.
Because of her, my life was saved.
I will never give Ninshubur to you."

The galla said:
"Walk on, Inanna,   50
We will accompany you to Umma."
In Umma, at the holy shrine,
Shara, the son of Inanna, was dressed in a soiled sackcloth
When he saw Inanna
Surrounded by the galla.   55
He threw himself in the dust at her feet.

The galla said:
"Walk on to your city, Inanna,
We will take Shara in your place."

Inanna cried: 60
"No! Not Shara!
He is my son who sings hymns to me.
He is my son who cuts my nails and smooths my hair.
I will never give Shara to you."

The galla said: 65
"Walk on, Inanna.
We will accompany you to Badtibira."

In Badtibira, at the holy shirine,
Lulah the son of Inanna, was in a soiled sackcloth.
When he saw Inanna   70

*sukkal: "supreme courier," official, or second in command; a valued advisor

Surrounded by the galla
He threw himself in the dust at her feet.

They said:
"Walk on to your city, Inanna.
We will take Lulal in your place."   75
Inanna cried:
"Not Lulal! He is my son.
He is a leader among men.
He is my right arm. He is my left arm.
I will never give Lulal to you."   80

The galla said:
"Walk on to your city, Inanna.
We will go with you to the big apple tree in Uruk."

In Uruk, by the big apple tree,
Dumuzi, the husband of Inanna, was dressed in his shining *me-* garments.*   85
He sat on his magnificent throne; (he did not move).

The galla seized him by his thighs.
They poured milk out of his seven churns.
They broke the reed pipe which the shepherd was playing.

Inanna fastened on Dumuzi the eye of death.   90
She spoke against him the word of wrath.
She uttered against him the cry of guilt:
"Take him! Take Dumuzi away!"

The galla, who know no food, who know no drink,
Who eat no offerings, who drink no libations,   95
Who accept no gifts, seized Dumuzi.
They made him stand up; they made him sit down.
They beat the husband of Inanna.
They gashed him with axes.

Dumuzi let out a wail.   100
He raised his hands to heaven to Utu, the God of Justice,
and beseeched him:
"O Utu, you are my brother-in-law,
I am the husband of your sister.
I brought cream to your mother's house,   105
I brought milk to Ningal's house.
I am the one who carried food to the holy shrine.
I am the one who brought wedding gifts to Uruk.
I am the one who danced on the holy knees, the knees
Inanna.   110

me: A concept in Mesopotamian religion concerning divine laws

Utu, you who are a just god, a merciful god,
Change my hands into the hands of a snake.
Change my feet into the feet of a snake.
Let me escape from my demons;
Do not let them hold me."   115
The merciful Utu accepted Dumuzi's tears.
He changed the hands of Dumuzi into snake hands.
He changed the feet of Dumuzi into snake feet.
Dumuzi escaped from his demons.
They could not hold him. . . .   120

At this point in the story, Dumuzi dreams of his own death and confides in his sister, Geshtinanna. He remains hidden, but she, and one of his friends, know his location. Geshtinanna will not tell the demons where he is, even when they torture her. The friend, however, reveals Dumuzi's location. Again, Dumuzi is pursued and evades the demons for a time, aided by his sister. But, eventually, they claim him and he is taken.

A lament was raised in the city: 1
"My Lady weeps bitterly for her young husband.
Inanna weeps bitterly for her young husband.
Woe for her husband! Woe for her young love!
Woe for her house! Woe for her city!

Dumuzi was taken captive in Uruk.   5
He will no longer bathe in Eridu.
He will no longer soap himself at the holy shrine.
He will no longer treat the mother of Inanna as his mother.
He will no longer perform his sweet task
Among the maidens of the city.   10

He will no longer compete with the young men of the city.
He will no longer raise his sword higher than the kurgarra priests.
Great is the grief of those who mourn for Dumuzi."

Inanna wept for Dumuzi:
"Gone is my husband, my sweet husband.   15
Gone is my love, my sweet love.
My beloved has been taken from the city.
O, you flies of the steppe,
My beloved bridegroom has been taken from me
Before I could wrap him with a proper shroud.   20

The wild bull lives no more.
The shepherd, the wild bull lives no more.
Dumuzi, the wild bull, lives no more.

I ask the hills and valleys:
'Where is my husband?'   25
I say to them:
'I can no longer bring him food.
I can no longer serve him drink.'

The jackal lies down in his bed.
The raven dwells in his sheepfold.   30
You ask me about his reed pipe?
The wind must play it for him.
You ask me about his sweet songs?
The wind must sing them for him."

Sirtur, the mother of Dumuzi, wept for her son: 35
"My heart plays the reed pipe of mourning.
Once my boy wandered so freely on the steppe,
Now he is captive.
Once Dumuzi wandered so freely on the steppe,
Now he is bound.   40

The ewe gives up her lamb.
The goat gives up her kid.
My heart plays the reed pipe of mourning.

O treacherous steppe!
In the place where he once said   45
'My mother will ask for me,'
Now he cannot move his hands.
He cannot move his feet.

My heart plays the reed pipe of mourning.
I would go to him,   50
I would see my child."

The mother walked to the desolate place.
Sirtur walked to where Dumuzi lay.
She looked at the slain wild bull.
She looked into his face. She said: 55
"My child, the face is yours.
The spirit has fled."

There is mourning in the house.
There is grief in the inner chambers.

The sister wandered about the city, weeping for her brother.   60
Geshtinanna wandered about the city, weeping for Dumuzi:
"O my brother! Who is your sister?
I am your sister.
O Dumuzi! Who is your mother?
I am your mother.   65
The day that dawns for you will also dawn for me.
The day that you will see I will also see.

I would find my brother! I would comfort him!
I would share his fate!"

When she saw the sister's grief,   70
When Inanna saw the grief of Geshtinanna,
She spoke to her gently:
"Your brother's house is no more.
Dumuzi has been carried away by the galla.
I would take you to him,   75
But I do not know the place."

Then a fly appeared.
The holy fly circled the air above Inanna's head and spoke:
"If I tell you where Dumuzi is,
What will you give me?"   80

Inanna said:
"If you tell me,
I will let you frequent the beer-houses and taverns.
I will let you dwell among the talk of the wise ones.
I will let you dwell among the songs of the minstrels."   85

The fly spoke:
"Lift your eyes to the edges of the steppe,
Lift your eyes to Arali.*

There you will find Geshtinanna's brother,
There you will find the shepherd Dumuzi."   90

Inanna and Geshtinanna went to the edges of the steppe.
They found Dumuzi weeping.
Inanna took Dumuzi by the hand and said:
"You will go to the underworld
Half the year.   95
Your sister, since she has asked,
Will go the other half.
On the day you are called,
That day you will be taken.
On the day Geshtinanna is called,   100
That day you will be set free."

Inanna placed Dumuzi in the hands of the eternal.

Holy Ereshkigal! Great is your renown!
Holy Ereshkigal! I sing your praises!

*Arali: a desert; alternately, Mt. Arali, "Home of the Gold"; also a name for the underworld

DISCUSSION QUESTIONS

1. Consider Inanna's choice between the farmer and the shepherd—her initial preference and the final decision. What can be learned about this culture based on this myth?

2. Explore the motif of the dying god and the vegetation cycle as it pertains to Inanna and Dumuzi (Ishtar and Tammuz). What does each of them represent?

3. Compare the "Descent of Ishtar" to similar myths from other cultures. What similarities and differences do you see, and what insight can be drawn from these myths? Why must Ishtar remove all her clothing and adornments before entering the underworld?

4. What can be inferred about the attitude toward women from reading these myths? What can be inferred about the values of these people? About relationships? Their general attitude toward life?

5. Explain the motif of the mother-son-consort in agricultural myths. How can a goddess be both mother and consort to the dying god?

Part 3: Journeys of Heroes and Heroines

The Epic of Gilgamesh (Sumerian/Babylonian)

In 1845, British archaeologists excavating the ruins of the ancient city of Nineveh (in present-day Iraq) discovered what turned out to be the oldest literary epic in the world. Preserved on twelve broken clay tablets was a story we now call *The Epic of Gilgamesh.*

The Epic of Gilgamesh is, more accurately, a collection of stories that were shared throughout Mesopotamian culture for nearly 1,000 years. In 1200 BCE a scribe named Sin-leqe-unnini combined the various stories into these twelve tablets, but we have no way of knowing if this was an original compilation or based on the work of other authors. It's likely a Sumerian story modified and adapted by Babylonians. Scholars estimate that oral traditions of the tale existed as far back as 2100 BCE.

Scholars have pieced together a basic story from three primary versions, although more than a dozen versions have been discovered. The most common version used is called the standard version, which was written in Akkadian, and dates between 1300–1000 BCE. This is the one discovered in Nineveh. The Sumerian and Akkadian versions of the epic do overlap, but there are some inconsistencies as well. Hittite and Hurrian versions have also been found; this presents some difficulty in deciphering the complete story.

The Epic of Gilgamesh presents several unique challenges for translators. One problem is that no single complete version exists. The story has been pieced together from broken fragments in cuneiform script and large portions are missing. Also, keep in mind that the epic was recorded in poetic verse, not prose, and there are more than 3,600 lines in the standard version.

But probably the most fascinating aspect of this tale is that the standard version contains a flood myth that is very similar to the account given in Genesis. In 1872, this story, which appears on the eleventh tablet, was translated by George Smith (see the Eleventh Tablet of the Epic of Gilgamesh—The Deluge).

Gilgamesh is said to have actually been a king of Uruk (present-day Warka), most likely around the twenty-seventh century BCE (2800–2600), although the character in the story is most likely more of a narrative figure than a historic one. In this case, myth, legend, and folklore have been blended together. At its peak, the city of Uruk is estimated to have had a population of around 50,000–80,000 people.

The tale of Gilgamesh was told for over a thousand years, then virtually forgotten until the tablets were found in the nineteenth century, renewing interest in this enduring tale. This story of the first epic hero, that is more than 4,000 years old, still has the power to captivate us. Its themes of civilization, mortality, companionship, legacy, and loss seem to have universal appeal.

Among the various translations of the epic, the woman sometimes named as Shamhat ("voluptuous one") hired to seduce Enkidu is referred to as a harlot, prostitute, courtesan, or priestess of Ishtar. This creates some ambiguity in our understanding of the story and the role this individual played in her society.

The notion that the Babylonians engaged in the practice of "sacred prostitution" has been cited by ancient historians for centuries. However, in recent decades, the idea that money was offered to temples in exchange for sexual favors has been debated by scholars. Confusion, undoubtedly, comes from the translation of words like "courtesan," "prostitute," and "harlot" and the connotation of these terms. In addition, "prostitute" implies a monetary transaction, whereas "courtesan" or "priestess" more appropriately indicates some kind of social or religious duty. We know that women worked in the temples and performed rituals, but they were not prostitutes. We should keep these ideas in mind as we read and realize the nature of this woman's role is not easy to define with perfect clarity.

In an effort to give a concise version of the story yet preserve some of the traditional language, we present here a prose version compiled from several prose and verse translations, both Akkadian and Babylonian.

THE EPIC OF GILGAMESH

The Arrival of Enkidu

Witness the great city of Uruk! Though made of brick, it shines like brilliant copper. Inside, too, the brick walls are perfect—eclipsed by no structure made by man or king. See how it was laid upon the foundation set by the Seven Counsellors. Gaze upon the Temple of Ishtar and the impressive city Gilgamesh built.

Hear now the story of how this king, once a tyrant, became beloved by his people and came to be a hero. Gilgamesh was the king of Uruk; upon stone he engraved the tale of his immense journey. Long were his labors; great was the wisdom he gained.

One-third man and two-thirds divine, Gilgamesh was the son of the goddess Ninsun and the mortal king Lugalbanda. Strong and perfect was Gilgamesh, beautiful and favored by the gods, yet he was mortal and arrogant. And, like all mortals, he feared death.

In all other things, Gilgamesh was fearless. But although a warrior, wrestler, and gifted in all things, he lacked respect and acted out of selfishness. He took wives from husbands, daughters from mothers, and sons from their fathers. A shepherd of the city should not conduct himself this way, but no one could rival his power. The nobles in the city grew weary of this behavior and professed their complaints to the gods. Anu heard this plea and said to the earth-goddess Aruru, "You made him; now make one to equal him." And so she created Enkidu. She cleansed her hands with water and using a pinch of clay, she fashioned a man and left him in the wilderness. Rough in body, long of hair, he was beast-like and adorned in animal skins. Enkidu lived among the creatures of the forest, ignorant of civilization.

One day a trapper discovered Enkidu at a water-hole. He observed this wild man for several days, terrified. The hunter was frustrated - Enkidu foiled all the traps he set for the animals; he reported this to Gilgamesh. Upon hearing this, Gilgamesh sent the courtesan Shamhat with the trapper and said, "This wild man will be drawn to her beauty, unable to resist." And so Enkidu again approached the water-hole and spied the woman. She disrobed before him and he succumbed to her charms. Fascinated, Enkidu forgot his savage ways and they spent six days and seven nights together. But when Enkidu tried to return to his wilderness home, the beasts rejected him, running swiftly away. And Enkidu found that his speed and strength were gone; yet he had gained understanding—the mind of a man. He sat at the woman's feet, confused.

Shamhat said to him, "You are now wise like a god. Why would you wish to remain among the beasts? Come with me to the city and meet the great king Gilgamesh; he is a mighty man and one you may come to call friend."

Meanwhile, Gilgamesh dreamed of Enkidu. He told his mother what he saw: A meteor fell from the sky but was too heavy to lift. The people of Uruk helped him drag it to her and she said it was his brother. She told him this meant the wild man was coming, and he would be a comrade, one made for him. In a second dream, Gilgamesh saw a strangely-shaped axe in the street; again, like the stone, he was drawn to it as a lover, and wore it at his side. She told him this, too, represented his destined friend and counselor—a man brave and strong, one he should embrace.

Enkidu agreed to accompany Shamhat, for he longed for the companionship of the one she mentioned. She brought him first to the community of shepherds. He tried to suckle from the animals, not understanding how to eat bread and drink wine. The woman reminded him that he must give up his wild ways and live like a man—eating their food, wearing clothes, and sleeping on a bed. When he learned to eat and drink, he was filled with joy. He drank seven goblets of wine. Then his hair was cut, and his body anointed with oil and he was dressed. He now appeared as a nobleman and warrior. He even helped the shepherds by chasing the wolves from the flocks.

When Enkidu arrived at Uruk, there was talk of an upcoming marriage. Enkidu overheard that the king, Gilgamesh, was insisting his right to bed the bride before the husband. Angered by this, Enkidu was determined to intervene. The people flocked around him, exclaiming that Gilgamesh would meet his match at last.

Later that night, as Gilgamesh proceeded to the temple, Enkidu blocked his way. The two men fought like bulls, destroying gateposts and shaking the very walls of the city. At last, Gilgamesh bent his knee, his rage dispelled. He realized this man was the companion his dreams foretold. They embraced as friends.

The Cedar Forest

One day Gilgamesh noticed tears in Enkidu's eyes and a sadness in his heart, and asked him the reason for his bitterness. Enkidu replied that it was sorrow over his lost strength. Gilgamesh had an answer. They would journey to the Cedar Forest and slay the giant, Humbaba, who terrorized the land. But Enkidu was dismayed. "I know of this giant," he replied, "and he is fierce. His roar is like a storm, his breath like fire, and his jaws are death. Humbaba was appointed by Enlil to guard the vast forest—why would you willingly commit to this task?"

But as a proud and mortal man, Gilgamesh wanted to leave a legacy. He believed this act would make him a hero so his name would live forever. "Only the gods can reach the heavens," he said. "Our days are but few. We will achieve glory that will live on after we are dead. I will go first, if you are afraid."

But Enkidu would not walk behind his friend. He offered to stay in the city and spread the word of Gilgamesh's journey, but he would not be convinced to join him. He was not ready to die. But Gilgamesh continued to encourage Enkidu until he reluctantly agreed. However, he insisted they first pay tribute to Shamash, the sun god, by offering prayer and sacrifice.

Gilgamesh made his case and Shamash accepted the offering of his tears as sacrifice. He was moved by Gilgamesh's plea, and vowed to help them on their journey. He quelled the floods and lightning so they would not trouble them. Then Gilgamesh ordered new weapons to be made for their quest—great axes, bows, and swords.

The Elders of Uruk also questioned this task. The Cedar Forest covered thirty-thousand square miles, and the wrath of Humbaba could not be defeated. But Gilgamesh remained undeterred and recruited volunteers to accompany them. He rallied single men who wished for a heroic adventure, and to rid the land of evil. Fifty young men agreed to join them.

Before they departed, the Elders offered some words of advice. They told Gilgamesh to avoid putting too much trust in his own strength, and to allow Enkidu to enter the forest first, since he was experienced in the wilderness. They reminded him to dig wells for water each night, make an offering of the water to Shamash, and to always honor his father. After killing Humbaba, they said he must wash his feet in the river, as required by the gods. They prayed to Shamash for victory and safe return of their king.

After receiving the blessings of the Elders, Gilgamesh and Enkidu went hand-in-hand to see his mother, Ninsun, a priestess of Shamash. He said to her, "Mother, though I am strong, I am determined to travel the unknown road to the Cedar Forest, facing a strange and uncertain battle. I attempt to rid the land of the evil Humbaba, which Shamash loathes. Pray to Shamash for me."

Ninsun cleansed herself and donned her ceremonial attire—a robe, jewels for her breast, and a tiara. She ascended to the roof of the temple and made an offering of burning incense to Shamash. Smoke rising, she raised her arms and said, "Shamash, why did you give my son this restless heart? Why has he been moved to such a journey? As he faces the unknown before him, I ask you to protect him until the day he returns, until he kills the evil which you hate. And at day's end when you rest, don't forget him, but give him to the watchmen of the night." She extinguished the incense and then said to Enkidu: "Though you are not my son, I receive you as such and adopt you." She placed a pendant around his neck. "I entrust my son to you," she said. "Go now with my blessing. May you both return safely."

After twenty leagues of travel, they stopped briefly for refreshment. After thirty leagues, they stopped to rest for the night. They walked fifty leagues in one day; in three days they traveled what would have taken six weeks.

They dug a well before the setting sun; Gilgamesh climbed up the mountainside and made his libation saying, "Bring me a dream, a favorable message from Shamash." That night, Gilgamesh slept deeply and dreamed. And when he awakened, he told Enkidu what he saw. "A crumbling mountain fell upon me. But I was rescued by a man who gave me drink and helped me to stand." Enkidu replied that this was a good dream for it foretold of the defeat of Humbaba. "Humbaba is the mountain."

The next night, after they traveled further into the forest, Gilgamesh once again asked for a dream. This time, as he told Enkidu, he dreamed he grabbed a wild bull and they fought so hard and stirred the dirt so the entire land became dark. "The bull stole my strength and I retreated. But then, the bull showed mercy and gave me food and drink." Enkidu replied, "The bull was surely Shamash watching over you."

The next night, Gilgamesh again awakened from a dream and said to Enkidu, "Why did I wake? Did you call? I am terrified. In this dream the earth and heavens roared and fire flashed from the sky—all was ash around us." Yet each disturbing dream was interpreted by Enkidu as a favorable omen.

Finally, after crossing seven mountains, they reached the forest gate. Before they entered, Enkidu cried out. "Let us not go deep into the forest! When I opened the gate, my hand failed and lost its strength." But Gilgamesh reassured him. "Do not be afraid, my friend, for you are experienced in battle. Take my hand, we will go together. There is no reason to fear death. Let your heart be roused by battle. Just stand beside me, and your strength will be restored."

They stood gazing at the deep, green forest, the magnificent cedars, and the trail Humbaba used—the path was well-marked. They looked upon the Cedar Mountain, the abode of the gods, the throne of Ishtar. The mountainside was lush with pleasant shade.

Gilgamesh and Enkidu agreed that felling one of the cedars would attract Humbaba's attention. Gilgamesh raised his axe, and chopped it down. Humbaba heard the noise and was enraged. He cried out: "Who is this who violates my woods and cuts down my precious trees?"

They then heard the voice of Shamash calling to them. "Do not be afraid. Go on. But do not allow him to enter his house."

But Gilgamesh was overcome by a sudden sleep and weakness and he lay speechless on the ground, as though in a trance. Enkidu tried to rouse him. "How long will you sleep? Do not let the mother who bore you be forced into mourning." At last Gilgamesh was awake and donned his breastplate. He said, "By the life of my mother Ninsun, and my father Lugalbanda, I swear I will not turn back!"

Then the sky darkened as Shamash hurled the thirteen winds upon Humbaba, immobilizing him, while Gilgamesh, Enkidu, and the other men felled the trees. When Gilgamesh cut down the seventh cedar he came face to face with Humbaba.

Humbaba then pleaded for his life. "Gilgamesh," he begged, "I am mountain-born, knowing no mother or father. Let me go and I will serve you; all the trees shall be yours, I will cut them for your palace." He took his hand, leading him to the house. "I swear by heaven and earth and by the dead."

Pity began to stir in Gilgamesh's heart. He said to Enkidu, "Should not the snared bird be allowed to return to its nest, as a captive man return to the arms of his mother?"

Enkidu replied, "Do not listen to him! If the snared bird is freed then you will not go home to Uruk, where the mother who gave you birth awaits your return!"

Humbaba dismissed Enkidu's words. "You are a servant and speak only evil."

But Gilgamesh heeded his friend's advice and drew his sword. He struck the monster upon the neck; Enkidu struck the second blow. A third blow severed Humbaba's head from his shoulders. When his body fell, the echo was heard for six miles.

They felled the remaining trees of Lebanon, and bundled them to bring home to Uruk.

Ishtar and Gilgamesh/The Death of Enkidu

Gilgamesh returned home, bathed, washed the long hair that fell over his shoulders, cleaned and polished his weapons, and changed back into his fine clothes. He donned his royal robes and placed the crown upon his head.

The goddess Ishtar noticed Gilgamesh adorned in his fine garments and admired his beauty. She said to him, "Come to me and be my husband and I will be your bride. I offer you a chariot of lapis lazuli with gold wheels and copper horns, drawn by mighty storm demons; our home will be perfumed with cedar. All will bow before you and pay tribute, your livestock will multiply, and your oxen and horses will be unrivaled in strength and speed."

Gilgamesh replied, "What could I offer you? What adornments for your body? I would give you gladly any food fit for gods and drink fit for queens, but to be my wife? What of your other bridegrooms? You once loved Tammuz, but left him weeping; you loved a bird but left him with a broken wing; you loved a stallion but whipped and beat him and forced him to drink muddy water; you loved the shepherd but made him a wolf. You are like half a door that fails to block the wind; a castle that crushes its warriors; pitch that blackens the hands of the bearer; a shoe that cuts the owner's feet; a water-skin that soaks the carrier. What would become of me?"

Ishtar became enraged at Gilgamesh's words. She complained bitterly in heaven, crying to her father, Anu. "He has insulted me! He threw my deeds into my face!" But Anu replied, "Did you not start the quarrel?" But she pleaded, "Father, give me the Bull of Heaven to kill Gilgamesh, or I will destroy the gates of the Netherworld and the dead will rise, outnumbering the living." Anu said, "If I grant this, there will be a drought for seven years in Uruk—have you saved enough grain to feed the people? Is there enough grass for the animals?" Ishtar said, "Yes, there is enough grain and grass for men and beasts."

And so Ishtar's desire was granted, and she led the Bull of Heaven into strong-walled Uruk. First the Bull went to the river. With one snort, a crack opened in the earth and 100 men fell to their deaths; with a second snort, 200 more fell dead. With his third snort, more cracks opened and Enkidu nearly fell in— but he recovered, and jumped upon the Bull, grabbing its horns. The Bull foamed and jerked, but Enkidu held on, shouting to Gilgamesh for help. Gilgamesh seized the Bull's tail and, with a thrust of his sword between its neck and horns, killed it. The two companions then cut out the Bull's heart and offered it to Shamash.

Ishtar was furious. She climbed upon the city wall and screamed a curse. "Woe to Gilgamesh, for he has scorned me by killing the Bull of Heaven!" Upon hearing these words, Enkidu tore off the Bull's right thigh and flung it into the goddess's face, saying "If I could do the same to you, I would, and drape the entrails over you!" Ishtar gathered her people, the courtesans and temple-girls, and lamented the great Bull.

Gilgamesh dispatched the smiths and craftsmen to take parts of the Bull for their use; he kept the horns for himself. They were plated with lapis two fingers thick and weighed thirty pounds each; he hung them on the palace wall.

That evening there was a great celebration in Uruk. But as he slept that night, Enkidu had a dream; he recounted it to Gilgamesh. "The gods held council and said that 'those who killed the Bull of Heaven and removed the cedars from the forest must die—Gilgamesh must not die; but Enkidu shall die.'" The dream caused Enkidu to be sick with fear. Gilgamesh cried to Shamash, "Why absolve me and not my brother?"

Enkidu cursed in his bitterness, shouting at the wooden gate, "If I had known my fate, I would have destroyed you!" He continued, "Shamash, foil the plans of that trapper who found me—may he catch no beasts and go hungry; and curse that courtesan to be without a home or comfort, sleeping in wastelands with thorns tearing her feet where she walks—may she be unwelcome wherever she goes!"

Shamash heard these words and reproached Enkidu from heaven: "Why do you curse the woman who taught you the ways of men, who gave you Gilgamesh for a brother, and gave you a comfortable home and glory in battle? When you are gone, Gilgamesh will lament by letting his hair grow long and wandering the world clad only in the skin of a lion."

These words eased Enkidu's heart. "I bless the temple-woman. May she be adored, receiving treasures of crystal, lapis, and gold, and enter the home of the gods." He then sat alone, still stricken and heart-sick. The next day, he told Gilgamesh of another dream he had. "I stood between earth and the heavens as they roared and rumbled, and a young man with somber face and eagle's talons fell upon me. He smothered me, and my arms became like wings. He led me to the Queen of the Underworld, where there is no light, where food is dust and clay, and from which none return. I saw there many who lived noble lives on earth, but now their crowns removed. In this House of Dust I saw Ereshkigal, the Queen, and Befit-Sheri, the scribe, kneeling before her, reading from the Tablet of Death in her hands. She saw me and spoke: 'Who has brought this one to me?' And then I awakened in terror."

Gilgamesh listened and wept and prayed, but by the end of the next day, Enkidu had fallen ill. Each day, for twelve days, his suffering grew. Then he said to Gilgamesh, "Ishtar has cursed me to die in shame, rather than in the glory of battle." Enkidu lay in bed, day after day, for twelve days, his flesh growing weaker.

Gilgamesh cried to his comrade, "May all the wild beasts weep for you—the gazelle, who was as a mother, and the wild ass, who was as a father; the bear, hyena, panther, tiger, jackal, lion, bull, stag, and ibex mourn you. May all the lands wail in mourning—the hills and pastures, the plains, the cypress and cedar we destroyed, and the rivers. May all those who knew you weep with mourning—the farmers and herders, nobles and warriors, those who fed and clothed you, and those who praised you."

When Enkidu died, Gilgamesh was overcome with grief. He cried out, pacing, "My swift friend, we fought the Bull of Heaven, we defeated the giant Humbaba, we climbed mountains and brought the cedars to Uruk! What is this evil slumber that has come upon you, so you no longer hear me?" He pulled at his hair, flung down his robes and raged like a lion, like a lioness stripped of her cubs. He touched Enkidu's chest, but no longer felt the beating heart. And so he placed a veil over his friend, like a bride.

He said to the Elders of Uruk: "I weep and mourn for Enkidu, my companion who was like a brother. He was to me like the axe at my side, a sword and shield, a comforting garment." He summoned all the smiths and craftsmen to create a statue of Enkidu, adorned with jewels and precious metals. He said, "My friend, I gave you a royal couch and seated you at my left hand for the princes of the world to kiss your feet; now all will mourn for you and joy be replaced with sorrow." And Gilgamesh let his hair grow long and set out to wander the world.

The Search for Everlasting Life

Gilgamesh roamed in bitterness, lamenting the loss of Enkidu and crying out in despair. "I share the fate of Enkidu—to die! How can I ever find peace, when I fear death? So now I must hurry. I must find Utanapishtim, the only man to find eternal life and join the gods. He can show me how to live forever."

All alone, Gilgamesh traveled, crossing grasslands and deserts. Then, upon a mountain pass one night, he prayed, "Long ago in these mountains I saw two lions; I was afraid. But I raised my eyes and prayed to Sin, the moon god, to protect me." That night he was roused by a dream; he saw the lions. He drew his axe and dagger, and fell upon the beasts like an arrow, tearing them apart and scattering them. He adorned his body in their skins, and made a meal of their flesh.

At last Gilgamesh came to the great mountains called Mashu, whose peaks rise to the heavens, and whose base reaches the Netherworld. Guarding the rising and setting sun, the Scorpion-men stood at the gate—half man, half dragon—it was death to look upon them. Gilgamesh felt terror in his heart and averted his eyes as he approached them. One of them said to the other, his wife, "This one who comes has the flesh of gods!" The woman answered, "Nay, only two-thirds is godlike; one-third is man." The Scorpion-man called out: "Why have you made this dangerous journey, child of the gods?"

Gilgamesh replied, "I seek my ancestor, Utanapishtim, for he has found everlasting life and I desire to accompany him."

The Scorpion-man answered, "Never has a mortal man done what you ask. None has crossed beneath the dark mountains, twelve leagues with no light."

But Gilgamesh was not to be deterred. He said, "In pain and sorrow I must go. In frigid cold or scorching heat, even gasping for breath, I will go. Open the gate."

The scorpion-man agreed to let him pass. "In safety may you travel, and return safely home," he said.

League after league Gilgamesh traversed the darkness of the mountain tunnel. Nothing ahead and nothing behind but the blackness of pitch. After eight leagues he cried out in the oppressive darkness. Still, nothing ahead and nothing behind but black. After nine leagues he felt a slight wind upon his face; after eleven leagues, a faint light appeared. At last, after twelve leagues, the sun shone brightly upon him.

When Gilgamesh emerged from the tunnel, he found himself in a glistening garden of jewels. The trees bore gems like fruit—leaves of lapis lazuli, carnelian hanging from vines. Instead of thorns and blossoms, there were pearls, agate, hematite, rubies, and emeralds. Then Shamash noticed Gilgamesh walking in wonder at the sparkling garden, and spoke to him. "No man has gone this way; you will not find what you seek."

Gilgamesh said, "Now that I have journeyed and toiled, am I to slumber in the earth forever? Though I be a dead man, let my eyes be dazzled with brightness."

Gilgamesh continued his journey, and eventually reached the sea. There he came upon Siduri, the tavern-keeper, who lived in a cottage on the shore. She was clothed in veils, with golden bowls and vats for her wine. She noticed Gilgamesh wearing skins on his body and despair on his face. She wondered at this stranger, thinking him a brigand who meant her harm, and bolted her door. But Gilgamesh called to her, "Alewife, why have you locked your door? I will shatter it, for I am Gilgamesh, who killed the lions in the mountain, defeated the Bull of Heaven, and overtook Humbaba, the guardian of the forest."

Siduri replied, "If you are Gilgamesh, the hero as you say, then why is your face so haggard and drawn? Why are you so wretched and your heart so sad? Why do you come such a distance, burned by heat and cold, roaming in the wilderness, searching the wind?"

Gilgamesh spoke to her, "Alewife, why should I not be worn and haggard? Why should I not feel despair? For I have crossed grasslands, deserts, and mountains. I have eaten wild beasts and wrapped my body in their skins. My friend, my brother, one I loved, who with me seized the Bull of Heaven and defeated the guardian of the forest, has been overtaken by mankind's fate. I wept for Enkidu for seven days and nights, until the worms crept over him. And now I fear death! How can I be still and silent? How can I bear the endless sleep? I cannot rest. I seek the way to Utanapishtim."

The tavern-keeper spoke to Gilgamesh, "You will not find what you seek. The gods keep everlasting life for themselves; it is not for us. Accept the fate we all share, Gilgamesh. Fill your life with good things—wash and dress yourself well; feast on fine foods; sing, dance, revel and rejoice every day and night. Cherish children and embrace your wife. This, too, is our fate."

Gilgamesh replied, "You give good advice, alewife, but you must know the way since you live on the shore. You must have seen a sign. I will swim the sea, if I must, or keep roaming the wild."

"There is no crossing," she said, "none but Shamash has done it. The waters are deep and deadly. But perhaps Urshanabi, the ferryman of Utanapishtim, would assist you. He lives in the forest and keeps sacred stones. But if he will not help you, you must turn back."

Gilgamesh became seized with anger at these words. Drawing his axe and dagger, he raced into the woods. He found the ferryman's home and, enraged, he smashed the sacred stone figures. Urshanabi, who was nearby, heard the destruction and ran to Gilgamesh. "Who are you, and why are you here?" He asked. "Why do you look so haggard? Why is your face so starved and your heart filled with despair?"

And Gilgamesh replied, "Urshanabi! I am Gilgamesh, king of Uruk. Why should I not be haggard and filled with despair? I have crossed mountains and deserts; I have been burned by heat and cold. My friend, my brother, with whom I defeated the Bull of Heaven and the guardian of the cedar forest, has been taken by the fate of all men. Why should I not wander? He has become clay. His fate lies upon me. How can I rest? Show me the way to Utanapishtim. I will swim the sea or wander the world forever."

Urshanabi said, "Gilgamesh, your own hands prevent the journey. In your anger, you destroyed the stones that allow for safe passage across the Waters of Death. Now you must go into the forest, and cut 300 poles, each one 60 cubits in length, and strip them. Then bring them to the boat."

Gilgamesh did as Urshanabi instructed, and they boarded the boat. For three days they traveled a journey that would normally take a month and a half. Then they reached the Waters of Death. Urshanabi said, "Use the poles you cut from the forest to propel us forward—but do not touch the water!" Each pole could only be used once; after Gilgamesh had used all the punting poles, Gilgamesh stripped off his garment and raised it in his arms as a sail.

Utanapishtim saw them coming and wondered, "Why have the sacred stones been broken? Why does the master not sail the boat?" When the boat reached the shore, Utanapishtim studied Gilgamesh and said, "Who are you and why have you come? Why is your face so gaunt and your cheeks so pale? Why does grief fill your heart? Why do you roam the wild and search for the wind?"

Gilgamesh answered, "I am Gilgamesh, king of Uruk. Why should my cheeks not be gaunt and my face pale? Why should I not roam over plains and mountains and search for the wind? Enkidu, my friend and brother, one I loved, who helped me conquer the Bull of Heaven and the guardian of the cedar forest, has been claimed by mortality. I wept over his body for seven days and watched the worms take him. My pleas did not awaken him. Am I not like him? I feel as though I'm already with him in the House of Dust. That is why I killed the beats and wear the skin of the lion, and why I came to the gate of the alewife; this is why I came to Urshanabi and crossed the Waters of Death. I wish to find everlasting life."

Utanapishtim said, "Gilgamesh, why are you filled with sadness? You are made of flesh and the divine, yet you have exhausted yourself. Nothing is permanent. Do we build homes to last forever? Does the river's flood endure? The great gods determine the fates of men—for both master and servant."

Gilgamesh said to Utanapishtim, "I see you, yet you appear no different from me; I thought to see a hero I should battle, but you rest easy. Tell me how you gained everlasting life."

Utanapishtim answered, "I will reveal the mystery to you—the secret of the gods."

The Story of the Flood

Utanapishtim told Gilgamesh the story of the great flood.

Enlil called the gods together and they complained that the people living upon the earth had become too noisy, disturbing the gods. They proposed a great flood to drown them. Ishtar agreed with Enlil's idea, but Ea did not. Ea appeared to Utanapishtim in a dream, urging him to leave behind his home and to build a giant ship. He instructed Utanapishtim to bring his wife and family aboard the ship, and craftspeople, and to gather his possessions, grains, and seeds of all living things, and also birds and beasts.

On the seventh day, the ship was complete and he waited for the time Ea pronounced—when the sky would grow dark and a storm would come. And so the storm came, and the ship set out. The gods watched. Ishtar regretted her part in the flood, seeing the suffering of the people. Even the gods were afraid. For seven days and nights the waters raged. On the eighth day, the winds stopped and the waters calmed. Shamash brought light to the sky. In gratitude, Utanapishtim sacrificed an ox and sheep to the gods. They floated for twelve days, then the ship grounded on a mountain. On the seventh day after landing, Utanapishtim sent out a dove, but it returned to the ship, finding no place to rest. Next, a swallow was sent. But it, too, returned. Then a raven was sent. It did not return, indicating the waters had receded.

Then all the creatures were set free and another sacrifice was made. Ishtar arrived and blessed them. All the gods came, except Enlil, who was furious. But the warrior god Ninurta said that this must be the work of Ea. Ea defended his decision, professing the unfairness of the flood. Ea then said that Utanapishtim had a dream that told him how to survive. Utanapishtim bowed to Enlil and he blessed them. Enlil said, "From now on Utanapishtim and his wife shall live like the gods. Utanapishtim has saved humanity and all the plants and animals. They shall have everlasting life."

And so Utanapishtim finished his tale. "Enlil gave us immortality," he said, "but Gilgamesh, though you are a king, who will assemble the gods for your sake?"

The Return

Utanapishtim said to Gilgamesh, "If you wish to become like the gods, you must possess strength and pass this test by remaining on your feet, awake for six days and seven nights." But Gilgamesh, squatting on his haunches, could not resist the sleep that came upon him. Utanapishtim said to his wife, "See this hero who seeks immortality. Sleep blows him over so easily, like mist." She said, "Wake him with a touch, so he may return to his home." But Utanapishtim said, "In time. For now we must prove that he sleeps, for he will deny it. Bake a loaf of bread each day he sleeps, and mark the day upon the wall." On the seventh day, Gilgamesh was still asleep. Near his head, six loaves of bread were lined in a row, and there were six marks on the wall. The first loaf of bread was shrunken; the second was spoiled; the third was soggy; the fourth was crusted with scaly white, the fifth had grayed with mold; the sixth was yet fresh, and the seventh was still warm from the fire.

Utanapishtim touched Gilgamesh who awakened and said, "I scarcely slept when you woke me." But Utanapishtim showed Gilgamesh the loaves of bread. "Count these loaves and see how long you slept." Gilgamesh exclaimed in misery, "O now what shall I do and where shall I go? Death dwells wherever I step!"

"Do not despair," Utanapishtim said. "You, as all others, cannot live forever. But other gifts have been granted to you. You have strength and might—recall your great deeds. You journeyed here, where no other has reached. And you have your kingdom and your people—the power to lead them and to teach. Return home, Gilgamesh, and cast away your sorrow. The gods have favored you. Rejoice! Do not fear!"

Then Utanapishtim said to Urshanabi, "Take this man to cleanse his body and hair; remove the animal skins and throw them to the sea. Adorn his body so his beauty is revealed and fit a new band for his head. Then accompany him to Uruk."

And so Gilgamesh was renewed and they prepared to sail. But then Utanapishtim's wife said, "Gilgamesh is weary from his dangerous journey to find you—is there no gift for his effort to take back to his city?" And Utanapishtim replied, "Because you made this journey, I will send with you a secret, a mystery created by the gods. There is plant that grows in the water—it flowers like a rose and its thorns will prick your hands, but if you can gather it, it will grant everlasting youth. You will not live forever, but you will remain strong and young."

And so Gilgamesh tied stones to his feet and sunk down into the deep water. He found the plant and picked it, though it cut his hands. Then he loosened the stones and surfaced. He climbed into the boat with Urshanabi and they crossed the Waters of Death. In three days they covered a distance of a month and a half's time. Gilgamesh exclaimed, "I name this plant 'the old man becomes young,' and I will bring it to Uruk so I may first share it with the old men, and then I will eat some myself to restore my youth."

They reached land and continued their journey. After twenty leagues they stopped to eat; after thirty leagues they stopped to rest. Gilgamesh carried the precious plant with him to keep it safe. He found a freshwater pool to bathe in, and left the plant with his clothing on the ground. But a serpent sensed the sweet plant and rose from the water, snatching it up. Instantly, the serpent's skin sloughed away, being renewed, and it returned to the pool.

Gilgamesh wept. As tears ran down his cheeks, he said to Urshanabi, "For this I toiled and labored? For this I have bled! For what, and why? I have gained nothing. I have no glory. The serpent now has the gift! The stream has now carried it beyond my reach."

Resolved, Gilgamesh carried on. They walked twenty leagues, then stopped to eat; after thirty leagues they rested. In three days they walked a journey of a month and a half. Then, at last, they arrived in Uruk.

Gilgamesh said to the ferryman, "Climb up the walls and see the glory of Uruk! See the city, gardens, fields, and the temple!"

This great city was the glory of Gilgamesh, who journeyed far and wide, who labored and toiled, and learned great mysteries and wisdom. He learned the tale of the flood, and engraved his story upon stone. Long after it was said of Gilgamesh that he brought light to his people. The people mourned and poured libations over his tomb. It is said he had no equal among men.

DISCUSSION QUESTIONS

1. What is the greatest lesson Gilgamesh learns on his journey? What does he gain? What does he lose?

2. Consider Enkidu's change when he becomes "civilized." In what ways is this change a metaphor for something far greater than one man's experience? What customs cause him to become civilized?

3. Trace the various points of the monomyth in this tale.

4. Why is it important that Gilgamesh does not immediately eat the plant of eternal youth?

5. What insights about human relationships can be gained from this story?

6. Identify motifs that recur throughout the tale and explore their meaning.

BIBLIOGRAPHY

Abdel Haleem, M. A. S. translator. *The Qur'an*. Introduction. Oxford UP, 2004.

"Ancient Mesopotamian Gods and Goddesses." AMGG Project.UK Higher Education Academy's Subject Centre for History, Classics, and Archaeology, 2011. http://oracc.museum.upenn.edu/amgg/index.html

Blenkinsopp, Joseph. *The Pentateuch: An Introduction to the First Five Books of the Bible*. Doubleday, 1992.

Breasted, James Henry. *Development of Religion and Thought in Ancient Egypt*. Hodder & Stoughton, 1912. http://www.sacred-texts.com/egy/rtae/rtae00.htm

Brown, Brian. *The Wisdom of the Egyptians*. Brentano's, 1923. http://www.sacred-texts.com/egy/woe/woe00.htm

Budge, E. A. Wallis. *Legends of the Gods*. Kegan Paul, Trench and Trübner & Co. Ltd., 1912. http://sacred-texts.com/egy/leg/leg00.htm

---. *The Literature of the Ancient Egyptians*. J.M. Dent & Sons, Ltd., 1914. http://www.gutenberg.org/files/15932/15932-h/15932-h.htm#Pg_51

---. *The Babylon Story of the Deluge as told by Assyrian Tablets Nineveh*. Pantianos, 1920.

Cohn, Norman. *Noah's Flood: The Genesis Story in Western Thought*. Yale UP, 1996.

Colavito, Jason. *The Epic of Gilgamesh*. http://www.jasoncolavito.com/epic-of-gilgamesh.html

Cotterell, Arthur, and Rachel Storm. *The Ultimate Encyclopedia of Mythology*. Hermes House, 1999.

In Search of History: Pyramids of Giza, 1997, A&E Television Networks.

Jastrow, M. "Descent of the Goddess Ishtar into the Lower World." *The Civilization of Babylonia and Assyria*, 1915. http://www.sacred-texts.com/ane/ishtar.htm

Kovacs, M. G. *The Epic of Gilgamesh*. Stanford University Press, 1989. http://jewishchristianlit.com/Texts/ANEmyths/gilgamesh00.html

Kramer, Samuel Noah. *Sumerian Mythology: A Study of Spiritual and Literary Achievement in the Third Millennium B.C.* Revised Edition. University of Pennsylvania Press, 1944, revised 1961. http://www.sacred-texts.com/ane/sum/sum01.htm

Leeming, David A. *The Handy Mythology Answer Book*. Visible Ink Press, 2015.

Lichtheim, Miriam. *Ancient Egyptian Literature*, Vol. 1, pp. 51–5. University of California Press, 1973.

MacKenzie, Donald. *Egyptian Myth and Legend*. Gresham Publishing, Co, 1907. http://www.sacred-texts.com/egy/eml/eml04.htm

---. *Myths of Babylonia and Assyria*. 1915. http://www.sacred-texts.com/ane/mba/mba11.htm. https://www.gutenberg.org/files/16653/16653-h/16653-h.htm

McClymond, Kathryn. "The World's Oldest Myth: Gilgamesh." *Great Mythologies of the World*. The Great Courses, 2015.

McCoy, Dan. "Creation Myths." *Egyptian Mythology*. http://egyptianmythology.org/stories/creation-myths/

Palmer, E. H. The Qur'an. Part 1: I-XVI in *Sacred Books of the East* Vol 6 & 9, 1880.

Plutarch, *De Iside et Osiride* Goodwin, editor. http://www.perseus.tufts.edu/hopper/text?doc=Perseus%3Atext%3A2008.01.0240%3Asection%3D18. http://data.perseus.org/citations/urn:cts:greekLit:tlg0007.tlg089.perseus-eng2:18

Powell, Barry B. *World Myth*. Pearson, 2014

Rodwell J. M., translator. *The Holy Qur'an*. 1876.

Rosenberg, Donna. *World Mythology*, 3rd. ed. NTC, 1999.

Sanders, N. K. *The Epic of Gilgamesh*. Assyrian International News Agency Books Online, last modified, January 8, 2017. http://www.aina.org/books/eog/eog.pdf

Shakir, M. H., translator. *The Holy Qur'an*. Tahrike Tarsile Qur'an, Inc., 1983.

Spence, Lewis. *Myths and Legends of Ancient Egypt*. Boston: David D. Nickerson & Co., 1915. https://www.gutenberg.org/files/43662/43662-h/43662-h.htm#CHAPTER_IV_THE_CULT_OF_OSIRIS

Spence, Lewis. *Myths and Legends of Babylonia and Assyria*. George G. Harrap & Co, Ltd., 1916.

The Egyptian Book of the Dead, A&E, 2010.

The King James Bible. http://www.gutenberg.org/files/10/10-h/10-h.htm

The New Oxford Annotated Bible: An Ecumenical Study Bible. Oxford UP, 1994.

Thompson, R. Campbell. *The Epic of Gilgamesh.*1928. http://www.sacred-texts.com/ane/eog/eog03.htm

Thury and Devinney. *Introduction to World Mythology*, 3rd ed. Oxford University Press, 2013.

Thury, Eva M., and Margaret K. Devinney. *Introduction to Mythology*, 4th ed. Oxford University Press, 2017.

Vandiver, Elizabeth. "The Epic of Gilgamesh." *Great Authors of the Western Literary Tradition*, 2nd ed. The Great Courses, 2004.

Voth, Grant. "Creation Myths." *Myth in Human History*. The Great Courses, 2010.

---. "The Goddess—Isis and Osiris." *Myth in Human History*. The Great Courses, 2010.

---. "Inanna and Dumuzi." *Myth in Human History*. The Great Courses, 2010.

---. "Mythic Heroes: Gilgamesh." *Myth in Human History*. The Great Courses, 2010.

Wilson, Epiphanius. *Sacred Books of the East Including Selections from the Vedic Hymns, Zend-Avesta, Dhammapada, Upanishads, the Koran, and the Life of Buddha.* "Selections from the Zend-Avesta." Translated by James Darmestetter, 1900.

Wolkstein, Diane, and Samuel Noah Kramer. *Inanna: Queen of Heaven and Earth*. Harper and Row, 1983.

Chapter 3

THE MYTHS OF THE MEDITERRANEAN

Source: Christina Gant

Introduction

© Bardocz Peter/Shutterstock.com

Greek myths have been made familiar to us through films, television, and popular literature, but the actual stories, written over 2,000 years ago, are even more fascinating than the Hollywood renderings. Aside from the major players such as Zeus, Poseidon, and Hades, their Roman counterparts and the rest of the pantheon were just as significant in the daily lives of the Greeks and Romans. And yet, while the gods certainly played a role in how people lived, they did not believe the gods controlled them—they were not puppets or pawns; however, they did believe sacrifice was crucial to ensuring the gods' favor.

Religious rites and worship were primarily local and regional affairs conducted within villages and households especially during certain times of the agricultural year. Offerings (typically animal sacrifices) were sometimes made at temples, but these were not places of actual worship. People also visited temples to consult oracles or seers for prophecies and advice. There was no official religious organization at this time, and the function of priests was mainly to perform certain rituals. Worship of the gods was not merely a personal act; it was a community endeavor as well. The gods were like an extended Greek family, each with specific personalities and attributes that helped people relate to them as individuals. These gods were not remote, but part of this world, accessible and familiar to the Greek people, believed to inhabit temples, shrines, and other sacred places on earth as well as their main dwelling place of Mt. Olympus.

© Volina/Shutterstock.com

Yet, despite the obvious attention people gave to the gods, the myths reveal that these gods did not have a particular love for humans, nor did they expect to be loved by the people, but rather honored and respected. In fact, aside from their role in the great epics, the gods did not appear to have much interest in the daily lives of human beings.

The gods were not perfect, and the Greeks didn't always take them seriously. In fact, the gods had many of the faults and flaws of human beings. Zeus was a philanderer, causing Hera to be jealous; Hades was an abductor. Comedic writers made fun of the gods and their dramatic exploits; philosophers were critical of their behavior, which was often immoral and violent—some even questioned their existence altogether.

Contemporary readers, especially those familiar with monotheism, may find it difficult to relate to not only a polytheistic system, but the notion of gods as imperfect beings, quarrelling amongst themselves. Greek religion didn't have specific rules, dogma, or the concept of sin. Additionally, the Greeks understood that the divine could be recognized as many facets of the same being, a concept that does not fit with the monotheistic perspective. It's important to keep this in mind while reading the myths. The stories are a product of their culture and the beliefs of the people at that time.

While Roman attitudes toward religion, economics, politics, and society differed greatly from that of the Greeks, they admired the Greek literary tradition and adopted not only their alphabet, but their myths. A study of this process is far too complex to address in the scope of this text, but one aspect to keep in mind is that the Romans used myth as legend which they tied closely to their history, which in turn conveyed and supported their values and ideals.

Many of the myths presented here were written by Romans, so names of the Roman gods and goddesses are used.

The Olympians			
God and Goddess (Greek, Roman, and other names)	Parentage	Traits	Sacred objects (animals, trees, etc.)
Zeus—Jupiter (Jove)	Kronos and Rhea	God of Sky, Rain, Clouds, Thunder	Eagle, Oak, Olive Tree, Lightning Bolt, Bull
Poseidon—Neptune	Kronos and Rhea	God of the Sea, Earthquakes, Horses, Floods	Trident, Horse, Bull, Golden Car, Dolphin, Pine Tree, Wild Celery
Hades—Pluto (Dis)	Kronos and Rhea	God of the Underworld, Wealth, Precious Metals	Invisible Helmet
Hera—Juno	Kronos and Rhea	Goddess of Marriage, the Sky, Married Women	Sceptre, Cow, Peacock, Lion, Pomegranate
Hephaestus— Vulcan (Mulciber)	Hera	God of Fire, Smithing, Metalworking, Volcanoes	Hammer & Tongs, Donkey
Aphrodite—Venus	Ouranos	Goddess of Love and Beauty, Procreation	Conch Shell, Myrtle, Dove, Sparrow, Swan, Rose
Athena—Minerva	Zeus and Metis	Goddess of Wisdom, War, Weaving, Crafts, Agriculture	Owl, Aegis, Olive Tree
Apollo (Phoebus)	Zeus and Leto	God of Music, Poetry, Prophecy, Truth, Healing	Lyre, Bow & Arrow, Laurel, Dolphin, Crow, Swan, Raven
Artemis—Diana	Zeus and Leto	Goddess of Hunting, Wilderness, Wild Animals, Children	Bow & Arrow, Bear, Deer, Cypress
Hermes—Mercury	Zeus and Maia	God of Travel, Messengers, Trade, Athletes, Thieves	Caduceus, Winged Sandals, Ram, Hare, Hawk, Crocus
Dionysus— Liber (Bacchus, Lyaeus)	Zeus and Semele	God of Wine, Festivity, Madness	Pinecone Staff, Serpent, Bull, Panther, Grapevine, Ivy
Ares—Mars	Zeus and Hera	God of War, Courage, Battlelust	Vulture, Dog, Serpent

Part 1: Creation and Destruction

Source: Christina Gant

The Homeric Hymn to Gaia

She is Mother Earth, she is the first Goddess of the Pantheon, she is Creator of the Universe. It is Gaia's creation of light and dark, sky and heavens that begins the world, and her coupling with heaven that leads to the creation of the Titans and Olympians, as Hesiod tells in his work *Theogony*.

Gaia, is found spelled and pronounced a variety of ways, including Gaia (GUY-uh), Gaea (JEE-uh), or Ge (JEE). For the purposes of consistency, we will call her "Gaia" throughout this chapter. This Homeric author calls her "Earth, the Mother of All" and Hesiod simply refers to her as "Earth" when explaining the creation of the universe.

Homer is famous for *The Iliad* and *The Odyssey*, which chronicle the Trojan War and Odysseus' long journey home. These epics come to us through oral poetry from around 750 BCE and have formed the backbone for what we know about the Greek tradition of storytelling. But after Homer, a host of poets were inspired in the seventh and sixth centuries BCE to emulate his style. These are the Hymnists, who would go on to write the Homeric Hymns anonymously, while giving the credit to Homer.

The Homeric Hymns are a collection of thirty-three odes (poems of praise) to individual gods and goddesses. They are anonymous, but written in what is called a "Homeric" style—that is, the same meter, cadence, and language that we find in a work like *The Odyssey*. They seem to have been performed: as songs, at religious festivals, as a kind of preface for larger storytelling events. They vary in length and many have likely been lost to us.

Homeric Hymn Number 30 invokes our praise and marvel of Gaia.

TO EARTH THE MOTHER OF ALL

I will sing of well-founded Earth, mother of all,   1
eldest of all beings. She feeds all creatures that are in the world,
all that go upon the goodly land, and all that are in the paths of the seas,
and all that fly: all these are fed of her store.
Through you, O queen, men are blessed in their children   5
and blessed in their harvests, and to you it belongs
to give means of life to mortal men and to take it away.
Happy is the man whom you delight to honor! He has all things abundantly:
his fruitful land is laden with corn, his pastures are covered
with cattle, and his house is filled with good things.   10
Such men rule orderly in their cities of fair women:
great riches and wealth follow them: their sons exult with ever-fresh delight,
and their daughters in flower-laden bands
play and skip merrily over the soft flowers of the field.
Thus is it with those whom you honor, O holy goddess, bountiful spirit.   15
Hail, Mother of the gods, wife of starry Heaven;
freely bestow upon me, for this my song substance that cheers the heart!
And now I will remember you and [sing] another song also.

DISCUSSION QUESTIONS

1. Think about the word "Hymn." When is it typically used? Why would a "Hymn" be directed toward Mother Earth?

2. Why does the author of the Hymn add that he will "remember you with another song also" as his last line?

3. Are there those who are not blessed by Gaia's "delight to honor"?

Source: Anonymous. *The Homeric Hymns and Homerica with an English Translation* by Hugh G. Evelyn-White. *Homeric Hymns.* 1914.

Orphic Hymn to Earth

The Orphic Hymns are similar to the Homeric Hymns as they are written by a group of devotees "in the style of" and who believed in the teachings of Orpheus, the son of Apollo by way of the Muse Calliope. Orpheus and his brother Linus were great musicians because of this alliance with the Muse. Linus was unfortunately killed by Heracles with his own lyre during a music lesson, but it is Orpheus' lyre who can charm to sleep the monsters of Hades: the Cerberus and the Furies. His talent, clearly noticed and praised, went on to be the foundation for the cult of Orphism.

The teachings of Orphism, which is not exactly a religion, but something to be considered more like a set of practices and beliefs related to the literature, is based on the idea that Zeus and Persephone are the parents of Dionysus and that humans are sprang from the ashes of the Titans. The Orphic mysteries say the soul of a human being continually attempts to attain spiritual enlightenment and reach the realm of the gods—later called the "Transmigration of Souls" and something that we associate with philosophers like Pythagoras and Plato.

Orphism tells the tales of the creation of the universe in ways very similar to Hesiod. This cult found its following between fifth century BCE through the second century CE. Many of the same characters, including Zeus and Earth and Kronos, appear in Orphic creation stories, though other characters like Light and Time are added as well.

The following Orphic Hymn is addressed to Earth, "To the Mother of the Gods."

HYMN 26 "TO THE MOTHER OF THE GODS"

Mother of Gods, great nurse of all, draw near, divinely honored, and regard my prayer:
Throned on a car, by lions drawn along, by bull-destroying lions, swift and strong,
Thou swayest the sceptre of the pole divine, and the world's middle seat, much-famed, is thine.
Hence earth is thine, and needy mortals share their constant food, from thy protecting care:
From thee at first both Gods and men arose; from thee, the sea and every river flows.
Hestia, and source of good, thy name we find to mortal men rejoicing to be kind;
For every good to give, thy soul delights; come, mighty power, propitious to our rites,
All-taming, blessed, Phrygian saviour, come, Kronos' great queen, rejoicing in the drum.
Celestial, ancient, life-supporting maid, fanatic Goddess, give thy suppliant aid;
With joyful aspect on our incense shine, and, pleased, accept the sacrifice divine.

DISCUSSION QUESTIONS

1. Compare the Orphic Hymn to the Homeric Hymn to Gaia. What do you see are the similarities and differences in tone, voice, style, rendering of Gaia?

2. Why do you think the names of other gods are mentioned in this hymn?

3. The last line mentions a "sacrifice divine." What can we glean about the practices associated with the Orphic cult from this hymn?

Source: *The Hymns of Orpheus*. Translated by Thomas Taylor, 1792.

Hesiod's *Theogony*

The ten-year war that waged between the Titans and Olympians, the birth of the cyclops and hundred handers, the fates and furies, the tale of Zeus' rise to power—it all comes down to us from the Greek poet Hesiod.

Writing between 750–650 BCE, the poet Hesiod is attributed to having passed down the oldest creation story of the Greeks. In his long work *Theogony*, he traces for us many concepts of the beginning of the creation of Greek culture. Much of the poem is considered a hymn to the Muses. Hesiod calls to them:

> From the Heliconian Muses let us begin to sing, who hold the great and holy mount of Helicon, and dance on soft feet about the deep-blue spring and the altar of the almighty son of Kronos, and, when they have washed their tender bodies in Permessus or in the Horse's Spring or Olmeius, make their fair, lovely dances upon highest Helicon and move with vigorous feet.

As was custom before a recitation, beginning with a call to the nine Muses of the arts would have ensured a divinely inspired story.

Hesiod continues his story of the *Theogony* with a chronology of births, beginning with Chaos, then Gaia and Ouranos, and the eventual birth of the pantheon of gods and goddesses we know. Interspersed between these immortal births are the stories of war, bravery, and cunning between the gods.

But as Edith Hamilton warns us, we can't read *Theogony* as a kind of "Greek bible." Hesiod's poem was not read as a step-by-step account of the gods' actions to be taken literally, but as a piece of a larger collection in which they learned about their gods and goddesses. We should instead think about *Theogony* as insight into the morals and social values that were present at the time of Hesiod's writing.

THEOGONY

Creation of the World (lines 105–154)

Hail, children of Zeus! Grant lovely song and celebrate the holy race of the deathless gods who are for ever, those that were born of Earth and starry Heaven and gloomy Night and them that briny Sea did rear. Tell how at the first gods and earth came to be, and rivers, and the boundless sea with its raging swell, and the gleaming stars, and the wide heaven above, and the gods who were born of them, givers of good things, and how they divided their wealth, and how they shared their honors amongst them, and also how at the first they took many-folded Olympus. These things declare to me from the beginning, you Muses who dwell in the house of Olympus, and tell me which of them first came to be.

In truth at first Chaos* came to be, but next wide-bosomed Earth, the ever-sure foundation of all the deathless ones who hold the peaks of snowy Olympus, and dim Tartarus in the depth of the wide-pathed Earth, and Eros,* fairest among the deathless gods, who unnerves the limbs and overcomes the mind and wise counsels of all gods and all men within them. From Chaos came forth Erebus* and

*Chaos here is void, nothingness
*Eros = Love
*Erebus = Darkness

Source: *Hesiod. The Homeric Hymns and Homerica with an English Translation* by Hugh G. Evelyn-White. *Theogony.* 1914.

black Night; but of Night were born Aether* and Day, whom she conceived and bore from union in love with Erebus. And Earth first bore starry Ouranos*, equal to herself, to cover her on every side, and to be an ever-sure abiding-place for the blessed gods. And she brought forth long hills, graceful haunts of the goddess Nymphs who dwell amongst the glens of the hills. She bore also the fruitless deep with his raging swell, Pontus,* without sweet union of love. But afterwards she lay with Heaven and bore deep-swirling Oceanus, Coeus and Crius and Hyperion and Iapetus,* Theia and Rhea, Themis and Mnemosyne and gold-crowned Phoebe and lovely Tethys.

After them was born Kronos the wily, youngest and most terrible of her children, and he hated his lusty sire. And again, she bore the Cyclopes, overbearing in spirit, Brontes, and Steropes and stubborn-hearted Arges,* who gave Zeus the thunder and made the thunderbolt: in all else they were like the gods, but one eye only was set in the midst of their foreheads. And they were surnamed Cyclopes because one orbed eye was set in their foreheads. Strength and might and craft were in their works. And again, three other sons were born of Earth and Heaven, great and doughty beyond telling, Cottus and Briareos and Gyes, presumptuous children. From their shoulders sprang a hundred arms, not to be approached, and fifty heads grew from the shoulders upon the strong limbs of each, and irresistible was the stubborn strength that was in their great forms.

The Plot to Kill Ouranos (lines 155–174)

For of all the children that were born of Earth and Heaven, these were the most terrible, and they were hated by their own father from the first. And he used to hide them all away in a secret place of Earth so soon as each was born, and would not suffer them to come up into the light: and Heaven rejoiced in his evil doing. But vast Earth groaned within, being straitened, and she thought a crafty and an evil wile. Forthwith she made the element of grey flint and shaped a great sickle, and told her plan to her dear sons. And she spoke, cheering them, while she was vexed in her dear heart: "My children, gotten of a sinful father, if you will obey me, we should punish the vile outrage of your father; for he first thought of doing shameful things." So she said; but fear seized them all, and none of them uttered a word.

But great Kronos the wily took courage and answered his dear mother: "Mother, I will undertake to do this deed, for I reverence not our father of evil name, for he first thought of doing shameful things." So he said: and vast Earth rejoiced greatly in spirit, and set and hid him in an ambush, and put in his hands a jagged sickle, and revealed to him the whole plot.

The Castration of Heaven/Creation of Aphrodite (lines 175–205)

And Heaven came, bringing on night and longing for love, and he lay about Earth spreading himself full upon her. Then the son from his ambush stretched forth his left hand and in his right took the great long sickle with jagged teeth, and swiftly lopped off his own father's members and cast them away to fall behind him. And not vainly did they fall from his hand; for all the bloody drops that gushed forth Earth received, and as the seasons moved round she bore the strong Erinyes* and the great Giants with gleaming armour, holding long spears in their hands and the Nymphs whom they call Meliae* all over the boundless earth.

*Aether = The Ether- the pure "upper" atmosphere
*Ouranos = Heaven
*Pontus = Sea
*Lapetus = Prometheus' father
*Brontes = Thunder, Steropes = Lightning, Arges = The Vivid One
*Erinyes = The Furies
*Meliae = Nymph of Ash Trees

And so soon as he had cut off the members with flint and cast them from the land into the surging sea, they were swept away over the main a long time: and a white foam spread around them from the immortal flesh, and in it there grew a maiden. First she drew near holy Cythera, and from there, afterwards, she came to sea-girt Cyprus, and came forth an awful and lovely goddess, and grass grew up about her beneath her shapely feet. Her gods and men call Aphrodite, and the foam-born goddess and rich-crowned Cytherea, because she grew amid the foam, and Cytherea because she reached Cythera, and Cyprogenes because she was born in billowy Cyprus, and Philommedes* because she sprang from the members. And with her went Eros, and comely Desire followed her at her birth at the first and as she went into the assembly of the gods. This honor she has from the beginning, and this is the portion allotted to her amongst men and undying gods,—the whisperings of maidens and smiles and deceits with sweet delight and love and graciousness.

The World of the Titans (lines 207–230)

But these sons whom he begot himself great Ouranos used to call Titans (Strainers) in reproach, for he said that they strained and did presumptuously a fearful deed, and that vengeance for it would come afterwards. And Night bore hateful Doom and black Fate and Death, and she bore Sleep and the tribe of Dreams. And again the goddess murky Night, though she lay with none, bare Blame and painful Woe, and the Hesperides who guard the rich, golden apples and the trees bearing fruit beyond glorious Ocean. Also she bore the Destinies and ruthless avenging Fates, Clotho and Lachesis and Atropos,* who give men at their birth both evil and good to have, and they pursue the transgressions of men and of gods: and these goddesses never cease from their dread anger until they punish the sinner with a sore penalty. Also deadly Night bore Nemesis (Indignation) to afflict mortal men, and after her, Deceit and Friendship and hateful Age and hard-hearted Strife. But abhorred Strife bore painful Toil and Forgetfulness and Famine and tearful Sorrows, Fightings also, Battles, Murders, Manslaughters, Quarrels, Lying Words, Disputes, Lawlessness and Ruin, all of one nature, and Oath who most troubles men upon earth when anyone willfully swears a false oath.

Kronos swallows the Olympians (lines 453–506)

But Rhea was subject in love to Kronos and bore splendid children, Hestia, Demeter, and gold-shod Hera and strong Hades, pitiless in heart, who dwells under the earth, and the loud-crashing Earth-Shaker, and wise Zeus, father of gods and men, by whose thunder the wide earth is shaken. These great Kronos swallowed as each came forth from the womb to his mother's knees with this intent, that no other of the proud sons of Heaven should hold the kingly office amongst the deathless gods. For he learned from Earth and starry Heaven that he was destined to be overcome by his own son, strong though he was, through the contriving of great Zeus. Therefore he kept no blind outlook, but watched and swallowed down his children: and unceasing grief seized Rhea.

But when she was about to bear Zeus, the father of gods and men, then she besought her own dear parents, Earth and starry Heaven, to devise some plan with her that the birth of her dear child might be concealed, and that retribution might overtake great, crafty Kronos for his own father and also for the children whom he had swallowed down. And they readily heard and obeyed their dear daughter, and told her all that was destined to happen touching Kronos the king and his stout-hearted son. So they sent her to Lyctus, to the rich land of Crete, when she was ready to bear great Zeus, the youngest of her children. Him did vast Earth receive from Rhea in wide Crete to nourish and to bring up. To that place came Earth carrying him swiftly through the black night to Lyctus first, and took him in her arms and hid him in a remote cave beneath the secret places of the holy earth on thick-wooded Mount Aegeum; but to the mightily ruling son of Heaven, the earlier king of the gods, she gave a great stone wrapped in

*Philommedes = Translates to "Member loving" or "Genital loving" since this is what she is created from
*Clotho = the Spinner, Lachesis = the Disposer of Lots, Atropos = she who cannot be averted

swaddling clothes. Then he took it in his hands and thrust it down into his belly: wretch! he knew not in his heart that in place of the stone his son was left behind, unconquered and untroubled, and that he was soon to overcome him by force and might and drive him from his honors, himself to reign over the deathless gods.

After that, the strength and glorious limbs of the prince increased quickly, and as the years rolled on, great Kronos the wily was beguiled by the deep suggestions of Earth, and brought up again his offspring, vanquished by the arts and might of his own son, and he vomited up first the stone which he had swallowed last. And Zeus set it fast in the wide-pathed earth at goodly Pytho under the glens of Parnassus, to be a sign thenceforth and a marvel to mortal men. And he set free from their deadly bonds the brothers of his father, sons of Heaven whom his father in his foolishness had bound. And they remembered to be grateful to him for his kindness, and gave him thunder and the glowing thunderbolt and lightning: for before that, huge Earth had hidden these. In them he trusts and rules over mortals and immortals.

War between Titans and Olympians (lines 617–728)

But when first their father was vexed in his heart with Obriareus and Cottus and Gyes*, he bound them in cruel bonds, because he was jealous of their exceeding manhood and comeliness and great size: and he made them live beneath the wide-pathed earth, where they were afflicted, being set to dwell under the ground, at the end of the earth, at its great borders, in bitter anguish for a long time and with great grief at heart. But the son of Kronos* and the other deathless gods whom rich-haired Rhea bore from union with Kronos, brought them up again to the light at Earth's advising. For she herself recounted all things to the gods fully, how with these they might gain victory and a glorious cause to vaunt themselves. For the Titan gods and as many as sprang from Kronos had long been fighting together in stubborn war with heart-grieving toil, the lordly Titans from high Othrys, but the gods, givers of good, whom rich-haired Rhea bore in union with Kronos, from Olympus.

So they, with bitter wrath, were fighting continually with one another at that time for ten full years, and the hard strife had no close or end for either side, and the issue of the war hung evenly balanced. But when he had provided those three with all things fitting, nectar and ambrosia which the gods themselves eat, and when their proud spirit revived within them all after they had fed on nectar and delicious ambrosia, then it was that the father of men and gods spoke amongst them: "Hear me, bright children of Earth and Heaven, that I may say what my heart within me bids. A long while now have we, who are sprung from Kronos and the Titan gods, fought with each other every day to get victory and to prevail. But show your great might and unconquerable strength, and face the Titans in bitter strife; for remember our friendly kindness, and from what sufferings you are come back to the light from your cruel bondage under misty gloom through our counsels." So he said.

And blameless Cottus answered him again: "Divine one, you speak that which we know well: no, even of ourselves we know that your wisdom and understanding is exceeding, and that you became a defender of the deathless ones from chill doom. And through your devising we have come back again from the murky gloom and from our merciless bonds, enjoying what we looked not for, O lord, son of Kronos. And so now with fixed purpose and deliberate counsel we will aid your power in dreadful strife and will fight against the Titans in hard battle." So he said: and the gods, givers of good things, applauded when they heard his word, and their spirit longed for war even more than before, and they all, both male and female, stirred up hated battle that day, the Titan gods, and all that were born of Kronos together with those dread, mighty ones of overwhelming strength whom Zeus brought up to the light from Erebus beneath the earth.

*Obriareus, Cottus, Gyes = The Hundred-Handers, Kronos' brothers
*Kronos = Zeus

A hundred arms sprang from the shoulders of all alike, and each had fifty heads growing from his shoulders upon stout limbs. These, then, stood against the Titans in grim strife, holding huge rocks in their strong hands. And on the other part the Titans eagerly strengthened their ranks, and both sides at one time showed the work of their hands and their might. The boundless sea rang terribly around, and the earth crashed loudly: wide Heaven was shaken and groaned, and high Olympus reeled from its foundation under the charge of the undying gods, and a heavy quaking reached dim Tartarus and the deep sound of their feet in the fearful onset and of their hard missiles. So, then, they launched their grievous shafts upon one another, and the cry of both armies as they shouted reached to starry heaven; and they met together with a great battle-cry.

Then Zeus no longer held back his might; but straight his heart was filled with fury and he showed forth all his strength. From Heaven and from Olympus he came immediately, hurling his lightning: the bolts flew thick and fast from his strong hand together with thunder and lightning, whirling an awesome flame. The life-giving earth crashed around in burning, and the vast wood crackled loud with fire all about. All the land seethed, and Ocean's streams and the unfruitful sea. The hot vapor lapped round the earthborn Titans: flame unspeakable rose to the bright upper air: the flashing glare of the thunderstone and lightning blinded their eyes for all that they were strong. Astounding heat seized Chaos: and to see with eyes and to hear the sound with ears it seemed even as if Earth and wide Heaven above came together; for such a mighty crash would have arisen if Earth were being hurled to ruin, and Heaven from on high were hurling her down; so great a crash was there while the gods were meeting together in strife. Also the winds brought rumbling earthquake and dust storm, thunder and lightning and the lurid thunderbolt, which are the shafts of great Zeus, and carried the clangor and the warcry into the midst of the two hosts. A horrible uproar of terrible strife arose: mighty deeds were shown and the battle inclined. But until then, they kept at one another and fought continually in cruel war.

And amongst the foremost Cottus and Briareos and Gyes insatiate for war raised fierce fighting: three hundred rocks, one upon another, they launched from their strong hands and overshadowed the Titans with their missiles, and hurled them beneath the wide-pathed earth, and bound them in bitter chains when they had conquered them by their strength for all their great spirit, as far beneath the earth as heaven is above earth; for so far is it from earth to Tartarus. For a brazen anvil falling down from heaven nine nights and days would reach the earth upon the tenth: and again, a brazen anvil falling from earth nine nights and days would reach Tartarus upon the tenth. Round it runs a fence of bronze, and night spreads in triple line all about it like a neck-circlet, while above grow the roots of the earth and unfruitful sea.

The Punishment of the Titans (lines 729–766)

There by the counsel of Zeus who drives the clouds the Titan gods are hidden under misty gloom, in a dank place where are the ends of the huge earth. And they may not go out; for Poseidon fixed gates of bronze upon it, and a wall runs all round it on every side. There Gyes and Cottus and great-souled Obriareus live, trusty warders of Zeus who holds the aegis*. And there, all in their order, are the sources and ends of gloomy earth and misty Tartarus and the unfruitful sea and starry heaven, loathsome and dank, which even the gods abhor. It is a great gulf, and if once a man were within the gates, he would not reach the floor until a whole year had reached its end, but cruel blast upon blast would carry him this way and that. And this marvel is awful even to the deathless gods. There stands the awful home of murky Night wrapped in dark clouds. In front of it the son of Iapetus stands immovably upholding the wide heaven upon his head and unwearying hands, where Night and Day draw near and greet one another as they pass the great threshold of bronze: and while the one is about to go down into the

*aegis = Protection or shield

house, the other comes out at the door. And the house never holds them both within; but always one is without the house passing over the earth, while the other stays at home and waits until the time for her journeying comes; and the one holds all-seeing light for them on earth, but the other holds in her arms Sleep the brother of Death, even evil Night, wrapped in a vaporous cloud. And there the children of dark Night have their dwellings, Sleep and Death, awful gods. The glowing Sun never looks upon them with his beams, neither as he goes up into heaven, nor as he comes down from heaven. And the former of them roams peacefully over the earth and the sea's broad back and is kindly to men; but the other has a heart of iron, and his spirit within him is pitiless as bronze: whomever of men he has once seized he holds fast: and he is hateful even to the deathless gods.

The Reign of Zeus (lines 885-1002)

Now Zeus, king of the gods, made Metis his wife first, and she was wisest among gods and mortal men. But when she was about to bring forth the goddess bright-eyed Athena, Zeus craftily deceived her with cunning words and put her in his own belly, as Earth and starry Heaven advised. For they advised him so, to the end that no other should hold royal sway over the eternal gods in place of Zeus; for very wise children were destined to be born of her, first the maiden bright-eyed Tritogeneia*, equal to her father in strength and in wise understanding; but afterwards she was to bear a son of overbearing spirit king of gods and men. But Zeus put her into his own belly first, that the goddess might devise for him both good and evil.

Next he married bright Themis [...] and Eurynome, the daughter of Ocean [...] Also he came to the bed of all-nourishing Demeter, and she bore white-armed Persephone whom Aidoneus* carried off from her mother; but wise Zeus gave her to him. And again, he loved Mnemosyne* with the beautiful hair: and of her the nine gold-crowned Muses were born who delight in feasts and the pleasures of song. And Leto was joined in love with Zeus who holds the aegis, and bore Apollo and Artemis delighting in arrows, children lovely above all the sons of Heaven.

Lastly, he made Hera his blooming wife: and she was joined in love with the king of gods and men, and brought forth Hebe and Ares and Eileithyia. But Zeus himself gave birth from his own head to bright-eyed Tritogeneia, the awful, the strife-stirring, the host-leader, the unwearying, the queen, who delights in tumults and wars and battles. But Hera without union with Zeus—for she was very angry and quarrelled with her mate—bare famous Hephaestus, who is skilled in crafts more than all the sons of Heaven. And of Amphitrite and the loud-roaring Earth-Shaker was born great, wide-ruling Triton, and he owns the depths of the sea, living with his dear mother and the lord his father in their golden house, an awful god. Also Cytherea* bore to Ares the shield-piercer Panic and Fear, terrible gods who drive in disorder the close ranks of men in numbing war, with the help of Ares, sacker of towns; and Harmonia whom high-spirited Cadmus made his wife. And Maia, the daughter of Atlas, bore to Zeus glorious Hermes, the herald of the deathless gods, for she went up into his holy bed. And Semele, daughter of Cadmus was joined with him in love and bore him a splendid son, joyous Dionysus,—a mortal woman an immortal son. And now they both are gods. And Alcmena was joined in love with Zeus who drives the clouds and bore mighty Heracles. And Hephaestus, the famous Lame One, made Aglaea, youngest of the Graces, his buxom wife. And golden-haired Dionysus made brown-haired Ariadne, the daughter of Minos, his buxom wife: and the son of Kronos made her deathless and unageing for him. And mighty Heracles, the valiant son of neat-ankled Alcmena, when he had finished his grievous toils, made Hebe the child of great Zeus and gold-shod Hera his shy wife in snowy Olympus. Happy he! For he has finished his great

*Tritogeneia = Athena, derives from the meaning "born from the head" as this is how Athena is
   born of Zeus
*Aidoneus = Hades
*Mnemosyne = Memory
*Cytherea = Aphrodite

work and lives amongst the undying gods, untroubled and unaging all his days. And Perseis, the daughter of Ocean, bore to unwearying Helios Circe and Aeetes the king. And Aeetes, the son of Helios who shows light to men, took to wife fair-cheeked Idyia, daughter of Ocean the perfect stream, by the will of the gods: and she was subject to him in love through golden Aphrodite and bore him neat-ankled Medea.

And now farewell, you dwellers on Olympus, and you islands and continents, and you briny sea within. Now sing the company of goddesses, sweet-voiced Muses of Olympus, daughter of Zeus who holds the aegis,—even those deathless ones who lay with mortal men and bore children like gods.

And the will of great Zeus was fulfilled.

DISCUSSION QUESTIONS

1. Why are Ouranos and Kronos scared of their children?

2. What does the symbolism of Kronos swallowing his children imply?

3. How would you characterize Gaia and Rhea?

4. Compare the generational fighting between Ouranos against Kronos and Kronos against Zeus to another creation myth.

5. What kinds of people are sent to Tartarus in this story? (By Ouranos? By Kronos? By Zeus?)

Ovid's *Metamorphoses*

The world had changed drastically between the time of Hesiod's mythmaking in Greece in the eighth century BCE and the Roman poet Ovid's writings in the first century. These changes can be seen by a comparison of the style and content of Hesiod's creation myth and the story of constant change that Ovid sets about writing in his *Metamorphoses*.

Ovid is not interested in the etiology—the explanations of why things are and how they came to be. This is his major departure from Hesiod. The very name of his fifteen-book poem clues the reader in at the onset—his is a work about change. Because of its extreme length and hexameter, Ovid's *Metamorphoses* is often called a "proem" (prose + poem = proem).

Ovid lived between 43 BCE and 17 CE, at a time of enormous change in the world of science, philosophy, and cultural understanding. His "chaos" at the beginning of *Metamorphoses* is an immediate indicator of this change—it brings together the elemental forms of earth, sea, dense air, and clear sky as the forms swirling around in chaotic mass before the creation of the universe and gods. This is different from the other forms of chaos that describe chaos as absolute void. While this may seem small, its implications are significant—it shows that Roman philosophers and scientists were questioning and transforming the belief systems and that the poets were listening. Ovid's *Metamorphoses* is as much a piece of scientific history as it is a piece of literary history.

METAMORPHOSES
(Book 1, Lines 1-88)

Mundi origo. (Creation of the World)   1
My soul is wrought to sing of forms transformed
to bodies new and strange! Immortal Gods
inspire my heart, for ye have changed yourselves
and all things you have changed! Oh lead my song   5
in smooth and measured strains, from olden days
when earth began to this completed time!
Before the ocean and the earth appeared—
before the skies had overspread them all—
the face of Nature in a vast expanse   10
was naught but Chaos uniformly waste.
It was a rude and undeveloped mass,
that nothing made except a ponderous weight;
and all discordant elements confused,
were there congested in a shapeless heap.   15
As yet the sun afforded earth no light,
nor did the moon renew her crescent horns;
the earth was not suspended in the air
exactly balanced by her heavy weight.
Not far along the margin of the shores   20
had Amphitrite stretched her lengthened arms,—
for all the land was mixed with sea and air.
The land was soft, the sea unfit to sail,
the atmosphere opaque, to naught was given
a proper form, in everything was strife,   25
and all was mingled in a seething mass—
with hot the cold parts strove, and wet with dry
and soft with hard, and weight with empty void.
But God, or kindly Nature, ended strife—
he cut the land from skies, the sea from land,   30
the heavens ethereal from material air;
and when were all evolved from that dark mass
he bound the fractious parts in tranquil peace.
The fiery element of convex heaven
leaped from the mass devoid of dragging weight,   35
and chose the summit arch to which the air
as next in quality was next in place.
The earth more dense attracted grosser parts
and moved by gravity sank underneath;
and last of all the wide surrounding waves   40
in deeper channels rolled around the globe.
And when this God —which one is yet unknown—
had carved asunder that discordant mass,
had thus reduced it to its elements,

Source: Ovid. *Metamorphoses*. Translated by Brookes More. 1922.

that every part should equally combine,   45
when time began He rounded out the earth
and moulded it to form a mighty globe.
Then poured He forth the deeps and gave command
that they should billow in the rapid winds,
that they should compass every shore of earth.   50
He also added fountains, pools and lakes,
and bound with shelving banks the slanting streams,
which partly are absorbed and partly join
the boundless ocean. Thus received amid
the wide expanse of uncontrolled waves,   55
they beat the shores instead of crooked banks.
At His command the boundless plains extend,
the valleys are depressed, the woods are clothed
in green, the stony mountains rise. And as
the heavens are intersected on the right   60
by two broad zones, by two that cut the left,
and by a fifth consumed with ardent heat,
with such a number did the careful God
mark off the compassed weight, and thus the earth
received as many climes.—Such heat consumes   65
the middle zone that none may dwell therein;
and two extremes are covered with deep snow;
and two are placed betwixt the hot and cold,
which mixed together give a temperate clime;
and over all the atmosphere suspends   70
with weight proportioned to the fiery sky,
exactly as the weight of earth compares
with weight of water.
And He ordered mist
to gather in the air and spread the clouds.   75
He fixed the thunders that disturb our souls,
and brought the lightning on destructive winds
that also waft the cold. Nor did the great
Artificer permit these mighty winds
to blow unbounded in the pathless skies,   80
but each discordant brother fixed in space,
although His power can scarce restrain their rage
to rend the universe. At His command
to far Aurora, Eurus took his way,
to Nabath, Persia, and that mountain range   85
first gilded by the dawn; and Zephyr's flight
was towards the evening star and peaceful shores,
warm with the setting sun; and Boreas
invaded Scythia and the northern snows;
and Auster wafted to the distant south   90

where clouds and rain encompass his abode.—
And over these He fixed the liquid sky,
devoid of weight and free from earthly dross.
And scarcely had He separated these
and fixed their certain bounds, when all the stars,   95
which long were pressed and hidden in the mass,
began to gleam out from the plains of heaven,
and traversed, with the Gods, bright ether fields:
and lest some part might be bereft of life
the gleaming waves were filled with twinkling fish;   100
the earth was covered with wild animals;
the agitated air was filled with birds.
But one more perfect and more sanctified,
a being capable of lofty thought,
intelligent to rule, was wanting still   105
man was created! Did the Unknown God
designing then a better world make man
of seed divine? or did Prometheus
take the new soil of earth (that still contained
some godly element of Heaven's Life)   110
and use it to create the race of man;
first mingling it with water of new streams;
so that his new creation, upright man,
was made in image of commanding Gods?
On earth the brute creation bends its gaze,   115
but man was given a lofty countenance
and was commanded to behold the skies;
and with an upright face may view the stars:—
and so it was that shapeless clay put on
the form of man till then unknown to earth.   120

DISCUSSION QUESTIONS

1. What is the role of the creator of the universe? Passive or active?

2. What differences are there between the "God" creator in Ovid's story and "Gaia" as creator in Hesiod's story?

3. How is the creation of man depicted?

The Ages of Man

Many cultures tell the story of a fall from grace, or a perfect race of man now in decline. Hesiod's *Works and Days* and Ovid's *Metamorphoses* posit two versions of the fall of man from the Golden Age to the Iron Age.

One interpretation of these stories of the "Ages" could simply be the inevitability of human suffering. "The Ages of Man" completes a cycle of a "golden race" without labor or death to that of the deplorable "race of iron" which toils in misery and consecrates injustice. Hesiod and Ovid both list the failures of morality and ethics within the races and ask readers to question exactly how far down the path to the Iron Age we have gone.

Hesiod's *Works and Days* lines 109–201	Ovid's *Metamorphoses* lines 89–162
First of all the deathless gods who dwell on Olympus made **a golden race** of mortal men who lived in the time of Kronos when he was reigning in heaven. And they lived like gods without sorrow of heart, remote and free from toil and grief: miserable age rested not on them; but with legs and arms never failing they made merry with feasting beyond the reach of all evils. When they died, it was as though they were overcome with sleep, and they had all good things; for the fruitful earth unforced bare them fruit abundantly and without stint. They dwelt in ease and peace upon their lands with many good things, rich in flocks and loved by the blessed gods. But after the earth had covered this generation—they are called pure spirits dwelling on the earth, and are kindly, delivering from harm, and guardians of mortal men; for they roam everywhere over the earth, clothed in mist and keep watch on judgements and cruel deeds, givers of wealth; for this royal right also they received;	First was **the Golden Age**. Then rectitude spontaneous in the heart prevailed, and faith. Avengers were not seen, for laws unframed were all unknown and needless. Punishment and fear of penalties existed not. No harsh decrees were fixed on brazen plates. No suppliant multitude the countenance of Justice feared, averting, for they dwelt without a judge in peace. Descended not the steeps, shorn from its height, the lofty pine, cleaving the trackless waves of alien shores, nor distant realms were known to wandering men. The towns were not entrenched for time of war; they had no brazen trumpets, straight, nor horns of curving brass, nor helmets, shields nor swords. There was no thought of martial pomp—secure a happy multitude enjoyed repose. Then of her own accord the earth produced a store of every fruit. The harrow touched her not, nor did the plowshare wound her fields. And man content with given food, and none compelling, gathered arbute fruits and wild strawberries on the mountain sides, and ripe blackberries clinging to the bush, and corners and sweet acorns on the ground, down fallen from the spreading tree of Jove. Eternal Spring! Soft breathing zephyrs soothed and warmly cherished buds and blooms, produced without a seed. The valleys, though unplowed gave many fruits; the fields though not renewed white glistened with the heavy bearded wheat: rivers flowed milk and nectar, and the trees, the very oak trees, then gave honey of themselves.

Source: *Hesiod. The Homeric Hymns and Homerica with an English Translation* by Hugh G. Evelyn-White. *Works and Days*. 1914.
Source: Ovid. *Metamorphoses*. Translated by Brookes More. 1922.

Hesiod's *Works and Days* lines 109–201	**Ovid's *Metamorphoses*** lines 89–162
—then they who dwell on Olympus made a second generation which was **of silver** and less noble by far. It was like the golden race neither in body nor in spirit. A child was brought up at his good mother's side a hundred years, an utter simpleton, playing childishly in his own home. But when they were full grown and were come to the full measure of their prime, they lived only a little time and that in sorrow because of their foolishness, for they could not keep from sinning and from wronging one another, nor would they serve the immortals, nor sacrifice on the holy altars of the blessed ones as it is right for men to do wherever they dwell. Then Zeus the son of Kronos was angry and put them away, because they would not give honor to the blessed gods who live on Olympus.	When Saturn had been banished into night and all the world was ruled by Jove supreme, **the Silver Age**, though not so good as gold but still surpassing yellow brass, prevailed. Jove first reduced to years the Primal Spring, by him divided into periods four, unequal,—summer, autumn, winter, spring.—then glowed with tawny heat the parched air, or pendent icicles in winter froze and man stopped crouching in crude caverns, while he built his homes of tree rods, bark entwined. Then were the cereals planted in long rows, and bullocks groaned beneath the heavy yoke.
But when earth had covered this generation also—they are called blessed spirits of the underworld by men, and, though they are of second order, yet honor attends them also—Zeus the Father made a third generation of mortal men, **a brazen race**, sprung from ash-trees; and it was in no way equal to the silver age, but was terrible and strong. They loved the lamentable works of Ares and deeds of violence; they ate no bread, but were hard of heart like adamant, fearful men. Great was their strength and unconquerable the arms which grew from their shoulders on their strong limbs. Their armor was of bronze, and their houses of bronze, and of bronze were their implements: there was no black iron. These were destroyed by their own hands and passed to the dank house of chill Hades, and left no name: terrible though they were, black Death seized them, and they left the bright light of the sun.	The third Age followed, called **The Age of Bronze**, when cruel people were inclined to arms but not to impious crimes.
But when earth had covered this generation also, Zeus the son of Kronos made yet another, the fourth, upon the fruitful earth, which was nobler and more righteous, a god-like race of hero-men who are called **demi-gods**, the race before our own, throughout the boundless earth. Grim war and dread battle destroyed a part of them, some in the land of Cadmus at seven-gated Thebes when they fought for the flocks of Oedipus, and some, when it had brought them in ships over the great sea gulf to Troy for rich-haired Helen's sake: there death's end enshrouded a part of them. But to the others father Zeus the son of Kronos gave a living and an abode apart from men, and made them dwell at the ends of earth. And they live untouched by sorrow in the islands of the blessed along the shore of deep-swirling Ocean, happy heroes for whom the grain-giving earth bears honey-sweet fruit flourishing thrice a year, far from the deathless gods, and Kronos rules over them; for the father of men and gods released him from his bonds. And these last equally have honor and glory.	[appears after the Iron Age] And lest ethereal heights should long remain less troubled than the earth, the throne of Heaven was threatened by **the Giants**; and they piled mountain on mountain to the lofty stars. But Jove, omnipotent, shot thunderbolts through Mount Olympus, and he overturned from Ossa huge, enormous Pelion. And while these dreadful bodies lay overwhelmed in their tremendous bulk, (so fame reports) the Earth was reeking with the copious blood of her gigantic sons; and thus replete with moisture she infused the steaming gore with life renewed. So that a monument of such ferocious stock should be retained, she made that offspring in the shape of man; but this new race alike despised the Gods, and by the greed of savage slaughter proved a sanguinary birth.

Hesiod's *Works and Days* lines 109–201	**Ovid's *Metamorphoses*** lines 89–162
And again far-seeing Zeus made yet another generation, the fifth, of men who are upon the bounteous earth. Thereafter, would that I were not among the men of the fifth generation, but either had died before or been born afterwards. For now truly is a **race of iron**, and men never rest from labor and sorrow by day, and from perishing by night; and the gods shall lay sore trouble upon them. But, notwithstanding, even these shall have some good mingled with their evils.	And last of all the ruthless and hard **Age of Iron** prevailed, from which malignant vein great evil sprung; and modesty and faith and truth took flight, and in their stead deceits and snares and frauds and violence and wicked love of gain, succeeded.—Then the sailor spread his sails to winds unknown, and keels that long had stood on lofty mountains pierced uncharted waves.
And Zeus will destroy this race of mortal men also when they come to have grey hair on the temples at their birth. The father will not agree with his children, nor the children with their father, nor guest with his host, nor comrade with comrade; nor will brother be dear to brother as aforetime. Men will dishonor their parents as they grow quickly old, and will carp at them, chiding them with bitter words, hard-hearted they, not knowing the fear of the gods. They will not repay their aged parents the cost of their nurture, for might shall be their right: and one man will sack another's city. There will be no favor for the man who keeps his oath or for the just or for the good; but rather men will praise the evil-doer and his violent dealing. Strength will be right, and reverence will cease to be; and the wicked will hurt the worthy man, speaking false words against him, and will swear an oath upon them. Envy, foul-mouthed, delighting in evil, with scowling face, will go along with wretched men one and all.	Surveyors anxious marked with metes and bounds the lands, created free as light and air: nor need the rich ground furnish only crops, and give due nourishment by right required,— they penetrated to the bowels of earth and dug up wealth, bad cause of all our ills,— rich ores which long ago the earth had hid and deep removed to gloomy Stygian caves: and soon destructive iron and harmful gold were brought to light; and War, which uses both, came forth and shook with sanguinary grip his clashing arms. Rapacity broke forth—the guest was not protected from his host, the father in law from his own son in law; even brothers seldom could abide in peace. The husband threatened to destroy his wife, and she her husband: horrid step dames mixed the deadly henbane: eager sons inquired their fathers, ages. Piety was slain: and last of all the virgin deity, Astraea vanished from the blood-stained earth.
And then Aidos and Nemesis, with their sweet forms wrapped in white robes, will go from the wide-pathed earth and forsake mankind to join the company of the deathless gods: and bitter sorrows will be left for mortal men, and there will be no help against evil.	

DISCUSSION QUESTIONS

1. Make a list of the similarities and differences in the ages between Hesiod and Ovid's telling of the Ages of Man.

2. Why do you think there is not a "demi-god" age in Ovid's writing?

3. Why is there such an emphasis on seasons and farming?

4. What age are we currently living in? Do you think Ovid and Hesiod offer an accurate portrayal?

5. Explain the emergence of evil or sinfulness in the Ages—is there anything that tells us <u>why</u> we are a fallen people?

Greek Flood Myth, as told by Apollodorus

This incredibly short flood myth was composed by an unknown author, but included in Apollodorus' *The Library* (which you can think of as the first Mythology textbook, written in about the second century CE).

In order to make sense of the myth that follows, we have to look for clues. The myth mentions the "Bronze Age," so we know that it likely follows Hesiod's rendering of the "Ages of Man." We can perhaps assume that Zeus was angered with the behavior of those men living in the Bronze Age and this may have been his punishment.

We know who Prometheus and his brother Epimetheus are, and that Pandora is given to Epimetheus as a punishment for Prometheus' misbehavior toward Zeus. Again, this may tell us about why these are the characters involved in this myth of destruction. But there is much we still do not know. Why does Prometheus interfere to warn them? When the couple was saved, why did Zeus give instructions for repopulating the earth?

"THE FLOOD"

And Prometheus had a son Deucalion. He reigning in the regions about Phthia, married Pyrrha, the daughter of Epimetheus and Pandora, the first woman fashioned by the gods. And when Zeus would destroy the men of the Bronze Age, Deucalion by the advice of Prometheus constructed a chest, and having stored it with provisions he embarked in it with Pyrrha. But Zeus by pouring heavy rain from heaven flooded the greater part of Greece, so that all men were destroyed, except a few who fled to the high mountains in the neighborhood. It was then that the mountains in Thessaly parted, and that all the world outside the Isthmus and Peloponnese was overwhelmed. But Deucalion, floating in the chest over the sea for nine days and as many nights, drifted to Parnassus, and there, when the rain ceased, he landed and sacrificed to Zeus, the god of Escape. And Zeus sent Hermes to him and allowed him to choose what he would, and he chose to get men. And at the bidding of Zeus he took up stones and threw them over his head, and the stones which Deucalion threw became men, and the stones which Pyrrha threw became women. Hence people were called metaphorically people (laos) from *laas*, "a stone. "And Deucalion had children by Pyrrha, first Hellen, whose father some say was Zeus, and second Amphictyon, who reigned over Attica after Cranaus; and third a daughter Protogenia, who became the mother of Aethlius by Zeus.

DISCUSSION QUESTIONS

1. Why do you think the flood was sent after the Bronze Age?

2. Why did Hermes choose to get men?

3. Does it surprise you that some men are allowed to escape the flood by fleeing to "high mountains in the neighborhood"? Does this accomplish Zeus' task?

4. What is the significance of men and women being created from stones?

Source: Apollodorus. *Apollodorus, The Library, with an English Translation* by Sir James George Frazer, 1921.

Ovid's Flood Myth: The Deluge

This story follows the Ages of Man in *The Metamorphoses*, when Jove (Jupiter) has decided that mankind has become deplorable and a flood must be sent to wipe out creation and begin again. But we must remember that Ovid's writing is about change, or the metamorphosizing of the order of the world and not a literal account. Thus we come into contact with a story about dolphins flying through trees, wolves swimming amongst sheep, and Triton blowing on a conch shell to signal the water's retreat.

Ovid's flood myth follows the same characters of the myth found in Apollodorus' collection, but Ovid has filled in some of the details. We are given more reasoning behind Jove's motives and a deeper understanding of what Deucalion and Pyrrha must have felt being the last two people alive.

THE DELUGE
(Lines 75–451)

"Thus fell one house, but not one house alone   1
deserved to perish; over all the earth
ferocious deeds prevail,—all men conspire
in evil. Let them therefore feel the weight
of dreadful penalties so justly earned,   5
for such hath my unchanging will ordained."
with exclamations some approved the words
of Jove and added fuel to his wrath,
while others gave assent: but all deplored
and questioned the estate of earth deprived   10
of mortals. Who could offer frankincense
upon the altars? Would he suffer earth
to be despoiled by hungry beasts of prey?
Such idle questions of the state of man
the King of Gods forbade, but granted soon   15
to people earth with race miraculous,
unlike the first.
And now his thunder bolts
would Jove wide scatter, but he feared the flames,
unnumbered, sacred ether might ignite   20
and burn the axle of the universe:
and he remembered in the scroll of fate,
there is a time appointed when the sea
and earth and Heavens shall melt, and fire destroy
the universe of mighty labour wrought.   25
Such weapons by the skill of Cyclops forged,
for different punishment he laid aside—
for straightway he preferred to overwhelm
the mortal race beneath deep waves and storms
from every raining sky. And instantly   30
he shut the Northwind in Aeolian caves,

Source: Ovid. *Metamorphoses.* Translated by Brookes More. 1922.

and every other wind that might dispel
the gathering clouds. He bade the Southwind blow:—
the Southwind flies abroad with dripping wings,
concealing in the gloom his awful face: 35
the drenching rain descends from his wet beard
and hoary locks; dark clouds are on his brows
and from his wings and garments drip the dews:
his great hands press the overhanging clouds;
loudly the thunders roll; the torrents pour;   40
Iris, the messenger of Juno, clad
in many coloured raiment, upward draws
the steaming moisture to renew the clouds.
The standing grain is beaten to the ground,
the rustic's crops are scattered in the mire,   45
and he bewails the long year's fruitless toil.
The wrath of Jove was not content with powers
that emanate from Heaven; he brought to aid
his azure brother, lord of flowing waves,
who called upon the Rivers and the Streams: 50
and when they entered his impearled abode,
Neptune, their ancient ruler, thus began;
        "A long appeal is needless; pour ye forth
        in rage of power; open up your fountains;
        rush over obstacles; let every stream   55
        pour forth in boundless floods."
Thus he commands, and none dissenting all the River Gods
return, and opening up their fountains roll
tumultuous to the deep unfruitful sea.
And Neptune with his trident smote the Earth,   60
which trembling with unwonted throes heaved up
the sources of her waters bare; and through
her open plains the rapid rivers rushed
resistless, onward bearing the waving grain,
the budding groves, the houses, sheep and men,—   65
and holy temples, and their sacred urns.
The mansions that remained, resisting vast
and total ruin, deepening waves concealed
and whelmed their tottering turrets in the flood
and whirling gulf. And now one vast expanse,   70
the land and sea were mingled in the waste
of endless waves—a sea without a shore.
One desperate man seized on the nearest hill;
another sitting in his curved boat,
plied the long oar where he was wont to plow;   75
another sailed above his grain, above
his hidden dwelling; and another hooked
a fish that sported in a leafy elm.
Perchance an anchor dropped in verdant fields,
or curving keels were pushed through tangled vines;   80

and where the gracile goat enjoyed the green,
unsightly seals reposed. Beneath the waves
were wondering Nereids, viewing cities, groves
and houses. Dolphins darting mid the trees,
meshed in the twisted branches, beat against   85
the shaken oak trees. There the sheep, affrayed,
swim with the frightened wolf, the surging waves
float tigers and lions: availeth naught
his lightning shock the wild boar, nor avails
the stag's fleet footed speed. The wandering bird,   90
seeking umbrageous groves and hidden vales,
with wearied pinion droops into the sea.
The waves increasing surge above the hills,
and rising waters dash on mountain tops.
Myriads by the waves are swept away,   95
and those the waters spare, for lack of food,
starvation slowly overcomes at last.
A fruitful land and fair but now submerged
beneath a wilderness of rising waves,
'Twixt Oeta and Aonia, Phocis lies,   100
where through the clouds Parnassus' summits twain
point upward to the stars, unmeasured height,
save which the rolling billows covered all:
there in a small and fragile boat, arrived,
Deucalion and the consort of his couch,   105
prepared to worship the Corycian Nymphs,
the mountain deities, and Themis kind,
who in that age revealed in oracles
the voice of fate. As he no other lived
so good and just, as she no other feared the Gods.   110
When Jupiter beheld the globe
in ruin covered, swept with wasting waves,
and when he saw one man of myriads left,
one helpless woman left of myriads lone,
both innocent and worshiping the Gods,   115
he scattered all the clouds; he blew away
the great storms by the cold Northwind.
Once more the earth appeared to heaven and the skies
appeared to earth. The fury of the main
abated, for the Ocean ruler laid   120
his trident down and pacified the waves,
and called on azure Triton.—Triton arose
above the waving seas, his shoulders mailed
in purple shells.—He bade the Triton blow,
blow in his sounding shell, the wandering streams   125
and rivers to recall with signal known:
a hollow wreathed trumpet, tapering wide
and slender stemmed, the Triton took amain
and wound the pearly shell at midmost sea.
Betwixt the rising and the setting suns   130

the wildered notes resounded shore to shore,
and as it touched his lips, wet with the brine
beneath his dripping beard, sounded retreat:
and all the waters of the land and sea
obeyed. Their fountains heard and ceased to flow;   135
their waves subsided; hidden hills uprose;
emerged the shores of ocean; channels filled
with flowing streams; the soil appeared; the land
increased its surface as the waves decreased:
and after length of days the trees put forth,   140
with ooze on bending boughs, their naked tops.
And all the wasted globe was now restored,
but as he viewed the vast and silent world
Deucalion wept and thus to Pyrrha spoke;
    "O sister! wife! alone of woman left!   145
    My kindred in descent and origin!
    Dearest companion of my marriage bed,
    doubly endeared by deepening dangers borne,—
    of all the dawn and eve behold of earth,
    but you and I are left—for the deep sea   150
    has kept the rest! And what prevents the tide
    from overwhelming us? Remaining clouds
    affright us. How could you endure your fears
    if you alone were rescued by this fate,
    and who would then console your bitter grief?   155
    Oh be assured, if you were buried in the waves,
    that I would follow you and be with you!
    Oh would that by my father's art I might
    restore the people, and inspire this clay
    to take the form of man. Alas, the Gods   160
    decreed and only we are living!"
Thus Deucalion's plaint to Pyrrha;—and they wept.
And after he had spoken, they resolved
to ask the aid of sacred oracles,—
and so they hastened to Cephissian waves   165
which rolled a turbid flood in channels known.
Thence when their robes and brows were sprinkled well,
they turned their footsteps to the goddess' fane:
its gables were befouled with reeking moss
and on its altars every fire was cold.   170
But when the twain had reached the temple steps
they fell upon the earth, inspired with awe,
and kissed the cold stone with their trembling lips, and said;
    "If righteous prayers appease the Gods,
    and if the wrath of high celestial powers   175
    may thus be turned, declare, O Themis! Whence
    and what the art may raise humanity?
    O gentle goddess help the dying world!"
Moved by their supplications, she replied;
    "Depart from me and veil your brows; ungird   180

your robes, and cast behind you as you go,
    the bones of your great mother."
Long they stood in dumb amazement: Pyrrha, first of voice,
refused the mandate and with trembling lips
implored the goddess to forgive—she feared   185
to violate her mother's bones and vex
her sacred spirit. Often pondered they
the words involved in such obscurity,
repeating oft: and thus Deucalion
to Epimetheus' daughter uttered speech   190
of soothing import;
        "Oracles are just
        and urge not evil deeds, or naught avails
        the skill of thought. Our mother is the Earth,
        and I may judge the stones of earth are bones   195
        that we should cast behind us as we go."
And although Pyrrha by his words was moved
she hesitated to comply; and both amazed
doubted the purpose of the oracle,
but deemed no harm to come of trial. They,   200
descending from the temple, veiled their heads
and loosed their robes and threw some stones
behind them. It is much beyond belief,
were not receding ages witness, hard
and rigid stones assumed a softer form,   205
enlarging as their brittle nature changed
to milder substance,—till the shape of man
appeared, imperfect, faintly outlined first,
as marble statue chiseled in the rough.
The soft moist parts were changed to softer flesh,   210
the hard and brittle substance into bones,
the veins retained their ancient name. And now
the Gods supreme ordained that every stone
Deucalion threw should take the form of man,
and those by Pyrrha cast should woman's form   215
assume: so are we hardy to endure
and prove by toil and deeds from what we sprung.

DISCUSSION QUESTIONS

1. Compare the two flood stories given by Apollodorus and Ovid.

2. Compare the flood stories of Ovid and the Hebrew story of "Genesis." Which is more condemning of the idea of human evil or sinfulness?

3. Does the flood seem like a fair punishment for the evils committed by the races of man described earlier in *The Metamorphoses*?

Part 2: Tricksters, Lovers, and Other Tales

Apollo and Daphne

The story of Apollo and Daphne is a story of passion, and scholars have interpreted it in many ways. Is it attempted rape? A tale of pride and arrogance? A tragic love story? It depends on how you read it.

There are numerous tales in Greek mythology involving what appears to be rape or abduction. What are we to make of such stories? Many blur the lines between love, passion, seduction, abduction, and submission. Some stories are clearer than others on these points, and each translation can also affect our reading. In most cases there is no correct interpretation; rather, there are layers of meaning to investigate and explore. The word "rape" in the context of Greek myth did not have the same meaning it has today—it did not always indicate a violent attack. Sometimes "rape" was the word used to describe passion and did not necessarily mean force or lack of consent. And sometimes such an encounter is described as a "ravishment" and even has spiritual connotations. Consider all aspects of the story and seek a variety of perspectives.

Apollo, twin brother of Artemis, is one of the most complex of the Greek gods. He is sometimes called Phoebus ("brilliant") and he's the only Greek god whose name remains the same in Rome. Depicted with a lyre as well as bow and arrows, he was associated with music and protection; he later became identified with the sun and referred to as the god of light.

Two important phrases associated with Apollo were "know thyself" and "nothing in excess." Apollo represented self-reflection and restraint, but his many attributes reflect the dual nature of humanity—he is both violent and compassionate; a healer and yet a bringer of plague. Apollo was also a god of prophecy. His sanctuary at Delphi was considered the world navel, the center of the earth. It is said that Zeus released an eagle in each direction and Delphi is the place where they met. It was here that people journeyed to consult one of the most famous oracles—the Pythia. Widely consulted by ordinary citizens and nobles alike, she sat on a tripod, breathing vapors from the pit inside the temple and entered a trancelike state. Priests would interpret her typically unintelligible words.

Apollo's pursuit of Daphne has been famously portrayed in art for centuries—especially the image of Daphne transforming into a tree to escape his advances. The story explains why the laurel tree was sacred to Apollo (*daphne* means "laurel"). This version of the story comes from Ovid's *Metamorphoses*.

APOLLO AND DAPHNE (PHOEBUS)

Daphne, the daughter of a River God	1
was first beloved by Phoebus, the great God	
of glorious light. 'Twas not a cause of chance	
but out of Cupid's vengeful spite that she	
was fated to torment the lord of light.	5
For Phoebus, proud of Python's death, beheld	
that impish god of Love upon a time	
when he was bending his diminished bow,	
and voicing his contempt in anger said;	

Source: Ovid. *Metamorphoses.* Translated by Brookes More. 1922.

"What, wanton boy, are mighty arms to thee,   10
great weapons suited to the needs of war?
The bow is only for the use of those
large deities of heaven whose strength may deal
wounds, mortal, to the savage beasts of prey;
and who courageous overcome their foes.—   15
It is a proper weapon to the use
of such as slew with arrows Python, huge,
whose pestilential carcase vast extent
covered. Content thee with the flames thy torch
enkindles (fires too subtle for my thought)   20
and leave to me the glory that is mine."
To him, undaunted, Venus, son replied;
"O Phoebus, thou canst conquer all the world
with thy strong bow and arrows, but with this
small arrow I shall pierce thy vaunting breast!   25
And by the measure that thy might exceeds
the broken powers of thy defeated foes,
so is thy glory less than mine." No more
he said, but with his wings expanded thence
flew lightly to Parnassus, lofty peak.   30
There, from his quiver he plucked arrows twain,
most curiously wrought of different art;
one love exciting, one repelling love.
The dart of love was glittering, gold and sharp,
the other had a blunted tip of lead;   35
and with that dull lead dart he shot the Nymph,
but with the keen point of the golden dart
he pierced the bone and marrow of the God.
Immediately the one with love was filled,
the other, scouting at the thought of love,   40
rejoiced in the deep shadow of the woods,
and as the virgin Phoebe (who denies
the joys of love and loves the joys of chase)
a maiden's fillet bound her flowing hair,—
and her pure mind denied the love of man.   45
Beloved and wooed she wandered silent paths,
for never could her modesty endure
the glance of man or listen to his love.
Her grieving father spoke to her, "Alas,
my daughter, I have wished a son in law,   50
and now you owe a grandchild to the joy
of my old age." But Daphne only hung
her head to hide her shame. The nuptial torch
seemed criminal to her. She even clung,
caressing, with her arms around his neck,   55
and pled, "My dearest father let me live
a virgin always, for remember Jove

did grant it to Diana at her birth."
But though her father promised her desire,
her loveliness prevailed against their will;   60
for, Phoebus when he saw her waxed distraught,
and filled with wonder his sick fancy raised
delusive hopes, and his own oracles
deceived him.—As the stubble in the field
flares up, or as the stacked wheat is consumed   65
by flames, enkindled from a spark or torch
the chance pedestrian may neglect at dawn;
so was the bosom of the god consumed,
and so desire flamed in his stricken heart.
He saw her bright hair waving on her neck;—   70
"How beautiful if properly arranged!"
He saw her eyes like stars of sparkling fire,
her lips for kissing sweetest, and her hands
and fingers and her arms; her shoulders white
as ivory;—and whatever was not seen   75
more beautiful must be.
Swift as the wind
from his pursuing feet the virgin fled,
and neither stopped nor heeded as he called;
"O Nymph! O Daphne! I entreat thee stay,   80
it is no enemy that follows thee—
why, so the lamb leaps from the raging wolf,
and from the lion runs the timid faun,
and from the eagle flies the trembling dove,
all hasten from their natural enemy   85
but I alone pursue for my dear love.
Alas, if thou shouldst fall and mar thy face,
or tear upon the bramble thy soft thighs,
or should I prove unwilling cause of pain!
"The wilderness is rough and dangerous,   90
and I beseech thee be more careful—I
will follow slowly.—Ask of whom thou wilt,
and thou shalt learn that I am not a churl—
I am no mountain dweller of rude caves,
nor clown compelled to watch the sheep and goats;   95
and neither canst thou know from whom thy feet
fly fearful, or thou wouldst not leave me thus.
"The Delphic Land, the Pataraean Realm,
Claros and Tenedos revere my name,
and my immortal sire is Jupiter.   100
The present, past and future are through me
in sacred oracles revealed to man,
and from my harp the harmonies of sound
are borrowed by their bards to praise the Gods.
My bow is certain, but a flaming shaft   105
surpassing mine has pierced my heart—

untouched before. The art of medicine
is my invention, and the power of herbs;
but though the world declare my useful works
there is no herb to medicate my wound,   110
and all the arts that save have failed their lord."

But even as he made his plaint, the Nymph
with timid footsteps fled from his approach,
and left him to his murmurs and his pain.
Lovely the virgin seemed as the soft wind   115
exposed her limbs, and as the zephyrs fond
fluttered amid her garments, and the breeze
fanned lightly in her flowing hair. She seemed
most lovely to his fancy in her flight;
and mad with love he followed in her steps,   120
and silent hastened his increasing speed.
As when the greyhound sees the frightened hare
flit over the plain:—With eager nose outstretched,
impetuous, he rushes on his prey,
and gains upon her till he treads her feet,   125
and almost fastens in her side his fangs;
but she, whilst dreading that her end is near,
is suddenly delivered from her fright;
so was it with the god and virgin: one
with hope pursued, the other fled in fear;   130
and he who followed, borne on wings of love,
permitted her no rest and gained on her,
until his warm breath mingled in her hair.
Her strength spent, pale and faint, with pleading eyes
she gazed upon her father's waves and prayed,   135
"Help me my father, if thy flowing streams
have virtue! Cover me, O mother Earth!
Destroy the beauty that has injured me,
or change the body that destroys my life."
Before her prayer was ended, torpor seized   140
on all her body, and a thin bark closed
around her gentle bosom, and her hair
became as moving leaves; her arms were changed
to waving branches, and her active feet
as clinging roots were fastened to the ground—   145
her face was hidden with encircling leaves.—
Phoebus admired and loved the graceful tree,
(For still, though changed, her slender form remained)
and with his right hand lingering on the trunk
he felt her bosom throbbing in the bark.   150
He clung to trunk and branch as though to twine.
His form with hers, and fondly kissed the wood
that shrank from every kiss.
And thus the God;

"Although thou canst not be my bride, thou shalt   155
be called my chosen tree, and thy green leaves,
O Laurel! shall forever crown my brows,
be wreathed around my quiver and my lyre;
the Roman heroes shall be crowned with thee,
as long processions climb the Capitol   160
and chanting throngs proclaim their victories;
and as a faithful warden thou shalt guard
the civic crown of oak leaves fixed between
thy branches, and before Augustan gates.
And as my youthful head is never shorn,   165
so, also, shalt thou ever bear thy leaves
unchanging to thy glory."
Here the God,
Phoebus Apollo, ended his lament,
and unto him the Laurel bent her boughs,   170
so lately fashioned; and it seemed to him
her graceful nod gave answer to his love.

DISCUSSION QUESTIONS

1. Consider the reason Apollo becomes infatuated with Daphne. What effect does this have on your interpretation of the story?

2. Are Daphne's actions an act of strength or desperation? Explain. How does the impact of her decision change when viewed from each of these perspectives?

3. Interpret the tale as a lesson in transformation rather than tragic love story. What lessons do the characters learn?

4. Compare a variety of artistic expressions of this tale. Include painting, sculpture, and modern literary retellings, especially contemporary poems.

5. Daphne states that she wishes to remain a virgin. Compare her to other virgin characters in mythology and explore the reasons and motivations for this choice.

6. Compare this story to other tales that suggest rape. For example, the "Rape of Persephone" and the "Rape of Helen." How do you interpret the term "rape" in each of these cases?

Cupid and Psyche

A myth that seems more like a fairy tale, "Cupid and Psyche" has been identified by scholars as the first "Beauty and the Beast" story. While Cupid is not really a beast, Psyche believes that he is; the idea of a beast as bridegroom is well established in fairy tales. In addition, it contains archetypes such as vain and jealous sisters, an overpowering mother, and magical helpers. Standard fairy tale motifs present in the story include keeping secrets, impossible tasks, and a happily ever after ending.

Cupid's Greek counterpart is Eros, a masculine version of Aphrodite, portrayed as a handsome young man, sometimes identified with male homosexuality. Eros is mentioned during creation, but he is also called the son of Aphrodite or sometimes described as her attendant. Eros means "love" but this can include all types of love—friendship and family, spiritual, romantic love, and sexual arousal. Today the name Cupid conjures up images of a chubby cherub with a bow, shooting people and causing them to fall in love. But as we see in the previous story of Apollo and Daphne, he did not always behave in such a manner.

Apuleius, a second-century Roman author, included the story in his *Metamorphoses*, often referred to as *The Golden Ass*. We've placed this myth here as a tale of love, but it would fit equally well in the category of hero stories portraying Psyche as a heroine.

CUPID AND PSYCHE

Lucius Apuleius

A certain king and queen had three daughters. The charms of the two elder were more than common, but the beauty of the youngest was so wonderful that the poverty of language is unable to express its due praise. The fame of her beauty was so great that strangers from neighboring countries came in crowds to enjoy the sight, and looked on her with amazement, paying her that homage which is due only to Venus herself. In fact Venus found her altars deserted, while men turned their devotion to this young virgin. As she passed along, the people sang her praises, and strewed her way with chaplets and flowers.

This homage to the exaltation of a mortal gave great offense to the real Venus. Shaking her ambrosial locks with indignation, she exclaimed, "Am I then to be eclipsed in my honors by a mortal girl? In vain then did that royal shepherd, whose judgment was approved by Jove himself, give me the palm of beauty over my illustrious rivals, Pallas and Juno. But she shall not so quietly usurp my honors. I will give her cause to repent of so unlawful a beauty."

Thereupon she calls her winged son Cupid, mischievous enough in his own nature, and rouses and provokes him yet more by her complaints. She points out Psyche to him and says, "My dear son, punish that contumacious beauty; give your mother a revenge as sweet as her injuries are great; infuse into the bosom of that haughty girl a passion for some low, mean, unworthy being, so that she may reap a mortification as great as her present exultation and triumph."

Cupid prepared to obey the commands of his mother. There are two fountains in Venus's garden, one of sweet waters, the other of bitter. Cupid filled two amber vases, one from each fountain, and suspending them from the top of his quiver, hastened to the chamber of Psyche, whom he found asleep. He shed a few drops from the bitter fountain over her lips, though the sight of her almost moved him to pity; then touched her side with the point of his arrow. At the touch she awoke, and opened eyes upon Cupid (himself invisible), which so startled him that in his confusion he wounded himself with his own arrow. Heedless of his wound, his whole thought now was to repair the mischief he had done, and he poured the balmy drops of joy over all her silken ringlets.

Source: Bulfinch, Thomas. *The Age of Fable; or, Stories of Gods and Heroes*, 3rd edition. 1855.

Psyche, henceforth frowned upon by Venus, derived no benefit from all her charms. True, all eyes were cast eagerly upon her, and every mouth spoke her praises; but neither king, royal youth, nor plebeian presented himself to demand her in marriage. Her two elder sisters of moderate charms had now long been married to two royal princes; but Psyche, in her lonely apartment, deplored her solitude, sick of that beauty which, while it procured abundance of flattery, had failed to awaken love.

Her parents, afraid that they had unwittingly incurred the anger of the gods, consulted the oracle of Apollo, and received this answer, "The virgin is destined for the bride of no mortal lover. Her future husband awaits her on the top of the mountain. He is a monster whom neither gods nor men can resist."

This dreadful decree of the oracle filled all the people with dismay, and her parents abandoned themselves to grief. But Psyche said, "Why, my dear parents, do you now lament me? You should rather have grieved when the people showered upon me undeserved honors, and with one voice called me a Venus. I now perceive that I am a victim to that name. I submit. Lead me to that rock to which my unhappy fate has destined me."

Accordingly, all things being prepared, the royal maid took her place in the procession, which more resembled a funeral than a nuptial pomp, and with her parents, amid the lamentations of the people, ascended the mountain, on the summit of which they left her alone, and with sorrowful hearts returned home.

While Psyche stood on the ridge of the mountain, panting with fear and with eyes full of tears, the gentle Zephyr raised her from the earth and bore her with an easy motion into a flowery dale. By degrees her mind became composed, and she laid herself down on the grassy bank to sleep.

When she awoke refreshed with sleep, she looked round and beheld near a pleasant grove of tall and stately trees. She entered it, and in the midst discovered a fountain, sending forth clear and crystal waters, and fast by, a magnificent palace whose august front impressed the spectator that it was not the work of mortal hands, but the happy retreat of some god. Drawn by admiration and wonder, she approached the building and ventured to enter.

Every object she met filled her with pleasure and amazement. Golden pillars supported the vaulted roof, and the walls were enriched with carvings and paintings representing beasts of the chase and rural scenes, adapted to delight the eye of the beholder. Proceeding onward, she perceived that besides the apartments of state there were others filled with all manner of treasures, and beautiful and precious productions of nature and art.

While her eyes were thus occupied, a voice addressed her, though she saw no one, uttering these words, "Sovereign lady, all that you see is yours. We whose voices you hear are your servants and shall obey all your commands with our utmost care and diligence. Retire, therefore, to your chamber and repose on your bed of down, and when you see fit, repair to the bath. Supper awaits you in the adjoining alcove when it pleases you to take your seat there."

Psyche gave ear to the admonitions of her vocal attendants, and after repose and the refreshment of the bath, seated herself in the alcove, where a table immediately presented itself, without any visible aid from waiters or servants, and covered with the greatest delicacies of food and the most nectareous wines. Her ears too were feasted with music from invisible performers; of whom one sang, another played on the lute, and all closed in the wonderful harmony of a full chorus.

She had not yet seen her destined husband. He came only in the hours of darkness and fled before the dawn of morning, but his accents were full of love, and inspired a like passion in her. She often begged him to stay and let her behold him, but he would not consent. On the contrary he charged her to make no attempt to see him, for it was his pleasure, for the best of reasons, to keep concealed.

"Why should you wish to behold me?" he said. "Have you any doubt of my love? Have you any wish ungratified? If you saw me, perhaps you would fear me, perhaps adore me, but all I ask of you is to love me. I would rather you would love me as an equal than adore me as a god."

This reasoning somewhat quieted Psyche for a time, and while the novelty lasted she felt quite happy. But at length the thought of her parents, left in ignorance of her fate, and of her sisters, precluded from sharing with her the delights of her situation, preyed on her mind and made her begin to feel her palace as but a splendid prison. When her husband came one night, she told him her distress, and at last drew from him an unwilling consent that her sisters should be brought to see her.

So, calling Zephyr, she acquainted him with her husband's commands, and he, promptly obedient, soon brought them across the mountain down to their sister's valley. They embraced her and she returned their caresses.

"Come," said Psyche, "enter with me my house and refresh yourselves with whatever your sister has to offer."

Then taking their hands she led them into her golden palace, and committed them to the care of her numerous train of attendant voices, to refresh them in her baths and at her table, and to show them all her treasures. The view of these celestial delights caused envy to enter their bosoms, at seeing their young sister possessed of such state and splendor, so much exceeding their own.

They asked her numberless questions, among others what sort of a person her husband was. Psyche replied that he was a beautiful youth, who generally spent the daytime in hunting upon the mountains.

The sisters, not satisfied with this reply, soon made her confess that she had never seen him. Then they proceeded to fill her bosom with dark suspicions. "Call to mind," they said, "the Pythian oracle that declared you destined to marry a direful and tremendous monster. The inhabitants of this valley say that your husband is a terrible and monstrous serpent, who nourishes you for a while with dainties that he may by and by devour you. Take our advice. Provide yourself with a lamp and a sharp knife; put them in concealment that your husband may not discover them, and when he is sound asleep, slip out of bed, bring forth your lamp, and see for yourself whether what they say is true or not. If it is, hesitate not to cut off the monster's head, and thereby recover your liberty."

Psyche resisted these persuasions as well as she could, but they did not fail to have their effect on her mind, and when her sisters were gone, their words and her own curiosity were too strong for her to resist. So she prepared her lamp and a sharp knife, and hid them out of sight of her husband. When he had fallen into his first sleep, she silently rose and uncovering her lamp beheld not a hideous monster, but the most beautiful and charming of the gods, with his golden ringlets wandering over his snowy neck and crimson cheek, with two dewy wings on his shoulders, whiter than snow, and with shining feathers like the tender blossoms of spring.

As she leaned the lamp over to have a better view of his face, a drop of burning oil fell on the shoulder of the god. Startled, he opened his eyes and fixed them upon her. Then, without saying a word, he spread his white wings and flew out of the window. Psyche, in vain endeavoring to follow him, fell from the window to the ground.

Cupid, beholding her as she lay in the dust, stopped his flight for an instant and said, "Oh foolish Psyche, is it thus you repay my love? After I disobeyed my mother's commands and made you my wife, will you think me a monster and cut off my head? But go; return to your sisters, whose advice you seem to think preferable to mine. I inflict no other punishment on you than to leave you for ever. Love cannot dwell with suspicion." So saying, he fled away, leaving poor Psyche prostrate on the ground, filling the place with mournful lamentations.

When she had recovered some degree of composure she looked around her, but the palace and gardens had vanished, and she found herself in the open field not far from the city where her sisters dwelt. She repaired thither and told them the whole story of her misfortunes, at which, pretending to grieve, those spiteful creatures inwardly rejoiced.

"For now," said they, "he will perhaps choose one of us." With this idea, without saying a word of her intentions, each of them rose early the next morning and ascended the mountain, and having reached the top, called upon Zephyr to receive her and bear her to his lord; then leaping up, and not being sustained by Zephyr, fell down the precipice and was dashed to pieces.

Psyche meanwhile wandered day and night, without food or repose, in search of her husband. Casting her eyes on a lofty mountain having on its brow a magnificent temple, she sighed and said to herself, "Perhaps my love, my lord, inhabits there," and directed her steps thither.

She had no sooner entered than she saw heaps of corn, some in loose ears and some in sheaves, with mingled ears of barley. Scattered about, lay sickles and rakes, and all the instruments of harvest, without order, as if thrown carelessly out of the weary reapers' hands in the sultry hours of the day.

This unseemly confusion the pious Psyche put an end to, by separating and sorting everything to its proper place and kind, believing that she ought to neglect none of the gods, but endeavor by her piety to engage them all in her behalf. The holy Ceres, whose temple it was, finding her so religiously employed, thus spoke to her, "Oh Psyche, truly worthy of our pity, though I cannot shield you from the frowns of Venus, yet I can teach you how best to allay her displeasure. Go, then, and voluntarily surrender yourself to your lady and sovereign, and try by modesty and submission to win her forgiveness, and perhaps her favor will restore you the husband you have lost."

Psyche obeyed the commands of Ceres and took her way to the temple of Venus, endeavoring to fortify her mind and ruminating on what she should say and how best propitiate the angry goddess, feeling that the issue was doubtful and perhaps fatal.

Venus received her with angry countenance. "Most undutiful and faithless of servants," said she, "do you at last remember that you really have a mistress? Or have you rather come to see your sick husband, yet laid up of the wound given him by his loving wife? You are so ill favored and disagreeable that the only way you can merit your lover must be by dint of industry and diligence. I will make trial of your housewifery." Then she ordered Psyche to be led to the storehouse of her temple, where was laid up a great quantity of wheat, barley, millet, vetches, beans, and lentils prepared for food for her pigeons, and said, "Take and separate all these grains, putting all of the same kind in a parcel by themselves, and see that you get it done before evening." Then Venus departed and left her to her task.

But Psyche, in a perfect consternation at the enormous work, sat stupid and silent, without moving a finger to the inextricable heap.

While she sat despairing, Cupid stirred up the little ant, a native of the fields, to take compassion on her. The leader of the anthill, followed by whole hosts of his six-legged subjects, approached the heap, and with the utmost diligence taking grain by grain, they separated the pile, sorting each kind to its parcel; and when it was all done, they vanished out of sight in a moment.

Venus at the approach of twilight returned from the banquet of the gods, breathing odors and crowned with roses. Seeing the task done, she exclaimed, "This is no work of yours, wicked one, but his, whom to your own and his misfortune you have enticed." So saying, she threw her a piece of black bread for her supper and went away.

Next morning Venus ordered Psyche to be called and said to her, "Behold yonder grove which stretches along the margin of the water. There you will find sheep feeding without a shepherd, with golden-shining fleeces on their backs. Go, fetch me a sample of that precious wool gathered from every one of their fleeces."

Psyche obediently went to the riverside, prepared to do her best to execute the command. But the river god inspired the reeds with harmonious murmurs, which seemed to say, "Oh maiden, severely tried, tempt not the dangerous flood, nor venture among the formidable rams on the other side, for as long as they are under the influence of the rising sun, they burn with a cruel rage to destroy mortals with their sharp horns or rude teeth. But when the noontide sun has driven the cattle to the shade, and the serene spirit of the flood has lulled them to rest, you may then cross in safety, and you will find the woolly gold sticking to the bushes and the trunks of the trees."

Thus the compassionate river god gave Psyche instructions how to accomplish her task, and by observing his directions she soon returned to Venus with her arms full of the golden fleece; but she received not the approbation of her implacable mistress, who said, "I know very well it is by none of your own doings that you have succeeded in this task, and I am not satisfied yet that you have any capacity to make yourself useful. But I have another task for you. Here, take this box and go your way to the infernal shades, and give this box to Proserpine and say, 'My mistress Venus desires you to send her a little of your beauty, for in tending her sick son she has lost some of her own.' Be not too long on your errand, for I must paint myself with it to appear at the circle of the gods and goddesses this evening."

Psyche was now satisfied that her destruction was at hand, being obliged to go with her own feet directly down to Erebus. Wherefore, to make no delay of what was not to be avoided, she goes to the top of a high tower to precipitate herself headlong, thus to descend the shortest way to the shades below. But a voice from the tower said to her, "Why, poor unlucky girl, do you design to put an end to your days in so dreadful a manner? And what cowardice makes you sink under this last danger who have been so miraculously supported in all your former?" Then the voice told her how by a certain cave she might reach the realms of Pluto, and how to avoid all the dangers of the road, to pass by Cerberus, the three-headed dog, and prevail on Charon, the ferryman, to take her across the black river and bring her back again. But the voice added, "When Proserpine has given you the box filled with her beauty, of all things this is chiefly to be observed by you, that you never once open or look into the box nor allow your curiosity to pry into the treasure of the beauty of the goddesses."

Psyche, encouraged by this advice, obeyed it in all things, and taking heed to her ways traveled safely to the kingdom of Pluto. She was admitted to the palace of Proserpine, and without accepting the delicate seat or delicious banquet that was offered her, but contented with coarse bread for her food, she delivered her message from Venus. Presently the box was returned to her, shut and filled with the precious commodity. Then she returned the way she came, and glad was she to come out once more into the light of day.

But having got so far successfully through her dangerous task a longing desire seized her to examine the contents of the box. "What," said she, "shall I, the carrier of this divine beauty, not take the least bit to put on my cheeks to appear to more advantage in the eyes of my beloved husband!" So she carefully opened the box, but found nothing there of any beauty at all, but an infernal and truly Stygian sleep, which being thus set free from its prison, took possession of her, and she fell down in the midst of the road, a sleepy corpse without sense or motion.

But Cupid, being now recovered from his wound, and not able longer to bear the absence of his beloved Psyche, slipping through the smallest crack of the window of his chamber which happened to be left open, flew to the spot where Psyche lay, and gathering up the sleep from her body closed it again in the box, and waked Psyche with a light touch of one of his arrows. "Again," said he, "have you almost perished by the same curiosity. But now perform exactly the task imposed on you by my mother, and I will take care of the rest."

Then Cupid, as swift as lightning penetrating the heights of heaven, presented himself before Jupiter with his supplication. Jupiter lent a favoring ear, and pleaded the cause of the lovers so earnestly with Venus that he won her consent. On this he sent Mercury to bring Psyche up to the heavenly assembly, and when she arrived, handing her a cup of ambrosia, he said, "Drink this, Psyche, and be immortal; nor shall Cupid ever break away from the knot in which he is tied, but these nuptials shall be perpetual."

Thus Psyche became at last united to Cupid, and in due time they had a daughter born to them whose name was Pleasure.

DISCUSSION QUESTIONS

1. Trace Psyche's journey using Campbell's monomyth. Which stages does she experience? Even though she has help and does not perform feats of physical strength, how does she display heroism?

2. In the book *The Uses of Enchantment*, Bruno Bettelheim suggests a Freudian interpretation of the story in which Psyche is experiencing marital anxiety and sexual repression, while Cupid is experiencing Oedipal difficulties. Examine these claims. To what extent do you agree or disagree? What other Freudian interpretations can you identify?

3. Explain importance of Cupid and Psyche giving birth to a daughter named Pleasure.

4. Consider the story using Jung's concept of individuation and the *animus*. How does Psyche develop throughout the myth?

5. What are the main themes in the story? What other fairy tale motifs are present?

Demeter and Persephone

The story of the daughter stolen away to be the bride of Hell itself comes to us from the anonymously written "Homeric Hymns." It is one of the most well-known of the Greek tales for its connection to the harvest and the simple fact that we as modern readers perhaps relate to the fear of a mother losing her child.

Demeter, the goddess of the harvest, would have been worshipped as a more important deity to everyday life, than say, Zeus. The very life cycle of birth, life, death—or childhood, fertility, sterility—or the moon cycle of waxing, full, waning—these all bear in mind the rotation of the seasons, the years, the lives that crops and animals and humans lead.

When Demeter realizes her daughter has been taken by Hades, and that Zeus was an accomplice, she punishes the humans with a lack of food, which in turn punishes those on Olympus by denying them the sacrifices they so crave. Her role as goddess of the harvest is powerful and closely tied to the rituals in the Eleusinian Mysteries, as described in the Hymn.

The following Homeric Hymn Number 2 journeys from Persephone's abduction to Demeter's efforts to get her back, and the trickery on Hades' part to keep Persephone for part of the year.

HOMERIC HYMN TO DEMETER

I sing of the beautiful goddess Demeter, she and her trim-ankled daughter Persephone whom Hades swept away, given to him by all-seeing, thundering Zeus.

Persephone is taken

Away from Demeter, lady of the golden sword and glorious fruits, Persephone was playing with the deep-bosomed daughters of Oceanus and gathering flowers over a soft meadow, roses and crocuses and beautiful violets, irises and hyacinths and the narcissus, which Gaia made to grow for Zeus and to please Hades, to be a snare for the bloom-like girl — a marvellous, radiant flower. It was a thing of awe for both deathless gods or mortal men to see: from its root grew a hundred blooms and it smelled most sweetly, so that heaven above and the whole earth and the sea's salt swell laughed for joy. The girl was amazed by the flower and reached out with both hands to take the lovely bloom; but there in the plain of Nysa, Hades with his immortal horses sprang out upon her.

He caught her against her will in his golden chariot and bore her away lamenting. She cried out shrilly, calling upon her father, Zeus. But no one, neither deathless gods or mortal men, heard her voice, not even the olive-trees bearing rich fruit: only tender-hearted Hecate, the daughter of Persaeus, heard the girl from her cave, and the lord Helios, Hyperion's bright son, as she cried to her father. But Zeus was sitting aloof, apart from the gods, in his temple where many pray, and receiving sweet offerings from mortal men. So Hades was bearing her away on his immortal chariot by leave of Zeus—his own brother's child and unwilling.

And so long as Persephone could still see the earth and starry heaven and the strong-flowing sea where fishes swim, and the rays of the sun stream, she still held hope to see her dear mother Demeter and the eternal gods; so long hope calmed her great heart for all her trouble ... and the heights of the mountains and the depths of the sea rang with her immortal voice: and her queenly mother heard her.

Demeter searches for Persephone

Bitter pain seized Demeter's heart, and she tore the covering upon her divine hair with her own hands: she ripped off her dark cloak from around both her shoulders and sped, like a wild-bird, over the firm land and yielding sea, seeking her child. But no one would tell her the truth, neither god nor mortal man; and of the birds of omen none came with true news for her. For nine days queenly Demeter wandered over the earth with flaming torches in her hands, so grieved that she did not eat the ambrosia or drink of the sweet nectar, nor did she sprinkle her body with water. But when the tenth dawn Hecate came with a torch in her hands, and told the news:

> "Queenly Demeter, bringer of seasons and the gift of the bountiful harvest, what god of heaven or what mortal man has rapt away Persephone and pierced your heart with sorrow? For I heard her voice, yet I did not see with my eyes who it was. But I tell you truly and shortly all I know."

Demeter did not reply, but sped swiftly with her, holding flaming torches in her hands. They came to Helios, who is watchman of both gods and men, and stood in front of his horses: and Demeter enquired of him if Helios had seen who had violently seized Persephone against her will. Helios answered her:

> "Queen Demeter, I will tell you the truth; for I greatly revere and pity you in your grief. Cloud-gathering Zeus gave Persephone to Hades, her father's brother, to be called his buxom wife. And Hades seized her and took her loudly crying in his chariot down to his realm of mist and gloom. But

Source: Anonymous. *The Homeric Hymns and Homerica with an English Translation* by Hugh G. Evelyn-White. *Homeric Hymns*. 1914.

cease your loud protests and keep your anger in: Hades is not an unseemly husband among the deathless gods for your child, being your own brother: also, for honor, he has that third share which he received when division was made between Zeus and Poseidon, and is the lord of his kingdom."

But Demeter's heart grieved more terribly, and she was so angry with Zeus that she avoided Olympus and went instead to the towns and rich fields of men in disguise.

Demeter nurses Demophon

No one noticed her until she came to the house of Celeus who then was lord of Eleusis. Vexed in her dear heart, she sat at the the Virgin's Well, where the women came to draw water, at a shady place over which grew an olive shrub. There the daughters of Celeus saw her, as they were coming for water, to carry to their father's house: these four were like goddesses in the flower of their adolescence. They did not know Demeter, but they spoke to her, asking who she was, where she came from, and why she was not among the other old women who would take care of her. Demeter, the queen among goddesses answered them:

"Hail, dear children, I will tell you my story; My mother named me Doso and I come unwillingly by way of pirates from Crete. They put men and women into a ship and fled secretly as my masters began to make a meal. Across the dark country I wandered and I come here: I know not at all what land this is or what people are in it. But may all those who dwell on Olympus give you husbands and children, so you take pity on me, maidens, and tell me the name of a house of what man and woman I may go, to work for them cheerfully at such tasks as belong to a woman of my age. I could nurse a newborn child, or keep house, or make my masters' bed, or teach the women their work."

Straightway one of the maidens answered:

"Mother, you are godlike. Stay here and we will go to our father's house and tell Metaneira, our deep-bosomed mother, so that she may bid you come to our home. She has an only son, who is being nursed. If you could bring him up until he reached the full measure of youth, any woman who should see you would straightway envy you, such gifts would our mother give for his upbringing."

Their mother invited the stranger to come for a measureless hire. When they arrived and met Metaneira, she was overcome with awe at seeing the stranger and offered a seat next to her. Demeter, bringer of seasons and giver of perfect gifts, would not sit upon the couch, but stayed silent with lovely eyes cast down until a stool with a fleece was brought for her instead. A long time she sat upon the stool without speaking because of her sorrow, and spoke to no one, but rested, never smiling, and tasting neither food nor drink, because she pined with longing for her deep-bosomed daughter. Then Metaneira filled a cup with sweet wine and offered it to her; but she refused it, for she said it was not lawful for her to drink red wine, but bade them mix meal and water with soft mint and give it to her to drink. Metaneira mixed the draught and gave it to the goddess as she was asked and the great queen Demeter received it to observe the sacrament. Metaneira began to speak:

"Hail, lady! For I think you are nobly born; truly dignity and grace are in your eyes as in the eyes of kings that deal justice. Yet we mortals bear what the gods send us, though we grieve; for a yoke is set upon our necks. But now, since you have come here, you shall have what I can give: and nurse me this child whom the gods gave me in my old age and beyond my hope, a son much prayed for. If you should bring him up until he reaches the full measure of youth, any one of woman-kind that sees you will straightway envy you, so great reward would I give for his upbringing."

Then rich-haired Demeter answered her:

"And to you, also, lady, all hail, and may the gods give you good! Gladly will I take the boy to my breast, as you bid me, and will nurse him. I shall ensure no witchcraft shall hurt him nor yet the misery of Undercutter [teething]: for I know a charm far stronger than toothache and I know an excellent safeguard against woeful witchcraft."

Demeter took the child in her fragrant bosom with her divine hands and his mother was glad in her heart. So the goddess nursed Demophon, the son of wise Celeus and Metaneira. And the child grew like some immortal being, not fed with food nor nourished at the breast: for by day rich-crowned Demeter would anoint him with ambrosia as if he were the offspring of a god and breathe sweetly upon him as she held him in her bosom. But at night she would hide him like a brand in the heart of the fire, unknown to his dear parents. And it brought great wonder in that he grew beyond his age; for he was like looking at a god's face. And she would have made him deathless and unageing, had not Metaneira kept watch by night from her sweet-smelling chamber and spied upon Demeter. Because she feared for her son and was greatly distraught in her heart, she lamented and uttered winged words:

"Demophon, my son, the strange woman buries you deep in fire and works grief and bitter sorrow for me!"

Demeter heard her, and was wrathful. With her divine hands she snatched from the fire the dear son whom Metaneira had born and cast him to the ground; for she was terribly angry in her heart. She said to Metaneira:

"Witless are you mortals and ignorant to understand the difference between the good and evil of your future. For now in your heedlessness you have wrought folly past healing; for I would have made your dear son deathless and unaging all his days and would have bestowed on him everlasting honor, but now he can in no way escape death and the fates. Yet shall unfailing honor always rest upon him, because he lay upon my knees and slept in my arms. But, as the years move round and when he is in his prime, the sons of the Eleusinians shall ever wage war and dread strife with one another continually. Lo! I am that Demeter who has share of honor and is the greatest help and cause of joy to the undying gods and mortal men. But now, let all the people build me a great temple and an altar below it and beneath the city and its sheer wall upon a rising hillock above Callichorus. And I myself will teach my rites, that hereafter you may reverently perform them and so win the favor of my heart."

When she had finished, the goddess thrust her costume of old age away from her: beauty spread round about her and a lovely fragrance was wafted from her sweet-smelling robes, and from the divine body of the goddess a light shone afar, while golden tresses spread down over her shoulders, so that Celeus was filled with brightness as with lightning.

All night long they sought to appease the glorious goddess, quaking with fear. Celeus called on countless people to an assembly and bade them make the temple for the goddess Demeter and an altar upon the rising hillock as she instructed. And they obeyed him speedily and harkened to his voice. As for the child, he grew like an immortal being.

Demeter ceases the harvest

Now when they had finished building and had drawn back from their toil, they went back to their houses. But golden-haired Demeter sat there apart from all the blessed gods and stayed, wasting with yearning for her daughter. Then she caused a most dreadful and cruel year for mankind over the all-nourishing earth: the ground would not make the seed sprout, for Demeter kept it hid. In the fields the oxen drew many a curved plough in vain, and many seeds were cast upon the land to no avail. She would have destroyed the whole race of man with cruel famine and have robbed those who dwell on Olympus of their glorious gifts and sacrifices, had not Zeus taken notice.

First he sent golden-winged Iris to call upon Demeter, lovely in form. She sped with swift feet to the stronghold of Eleusis, and there, finding dark-cloaked Demeter in her temple, spoke to her and uttered winged words:

"Demeter, father Zeus, whose wisdom is everlasting, calls you to come join the eternal gods on Olympus: come therefore, and let not the message I bring from Zeus pass unobeyed."

But Demeter's heart was not moved. Zeus tried again; he sent forth all the rest of the blessed and eternal gods: and they came, one after the other, and kept calling her and offering many very beautiful gifts and whatever rights she might be pleased with. Yet no one was able to persuade her mind or will, so angry was she in her heart; she stubbornly rejected all their words: for she vowed that she would never set foot on Olympus, nor would she let fruit spring out of the ground, until she beheld with her own eyes her fair-faced daughter Persephone. When Zeus heard this, he sent Hermes to Hades, hoping to speak to Hades with gentle words. Hermes found the lord Hades in his house seated upon a couch, and his shy mate with him, much reluctant, because she yearned for her mother. Hermes drew near and said:

"Hades, ruler over the departed, father Zeus bids me bring noble Persephone forth from Erebus to the gods, that her mother may see her with her eyes and cease from her dread anger with the immortals; for now she plans an awful deed, to destroy the earth-born men by keeping seed hidden beneath the earth, and so she makes an end of the sacrifices to the immortal gods. She is fearfully angry and does not consort with the gods on Olympus, but sits aloof in her fragrant temple at Eleusis."

Hades tricks Persephone with the pomegranate

Hades smiled grimly and obeyed the behest of Zeus the king. He straightway urged wise Persephone, saying:

"Go now, Persephone, to your dark-robed mother, go, and feel kindly in your heart towards me: do not be exceedingly downcast; for I am not an unfitting husband for you among the deathless gods, as I am your father's brother. If you are to stay here with me, you shall rule all that lives and moves and shall have the greatest rights among the deathless gods: those who do not appease your power with offerings and reverently perform rites give you gifts, they shall be punished."

Persephone was filled with joy and hastily sprang up to leave. But Hades secretly gave her sweet pomegranate seed to eat, taking care for himself that she might not remain forever above with Demeter. Hades got ready his deathless horses and she mounted on the chariot, and Hermes took reins and whip in his hands and drove from the hall, the horses speeding readily.

When Demeter saw them, she rushed forth, and when Persephone saw her mother's sweet eyes, she left the chariot and horses, and leaped down to run to her, and falling upon her neck, and embracing her. But while Demeter was still holding her dear child in her arms, her heart suddenly told her there was something wrong--she feared greatly and ceased hugging her daughter and asked of her at once:

"My child, tell me, surely you have not tasted any food while you were below? Speak out and hide nothing, but let me know. For if you have not, you shall come back from loathly Hades and live with me and your father at Olympus and be honored by all the deathless gods; but if you have tasted food, you must go back again beneath the secret places of the earth, to dwell a third part of the seasons every year: for the other two parts you shall be with me and the other deathless gods. When the earth blooms with the fragrant flowers of spring, then from the realm of darkness and gloom will you emerge to be with me. Now tell me how he rapt you away to the realm of darkness and gloom, and by what trick did the strong Hades beguile you?"

The beautiful Persephone answered her:

"Mother, he secretly put in my mouth sweet food, a pomegranate seed, and forced me to taste against my will. It was my father's plan to carry me off beneath the depths of the earth to become the bride of Hades. I was playing in a lovely meadow, gathering sweet flowers I plucked the narcissus but the earth parted beneath, and there the strong lord Hades sprang forth and in his golden chariot he bore me away, all unwilling, beneath the earth: then I cried with a shrill cry. All this is true, though it grieves me to tell the tale."

So did they feel with one heart, and greatly cheer each the other's soul and spirit with many an embrace: their hearts had relief from their griefs while each took and gave back joyousness. Lady Hecate came then, and became from then on minister and companion to Persephone.

Demeter relents and teaches the people her mysteries

All-seeing Zeus sent a messenger to them, rich-haired Rhea, to bring Demeter to join the families of the gods: Rhea swiftly rushed down from the peaks of Olympus and came to the plain of Rharus, which was once rich, fertile corn-land, but had in Demeter's anger lay idle and utterly leafless. As spring-time came, it was soon to be waving with long ears of corn, and its rich furrows to be loaded with grain upon the ground, while others would already be bound in sheaves. This occurred from the time Rhea landed from the fruitless upper air. Rhea and Demeter met and the goddesses were glad to see each other and cheered in hearts. Rhea said to Demeter:

> "Come, my daughter; for far-seeing Zeus the loud-thunderer calls you to join the families of the gods, and has promised to give you what rights you please among the deathless gods, and has assented that for a third part of the circling year your daughter shall go down to darkness and gloom, but for the two parts she shall be with you and the other deathless gods: so has he declared it shall be and has bowed his head in token. But come, my child, obey, and be not too angry with him; but rather increase the harvest for men that which gives them life."

Rich-crowned Demeter did not refuse, but straightway made fruit to spring up from the rich lands, so that the whole wide earth was laden with leaves and flowers. Then she went to the kings who deal justice and leaders of the people, to show them the conduct of her rites and taught them all her mysteries,— mysteries full of awe which no one may in any way transgress or pry into or utter, for deep awe of the gods checks the voice. Happy is he among men upon earth who has seen these mysteries; but he who is uninitiated and who takes no part in them, has no part in the gifts of the mysteries once he is dead.

When the bright goddess had taught them all, Demeter and Persephone went to Olympus to the gathering of the other gods. And there they dwell beside Zeus who delights in thunder, aweful and reverend goddesses. Blessed are the men on earth whom they freely love: soon they do send wealth as guest to his great house.

And now, queen of the land of sweet Eleusis, giver of good gifts, bringer of seasons, queen Demeter, be gracious, you and your daughter, all beauteous Persephone, and for my song grant me heart-cheering substance. And now I will remember you with another song also.

DISCUSSION QUESTIONS

1.   Why was a pomegranate used as the instrument for keeping Persephone in Hades' realm?

2.   Why do both Zeus and Hades use the argument that Hades is not a bad husband to have, all things considered?

3.   What do you think is the significance for including the nursing of Demophon?

4.   What can we glean about Zeus' personality from this story?

Prometheus

The character of Prometheus, written about by Hesiod in both *Theogony* and in *Works and Days* does not "fit in." He does not belong with the gods on Mt. Olympus, but nor is he human, though he admittedly saved their race. He is instead a "liminal" figure, occupying the space between the mortal and immortal, as most tricksters do.

Prometheus' story has been written about by so many authors that it is difficult to parse the original from its sequels and to determine exactly what happened to him while he was chained up on that rock. We know that it was during one of Heracles' labors that Prometheus was freed, but there is contrasting information about which of the labors and even Heracles' motivations for freeing Prometheus is in question. The story is in Apollodorus' *The Library* and has been reprinted in seemingly every anthology of mythology since.

Here we give Hesiod's two stories of Prometheus, which are not identical, but tell different parts of the same story. Pay attention to the order that Hesiod tells the story—he tells us the end before he tells us *why* it happened.

PROMETHEUS
From Hesiod's *Theogony* lines 507–616

Now Iapetus took to wife the neat-ankled maid Clymene, daughter of Ocean, and went up with her into one bed. And she bore him a stout-hearted son, Atlas: also she bore very glorious Menoetius and clever Prometheus, full of various wiles, and scatter-brained Epimetheus who from the first was a mischief to men who eat bread; for it was he who first took of Zeus the woman, the maiden whom he had formed. But Menoetius was outrageous, and farseeing Zeus struck him with a lurid thunderbolt and sent him down to Erebus because of his mad presumption and exceeding pride. And Atlas through hard constraint upholds the wide heaven with unwearying head and arms, standing at the borders of the earth before the clear-voiced Hesperides; for this lot wise Zeus assigned to him.

And ready-witted Prometheus he bound with inextricable bonds, cruel chains, and drove a shaft through his middle, and set on him a long-winged eagle, which used to eat his immortal liver; but by night the liver grew as much again everyway as the long-winged bird devoured in the whole day. That bird Heracles, the valiant son of shapely-ankled Alcmene, slew; and delivered the son of Iapetus from the cruel plague, and released him from his affliction—not without the will of Olympian Zeus who reigns on high, that the glory of Heracles the Theban-born might be yet greater than it was before over the plenteous earth. This, then, he regarded, and honored his famous son; though he was angry, he ceased from the wrath which he had before because Prometheus matched himself in wit with the almighty son of Kronos.

For when the gods and mortal men had a dispute at Mecone, even then Prometheus was forward to cut up a great ox and set portions before them, trying to deceive the mind of Zeus. Before the rest he set flesh and inner parts thick with fat upon the hide, covering them with an ox paunch; but for Zeus he put the white bones dressed up with cunning art and covered with shining fat. Then the father of men and of gods said to him:

"Son of Iapetus, most glorious of all lords, good sir, how unfairly you have divided the portions!"

So said Zeus whose wisdom is everlasting, rebuking him. But wily Prometheus answered him, smiling softly and not forgetting his cunning trick:

Source: Hesiod. *The Homeric Hymns and Homerica with an English Translation* by Hugh G. Evelyn-White. *Theogony.* 1914.

"Zeus, most glorious and greatest of the eternal gods, take which ever of these portions your heart within you bids."

So he said, thinking trickery. But Zeus, whose wisdom is everlasting, saw and failed not to perceive the trick, and in his heart he thought mischief against mortal men which also was to be fulfilled. With both hands he took up the white fat and was angry at heart, and wrath came to his spirit when he saw the white ox-bones craftily tricked out: and because of this the tribes of men upon earth burn white bones to the deathless gods upon fragrant altars. But Zeus who drives the clouds was greatly vexed and said to him:

"Son of Iapetus, clever above all! So, sir, you have not yet forgotten your cunning arts!"

So spake Zeus in anger, whose wisdom is everlasting; and from that time he was always mindful of the trick, and would not give the power of unwearying fire to the Melian race of mortal men who live on the earth.

But the noble son of Iapetus outwitted him and stole the far-seen gleam of unwearying fire in a hollow fennel stalk. And Zeus who thunders on high was stung in spirit, and his dear heart was angered when he saw amongst men the far-seen ray of fire. Forthwith he made an evil thing for men as the price of fire; for the very famous Limping God formed of earth the likeness of a shy maiden as the son of Kronos willed. And the goddess bright-eyed Athena girded and clothed her with silvery raiment, and down from her head she spread with her hands an embroidered veil, a wonder to see; and she, Pallas Athena, put about her head lovely garlands, flowers of new-grown herbs. Also she put upon her head a crown of gold which the very famous Limping God made himself and worked with his own hands as a favor to Zeus his father. On it was much curious work, wonderful to see; for of the many creatures which the land and sea rear up, he put most upon it, wonderful things, like living beings with voices: and great beauty shone out from it.

But when he had made the beautiful evil to be the price for the blessing, he brought her out, delighting in the finery which the bright-eyed daughter of a mighty father had given her, to the place where the other gods and men were. And wonder took hold of the deathless gods and mortal men when they saw that which was sheer guile, not to be withstood by men.

For from her is the race of women and female kind: of her is the deadly race and tribe of women who live amongst mortal men to their great trouble, no help meets in hateful poverty, but only in wealth. And as in thatched hives bees feed the drones whose nature is to do mischief—by day and throughout the day until the sun goes down the bees are busy and lay the white combs, while the drones stay at home in the covered hives and reap the toil of others into their own bellies—even so Zeus who thunders on high made women to be an evil to mortal men, with a nature to do evil. And he gave them a second evil to be the price for the good they had: whoever avoids marriage and the sorrows that women cause, and will not wed, reaches deadly old age without anyone to tend his years, and though he at least has no lack of livelihood while he lives, yet, when he is dead, his kinsfolk divide his possessions amongst them. And as for the man who chooses the lot of marriage and takes a good wife suited to his mind, evil continually contends with good; for whoever happens to have mischievous children, lives always with unceasing grief in his spirit and heart within him; and this evil cannot be healed. So it is not possible to deceive or go beyond the will of Zeus: for not even the son of Iapetus, kindly Prometheus, escaped his heavy anger, but of necessity strong bands confined him, although he knew many a wile.

From Hesiod's *Works and Days* lines 42–108

For the gods keep hidden from men the means of life. Else you would easily do work enough in a day to supply you for a full year even without working; soon would you put away your rudder over the smoke, and the fields worked by ox and sturdy mule would run to waste. But Zeus in the anger of his heart hid it, because Prometheus the crafty deceived him; therefore he planned sorrow and mischief against men.

He hid fire; but that the noble son of Iapetus stole again for men from Zeus the counsellor in a hollow fennel-stalk, so that Zeus who delights in thunder did not see it. But afterwards Zeus who gathers the clouds said to him in anger:

> "Son of Iapetus, surpassing all in cunning, you are glad that you have outwitted me and stolen fire—a great plague to you yourself and to men that shall be. But I will give men as the price for fire an evil thing in which they may all be glad of heart while they embrace their own destruction."

So said the father of men and gods, and laughed aloud. And he bade famous Hephaestus make haste and mix earth with water and to put in it the voice and strength of human kind, and fashion a sweet, lovely maiden-shape, like to the immortal goddesses in face; and Athena to teach her needlework and the weaving of the varied web; and golden Aphrodite to shed grace upon her head and cruel longing and cares that weary the limbs. And he charged Hermes the guide, the Slayer of Argus, to put in her a shameless mind and a deceitful nature. So he ordered. And they obeyed the lord Zeus the son of Kronos.

Forthwith the famous Lame God moulded clay in the likeness of a modest maid, as the son of Kronos purposed. And the goddess bright-eyed Athena girded and clothed her, and the divine Graces and queenly Persuasion put necklaces of gold upon her, and the rich-haired Hours crowned her head with spring flowers. And Pallas Athena bedecked her form with all manner of finery. Also the Guide, the Slayer of Argus, contrived within her lies and crafty words and a deceitful nature at the will of loud thundering Zeus, and the Herald of the gods put speech in her. And he called this woman Pandora ["all gifts"], because all they who dwelt on Olympus gave each a gift, a plague to men who eat bread. But when he had finished the sheer, hopeless snare, the Father sent glorious Argus-Slayer, the swift messenger of the gods, to take it to Epimetheus as a gift. And Epimetheus did not think on what Prometheus had said to him, bidding him never take a gift of Olympian Zeus, but to send it back for fear it might prove to be something harmful to men. But he took the gift, and afterwards, when the evil thing was already his, he understood. For ere this the tribes of men lived on earth remote and free from ills and hard toil and heavy sicknesses which bring the Fates upon men; for in misery men grow old quickly.

But the woman took off the great lid of the jar with her hands and scattered, all these and her thought caused sorrow and mischief to men. Only Hope remained there in an unbreakable home within under the rim of the great jar, and did not fly out at the door; for ere that, the lid of the jar stopped her, by the will of Aegis-holding Zeus who gathers the clouds. But the rest, countless plagues, wander amongst men; for earth is full of evils, and the sea is full. Of themselves diseases come upon men continually by day and by night, bringing mischief to mortals silently; for wise Zeus took away speech from them. So is there no way to escape the will of Zeus. Or if you will, I will sum you up another tale well and skillfully—and do you lay it up in your heart,—how the gods and mortal men sprang from one source.

DISCUSSION QUESTIONS

1. Why is the story told out of order? Make a quick outline of the key moments and think about the significance of the beginning and ending that Hesiod chose.

2. What are the differences between Hesiod's telling in *Theogony* and in *Works and Days*?

3. How does the character of Pandora change the world?

4. What is the significance of "hope"?

5. What are the differences between Epimetheus and Prometheus?

Part 3: Journeys of Heroes and Heroines

Heracles

All cultures have heroes, and the Greeks and Romans claim some of the most well-known and well-loved. The great epics of Greece and Rome tell of wars and adventures, monsters and quests. Although Heracles (Latin, Hercules) is not the star of a great epic like *The Iliad*, *The Odyssey*, or *The Aeneid*, he is one of the first names we think of as a Greek heroic figure. His legendary labors have long been celebrated and are still being adapted in modern fiction and film.

Dozens of Greek and Roman historians, scholars, and poets wrote about Heracles in the Classical Age. And, as all myths, there are different versions of the tales. Our main source for the tale of Heracles is Apollodorus, but there are many other accounts; Ovid also wrote about the life of Heracles. His death is told by Sophocles; in drama, Euripides highlights his tragic madness. Aristophanes portrays him as a comic figure. The poets Pindar and Theocritus both wrote about his birth and training, and Hesiod wrote about him as well. With so much source material, naturally each author's treatment offers a slightly different perspective on the hero. Even the chronology of his exploits varies from source to source—the play by Euripides places his madness after the labors, rather than before. Some accounts of his behavior suggest a burlesque side of Heracles—prone to drunken foolishness and folly. But the majority of the literature centers on his many heroic deeds. He was viewed as a role model in ancient Greece and many shrines were dedicated to him. Young men, especially, revered him for his strength and courage. In fact, some scholars focus solely on Heracles' brute strength and lack of cleverness, especially when compared to other Greek heroes, showing him to be a character of pure strength but lacking in intelligence. Perhaps if we look more closely he becomes a man driven simply by emotion—reacting quickly, even rashly at times—making him a dangerous and formidable opponent.

What he lacks in complexity, Heracles makes up for in sheer number and impressiveness of heroic feats. He performed other great deeds in addition to the twelve labors. The Greek poet Pindar tells that Heracles founded the first Olympic Games. Heracles was mentioned in *The Argonautica* (he was briefly part of the journey with Jason), and in *The Iliad* and *The Odyssey* as well. In *The Odyssey*, Odysseus meets Heracles' ghost.

Attitudes toward Heracles changed over the centuries from depicting him as simply a strong man into a more virtuous one. Yet he's clearly not what we call a Homeric hero; he does not typically battle other warriors, but deals mainly with animals and monsters. Eventually, though, he became known as a benefactor to humans, performing good deeds to benefit others. Despite the mixed portrayals there is always a common thread—his bravery and strength.

In the monomyth, the Road of Trials marks a stage in the hero's journey. In some stories this is just a small part of the journey; in others, the Road of Trials can take up all or most of the hero's quest, as it does in this case. Tests and trials can symbolize rites of passage—they can represent maturity and the demands of reaching adulthood. In addition, accomplishing great deeds and completing tasks suggests a way of making one's mark on the world, leaving a legacy, or proving one's worth.

The Birth of Heracles

In *The Library*, Apollodorus tells of Zeus visiting the bedchamber of Alcmene disguised as her husband Amphitryon, and lengthening one night into three. Amphitryon learned the truth, of course, but Alcmene became pregnant with twin boys—one the son of Zeus (Heracles), and the other (Iphicles) by her husband. Heracles was born one day before Iphicles, making him the heir. When the boys were eight months old, Hera sent two large snakes to attack them, hoping to destroy Heracles. But Heracles, already displaying the strength of a demi-god, strangled both snakes—one in each hand.

As a young boy, Heracles was taught to wrestle, use both sword and bow, throw a javelin, drive a chariot, and even play the lyre. But Heracles killed his music tutor, Linus, son of Apollo. Linus struck him and Heracles struck back, hitting him with the lyre and killing him. For this act, Heracles was exiled to tend the cattle. When Heracles was eighteen he set out to kill a lion that was preying on the cattle and, during the hunt, Heracles stayed with Thespius, another ruler who lived nearby. Thespius had 50 daughters and hoped one of them would bear the child of Heracles, so he sent one of his daughters to Heracles's bed each night (Heracles thought he was with the same girl each night). Some stories say he was with all 50 girls in one night. He did eventually kill the lion. Additionally, Heracles led the Theban army into a battle and among the many prizes he was granted from the gods (a golden breastplate, bow and arrow, sword) he was given Megara, the daughter of Creon, as his wife. They had three children.

TWELVE LABORS OF HERACLES

[2.4.12] Now it came to pass that after the battle with the Minyans Heracles was driven mad through the jealousy of Hera and flung his own children, whom he had by Megara, and two children of Iphicles into the fire; wherefore he condemned himself to exile, and was purified by Thespius, and repairing to Delphi he inquired of the god where he should dwell. The Pythian priestess then first called him Heracles, for hitherto he was called Alcides. And she told him to dwell in Tiryns, serving Eurystheus for twelve years and to perform the ten labours imposed on him, and so, she said, when the tasks were accomplished, he would be immortal.

[2.5.1] When Heracles heard that, he went to Tiryns and did as he was bid by Eurystheus. First, Eurystheus ordered him to bring the skin of the Nemean lion; now that was an invulnerable beast begotten by Typhon. On his way to attack the lion he came to Cleonae and lodged at the house of a day-laborer, Molorchus; and when his host would have offered a victim in sacrifice, Heracles told him to wait for thirty days, and then, if he had returned safe from the hunt, to sacrifice to Saviour Zeus, but if he were dead, to sacrifice to him as to a hero. And having come to Nemea and tracked the lion, he first shot an arrow at him, but when he perceived that the beast was invulnerable, he heaved up his club and made after him. And when the lion took refuge in a cave with two mouths, Heracles built up the one entrance and came in upon the beast through the other, and putting his arm round its neck held it tight till he had choked it; so laying it on his shoulders he carried it to Cleonae.

* * *

[2.5.2] As a second labour he ordered him to kill the Lernaean hydra. That creature, bred in the swamp of Lerna, used to go forth into the plain and ravage both the cattle and the country. Now the hydra had a huge body, with nine heads, eight mortal, but the middle one immortal. So mounting a chariot driven by Iolaus, he came to Lerna, and having halted his horses, he discovered the hydra on a hill beside the

Source: Apollodorus. *Apollodorus, The Library, with an English Translation* by Sir James George Frazer, 1921.

springs of the Amymone, where was its den. By pelting it with fiery shafts he forced it to come out, and in the act of doing so he seized and held it fast. But the hydra wound itself about one of his feet and clung to him. Nor could he effect anything by smashing its heads with his club, for as fast as one head was smashed there grew up two. A huge crab also came to the help of the hydra by biting his foot. So he killed it, and in his turn called for help on Iolaus who, by setting fire to a piece of the neighboring wood and burning the roots of the heads with the brands, prevented them from sprouting. Having thus got the better of the sprouting heads, he chopped off the immortal head, and buried it, and put a heavy rock on it, beside the road that leads through Lerna to Elaeus. But the body of the hydra he slit up and dipped his arrows in the gall. However, Eurystheus said that this labour should not be reckoned among the ten because he had not got the better of the hydra by himself, but with the help of Iolaus.

[2.5.3] As a third labour he ordered him to bring the Cerynitian hind alive to Mycenae. Now the hind was at Oenoe; it had golden horns and was sacred to Artemis; so wishing neither to kill nor wound it, Heracles hunted it a whole year. But when, weary with the chase, the beast took refuge on the mountain called Artemisius, and thence passed to the river Ladon, Heracles shot it just as it was about to cross the stream, and catching it put it on his shoulders and hastened through Arcadia. But Artemis with Apollo met him, and would have wrested the hind from him, and rebuked him for attempting to kill her sacred animal. Howbeit, by pleading necessity and laying the blame on Eurystheus, he appeased the anger of the goddess and carried the beast alive to Mycenae.

[2.5.4] As a fourth labour he ordered him to bring the Erymanthian boar alive; now that animal ravaged Psophis, sallying from a mountain which they call Erymanthus.

. . .

And when he had chased the boar with shouts from a certain thicket, he drove the exhausted animal into deep snow, trapped it, and brought it to Mycenae.

[2.5.5] The fifth labour he laid on him was to carry out the dung of the cattle of Augeas in a single day. Now Augeas was king of Elis; some say that he was a son of the Sun, others that he was a son of Poseidon, and others that he was a son of Phorbas; and he had many herds of cattle. Heracles accosted him, and without revealing the command of Eurystheus, said that he would carry out the dung in one day, if Augeas would give him the tithe of the cattle. Augeas was incredulous, but promised. Having taken Augeas's son Phyleus to witness, Heracles made a breach in the foundations of the cattle-yard, and then, diverting the courses of the Alpheus and Peneus, which flowed near each other, he turned them into the yard, having first made an outlet for the water through another opening. When Augeas learned that this had been accomplished at the command of Eurystheus, he would not pay the reward; nay more, he denied that he had promised to pay it, and on that point he professed himself ready to submit to arbitration. . . . But Eurystheus would not admit this labour either among the ten, alleging that it had been performed for hire.

[2.5.6] The sixth labour he enjoined on him was to chase away the Stymphalian birds. Now at the city of Stymphalus in Arcadia was the lake called Stymphalian, embosomed in a deep wood. To it countless birds had flocked for refuge, fearing to be preyed upon by the wolves. So when Heracles was at a loss how to drive the birds from the wood, Athena gave him brazen castanets, which she had received from Hephaestus. By clashing these on a certain mountain that overhung the lake, he scared the birds. They could not abide the sound, but fluttered up in a fright, and in that way Heracles shot them.

[2.5.7] The seventh labour he enjoined on him was to bring the Cretan bull. Acusilaus says that this was the bull that ferried across Europa for Zeus; but some say it was the bull that Poseidon sent up from the sea when Minos promised to sacrifice to Poseidon what should appear out of the sea. And they say that when he saw the beauty of the bull he sent it away to the herds and sacrificed another to Poseidon; at which the god was angry and made the bull savage. To attack this bull Heracles came to Crete, and when, in reply to his request for aid, Minos told him to fight and catch the bull for himself, he caught it and brought it to Eurystheus, and having shown it to him he let it afterwards go free. But the bull roamed to Sparta and all Arcadia, and traversing the Isthmus arrived at Marathon in Attica and harried the inhabitants.

[2.5.8] The eighth labour he enjoined on him was to bring the mares of Diomedes the Thracian to Mycenae. Now this Diomedes was a son of Ares and Cyrene, and he was king of the Bistones, a very warlike Thracian people, and he owned man-eating mares. So Heracles sailed with a band of volunteers, and having overpowered the grooms who were in charge of the mangers, he drove the mares to the sea. When the Bistones in arms came to the rescue, he committed the mares to the guardianship of Abderus, who was a son of Hermes, a native of Opus in Locris, and a minion of Heracles; but the mares killed him by dragging him after them. But Heracles fought against the Bistones, slew Diomedes and compelled the rest to flee. And he founded a city Abdera beside the grave of Abderus who had been done to death, and bringing the mares he gave them to Eurystheus. But Eurystheus let them go, and they came to Mount Olympus, as it is called, and there they were destroyed by the wild beasts.

[2.5.9] The ninth labour he enjoined on Heracles was to bring the belt of Hippolyte. She was queen of the Amazons, who dwelt about the river Thermodon, a people great in war; for they cultivated the manly virtues, and if ever they gave birth to children through intercourse with the other sex, they reared the females; and they pinched off the right breasts that they might not be trammelled by them in throwing the javelin, but they kept the left breasts, that they might suckle. Now Hippolyte had the belt of Ares in token of her superiority to all the rest. Heracles was sent to fetch this belt because Admete, daughter of Eurystheus, desired to get it. So taking with him a band of volunteer comrades in a single ship he set sail and put in to the island of Paros, which was inhabited by the sons of Minos, to wit, Eurymedon, Chryses, Nephalion, and Philolaus. But it chanced that two of those in the ship landed and were killed by the sons of Minos. Indignant at this, Heracles killed the sons of Minos on the spot and besieged the rest closely, till they sent envoys to request that in the room of the murdered men he would take two, whom he pleased. So he raised the siege, and taking on board the sons of Androgeus, son of Minos, to wit, Alcaeus and Sthenelus, he came to Mysia, to the court of Lycus, son of Dascylus, and was entertained by him; and in a battle between him and the king of the Bebryces Heracles sided with Lycus and slew many, amongst others King Mygdon, brother of Amycus. And he took much land from the Bebryces and gave it to Lycus, who called it all Heraclea.

Having put in at the harbor of Themiscyra, he received a visit from Hippolyte, who inquired why he had come, and promised to give him the belt. But Hera in the likeness of an Amazon went up and down the multitude saying that the strangers who had arrived were carrying off the queen. So the Amazons in arms charged on horseback down on the ship. But when Heracles saw them in arms, he suspected treachery, and killing Hippolyte stripped her of her belt. And after fighting the rest he sailed away and touched at Troy.

* * *

[2.5.10] As a tenth labour he was ordered to fetch the kine* of Geryon from Erythia. Now Erythia was an island near the ocean; it is now called Gadira. This island was inhabited by Geryon, son of Chrysaor by Callirrhoe, daughter of Ocean. He had the body of three men grown together and joined in one at the waist, but parted in three from the flanks and thighs. He owned red kine, of which Eurytion was the herdsman and Orthus, the two-headed hound, begotten by Typhon on Echidna, was the watchdog. So journeying through Europe to fetch the kine of Geryon he destroyed many wild beasts and set foot in Libya, and proceeding to Tartessus he erected as tokens of his journey two pillars over against each other at the boundaries of Europe and Libya. But being heated by the Sun on his journey, he bent his bow at

*kine = cows

the god, who in admiration of his hardihood, gave him a golden goblet in which he crossed the ocean. And having reached Erythia he lodged on Mount Abas. However, the dog, perceiving him, rushed at him; but he smote it with his club, and when the herdsman Eurytion came to the help of the dog, Heracles killed him also. But Menoetes, who was there pasturing the kine of Hades, reported to Geryon what had occurred, and he, coming up with Heracles beside the river Anthemus, as he was driving away the kine, joined battle with him and was shot dead. And Heracles, embarking the kine in the goblet and sailing across to Tartessus, gave back the goblet to the Sun.

And passing through Abderia he came to Liguria, where Ialebion and Dercynus, sons of Poseidon, attempted to rob him of the kine, but he killed them and went on his way through Tyrrhenia. But at Rhegium a bull broke away and hastily plunging into the sea swam across to Sicily, and having passed through the neighboring country since called Italy after it, for the Tyrrhenians called the bull *italus*, came to the plain of Eryx, who reigned over the Elymi. Now Eryx was a son of Poseidon, and he mingled the bull with his own herds. So Heracles entrusted the kine to Hephaestus and hurried away in search of the bull. He found it in the herds of Eryx, and when the king refused to surrender it unless Heracles should beat him in a wrestling bout, Heracles beat him thrice, killed him in the wrestling, and taking the bull drove it with the rest of the herd to the Ionian Sea. But when he came to the creeks of the sea, Hera afflicted the cows with a gadfly, and they dispersed among the skirts of the mountains of Thrace. Heracles went in pursuit, and having caught some, drove them to the Hellespont; but the remainder were thenceforth wild. Having with difficulty collected the cows, Heracles blamed the river Strymon, and whereas it had been navigable before, he made it unnavigable by filling it with rocks; and he conveyed the kine and gave them to Eurystheus, who sacrificed them to Hera.

[2.5.11] When the labours had been performed in eight years and a month, Eurystheus ordered Heracles, as an eleventh labour, to fetch golden apples from the Hesperides, for he did not acknowledge the labour of the cattle of Augeas nor that of the hydra. These apples were not, as some have said, in Libya, but on Atlas among the Hyperboreans. They were presented (by Earth) to Zeus after his marriage with Hera, and guarded by an immortal dragon with a hundred heads, offspring of Typhon and Echidna, which spoke with many and diverse sorts of voices. With it the Hesperides also were on guard, to wit, Aegle, Erythia, Hesperia, and Arethusa.

. . .

Now Prometheus had told Heracles not to go himself after the apples but to send Atlas, first relieving him of the burden of the sphere; so when he was come to Atlas in the land of the Hyperboreans, he took the advice and relieved Atlas. But when Atlas had received three apples from the Hesperides, he came to Heracles, and not wishing to support the sphere (he said that he would himself carry the apples to Eurystheus, and bade Heracles hold up the sky in his stead. Heracles promised to do so, but succeeded by craft in putting it on Atlas instead. For at the advice of Prometheus he begged Atlas to hold up the sky till he should) put a pad on his head. When Atlas heard that, he laid the apples down on the ground and took the sphere from Heracles. And so Heracles picked up the apples and departed. But some say that he did not get them from Atlas, but that he plucked the apples himself after killing the guardian snake. And having brought the apples he gave them to Eurystheus. But he, on receiving them, bestowed them on Heracles, from whom Athena got them and conveyed them back again; for it was not lawful that they should be laid down anywhere.

[2.5.12] A twelfth labour imposed on Heracles was to bring Cerberus from Hades. Now this Cerberus had three heads of dogs, the tail of a dragon, and on his back the heads of all sorts of snakes. When Heracles was about to depart to fetch him, he went to Eumolpus at Eleusis, wishing to be initiated. However it was not then lawful for foreigners to be initiated: since he proposed to be initiated as the adoptive son of Pylius. But not being able to see the mysteries because he had not been cleansed of the slaughter of the centaurs, he was cleansed by Eumolpus and then initiated. And having come to Taenarum in Laconia, where is the mouth of the descent to Hades, he descended through it. But when the souls saw him, they fled, save Meleager and the Gorgon Medusa. And Heracles drew his sword against the Gorgon, as if she were alive, but he learned from Hermes that she was an empty phantom. And being come near to the gates of Hades he found Theseus and Pirithous, him who wooed Persephone in wedlock and was therefore bound fast. And when they beheld Heracles, they stretched out their hands as if they should be raised from the dead by his might. And Theseus, indeed, he took by the hand and raised up, but when he would have brought up Pirithous, the earth quaked and he let go. And he rolled away also the stone of Ascalaphus. And wishing to provide the souls with blood, he slaughtered one of the kine of Hades. But Menoetes, son of Ceuthonymus, who tended the king, challenged Heracles to wrestle, and, being seized round the middle, had his ribs broken; howbeit, he was let off at the request of Persephone. When Heracles asked Pluto for Cerberus, Pluto ordered him to take the animal provided he mastered him without the use of the weapons which he carried. Heracles found him at the gates of Acheron, and, cased in his cuirass and covered by the lion's skin, he flung his arms round the head of the brute, and though the dragon in its tail bit him, he never relaxed his grip and pressure till it yielded. So he carried it off and ascended through Troezen. But Demeter turned Ascalaphus into a short-eared owl, and Heracles, after showing Cerberus to Eurystheus, carried him back to Hades.

[2.6.1] After his labours Heracles went to Thebes and gave Megara to Iolaus, and, wishing himself to wed, he ascertained that Eurytus, prince of Oechalia, had proposed the hand of his daughter Iole as a prize to him who should vanquish himself and his sons in archery. So he came to Oechalia, and though he proved himself better than them at archery, yet he did not get the bride; for while Iphitus, the elder of Eurytus's sons, said that Iole should be given to Heracles, Eurytus and the others refused, and said they feared that, if he got children, he would again kill his offspring.

DISCUSSION QUESTIONS

1. If the Greeks did not believe the gods controlled the will of human beings, how do we account for Heracles' madness, delivered upon him by Hera? What role does this play in the story?

2. What difference does it make if Heracles goes mad before or after his labors? How does this change your interpretation of the story? Consider Heracles' motivation for the twelve labors. How does this influence your interpretation? Is he seeking glory, immortality, or redemption? Or is he simply obeying orders from the gods?

3. Besides the obvious Road of Trials, explain other aspects of the monomyth you see in this story.

4. Heracles has some assistance from others—both gods and humans—in completing his tasks. How does this color your view of him as a hero?

5. Heracles is half-human, half-god. How would your view of him change if he were completely human or a god? Is he a relatable or sympathetic character? Why or why not?

6. The name Heracles means "glory of Hera," and yet her manipulations are the cause of much of his suffering. Discuss the meaning of his name.

Perseus

Source: Christina Gant

Another favorite hero in Greek mythology is Perseus. Like Heracles, he is an illegitimate son of Zeus and, also like Heracles, there are many tales of his great accomplishments—most famously, his encounter with Medusa and his rescue of the princess Andromeda. The story of Perseus also gives us a glimpse of some other characters of Greek myth, including Atlas and Medusa.

Very few Greek literary sources on Perseus remain; for this myth we'll use Apollodorus and the Roman poet Ovid as our main sources, as they provide the most complete accounts. There is little mention of Perseus' death in ancient literature, although sites where he was worshipped are reported in Athens, Seriphos, and Argos. Pausanias, a Greek author who lived in the Roman Empire, wrote briefly about this, also including Argos as the place where Medusa's head was eventually buried, alongside one of Perseus' daughters. Pausanias claims she was the first woman to remarry following the death of her husband, violating the custom of remaining a widow.

It's interesting that while comparatively less material exists about Perseus, as compared to other Greek heroes, he remains a popular figure. Like Heracles, tales about Perseus in the form of novels and films continue to entertain us.

Birth of Perseus

Acrisius, King of Argos, had only one child—a daughter named Danae. The oracle at Delphi prophesied that he would never have a son and, furthermore, his daughter's future son would kill him. Dreading this prophecy, he desperately wanted to get rid of his daughter. Rather than kill her, for he feared punishment by the gods, he instead imprisoned her in a bronze chamber and buried it. He did, however, leave an opening in the roof for air and light.

It was through this opening that Zeus came to Danae as a shower of golden light falling into her lap and she bore his child, Perseus. She tried to keep his existence a secret, but her father eventually discovered the child

Source: Anonymous. *The Homeric Hymns and Homerica with an English Translation* by Hugh G. Evelyn-White. *Homeric Hymns.* 1914.

because of the noise he made while playing. He did not believe her claim that the child was the son of Zeus. Yet again, out of fear, he didn't kill the child. He locked both of them in a chest and floated them out to sea.

By chance a fisherman named Dictys found them and took them to his home on the island of Seriphos. He and his wife were childless, so they cared for Danae and Perseus as family. The fisherman's cruel brother Polydectes ruled the island and wanted Danae for his wife but she did not return his affection. By this time Perseus was a grown man and Polydectes thought he could possess Danae if he could get her son out of the way.

In the guise of pretending to be a suitor for another woman, Polydectes invited all the men on the island to a banquet. Each was required to give Polydectes a gift (typically a horse); Perseus boasted he could do better than that—he could give Polydectes the head of a Gorgon. Polydectes then ordered Perseus to do just that. Other versions of the story say that Polydectes tricked Perseus by telling him how he desired a Gorgon's head above any prize; shortly after this he announced his upcoming marriage plans. Perseus decided to fetch Medusa's head as a gift, unknowingly falling into the trap that this task would prove fatal. Either way, pursuing the Gorgon was his quest.

Perseus and Medusa

After many unsuccessful attempts to gain advice on how to find the Gorgons, Hermes and Athena helped Perseus. Hermes told him about some nymphs who could assist him by providing directions and magical objects, but to find them he first needed the sisters of the Gorgons, the Graeae (Graiai/the Gray Ones) to tell him the way. These were three women who were born old and blind. They had a single eye and one tooth that they shared, passing it back and forth between them; Perseus was able to steal these items as they changed hands and would only return them in exchange for information about the nymphs. From the nymphs he not only received directions to the Gorgons, but three special objects: a Cap of Invisibility, winged sandals, and a special wallet, called a *kibisis*. This item was like a satchel that was small but could magically hold many large items. In addition, Hermes gave Perseus a sword and in some versions Athena provides him with a polished shield that acts as a mirror.

The Gorgons, of whom there were three, were hideous immortal creatures with "heads twined about with the scales of dragons, and great tusks like swine's, and brazen hands, and golden wings, by which they flew; and they turned to stone such as beheld them." But only Medusa was mortal. She was once a beautiful woman and her hair was her most glorious feature. She lost her virginity in Athena's temple where Poseidon seduced her. Offended and outraged, Athena punished Medusa by transforming her into a Gorgon, writhing snakes replacing her lovely hair.

Since Medusa was the only mortal Gorgon, she was Perseus' target. Luckily, he came upon her while she was sleeping. Athena guided him and, using his shield to look at her only by reflection, he cut off her head. When Medusa's head was severed, two creatures sprang forth from her body—children of the union between Medusa and Poseidon—the monster Chrysaor and the winged steed Pegasus. It is said that when Pegasus' hoof struck Mt. Helicon the fountain Hippocrene (Horses' Fountain) was created; this fountain became sacred to the Muses as the source of poetic inspiration. Also following the decapitation of Medusa, it is said that her sisters wailed in agony so beautifully that Athena created a flute to recreate the sound.

Perseus was able to escape the other Gorgons by wearing the Cap of Invisibility and the winged sandals. As he traveled the sky over the Libyan desert with Medusa's head, drops of blood that fell upon the ground turned into venomous snakes.

As Perseus journeyed home, his adventures continued, including his meeting with the princess Andromeda. Here is the account as told by Ovid:

PERSEUS AND ANDROMEDA

In their eternal prison, Aeous,	1
grandson of Hippotas, had shut the winds;	
and Lucifer,* reminder of our toil,	
in splendour rose upon the lofty sky:	
and Perseus bound his wings upon his feet,	5
on each foot bound he them; his sword he girt	
and sped wing-footed through the liquid air.	
Innumerous kingdoms far behind were left,	
till peoples Ethiopic and the lands	
of Cepheus were beneath his lofty view.	10
There Ammon, the Unjust, had made decree	
Andromeda, the Innocent, should grieve	
her mother's tongue. They bound her fettered arms	
fast to the rock. When Perseus her beheld	
as marble he would deem her, but the breeze	15
moved in her hair, and from her streaming eyes	
the warm tears fell. Her beauty so amazed	
his heart, unconscious captive of her charms,	
that almost his swift wings forgot to wave.—	
Alighted on the ground, he thus began;	20
"O fairest! whom these chains become not so,	
but worthy are for links that lovers bind,	
make known to me your country's name and your's	
and wherefore bound in chains." A moment then,	
as overcome with shame, she made no sound:	25
were not she fettered she would surely hide	
her blushing head; but what she could perform	
that did she do—she filled her eyes with tears.	
So pleaded he that lest refusal seem	
implied confession of a crime, she told	30
her name, her country's name, and how her charms	
had been her mother's pride. But as she spoke	
the mighty ocean roared. Over the waves	
a monster fast approached, its head held high,	
abreast the wide expanse.—The virgin shrieked;—	35
no aid her wretched father gave, nor aid	
her still more wretched mother; but they wept	
and mingled lamentations with their tears—	
clinging distracted to her fettered form.	
And thus the stranger spoke to them, "Time waits	40
for tears, but flies the moment of our need:	
were I, who am the son of Regal Jove	
and her whom he embraced in showers of gold,	
leaving her pregnant in her brazen cell, —	
I, Perseus, who destroyed the Gorgon, wreathed	45
with snake-hair, I, who dared on waving wings	
to cleave etherial air—were I to ask	

*Lucifer: "light-bringer" (Latin); a personification of the morning star as a man bearing a torch.

Source: Ovid. *Metamorphoses.* Translated by Brookes More. 1922.

the maid in marriage, I should be preferred
above all others as your son-in-law.
Not satisfied with deeds achieved, I strive   50
to add such merit as the Gods permit;
now, therefore, should my velour save her life,
be it conditioned that I win her love."
To this her parents gave a glad assent,
for who could hesitate? And they entreat,   55
and promise him the kingdom as a dower.
As a great ship with steady prow speeds on;
forced forwards by the sweating arms of youth
it plows the deep; so, breasting the great waves,
the monster moved, until to reach the rock   60
no further space remained than might the whirl
of Balearic string encompass, through
the middle skies, with plummet-mold of lead.
That instant, spurning with his feet the ground,
the youth rose upwards to a cloudy height;   65
and when the shadow of the hero marked
the surface of the sea, the monster sought
vainly to vent his fury on the shade.
As the swift bird of Jove, when he beholds
a basking serpent in an open field,   70
exposing to the sun its mottled back,
and seizes on its tail; lest it shall turn
to strike with venomed fang, he fixes fast
his grasping talons in the scaly neck;
so did the winged youth, in rapid flight   75
through yielding elements, press down
on the great monster's back, and thrust his sword,
sheer to the hilt, in its right shoulder—loud
its frightful torture sounded over the waves.—
So fought the hero-son of Inachus.   80
Wild with the grievous wound, the monster rears
high in the air, or plunges in the waves;—
or wheels around as turns the frightened boar
shunning the hounds around him in full cry.
The hero on his active wings avoids   85
the monster's jaws, and with his crooked sword
tortures its back wherever he may pierce
its mail of hollow shell, or strikes betwixt
the ribs each side, or wounds its lashing tail,
long, tapered as a fish.   90
The monster spouts
forth streams—incarnadined with blood—
that spray upon the hero's wings; who drenched,
and heavy with the spume, no longer dares
to trust existence to his dripping wings;   95
but he discerns a rock, which rises clear
above the water when the sea is calm,
but now is covered by the lashing waves.

On this he rests; and as his left hand holds
firm on the upmost ledge, he thrusts his sword,   100
times more than three, unswerving in his aim,
sheer through the monster's entrails.—Shouts of praise
resound along the shores, and even the Gods
may hear his glory in their high abodes.
Her parents, Cepheus and Cassiope,   105
most joyfully salute their son-in-law;
declaring him the saviour of their house.
And now, her chains struck off, the lovely cause
and guerdon of his toil, walks on the shore.
The hero washes his victorious hands   110
in water newly taken from the sea:
but lest the sand upon the shore might harm
the viper-covered head, he first prepared
a bed of springy leaves, on which he threw
weeds of the sea, produced beneath the waves.   115
On them he laid Medusa's awful face,
daughter of Phorcys;—and the living weeds,
fresh taken from the boundless deep, imbibed
the monster's poison in their spongy pith:
they hardened at the touch, and felt in branch   120
and leaf unwonted stiffness. Sea-Nymphs, too,
attempted to perform that prodigy
on numerous other weeds, with like result:
so pleased at their success, they raised new seeds,
from plants wide-scattered on the salt expanse.   125
Even from that day the coral has retained
such wondrous nature, that exposed to air
it hardens.—Thus, a plant beneath the waves
becomes a stone when taken from the sea.
Three altars to three Gods he made of turf.   130
To thee, victorious Virgin, did he build
an altar on the right, to Mercury
an altar on the left, and unto Jove
an altar in the midst. He sacrificed
a heifer to Minerva, and a calf   135
to Mercury, the Wingfoot, and a bull
to thee, O greatest of the Deities.
Without a dower he takes Andromeda,
the guerdon of his glorious victory,
nor hesitates.—Now pacing in the van,   140
both Love and Hymen wave the flaring torch,
abundant perfumes lavished in the flames.
The houses are bedecked with wreathed flowers;
and lyres and flageolets resound, and songs—
felicit notes that happy hearts declare.   145
The portals opened, sumptuous halls display
their golden splendours, and the noble lords
of Cepheus' court take places at the feast,
magnificently served.

Perseus returned to the island of Seriphos with Andromeda and learned that Danae and Dictys, now a widower, had escaped from Polydectes and were hiding in a temple. Perseus used Medusa's head to turn Polydectes and all his followers to stone. Danae returned home and Perseus declared Dictys to be the king of the island. He returned the magical objects to the nymphs and gods and gave Athena the head of Medusa—it is said that she wore the head on her shield (aegis) to arouse fear in her enemies.

Acrisius, hearing of Perseus's return, fled to Thessaly, but Perseus followed him; there Perseus competed in athletic games as part of the king's celebration to honor his late father. Here, the prophecy came true—Perseus threw a discus and killed Acrisius by accident. Since he killed his own grandfather, Perseus was too ashamed to return to his ancestral home of Argos; he buried Acrisius and went to Tiryns and exchanged kingdoms with Megapenthes, son of Proetus. Perseus founded Mycenae and he and Andromeda had two daughters and seven sons.

DISCUSSION QUESTIONS

1. Consider the brief story of Medusa and Pegasus and what this encounter adds to the myth.

2. Which parts of Campbell's monomyth are present in the tales of Perseus and how do they add to your interpretation of the story?

3. What are the various etiological aspects of the Perseus myth?

Theseus

Theseus is another widely celebrated hero, beloved by the people of Athens. In some ways he is similar to Heracles; in fact, they were cousins. The main sources for the heroic tales of Theseus are Plutarch and Apollodorus. Despite some less appealing aspects of his behavior, behavior, the Athenians regarded the character of Theseus as the ideal hero—honorable and virtuous, a model citizen.

Birth, Homecoming, and Labors of Theseus

The story begins with Aegeus, the father of Theseus, a king of Athens. Aegeus was childless and, like so many other leaders, sought advice from the oracle at Delphi. He was told, "The bulging mouth of the wineskin, O best of men, loose not until thou hast reached the height of Athens." On his journey home Aegeus stayed with king Pittheus of Troezen and asked his advice about this mysterious instruction. Pittheus understood. He knew the oracle was instructing Aegeus to wait until returning home to Athens to have intercourse; he took advantage of the situation and persuaded Aegeus to become intoxicated and spend the night with his daughter, Aethra (in Apollodorus's version of the tale, Poseidon was also with Aethra on the same night, so sometimes Poseidon is named as Theseus' father).

Source: Apollodorus. *The Library.* Translated by J.G. Frazer. 1921.

"Now Aegeus charged Aethra that, if she gave birth to a male child, she should rear it, without telling whose it was; and he left a sword and sandals under a certain rock, saying that when the boy could roll away the rock and take them up, she was then to send him away with them." When Theseus came of age, and moved the stone to discover the sword and sandals, he made his way to Athens and his adventures began.

Theseus is generally credited with six labors on his journey to Athens, although the number of deeds and their particular order can vary depending on the version of the story. Theseus's labors consist mainly of ridding the land of bandits and outlaws. Theseus chose to take the route over land to Athens, knowing it would be more dangerous but desiring to prove himself.

First he killed a brigand named Periphetes, also called Corynetes (Club Man) for his choice of weapon, and kept the club for his own. Next, he encountered another bandit, Sinis, nicknamed Pityocamptes (Pine Bender) because he would bend pine saplings, tie one end of a victim to each tree, and then release the trees, tearing his victims in half. Theseus inflicted this same torture upon him. His third labor was killing a giant sow that was terrorizing the village of Crommyon. After that, he met another outlaw, a man called Sciron, who was preventing him from traveling the path he desired. Sciron demanded all travelers to stop and wash his feet before passing. When they bent over to do so, he would kick them into the sea where they were devoured by an enormous sea turtle. Again, Theseus uses the villain's own methods to kill him. For his fifth labor, Theseus defeated Cercyon, another man who barred his way. Cercyon forced all travelers to wrestle him to the death. Naturally, Theseus was victorious. For his final deed, Theseus came upon the outlaw Procurstes (The Stretcher), yet another menace to travelers. He would force his victims to lie upon a bed and if they were too long to fit, he would cut them to the proper size with a saw; those who were too short he hammered out their body until they fit perfectly. And again, Theseus dispatched this enemy using his own methods.

When Theseus arrived in Athens, he still had more to endure. Aegeus was now married to Medea, and she expected their son Medus to be the heir; Medea discovered Theseus' true identity as a rival to her son so she attempted to poison him, convincing Aegeus that this stranger was a threat. But at the banquet where she planned to carry out her plan, Theseus drew his sword as though to cut his meat with it. Aegeus recognized the sword and, realizing Theseus was his son, knocked the poisoned cup of wine from his hand. Still, Theseus was not out of danger. Aegeus' brother Pallas and his sons were plotting to overthrow Aegeus and when Theseus was revealed as the heir, they attacked him. Theseus killed most of them and Pallas and the remainder of his sons withdrew.

In addition, Theseus captured the bull of Marathon, believed to have been brought from Crete by Heracles, and took the bull back to Athens, sacrificing it to Apollo. Apollodorus' account cites this act as Medea's attempt to be rid of Theseus, convincing Aegeus to send him on this quest, but he succeeds.

The Minotaur

And yet, after all these great deeds, we still have not come to the greatest of Theseus' acts—his defeat of the famous Minotaur.

King Minos of Crete prayed to Poseidon for a special sacrificial bull. But he coveted the bull he received and sacrificed a lesser bull, keeping Poseidon's bull for himself. Poseidon punished Minos by causing his wife to become infatuated with the bull. She mated with it and bore a half-man, half-bull creature—the Minotaur. It is said to have a man's body and a bull's head. Rather than kill it, Minos imprisoned it in a vast labyrinth, created by the craftsman Daedalus. And this is where Theseus again displays his heroism.

THE TRIBUTE

Years passed by. Every spring when the roses began to bloom seven youths and seven maidens were put on board of a black-sailed ship and sent to Crete to pay the tribute which King Minos required. In every house in Athens there was sorrow and dread, and the people lifted up their hands to Athena on the hilltop and cried out, "How long, O Queen of the Air, how long shall this thing be?"

In the meanwhile the little child at Troezen on the other side of the sea had grown to be a man. His name, Theseus, was in everybody's mouth, for he had done great deeds of daring; and at last he had come to Athens to find his father, King Aegeus, who had never heard whether he was alive or dead; and when the youth had made himself known, the king had welcomed him to his home and all the people were glad because so noble a prince had come to dwell among them and, in time, to rule over their city.

The springtime came again. The black-sailed ship was rigged for another voyage. The rude Cretan soldiers paraded the streets; and the herald of King Minos stood at the gates and shouted:

"Yet three days, O Athenians, and your tribute will be due and must be paid!"

Then in every street the doors of the houses were shut and no man went in or out, but every one sat silent with pale cheeks, and wondered whose lot it would be to be chosen this year. But the young prince, Theseus, did not understand; for he had not been told about the tribute.

"What is the meaning of all this?" he cried. "What right has a Cretan to demand tribute in Athens? And what is this tribute of which he speaks?"

Then Aegeus led him aside and with tears told him of the sad war with King Minos, and of the dreadful terms of peace. "Now, say no more," sobbed Aegeus, "it is better that a few should die even thus than that all should be destroyed."

"But I will say more," cried Theseus. "Athens shall not pay tribute to Crete. I myself will go with these youths and maidens, and I will slay the monster Minotaur, and defy King Minos himself upon his throne."

"Oh, do not be so rash!" said the king; "for no one who is thrust into the den of the Minotaur ever comes out again. Remember that you are the hope of Athens, and do not take this great risk upon yourself."

"Say you that I am the hope of Athens?" said Theseus. "Then how can I do otherwise than go?" And he began at once to make himself ready.

On the third day all the youths and maidens of the city were brought together in the market place, so that lots might be cast for those who were to be taken. Then two vessels of brass were brought and set before King Aegeus and the herald who had come from Crete. Into one vessel they placed as many balls as there were noble youths in the city, and into the other as many as there were maidens; and all the balls were white save only seven in each vessel, and those were black as ebony.

Then every maiden, without looking, reached her hand into one of the vessels and drew forth a ball, and those who took the black balls were borne away to the black ship, which lay in waiting by the shore. The young men also drew lots in like manner, but when six black balls had been drawn Theseus came quickly forward and said:

"Hold! Let no more balls be drawn. I will be the seventh youth to pay this tribute. Now let us go aboard the black ship and be off."

Source: Baldwin, James. *Old Greek Stories.*

Then the people, and King Aegeus himself, went down to the shore to take leave of the young men and maidens, whom they had no hope of seeing again; and all but Theseus wept and were brokenhearted.

"I will come again, father," he said.

"I will hope that you may," said the old king. "If when this ship returns, I see a white sail spread above the black one, then I shall know that you are alive and well; but if I see only the black one, it will tell me that you have perished."

And now the vessel was loosed from its moorings, the north wind filled the sail, and the seven youths and seven maidens were borne away over the sea, towards the dreadful death which awaited them in far distant Crete.

THE PRINCESS

At last the black ship reached the end of its voyage. The young people were set ashore, and a party of soldiers led them through the streets towards the prison, where they were to stay until the morrow. They did not weep nor cry out now, for they had outgrown their fears. But with paler faces and firm-set lips, they walked between the rows of Cretan houses, and looked neither to the right nor to the left. The windows and doors were full of people who were eager to see them.

"What a pity that such brave young men should be food for the Minotaur," said some.

"Ah, that maidens so beautiful should meet a fate so sad!" said others.

And now they passed close by the palace gate, and in it stood King Minos himself, and his daughter Ariadne, the fairest of the women of Crete.

"Indeed, those are noble young fellows!" said the king.

"Yes, too noble to feed the vile Minotaur," said Ariadne.

"The nobler, the better," said the king; "and yet none of them can compare with your lost brother Androgeos."

Ariadne said no more; and yet she thought that she had never seen any one who looked so much like a hero as young Theseus. How tall he was, and how handsome! How proud his eye, and how firm his step! Surely there had never been his like in Crete.

All through that night Ariadne lay awake and thought of the matchless hero, and grieved that he should be doomed to perish; and then she began to lay plans for setting him free. At the earliest peep of day she arose, and while everybody else was asleep, she ran out of the palace and hurried to the prison. As she was the king's daughter, the jailer opened the door at her bidding and allowed her to go in. There sat the seven youths and the seven maidens on the ground, but they had not lost hope. She took Theseus aside and whispered to him. She told him of a plan which she had made to save him; and Theseus promised her that, when he had slain the Minotaur, he would carry her away with him to Athens where she should live with him always. Then she gave him a sharp sword, and hid it underneath his cloak, telling him that with it alone could he hope to slay the Minotaur.

"And here is a ball of silken thread," she said. "As soon as you go into the Labyrinth where the monster is kept, fasten one end of the thread to the stone doorpost, and then unwind it as you go along. When you have slain the Minotaur, you have only to follow the thread and it will lead you back to the door. In the meanwhile I will see that your ship, is ready to sail, and then I will wait for you at the door of the Labyrinth."

The jailer opened the door at her bidding. Theseus thanked the beautiful princess and promised her again that if he should live to go back to Athens she should go with him and be his wife. Then with a prayer to Athena, Ariadne hastened away.

THE LABYRINTH

As soon as the sun was up the guards came to lead the young prisoners to the Labyrinth. They did not see the sword which Theseus had under his cloak, nor the tiny ball of silk which he held in his closed hand. They led the youths and maidens a long way into the Labyrinth, turning here and there, back and forth, a thousand different times, until it seemed certain that they could never find their way out again. Then the guards, by a secret passage which they alone knew, went out and left them, as they had left many others before, to wander about until they should be found by the terrible Minotaur.

"Stay close by me," said Theseus to his companions, "and with the help of Athena who dwells in her temple home in our own fair city, I will save you."

Then he drew his sword and stood in the narrow way before them; and they all lifted up their hands and prayed to Athena.

For hours they stood there, hearing no sound, and seeing nothing but the smooth, high walls on either side of the passage and the calm blue sky so high above them. Then the maidens sat down upon the ground and covered their faces and sobbed, and said:

"Oh, that he would come and put an end to our misery and our lives."

At last, late in the day, they heard a bellowing, low and faint as though far away. They listened and soon heard it again, a little louder and very fierce and dreadful.

"It is he! it is he!" cried Theseus; "and now for the fight!"

Then he shouted, so loudly that the walls of the Labyrinth answered back, and the sound was carried upward to the sky and outward to the rocks and cliffs of the mountains. The Minotaur heard him, and his bellowings grew louder and fiercer every moment.

"He is coming!" cried Theseus, and he ran forward to meet the beast. The seven maidens shrieked, but tried to stand up bravely and face their fate; and the six young men stood together with firm-set teeth and clinched fists, ready to fight to the last.

Soon the Minotaur came into view, rushing down the passage towards Theseus, and roaring most terribly. He was twice as tall as a man, and his head was like that of a bull with huge sharp horns and fiery eyes and a mouth as large as a lion's; but the young men could not see the lower part of his body for the cloud of dust which he raised in running. When he saw Theseus with the sword in his hand coming to meet him, he paused, for no one had ever faced him in that way before. Then he put his head down, and rushed forward, bellowing. But Theseus leaped quickly aside, and made a sharp thrust with his sword as he passed, and hewed off one of the monster's legs above the knee.

The Minotaur fell upon the ground, roaring and groaning and beating wildly about with his horned head and his hoof-like fists; but Theseus nimbly ran up to him and thrust the sword into his heart, and was away again before the beast could harm him. A great stream of blood gushed from the wound, and soon the Minotaur turned his face towards the sky and was dead.

Then the youths and maidens ran to Theseus and kissed his hands and feet, and thanked him for his great deed; and, as it was already growing dark, Theseus bade them follow him while he wound up the silken thread which was to lead them out of the Labyrinth. Through a thousand rooms and courts and winding ways they went, and at midnight they came to the outer door and saw the city lying in the moonlight before them; and, only a little way off, was the seashore where the black ship was moored which had brought them to Crete. The door was wide open, and beside it stood Ariadne waiting for them.

"The wind is fair, the sea is smooth, and the sailors are ready," she whispered; and she took the arm of Theseus, and all went together through the silent streets to the ship.

When the morning dawned they were far out to sea, and, looking back from the deck of the little vessel, only the white tops of the Cretan mountains were in sight.

Minos, when he arose from sleep, did not know that the youths and maidens had gotten safe out of the Labyrinth. But when Ariadne could not be found, he thought that robbers had carried her away. He sent soldiers out to search for her among the hills and mountains, never dreaming that she was now well on the way towards distant Athens.

Many days passed, and at last the searchers returned and said that the princess could nowhere be found. Then the king covered his head and wept, and said:

"Now, indeed, I am bereft of all my treasures!"

In the meanwhile, King Aegeus of Athens had sat day after day on a rock by the shore, looking and watching if by chance he might see a ship coming from the south. At last the vessel with Theseus and his companions hove in sight, but it still carried only the black sail, for in their joy the young men had forgotten to raise the white one.

"Alas! alas! my son has perished!" moaned Aegeus; and he fainted and fell forward into the sea and was drowned. And that sea, from then until now, has been called by his name, the Aegean Sea.

Thus Theseus became king of Athens.

At this point in the story the accounts diverge. On the way to Athens they stopped on the island of Naxos. Here is it said that Theseus abandoned Ariadne. One version says he simply sailed away without her while she slept. However, Dionysus discovered her and they eventually fell in love; the alternate story is that Dionysus fell in love with her and carried her away.

The other account reports that Ariadne became ill and she was resting on shore to recover. The wind carried the ship away without her and when Theseus was finally able to return for her, he learned that she had died. In his grief over losing Ariadne, Theseus neglected to change the ship's sail from black to white.

Other exploits of Theseus include his joining Heracles against the Amazons and winning for his wife an Amazon named Antiope (Hippolyta)—they eventually had a son, Hippolytus. Theseus again battled the Amazons when, in vengeance, they attacked Attica; Antiope was killed during the attack.

In Euripides's tragic drama *Hippolytus*, Theseus is married to Phaedra, a daughter of Minos. They had two sons of their own, but Phaedra fell in love with Theseus' son Hippolytus; she hung herself in shame. However, she left a letter that claimed Hippolytus tried to seduce her. Theseus, who had been away from home, returns to discover the letter and Phaedra dead. He sends Hippolytus into exile and pleads with Poseidon to kill him. Hippolytus is fatally wounded but is able to make peace with Theseus before he dies.

In another story, Theseus is involved in a plot to abduct Helen and assisted his friend Pirithous in trying to take Persephone. While Theseus' attempt to steal the young Helen was ultimately unsuccessful, he did go with Pirithous to the Underworld; this venture failed as well. They were both bound in magical chains, but Heracles negotiated for Theseus' release.

DISCUSSION QUESTIONS

1. Many heroic tales reveal that heroes are not perfect. How do you reconcile a hero's misdeeds with his great accomplishments?

2. Compare Theseus to the other Greek heroes. Which of these characters do you think best embodies the qualities of a hero? Explain.

3. Research some of the lesser-known adventures of Theseus. How do these stories change your opinion of him as a hero?

4. Investigate Theseus' association with bulls. What meaning does this have? What does the bull symbolize?

5. Use Campbell's monomyth to analyze the adventures of Theseus. What interpretations can you draw from this analysis?

BIBLIOGRAPHY

Anonymous. *The Homeric Hymns and Homerica with an English Translation* by Hugh G. Evelyn-White. *Homeric Hymns.* Harvard University Press; William Heinemann Ltd., 1914.

Apollodorus. *Epitome.* Translated by J.G. Frazer. Harvard University Press; London, William Heinemann Ltd. 1921.

---. *The Library.* Translated by J.G. Frazer. Harvard University Press; London, William Heinemann Ltd. 1921.

Apuleius, Lucius. "Cupid and Psyche." *Folklore and Mythology Electronic Texts.* University of Pittsburgh. http://www.pitt.edu/~dash/cupid.html

Baldwin, James. *Old Greek Stories.* American Book Co. http://www.gutenberg.org/files/11582/11582-h/11582-h.htm

Bulfinch, Thomas. *The Age of Fable; or, Stories of Gods and Heroes,* 3rd edition. Sanborn, Carter, Bazin and Company, 1855.

Hamilton, Edith. *Mythology: Timeless Tales of Gods and Heroes.* Grand Central Publishing, 1942.

Holzberg, Niklas. *Ovid: The Poet and His Work.* Trans. G. M. Goshgarian. Cornell University Press, 2002.

The Homeric Hymns. Translated by Michael Crudden. Oxford University Press, 2001.

Maurizio, Lisa. *Classical Mythology in Context.* Oxford University Press, 2016.

Morford, Mark, and Robert Lenardon. *Classical Mythology,* 7th ed. Oxford University Press, 2003.

Leeming, David. *Mythology: The Voyage of the Hero,* 3rd ed. Oxford University Press, 1998.

---. *The World of Myth: An Anthology.* Oxford University Press, 1990.

---. *The World of Myth: An Anthology.* 2nd ed. Oxford University Press, 2014.

Ovid. *Metamorphoses.* Translated by Brookes More. Cornhill Publishing Co., 1922.

Plutarch. *Lives, Vol 1. Life of Theseus.* Translated by Perrin, Bernadotte. Loeb Classical Library Vol. 46. Harvard University Press; William Heinemann Ltd., 1914. http://www.theoi.com/Text/PlutarchTheseus.html

Rosenberg, Donna. *Mythology: An Anthology of the Great Myths and Epics*, 3rd ed. McGraw Hill, 1999.

The Hymns of Orpheus. Translated by Taylor, Thomas (1792). University of Pennsylvania Press, 1999.

Thury, Eva M., and Margaret K. Devinny. *Introduction to Mythology*, 3rd ed. Oxford University Press, 2013.

Whitmarsh, Tim. *Battling the Gods: Atheism in the Ancient World*. Knopf, 2015.

Works of Hesiod and the Homeric Hymns. Translated by Daryl Hine. University of Chicago Press, 2005.

Chapter 4

THE MYTHS OF SCANDINAVIAN AND SLAVIC COUNTRIES

© Nell Novara

INTRODUCTION

Part 1: Creation and Destruction

Greenland Creation
Slovenian Creation
Buriat Creation
The *Kalevala* (Finnish)
Prose Edda (Norse)

Part 2: Tricksters, Lovers, and Other Tales

How the Fog Came and The Thunder Spirits (Greenland)
The Legend of the Reindeer (Sami)
The Witch and the Sister of the Sun (Russian)
How Thor Lost His Hammer (Norse)

Part 3: Journeys of Heroes and Heroines

Sigurd the Volsung (Norse)
Thor and the Giants of Utgardr (Norse)
Ivan Tsarevich, The Fire-bird, and the Gray Wolf (Russian)

163

Introduction

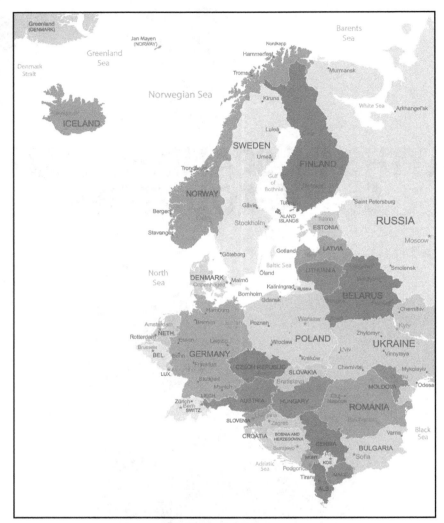

© ekler/Shutterstock.com

Northern and Eastern European mythology consists mainly of two groups: people of Germanic and Slavic descent. This group includes Germans, Dutch, Danes, Swedes, Norwegians, and Icelanders as well as Russians, Serbs, Croats, Bulgarians, Romanians, Slovacs, and Poles; in addition, Greenlanders, Prussians, Lithuanians, Letts, Finns, and Lapps are part of these groups. The majority of myths that have survived from these areas is from the Scandinavian and Icelandic people. Some of the Germanic peoples are categorized under the label of Norse, which contains some of the most well-known myths in the world. However, in an effort to draw attention to some lesser-known stories, we have included several myths from Slavic groups in addition to regions such as Finland, Greenland, and stories from indigenous tribes from these areas.

A majority of these people practiced shamanism, and traces of animism and a spiritual connection to nature is illustrated in many of these myths. Due to the great variety of cultures and types of myths presented here, detailed introductory material precedes the individual stories. Prominent features found in these tales are quests and journeys, death and rebirth, family relationships, and creation stories, including the roles human beings play in ordering the cosmos.

Part 1: Creation and Destruction

© Nell Novara

Greenland Creation

The stories of Greenland's heroes, folklore, and mythology have been documented by many of the explorers of the nineteenth century. Probably the most conscientious record of these tales comes to us from Danish-Eskimo explorer and ethnographer Knud Rasmussen. Knud, or Kunúnguaq, as his native name was given to him, was born in Ilulissat, Greenland, in 1879 and spent his life exploring the country by dogsled, collecting myths from nearly every native tribe from Greenland to the Bering Strait.

Because he was able to speak the language, Rasmussen's accounts are some of the most compelling. His books are full of sketches completed by native artists, and his translations were compiled into fifteen volumes on native life and stories.

It is worth noting that while many of Rasmussen's books and the older translations refer to the people living near the Arctic as "Eskimos," that the word has fallen out of usage due to its derogatory meaning. Lawrence Kaplan of the Alaska Native Language Center writes that "Eskimo" was thought to mean "eater of raw meat" and referred to all native people, regardless of their tribal identity. It is a lumping together of unique cultures. The proper term to use is "Inuit," which means "people," or many Greenlanders call themselves "Kalaallit," meaning "Greenlandic."

The following creation story tells how men, children, dogs, and death come to be in the world. The Angmagssalik person who told Rasmussen this story begins by acknowledging the old age of the tale.

THE COMING OF MEN, A LONG, LONG WHILE AGO

Our forefathers have told us much of the coming of earth, and of men, and it was a long, long while ago. Those who lived long before our day, they did not know how to store their words in little black marks, as you do; they could only tell stories. And they told of many things, and therefore we are not without knowledge of these things, which we have heard told many and many a time, since we were little children. Old women do not waste their words idly, and we believe what they say. Old age does not lie.

A long, long time ago, when the earth was to be made, it fell down from the sky. Earth, hills and stones, all fell down from the sky, and thus the earth was made.

And then, when the earth was made, came men. It is said that they came forth out of the earth. Little children came out of the earth. They came forth from among the willow bushes, all covered with willow leaves. And there they lay among the little bushes: lay and kicked, for they could not even crawl. And they got their food from the earth.

Then there is something about a man and a woman, but what of them? It is not clearly known. When did they find each other, and when had they grown up? I do not know. But the woman sewed, and made children's clothes, and wandered forth. And she found little children, and dressed them in the clothes, and brought them home.

And in this way men grew to be many. And being now so many, they desired to have dogs. So a man went out with a dog leash in his hand, and began to stamp on the ground, crying, "Hok—hok—hok!" Then the dogs came hurrying out from the hummocks, and shook themselves violently, for their coats were full of sand. Thus men found dogs.

But then children began to be born, and men grew to be very many on the earth. They knew nothing of death in those days, a long, long time ago, and grew to be very old. At last they could not walk, but went blind, and could not lie down.

Neither did they know the sun, but lived in the dark. No day ever dawned. Only inside their houses was there ever light, and they burned water in their lamps, for in those days water would burn.

But these men who did not know how to die, they grew to be too many, and crowded the earth. And then there came a mighty flood from the sea. Many were drowned, and men grew fewer. We can still see marks of that great flood, on the high hill-tops, where mussel shells may often be found.

And now that men had begun to be fewer, two old women began to speak thus:

"Better to be without day, if thus we may be without death," said the one.

"No; let us have both light and death," said the other.

And when the old woman had spoken these words, it was as she had wished. Light came, and death.

It is said, that when the first man died, others covered up the body with stones. But the body came back again, not knowing rightly how to die. It stuck out its head from the bench, and tried to get up.

But an old woman thrust it back, and said: "We have much to carry, and our sledges are small."

For they were about to set out on a hunting journey. And so the dead one was forced to go back to the mound of stones.

And now, after men had got light on their earth, they were able to go on journeys, and to hunt, and no longer needed to eat of the earth. And with death came also the sun, moon and stars.

For when men die, they go up into the sky and become brightly shining things there.

Source: Rasmussen, Knud. *Eskimo Folk Tales.* Trans. W. Worster. 1921.

DISCUSSION QUESTIONS

1. What is the role of the women in this story?

2. Why are dogs important to the creation myth?

3. How does death come into the world?

4. There is reference of a flood and mussel shells—what might this be explaining?

Slovenian Creation

A relatively understudied group of mythologies, the Slavonic peoples make up the crossroads of Central, Southern, and Eastern European culture. A. H. Wratislaw of Christ's College, Cambridge, took on the task of collecting and translating a compendium of Slavonic myths that covered the stories of Bohemians, Moravians, Hungarians, Lusatians, Kashubians, Polish, Russians, Bulgarians, Serbians, Bosnians, Carniolans, Croatians, and Illyrians.

Much of the current religious practice of these people is Christianity (Catholicism, specifically), which may account for some of the religious undertones present in the following stories. The collector of these myths remarked about the nature of the religiousness of these stories that he believed them to possess, "A mixture of heathen-Slavonic and Christian elements; but I think the basis is entirely indigenous."

Christianity had been introduced in the ninth century, and these myths have adapted to the cultural pressures, while preserving the spirit of their intent. The people living in this region before Christianization were polytheistic pagans, who retain many of these elements in their current creation and destruction myths.

The two myths here represent a creation myth and flood/destruction myth from former Carniola (present-day Slovenia).

THE ORIGIN OF MAN

In the beginning there was nothing but God, and God slept and dreamed. For ages and ages did this dream last. But it was fated that he should wake up.

Having roused himself from sleep, he looked round about him, and every glance transformed itself into a star. God was amazed, and began to travel to see what he had created with his eyes. He travelled and travelled, but nowhere was there either end or limit.

As he travelled, he arrived at our earth also; but he was already weary; sweat clung to his brow. On the earth fell a drop of sweat: the drop became alive, and here you have the first man.

He is God's kin, but he was not created for pleasure: he was produced from sweat; already in the beginning it was fated for him to toil and sweat.

God's Cock

The earth was waste: nowhere was there aught but stone. God was sorry for this, and sent his cock to make the earth fruitful, as he knew how to do. The cock came down into a cave in the rock, and fetched out an egg of wondrous power and purpose.

Source: *Sixty Folk Tales from Exclusively Slavonic Sources*. Trans. A. H. Wratislaw. 1889.

The egg chipped, and seven rivers trickled out of it. The rivers irrigated the neighbourhood, and soon all was green: there were all manner of flowers and fruits; the land, without man's labour, produced wheat, the trees not only apples and figs, but also the whitest and sweetest bread. In this paradise men lived without care, working, not from need, but for amusement and merriment. Round the paradise were lofty mountains, so that there was no violence to fear, nor devilish storm to dread.

But further: that men, otherwise their own masters, and free, might not, from ignorance, suffer damage, God's cock hovered high in the sky, and crowed to them every day, when to get up, when to take their meals, and what to do, and when to do it. The nation was happy, only God's cock annoyed them by his continual crowing. Men began to murmur and pray God to deliver them from the restless creature: "Let us now settle for ourselves," said they, "when to eat, to work, and to rise."

God hearkened to them; the cock descended from the sky, but crowed to them just once more: "Woe is me! Beware of the lake!"

Men rejoiced, and said that it was never better; no one any more interfered with their freedom. After ancient custom, they ate, worked, and rose, all in the best order, as the cock had taught them. But, little by little, individuals began to think that it was unsuitable for a free people to obey the cock's crowing so slavishly, and began to live after their own fashion, observing no manner of order. Through this arose illnesses, and all kinds of distress; men looked again longingly to the sky, but God's cock was gone for ever.

They wished, at any rate, to pay regard to his last words. But they did not know how to fathom their meaning. The cock had warned them to dread the lake, but why? For they hadn't it in their valley; there flowed quietly, in their own channel, the seven rivers which had burst out of the egg. Men therefore conjectured that there was a dangerous lake somewhere on the other side of the mountains, and sent a man every day to the top of a hill to see whether he espied aught. But there was danger from no quarter; the man went in vain, and people calmed themselves again.

Their pride became greater and greater; the women made brooms from the wheat-ears, and the men straw mattresses. They would not go any more to the tree to gather bread, but set it on fire from below, that it might fall, and that they might collect it without trouble. When they had eaten their fill, they lay down by the rivers, conversed, and spoke all manner of blasphemies.

One cast his eyes on the water, wagged his head, and jabbered: "Eh! brothers! A wondrous wonder! I should like to know, at any rate, why the water is so much, neither more nor less."

"This, too," another answered, "was a craze of the cock's; it is disgraceful enough for us to be listening to orders to beware of a lake, which never was, and never will be. If my opinion is followed, the watcher will go today for the last time. As regards the rivers, I think it would be better if there more water."

His neighbour at first agreed, but thought, again, that there was water in abundance; if more, would be too much. A corpulent fellow put in energetically that undoubtedly both were right; it would, therefore, be the most sensible thing to break the egg up, and drive just as much water as was wanted into each man's land, and there was certainly no need of a watchman to look out for the lake.

Scarcely had these sentiments been delivered, when an outcry arose in the valley; all rushed to the egg to break it to pieces; all men deplored nothing but this, that the disgraceful look out could not put a stop to before the morrow. The people stood round the egg, the corpulent man took up a stone, and banged it against the egg. It split up with a clap of thunder, and so much water burst out of it that almost the whole human race perished.

The paradise was filled with water, and became one great lake. God's cock warned truly, but in vain, for the lawless people did not understand him. The flood now reached the highest mountains, just to the place where the watchman was standing, who was the only survivor from the destruction of mankind. Seeing the increasing waters he began to flee.

DISCUSSION QUESTIONS

1. What do these two tales tell us about human nature?

2. What do these two tales say about God's opinion of human's role on the earth?

3. In "God's Cock," who/what does the cock represent?

Buriat Creation

The Buriat are the indigenous inhabitants of the Southwestern Siberian area of Russia. The Buriat (sometimes spelled Buryat), are a culmination of the Turkic tribe called the Kurikan, and the Mongol tribal people who had settled together on the Eastern bank of Lake Baikal near the end of the seventeenth century. The Buriat still live at Lake Baikal, speak their own language, are accomplished artists, and number near 500,000.

The Buriat people practice shamanism, a kind of belief in spirits and the ability to interact with those spirits through the aid of a member of the tribe who is a shaman. A shaman is a chosen, very gifted person in the art of communicating with the spirits, the healing arts, and in leading the community. There are many forms of shamanism unique to each tribe and area of the world. A Buriat shaman is equipped with drum, staff, amulets, and a costume with many bells and swinging pendants used to call or send away spirits. The drum is an integral part of the ritualized trance that the shaman achieves to connect with the spirits.

The following myths of creation show some of these principles of communication with spirits and the natural world. This translation is from Jeremiah Curtin, following a year spent in the Buriat region, during which he learned the language and mythology and set about writing a history of the people, their culture, and much of their folklore.

THE CREATION

In the beginning there were Esege Malan, the highest god, and his wife, Ehé Ureng Ibi.

At first it was dark and silent; there was nothing to be heard or seen. Esege took up a handful of earth, squeezed moisture out of it, and made the sun of the water; he made the moon in the same way.

Next he made all living things and plants. He divided the world into East and West, and gave it to the highest order of gods. These gods are very strict, and people must sacrifice horses and rams to them. If angered, they punish by bringing sickness, especially to children. Some of the higher gods punish with disease or bring misfortune to people who offend local gods. For instance, if a man calls to witness or swears by a local god either he is punished by that local god, or judgment is rendered by one of the superior gods, for it is a great sin to swear by any Burkan (God), whether the man swears truly or falsely.

Among these principal gods are the bird gods of the South-west. Many of them take the form of swans. They are very kind to good people. To these bird gods offerings are made twice each year. In the autumn a wether (castrated ram) is offered, and in the spring mare's milk, tea, millet, and tobacco. Between these two higher orders and the Ongon gods there is a secondary order of Burkans of both sexes. Some of these descended from the higher Burkans, and others were in the old, old time people who by the favor of the divinities were made Shamans.

Source: Curtin, Jeremiah. *A Journey in Southern Siberia: The Mongols, Their Religion, and Their Myths.* 1909.

Esege Malan and Mother Earth

After Esege Malan had straightened out all things, Ehé Tazar, Mother Earth, went to visit him, and they spent several days very pleasantly. When Ehé Tazar's visit was ended and she was ready to go, she asked Esege Malan to give her the sun and the moon, and he gave them gladly; but he soon found that it was very difficult to get them for her. He called a thousand Burkans together and asked how he was to accomplish the feat, and though they studied long and seriously over it they could not tell him. Then Esege Malan sent for Zarya Azergesha (the hedgehog), and Zarya went up to the sky to the dwelling of Esege Malan.

Esege Malan had three daughters who often came down to the earth, removed their clothing, turned themselves into swans, and sported in the sea. It happened that the three were at home when Zarya Azergesha came. Esege had told his daughters that Zarya was a queer fellow, that he was lame and hairy, but he was very wise, and they must not laugh at him.

Notwithstanding this, when Zarya walked in Esege's daughters looked sidewise and laughed; they could not help it, he was so droll. He saw them laugh and said to himself, "Esege Malan has called me up here for his daughters to laugh at and ridicule!" He was terribly angry, and left so quickly that Esege had not time to say a word.

Zarya knew, however, what Esege wanted, for the messenger had told him. He came down from the sky very quickly, but two Shalmos (invisible spirits) followed, sent by Esege Malan to listen and hear what Zarya said as he traveled. For Esege knew that Zarya was raging, and he thought that he might say something about the sun and the moon.

The first thing Zarya saw as he came to earth was a herd of cows and bulls. When they caught sight of him they were frightened, put up their tails and ran. Zarya , angry that they should be frightened at him, cursed them, saying: "May the hair rope never leave your nostrils, and the yoke never leave your necks!" And so it has been.

He went farther and came to a herd of horses. They were frightened also, raised their tails, and ran away. Zarya, terribly angry, cursed them, saying: "May the bit never leave your mouths and the saddle never leave your backs!" And so it has been.

The Shalmos followed him always, listening to what he said. After a time Zarya began to talk to himself and abuse Esege Malan. "What sort of a ruler is that Esege Malan?" asked he. "What sort of a master of the world? He manages everything, fixes everything. He has given away the sun and the moon, but does not know how to get them! If he is so wise, why does he not come to visit Mother Earth, and when the visit is ended and he is ready to go, ask her for the hot dancing air of summer and the echo. She would give them to him gladly, but how could she get them for him?"

When the Shalmos heard this they followed no farther, but went to the sky very quickly and told Esege Malan all that Zarya had said. Esege waited until a sufficient time had passed; then he came to return Mother Earth's visit, and while they were walking around he said: "When you came to visit me I gave you the sun and the moon, now I ask for a present. Give me the hot dancing air of summer and echo." She gave them, but try as she would she could not get them for him.

When she found that it was impossible to get them, and no one could tell her how to do it, Esege said: "Let the sun and the moon remain where they are and the hot dancing air of summer and echo stay here!"

And so it is that though the sun and the moon belong to the earth, they are in the sky, and the hot dancing air and the echo, though they belong to Esege Malan, remain with Mother Earth.

DISCUSSION QUESTIONS

1. What do the Shalmos represent?

2. Why does Esege Malan go to such length to give Mother Earth the Sun and Moon?

3. What is Zarya's role in the story? And why is he the embodiment of a hedgehog?

The *Kalevala* (Finnish)

Introduction

The *Kalevala* is considered the national epic of Finland. It was first published in 1835, compiled by Finnish scholar and folklorist Elias Lönnrot. The epic was enthusiastically received, but was not without its critics. Some claimed that the work was more of Lönnrot's invention than actual folklore. Yet research into Lönnrot's process proved that only two percent of the epic was his creation—the rest of the material is based on authentic verses that he collected. It's important to keep in mind that while this work can be considered myth, it is primarily a combination of literature and folklore.

The epic poem is a collection of stories called runes or runos—not to be confused with the runic script of the Norse or Celts. The runos were sung or chanted, passed down orally, and, naturally, changed over time. Lönnrot traveled the region on nearly a dozen rune-collecting journeys, listening to the rune-singers as they shared chants and songs handed down for generations. It's not surprising that these runos were still remembered; because of its geographically remote location, Finland was able to preserve its traditions a bit longer than some other areas, before indigenous beliefs were influenced and eventually displaced by Christianity.

In similar fashion to the Grimm brothers collecting tales, Lönnrot collected and edited, added and rearranged the material; he kept detailed records of his visits and his process. But as his collection of runos continued to grow, his role began to change. He was no longer merely collecting, but creating. In addition, as he studied, his view of the material changed.

According to Juha Pentikäinen,

> For Lönnrot, the *Kalevala* was 'mythology' in two regards: it was, on the one hand, a collection of pre-Christian, mythological subject matter, mediated by folklore, and, on the other hand, a synthesis achieved by him as its compiler, the result of his own scholarship. (Pentikäinen 6)

There are two versions of the *Kalevala*—the "old" and the "new." By 1849, Lönnrot had collected fifty runos, containing 23,000 lines—this was the "new" version; the old version, published in 1835, had thirty-two runos. The first two runos which we've included here, tell the story of creation, and are followed by a variety of stories concerning several heroic and magical characters.

Today the *Old Kalevala* has nearly been forgotten. The new version is longer, and the runos are ordered differently. Both versions begin with the story of creation, but even that account has been changed. The *Old*

Kalevala describes Väinämöinen's birth and his role as creator of the world. However, in the *New Kalevala*, which still concerns Väinämöinen's birth, his mother creates the world before he is born.

Water is a primary element in creation, as well as the egg. The egg creation story found in Finnish oral poetry is also popular in other Central Eurasian myths. These motifs are also seen in the creation epic in India. It is believed that Lönnrot was influenced by these similarities and changed his focus to Ilmatar as a creator, akin to Brahma in Hindu mythology. Lönnrot also defended this change by explaining that the etymology of the name Väinämöinen is "vein emoinen," mother of waters or guardian spirit of the water (Pentikäinen 142). He understood this to mean that the name Väinämöinen grew out of its original meaning of the mother creator— the mother of waters—and eventually became the name of her child, Väinämöinen.

The name *Kalevala* (land of heroes) comes from Kaleva's region as home of the sons of Kaleva, the land of his people, Kaleva being an ancient Finnish hero—perhaps the first settler. There is also much debate over the exact role of many characters in the epic—the main characters, Väinämöinen, Ilmarinen, and Lemminkäinen, each have multiple roles in the epic. "They appear as mythical gods of creation and culture heroes, as well as prototypes of the first shamans, healers, and sages" (Pentikäinen 154). The runos also illustrate the importance of chanting incantations and spells and, in addition, the skill of rune singers as magicians. Singing contests and magical charms are prevalent throughout.

Language reveals evidence that "the ancient religion of the Finns is inseparable from Arctic shamanism" (Pentikäinen 179). The Finns speak a Finno-Ugric language shared only by Estonians and a few groups in northwestern Russia and Siberia. In addition, there are many parallels with Asian shamanism in many ancient Finnish beliefs. The ancient Finns were animists, and this region was long considered a mysterious and magical place. Sailors in the Middle Ages feared the conjuring skills of Finnish magicians whom they believed could wreck their ships. Some called it "the land of witches"; the Scotch word "finn" means "powerful sage" (Pentikäinen 182–3).

While Lönnrot did try to preserve the meaning of the runos, it's inevitable that some of his Christian worldview seeped into his adaptation of the story. He saw the characters as more heroic than godly, and emphasized a belief in a supreme deity, as he believed the ancient people were progressing toward Christianity; yet he believed the stories were rooted in a historical past. But, "the conflict between Lönnrot's own Christian-based, linear worldview and the cyclical worldview of the singers . . . remains apparent. It is also apparent in the *Kalevala* that, although the intricate plot of the epic is linear, individual poems continue to transmit a shamanistic, cyclical concept . . . " (Pentikäinen 237).

There is some debate regarding the age of the runos. While some scholars maintain they are of pre-Christian origin, others believe they are more recent and reflect the influence of Christianity. In fact, the ages of the stories do vary—some runos may be a great deal older than others. The oldest are believed to be the stories of creation. Lönnrot, in determining the order of the runos in the published epic, tried to organize them by this structure—oldest to newest. The last runo may even derive from a period of transition between paganism and Christianity. But while Lönnrot was firm in his belief that the *Kalevala* reflected the worldview of the ancient Finnish people, it cannot be denied that some intermingling has occurred. Yet while the influence of the Catholic Middle Ages can be seen in some places, "numerous mythical incantations contain aspects which seem to greatly predate the Middle-Ages . . . [and] many of the elements preserved in this poetic form are so archaic that they are not found in the prose tradition which was recorded at the same time" (Pentikäinen 83). The tradition of rune-singing is believed to be 2,500–3,000 years old, and the actual content of the runos is speculated to be even older than the tradition of singing.

RUNO I.—BIRTH OF VÄINÄMÖINEN

Argument

Prelude (1–102). The Virgin of the Air descends into the sea, where she is fertilized by the winds and waves and becomes the Water-Mother (103–176). A teal builds its nest on her knee, and lays eggs (177–212). The eggs fall from the nest and break, but the fragments form the earth, sky, sun, moon and clouds (213–244). The Water-Mother creates capes, bays, sea-shores, and the depths and shallows of the ocean (245–280). Väinämöinen is born from the Water-Mother, and is tossed about by the waves for a long time until he reaches the shore (281–344).

The first 102 lines set the stage for the reciting of the poem in a sort of "call" to gather listeners together. The narrator expresses the importance of preserving and sharing stories: "Of the rising generation, / Let them learn the words of magic, / And recall our songs and legends . . ." (lines 28–30). We begin with line 103.

I have often heard related,	
And have heard the song recited,	
How the nights closed ever lonely,	105
And the days were shining lonely.	
Only born was **Väinämöinen***,	
And revealed the bard immortal,	
Sprung from the divine Creatrix,	
Born of **Ilmatar***, his mother.	110
Air's young daughter was a virgin,	
Fairest daughter of Creation.	
Long did she abide a virgin,	
All the long days of her girlhood,	
In the Air's own spacious mansions,	115
In those far extending regions.	
Wearily the time passed ever.	
And her life became a burden,	
Dwelling evermore so lonely,	
Always living as a maiden,	120
In the Air's own spacious mansions,	
In those far-extending deserts.	
After this the maid descending,	
Sank upon the tossing billows,	
On the open ocean's surface,	125
On the wide expanse of water.	

*Väinämöinen = shaman, culture hero; revered as a deity
*Ilmatar = Daughter of the sky; New Kalevala, she creates the universe

---

Source: Anonymous. *Kalevala: The Land of the Heroes.* Translated by W.F. Kirby. 1907.

Then a storm arose in fury,
From the East a mighty tempest,
And the sea was wildly foaming,
And the waves dashed ever higher.   130

Thus the tempest rocked the virgin,
And the billows drove the maiden,
O'er the ocean's azure surface,
On the crest of foaming billows,
Till the wind that blew around her,   135
And the sea woke life within her.

Then she bore her heavy burden,
And the pain it brought upon her,
Seven long centuries together,
Nine times longer than a lifetime.   140
Yet no child was fashioned from her,
And no offspring was perfected.

Thus she swam, the Water-Mother,
East she swam, and westward swam she,
Swam to north-west and to south-west,   145
And around in all directions,
In the sharpness of her torment,
In her body's fearful anguish;
Yet no child was fashioned from her,
And no offspring was perfected.   150

Then she fell to weeping gently,
And in words like these expressed her:
"O how wretched is my fortune,
Wandering thus, a child unhappy!
I have wandered far already,   155
And I dwell beneath the heaven,
By the tempest tossed for ever,
While the billows drive me onward.
O'er this wide expanse of water,
On the far-extending billows.   160

"Better were it had I tarried,
Virgin in aerial regions,
Then I should not drift for ever,
As the Mother of the Waters.
Here my life is cold and dreary,   165
Every moment now is painful,
Ever tossing on the billows,
Ever floating on the water.

"**Ukko***, thou of Gods the highest,
Ruler of the whole of heaven,   170
Hasten here, for thou art needed;
Hasten here at my entreaty.
Free the damsel from her burden,
And release her from her tortures.
Quickly haste, and yet more quickly,   175
Where I long for thee so sorely."

Short the time that passed thereafter,
Scarce a moment had passed over,
Ere a beauteous **teal** came flying
Lightly hovering o'er the water,   180
Seeking for a spot to rest in,
Searching for a home to dwell in.

Eastward flew she, westward flew she.
Flew to north-west and to southward,
But the place she sought she found not,   185
Not a spot, however barren,
Where her nest she could establish,
Or a resting-place could light on.

Then she hovered, slowly moving,
And she pondered and reflected,   190
"If my nest in wind I 'stablish
Or should rest it on the billows,
Then the winds will overturn it,
Or the waves will drift it from me."

Then the Mother of the Waters,   195
Water-Mother, maid aerial,
From the waves her knee uplifted,
Raised her shoulder from the billows,
That the teal her nest might 'stablish,

And might find a peaceful dwelling.   200
Then the teal, the bird so beauteous,
Hovered slow, and gazed around her,
And she saw the knee uplifted
From the blue waves of the ocean,
And she thought she saw a hillock,   205
Freshly green with springing verdure.
There she flew, and hovered slowly,
Gently on the knee alighting,
And her nest she there established,
And she laid her eggs all golden,   210

   Ukko = God of thunder; supreme deity
   teal = a type of duck

Six gold eggs she laid within it,
And a seventh she laid of iron.

O'er her eggs the teal sat brooding,
And the knee grew warm beneath her;
And she sat one day, a second,   225
Brooded also on the third day;
Then the Mother of the Waters,
Water-Mother, maid aerial,
Felt it hot, and felt it hotter,
And she felt her skin was heated,   220
Till she thought her knee was burning,
And that all her veins were melting.
Then she jerked her knee with quickness,
And her limbs convulsive shaking,
Rolled the eggs into the water,   225
Down amid the waves of ocean,
And to splinters they were broken,
And to fragments they were shattered.

In the ooze they were not wasted,
Nor the fragments in the water,   230
But a wondrous change came o'er them,
And the fragments all grew lovely.
From the cracked egg's lower fragment,
Now the solid earth was fashioned,
From the cracked egg's upper fragment,   235
Rose the lofty arch of heaven,
From the yolk, the upper portion,
Now became the sun's bright lustre;
From the white, the upper portion,
Rose the moon that shines so brightly;   240
Whatso in the egg was mottled,
Now became the stars in heaven,
Whatso in the egg was blackish,
In the air as cloudlets floated.

Now the time passed quickly over,   241
And the years rolled quickly onward,
In the new sun's shining lustre,
In the new moon's softer beaming.
Still the Water-Mother floated,
Water-Mother, maid aerial,   250
Ever on the peaceful waters,
On the billows' foamy surface,
With the moving waves before her,
And the heaven serene behind her.

When the ninth year had passed over,   255
And the summer tenth was passing,

From the sea her head she lifted,
And her forehead she uplifted,
And she then began Creation,
And she brought the world to order,   260
On the open ocean's surface,
On the far extending waters.
Wheresoe'er her hand she pointed,
There she formed the jutting headlands;
Wheresoe'er her feet she rested,   265
There she formed the caves for fishes;
When she dived beneath the water,
There she formed the depths of ocean;
When towards the land she turned her,
There the level shores extended,   270
Where her feet to land extended,
Spots were formed for salmon-netting;
Where her head the land touched lightly,
There the curving bays extended.
Further from the land she floated,   275
And abode in open water,
And created rocks in ocean,
And the reefs that eyes behold not,
Where the ships are often shattered,
And the sailors' lives are ended.   280

Now the isles were formed already,
In the sea the rocks were planted;
Pillars of the sky established,
Lands and continents created;
Rocks engraved as though with figures,   285
And the hills were cleft with fissures.
Still unborn was Väinämöinen;
Still unborn, the bard immortal.

Väinämöinen, old and steadfast,
Rested in his mother's body   290
For the space of thirty summers,
And the sum of thirty winters,
Ever on the placid waters,
And upon the foaming billows.

So he pondered and reflected   295
How he could continue living
In a resting-place so gloomy,
In a dwelling far too narrow,
Where he could not see the moonlight,
Neither could behold the sunlight.   300

Then he spake the words which follow,
And expressed his thoughts in this wise:

"Aid me Moon, and Sun release me,
And the Great Bear lend his counsel,
Through the portal that I know not,   305
Through the unaccustomed passage.
From the little nest that holds me,
From a dwelling-place so narrow,
To the land conduct the roamer,
To the open air conduct me,   310
To behold the moon in heaven,
And the splendour of the sunlight;
See the Great Bear's stars above me,
And the shining stars in heaven."

When the moon no freedom gave him,   215
Neither did the sun release him,
Then he wearied of existence,
And his life became a burden.
Thereupon he moved the portal,
With his finger, fourth in number,   320
Opened quick the bony gateway,
With the toes upon his left foot,
With his nails beyond the threshold,
With his knees beyond the gateway.

Headlong in the water falling,   325
With his hands the waves repelling,
Thus the man remained in ocean,
And the hero on the billows.

In the sea five years he sojourned,
Waited five years, waited six years,   330
Seven years also, even eight years,
On the surface of the ocean,
By a nameless promontory,
Near a barren, treeless country.

On the land his knees he planted,   335
And upon his arms he rested,
Rose that he might view the moonbeams,
And enjoy the pleasant sunlight,
See the Great Bear's stars above him,
And the shining stars in heaven.   340

Thus was ancient Väinämöinen,
He, the ever famous minstrel,
Born of the divine Creatrix,
Born of Ilmatar, his mother.

RUNO II.—BIRTH OF VÄINÄMÖINEN (THE SOWING)

Argument

Väinämöinen lands on a treeless country and directs Sampsa Pellervoinen to sow trees (1–42). At first the oak will not grow, but after repeated sowings it springs up, overshadows the whole country, and hides the sun and moon (43–110). A little man rises from the sea, who fells the oak, and permits the sun and moon to shine again (111–224). Birds sing in the trees; herbs, flowers and berries grow on the ground; only the barley will not spring up (225–256). Väinämöinen finds some barleycorns in the sand on the shore, and fells the forest, leaving only a birch-tree as a resting-place for the birds (257–264). The eagle, grateful for this, strikes fire, and the felled trees are consumed (265–284). Väinämöinen sows the barley, prays to Ukko for its increase, and it grows and flourishes (285–378).

Then did Väinämöinen, rising,
Set his feet upon the surface
Of a sea-encircled island,
In a region bare of forest.

There he dwelt, while years passed over,   5
And his dwelling he established
On the silent, voiceless island,
In a barren, treeless country.

Then he pondered and reflected,
In his mind he turned it over,   10
"Who shall sow this barren country,
Thickly scattering seeds around him?"

Pellervoinen, earth-begotten,
Sampsa, youth of smallest stature,
Came to sow the barren country,   15
Thickly scattering seeds around him.

Down he stooped the seeds to scatter,
On the land and in the marshes,
Both in flat and sandy regions,
And in hard and rocky places.   20
On the hills he sowed the pine-trees,
On the knolls he sowed the fir-trees,
And in sandy places heather;
Leafy saplings in the valleys.

In the dales he sowed the birch-trees,   25
In the loose earth sowed the alders,
Where the ground was damp the cherries,
Likewise in the marshes, sallows.
Rowan-trees in holy places,
Willows in the fenny regions,   30

Juniper in stony districts,
Oaks upon the banks of rivers.

Now the trees sprang up and flourished,
And the saplings sprouted bravely.
With their bloom the firs were loaded,   35
And the pines their boughs extended.
In the dales the birch was sprouting,
In the loose earth rose the alders,
Where the ground was damp the cherries,
Juniper in stony districts,   40
Loaded with its lovely berries;
And the cherries likewise fruited.

Väinämöinen, old and steadfast,
Came to view the work in progress,
Where the land was sown by Sampsa,   45
And where Pellervoinen laboured.
While he saw the trees had flourished,
And the saplings sprouted bravely,
Yet had **Jumala's*** tree, the oak-tree,
Not struck down its root and sprouted.   50

Therefore to its fate he left it,
Left it to enjoy its freedom,
And he waited three nights longer,
And as many days he waited.
Then he went and gazed around him,   55
When the week was quite completed.
Yet had Jumala's tree, the oak-tree,
Not struck down its root and sprouted.

Then he saw four lovely maidens;
Five, like brides, from water rising;   60
And they mowed the grassy meadow,
Down they cut the dewy herbage,
On the cloud-encompassed headland,
On the peaceful island's summit,
What they mowed, they raked together,   65
And in heaps the hay collected.

From the ocean rose up **Tursas***,
From the waves arose the hero,
And the heaps of hay he kindled,
And the flames arose in fury.   70
All was soon consumed to ashes,
Till the sparks were quite extinguished.

*Jumala = Sky god/supreme god (sometimes equated to Ukko)
*Tursas = a gnome

Then among the heaps of ashes,
In the dryness of the ashes,
There a tender germ he planted,   75
Tender germ, of oak an acorn
Whence the beauteous plant sprang upward,
And the sapling grew and flourished,
As from earth a strawberry rises,
And it forked in both directions.   80
Then the branches wide extended,
And the leaves were thickly scattered,
And the summit rose to heaven,
And its leaves in air expanded.

In their course the clouds it hindered,   85
And the driving clouds impeded,
And it hid the shining sunlight,
And the gleaming of the moonlight.

Then the aged Väinämöinen,
Pondered deeply and reflected,   90
"Is there none to fell the oak-tree,
And o'erthrow the tree majestic?
Sad is now the life of mortals,
And for fish to swim is dismal,
Since the air is void of sunlight,   95
And the gleaming of the moonlight."

But they could not find a hero,
Nowhere find a man so mighty,
Who could fell the giant oak-tree,
With its hundred spreading branches.   100

Then the aged Väinämöinen,
Spoke the very words which follow;
"Noble mother, who hast borne me,
Luonnotar*, who me hast nurtured;
Send me powers from out the ocean: 105
(Numerous are the powers of ocean)
So that they may fell the oak-tree,
And destroy the tree so baneful,
That the sun may shine upon us.
And the pleasant moonlight glimmer."   110

Then a man arose from ocean,
From the waves a hero started,
Not the hugest of the hugest,
Nor the smallest of the smallest.
As a man's thumb was his stature;   115
Lofty as the span of woman.

*Luonnotar = one of three maidens who nursed Väinämöinen

Decked his head a helm of copper,
On his feet were boots of copper,
On his hands were copper gauntlets.
Gloves adorned with copper tracings;   120
Round his waist his belt was copper;
In his belt his axe was copper;
And the haft thereof was thumb-long,
And the blade thereof was nail-long.

Väinämöinen, old and steadfast,   125
Deeply pondered and reflected:
"While he seems a man in semblance,
And a hero in appearance,
Yet his height is but a thumb-length,
Scarce as lofty as an ox-hoof."   130

Then he spoke the words which follow,
And expressed himself in this wise:
"Who are you, my little fellow,
Most contemptible of heroes,
Than a dead man scarcely stronger;   135
And your beauty all has vanished."

Then the puny man from ocean,
Hero of the floods, made answer:

"I'm a man as you behold me,
Small, but mighty water-hero,   140
I have come to fell the oak-tree,
And to splinter it to fragments."

Väinämöinen, old and steadfast,
Answered in the words which follow:
"You have hardly been created,   145
Neither made, nor so proportioned,
As to fell this mighty oak-tree,
Overthrow the tree stupendous."

Scarcely had the words been spoken,
While his gaze was fixed upon him,   150
When the man transformed before him,
And became a mighty hero.
While his feet the earth were stamping,
To the clouds his head he lifted,
To his knees his beard was flowing,   155
To his spurs his locks descended.
Fathom-wide his eyes were parted,
Fathom-wide his trousers measured;
Round his knee the girth was greater,

And around his hip 'twas doubled.   160
Then he sharpened keen the axe-blade,
Brought the polished blade to sharpness;
Six the stones on which he ground it,
Seven the stones on which he whet it.

Then the man stepped forward lightly,   165
Hastened on to do his mission;
Wide his trousers, and they fluttered
Round his legs as onward strode he,
And the first step taken, brought him
To the shore so soft and sandy;   170
With the second stride he landed
On the dun ground further inland,
And the third step brought him quickly,
Where the oak itself was rooted.

With his axe he smote the oak-tree,   175
With his sharpened blade he hewed it;
Once he smote it, twice he smote it,
And the third stroke wholly cleft it.
From the axe the flame was flashing,
Flame was bursting from the oak-tree,   180
As he strove to fell the oak-tree,
Overthrow the tree stupendous.
Thus the third blow was delivered,
And the oak-tree fell before him,
For the mighty tree was shattered,   185
And the hundred boughs had fallen,
And the trunk extended eastward,
And the summit to the north-west,
And the leaves were scattered southwards,
And the branches to the northward.   190

He who took a branch from off it,
Took prosperity unceasing,
What was broken from the summit,
Gave unending skill in magic;
He who broke a leafy branchlet,   195
Gathered with it love unending.
What remained of fragments scattered,
Chips of wood, and broken splinters,
On the bright expanse of ocean,
On the far-extending billows,   200
In the breeze were gently rocking,
On the waves were lightly drifted.
Like the boats on ocean's surface,
Like the ships amid the sea-waves.

Northward drove the wind the fragments,   205
Where the little maid of Pohja,
Stood on beach, and washed her head-dress,
And she washed her clothes and rinsed them,
On the shingle by the ocean,
On a tongue of land projecting.   210

On the waves she saw the fragments,
Put them in her birchbark wallet,
In her wallet took them homeward;
In the well-closed yard she stored them,
For the arrows of the sorcerer,   215
For the chase to furnish weapons.

When the oak at last had fallen,
And the evil tree was levelled,
Once again the sun shone brightly,
And the pleasant moonlight glimmered,   220
And the clouds extended widely,
And the rainbow spanned the heavens,
O'er the cloud-encompassed headland,
And the island's misty summit.

Then the wastes were clothed with verdure,   225
And the woods grew up and flourished;
Leaves on trees and grass in meadows.
In the trees the birds were singing,
Loudly sang the cheery throstle;
In the tree-tops called the cuckoo.   230

Then the earth brought forth her berries;
Shone the fields with golden blossoms;
Herbs of every species flourished;
Plants and trees of all descriptions;
But the barley would not flourish,   235
Nor the precious seed would ripen.

Then the aged Väinämöinen,
Walked around, and deeply pondered,
By the blue waves' sandy margin,
On the mighty ocean's border,   240
And six grains of corn he found there,
Seven fine seeds of corn he found there,
On the borders of the ocean,
On the yielding sandy margin.
In a marten's skin he placed them,   245
From the leg of summer squirrel.

Then he went to sow the fallows;
On the ground the seeds to scatter,

Near to Kaleva's own fountain,
And upon the field of **Osmo***.   250

From a tree there chirped the titmouse:
"Osmo's barley will not flourish,
Nor will Kaleva's oats prosper,
While untilled remains the country,
And uncleared remains the forest,   255
Nor the fire has burned it over."

Väinämöinen, old and steadfast,
Ground his axe-blade edge to sharpness
And began to fell the forest,
Toiling hard to clear the country.   260
All the lovely trees he levelled,
Sparing but a single birch-tree,
That the birds might rest upon it,
And from thence might call the cuckoo.

In the sky there soared an eagle,   265
Of the birds of air the greatest,
And he came and gazed around him.
"Wherefore is the work unfinished,
And the birch-tree still unfallen?
Wherefore spare the beauteous birch-tree?"   270

Said the aged Väinämöinen,
"Therefore is the birch left standing,
That the birds may perch upon it;
All the birds of air may rest there."

Said the bird of air, the eagle,   275
"Very wisely hast thou acted,
Thus to leave the birch-tree standing
And the lovely tree unfallen,
That the birds may perch upon it,
And that I myself may rest there."   280

Then the bird of air struck fire,
And the flames rose up in brightness,
While the north wind fanned the forest,
And the north-east wind blew fiercely.
All the trees were burned to ashes,   285
Till the sparks were quite extinguished.

Then the aged Väinämöinen,
Took the six seeds from his satchel,
And he took the seven small kernels,
From the marten's skin he took them,   290

Osmo/Osmoinen = a young man

From the leg of summer squirrel,
From the leg of summer ermine.

Then he went to sow the country,
And to scatter seeds around him,
And he spoke the words which follow;   295
"Now I stoop the seeds to scatter,
As from the Creator's fingers,
From the hand of Him Almighty,
That the country may be fertile,
And the corn may grow and flourish.   300

"Patroness of lowland country,
Old one of the plains; Earth-Mother,
Let the tender blade spring upward,
Let the earth support and cherish.
Might of earth will never fail us,   305
Never while the earth existeth,
When the Givers are propitious.
And Creation's daughters aid us.

"Rise, O earth; from out thy slumber,
Field of the Creator, rouse thee,   310
Make the blade arise and flourish.
Let the stalks grow up and lengthen,
That the ears may grow by thousands,
Yet a hundredfold increasing,
By my ploughing and my sowing,   315
In return for all my labour.

"Ukko, thou of Gods the highest.
Father, thou in heaven abiding,
Thou to whom the clouds are subject.
Of the scattered clouds the ruler,   320
All thy clouds do thou assemble,
In the light make clear thy counsel,
Send thou forth a cloud from eastwards
In the north-west let one gather,
Send thou others from the westward,   325
Let them drive along from southward.
Send the light rain forth from heaven,
Let the clouds distil with honey,
That the corn may sprout up strongly,
And the stalks may wave and rustle."   330

Ukko, then, of Gods the highest,
Father of the highest heaven,
Heard, and all the clouds assembled.

In the light made clear his counsel,
And he sent a cloud from eastward.   335
In the north-west let one gather,
Others, too, he sent from westward,
Let them drive along from southward,
Linked them edge to edge together,
And he closed the rifts between them.   340
Then he sent the rain from heaven,
And the clouds distilled sweet honey,
That the corn might sprout up stronger,
And the stalks might wave and rustle.
Thus the sprouting germ was nourished,   345
And the rustling stalks grew upward,
From the soft earth of the cornfield.
Through the toil of Väinämöinen.

After this, two days passed over,
After two nights, after three nights,   350
When the week was full completed,
Väinämöinen, old and steadfast,
Wandered forth to see the progress;
How his ploughing and his sowing
And his labours had resulted.   355
There he found the barley growing,
And the ears were all six-cornered,
And the stalks were all three-knotted.

Then the aged Väinämöinen
Wandered on and gazed around him,   360
And the cuckoo, bird of springtime,
Came and saw the birch-tree growing.
"Wherefore is the birch left standing,
And unfelled the slender birch-tree?"

Said the aged Väinämöinen,   365
"Therefore is the birch left standing,
And unfelled the slender birch-tree,
As a perch for thee, O Cuckoo;
Whence the cuckoo's cry may echo.
From thy sand-hued throat cry sweetly,   370
With thy silver voice call loudly,
With thy tin-like voice cry clearly,
Call at morning, call at evening,
And at noontide call thou likewise,
To rejoice my plains surrounding,   375
That my woods may grow more cheerful,
That my coast may grow more wealthy,
And my region grow more fruitful."

LINE NOTES

(These are by the translator, when not otherwise stated. K. K. indicates Prof. Kaarle Krohn, and A. M. Madame Aino Malmberg)

RUNO I

110. Ilmatar, the Daughter of the Air; —tar is the usual feminine suffix in Finnish, and is generally to be understood to mean "daughter of ——." In the following passages we have the combined Finnish version of the widespread cosmogonical myths of the Divine Spirit brooding over the waters of Chaos; and the Mundane Egg. In the First Recension of the *Kalevala* however, and in many Finnish ballads, an eagle is said to have built her nest on the knees of Väinämöinen after he was thrown into the sea by the Laplander, and the Creation-Myth is thus transferred to him.

229–244. In the Scandinavian Mythology the world was created in a similar manner by Othin and his brothers from the body of the giant Ymir.

289. Vaka vanha Väinämöinen—these are the usual epithets applied to Väinämöinen in the *Kalevala*. "Vanha" means old; "vaka" is variously interpreted: I have used "steadfast" by Prof. Krohn's advice, though I think "lusty" might be a better rendering.

320. The ring-finger is usually called the "nameless finger" in Finnish.

RUNO II

27. The Bird Cherry (*Prunus Padus*).

29. The Mountain Ash, or Rowan Tree, is a sacred tree in Finland, as in Scotland.

83. The Great Oak-tree is a favorite subject in Finnish and Esthonian ballads.

117. Finnish, and Esthonian water-heroes are sometimes described as entirely composed of copper.

211. Compare the account of the breaking up of the Sampo, and the dispersal of its fragments, in Runo XLIII.

245. The summer ermine is the stoat, which turns white in winter in the North, when it becomes the ermine. The squirrel also turns grey in the North in winter.

376. The cuckoo is regarded as a bird of good omen.

DISCUSSION QUESTIONS

1. Explain the conflict that occurs when trees begin to grow and what this situation, and Väinämöinen's actions, reveal about this culture.

2. This part of the epic concerns creation, but in what ways is it also a hero's story?

3. What features of the oral tradition can you identify in this piece?

4. In what category of creation myths would you place this story? What motifs or archetypes can you identify?

© Miranda Carter.

Prose Edda (Norse)

When Snorri Sturluson wrote the Norse stories of his people in the 1220s CE, he understood that these tales were in danger of being lost. The oldest texts tell us that Iceland was not inhabited until the ninth century CE, when explorers from Norway and Celts began to populate the island; we now know these explorers and settlers as Vikings. From the beginning of settlement, the Vikings created pagan rituals and beliefs, and worshipped the many gods, or Æsir, who inhabited many mythological realms. At the same time, the religion of Christianity began to spread from the Middle East, through the Roman Empire, and continued north to Norway and Iceland. By 1000 CE, the "Althing," an elected assembly of Icelanders, declared that a peaceful transition to adopting Christianity would take place for all Icelanders.

Sturluson was a historian, elected leader to the Althing assembly in Iceland, and the descendant of a great poet and writer. Having grown up around the fantastic mythology of Iceland, Sturluson began to write many books on the folklore of his people. The *Prose Edda* is set as a conversation between a visiting Swedish king, Gylfi, and the Æsir: The High One, Just As High, and The Third One. Through this conversation, Gylfi learns about the creation of the world, the many realms and the fantastic creatures that inhabitant them, and of the end of the world, or Ragnarok. Sturluson was smart in his writing; many Christian themes are present and allusions made to Biblical stories, which likely kept him from being assassinated for heresy. The knowledgeable reader can see both the pagan origins of the stories, and the Christian subtext that allow for a rich chronicle of early Icelander belief.

THE DELUDING OF GYLFI

King Gylfi was a wise man and skilled in magic. He was much troubled that the Æsir-people were so cunning that all things went according to their will. He pondered whether this might proceed from their own nature, or whether the divine powers which they worshipped might ordain such things. He set out on his way to Ásgard, going secretly, and clad himself in the likeness of an old man, with which he dissembled. But the Æsir were wiser in this matter, having second sight; and they saw his journeying before ever he came, and prepared against him deceptions of the eye. When he came into the town, he saw there a hall so high that he could not easily make out the top of it: its thatching was laid with golden shields after the fashion of a shingled roof. So also says Thjódólfr of Hvin, that Valhalla was thatched with shields:

On their backs they let beam,
sore battered with stones,
Odin's hall-shingles,
the shrewd sea-farers.

In the hall-doorway Gylfi saw a man juggling with anlaces, having seven in the air at one time. This man asked of him his name. He called himself Gangleri, and said he had come by the paths of the serpent, and prayed for lodging for the night, asking: "Who owns the hall?" The other replied that it was their king; "and I will attend thee to see him; then shalt thou thyself ask him concerning his name"; and the man wheeled about before him into the hall, and he went after, and straightway the door closed itself on his heels. There he saw a great room and much people, some with games, some drinking; and some had weapons and were fighting. Then he looked about him, and thought unbelievable many things which he saw; and he said:

All the gateways
ere one goes out
Should one scan:
For 't is uncertain
where sit the unfriendly
On the bench before thee.

He saw three high-seats, each above the other, and three men sat thereon, one on each. And he asked what might be the name of those lords.

He who had conducted him in answered that the one who, sat on the nethermost high-seat was a king, "and his name is The High One; but the next is named Just As High; and he who is uppermost is called The Third One." Then The High One asked the newcomer whether his errand were more than for the meat and drink which were always at his command, as for every one there in the Hall of the High One. He answered that he first desired to learn whether there were any wise man there within. The High One said, that he should not escape whole from thence unless he were wiser.

And stand thou forth
who speirest;
Who answers,
he shall sit.

Gangleri began his questioning thus: "Who is foremost, or oldest, of all the gods?"

The High One answered: "He is called in our speech Allfather, but in the Elder Ásgard he had twelve names: one is Allfather; the second is Lord, or Lord of Hosts; the third is Nikarr, or Spear-Lord; the fourth

Source: Sturulson, Snorri. *Prose Edda.* Trans. Arthur Gilchrist Brodeur. 1916.

is Nikudr, or Striker; the fifth is Knower of Many Things; the sixth, Fulfiller of Wishes; the seventh, Far-Speaking One; the eighth, The Shaker, or He that Putteth the Armies to Flight; the ninth, The Burner; the tenth, The Destroyer; the eleventh, The Protector; the twelfth, Gelding."

Then asked Gangleri: "Where is this god, or what power hath he, or what hath he wrought that is a glorious deed?"

The High One made answer: "He lives throughout all ages and governs all his realm, and directs all things, great and small."

Then said Just As High: "He fashioned heaven and earth and air, and all things which are in them."

Then spake The Third One: "The greatest of all is this: that he made man, and gave him the spirit, which shall live and never perish, though the flesh-frame rot to mould, or burn to ashes; and all men shall live, such as are just in action, and be with himself in the place called Gimlé. But evil men go to Hel and thence down to the Misty Hel; and that is down in the ninth world."

Then said Gangleri: "What did he before heaven and earth were made?"

And The High One answered: "He was then with the frost-Giants."

Gangleri said: "What was the beginning, or how began it, or what was before it?"

The High One answered: "As is told in *Völuspá*:

Erst was the age
when nothing was:
Nor sand nor sea,
nor chilling stream-waves;
Earth was not found,
nor Ether-Heaven,--
A Yawning Gap,
but grass was none."

Then said Just As High: "It was many ages before the earth was shaped that the Mist-World was made; and midmost within it lies the well that is called Hvergelmir, from which spring the rivers called Svöl, Gunnthrá, Fjörm, Fimbulthul, Slídr and Hríd, Sylgr and Ylgr, Víd, Leiptr; Gjöll is hard by Hel-gates."

And The Third One said: "Yet first was the world in the southern region, which was named Múspell; it is light and hot; that region is glowing and burning, and impassable to such as are outlanders and have not their holdings there. He who sits there at the land's-end, to defend the land, is called Surt; he brandishes a flaming sword, and at the end of the world he shall go forth and The High One, and overcome all the gods, and burn all the world with fire; thus is said in *Völuspá*:

Surt fares from the south
with switch-eating flame,--
On his sword shimmers
the sun of the War-Gods;
The rock-crags crash;
the fiends are reeling;
Heroes tread Hel-way;
Heaven is cloven."

Gangleri asked: "How were things wrought, ere the races were and the tribes of men increased?"

Then said The High One: "The streams called Ice-waves, those which were so long come from the fountain-heads that the yeasty venom upon them had hardened like the slag that runs out of the fire,— these then became ice; and when the ice halted and ceased to run, then it froze over above. But the drizzling rain that rose from the venom congealed to frost, and the frost increased, frost over frost, each over the other, even into Ginnungagap, the Yawning Void."

Then spake Just As High: "Ginnungagap, which faced toward the northern quarter, became filled with heaviness, and masses of ice and frost, and from within, drizzling rain and gusts; but the southern part of the Yawning Void was lighted by those sparks and glowing masses which flew out of Múspellheim."

And The Third One said: "Just as cold arose out of Niflheim, and all terrible things, so also all that looked toward Múspellheim became hot and glowing; but Ginnungagap was as mild as windless air, and when the breath of heat met the frost, so that it melted and dripped, life was quickened from the yeast-drops, by the power of that which sent the heat, and became a man's form. And that man is named Ymir, but the frost-Giants call him Aurgelimir; and thence are come the races of the frost-Giants, as it says in *Völuspá the Less*:

All the witches
spring from Witolf,
All the warlocks
are of Willharm,
And the spell-singers
spring from Swarthead;
All the ogres
of Ymir come.

But concerning this says Vafthrúdnir the giant:

Out of the Ice-waves
issued venom-drops,
Waxing until
a giant was;
Thence are our kindred
come all together,--
So it is
they are savage forever."

Then said Gangleri: "How did the races grow thence, or after what fashion was it brought to pass that more men came into being? Or do ye hold him God, of whom ye but now spake?"

And Just As High answered: "By no means do we acknowledge him God; he was evil and all his kindred: we call them frost-Giants. Now it is said that when he slept, a sweat came upon him, and there grew under his left hand a man and a woman, and one of his feet begat a son with the other; and thus the races are come; these are the frost-Giants. The old frost-Giant, him we call Ymir."

Then said Gangleri: "Where dwelt Ymir, or wherein did he find sustenance?"

The High One answered: "Straightway after the frost dripped, there sprang from it the cow called Audumla; four streams of milk ran from her udders, and she nourished Ymir."

Then asked Gangleri: "Wherewithal was the cow nourished?"

And The High One made answer: "She licked the ice-blocks, which were salty; and the first day that she licked the blocks, there came forth from the blocks in the evening a man's hair; the second day, a man's head; the third day the whole man was there. He is named Búri: he was fair of feature, great and mighty. He begat a son called Borr, who wedded the woman named Bestla, daughter of Bölthorn the giant; and they had three sons: one was Odin, the second Vili, the third Vé. And this is my belief, that he, Odin, with his brothers, must be ruler of heaven and earth; we hold that he must be so called; so is that man called whom we know to be mightiest and most worthy of honor, and ye do well to let him be so called."

Then said Gangleri: "What covenant was between them, or which was the stronger?"

And The High One answered: "The sons of Borr slew Ymir the giant; lo, where he fell there gushed forth so much blood out of his wounds that with it they drowned all the race of the frost-Giants, save that one, whom giants call Bergelmir, escaped with his household; he went upon his ship, and his wife with him, and they were safe there. And from them are come the races of the frost-Giants, as is said here:

Untold ages
ere earth was shapen,
Then was Bergelmir born;
That first I recall,
how the famous wise giant
On the deck of the ship was laid down."

Then said Gangleri: "What was done then by Borr's sons, if thou believe that they be gods?"

The High One replied: "In this matter there is no little to be said. They took Ymir and bore him into the middle of the Yawning Void, and made of him the earth: of his blood the sea and the waters; the land was made of his flesh, and the crags of his bones; gravel and stones they fashioned from his teeth and his grinders and from those bones that were broken."

And Just As High said: "Of the blood, which ran and welled forth freely out of his wounds, they made the sea, when they had formed and made firm the earth together, and laid the sea in a ring round about her; and it may well seem a hard thing to most men to cross over it."

Then said The Third One: "They took his skull also, and made of it the heaven, and set it up over the earth with four corners; and under each corner they set a dwarf: the names of these are East, West, North, and South. Then they took the glowing embers and sparks that burst forth and had been cast out of Múspellheim, and set them in the midst of the Yawning Void, in the heaven, both above and below, to illumine heaven and earth. They assigned places to all fires: to some in heaven, some wandered free under the heavens; nevertheless, to these also they gave a place, and shaped them courses. It is said in old "songs, that from these the days were reckoned, and the tale of years told, as is said in *Völuspá*:

The sun knew not
where she had housing;
The moon knew not
what Might he had;
The stars knew not
where stood their places.
Thus was it ere
the earth was fashioned."

Then said Gangleri: These are great tidings which I now hear; that is a wondrous great piece of craftsmanship, and cunningly made. How was the earth contrived?"

And The High One answered: "She is ring-shaped without, and round about her without lieth the deep sea; and along the strand of that sea they gave lands to the races of giants for habitation. But on the inner earth they made a citadel round about the world against the hostility of the giants, and for their citadel they raised up the brows of Ymir the giant, and called that place Midgard. They took also his brain and cast it in the air, and made from it the clouds, as is here said:

Of Ymir's flesh
the earth was fashioned,
And of his sweat the sea;
Crags of his bones,
trees of his hair,
And of his skull the sky.
Then of his brows
the blithe gods made
Midgard for sons of men;
And of his brain
the bitter-mooded
Clouds were all created."

Then said Gangleri: "Much indeed they had accomplished then, methinks, when earth and heaven were made, and the sun and the constellations of heaven were fixed, and division was made of days; now whence come the men that people the world?"

And The High One answered: 'When the sons of Borr were walking along the sea-strand, they found two trees, and took up the trees and shaped men of them: the first gave them spirit and life; the second, wit and feeling; the third, form, speech, hearing, and sight. They gave them clothing and names: the male was called Ask, and the female Embla, and of them was mankind begotten, which received a dwelling-place under Midgard. Next they made for themselves in the middle of the world a city which is called Ásgard. There dwelt the gods and their kindred; and many tidings and tales of it have come to pass both on earth and aloft. There is one abode called Hlidskjálf, and when Allfather sat in the high-seat there, he looked out over the whole world and saw every man's acts, and knew all things which he saw. His wife was called Frigg daughter of Fjörgvinn; and of their blood is come that kindred which we call the races of the Æsir, that have peopled the Elder Ásgard, and those kingdoms which pertain to it; and that is a divine race. For this reason must he be called Allfather: because he is father of all the gods and of men, and of all that was fulfilled of him and of his might. The Earth was his daughter and his wife; on her he begot the first son, which is Ása-Thor: strength and prowess attend him, wherewith he overcometh all living things."

DISCUSSION QUESTIONS

1. Why is this story told through the lens of "Gangleri" asking the Aesir a string of questions about their world?

2. Consider the title "The Deluding of Gylfi"—what might be its significance?

3. How do the world and mankind become fashioned?

4. What Christian imagery are you able to pick up in this story?

RAGNAROK

Then said Gangleri: "What tidings are to be told concerning the End of the Gods? Never before have I heard aught said of this."

The High One answered: "Great tidings are to be told of it, and much. The first is this, that there shall come that winter which is called the Awful Winter: in that time snow shall drive from all quarters; frosts shall be great then, and winds sharp; there shall be no virtue in the sun. Those winters shall proceed three in succession, and no summer between; but first shall come three other winters, such that over all the world there shall be mighty battles. In that time brothers shall slay each other for greed's sake, and none shall spare father or son in manslaughter and in incest; so it says in *Völuspá*:

Brothers shall strive
and slaughter each other;
Own sisters' children
shall sin together;
Ill days among men,
many a whoredom:
An axe-age, a sword-age,
shields shall be cloven;
A wind-age, a wolf-age,
ere the world totters.

Then shall happen what seems great tidings: the Wolf shall swallow the sun; and this shall seem to men a great harm. Then the other wolf shall seize the moon, and he also shall work great ruin; the stars shall vanish from the heavens. Then shall come to pass these tidings also: all the earth shall tremble so, and the crags, that trees shall be torn up from the earth, and the crags fall to ruin; and all fetters and bonds shall be broken and rent. Then shall Fenrir-Wolf get loose; then the sea shall gush forth upon the land, because the Midgard Serpent stirs in giant wrath and advances up onto the land. Then that too shall happen, that Naglfar shall be loosened, the ship which is so named. (It is made of dead men's nails; wherefore a warning is desirable, that if a man die with unshorn nails, that man adds much material to the ship Naglfar, which gods and men were fain to have finished late.) Yet in this sea-flood Naglfar shall float. Hrymr is the name of the giant who steers Naglfar.

Fenrir-Wolf shall advance with gaping mouth, and his lower jaw shall be against the earth, but the upper against heaven,--he would gape yet more if there were room for it; fires blaze from his eyes and nostrils. The Midgard Serpent shall blow venom so that he shall sprinkle all the air and water; and he is very terrible, and shall be on one side of the Wolf. In this din shall the heaven be cloven, and the Sons of Múspell ride thence: Surt shall ride first, and both before him and after him burning fire; his sword is exceeding good: from it radiance shines brighter than from the sun; when they ride over Bifröst, then the bridge shall break, as has been told before.

The Sons of Múspell shall go forth to that field which is called Vígrídr, thither shall come Fenrir-Wolf also and the Midgard Serpent; then Loki and Hrymr shall come there also, and with him all the frost-Giants. All the champions of Hel follow Loki; and the Sons of Múspell shall have a company by themselves, and it shall be very bright. The field Vígrídr is a hundred leagues wide each way.

"When these tidings come to pass, then shall Heimdallr rise up and blow mightily in the Gjallar-Horn, and awaken all the gods; and they shall hold council together. Then Odin shall ride to Mímir's Well and take counsel of Mímir for himself and his host. Then the Ash of Yggdrasill shall tremble, and nothing then shall be without fear in heaven or in earth. Then shall the Æsir put on their war-weeds, and all the Champions, and advance to the field:

Source: Sturulson, Snorri. *Prose Edda*. Trans. Arthur Gilchrist Brodeur. 1916.

Odin rides first with the gold helmet and a fair birnie, and his spear, which is called Gungnir. He shall go forth against Fenrir-Wolf, and Thor stands forward on his other side, and can be of no avail to him, because he shall have his hands full to fight against the Midgard Serpent.

Freyr shall contend with Surt, and a hard encounter shall there be between them before Freyr falls: it is to be his death that he lacks that good sword of his, which he gave to Skírnir. Then shall the dog Garmr be loosed, which is bound before Gnipa's Cave: he is the greatest monster; he shall do battle with Týr, and each become the other's slayer.

Thor shall put to death the Midgard Serpent, and shall stride away nine paces from that spot; then shall he fall dead to the earth, because of the venom which the Snake has blown at him.

The Wolf shall swallow Odin; that shall be his ending. But straight thereafter shall Vídarr stride forth and set one foot upon the lower jaw of the Wolf: on that foot he has the shoe, materials for which have been gathering throughout all time. (They are the scraps of leather which men cut out: of their shoes at toe or heel; therefore he who desires in his heart to come to the Æsir's help should cast those scraps away.) With one hand he shall seize the Wolf's upper jaw and tear his gullet asunder; and that is the death of the Wolf.

Loki shall have battle with Heimdallr, and each be the slayer of the other. Then straightway shall Surt cast fire over the earth and burn all the world; so is said in *Völuspá*:

High blows Heimdallr,	1
the horn is aloft;	
Odin communes	
with Mimir's head;	
Trembles Yggdrasill's	5
towering Ash;	
The old tree wails	
when the Ettin is loosed.	
What of the Æsir?	
What of the Elf-folk?	10
All Jötunheim echoes,	
the Æsir are at council;	
The dwarves are groaning	
before their stone doors,	
Wise in rock-walls;	15
wit ye yet, or what?	
Hrymr sails from the east,	
the sea floods onward;	
The monstrous Beast	
twists in mighty wrath;	20
The Snake beats the waves,	
the Eagle is screaming;	
The gold-neb tears corpses,	
Naglfar is loosed.	
From the east sails the keel;	25
come now Múspell's folk	
Over the sea-waves,	
and Loki steereth;	
There are the warlocks	
all with the Wolf,--	30

With them is the brother
of Býleistr faring.
Surt fares from southward
with switch-eating flame;
On his sword shimmers   35
the sun of the war-gods;
The rocks are falling,
and fiends are reeling,
Heroes tread Hel-way,
heaven is cloven.   40
Then to the Goddess
a second grief cometh,
When Odin fares
to fight with the Wolf,
And Beli's slayer,   45
the bright god, with Surt;
There must fall
Frigg's beloved.
Odin's son goeth
to strife with the Wolf,--   50
Vídarr, speeding
to meet the slaughter-beast;
The sword in his hand
to the heart he thrusteth
Of the fiend's offspring;   55
avenged is his Father.
Now goeth Hlödyn's
glorious son
Not in flight from the Serpent,
of fear unheeding;   60
All the earth's offspring
must empty the homesteads,
When furiously smiteth
Midgard's defender.
The sun shall be darkened,   65
earth sinks in the sea,--
Glide from the heaven
the glittering stars;
Smoke-reek rages
and reddening fire: 70
The high heat licks
against heaven itself.

And here it says yet so:

Vígrídr hight the field
where in fight shall meet   75
Surt and the cherished gods;
An hundred leagues
it has on each side:
Unto them that field is fated."

Regeneration

Then said Gangleri: "What shall come to pass afterward, when all the world is burned, and dead are all the gods and all the champions and all mankind? Have ye not said before, that every man shall live in some world throughout all ages?"

Then The Third One answered: "In that time the good abodes shall be many, and many the ill; then it shall be best to be in Gimlé in Heaven. Moreover, there is plenteous abundance of good drink, for them that esteem that a pleasure, in the hall which is called Brimir: it stands in Ókólnir. That too is a good hall which stands in Nida Fells, made of red gold; its name is Sindri. In these halls shall dwell good men and pure in heart.

"On Nástrand is a great hall and evil, and its doors face to the north: it is all woven of serpent-backs like a wattle-house; and all the snake-heads turn into the house and blow venom, so that along the hall run rivers of venom; and they who have broken oaths, and murderers, wade those rivers, even as it says here:

I know a hall standing
far from the sun,
In Nástrand: the doors;
to northward are turned;
Venom-drops fill
down from the roof-holes;
That hall is bordered
with backs of serpents.
There are doomed to wade
the weltering streams
Men that are mansworn,
and they that murderers are.

But it is worst in Hvergelmir:

There the cursed snake
tears dead men's corpses."

Then spake Gangleri: "Shall any of the gods live then, or shall there be then any earth or heaven?"

The High One answered: "In that time the earth shall emerge out of the sea, and shall then be green and fair; then shall the fruits of it be brought forth unsown. Vídarr and Váli shall be living, inasmuch as neither sea nor the fire of Surt shall have harmed them; and they shall dwell at Ida-Plain, where Ásgard was before. And then the sons of Thor, Módi and Magni, shall come there, and they shall have Mjöllnir there. After that Baldr shall come thither, and Hödr, from Hel; then all shall sit down together and hold speech with one another, and call to mind their secret wisdom, and speak of those happenings which have been before: of the Midgard Serpent and of Fenrir-Wolf. Then they shall find in the grass those golden chess-pieces which the Æsir had had; thus is it said:

In the deities' shrines
Shall dwell Vídarr and Váli
When the Fire of Surt is slackened;
Módi and Magni
shall have Mjöllnir
At the ceasing of Thor's strife.

In the place called Hoddmímir's Holt there shall lie hidden during the Fire of Surt two of mankind, who are called thus: Líf and Lífthrasir, and for food they shall have the morning-dews. From these folk shall come so numerous an offspring that all the world shall be peopled, even as is said here:

Líf and Lífthrasir,
these shall lurk hidden
In the Holt of Hoddmímir;
The morning dews
their meat shall be;
Thence are gendered the generations.

And it may seem wonderful to thee, that the sun shall have borne a daughter not less fair than herself; and the daughter shall then tread in the steps of her mother, as is said here:

The Elfin-beam
shall bear a daughter,
Ere Fenrir drags her forth;
That maid shall go,
when the great gods die,
To ride her mother's road.

But now, if thou art able to ask yet further, then indeed I know not whence answer shall come to thee, for I never heard any man tell forth at greater length the course of the world; and now avail thyself of that which thou hast heard."

Thereupon Gangleri heard great noises on every side of him; and then, when he had looked about him more, lo, he stood out of doors on a level plain, and saw no hall there and no castle. Then he went his way forth and came home into his kingdom, and told those tidings which he had seen and heard; and after him each man told these tales to the other.

DISCUSSION QUESTIONS

1. According to the story of Ragnarok, what brings about the destruction of their world?
2. What role does each god play in the battle of Ragnarok?
3. How will the gods continue to live?

Part 2: Tricksters, Lovers, and Other Tales

How the Fog Came and The Thunder Spirits (Greenland)

The two stories that follow are from Knud Rasmussen's collection *Eskimo Folk-Tales* and explain two of the earth's elements: Fog and Thunder. As Rasmussen traveled Greenland, collecting oral stories from native Inuit, he undoubtedly found himself laughing at some of their more illustrious explanations for the way the world worked.

The first story "How the Fog Came," certainly qualifies as a tongue-in-cheek punishment for the Mountain Spirit's wife. The second story, "The Thunder Spirits," is a sort of cautionary tale about the sisters who were scolded too often by their father.

HOW THE FOG CAME

There was a Mountain Spirit, which stole corpses from their graves and ate them when it came home. And a man, wishing to see who did this thing, let himself be buried alive. The Spirit came, and saw the new grave, and dug up the body, and carried it off.

The man had stuck a flat stone in under his coat, in case the Spirit should try to stab him.

On the way, he caught hold of all the willow twigs whenever they passed any bushes, and made himself as heavy as he could, so that the Spirit was forced to put forth all its strength.

At last the Spirit reached its house, and flung down the body on the floor. And then, being weary, it lay down to sleep, while its wife went out to gather wood for the cooking.

"Father, father, he is opening his eyes," cried the children, when the dead man suddenly looked up.

"Nonsense, children, it is a dead body, which I have dropped many times among the twigs on the way," said the father.

But the man rose up, and killed the Mountain Spirit and its children, and fled away as fast as he could. The Mountain Spirit's wife saw him, and mistook him for her husband.

"Where are you going?" she cried.

The man did not answer, but fled on. And the woman, thinking something must be wrong, ran after him.

And as he was running over level ground, he cried: "Rise up, hills!"

And at once many hills rose up.

Then the Mountain Spirit's wife lagged behind, having to climb up so many hills. The man saw a little stream, and sprang across.

"Flow over your banks!" he cried to the stream. And now it was impossible for her to get across.

"How did you get across?" cried the woman.

"I drank up the water. Do you likewise." And the woman began gulping it down.

Source: Rasmussen, Knud. *Eskimo Folk Tales*. Trans. W. Worster. 1921.

Then the man turned round towards her, and said: "Look at the tail of your tunic; it is hanging down between your legs."

And when she bent down to look, her belly burst. And as she burst, a steam rose up out of her, and turned to fog, which still floats about to this day among the hills.

The Thunder Spirits

Two sisters, men say, were playing together, and their father could not bear to hear the noise they made, for he had but few children, and was thus not wont to hear any kind of noise. At last he began to scold them, and told them to go farther away with their playing.

When the girls grew up, and began to understand things, they desired to run away on account of their father's scolding. And at last they set out, taking with them only a little dogskin, and a piece of boot skin, and a fire stone. They went up into a high mountain to build themselves a house there.

Their father and mother made search for them in vain, for the girls kept hiding themselves; they had grown to be true mountain dwellers, keeping far from the places of men. Only the reindeer hunters saw them now and again, but the girls always refused to go back to their kin.

And when at last the time came when they must die of hunger, they turned into evil spirits, and became thunder.

When they shake their dried boot skin, then the gales come up, the south-westerly gales. And great fire is seen in the heavens whenever they strike their fire stone, and the rain pours down whenever they shed tears.

Their father held many spirit callings, hoping to make them return. But this he ceased to do when he found that they were dead.

But men say that after those girls had become spirits, they returned to the places of men, frightening many to death. They came first of all to their father and mother, because of the trouble they had made. The only one they did not kill was a woman bearing a child on her back. And they let her live, that she might tell how terrible they were. And tales are now told of how terrible they were.

When the thunder spirits come, even the earth itself is stricken with terror. And stones, even those which lie on level ground, and not on any slope at all, roll in fear towards men.

Thus the thunder comes with the south-westerly gales; there is a noise and crackling in the air, as of dry skins shaken, and the sky glows from time to time with the fire from their firestone. Great rocks, and everything which stands up high in the air, begin to glow.

When this happens, men use to take out a red dog, and cut its ear until the blood comes, and then lead the beast round about the house, letting the blood drip everywhere, for then the house will not take fire.

A red dog was the only thing they feared, those girls who were turned to thunder.

DISCUSSION QUESTIONS

1. How does magic play a role in the two stories?

2. How are common earthly elements anthropomorphized?

3. What is the lesson of each story?

The Legend of the Reindeer (Sami)

The Sami are the Northernmost indigenous peoples in Europe, living in parts of Norway, Sweden, Finland, and the Russian Kola Peninsula. They are sometimes known as the "Sami-Lapp" people, but that is an Anglicized version of their tribal name. They belong to the Finno-Urgic language family which is considered a severely to critically endangered language, with roughly 70,000 people identifying as being of Sami descent, and many fewer speaking the language.

Like many of the surrounding indigenous people, the Sami people practice shamanism. Each culture approaches the practice of shamanism distinctly, and the Sami traditions of animism and death rituals are particularly interesting, as they tie into "The Legend of the Reindeer."

Totems are used to depict sacred animals to the communities. The bird and bear are the most prominent figures in these carvings. In their stories, there are evil spirits, called "Ulda," who are responsible for the kidnapping of small children. As you read the following myth, you may notice similarities between the Ulda and the greedy character of Attjis-ene. The importance of one's hair is also highlighted in the shamanistic practice, which you may see connections to during the burial of the daughter of the Sun.

The story of the daughters of the Sun and Moon and the taming of the Reindeer is from a 1918 article published in *Folklore Journal* and recounts A. Fjellner's lifelong collections of the Sami mythology.

THE LEGEND OF THE REINDEER

Njawis and Attjis hunted and caught reindeer. They established marriage, binding their wives by sacred oaths. The wife of Njavvis, Njavvis-ene, was a daughter of the Sun; the wife of Attjis, Attjis-ene, was a daughter of the Moon. Both Njavvis and Attjis were murdered, and, at the time of their murder, their two wives were both pregnant. Their widows did not fish nor hunt, but they tethered the reindeer that were caught, and looked after them, and tamed them.

And because the reindeer were tamed by women, women have always had the largest share of the herd. But men first hunted and caught reindeer, and still it was their part to kill them, and to cut them up and cook them. Men have, therefore, the first portion at meals, and the master of the household has his portion cut off nearest the head.

Njavvis-ene had a fair, smiling countenance, long flowing hair, a lofty forehead, dark regular eyebrows and gentle eyes. Her nose was small and aquiline, her neck of dazzling whiteness, her hands soft, and her body plump and well-liking. She walked erect, with graceful gait, and wore fine, dark skins.

Attjis-ene, on the contrary, had a long, dark, morose-looking face, loose, tangled hair, a broad wrinkled forehead, a pointed chin, broad mouth, big teeth and a tall, thin body. Her voice was particularly piercing and unpleasant, and she was thinly clad in white clothes.

Both widows bore children. Njavvis-ene had a son; Attjis-ene a daughter. The children grew up. One day the widows went together to gather cloud-berries. "Whoever fills her basket first shall have the boy," said Attjis-ene. Njavvis-ene would not agree to this proposal at first, but at last she consented. Then Attjis-ene put some moss and twigs into her basket, gathered a few cloud-berries, and pretended to have filled the basket.

Source: Bilson, Charles J. "Some Mythical Tales of the Lapps," 1918.

"Now my basket is full first," she said. "The boy is mine: you must take the girl." When Njavvis-ene found that she had been cheated, she would not let the boy go, but Attjis-ene took him away from her by force, and gave her own daughter to her instead.

As soon as the boy grew big enough to be of use, Attjis-ene went off, taking her herd of reindeer away from that of Njavvis-ene; because she thought that her herd would thrive better with the help of the boy.

"I shall soon be much richer than you," she said, boastfully. "I shall kill lots of reindeer."

It happened one spring-time that there was a very great flood. Njavvis-ene was without any food. Her foster-daughter was hungry, and cried for something to eat. Then Njavvis-ene put a pot of water on the fire, and placed in it some dry bones, and a piece of bark, which she pretended to cook, in order to deceive the girl. The boy learned of his old playmate's sad plight, and took a piece of meat from Attjis-ene, went to Njavvis-ene's hut, climbed up onto the roof, and let the piece of meat down by a string into the pot.

Njavvis-ene saw the boy's reflection in the water that was in the pot, lifted up her eyes and said, "Hullo! my son!"

"What?" said he. "Am I your son?"

She answered: "Follow me to a spring of water; and we will look at our reflections." They did so.

The boy exclaimed, "Yes, indeed, my mother!" and embraced her.

Then she told him how when young he had been fraudulently obtained and forcibly taken away by Attjis-ene.

He said, "It is right that those who steal men should die!"

So he went home and killed Attjis-ene. While she was dying, she seized him round the thigh, squeezed him so hard that the sinews of the hip were strained, and said:

> "Though I helped to tame reindeer,
> I am slain ungratefully by thee;
> But one heritage I leave thy race; --
> When among kinsmen far removed
> Some one's hip aches, and is tortured with cramp,
> It is I who squeeze the sinews."

Therefore the Laplanders say to this day, when they feel cramping pains, *"Attjis-ene suonab tuorela,"* "Attjis-ene is pulling the sinew."

Yet no blessing came with Attjis-ene's herd, from which she expected so much profit; for her evil influence extended even to that. When she was dying, she spitefully caused her reindeer to disperse, and changed them into other animals. Some became frogs and toads, and therefore these creatures must not be disturbed. One kind of beetle is also a descendant of her herd.

Njavvis-ene's herd of reindeer increased so fast that she could not tend them all, and a great number escaped. Mankind multiplied, and food became insufficient. In the Golden Age men had taken milk from the springs; now they learned to milk reindeer. And, as milk was the gift of God, none must be thrown away. If any is spilt, it must be gathered up again. Still one may, with impunity, throw a little milk on the ground for the beetles who represent the herd of Attjis-ene, for they must be fed.

As reindeer increased, they wandered further afield, and became more shy. So the Dog was installed in the service of men, the Laplander's best friend. In one case, however, he threatens misfortune,--if he is neglected in his old age; and therefore the Laplanders are very careful to kill their dogs when they are old, but before they are too old.

It is also told of Attjis-ene that, after her departure from Njavvis-ene, when she became more wicked every day, she was impregnated by the North Wind, and bore a son, Atsits, who is also called Attjevits and Askevits, and whom the Swedes call Askfis. He was harsh and strong like his father; jealous, arrogant and sly like his mother. He ill-treated reindeer, pulling off their horns, and playing all manner of tricks.

At last he even bantered the Moon, his mother's father, because he was paler than the Sun. And therefore he was cast up into the Moon, and sits there still, with a reindeer's horn in one hand, while in the other he holds his own head, which was cut off as a punishment for his crimes. Anyone who has good eyes can see him.

The good daughter of the Sun, Njavvis-ene, lived long. When she felt that death was drawing near, she asked to be buried on the top of a high mountain. And this was done, and the mountain is called "The Mount of the Sun's Daughter" to this day. She was shrouded in birch-bark, but lay upon a bed of njavvi, the long hairs on a reindeer's neck, from which her husband took his name. She was covered over with njavvi, with sand on the top of that; and flat stones were placed round her grave, a marking-stone at her head, another at her feet, and another at each arm.

The headstone and the covering slabs were engraved; the slabs were covered with turf, and on the foot-stone was written: "Lift the turf; read the epitaph." The grave is still on the Mount of the Sun's Daughter. But she herself is not there. Her spirit wanders abroad in the likeness of a beautiful damsel, with a spirit-herd, throughout all Lapland. When she is awake, she is invisible; but, when she is asleep, she can be seen, and her herd too.

"Under wet black rocks,
In green and grassy mountain places,
The Sun's Daughter is seen slumbering.
Whoso shall awake the Sun's Daughter with his embrace,
Kiss the dreamer out of her slumber,
He shall obtain the fair sleeper,
Obtain her strong and fertile herd."

But, in trying to take Njavvis-ene and her herd, one is not always successful.

DISCUSSION QUESTIONS

1. What do you think the headstone's engraving is meant to suggest?

2. How are gender roles a part of this myth?

3. What is the significance of the reindeer?

The Witch and the Sister of the Sun (Russian)

The word "Skazka" is English for the Russian word "story" or "folktale." Russia and its vast country of inhabitants are a wealth of native stories. Some have been adapted or influenced by Asian or European lore, but many retain a particular Russian flair for personifying animals, sending off the sons of Tsars on journeys, and explaining the climate through means of witchcraft and trickery.

Russian Shamanism is closely tied to its oral tradition and full of incantations, ritual songs, and epic poetry which explains human ability to interact with the natural world. In many of these oral stories, humans can talk to animals (horses in particular), trees (the oak is a favorite), or to the Earth itself (personified as feminine).

The following story was written by Edith M. S. Hodgett, a woman who grew up in Russia and emigrated to England in the mid-1800s. She wanted to capture the stories of her childhood, which she heard from her nurse and those she grew up around, and bring them to light as a published collection.

THE WITCH AND THE SISTER OF THE SUN

In a distant kingdom, near the World's End, lived a king and queen who had an only son, named Prince Nekita. When this prince had arrived at the age of fourteen, he went to "look up" a favourite groom of his. Now this groom had been in the habit of always telling Prince Nekita (when quite a child) some very pretty fairy tales, which the young prince had greatly enjoyed but since the prince had come into his "teens," he had had other things to do, and had not had time to listen to these stories; but on this particular day it so happened that he had a half holiday, and thought it would be rather a good idea to go and spend it in the stables.

Away he went, and this is what the groom had to say:-- "I have something far more important than a fairy tale to tell you today, Prince Nekita," said the groom gravely, "and am right glad that you have come to me, for you are in great danger. Listen-- the queen, your mother, will soon have a daughter, but by no means a good one; the child will grow into a dreadful old witch, and will kill your father and mother and all the grand people at court, and if you stay in the palace, she will kill you, too; so if you wish to save your life and become a great man, you must go to the king, your father, and tell him what you have just heard-- but you need not mention my name-- and ask him for a certain horse, which runs faster than any bird can fly; get upon this horse and go whithersoever your eyes take you. That is all I have to say, so go at once to the king and lose not a moment. Farewell!"

After that the wonderful groom disappeared and no one ever saw him again. Meanwhile Prince Nekita went to the king, his father, and told him everything, not forgetting to ask for the flying horse. The king was delighted at the idea of having a daughter, but could not believe that she could turn out to be a wicked old witch; he ordered the flying horse to be brought and given to the prince, wished his handsome young son luck, and left him to mount the splendid animal, but forgot to ask whither he intended going. The prince mounted his horse, bid all the courtiers and servants farewell, and away he flew.

Long, long, did he ride, until it suddenly struck him that he could not possibly go on riding for ever, besides he was hungry and sleepy. What was he to do? Suddenly he came upon a little hut, at the door of which sat two old women, busy embroidering. He stopped his horse and asked them whether they would let him stay with them for a day or two to rest but they shook their old heads, saying-- "Nay, prince, though we should be very glad indeed to let you stay with us and rest for awhile we cannot possibly ask you in, for we have unfortunately not very long to live. Death is already knocking at our door. But that you should not think us unkind, take this little box of needles and remember us. It may prove useful to you, for the needles are not of the common kind."

Source: *Tales and Legends from the Land of the Tzar: Collection of Russian Stories.* 2nd ed. Trans by Edith M. S. Hodgetts. 1891.

Prince Nekita took the little box, thanked the old women, and wept bitterly as he rode away, for besides feeling hungry and tired, he was very sorry for these two poor creatures. On rode the prince for a long time without meeting any one whom he could ask for something to eat, and without seeing any place where he could rest himself and his horse. At last he saw an old oak tree; he went up to it, and asked it to shelter him for a few days; but the tree shook its branches, and replied,-- "Nay Prince Nekita, I cannot shelter you, much as I should like to do so, for I have not long to live; death is knocking at my door!"

Prince Nekita again wept; it seemed to him that no one and nothing were to live very long. On he rode, till at length he came to the noble dwelling of the Sister of the Sun. He stopped before the golden palace, and knocked at the door. The Sun's sister ran out to him and welcomed him warmly. She took him into her palace and gave him most delicious things to eat and drink, so that Prince Nekita felt himself in the seventh heaven of bliss, and in no hurry to leave. In fact, when the beautiful Sister of the Sun asked him to stay in her palace and make it his home, he did not think twice about it, but gratefully accepted her kind invitation; and as the years rolled on, the Sister of the Sun loved him as dearly as if he had been her own child. She took great care of him, fed him, and clothed him in rich garments, and made a regular pet of the young prince.

But one day after the lapse of a great many years, the prince, who had now grown into a tall handsome man, with golden hair, and a long drooping moustache, wished very much to see how things were getting on in his father's kingdom, so he got on to his flying horse and flew to the top of a great mountain, where he could see everything that was going on at home. He looked, and behold! everybody had been eaten up; there was not a soul alive, all the houses, shops, and streets were one mass of ruin. Even the very palace, in which he had spent his childhood, was torn down with the exception of one wing in which dwelt his sister, the witch, by herself. He looked and wept, a thing which he had not indulged in for many a long year. He returned with a sad face and tearful eyes, to the Sister of the Sun, who felt very sorry and anxious about him, and wondered greatly what had happened.

"What is the matter?" she asked. "I don't like to see you look so sad."

"The wind was a little too much for my eyes, madam, that is all," he replied.

But the Sister of the Sun did not believe him, and as he continued going up the mountain every day, and returning with a tearful face, she wondered more and more what the reason could be; but she could get nothing out of him, all he answered was that the wind had been too much for his eyes. At last the Sister of the Sun could stand it no longer, she was determined to find out the cause and help him if she could. So she commanded what little wind there was to stop, and when the prince returned from his journey up the mountain with a tearful face, he did not know how to answer her inquiries, and was at last obliged to tell the truth. The Sister of the Sun was very sorry and tried to comfort him, but all in vain, he felt too wretched, and would do nothing but go to the mountain and weep for the loss of his friends and his country.

One day he came to the Sister of the Sun and told her that he intended to visit his father's kingdom and see what had been done to it. At first the Sister of the Sun would not hear of it, but on seeing that the prince looked greatly disappointed, she consented, and gave him a comb, two apples, and a blessing as parting gifts.

"Take this comb and these apples, for they are useful things to have; when you throw the comb on the ground an oak forest will spring up; as to the apples, if you give them to some very, very old people, they will instantly become young, and my blessing will keep you from harm. Good bye, dear prince, and come back to me soon."

Prince Nekita, after embracing her, rode off on his flying horse. He soon came to the old oak tree, and found it nearly dead, with the exception of a few branches; he felt sorry for the old tree, and remembering the comb he threw it down on the ground and up sprang a large and beautiful oak forest. The tree was delighted, it thanked the prince for his kindness, and promised to help him if it could. Away went the prince until he reached the hut where he had found the two old women, who were now lying on their death beds. He gave them each an apple, which they ate and became quite young and well again. They almost embraced the prince in their joy, and gave him a handkerchief which would turn into a large lake when thrown down on the ground. At last Prince Nekita arrived at his skeleton home, and the witch, his sister, came out to meet him, smiling and after kissing him most affectionately, led him into a chamber in the remaining wing of the palace.

"Sit down, dear brother," she said, "and amuse yourself just as much as you like, while I go and get the dinner ready; for I have no servants here, I hate to have them about me."

So saying, the witch disappeared, while Prince Nekita went to the window and looked out. How changed everything was, and how horrid all looked; the streets were covered with dead bodies, and human bones, skulls, and ruined houses lay all over the place in hopeless confusion. The poor prince shuddered, and turned his back on the window, when suddenly his eyes fell upon a harp standing in the corner of the room. He went up to it, threw off his cloak, and began playing a Russian air, when out came a little mouse from under the floor, and said in a human voice,--

"Save yourself, Prince Nekita, fly for your life! Your sister has just gone to sharpen her teeth, and unless you wish to be eaten up, you had better leave this wretched place."

Prince Nekita did not wait to be told a second time; he mounted his horse and flew, while the mouse taking the prince's place by the harp, played away at it, so that the witch might not know that the prince had left. After having sharpened her teeth the witch returned, but could see no one; even the mouse had run away into its little hole on hearing the witch approach, and was now running up and down there just as if nothing had happened. The witch was in a great rage, she howled and growled until she came to the conclusion that she had better go after her brother, so off she went in her mortar.

The prince, on hearing a noise behind him, looked round and saw the witch coming after him; on he rode faster and faster, and she came closer and closer to him. At last Prince Nekita, on seeing his danger, threw down the handkerchief, and there appeared a very large lake. While the witch was crossing this lake, the prince managed to get at a good distance off, and for some time did not see her, but after awhile he looked round and beheld her coming nearer and nearer. He was now not very far from the oak forest, which, when it saw that the prince was in danger, spread out its branches so thickly that the witch lost some time in biting her way through, while the prince neared the dwelling of the Sister of the Sun. But the witch after having got through the forest, began her pursuit once more.

"Ah!" she cried as she came close behind the prince, "I shall catch you, you have no means of saving yourself *now*."

But she was mistaken, for after flying on and on as fast as ever he could, Prince Nekita at last reached the dwelling of the Sister of the Sun; he rode in and the big golden gates were closed after him. Meanwhile, the witch began thinking what she had better do to get at him. She knocked at the gates, and the Sister of the Sun, in all her dazzling beauty, came out to her.

"Let me have a pair of scales, great Sister of the Sun," said the witch, "and see who is heavier, my brother or I; if I am heavier, I will eat him; if *he* is heavier, he can eat me, or do whatever he likes with me!"

The Sister of the Sun laughed at this, but, nevertheless she agreed to the proposal, for she knew what would happen. The prince jumped onto the scales first, but hardly had the witch put her foot upon the scales, when up went the prince high in the air, and would certainly have fallen had the Sun not caught him in his arms, and taken him to his glorious home in the sky, where, to the prince's delight, the Sister of the Sun soon joined them, leaving the witch to stamp about in a tremendous rage at not having been able to eat her brother; and I believe she is still alive, reigning near the World's End, unless some brave knight has been able to kill her.

DISCUSSION QUESTIONS

1. How does Prince Nekita's encounters help him along his journey?

2. How are the Witch and the Sister of the Sun two common tropes in fairy tales?

3. How does the prophecy of the groom set the story in motion? If Prince Nekita hadn't listened to it, would the Witch have reached her power?

How Thor Lost His Hammer (Norse)

The hammer, Mjölnir, was originally owned by Odin, who we met in "The Prose Edda" as the King of the Gods in Asgard. Odin passed down this object to his son, Odinson, or Thor, as he is more familiarly known. Sturluson tells us that the hammer is created by the dwarf brothers, Eitri and Brokkr. This story of Thor's lost hammer comes from the Elder Edda, or "The Poetic Edda," and is often a favorite for its use of cross-dressing and trickery.

HOW THOR LOST HIS HAMMER

"Come, Loki, are you ready? My goats are eager to be off!" cried Thor, as he sprang into his chariot, and away they went, thundering over the hills. All day long they journeyed, and at night they lay down to rest by the side of a brook.

When Baldur, the bright sun-god, awoke them in the morning, the first thing Thor did was to reach out for Mjolnir, his magic hammer, which he had carefully laid by his side the night before.

"Why, Loki!" cried he. "Alas, my hammer is gone! Those evil frost giants must have stolen it from me while I slept. How shall we hold Asgard against them without my hammer? They will surely take our stronghold!"

"We must go quickly and find it!" replied Loki. "Let us ask Freyja to lend us her falcon garment."

Now the goddess, Freyja, had a wonderful garment made of falcon feathers, and whoever wore it looked just like a bird. As you may suppose, this was sometimes a very useful thing. So Thor and Loki went quickly back to Asgard, and drove with all speed to Freyja's palace, where they found her sitting among her maidens.

"Asgard is in great danger!" said Thor, "and we have come to you, fair goddess, to ask if you will lend us your falcon garment, for my hammer has been carried off, and we must go in search of it."

Source: Foster, Mary H., and Mabel H. Cummings. "Asgard Stories: Tales from Norse Mythology," 1901.

"Surely," answered Freyja, "I would lend you my falcon cloak, even if it were made of gold and silver!"

Then Loki quickly dressed himself in Freyja's garment and flew away to the land of the frost giants, where he found their king making collars of gold for his dogs, and combing his horses.

As Loki came near, he looked up and said, "Ah, Loki, how fare the mighty gods in Asgard?"

"The Æsir are in great trouble," replied Loki, "and I am sent to fetch the hammer of Thor."

"And do you think I am going to be foolish enough to give it back to you, after I have had all the trouble of getting it into my power?" said the king. "I have buried it deep, deep, down in the earth, and there is only one way by which you can get it again. You must bring me the goddess Freyja to be my wife!"

Loki did not know what to say to this, for he felt sure that Freyja would never be willing to go away from Asgard to live among the fierce giants; but as he saw no chance of getting the hammer, he flew back to Asgard, to see what could be done.

Thor was anxiously looking out for him. "What news do you bring, Loki?" cried he. "Have you brought me my hammer again?"

"Alas, no!" said Loki. "I bring only a message from the giant king. He will not give up your hammer until you persuade Freyja to marry him!"

Then Thor and Loki went together to Freyja's palace, and the fair goddess greeted them kindly, but when she heard their errand, and found they wished her to marry the cruel giant, she was very angry, and said to Thor, "You should not have been so careless as to lose your hammer; it is all your own fault that it is gone, and I will never marry the giant to help you get it again."

Thor then went to tell Father Odin, who called a meeting of all the Æsir, for it was a very serious matter they were to consider. If the king of the giants only knew the power of the mighty hammer, he might storm Asgard, and carry off the fair Freyja to be his bride.

So the Æsir met together in their great judgment hall, in the palace of Gladsheim; long and anxiously they talked over their peril, trying to find some plan for saving Asgard from these enemies. At last Heimdall, the faithful watchman of the rainbow bridge, proposed a plan.

"Let us dress Thor," said he, "in Freyja's robes, braid his hair, and let him wear Freyja's wonderful necklace, and a bridal veil!"

"No, indeed!" cried Thor, angrily, "you would all laugh at me in a woman's dress; I will do no such thing! We must find some other way."

But when no other way could be found, at last Thor was persuaded to try Heimdall's plan, and the Æsir went to work to dress the mighty thunder-god like a bride. He was the tallest of them all, and, of course, he looked very queer to them in his woman's clothes, but he would be small enough beside a giant. Then they dressed Loki to look like the bride's waiting-maid, and the two set off for Utgard, the stronghold of the giants.

When the giant king saw them coming he bade his servants make ready the wedding feast, and invited all his giant subjects to come and celebrate his marriage with the lovely goddess Freyja. So the wedding party sat down to the feast, and Thor, who was always a good eater, ate one ox and eight salmon, and drank three casks of mead. The king watched him, greatly surprised to see a woman eat so much, and said:—

"Where hast thou seen such a hungry bride!"

But the watchful Loki, who stood near by, as the bride's waiting-maid, whispered in the king's ear, "Eight nights has Freyja fasted and would take no food, so anxious was she to be your bride!"

This pleased the giant, and he went toward Thor, saying he must kiss his fair bride. But when he lifted the bridal veil, such a gleam of light shot from Thor's eyes that the king started back, and asked why Freyja's eyes were so sharp.

Again Loki replied, "For eight nights the fair Freyja has not slept, so greatly did she long to reach here!"

This again pleased the king, and he said, "Now let the hammer be brought and given to the bride, for the hour has come for our marriage!"

All this time Thor was so eager to get his treasure back that he could hardly keep still, and if it had not been for what the wily Loki said, he might have been found out too soon. But at last the precious hammer was brought and handed to the bride, as was always the custom at weddings; as soon as Thor grasped it in his hand, he threw off his woman's robes and stood out before the astonished giants.

Then did the mighty Thunderer sweep down his foes, and many of the cruel frost giants were slain. Once more the sacred city of Asgard was saved from danger, for Thor was its defender, and he was careful never again to let his magic hammer be taken from him.

DISCUSSION QUESTIONS

1. How is Loki a Trickster figure in this story?

2. How would you characterize Freyja? What do the men see when they look at her?

3. Why does it matter that Thor lost his hammer?

Part 3: Journeys of Heroes and Heroines

© Miranda Carter

Sigurd the Volsung (Norse)

The "Viking Age" can be classified by the interaction of Scandinavians and Europeans (circa 800–1000 CE). The original meaning of the word "Viking" is uncertain. But we do know that European writers, mainly clergymen, used it to refer to pagan invaders. It is true that the Scandinavian sailors had impressive ships and conducted a variety of expeditions involving trading and settling as well as military might. Inevitably, pagan beliefs encountered Christianity and over time conversion occurred, in some cases to facilitate the trading process. Iceland was the slowest to embrace Christianity and the old tales persisted longer in this area. But as with the myths of many other areas, the stories were recorded by Christians.

The word "saga" in old Icelandic means both "history" and "narrative," as well as being related to the verb "to say" (Lindow 26). Mythic-heroic sagas recount the deeds of heroes, sometimes with gods and goddesses playing small parts in the tale, and generally involve great battles and sometimes the use of magic or magical objects.

The *Volsunga Saga* (or Saga of the Volsungs) is the most complete version of the heroic epic of Sigurd the Volsung, written in Icelandic, and dates to the thirteenth century CE; the author's identity is unknown. But the story existed in earlier versions and other languages; the oldest is believed to have been written between 700–750 CE. In fact, in the epic story of *Beowulf* a minstrel performs this legend.

Norse myths and legends grew from the punishing and brutal environment in which these people lived. In addition to harsh living conditions, faced with the inevitability of death and no comfort from the gods, leaving a legacy of great deeds was of utmost importance. For the warrior, death on the field of battle was accepted and was to be faced with courage; the bravest would be taken to Valhalla to await the final battle at Ragnarok—where even the gods would perish—but this was not believed to be the end of the world. To be remembered for one's actions was the only immortality—to earn honor in battle by enemies conquered and wealth acquired—and the sharing of one's wealth was highly regarded. Loyalty to the king was of prime importance, even before family or friends. Justice and retribution for wrongs was expected, and feuds between families were not uncommon. A *wergild* (man-price) could be offered as a kind of payment for the cause of an accidental death, but the recipient did not have to agree to the payment. Punishment for wrongdoing was to be expected and accepted.

This version of the tale is from *Stories From Northern Myths* by Emilie Kip Baker. It is a blending of the *Volsunga Saga* and a German rendering of the tale called *Nibelungenlied*. Portions of the tale have been condensed or adapted by the authors, as noted.

SIGURD THE VOLSUNG

Andvari's Hoard

Once Odin and Hœnir and Loki went on a visit to the earth, and in order to mingle freely with people without being recognized as gods, they laid aside all their divine powers and became, even in appearance, like ordinary men. When they had wandered about the earth many days, and talked with many people,— who never knew, of course, that the gods were among them,—they grew tired of the busy life of the world, and longed to find some place of quiet and rest. So they went far into the heart of the forest, and sat down beside a brook where many fish were leaping about and darting through the sparkling water. The gods lay idly upon the grass and watched them for a long time. Presently, they spied an otter sitting on the bank of the stream, lazily eating a fish which he had just caught. The gods looked on at the meal, and it made them remember that they too were hungry. Odin therefore proposed that they journey on in search of food, and to this the others readily consented; but as they rose to go, Loki suddenly took up a large stone, and, throwing it at the otter, killed him instantly. At this wanton cruelty Odin became angry, and rebuked Loki for his act[1]; but Loki only laughed, while he skinned the otter and cast its body back into the stream.

The gods then wandered on until almost nightfall before they came to any dwelling, and this was only a rude hut built on the side of a mountain. But they were too weary to look further, so they stopped to beg food and a lodging for the night. The old man[2] who lived in the hut bade them enter and share his simple fare, and in return he asked them to tell him of their adventures. Without revealing their identity, Odin told him of their wanderings among men, and of the strange things they had seen. Hœnir also related many stories; but his were of brave heroes who had wrought the mightiest deeds on bloody battlefields. When it came Loki's turn, they asked him to tell all he knew of the life lived by the bright dwellers in Asgard, but Loki laughed and threw upon the ground his otter's skin. When the old man saw this, he cried out:—

"O wicked, cruel man, you have killed my son. He was fishing to-day in the stream, and at this sport he always takes the form of an otter. Alas, this is indeed he, and you have slain him."

Then he raised a loud cry, and called for help to his two sons, Fafnir and Regin, who came running in from the woods nearby. As soon as they heard of the killing of their brother, they seized the three gods and bound them hand and foot, for, in becoming men, the gods had lost all their divine powers, and they had no choice but to yield.

When Odin begged the old man to ask whatever he would in payment for their ransom, both Fafnir and Regin demanded the life of one of the gods in return for their brother's. But their father spread the otter's skin upon the ground, and, turning to Odin, said,—

"You and your wicked companions shall be free when you have covered every hair of this hide with a piece of gold or a precious stone."

"We will do this," answered Odin; "but first you must set one of us free that he may go and procure the treasure. Let the other two stay bound as hostages until he returns."

Source: Baker, Emilie Kip. *Stories From Northern Myths*. The MacMillan Co., 1914.

To this the old man and his sons agreed, and Odin bade them unbind Loki, for he alone would know where to find such vast treasure as they needed. Accordingly Loki was freed, and promising his companions to return with their ransom, he hurried away. There was only one place where a hoard of gold and precious stones might be found, and thither Loki directed his steps. There were many mountains to climb and rivers to cross before he reached the place he sought, and night coming on made the journey more difficult and wearisome.

At last he spied upon a rocky mountainside the thing he had come so far to find, a small, deep cavern in the rocks. As Loki drew nearer, the moonlight revealed a little brook gushing from the mouth of the cavern and winding in and out among the rocks below. It was small, but beautifully clear, and the pebbles in its bed shone in the moonlight like diamonds. Just where it issued from the cave, the water flowed swiftly over a deep pool, and here it was so dark that only the sharp eyes of Loki could have caught the faint shimmer of a salmon which lay lurking in its depths.

Loki saw it, however, and his heart leaped for joy, for this salmon was no other than the cunning dwarf Andvari, the owner of a wonderful hoard of gold and gems. The treasure was buried somewhere near the cavern, and it was to gain this glittering hoard that Loki had come so far. So he now put forth all his skill to catch the wily salmon as it darted to and fro in the stream. The dwarf knew, however, who the fisherman was, and why he had come, and he had no intention of being caught and made to yield up his treasures. Loki spent many hours trying to lure the salmon into the shallows, but all his efforts were in vain. The crafty fish never moved from his deep, dark pool. Then Loki saw that further attempts would be useless unless he had help from someone with magic skill, so he determined to seek the aid of Queen Ran and her wonderful net.

Leaving the cave, he hurried down to the sea, and for many hours he walked along the shore, searching carefully among the rocks for the hiding place of the cruel ocean queen. Somewhere here, or upon the jagged reefs, he would be sure to find her spreading a net for her prey. But though he wandered for miles along the water's edge, he caught no glimpse of her anywhere; and, wearied and disheartened, he was about to give up his search, when he heard a low, rippling laugh just behind him, and turning he saw the beautiful daughters of the sea-king seated on the rocks combing their golden hair. Loki went over to them and begged them to tell him where he could find their mother, Queen Ran.

"Why do you seek her?" one of the maidens asked.

"Because I am a fisherman, and would like to ask her where the big fish are gathering now," replied Loki.

The sea-maidens laughed again and said:—

"O crafty, cunning Loki, do not think to deceive us who know well who you are, and why you have come hither. Play no tricks, then, and tell no lies to our mother, or you will not gain the object of your journey."

Loki promised, and begged the nymphs to tell him where to find Queen Ran, since no other than Odin himself needed her help.

"You must go about ten miles farther," answered one of the maidens, "until you come to a place where the rocks are high, and project in sharp, dangerous reefs far out into the sea. Here the waves dash with tremendous fury, and here is many a good ship wrecked and all her cargo lost. Look among the shadows of the rocks, and you will find our mother sitting there mending her net."

Loki thanked the nymphs and hurried on, for the night was growing black and the moon was completely hidden, and he had yet far to go. When he felt sure that ten miles lay between him and the daughters of the sea, he stopped and looked carefully about him. Near by was a group of tall, jagged rocks over which the waves dashed with great force; but there was one spot so protected that even the spray from the water did not reach it, and here Loki spied Queen Ran, long-fingered, greedy and cruel, mending her magic net. When she saw Loki, she tried to hide in the shadow of the rocks, for she knew him and feared he had come with some unfriendly message from Odin. But Loki called to her and said:—

"Be not afraid, O Queen, for I come as a petitioner to beg a great boon of thee;" and Ran replied, "What does Loki wish, that he leaves the shining halls of Asgard to travel over the earth to speak to the wife of Æger?"

"I have journeyed thus far," answered Loki, "because I have heard of your wonderful net. They say that it will catch whatever you wish, and that anything once caught cannot escape from its magic meshes. Therefore I have come to ask your help, for there is a certain salmon which I have long tried to snare, but which is too cunning to be caught by ordinary means. Lend me, I beg, your magic net."

"I cannot! I cannot!" cried Ran, "there is a ship sailing hither which will reach these rocks in the morning, and it is full of great treasure—jewels, and gold, and rich apparel. I have sent my mermaids to lure it to the reefs, where it will be dashed to pieces, and the prize be gathered into my net. No, I cannot lend it to you."

"But let me have it for just one hour," pleaded Loki, "and I will promise to return it in that time. I swear it on the word of a god."

The oath was reassuring, but still Ran hesitated to let the precious net leave her hands. At length, however, she was persuaded, and with many expressions of gratitude, Loki said good-bye and hastened back to the cave of Andvari, for the night was now far spent, and at daylight the salmon would be sure to leave his haunts.

When he reached the cavern, the fish was still lying idly in the water, but upon seeing the net in Loki's hand it darted like a flash down the stream. Then Loki quickly cast his net, and though the cunning fish swam with wonderful swiftness, it could not escape the magic net which began to close slowly and surely about it. As soon as Loki thought that his prize was secure, he drew the net on land, and, after slowly loosening the meshes, he at last grasped the struggling fish in his hand. Now, however, it was no longer a salmon fighting for its freedom, but the crafty dwarf Andvari. Any one less wise than Loki would have dropped him immediately in surprise at the transformation, but Loki only held on the tighter, and shook the poor dwarf until he cried for mercy.

"No mercy will I grant thee, thou master thief," exclaimed the god, "until thou hast revealed to me the hiding place of thy ill-gotten treasures. Show me where it lies, or I will dash thee to pieces upon these rocks."

Seeing that there was no hope of escape, Andvari promised to yield up his hoard, and pointing to a large rock nearby bade Loki raise it and look beneath. Without loosening his hold of the dwarf, Loki tried to lift the stone, but though it was far from being heavy or beyond his strength, he found that he could not move it. Then he knew that he was being tricked, and, grasping the dwarf still tighter, he shook him fiercely and commanded him to give his help. Andvari laid his finger on the stone and immediately it turned over and disclosed a large pit beneath.

It was quite dark now and the moon was completely hidden; yet even in the dim light Loki saw the sparkle of thousands of precious gems and the shimmer of many dazzling heaps of gold. It was truly a wonderful sight, and would have bewildered the ordinary finder of such wealth; but Loki had no time to spend in admiration. He gathered all the treasure together in the net, which, by its magic power, grew larger and larger as he continued to fill it.

The dwarf meanwhile stood by sullen and angry, watching the gold and gems being poured into the net. Had it been Odin who was robbing him of his hoard, he would have begged that some small portion of it might be left him, but he knew better than to make such a request of Loki. So when the last of the treasure had been gathered up, he turned away and was disappearing into the woods when Loki caught the glitter of something upon his finger, and seizing him roughly, cried out: "Ho, ho, my cunning elf. So you would keep back some of the gems, I see. Yield me that ring upon your finger, or you shall not have one moment more to live."

Andvari's face grew black with rage, and he refused to give up his ring, stamping his foot all the while upon the ground and cursing Loki for his avarice and greed. Yet he knew too well that his fury was in vain, and soon he changed his tone, begging Loki, humbly, to leave him his one poor gem. This appeal would have moved any other of the gods, but Loki was never known to do a generous thing in all his life. He only gave a mocking, hateful laugh, and, seizing the dwarf, tore the ring from his finger.

It was a wonderful ring, shaped like a serpent, coiled, with its tail in its mouth. It had two blood-red rubies for eyes, and in the dim light they seemed to Loki to glow with all the cunning and cruelty of a living serpent. But this did not deter him from slipping the ring on his finger, and laughing triumphantly at the dwarf, who was now foaming with helpless rage. Then Andvari cursed the ring and said: "May this ring be your bane, and the bane of all who shall possess it. May it bring sorrow and evil upon him who shall wear it, and from this day be the source of envy and hatred and bloodshed."

To these dreadful words Loki paid no heed, and, throwing his precious burden upon his shoulder, he hurried down the mountain side and sped swiftly on to the old man's cottage. Odin and Hœnir were still bound, and they had almost given up hope of Loki's return. But they forgot the tediousness of their captivity when they saw the great heap of gold and gems which Loki poured out of the net; for here was surely more than enough to cover ten otters' skins, and the remainder of the treasure would be their own.

Fafnir and Regin stretched the skin upon the ground, and bade Loki cover every hair. This seemed at first an easy thing to do; but the more gold and precious stones that Loki spread upon it, the larger the skin seemed to grow, until it covered the entire floor of the hut; and though Loki still added handfuls of gold, the brothers always found some spot uncovered. At last every hair of the hide was completely hidden beneath some coin or gem, and the gods demanded their release. The old man unloosed the cords which bound them and was bidding them depart, when Regin uttered a loud cry and declared that there was one hair yet uncovered upon the otter's head.

Odin and Hœnir looked at each other in dismay, for the net was now empty, and there was no way to procure further treasure. Meanwhile, the old man and his sons were clamouring loudly for the gods to fulfil their promise. The case seemed indeed desperate; until Loki drew from his finger the serpent ring of Andvari, and laid it upon the hair. The brothers being now satisfied, the gods left the hut with all speed. Odin and Hœnir returned at once to Asgard, while Loki took back the net to Queen Ran, who was anxiously waiting, and reached her just as the dawn was breaking.

The treasure soon became, according to Andvari's words, a source of hatred and bloodshed; for the old man, wishing to keep the wealth for himself, drove his sons from the house, and shut himself up with his treasure. All day long he sat poring greedily over the heap of glittering gems, and running his fingers through the shining gold. Above all, he loved to watch the serpent ring, with its glowing ruby eyes.

Then one night Fafnir came suddenly upon him, demanding his share of the gold; and when the old man refused to yield up even one stone, Fafnir slew him in his anger, and took possession of all the treasure. Soon he grew fearful that his brother might steal upon him sometime and rob, or perchance kill him; so he changed himself into a monstrous dragon which breathed forth fire and spat deadly poison. Thus secured, he coiled himself about the hoard, and no one dared to approach him. Regin meanwhile fled to a neighbouring city, and became the king's master-smith, the maker of strong swords.

The Story of Siegmund

The king whose protection Regin sought was named Alf, and when he learned of the great skill that belonged to this stranger in his realm, he gave Regin a place of honour among the sword-makers, and soon promoted him to be master-smith. Before many years passed the fame of Regin's smithy had spread far and wide; for here men gathered not only to learn the master's craft, but to share in that wisdom which he seemed to have gathered from all the ages. Even the noted wise men of the kingdom came to him, wondering at his great knowledge; and the king sought his counsel in all the difficult affairs of state.

At the court of King Alf lived his foster-son Sigurd,[3] who was much beloved by the king, although he was not of his own blood. The youth was tall and strong, of fearless bearing, and with so keen an eye that men often quailed before his glance. His hair was golden red, and fell down in long locks over his shoulders; and his body was of a strength that matched the beauty of his face. Men said of him that "never did he lose heart, and of naught was he afraid." When Sigurd grew to manhood, King Alf sent him to Regin's smithy that he might not only profit by the wisdom of this wisest of teachers, but also be taught to fashion a sword that could be worthily borne by one of his name and race, for Sigurd was the last of the Volsungs—a race of warriors whose fame was still fresh in the minds of men.

At first Sigurd did not like to wear the woollen coat and rough leather apron of a smith, for he was a prince's son and he thought the work menial; but he soon learned to respect his great teacher so much that the place took on a new dignity in his eyes and he no longer chafed at the hard work or the simple fare he shared with Regin. Early in the morning the sound of Sigurd's hammer could be heard as he worked blithely at his trade, and he almost forgot that he had ever known any other life than this one by Regin's side. When the long day was over and he sat with his master by the glowing light of the forge, Regin would tell him wonderful tales of gods and heroes and especially of the warrior race from which Sigurd sprang. Many times they sat until the last bit of fire in the forge sank into lifeless embers, and still the youth listened eagerly to the stories of brave deeds wrought by the long-dead Volsungs. The story which he never tired of hearing was that of his own birth, and in this wise did Regin always begin the tale:—

There was once a mighty king named Volsung,[4] who built a lordly palace such as men never saw before nor will ever see again; for its walls glistened with thousands of shields taken from his enemies in battle, and in the centre of the palace was a large courtyard in which grew a wonderful tree. This tree was so high that it towered above the castle walls, and its branches grew so thick that they spread like a roof over the whole palace. The king called this tree Branstock, and about its mighty trunk the Volsungs gathered to feast and sing songs in praise of their king and their race.

[Here, in abridged form, are the tales Regin told to Sigurd regarding the vengeance of the Volsungs and the magic sword.]

The King had ten sons, each strong and brave, and one daughter, Signy, who was so beautiful that suitors flocked from all over the world to meet her. One of these suitors, Siggeir, who rules the Goths, offered her many costly gifts, but she did not trust him. However, her father was impressed by his wealth and encouraged Signy to marry him. At last she did, but she did not love him.

At the wedding feast an old, one-eyed man appeared, with a long white beard, clad in a blue cloak. He drew a sword and thrust it up to the hilt into the trunk of the great tree. He said, "Whoso draweth this sword from the tree shall have it as a gift from me; and he shall find that he never bore in his hand a better sword than this." So saying, the old man went forth from the hall, and none knew who he was nor whither he went; but some whispered that it was Odin himself who had been among them.

The guests each tried but no one could draw the sword—not even the king himself. After some urging by his warriors, the king summoned the young Siegmund[5] to try. To everyone's astonishment, he drew the sword. Everyone rejoiced, except King Siggeir, who vowed hatred for Siegmund. Siggeir even tried to buy the sword from him, but Siegmund replied: "You might have had the sword if it were Odin's will that you should bear it. But now it shall stay mine, though you offered me all the gold you have." And so King Siggeir was angered and secretly vowed revenge on Siegmund and all the Volsungs.

After the wedding, as Signy departed with King Siggeir, he invited King Volsung and his ten sons to visit them in Gothland. Signy begged her father to not allow her to go—she dreaded the marriage and felt no good would come of it. But King Volsung answered: "Speak not so, my daughter; and go with thy husband, for it will bring great shame to us if we fail to trust him without reason. Moreover, he will pay us back most evilly if we break faith with him for no cause." And so the couple sailed away.

The time eventually came for the visit and the Volsungs arrived with a company of men. Signy came secretly to her family, begging them to return home because Siggeir had vowed to kill them all. But the king of the Volsungs would not run from a fight, and had no fear. However, when they arrived at the palace, each carried a sword under his cloak, just in case.

Upon their arrival, King Siggeir met them with his army and the Volsungs, though they fought valiantly, were greatly outnumbered. All the men of the Volsungs were slain, including the king; however, his ten sons were alive, yet wounded, and led in chains to Siggeir.

Signy begged for the lives of her brothers, but Siggeir laughed at her and ordered them to be killed before her eyes. But first he took the coveted sword from Siegmund, stating that he should die by this blade. Again, Signy begged, asking that Siggeir give them but a few more days to live, then she would give up. To prove her sincerity, she asked that they be chained to a fallen oak in the forest. This way they would be out of Siggeir's sight and she could visit them. Siggeir agreed, mainly because the men were wounded and he wanted to prolong their pain. A watch was put on Signy.

At midnight a she-wolf[6] in the forest ate one of her brothers. When Signy found out, she begged for Siggeir to put them in a prison. But he only laughed at her and left them in the woods. Each night at midnight the she-wolf returned and ate one of the brothers until only Siegmund remained. Signy asked a servant whom she trusted to take honey to her brother and smear it on his face and hands. That night, the wolf licked the honey, but did not eat Siegmund.

Some of the honey dripped onto Siegmund's mouth and when the she-wolf licked him, he bit down on her tongue. She pulled away so hard that the chain that bound Siegmund snapped, and he was free. He strangled the wolf with his bare hands, and fled.

King Siggeir thought all the Volsungs were now dead, but Signy believed Siegmund had escaped. Her trusted servant eventually told her that Siegmund was alive and needed her help, so she sent food to him and vowed to always take care of him. He built himself a secret underground dwelling in the forest, living as a wild-man. Since the king believed all the Volsungs were dead, he allowed Signy some freedom, and she visited Siegmund at night. They wanted to avenge their family, but didn't know how they could succeed against the king's army.

The Vengeance of the Volsungs

Many years passed and King Siggeir and Signy had two sons; Signy hoped one of them might have the Volsung spirit. When the eldest son was ten, Signy sent him to the forest to meet Siegmund and possibly be trained. Siegmund welcomed the boy and they prepared to share a meal; but something was moving in the flour sack, and the boy feared to reach in for flour to make the bread. Therefore, Siegmund believed the lad too faint-hearted and unworthy to aid their vengeance. The next year the second son was sent, but the result was the same. But then, a third son was born who had a face like that of Siegmund. When he was old enough, she tested him by sewing a shirt to his skin—he laughed, tearing it off, saying "How little would a Volsung care for such a smart as that!" Then Signy knew she could send this boy to her brother.

When the boy, named Sinfiotli, came to Siegmund's hut, he was told to knead the meal for the baking, just as his brothers had been. Then he was left alone, and when Siegmund returned from gathering firewood, the bread was ready baked and lying on the hearth. When asked if he had seen anything move in the meal, the lad replied, "Yes, I felt there was something alive in the sack, but whatever it was I have kneaded it all together with the meal."

Then Siegmund laughed and said:—

"Naught wilt thou eat of bread this night, for thou hast kneaded up the most deadly of serpents. Though I may eat of any poison and live, there is no venom which thou mayst take and remain alive."

Sinfiotli remained with Siegmund and was trained as a warrior of the Volsungs. On one of their excursions they came across two men asleep in a cottage; their wrists and ankles adorned with golden rings and wolfskins over their heads. Siegmund knew by these signs that they were werewolves and this was the tenth night—a time when they could regain human form. Siegmund and Sinfiotli put on the wolf skins, becoming enchanted. They ran howling through the forest, each on their own but agreeing to help each other if necessary. Siegmund was attacked by a band of men but Sinfiotli heard his howl and together they killed the men. Once again they went their own ways. Yet it wasn't long before Sinfiotili was attacked by eleven hunters; he fought them off alone, killing them all. As he rested under an oak tree, Siegmund found him and asked why he did not howl for help. Sinfiotili answered, "I was loath to call on you for the killing of only eleven men."

Suddenly, in wolfish anger, Siegmund sprang upon Sinfiotli, biting his throat. But the instant he saw his friend lying dead, he was filled with sorrow and bore his body back to the earth-dwelling. The next day Siegmund saw to weasels fighting and one killed the other. But the attacker returned with a leaf in his mouth and, laying the leaf on the wound, the weasel recovered. Just then a raven flew overhead with the same leaf, dropping it at the werewolf's feet. Siegmund placed the leaf on Sinfiotli's wound, and his life was restored. When their enchantment ended, they burned the wolf skins to prevent anyone else from using them.

Once Sinfiotli reached manhood, Siegmund felt it was time for the long-awaited vengeance. They came one evening to King Siggeir's palace, hiding themselves among casks of ale in the hall. Signy was aware of their arrival and found them as the King sat drinking; they plotted how to slay the king.

But that night two of Signy's children were playing and their ball rolled among the casks where Siegmund and Sinfiotli were hiding. The children spotted them and ran screaming to their father. As the fearful king pondered what to do, Signy led the children to the hall and said to her brother, "See, these two have betrayed you. Kill them, therefore." But Siegmund answered, "Never will I slay thy children for telling where I lay hid." But no sooner had he spoken than Sinfioltil drew his sword and killed them, taking the bodies and casting them at the king's feet. Enraged, the king ordered his men to seize the strangers and bind them.

Siegmund and Sinfiotli fought bravely, but they were outnumbered and thrown into the dungeon while the king pondered how to kill them. In the morning, the king ordered a great pit to be dug and with a tall, flat stone placed in the middle to serve as a wall. Siegmund was placed on one side and Sinfiotli on the other. He ordered his men to cover the pit with turf, burying the prisoners alive. But Signy threw a bundle of straw to Sinfiotli, commanding the servants to silence.

Later that night, Sinfiotli unwrapped the bundle to make a bed—he found within a swine's flesh to eat and, as he tore apart the meat, he found his sword hidden inside. He drove the sword into the rock, creating a gap to Siegmund on the other side. They worked together to cut the great stone in half. By dawn, they had worked so vigorously that the sword glowed red, yet it remained sharp. Eventually they cut through the turf and stones over the pit and were free.

All were still asleep in the palace, so they crept into the hall with armfuls of wood. They piled the wood around the sleepers and, kindled a fire using dry leaves. The smoke awakened the inhabitants and the king heard the screams. He shouted, "Who has kindled this fire in which I burn?"

And Siegmund answered him from without the hall, "It is I, Siegmund the Volsung, with Sinfiotli, my sister's son; and now thou mayst know at last that all of my race are not dead." Then he barred the palace doors, imprisoning everyone. He begged Signy to come out but she stood by the king and said,

"I have kept well in memory the slaying of the Volsungs, and that it was King Siggeir who wrought the shameful deed. I sent two of my sons into the forest to learn how to avenge the wrong, and then came unto thee Sinfiotli who is a Volsung and none of King Siggeir's race. I also bade thee kill my young children, since their words had betrayed thee. For this and naught else have I wrought all these years that Siggeir might get his bane at last. Now vengeance has fallen upon him, but let the end come also to me, for merrily will I die with King Siggeir, though I was not merry to wed with him."

And so Signy died in the fire with her husband. Siegmund then gathered a company of folk and filled ships with the king's treasures and they set sail for home. Upon arrival, however, they found that a neighboring king had usurped the throne. Siegmund drove him from the country and took the throne of his father, where he ruled for many years. He and Sinfiotli waged war with other kings, and their fame spread abroad throughout the land. None could equal them in strength and valour, and of all the Volsungs King Siegmund bade fair to be greatest in renown.

As Regin spoke these last words, he turned to the youth at his side and smiled when he saw the glow of pride that shone in Sigurd's face as the master spoke of the brave deeds of the Volsungs.

"Shall I tell you the rest of the tale, and of how the sword of Odin failed your father in his need?" he asked, knowing well the answer Sigurd would make. Then the youth laid new coals on the fire; and the master resumed the oft-told tale.

The Magic Sword

Siegmund became a mighty king, known as a giver of rich gifts, and Sinfiotli sat in a seat of honor at his side. Now Sinfiotli loved a fair woman who was also wooed by the brother of Borghild, Siegmund's queen. They fought, and Sinfiotli killed the queen's brother, taking the maiden for his wife. Borghild demanded that Sinfiotli be banished for his deed, but Sigemund said the fight was fair; he offered her great treasure as payment for her brother's life. This did not appease her. But she pretended forgiveness, asking Siegmund and Sinfiotli to attend her brother's funeral feast.

Borghild brought drink to each guest at the feast. When she came to Sinfiotli bearing the great horn, she said, "Drink now, fair stepson." But when the youth looked into the horn he answered, "Nay, I will not, for the drink is charmed." Then the queen laughed and handed the horn to Siegmund, who drank the ale to the last drop, for no poison nor charmed drink could work him any harm. Two more times Borghild came to Sinfiotli with the horn and each time he refused. And each time Siegmund drank. But by this time Siegmund had become so intoxicated that he forgot the queen's hatred for her brother's slayer. He said to Sinfiotli, "Drink and fear naught."

So Sinfiotli drank, and straightway fell down dead. Upon seeing this Siegmund's senses returned and he regretted his words. He took Sinfiotli's body through the woods until he reached the seashore. There he found a little boat with an old man seated at the oars. The man wore a dark blue cloak, and his hat was drawn down over his face; but in his sorry Siegmund saw none of this. The old man asked if they would be ferried to the other side of the bay, and Siegmund came with his burden to the water's edge. The little boat could not hold them all, so Siegmund laid the body of Sinfiotli beside the ferryman. But as soon as it was placed within, both the boat and the old man vanished, and Siegmund found himself alone. Yet his heart was full of gladness, for he knew that it was Odin himself who had come to take another Volsung to join the heroes in Valhalla. Then Siegmund returned to his own hall, and so hateful did the queen become in his eyes that he could bear the sight of her no longer and drove her forth from the palace. Soon after, word was brought to him that Borghild was dead.

Now in a neighbouring country lived a wealthy king with a daughter named Hiordis—the fairest and wisest among women. Siegmund, though he was well on in years, desired to wed her. He chose his best warriors to accompany him and he set forth, bearing great gifts. He was welcomed at the palace, but there was another king seeking the maiden's hand. Hiordis's father feared that the rejected suitor would cause trouble so he said to his daughter, "You are a wise woman, and I will let this matter rest in your hands. Choose a husband for yourself, and I will abide by your choice though my whole kingdom be plunged into warfare." Then Hiordis answered, "Though King Lyngi is far younger than Siegmund, yet I will choose Siegmund for my husband, for his fame as a warrior is greater and we can rely upon his strength." So Hiordis wedded Siegmund the Volsung and the feasting lasted many days. After the Volsungs returned home, they received word, as Siegmund expected, that King Lyngi, with a host of followers, demanded the Volsungs meet him in battle.

Siegmund and his men fought valiantly against the enemy horde, even though they were outnumbered. No helmet or shield could withstand his sword; his arms were red up to the shoulders with blood. Now after the battle had raged a long while, a strange man suddenly appeared amidst the fight. He wore a blue cloak and slouched hat pulled down to conceal his face and the fact he only had one eye. He advanced upon Siegmund, shield held aloft, and the battle-weary Siegmund, not knowing the stranger, struck the shield with all his strength. The magic sword, which had never failed him, broke in half. As the pieces fell, the stranger disappeared, but Siegmund knew who had stood before him and he lost his heart for the fight. His men fell around him, and even though Siegmund still fought, he knew the battle was lost. At last, Siegmund was mortally wounded. His men saw him fall, and died fighting half-heartedly around him.

Hiordis had left the palace with her handmaid, hiding in the forest. They brought as much treasure with them as they could carry, to keep it from King Lyngi. When most of the Volsungs were defeated, King Lyngi entered the palace to take possession of Siegmund's wealth and his queen. But he found most of the treasure chests empty and no one knew the whereabouts of the queen. King Lyngi contented himself with what riches he found and that night he and his followers celebrated their victory.

During the revelry, Hiordis crept from her hiding-place and sought for Siegmund among the dead on the gruesome battle-field. At last she found him, but could not staunch the blood of his wounds. He said, "I will not suffer myself to be healed, since Odin wills that I should never draw sword again." Then the queen wept softly and answered, "If thou diest, who will then avenge us?" And Siegmund said: "Fear not that the last of the Volsungs has stood to do mighty deeds, for a son will be born to thee and me who shall be greater than all those who have been before him. Cherish carefully the pieces of Odin's sword which lie here beside me, for of these shall a goodly sword be made, and our son shall bear it, and with it he shall work many a great work so that his name shall be honoured as long as the world endures. Go now, for I grow weary with my wounds and would fain follow my kinsmen. Soon I shall be with all the Volsungs who have gone before me."

So Hiordis the queen kept silent, but stayed beside Siegmund until the dawn; and when she knew he was dead, she carried pieces of the broken sword into the forest. Then she said to her handmaid: "Let us now change raiment, and do thou henceforth be called by my name and say that thou art the king's daughter. Look over there to the sea, where some ships are now sailing toward our shores. Neither to

King Lyngi nor to the strangers that are approaching would I be known as Siegmund's queen." Then the women watched the ships as they neared the land.

The newcomers were not of King Lyngi's following, but were Vikings who had put into that coast on account of the high seas; and when they made a landing they came up over the shore and looked with wonder at the battle-field and the great number of the dead. The leader of the Vikings was Alf, the son of Hjalprek, king of Denmark, and as he gazed across the battle-field he saw the two women watching him, so he sent his men to bring them to him. When Hiordis and her handmaid stood before Alf, he asked them why they were standing thus alone, and why so many men lay dead upon the field. Then Hiordis, remembering the lowly position she had assumed, kept silent, but the handmaid spoke to him as befitted a king's daughter, and told him of the fall of Siegmund and the death of the Volsungs at the hand of King Lyngi and his hosts.

When Alf learned that the woman to whom he was speaking was of the royal household, he asked if she knew where the Volsungs' treasure was hid; and the bondmaid answered that she had the greater part of it with her in the forest. So she led him to the spot where the gold and silver lay; and such a wonder of wealth was there that the men thought they had never seen so many priceless things heaped together in one place. All this treasure the Vikings carried to their ships; and when they set sail it was with the wealth of Siegmund on board as well as Queen Hiordis and her handmaid. During the voyage Alf spoke frequently with Hiordis and her maiden, but often he sat by the bondwoman's side, believing her to be the king's daughter.

Upon returning home the Vikings were met by the queen mother, who listened gladly to their tale and welcomed the strangers. But after a few days, she asked King Alf why the fairer of the two women had fewer rings and meaner attire than her companion. "For," she said, "I deem the one whom you have held of least account to be the nobler born." And Alf answered: "I, too, have doubted that she is really a bondmaid; for though she spoke but little when I first greeted her, she bore herself proudly like a king's daughter. But now let us make a trial of the two." So when the men were feasting that night, Alf left his companions and came and sat down by the women. Turning to the handmaiden, he said, "How do you know what is the hour for rising in winter when there are no lights in the heavens?" And the bondwoman answered, "In my youth I was wont to get up at dawn to begin my tasks, and now I waken as soon as the day breaks."

"Ill manners for a king's daughter," laughed Alf, and, turning to Hiordis, he asked her the same question.

The queen then unhesitatingly replied: "My father once gave me a little gold ring, and this always grows cold on my finger as the day dawns. Thus I know it is soon time to rise."

At these words King Alf sprang up, crying: "Gold rings are not given to bondmaids. Thou art the king's daughter."

Then Hiordis the queen, seeing that she could deceive Alf no longer, told him the truth. And when he knew she was the wife of Siegmund he decreed that she should be held in great honour. Not long after this the son of Hiordis and Siegmund was born, and great rejoicing was made throughout the kingdom, for when the child was but a few days old, King Alf wedded Hiordis, whom he had found the worthiest of women. The boy was much beloved by his stepfather, and no one who looked upon him desired any other to succeed King Alf upon the throne, for the child was beautiful to see, brave and bold-looking, even as an infant. His eyes had already the keenness of a falcon, and so straight and strong he grew that the heart of King Alf was filled with joy.

[The abridged version of the story ends here.]

When Regin reached this part of his story, he turned to Sigurd and laid his hand on the youth's shoulder, saying: "The gods have placed you among a kindly people, and given you a foster-father that has ever sought to train you in wisdom and in strength. But you are not of this people, and your place is not among them. Great deeds are in store for you, and you are to be worthy of your race. All that I could teach you, you have learned. Go forth, therefore, and by your own hand win fame that shall add to the glory of the Volsungs. Tomorrow you shall fashion a sword for your use, and it shall be mightier than any that has come from our hands. But let us drop the tale now and sleep, for it is almost daylight, and only a spark glimmers in the forge."

The next day Sigurd made ready the fire, but before he laid the steel in it he asked Regin what had become of the pieces of Odin's famous sword. "No one knows where they are hidden,"[7] answered the master, "for on the death of your mother Hiordis, the secret was lost, and no man can tell where the place of their hiding may be." So Regin selected the very finest steel for Sigurd's sword, and the youth set to work eagerly, for Regin's story had filled him with a burning desire to go out into distant lands and do great deeds worthy of his name and race. For seven days and nights he never left his forge, but stood tempering and testing his steel, and throwing aside every piece that did not seem perfect. At last a blade was finished that promised to be worthy of a Volsung. Regin praised it highly and said he had never felt a finer edge. But Sigurd only said, "Let us prove it." So he took the sword and smote with all his strength upon the anvil. The blade shivered into a dozen pieces.

Nothing disheartened, Sigurd set to work again, and spent many days and nights at his forge, often forgetting to eat or sleep in his eagerness to finish his task. When at last the steel had been finely tempered and seemed of perfect workmanship, he called to Regin and bade him try its strength. "Nay, let us not dull the edge," replied the master; "there is no need to put it to the test, for I can see that it is true and strong." But Sigurd took the sword and smote again upon the anvil; this time the blade was blunted, though it did not break in pieces. Then Regin besought him to try no longer, but the youth, grim and determined, returned to the forge and made ready his tools for another effort.

That night he paused many times in his work, and often felt so discouraged that he was tempted to give up the task; but each time he became ashamed of his weakness, and bravely set to work again. Once when he sat down by the fire to rest, he was conscious of some one's being in the room, but thinking it was Regin who had come to inspect his work, he did not look up to see. At length, however, the silence grew uncomfortable, and Sigurd turned around. Close beside him was standing a tall man wrapped in a dark blue mantle. His beard and hair were very long and very white, and by the dim light of the fire Sigurd noticed that he had only one eye. His face was kindly, and his whole presence had an air both gentle and reassuring, yet something about him filled the youth with a strange awe. He waited for the stranger to speak, but no word came, and Sigurd began to tremble with nervous fear. At this the old man smiled, and handed him the pieces of a broken sword. Sigurd took them in wonder, but before he could frame a question he found himself suddenly alone; the stranger had disappeared.

The next morning Sigurd hastened to Regin and told him of his strange visitor. Regin thought at first that the lad had been dreaming, but when he saw the pieces of broken sword, he cried out joyfully:

"Fortune now be with you, Sigurd; for it was no other than Odin who visited you, and these pieces are of the famous sword which in former days the ruler of the gods gave to your father. There is no fear for your future now, since Odin has chosen to watch over your welfare; and by his decree you will stand or fall."

Grasping the pieces of Odin's sword firmly in his hand, Sigurd welded them together into a mighty weapon, the strongest that had ever come from the hand of man. And he called the sword Gram.[8] Then he bade Regin test the mettle of the new blade, and when the master looked upon it, it seemed as though a fire burned along the edges of the sword. Now Sigurd grasped the weapon in his two hands and smote with all his strength upon the anvil, but no pieces of steel fell shattered at his feet, for the sword had cut the anvil in two as easily as if it had been a feather. So Sigurd was satisfied.

The Slaying of Fafnir[9]

One day Regin said to Sigurd, "You have forged for yourself the famous sword Gram as your father Siegmund foretold. Now it remains for you to fulfil the rest of the prophecy and win fame that will add glory to the name of the Volsungs. Of my celebrated wisdom you have already learned all there is of worth, and there are no ties to hold you to this people; but before you leave the land which has nourished you, there is one more task which I would fain lay upon you—the slaying of the dragon which guards a wonderful treasure."

"How can I start out upon adventures with nothing but a sword, even though that sword be Odin's gift?" asked Sigurd. "I have no horse, and I should make a sorry appearance if I went on foot."

"Go out into yonder meadow," said Regin, "and there you will find the best steeds that King Alf has gathered either by purchase or as the spoil of battle. Choose yourself one from among them; they are all of noble race."

Sigurd went over to the meadow where the stately horses were grazing, and saw that each one of them was truly fine enough to be the charger of a king's son. Indeed, they all seemed to him so desirable that there was none which he would prefer above another. While he was hesitating, he heard a voice at his side ask, "Would you choose a steed, Sir Sigurd?"

Sigurd turned quickly around, for he had not heard any one approaching, and his heart beat fast when he saw beside him a tall form wrapped in a blue mantle. He dared not look closer, and he trembled now with both fear and joy, for the form and voice were strangely familiar. Then falteringly he answered:—

"I would indeed choose, but all the horses seem to me to be of equal beauty and strength."

The stranger shook his head and said: "There is one horse here which far surpasses all the rest, for he came from Odin's pastures on the sunny slopes of Asgard. He it is you must choose."

"Gladly would I do so," replied Sigurd, "but I am too ignorant to know which he is."

"Drive all the horses into the river," said the old man, "and I think you will then find the choice easy."

So Sigurd drove them out of the meadow, and down a steep bank into the stream below. They all plunged in boldly, but soon began to struggle frantically against the current which was bearing them rapidly down the river upon a bank of rocks below. Some of the horses turned back when they felt the force of the water; some fought helplessly against it and were carried down toward the rocks; but one swam to the other side and sprang up on the green bank. Here he stopped a moment to graze, then he plunged again into the stream, and, breasting the current with apparent ease, he swam to the shore and stood at Sigurd's side.

The youth stroked the stately head and looked into the large, beautiful eyes. Then turning to the stranger he said, "This is he."

"Yes," replied the old man, "this is he, and a better steed did man never have. His name is Greyfel,[10] and he is yours as a gift from Odin."

So saying, the strange visitor disappeared, and Sigurd returned to his forge full of joy and pride, for he knew that no other than the Father of the Gods himself had come to direct his choice.

When Regin heard of this second visit of Odin's he said to Sigurd: "You are truly blest and favoured of the gods, and it may be that you are the one chosen to perform the task of which I have already spoken to you. I have cherished the hope for many years that in you I might find one brave enough to face the dragon, and restore the treasure to its rightful owner." Then he told Sigurd of Andvari's hoard, and of how it came to be guarded by the dragon Fafnir. "This monster," he continued, "does not rest satisfied with the possession of his treasure, but must needs live upon the flesh of men; and he has thus become the terror of all the country round. Many brave men have sought to slay him for the sake of the gold, but they have only miserably perished; for the dragon breathes out fire which will consume ten men at a breath; and he spits forth poison so deadly that one drop of it can kill. He is, as I have told you, my brother, but nevertheless I bid you slay him."

"I will go," cried Sigurd, eagerly; "for though the monster be all that you have said, with Greyfel and my sword Gram I fear neither man nor beast."

The following day Sigurd bade farewell to King Alf and started on his journey, taking Regin with him, since the latter knew the road so well and could guide him to the dragon's cave. They travelled for many days and nights, and at last came to a narrow river whose current was so fierce that no boat, Regin said, was ever known to brave its waters. But neither Sigurd nor Greyfel felt a touch of fear, and the noble horse carried both riders safely to the opposite bank. Here they found themselves at the foot of a tall mountain, which seemed to rise straight up like a wall from the river's edge. It was apparently of solid rock, for no tree or shrub or blade of grass grew upon its steep side. There were no sounds of birds in the air, no sign of any living thing inhabiting this dreary place; nothing to see but the rushing river over which the mountain cast its gloomy shadow. It was enough to dishearten the stoutest hero, but Sigurd refused to turn back, though Regin, now trembling and fearful, besought him to give up the adventure.

They went on some distance farther along the river bank, to a place where the mountain appeared less rocky and forbidding. There were patches of earth to be seen here and there, and occasionally a straggling tree sought to strike its roots into the unfriendly soil. Pointing up through the trees, Regin said:—

"Look close and you will see what seems to be a path worn in the earth. It reaches from the mountain top down to the water's edge, and it is the trail of the dragon. Over this he will come to-morrow at sunrise, but think not to encounter him face to face, for you could not do it and live. You must depend upon stratagem if you would hope to slay him. Dig, therefore, a series of pits and cover them with boughs, so that the dragon, as he rushes down the mountain side, may fall into one of them and not get out until you have slain him. As for me, I will go some distance below, where the view of Fafnir's cave is plainer, and I can warn you of his approach." So saying, he went away, and Sigurd remained alone, wondering at Regin's cowardice, but content to face the danger with only the help of Gram.

It was now night, and the place became full of unknown terrors. Even the stars and the moon were hidden by thick clouds, and Sigurd could hardly see to dig his pits. Every time he struck the earth, the blow brought a deep echo from the mountain, and now and then he heard the dismal hoot of an owl. There was no other sound save the noise of the swiftly running river, and his own heavy breathing as he worked away at his task.

Suddenly he was aware that someone was standing beside him, and when he turned to look, his heart beat fast with joy, for even in the darkness he fancied he saw the blueness of the stranger's coat, and his long, white beard beneath the hood.

"What are you doing in this dismal country, Sir Sigurd?" asked the old man.

"I have come to slay Fafnir," replied the youth.

"Have you no fear, then?" continued the stranger, "or no love for your life that you risk it thus boldly? Many a brave man has met death ere this in the perilous encounter you would try. You are young yet, and life is full of pleasures. Give up this adventure, then, and return to your father's hall."

"No, I cannot," answered Sigurd. "I am young, it is true, but I have no fear of the dragon, since Odin's sword is in my hands."

"It is well said," replied the old man; "but if you are to accomplish the slaying of Fafnir, do not dig any pits here on the river's bank, for it will be of no avail. But go up on the mountain side until you have found a narrow path worn deep into the earth. It is Fafnir's trail, and over it he is sure to come. Dig there a deep pit, and hide in it yourself, first covering the top with a few boughs. As the dragon's huge body passes over this, you can strike him from beneath with your sword."

As the stranger finished speaking, Sigurd turned to thank him, but he saw no one there; only Greyfel was standing at his side. But his courage now rose high, for he knew that it was Odin who had talked with him. He hurried up the mountain side and soon found the dragon's trail. Here he dug a deep pit and crept into it himself, covering the top as Odin had directed. For hours he lay still and waited, and it seemed to him that the night would never end. At last a faint streak of light appeared in the east, and it soon grew bright enough for Sigurd to see plainly about him. He raised one corner of his roof of boughs and peeped cautiously out. Just then there came a terrible roar which seemed to shake the whole mountain. This was followed in a moment by a loud rushing sound like some mighty wind, and the air was full of heat and smoke as from a furnace. Sigurd dropped quickly back into his hiding-place, for he knew that the dragon had left his cave.

Louder and louder grew the fearful sound, as the monster rushed swiftly down the mountain side, leaving smoke and fire in his trail. His claws struck deep into the ground, and in his rapid descent he sometimes tore up the roots of trees. His huge wings flapping at his side made a frightful noise, while the black scaly tail left behind it a track of deadly slime. On he went until, all unknowing, he glided over the loosely strewn boughs which covered the pit, and Sigurd struck with his good sword Gram. It seemed to him that he had struck blindly. Yet in a moment he knew that the blow was sure and had pierced the monster's heart, for he heard it give one roar of mortal pain. Then, as he drew out his sword, the huge body quivered an instant and rolled with a crash down the mountain side. But in drawing out his sword from the dragon's heart, a great gush of blood followed which bathed Sigurd from head to foot in its crimson stream. He did not heed this, however, but sprang out of the pit and hurried down to where the dragon, so lately a thing of dread and horror, now lay apparently lifeless at the foot of the mountain.

When Fafnir was aware that he had received his death-wound, he began to lash out fiercely with his head and tail, in hopes that he would thereby kill the thing which had destroyed him. But Sigurd stayed at a safe distance; and when he saw the dragon cease its frantic struggles and lie quiet on the ground, he came nearer and gazed at it in wonder and half in fear—for Fafnir, though dying, was still a terrible creature to look upon.

The dragon slowly raised its head as Sigurd approached, and said, "Who art thou, and who is thy father and thy kin that thou wert so bold as to come against me?" At first Sigurd was loath to tell his name[11]; but soon he felt ashamed of his fears and answered boldly: "Sigurd I am called, and my father was Siegmund the Volsung." Then said Fafnir, "Who urged thee to this deed?" and Sigurd answered, "A bold heart urged me; and my strong hand and good sword aided me to do the deed."

Now Fafnir knew well who it was that had set the youth upon this adventure, and he said: "Of what use is it to lie? Regin, my brother, hath sent thee to work my death, for he is eager to gain the treasure which I guarded these many years. Go, therefore, and seek it out, but first I will give thee this counsel; turn away thy steps from this ill-fated gold, for a curse rests upon it, and it shall be the bane of every one that possesses it." As he spoke these words, Fafnir gave a fearful shudder that seemed to make the trees around him tremble; and in a moment Sigurd saw that the great dragon was dead.

Then Regin crept out of his hiding-place, and drew near to the dead creature, peering closely into the dull, glazed eyes to see if it were really a thing no longer to be feared. A look of hatred came into his face, but it disappeared quickly when he turned to the youth at his side and said:—

"Bravely done, Sigurd! You have this day wrought a great deed which shall be told and sung as long as the world stands fast." Then he added eagerly, "Have you found the hoard?"

"I did not look for it," answered Sigurd; "for after what you have told me of the curse which rests upon it, I had no desire to touch it."

Regin seemed now to be trembling with excitement, and he exclaimed hurriedly: "We must seek it at once, yes, at once, before anyone can come to claim it and we thereby lose a wonderful treasure. But let me go alone to find it, for you would surely lose your way." Then as he saw Sigurd wiping his blood-stained sword on the earth, he grasped the youth's arm fiercely and said: "Do not put the blade into its sheath until you have done one thing further. While I am searching for the cave, do you cut out Fafnir's heart and roast it, that I may eat it upon my return."

While he was speaking, Regin's face had lost its usual gentle and kindly look, and had become crafty and sly and full of cruel cunning. He looked now and then suspiciously at Sigurd, but the youth turned his head away, for he could not bear to look on at such a dreadful transformation. Meanwhile Regin was muttering to himself: "The gold! the gold! and precious gems in great glittering heaps! All of Andvari's hoard is mine now,—all mine." And he hurried away, leaving Sigurd surprised and sorrowing to find how soon the curse of that ill-fated gold had fallen on its would-be possessor.

When Regin had gone, Sigurd set to work to roast Fafnir's heart, and when the dreadful meal was cooked, he laid it upon the grass, but in so doing, some of the blood dropped upon his hand. Wondering what taste there could be in the dragon's heart to make Regin desire to eat it, Sigurd put the finger, on which the blood had dropped, to his lips. All at once he heard a hum of voices in the air. It was only a flock of crows flying overhead and chattering to themselves, but it sounded like human voices, and Sigurd could plainly tell what the crows were saying. A moment later two ravens came flying by, and he heard one of them say, "There sits Sigurd roasting Fafnir's heart that he may give it to Regin, who will taste the blood, and so be able to understand the language of birds."

"Yes," replied the other raven, "and he is waiting for Regin to return, not knowing that when Regin has taken possession of the hoard, he will come back and slay Sigurd."

The youth listened to these words in sorrow and surprise, for in spite of the look which he had seen on Regin's face, he could not believe his master guilty of such murderous thoughts.

Soon Regin returned, but what a change had come over him. Sigurd saw that the raven's words were indeed true, and that the curse of Andvari had fallen upon the new possessor of the hoard. If Regin's face had been mean and crafty before, it was now ten times more dreadful, and his mouth wore an evil smile which made Sigurd shudder. It seemed, too, as if his body had shrunk, and its motion was not unlike the gliding of a serpent. He was talking to himself as he came along, and appeared to be counting busily on his fingers. When Sigurd spoke, he looked up and eyed him furtively, then his face became suddenly black with rage, and he sprang at the youth, crying: "Fool and murderer, you shall have none of the gold. It is mine, all mine."

With the strength of a madman he dashed Sigurd upon the ground, and seizing a large stick struck him with all his force. But Sigurd sprang up quickly and, drawing Gram, prepared to defend himself against Regin's attack. Enraged now to the point of frenzy, Regin struck again and again, and suddenly, in his blind fury, rushed upon Sigurd's sword. Sigurd uttered a cry of horror and closed his eyes, for he could not look upon the painful sight. When he opened them again, Regin was lying dead at his feet. Then he drew out his sword, and, sitting down beside his slain friend, wept bitterly. At length he arose, and mounting Greyfel rode sorrowfully away.

The good horse bore him straight to Glistenheath—to the cave where Fafnir had hidden the ill-fated hoard. Here he found gold and gems in such heaps that his eyes were dazzled, and he turned away fearing to burden himself with the treasure and the curse which rested upon it. But from the pile he took Andvari's ring, which he placed upon his finger, and a gold helmet. He also chose from the treasures of the hoard a magic cape and a shield. Then he remounted Greyfel, after placing upon him as many sacks of gold as the horse could well carry.

The Valkyrie[12]

For many days Sigurd travelled on, saddened and discouraged, and having no heart for further adventures, since his first one had ended so sadly. He felt that he cared but little what became of him, and, letting the reins lie loose on Greyfel's neck, he allowed the horse to carry him wherever it would. At night he rested under the shade of the forest trees, and by day he wandered aimlessly over the country, too disheartened even to wish to return to King Alf's court again. But although he did not care to guide Greyfel, the horse was being led by a hand far wiser than his own, for Odin had other tasks in store for Sigurd, and it was he who now directed the young hero's path.

One day at nightfall they came to the foot of a mountain[13] and Greyfel stopped, as if waiting for his master to dismount. Sigurd, not wishing to rest here, urged his horse forward; but, for the first time, Greyfel refused to obey. His master, wondering at this stubbornness, but too tired and indifferent to force him further, dismounted and prepared to remain where he was for the night. Something about the place, its loneliness and silence, recalled the other mountain side where his first deed of glory and his first great sorrow had come to him. He could not sleep, so he wandered about among the trees, now and then stopping to listen as some sound broke the stillness of the night.

Once when he was looking toward the mountain top, he fancied he caught the glimmer of a light somewhere among the trees; and as he watched it longer, he saw what appeared to be tongues of flame leaping up and then disappearing. Alert now, and eager to get nearer this strange sight, he mounted Greyfel and directed him toward the fire. The horse obeyed readily, seeming to know the way; and when Sigurd drew nearer, he found that this was no common fire, but a circle of flames enclosing a large rock. There was no path up the mountain, and Sigurd felt uncertain whether to proceed. The horse, however, did not hesitate, but began the ascent boldly, picking his way among the trees and over the fallen trunks; sometimes stumbling and sometimes bruising his legs, but never once faltering or showing a desire to turn back.

Suddenly Sigurd felt upon his face a scorching wind followed by thick smoke that blinded his eyes. A quick turn of Greyfel's had brought them almost upon a wall of leaping flames, which rose so high that Sigurd could see nothing beyond them. The intense heat burned his face, and he dared not open his eyes to look about him. Greyfel snorted and pawed the ground, then suddenly made a movement forward as if to plunge into the flames. For an instant Sigurd thought of the prophecy made by his father Siegmund that he should be the greatest of the Volsungs, and he hesitated to risk his life thus lightly. Then he felt ashamed of the momentary cowardice, and with but one quick throb of fear at the peril he was rushing into, he bent forward and spurred Greyfel into the fire.

It was all over in an instant. He felt the scorching flames lick his face, and then he heard the horse's feet strike upon solid rock. When he opened his eyes to look about him, he realized that he had ridden through the fire all unharmed, and he was full of wonder at his safety. Greyfel, too, was unhurt; not a single hair upon his mane was singed; and Sigurd offered a silent prayer to Odin, who had guided them through such peril.

He dismounted and looked about, and found that he was standing upon the rock which he had seen from below, and which he now discovered to be completely encircled by the wall of fire. But stranger even than this was the sight of a man lying full length upon the rock, and seemingly unconscious of the fire which was raging all around him.[14] His shield was on the ground beside him, but his helmet covered his face so that Sigurd could not tell whether he was dead or sleeping. His figure was youthful and his dress of richest texture, while the armor which he bore seemed too fine to bear the brunt of warfare.

For a long time Sigurd stood beside the unconscious figure, wondering whether he had best awake the sleeper, or go away and leave him undisturbed. At last his curiosity became too strong, and, lifting the youth gently, he raised the helmet and gazed with wonder and delight at the beautiful face beneath. Then, as the sleeper did not awake, Sigurd took off his helmet, hoping thus to rouse him; but what was his surprise to see a shower of long golden hair fall down over the shoulders of the seeming youth. He started back so suddenly that the maiden awoke, and looking up at Sigurd said softly, "So you have come at last."

The young hero was too astonished to make any reply, but remained kneeling beside her, waiting for her to speak again. He wondered whether she was really human, or only some spirit of the night. Seeing his surprise, the maiden smiled, and, seating herself upon the rock, she pointed to a place beside her and said:—

"Sit down, Sir Sigurd, and I will tell you my story, and how I came to be sleeping in this strange place."

Still wondering, especially at hearing himself thus addressed, Sigurd obeyed, and the maiden began:—

"My name is Brunhilde, and I am one of Odin's Valkyries, or choosers of the slain. There are eight of us who do this service, and we ride to battle on swift-winged horses, wearing such armor as warriors carry, except that it is invulnerable.[15] We go into the midst of the fight even when it is fiercest, and when any of the heroes whom Odin has chosen are slain, we raise him from the battle-field, lay him before us on the horse, and ride with him to Asgard, to the place called Valhalla. This is a beautiful hall made of gold and marble, and it has five and forty doors wide enough for eight hundred warriors to march in abreast. Inside, its roof is made of golden shields, and its walls are hung with spears of polished steel that give a wonderful bright light to all the hall. Every day the warriors drink of the mead which is prepared for the gods themselves, and they feast on the meat of a wonderful boar[16] which is daily slain and boiled in the great cauldron, and which always comes to life again just before the heroes are ready to eat.

"Sometimes Odin sits at the board and shares the feast with them, and when the Valkyries are not doing service on the battle-field, they lay aside their armor and clothe themselves in pure white robes, to wait upon the heroes. When the feast is over, the warriors call for their weapons, and spear in hand they go out into the great courtyard, where they fight desperate battles and deal terrible wounds, performing deeds of valour such as they achieved while on the earth. Since in Asgard there is no dying, every combatant who receives some terrible wound is healed at once by magic power. Thus the heroes share the blessings and privileges of the gods, and live forever, having won great fame and glory.

"Now there was a certain battle being waged in a country far from here, in which the combatants were an old warrior named Helm Gunnar, and a youth called Agnar. Odin had commanded me to bear Helm Gunnar to Valhalla, and leave the other to the mercy of the conquerors. The youth of Agnar moved me, however, to pity; so I left the old warrior upon the battle-field, though he was already sore wounded. Then I lifted Agnar from the ground, and, laying him upon my horse, I carried him to Asgard.

"In punishment for my disobedience and daring, the All-father took from me forever my privilege of being a Valkyrie, or shield-maiden. He also condemned me to the life of a mortal, and then he brought me to this rock, where he stung me with the sleep-thorn, and made this my sleeping place. But first he surrounded the rock with a wall of fire, and he decreed that I should sleep here until a hero who knew no fear should ride through the flames and waken me. I am well versed in the lore of runes, and I read there long ago that he who knows no fear is Sigurd, the slayer of Fafnir. Therefore thou art Sigurd and my deliverer."

For a long time Brunhilde talked with him, and told him many wonderful things, of the noble deeds of heroes and of bloody battles fought in far-off lands. Then, knowing that he was but a youth in spite of his brave acts, she imparted to him something of the wisdom she had gained as "one of the greatest among great women"—for thus it was that men spoke of her. She warned Sigurd of the dangers he would encounter on his journey, and bade him beware of the wiles of those who would call themselves his friends. She charged him to abide always by his oath, "for great and grim is the reward for the breaking of plighted troth."

"Bear and forbear, and so win for thyself long, enduring praise of men.

"Give kind heed to dead men—sick-dead, sea-dead, or sword-dead."

Thus spoke Brunhilde, and Sigurd listened, and ever, as she stopped speaking, he begged to hear still more. Then she read for him many things written in the runes, and Sigurd listened, marvelling at her wisdom.

The circle of fire had now burnt itself out, but daylight had come, and Sigurd could plainly see the perilous ascent he had made up the mountain. Brunhilde took his hand and bade him farewell, but, before she left him, Sigurd put upon her finger the ring which he had taken from Andvari's hoard. Then he watched her depart toward her castle in Isenland, feeling very lonely, and wishing he might follow her. But Greyfel's head was turned a different way, and Sigurd knew that Odin had other things for him to do, so he allowed the horse to carry him away from Brunhilde's country, though he would fain have gone thither. And Sigurd longed for the maiden, and sorrowed at parting from her; but Brunhilde, though she loved him well, bade him go his way, since thus it was written in the runes that not she, but another, should be the wife of Sigurd.

Sigurd at Gunther's Court (abridged)

Sigurd rode on, weary of solitude and wondering what adventures awaited him. Hoping that his destiny would guide him, he rested the reins on Greyfel's neck, trusting Odin to lead them in the right direction. One day, as he rode through a dense forest, he encountered a man on horseback. Sigurd asked him their location. The man replied the land was called Burgundy, the land of King Gunther (17). He encouraged Sigurd to continue, for he would find shelter at the palace. A great feast was being held—meat served on gold platters and wine in silver goblets.

The King's mother, Queen Ute (18), and her daughter, Kriemhild (19), spotted Sigurd from a high window as he arrived. The queen was a wise-woman, skilled in magic and interpreting dreams. Once when Kriemhild was young she dreamt that a golden hawk alighted on her wrist, becoming so dear to her that she would cast aside all riches. The queen told her that this dream meant that a hero was coming to court her some day, to remain at her side as the hawk at her wrist. On this day, when Kriemhild exclaimed that a wandering minstrel was approaching, the queen rose from her loom and watched him approach. "That is no wandering harper, child, but a knight with tidings from far away." She instructed her to summon Hagen (20) their formidable warrior, and question him about this stranger.

Hagen was tall, strong, and powerful, despite his gray hairs. His dark, deeply furrowed face revealed one grim and stern, loyal only to Gunther, his liege lord. He was always at Gunther's side, and famous for his wisdom and skill in matters of state. His memory was long and his knowledge was great. When he was summoned about the stranger, and looked out the queen's window at him, he replied, "That is Sigurd, slayer of Fafnir, possessor of a famous hoard (21). It would be well for the king to welcome his guest."

Sigurd was pleased and surprised by the warm reception and was glad to accept the king's invitation to stay with them for a time. There were many feasts and games held in Sigurd's honor, and all the princes of Burgundy came to visit, so Sigurd was persuaded to remain at the palace longer. He became friend and companion to the king, and spent much time talking with the lovely Kriemhild. Only Hagen kept his distance.

Just before Sigurd arrived, Gunther had been involved in war with a neighboring prince. Gunther's forces were inferior, and he feared defeat and the loss of his kingdom. Hagen pressed the king to ask Sigurd for assistance. But the king resisted, stating that he was a guest. But Hagen protested, stating, "He holds himself as your friend, so your cause should be his as well. We need help, and he alone is powerful enough to turn the tide of battle in our favor. He has a magic cloak, and the mighty Gram, forged from the pieces of Odin's legendary sword. With Sigurd as an ally, no enemy can stand against us." And so Gunther asked Sigurd for aid.

Sigurd agreed, and willingly fought beside the king achieving victory after victory. Enemies fell or fled in terror from their army, and eventually the war was ended. Soon after, Hagen asked King Gunther to keep Sigurd with them, as he was a strong ally. "Let us bind him to our house by some close tie, and as no bond is closer than marriage, you must wed him to your sister Kriemhild, who already looks upon him with favor." But the king replied, "That cannot be, much as I desire it, for Sigurd will not wed with my sister since his heart still yearns for Brunhilde. He is even now planning to seek her."

"All this is true," answered Hagen, "and while Sigurd longs for the shield-maiden nothing can be done. But summon your mother and bade her mix for him a draught of forgetfulness." Gunther agreed, and the queen mother willingly offered her help. Later that night, when Sigurd returned from a journey to a nearby city, she offered him a cup that contained a potion which made him forget Brunhilde and his ride through the wall of fire. And so he turned his favor upon the lovely Kriemhild and sought her hand in marriage. All the people rejoiced at the union, for Sigurd was both loved and feared. The wedding celebration lasted many weeks and costly gifts were distributed by the king among his vassals. Yet in the midst of the rejoicing, a strange and uneasy feeling crept upon Sigurd. He felt himself struggling with some memory, and his troubled mind worried the gentle Kriemhild so he banished the thought and joined in the merriment.

Soon, the wily Hagen, who knew Sigurd possessed Andvari's hoard, began whispering that the young hero brought no gift to his bride and word spread that Sigurd lived on the king's bounty. When Sigurd heard this rumor, he paled with anger. In the presence of the court, he formally presented Kriemhild the gift of all his treasure—the chests of gold he carried on his horse, and the hoard that still remained in Fafnir's lair. In his pride and resentment, he forgot about the curse that lay upon the treasure. And because of the drink of forgetfulness, he no longer remembered the ring he placed on Brunhilde's finger. King Gunther and his people rejoiced at the gift and even Hagen was satisfied, for he was unaware of the curse and hoped Sigurd would bring the great treasure to Burgundy.

The Wooing of Brunhilde (abridged)

Sigurd lived happily at Gunther's court and now, married to the lovely Kriemhild, he was content, and desired nothing more than to spend his days with her in Burgundy. Ever since his marriage, it seemed all the events of his past were veiled in mist. He only dimly recalled the forging of Gram and his defeat of the dragon Fafnir, and Brunhilde had passed completely from his memory. Kriemhild, who believed she had truly won the hero's heart, knew nothing of Brunhilde or the magic potion her mother gave to Sigurd.

One day, an old harper came to the palace. He was white-haired and stooped with age, but was still skilled in his craft and sung of the brave deeds of heroes. One night he told of a place called Isenland, the home of a beautiful maiden who was sought after by kings and princes. "But she refuses to wed; she has never yet been won," the old man continued, "for she is a warrior queen, and to those who seek her hand she proposes a trial of strength. Those who lose the contest lose their lives."

Gunther asked, "Then why is she willing to marry if she has more than a man's strength and go to battle like any warrior?" The harper replied, "She does not wish to do so, but it is written in the runes that she must wed. But she is determined only to yield to the hero whose strength can surpass her own." The king asked, "What is her name?"

"Brunhilde," the old man replied. Gunther glanced at Sigurd, afraid the name would recall some memory, but he appeared unconcerned. But Sigurd noticed a flush on the king's face and said "Look now, sir harper, and see how quickly another victim has been found! Perhaps our king is eager to behold her beauty and win her for his queen. What say you, friend Gunther?"

And the king replied, "I would risk my life to gain this magnificent maiden." The king was so determined that even Hagen could not deter him. His sister's gentle plea was also ignored. When the matter was settled, Hagen came to him in secret and said, "If you are truly set on this foolish journey, take Sigurd with you. He has the sword and cloak that makes him invisible. This can help you." Gunther took this advice. In fact, Sigurd was eager to go, for he was growing tired of the quiet life at court and longed for an adventure. He reassured the lovely Kriemhild, who begged him not to go.

Sigurd's only condition was that Gunther take only himself, Hagen, and his brother Dankwart on the journey. Hagen disagreed, but Gunther trusted Sigurd and consented. Queen Ute, Kriemhild, and her maidens, spent long days making fine garments for the men to wear, adorned with jewels, so that they would make an impressive appearance. But the queen was troubled that no retinue of lords would be accompanying them, as was customary for a king. She resented Sigurd for compelling the king to travel to a foreign land with only three of his own kinsmen.

A ship was made ready, and the most skilled men placed at the oars. At last, they set sail. And while many who watched weeped at their departure, the heroes were eager for the voyage and a successful adventure—all but Hagen who, even though he would follow his king anywhere, had no confidence in the journey. It was a long but uneventful voyage, when at last they saw the forbidding towers of a castle upon a rocky cliff. Before they reached it, Sigurd said to Gunther, "Tell everyone that I'm here to attend you as your vassal." Gunther was surprised, but agreed.

From a chamber window in the castle (22) the queen watched the knights approach. She did not believe them to be royalty, for they had no attendants. She sent a maiden to meet them, and she returned with much excitement. "It is Gunther, king of Burgundy, my lady, and with him are his kinsmen, and a noble youth named Sigurd. I hear that they have come to match strength with you in the games."

Brunhilde trembled with delight to learn that Sigurd was at her castle gates. She remembered well how this brave youth had ridden through the wall of fire and awakened her from sleep. For the first time since Odin took her shield she was glad to be a mortal maiden. She hoped his strength was equal to his valor.

The visitors were made welcome and, at last, Brunhilde descended to the great hall in her costliest robes to receive her guests. Each approached the marble throne in turn, and to Gunther, Dankwart, and Hagen she offered her hand and greeted them. But when Sigurd approached she rose, took both his hands in hers and said softly, "So you have come again to seek me, Sir Sigurd. But this time it is not through a circle of fire. It is long since we last met, but I have not forgotten you, nor have I lost the ring you placed upon my finger. There is no one I would be happier to see within my halls."

At first, Sigurd was bewildered by her words. A troubled look passed across his face, and he rubbed his eyes as though waking from sleep. He gazed long into the queen's face, murmuring, "Brunhilde—the Valkyrie—the wall of fire." Then, the mist was lifted from his eyes. He remembered his ride through the fire, the sleeping maiden, and all of the forgotten past that had been taken from him.

Brunhilde saw the change in his face, but mistook its meaning. She thought he had carelessly forgotten her, and was now trying to recall some memory. Her soft manner turned to hardness; her pride was hurt, and shame forbade her from showing favours to one who could so easily forget her. Sigurd understood that something had happened to cause his forgetfulness. He knew now that if he could choose his bride it would be Brunhilde. But he was here as Gunther's vassal to help him win Brunhilde for his wife, and he was determined to remain true to him.

And so the day was set and the contest was arranged. Brunhilde was adorned in a coat of mail, golden helmet, and corselet of finely wrought silver; she carried a shield heavy enough for the most powerful warrior and her spear was carried on the shoulders of three strong men—no one but Brunhilde had ever been known to lift it. The men of Burgundy watched in mingled fear and amazement, but Sigurd told his king to show no fear, then he secretly donned the Tarnkappe and crept into the courtyard. He stood close to the king and whispered for him to follow his instructions. Sigurd placed himself between Brunhilde and Gunther, taking what would have been a fatal blow from her spear with the magic shield from Andvari's hoard. Sigurd returned a blow with the spear, making it appear to be in Gunther's hand. The tremendous blow hit her shield and sent her to the ground. She rose, flushed with shame and anger, and approached the king. She said, "That was a noble blow, King Gunther, and I count myself fairly beaten at this first game, but you must also win in casting the stone and in leaping." But just as before, Sigurd secretly helped the king. The warrior maiden at last declared herself beaten and, though her face revealed her disappointment, she said, "From henceforth Brunhilde is no longer her own master, but the wife and vassal of the king of Burgundy."

There was feasting that night, though hearts were heavy for the loss of their queen. Brunhilde strove to be happy and proud, but though she appeared to honor her liege lord, her heart longed for Sigurd, and she rued the day that brought the Burgundians to Isenland.

How Brunhilde Came to Burgundy

So Brunhilde and the Lord of Burgundy were wedded, and, after many days spent in feasting and merriment, Gunther told his queen that they must prepare for the return voyage. It was some time since he and his friends had set out on their journey to Isenland, and he feared that if he stayed much longer at Brunhilde's palace, his own people would give them up for dead. Then he went secretly to Sigurd, and with a shamed, flushed face he said: "My friend and brother, I have come to ask your help in a strange matter. I cannot return to Burgundy with a wife who is my master, even as Brunhilde is now, for I shall become the laughing-stock of all my people. The queen of Isenland does not love me, and she treats me each day with more contempt. She does not scruple to insult me by making me the victim of her great strength, which I am powerless to meet. Her might—which no other woman has ever equalled—depends on a wonderful girdle which she wears; and when I tried to wrest this from her, she tied me hand and foot and hung me on a nail in the chamber wall. Only by my promising never to trouble her again was I able to get release."

Sigurd felt sorry indeed for Gunther's plight, and he offered to try and subdue the warrior queen to her husband's will. So that night he assumed the form of Gunther, and wrestled with Brunhilde until he had taken from her the wonderful girdle in which lay all her unwomanly strength. He also took from her finger the serpent ring of Andvari which he himself had given her when they had talked together on the mountain. Brunhilde, being now quite ready to obey her lord, believing that he was truly her master by virtue of his superior strength, prepared for her departure from Isenland, and took with her as many of her own followers as Gunther would allow. He besought her not to overburden the good ship which had brought them thither with chests of raiment and household goods, since Queen Ute could amply provide all that Brunhilde might desire.

As to the wealth she had at her command, he bade her leave all that behind, for the rich lands of Burgundy yielded more than enough to satisfy the proudest heart. The queen therefore opened her chests full of gold and silver and divided them among her knights and among the poor of her kingdom. Her rich robes, and all the costly apparel she had worn, she gave to her maidens, and arranged to take with her only a small part of her possessions. While preparations were being made for the departure of Brunhilde to the country of her liege lord and husband, Hagen was fuming uneasily at the long delay, and predicting all manner of misfortunes if they did not speedily leave Isenland. Gunther tried to allay his fears and said:—

"You are restless, Hagen, because you are old, and cannot share your lord's joy in having won this peerless maiden for his queen. There is really no cause for alarm, for the people here are friendly to us now that I am their acknowledged king. Besides, have we not Sigurd with us, and how can we fear any harm when he is here to protect us?"

"Yes, yes," answered Hagen, angrily, "to be sure we have Sigurd with us, but it is always Sigurd whom we have to lean on like a babe on its mother. Before he came among us, we ourselves were counted warriors worthy to be feared; but now it is always Sigurd who fights our battles, guides our ship, and brings us out of all our difficulties. It is Sigurd, too, who wins us a warrior maiden whom we would never have conquered alone, weak and nerveless men that we are. It is Sigurd, always Sigurd, and I hate his very name."

"Nay, now, good Hagen," said the king, soothingly, "these things should not provoke you to jealousy, but rather make you hold the youth in respect and honour. What would Burgundy do without Sigurd?"

"That is just it," retorted Hagen, bitterly. "Burgundy is naught except as she holds this foreign prince in her court. She boasts no warrior so valiant, no soldier so dear to her people, as this man who came to us a stranger. Better far that he should return to his own country than to stay longer among us."

"Nay, nay," answered Gunther; "if Sigurd is so beloved by our people, it is a greater reason for his remaining with them." But Hagen shook his head, and muttered something which the king did not understand.

Everything was at last ready for Brunhilde's departure, and she bade a sorrowful farewell to all her household and to all the people of Isenland. Then she embarked on the white-sailed ship with the four Burgundian warriors. In a few days she was far out of sight of the land she loved, and was being borne toward a country unfamiliar and unwelcome. For even though she had been forced to own herself conquered in the games, Brunhilde had never been willing to become Gunther's wife, or to go with him to his home across the sea.

The voyage was quickly and pleasantly spent to all except the queen, who sat upon the deck, moody and silent, ignoring all Gunther's efforts to divert her. Sigurd felt happy at the thought of returning to the beautiful Kriemhild, though his heart was heavy with fear that the coming of Brunhilde to Burgundy would bring trouble and sorrow in its train. The evident dislike which the queen felt for King Gunther boded no good for the future to him or to his friends. Only toward Hagen did she show any kindness, and her overtures of friendship were, strange to say, very willingly met by the grim, reserved man. She would talk for hours with Hagen when no one else could get from her a moment's notice, and the gray-haired old warrior seemed ever ready to please and serve her.

At last the voyage was over, and the king was again in his own land and among his own people. Great rejoicing was made over his return, and feasts were held for many days in honour of the wonderful maiden who was now King Gunther's wife. But though everything was done for her pleasure, and many princes of the provinces of Burgundy came to do homage to their queen, Brunhilde remained ever moody and silent. The gentle Kriemhild tried in vain to induce her to join in the feasting and merriment, but Brunhilde refused, almost angrily, and sat apart, brooding over her unhappy lot. After a time Gunther sought his mother, Queen Ute, and begged her to give Brunhilde some drink which would make her forget Isenland, and so be content to dwell with him. Queen Ute shook her head, and said sadly that she had nothing which could accomplish this for him.

The king went next to Hagen and said: "You have won Brunhilde's confidence, my uncle. Tell me, therefore, why the queen is silent and unhappy."

At this Hagen laughed mockingly and whispered: "Ask your noble friend Sigurd whom you love and trust so fully what it is that makes Brunhilde's heart so heavy with longing, and so full of bitterness. He can tell you far better than I." But shame and pride forbade Gunther to go again with his troubles to Sigurd, so he kept silent, and waited for time to cure the queen's grief.

Things went on in this way for some time, for nothing seemed to change the haughty queen, or soften her dislike for all of Gunther's household except Hagen. He remained her devoted follower, and her one confidant and friend. Toward the gentle Kriemhild she showed both jealousy and aversion, though the sweet, friendly wife of Sigurd was at a loss to understand the reason for her sister-in-law's behaviour.

On his return to Burgundy, Sigurd had been unwise enough to tell Kriemhild of the stratagem by which he had won Brunhilde for the king, and how later he had wrestled with the mighty queen, and taken from her the magic girdle. He also gave Kriemhild the serpent ring which Brunhilde had prized more than all her possessions, but which she had yielded when—as she supposed—Gunther had outmatched her in strength. All this trickery Brunhilde did not as yet even suspect, so Kriemhild wondered at her ill-concealed hatred of the king.

One day Brunhilde and Kriemhild were walking together in the palace garden, and as they were about to enter the great feasting hall, Kriemhild, being a little in advance of the queen, was just crossing the doorway when Brunhilde called out angrily,—

"Do you presume to enter before me, your queen? you who are the wife of a vassal?"

"I am no vassal," retorted Kriemhild, quickly, "for Sigurd owns allegiance neither to you nor to any other."

"That is a lie," cried Brunhilde, wrathfully, "for when Sigurd came to Isenland, he declared that Gunther was his liege lord, and himself a humble vassal."

"That was only to save your pride," answered Kriemhild, now dropping her angry tone, for she saw that the queen was in a towering rage.

"Gunther deceived me, then," stormed Brunhilde, furiously; then she added mockingly, "Since Sigurd is no vassal of the king's, I suppose he is a much greater and richer prince; that he is braver also, and stronger, and could outstrip the king in a contest of strength such as that in which Gunther won me for his wife."

"Even so," replied Kriemhild, "for it was really Sigurd who outdid you in the games, and not Gunther at all. It was Sigurd, too, who wrested from you the girdle and the ring, and he gave them to me as a trophy dearly won." As she said this, Kriemhild showed her two possessions and then passed quietly into the hall, while Brunhilde stood at the door too bewildered by her words to speak.

At length she realized the meaning of Kriemhild's speech. Full of anger and fearful suspicion, she sought out Hagen, and demanded that he should tell her all he knew of Sigurd's part in the contest. And Hagen told her how Sigurd had put on his Tarnkappe and stood before the king unseen; how he, and not Gunther, had flung the spear, and hurled the stone and made the wonderful leap; how it was Sigurd alone who had gained the victory, and he who should rightfully have won her.

Upon hearing this, Brunhilde wept in anger and sorrow, and said bitterly: "I might have known that none but Sigurd could claim the warrior queen for his bride. That fool and weakling, King Gunther, is no mate for Brunhilde, and never would he have called me wife had I not been tricked and deceived. He is a coward, and merits all the hatred and contempt I have shown him." Then her anger grew fiercer than ever, and she swore vengeance upon those who had wronged her.

"Cherish not your wrath against the king," said Hagen, "for it is Sigurd who has brought this shame upon you. He has been a source of evil ever since he came among us, and he will yet be the king's bane; yea, and thine also. It were better that he died,—and soon."

"He shall die," cried Brunhilde. "I will call Gunther hither and taunt him with his weakness and cowardice. Then if he is a man, he will avenge me of this insult which Kriemhild has put upon me."

So she summoned the king to her presence and poured forth the story of her wrongs, bidding him slay Sigurd if he ever hoped to merit anything but her hatred and contempt. The king listened to her words, but though he felt ashamed of the sorry part he had played, he would not give her the promise she desired, for he loved Sigurd, and could not find it in his heart to kill him, even to win Brunhilde's love.

Seeing that neither threats nor pleading would move the king to do what she desired, Hagen begged the queen to leave them, and give Gunther more time to make his decision. So Brunhilde went away, and when Hagen was sure that there was no danger of her returning, he came close to the king and whispered:—

Blind fool that you are! Do you not see even yet why the queen has been unhappy ever since she came to Burgundy? She loves your friend Sigurd, and it is he whom she would fain call husband and lord!" Then he left the king alone, and Gunther sat for a long time thinking over what Hagen had said. He felt discouraged and sick at heart; for he knew that he was unable to solve the difficulties before him, or to avert the dreadful fate which seemed to be overshadowing him and all his household.

The Death of Sigurd (abridged)

Shortly after this Hagen came one day to the king, and said: "As long as Sigurd lives, there is naught that will appease the wrath of Brunhilde, or make her cease to weep. If you would have peace for yourself and would win the queen's love, it must be by Sigurd's death."

"But I cannot slay him, Hagen," answered Gunther, sadly; "he is my friend, and also my brother, and I cannot do such a treacherous thing."

"There is no need for you to perform the deed yourself. Only consent to having Sigurd killed, and another hand than yours will carry it out. It is useless to try and pacify the queen so long as Sigurd lives to arouse daily her jealous wrath. Consent, therefore, to his death," urged Hagen, "and I myself will slay him and take all the burden of the guilt upon my shoulders."

For many hours he talked with the king, working upon a weak will and unsteady purpose, and rousing in Gunther the jealous fear that Sigurd would play him false. There seemed, indeed, only one way out of the difficulty, and at last Gunther consented to Hagen's wish and promised to aid him in carrying out his plans.

"If I cannot win Brunhilde's love except by Sigurd's death, then he had better die," cried the king; "for there is ever raging in my ears the queen's words: 'Never will I live to be mocked by Kriemhild. This thing must be ended by Sigurd's death, or my death, or yours. Would that I were again in Odin's hall—a shield-maiden starting for battle or returning with my weapons stained with red blood.' Do what you will then, my uncle, for I would lay down my life to win Brunhilde's love."

Having won over the king, Hagen went away, determined to avenge Brunhilde's wrongs and rid the kingdom of one whom he had long feared and hated. His plans were then quickly made. He remembered that he had often heard it whispered about the palace that some magic charm kept Sigurd from ever being wounded in battle, since no weapon had the power to harm him. So before he could carry out his plans, he must learn with certainty whether the report was true or false. There was but one person who would be likely to know this; and accordingly on a certain day when Sigurd had gone hunting with the king, Hagen went to Kriemhild, and seating himself beside her he inquired kindly if she were very happy as the wife of Sigurd.

Kriemhild looked surprised at this unexpected visit from her uncle, for he seldom took any notice of her; but she thought that he was prompted to a show of interest in her by his fondness for Sigurd. So she welcomed him gladly and answered his question in a way to settle all doubts concerning her happiness, had her uncle really felt any friendly interest. Hagen smiled at her reply, and said,—

"Then what will you do if Sigurd is wounded in battle, and brought home dead upon his shield?"

"That cannot happen," answered Kriemhild, betrayed into further confidence by Hagen's seemingly affectionate concern.

"But such things do happen, even to the bravest warrior," persisted Hagen, "unless it be true, as I have sometimes heard, that Sigurd is invulnerable."

Not dreaming of his purpose in asking this question, Kriemhild proudly replied, "It is indeed true, and that is why I have no fears when my lord goes to battle."

"Was this great gift from Odin?" asked Hagen.

Now Kriemhild knew that Sigurd had forbidden her to speak of this matter to any one, but she thought there could surely be no harm in revealing the secret to one so devoted and loyal as her uncle, so she told Hagen all about the slaying of Fafnir. She said also that Sigurd had been bathed in the dragon's blood, and that this was supposed to render him invulnerable.

"Was he completely covered by the stream of blood?" asked Hagen, with great interest.

"Yes," answered Kriemhild, "he was bathed from head to foot, except one small spot upon his shoulder, on which a leaf happened to fall."

"Are you not afraid that he may be struck in that place by a spear or arrow, and so meet his death?"

"It might indeed be so," said Kriemhild, "but I do not fear it."

"Still," persisted Hagen, "it would be well to have someone always near Sigurd in battle, to guard him against any death-blow, and since I alone know of his point of weakness, let me be the one to protect him. This service I shall be better able to render if you will sew a mark upon his coat over the exact spot on his shoulder where the leaf fell, so that when we are beset by enemies upon the road, or go forth to battle, I may keep beside him and shield him from a possible death blow."

Kriemhild was greatly moved by this evidence of loyalty in Hagen, and thanking him warmly for his devotion, she promised to sew upon Sigurd's coat some mark by which the vulnerable spot could be known. Then she hurried away to begin her task, not dreaming of Hagen's wicked purpose in obtaining her secret.

Some days later Hagen proposed that there should be a great hunt given in one of the neighbouring forests, and Gunther, who had promised to aid him in his plans, urged Sigurd to accompany them. Sigurd gladly consented, for he had greatly enjoyed this sport since his first coming to Burgundy. His superiority in the chase added much to Hagen's anger and jealousy, for as Sigurd had proved himself the greatest of warriors on the battlefield, so in the hunt he was the peer of all the knights of Burgundy.

A day was set for the great hunt, and a forest was chosen which was famous for the number and fierceness of its wild beasts. Then early one morning Gunther, Hagen, and Sigurd set forth with their knights, in full expectation of having a profitable as well as exciting day. It was a beautiful morning in early spring, and the spirits of the hunting party rose high as they cantered out of the city gates and made their way toward the forest.

Sigurd rode ahead of the party, with Gunther and Hagen beside him. His suit was of royal purple, embroidered richly by Kriemhild's loving fingers, and his spear shone bright in the sunlight as he galloped along, light-hearted and unsuspicious of the black thoughts which were harboured in Hagen's wicked heart. He looked so brave and joyous, so beautiful as a youth and so gallant as a knight, that all the warriors in Gunther's train said among themselves that no one in Burgundy was fit to be compared to Sigurd.

These remarks soon came to Hagen's ears, and hardened him in his determination to slay this foreign prince whom all his own countrymen would so gladly make their king in place of the weak and unwarlike Gunther. He hid this feeling, however, and kept close to Sigurd's side, looking eagerly for the spot upon his shoulder where the loving but foolish Kriemhild had sewed the fatal mark.

The hunting party soon came to the edge of the forest, where they divided into three groups. Each leader took with him a party of followers, and they set out in different directions, with the agreement that when the sun was overhead they should meet at a well-known place where Gunther had arranged that their dinner was to be set out. Sigurd galloped away, and a greater part of the knights followed him. Hagen saw this and frowned darkly, but he said nothing, only waited for Sigurd to get out of sight. Then he whispered to the king:—

"Today is the day for our deed. This must be the last time that your friend Sigurd flaunts his superiority over the king."

Gunther trembled and answered weakly:—
"Must it be done, Hagen? Is there no other way to rid our kingdom of him?"

"No way but by his death," replied Hagen, firmly; then he added: "and do not you give way to foolish fancies, or my plans may fail. I have no womanish scruples, and Sigurd must die today."

Not wishing to have it appear that anything unusual was in preparation, Hagen ceased to confer with the king, but summoned his knights to the chase. But something in the faces of the leaders made the men only half-hearted in their eagerness for the hunt, and a spirit of silence and gloom spread over the whole party. They hunted all the morning, but their success was small, and when they finally drew up at the meeting place, they found that they had very little game to boast of. The men had already come from the castle with great baskets of provisions, so the knights dismounted, and sat upon the grass to await the coming of Sigurd.

Soon they heard the loud blast of horns, and the joyous shouting of men mingled with the barking and yelping of hounds; and in a moment Sigurd and his followers came in sight. They shouted merrily to their comrades, and galloped forward to join them, while those seated upon the ground looked with delight and surprise at the beasts which had been slain by Sigurd's skilful hand. There was a large black bear of the kind which was known to be so fierce that it was well-nigh impossible to kill or capture him. There was also a huge wild boar and three shaggy wolves, besides a great number of smaller animals, such as the fox and deer. The knights were all loud in their praises of Sigurd's wonderful skill, and he took their homage gladly, seeming wholly unconscious of Hagen's cruel face or Gunther's averted eyes.

Soon the midday feast was ready, and the men sat down to eat. Some of the game they had caught that morning was roasted and placed before them, and they ate almost greedily, for the sport had given them sufficient excuse for hunger. Gunther asked for wine, and Hagen replied that they had no need of wine with such a clear, beautiful stream nearby whose water was finer than wine. "Let us go there and quench our thirst, he said." Gunther agreed. Sigurd offered to go ahead and test the water. Hagen offered to show him the way, then added—"Will you run a race with me, Sir Sigurd, to see which of us will reach the stream first? For though I am much older than you in years, I was accounted a famous runner in my time."

"Gladly," replied Sigurd; and they started off toward the stream. But although Hagen went with wonderful swiftness considering his years, he could not outrun the fleet-footed Sigurd, who reached the goal some minutes before Hagen came up.

"You are truly a swift runner, even now, friend Hagen," he cried gayly, "and I can easily believe your boast that you were once the most famous runner in the kingdom."

At this Hagen smiled and said, "But what are we poor men, even the best of us, beside the noble Sigurd, who can outstrip all the warriors of Burgundy, no matter what the contest may be?"

"Nay, you are overzealous in your praise," laughed Sigurd, but he was pleased with Hagen's friendly words, for he did not detect the undertone of jealousy and anger. Then courteously he bade Hagen drink of the stream, but Hagen answered:—

"Do you drink first, and let me follow you, for though you would yield the courtesy to me because of my age, I would rather give precedence to you as the better runner. Drink, therefore, but first lay aside your armour, for the weight of it might throw you into the stream."

Sigurd, ever trustful and unsuspicious, threw off his coat of mail and laid his spear beside it, thus leaving unprotected the inner coat on which Kriemhild had sewed the fatal mark. Then he knelt upon the ground, and stooping over put his hand into the stream and prepared to raise the water to his lips. At this moment Hagen, with catlike swiftness, caught up Sigurd's shining spear, and, aiming it directly toward the mark, hurled it with all his force. [23]

The weapon sank into the stooping body, and with a groan Sigurd rolled over upon the ground. As soon as he was able, he turned to see who had done this cowardly deed; and only when he saw Hagen fleeing in guilty haste, could he believe that the blow was dealt by one who so lately seemed his friend. Sigurd put his hand feebly to his shoulder, and when he found where the spear had struck, he knew that his wound was mortal. He made one great effort to rise, and gathering together all his strength, he drew out the spear and started in pursuit of Hagen.

The treacherous murderer had fled for protection to the king, and thither Sigurd followed him; but before he reached the astonished and horror-stricken group who were watching his approach, the blood began to gush forth from his wound, and he sank helplessly to the ground. The whole company of knights knelt down beside him, weeping and lamenting over the loss of their leader. One of them raised the dying hero's head and placed it upon his knee, while others tried to stanch the blood from his wound. Sigurd, however, bade them cease their efforts, for his end had now come.

Then he turned to Hagen, and upbraided him for his cowardly deed, and for his treachery in obtaining the secret of his vulnerability from Kriemhild to use it in such a dastardly way. His strength was now almost exhausted, and his eyes began to close; but suddenly he roused again, and said to the trembling and terrified king:—

"Thou hast played a coward's part to thy friend who trusted thee, O Gunther, and some day thou wilt bitterly repent of having aided thine uncle in his wickedness. But for this I will not reproach thee, for thou art already sorrowing. One thing only I ask of thee, and do thou promise it, and make what amends thou canst. Take care of thy sister Kriemhild, and do not let Hagen's vengeance extend to her. Though thou hast proved an unworthy friend to me, yet I commend my wife to thy keeping. Wilt thou swear to protect and cherish her?"

"I swear it," replied Gunther, now weeping remorseful tears.

"Then see that thou play the man, nay, be for once the king, and keep thine oath to the dying."

As he finished these words, Sigurd sank back lifeless into the arms of the knight who supported him. All at once the clouds overhead grew fearfully dark, and the air seemed full of a strange, ominous stillness. The birds stopped their singing, and the forest was silent with the hush of night. The warriors stood weeping beside the body of their slain leader, but no one dared to speak. Slowly and sadly they raised Sigurd from the ground and, placing him on their shoulders, bore him to the place where the faithful Greyfel was standing, patiently awaiting the coming of his master. One of the knights led the horse, while a solemn group of mourners followed, and not even the sternest old warrior among them felt ashamed of the tears he shed for the dead hero.

When the sorrowful procession reached the city gates, the news was quickly spread that Sigurd was slain, and by the hand of Hagen. There was great mourning throughout the city, and beneath the wail of sorrow was a muttered undertone of threats towards the man who could do such a cowardly and treacherous thing as to kill the friend who trusted him. But Hagen faced the people, calm and grim as ever, and said boldly:—

"Let all the guilt of this deed rest upon me, for it was by my hand that Sigurd died. Now there is but one lord of Burgundy, King Gunther, and no longer shall Brunhilde sit in tears, for the insult put upon her is avenged."

The Last of the Hoard (abridged)

Though the news of the death of Sigurd had spread throughout the city, no one dared to bring the dreadful tidings to Kriemhild, who sat in her bower with her maidens, waiting her lord's return. The day was now far spent, and she began to wonder at his long delay, when the sound of some disturbance in the street reached her chamber windows, and she looked out to see what the unusual noise might be. At first she feared it was an outbreak of war, but the solemn procession which was wending its way toward the palace was not martial in its bearing, but full of the awful stillness of a funeral march. She saw that someone was being borne on the shoulders of the men—someone dead—and the others were his mourning followers. She wondered who it could be, and why they were bringing him to the palace.

Kriemhild trembled with fear and dread as she saw the figures of Gunther and Hagen return without Sigurd. Unable to bear the suspense any longer, she left the room and hurried down to meet her brother and learn tidings of Sigurd. But the moment she entered the hall, the faces of the men told her all she wished to know, and she did not need to inquire who the dead might be.

Everyone in the palace shared the grief of Sigurd's gentle wife, and all the city mourned with her in the loss of one so greatly beloved as the hero whom Hagen called a "stranger." As long as the first shock of Sigurd's tragic death engrossed all of Kriemhild's thought and feeling, she did not realize the part which Hagen had played in the event; but as the days went by and she had time to think of all that had gone before, she remembered how her uncle had traitorously obtained the secret of Sigurd's vulnerable spot from her, and how she herself had, at his request, sewed the fatal mark upon her husband's coat. She had heard that it was by Hagen's hand that Sigurd met his death, yet she could not believe him guilty of such a terrible deed. So one day she went weeping to Hagen, and asked him to tell her by whom Sigurd was slain.

"The story of such things is not for a woman's ears," replied Hagen, "and whether he died by my hand or another's is of small moment. It was the will of the Norns, who rule the life of every man, that he should die, and their decrees no one of us can change or avert."

When the day was set for the great funeral fires to be lit, all the princes of Burgundy came to attend the solemn festival, and sought to do homage to the dead hero by bringing rich gifts to be laid upon the funeral pyre. This imposing structure was erected in front of the palace, and on the appointed day the foremost lords of Gunther's household brought the body of Sigurd from the palace where it had lain in state, and placed it sorrowfully upon the funeral pyre. Beside him was laid his armour and his magic Tarnkappe, and last of all the famous sword Gram. The king had ordered that Greyfel be carefully guarded for fear that if he were brought upon the scene, he would leap into the flames and perish with his master.

Around these things, which were sacred to the memory of Sigurd, the princes of Burgundy piled their most costly gifts, and everything was ready for the fires to be lit. But no one of Gunther's men could bear to place a torch to the wood, and a dreadful stillness fell over the whole assembly. At length Hagen came boldly forward and laid a burning brand to the pile of logs which formed the funeral pyre. In a moment the whole structure was ablaze, and the hungry flames leaped upward toward the sky.

Gunther stood by, trembling and fearful, lest Odin should send some terrible retribution upon the one who had slain his chosen hero. Kriemhild, weeping, hid her face in her hands, for she could not watch the dreadful fires. On the faces of all the watchers was reflected a great sorrow, for no prince of Burgundy was so dear to them as Sigurd, even though he came from a foreign land. Only Hagen showed no grief or any sign of repentance for his deed, but stood by unmoved, like a grim, avenging god.

Then suddenly a figure appeared in their midst, wild and dishevelled, and seemingly mad with grief. It was Brunhilde, once a Valkyrie, come to claim her slain. Turning to the astonished group of mourners, she cried exultingly:—

"Look, you people of Burgundy, for the last time upon your queen whom you have ever seen fulfilling the common lot of mortal woman, and know that I was once a shield-maiden, one of Odin's Valkyries. I was condemned to eternal sleep by the great All-father, but was rescued by Sigurd, the hero who knows no fear. And here he lies who rode through the wall of fire to waken me, and who won me in the games by his godlike strength, though your cowardly King Gunther made false claim to me. Here lies Sigurd, the chosen hero of Odin and the true mate of Odin's warrior maiden. Therefore for him alone does Brunhilde own her love, and to him alone will she be wed. The Valkyrie yields only to the greatest hero." Saying this she leaped upon the funeral pyre, and in a moment had perished beside Sigurd in the flames. [24]

And what of the ill-fated hoard upon which still rested Andvari's curse?

When the shock of the terrible events connected with Sigurd's death was over, and quiet was once more restored to Gunther's palace, Hagen came one day to the king and said:—

"You remember that Sigurd gave all of his treasure to Kriemhild on their wedding day, and although the hoard was never brought to Burgundy it still remains in the possession of your sister. Entreat her, therefore, to have it conveyed here; and, to accomplish your end more easily, tell her that she can honour Sigurd's memory by distributing his wealth among the poor. When we get the treasure into our hands, we will see, however, that nothing so foolish is done."

The weak-willed Gunther, always under the control of Hagen, accordingly sought Kriemhild and told her what great things could be done in honour of Sigurd, if only the treasure in the dragon's cave could be placed at her disposal. Kriemhild was not suspicious of her brother, for she did not know what part he had played in Sigurd's death, so she listened readily to his words, and said,—

"It shall be done even as you say, for naught can now bring me solace in my grief save some way to make the name of Sigurd dearer to the hearts of the people."

Then she handed Gunther the serpent ring which Sigurd had given her, and told him where to find the famous hoard in the cave of Glistenheath. She bade him keep the ring carefully, for Andvari might again have taken possession of the treasure, though he would yield it to the wearer of the ring.

The king took the ring from Kriemhild, and hastened with it to Hagen, who at once set to work to make preparations for conveying the hoard to Burgundy. In a few days a great number of wagons were fitted up, and with these a hundred men were despatched to gather all the treasure and bring it back to the palace. Although most of the men were Hagen's own followers, he could not trust them to go alone on this important mission, so he placed Sigurd's ring upon his own finger and led the expedition himself.

The hoard was found securely stowed away in Fafnir's cave, and not a single piece of gold had been taken since Sigurd rode away after slaying the dragon. The dwarf Andvari still guarded the treasure which had once been his; but when Hagen showed the serpent ring, he allowed the stranger to enter the cave. He would have preferred to deliver the hoard to Sigurd himself, but the possession of the serpent ring made its wearer the rightful owner of all the treasure. So Andvari was obliged to admit Hagen's claim, and assist him in bearing away the gold.

Some days later, the company which had set out from Gunther's palace empty-handed came back laden with such wealth of gold and precious stones that all the riches of Burgundy seemed nothing in comparison. This great hoard was stored safely in Gunther's palace, and Kriemhild was very glad to find so much wealth at her disposal.

She became very lavish in her gifts, and eager to pour out all her riches, if only it brought added honour upon Sigurd's memory. No one who came to beg alms of her ever went away empty-handed, and the palace was always full of suppliants for her bounty. This extravagant giving went on for some time, until one day Hagen came to the king and said:—

"If your sister continues to distribute so much gold among the people, we will soon have them idle and rebellious, and then they will be useless to us in time of warfare. Bid her, therefore, to cease her giving."

But Gunther answered, "I have brought enough sorrow upon her through my evil deeds, and if this lavish giving can soften her grief, let her continue to dispose of her wealth as it pleases her, even though she should exhaust all the treasure that is in the hoard."

Hagen determined, however, that it must not be so, and seeing that he could get no help from the king, he planned to gain his end by other means. So he made every appearance of approving Kriemhild's lavish gifts, and in time prevailed upon her to give him access to the treasure, that he might help her in disposing of it. Then one dark night he gathered together a band of his own followers, and stole all that remained of the hoard. They carried it from the palace by a secret passage, and brought it down to the river, where Hagen sunk it many fathoms deep. Neither he nor anyone else could ever regain it, but at least it was out of Kriemhild's hands.

Thus was the hoard of Andvari, with its fateful curse, placed forever beyond the reach of men; but the charm and the mystery which hung around its very name still lingered through all the centuries that followed, and today the sailors upon the river Rhine are still looking for some glimpse of the sunken treasure.

The Punishment of Loki (abridged)

The curse which the dwarf Andvari had placed upon the hoard, and particularly upon the serpent ring which Loki had wrested from him, did not end with the sinking of the treasure in the river. Both Hagen and Kriemhild had been wearers of the ring, and evil soon fell upon them as it had upon Fafnir, Regin, Sigurd, and Brunhilde. Some years after Sigurd's death, Kriemhild married Etzel, king of the Huns, and was slain by one of his knights. Before this, however, she herself had struck the blow that killed the treacherous and cruel Hagen. With the burial of Kriemhild, the ill-fated ring passed forever from the sight of men, and the curse of Andvari was never again visited upon its unfortunate possessors.

Any other of the gods than Loki would have regretted the greed which made him tear the serpent ring from Andvari's finger, and thus bring misfortune upon so many innocent people; but Loki did not care whether human lives were wrecked by his misdoing any more than he felt one moment's remorse for having slain the shining Balder.

The gods had never forgiven Loki for this wicked deed, and they longed very much to drive him out of their beautiful city, which had never harboured any other evil thing. But Loki was Odin's brother, and they dared not punish him until the All-Wise One was ready to give his consent. Odin knew as well as they, that the slayer of Balder was not fit to live among the gods; but he waited for Loki to commit one more act of cruelty before he drove the offender out of Asgard. This occasion came, at last, sooner than Odin expected.

One day all the gods were invited to a feast in the halls of Æger, the sea-king; Thor was not present at the feast, for he had been obliged to go on a long journey, but Loki was there, looking sullen and angry. The palace of the sea-god was very beautiful, with its walls and ceiling made of mother-of-pearl so delicately laid that the light filtered softly through it. On the floor was strewn the finest golden sand, and all the food was placed in opal-tinted seashells. The only thing that marred the beauty of the scene was Loki's ugly, wicked face.

As the meal progressed and the gods grew merry over their cups, they almost forgot the presence of the unwelcome guest; but Loki brooded in angry silence, waiting for some chance to wreak his ill will upon the whole company. A servant stopped beside him to refill his horn with the foaming ale; and one of the gods, as he watched this, said to old Æger: "Your servants have been well instructed. They are as careful to wait upon Loki as if he were an honoured guest." When Loki heard these words, he flew into a mad rage and, seizing a knife that was lying on the table, he struck the unoffending servant dead.

At this wanton cruelty the gods sat speechless; but Odin rose, looking stern and awful in his wrath, and with a relentless voice he bade Loki be gone. "Never dare to tread our sacred halls again, nor pollute the pure air of Asgard with your presence," he cried. So terrible did Odin look that Loki slunk away out of the hall, and the gods returned again to their feasting. Soon a great noise was heard outside the hall, and all the servants came running in, looking very much frightened. Behind them walked Loki, who came boldly up to the table and dared Odin to send him out before he had spoken the words he had come back to say.

Then he began to talk to each one of the gods in turn, telling them of all the foolish or mean or wicked things they had ever done—ridiculing their mistakes, and laying bare all their faults in such a dishonest way that each small offence seemed an act of monstrous wickedness. Not content with trying to shame the heroes of Asgard, Loki began to speak slightingly of the goddesses and attributed to them all the hateful things that his malicious imagination could invent. He was just telling some shameful lie about Sif when a rumbling of chariot wheels was heard outside, and in a moment Thor rushed into the hall brandishing his hammer. He had heard Loki's last words, and he made straight for the slanderer, intending to crush him with one blow of Mjolnir. Loki, however, quickly changed himself into a sea serpent, and slid out of the room before Thor's vengeful hammer could descend upon his head.

Taking his own shape, he made his way to the mountains of the north, and there he built a hut with four doors, opening north, east, south, and west, so that he could see anyone approaching and could easily make his escape. The hut was close beside a swift mountain stream, and here Loki spent many days in fishing—for there was little else to do to beguile the long hours. Remembering how easy it had been to catch Andvari after he had obtained the help of Ran, Loki made himself a net like the one which he had borrowed from the ocean queen. It took him a long time to weave the net; and one day, just as it was nearly finished, he saw two figures standing on the brow of the hill and knew Thor and Odin had come to punish him for his many evil deeds—but he did not intend to be caught without making every possible effort to escape. So he threw the net which he was making into the fire, and, hurrying down to the stream, he quickly changed himself into a salmon.

When Odin and Thor reached the hut where they knew Loki had been in hiding, they found that he had escaped them. Then Thor by chance stumbled over the logs on the hearth, and, in doing so, he discovered the half-burnt net. Picking it up, he cried to Odin: "So this is what our crafty Loki has been doing to fill his idle hours. There must be some brook nearby."

"Yes," replied Odin, "and that is where he has just gone. He has changed himself into a fish."

So the two gods went to the mountain stream, and there they saw a salmon lurking in the depths of a pool. Odin had already mended the burnt net so that it was serviceable. After several attempts, they caught the salmon as it leapt into the air.

Then, finding itself caught, with incredible quickness it began to work its way through the meshes of the net, and would have slid out of the gods' hands had not Thor suddenly caught it by the tail. Since that time, so the story goes, all salmon have their tails pointed.

Odin now changed Loki into his proper form, and he and Thor dragged the wicked god to a cave in the mountain. Here they bound Loki hand and foot with iron chains, and fastened these firmly to the rock. Then Odin placed over his head a venomous serpent which dropped its poison upon the face of the fettered god, causing him great pain. So, chained and suffering, he lay there in the cave, unpitied by either gods or men. Only Sigyn, his faithful wife, felt any sorrow for his pain, and she sat always beside him to catch the venom in a cup so that it should not fall on the captive's face. When she was obliged to turn away to empty the cup, the drops of poison fell upon Loki, and he shook and writhed so terribly in his agony that the whole earth trembled.

So Loki lay chained in the cave until the day when, according to the decree of the Norns, he was allowed to break his fetters and become the leader in that terrible battle which ushered in the last great day—Ragnarok, the Twilight of the Gods.

NOTES

1. The otter was held sacred by the Norsemen, and it figures in the myths of many races. Even today the killing of an otter is considered a great crime by the Parsees.

2. The old man's name was Hreidmar (Rodmar).

3. In the *Volsunga Saga* his name is Sigurd; however, the original version of this text used the Germanic name of Siegfried. The name has been changed to Sigurd throughout this version.

4. Volsung was the son of Rerir, who was the son of Sigi, the son of Odin.

5. Spelled Sigmund in the *Volsunga Saga*.

6. The she-wolf was supposed to be the mother of King Siggeir, who had been turned into a wolf by a troll.

7. In the *Volsunga Saga* the queen, who is still living, gives the pieces of the sword to Sigurd.

8. In the *Volsunga Saga* the sword is called Gram. Balmung was used in the original version of this tale; it has been changed to Gram throughout this version.

9. In the *Volsunga Saga* the hero is now often called Fafnir's bane.

10. The horse is called Grani in the *Volsunga Saga*.

11. There is an old superstition that the curse of the dying is sure to be fulfilled if he knows his enemy's name.

12. From this chapter on, the incidents follow the story in the *Nibelungenlied*.

13. The mountain was called Hindfell.

14. In the *Volsunga Saga*, Brunhilde lies asleep in a shield-hung castle surrounded by fire.

15. The light made by the gleaming shields of the Valkyries was the Aurora Borealis.

16. The boar was called Serimnir.

17.–19. In the *Volsunga Saga*, Gunther is called Gunnar, Ute is called Grimhild, and Kriemhild is called Gudrun.

20. Called Hogni, in the *Volsunga Saga*. He is the king's brother—not his uncle, as in the *Nibelungenlied*.

21. In the *Nibelungenlied*, Sigurd (Siegfried) took the treasure from two princes, the sons of King Niblung.

22. In the *Volsunga Saga*, the castle is called Hlymdale, and Gunnar has to ride through the flames, with Sigurd's help, to win Brunhilde.

23. In the *Volsunga Saga*, Guttorm, the younger brother, is incited to slay Sigurd (Siegfried) while the hero is sleeping in bed.

24. In the *Volsunga Saga*, Brunhilde kills herself with a sword.

DISCUSSION QUESTIONS

1. Comment on the role of the gods in this story. In what ways do they help or hinder the actions of human beings?

2. Are all of the actions of Sigurd and his family truly heroic? Explain.

3. Discuss the function of treasure in the story. How does the story illustrate the attitude these people had toward wealth?

4. Sigurd knows the dragon's treasure is cursed, so why does he take it? Did he do the right thing? Defend your response.

Thor and the Giants of Utgardr (Norse)

As a part of the "Prose Edda," The Third One tells this story. Thor and Loki stop in the forest and have dinner with Thor's magical goats that regenerate overnight to provide a never-ending food supply. The son of the farmer cuts off one of the legs of the goat and ruins the spell. The parents give the son (Thjálfi) and daughter (Röskva) to Thor as servants. The story picks up the next morning when they begin their travels again with nothing to eat.

THOR AND THE GIANTS OF UTGARDR

Thor and Loki Meet Skrymir

Thereupon he left his goats behind, and began his journey eastward toward Jötunheim and clear to the sea; and then he went out over the sea, that deep one; but when he came to land, he went up, and Loki and Thjálfi and Röskva with him. Then, when they had walked a little while, there stood before them a great forest; they walked all that day till dark. Thjálfi was swiftest-footed of all men; he bore Thor's bag, but there was nothing good for food. As soon as it had become dark, they sought themselves shelter for the night, and found before them a certain hall, very great: there was a door in the end, of equal width with the hall, wherein they took up quarters for the night.

But about midnight there came a great earthquake: the earth rocked under them exceedingly, and the house trembled. Then Thor rose up and called to his companions, and they explored farther, and found in the middle of the hall a side-chamber on the right hand, and they went in thither. Thor sat down in the doorway, but the others were farther in from him, and they were afraid; but Thor gripped his hammer-shaft and thought to defend himself. Then they heard a great humming sound, and a crashing.

But when it drew near dawn, then Thor went out and saw a man lying a little way from him in the wood; and that man was not small; he slept and snored mightily. Then Thor thought he could perceive what kind of noise it was which they had heard during the night. He girded himself with his belt of strength, and his divine power waxed; and on the instant the man awoke and rose up swiftly; and then, it is said, the first time Thor's heart failed him, to strike him with the hammer.

He asked him his name, and the man called himself Skrýmir, "but I have no need," he said, "to ask thee for thy name; I know that thou art Thor. But what? Hast thou dragged away my glove?"

Then Skrýmir stretched out his hand and took up the glove; and at once Thor saw that it was that which he had taken for a hall during the night; and as for the side-chamber, it was the thumb of the glove. Skrýmir asked whether Thor would have his company, and Thor assented to this. Then Skrýmir took and unloosened his provision wallet and made ready to eat his morning meal, and Thor and his fellows in another place. Skrýmir then proposed to them to lay their supply of food together, and Thor assented. Then Skrýmir bound all the food in one bag and laid it on his own back; he went before during the day, and stepped with very great strides; but late in the evening Skrýmir found them night-quarters under a certain great oak.

Then Skrýmir said to Thor that he would lay him down to sleep,—"and do ye take the provision-bag and make ready for your supper."

Thereupon Skrýmir slept and snored hard, and Thor took the provision-bag and set about to unloose it; but such things must be told as will seem incredible: he got no knot loosened and no thong-end stirred, so as to be looser than before. When he saw that this work might not avail, then he became angered, gripped the hammer Mjöllnir in both hands, and strode with great strides to that place where Skrýmir lay, and smote him in the head.

Source: Foster, Mary H., and Mabel H. Cummings. "Asgard Stories: Tales from Norse Mythology," 1901.

Skrýmir awoke, and asked whether a leaf had fallen upon his head; or whether they had eaten and were ready for bed? Thor replied that they were just then about to go to sleep; then they went under another oak. It must be told thee, that there was then no fearless sleeping. At midnight Thor heard how Skrýmir snored and slept fast, so that it thundered in the woods; then he stood up and went to him, shook his hammer eagerly and hard, and smote down upon the middle of his crown: he saw that the face of the hammer sank deep into his head.

And at that moment Skrýmir awoke arid said: "What is it now? Did some acorn fall on my head? Or what is the news with thee, Thor?" But Thor went back speedily, and replied that he was then but new-wakened; said that it was then midnight, and there was yet time to sleep.

Thor meditated that if he could get to strike him a third blow, never should the giant see himself again; he lay now and watched whether Skrýmir were sleeping soundly yet. A little before day, when he perceived that Skrýmir must have fallen asleep, he stood up at once and rushed over to him, brandished his hammer with all his strength, and smote upon that one of his temples which was turned up.

But Skrýmir sat up and stroked his cheek, and said: "Some birds must be sitting in the tree above me; I imagined, when I awoke, that some dirt from the twigs fell upon my head. Art thou awake, Thor? It will be time to arise and clothe us; but now ye have no long journey forward to the castle called Útgardr. I have heard how ye have whispered among yourselves that I am no little man in stature; but ye shall see taller men, if ye come into Útgardr. Now I will give you wholesome advice: do not conduct yourselves boastfully, for the henchmen of Útgard-Loki will not well endure big words from such swaddling-babes. But if not so, then turn back, and I think it were better for you to do that; but if ye will go forward, then turn to the east. As for me, I hold my way north to these hills, which ye may how see."

Skrýmir took the provision-bag and cast it on his back, and turned from them across the forest; and it is not recorded that the Æsir bade him god-speed.

The Games at Útgardr

Thor turned forward on his way, and his fellows, and went onward till mid-day. Then they saw a castle standing in a certain plain, and set their necks down on their backs before they could see up over it. They went to the castle; and there was a grating in front of the castle-gate, and it was closed. Thor went up to the grating, and did not succeed in opening it; but when they struggled to make their way in, they crept between the bars and came in that way. They saw a great hall and went thither; the door was open; then they went in, and saw there many men on two benches, and most of them were big enough.

Thereupon they came before the king Útgard-Loki and saluted him; but he looked at them in his own good time, and smiled scornfully over his teeth, and said: "It is late to ask tidings of a long journey; or is it otherwise than I think: that this toddler is Thor? Yet thou mayest be greater than thou appearest to me. What manner of accomplishments are those, which thou and thy fellows think to be ready for? No one shall be here with us who knows not some kind of craft or cunning surpassing most men."

Then spoke Loki, who came last: "I know such a trick, which I am ready to try: that there is no one within here who shall eat his food more quickly than I."

Then Útgard-Loki answered: "That is a feat, if thou accomplish it; and this feat shall accordingly be put to the proof."'

He called to the farther end of the bench, that he who was called Logi should come forth on the floor and try his prowess against Loki. Then a trough was taken and borne in upon the hall-floor and filled with flesh; Loki sat down at the one end and Logi at the other, and each ate as fast as he could, and they met in the middle of the trough. By that time Loki had eaten all the meat from the bones, but Logi likewise had eaten all the meat, and the bones with it, and the trough too; and now it seemed to all as if Loki had lost the game.

Then Útgard-Loki asked what yonder young man could play at; and Thjálfi answered that he would undertake to run a race with whomsoever Útgard-Loki would bring up. Then Útgard-Loki said that that was a good accomplishment, and that there was great likelihood that he must be well endowed with fleetness if he were to perform that feat; yet he would speedily see to it that the matter should be tested.

Then Útgard-Loki arose and went out; and there was a good course to run on over the level plain. Then Útgard-Loki called to him a certain lad, who was named Hugi, and bade him run a match against Thjálfi. Then they held the first heat; and Hugi was so much ahead that he turned back to meet Thjálfi at the end of the course.

Then said Útgard-Loki: "Thou wilt need to lay thyself forward more, Thjálfi, if thou art to win the game; but it is none the less true that never have any men come hither who seemed to me fleeter of foot than this."

Then they began another heat; and when Hugi had reached the course's end, and was turning back, there was still a long bolt-shot to Thjálfi.

Then spake Útgarda-Loki: "Thjálfi appears to me to run this course well, but I do not believe of him now that he will win the game. But it will be made manifest presently, when they run the third heat."

Then they began the heat; but when Hugi had come to the end of the course and turned back, Thjálfi had not yet reached mid-course. Then all said that that game had been proven.

Next, Útgarda-Loki asked Thor what feats there were which he might desire to show before them: such great tales as men have made of his mighty works. Then Thor answered that he would most willingly undertake to contend with any in drinking. Útgard-Loki said that might well be; he went into the hall and called his serving-boy, and bade him bring the sconce-horn which the henchmen were wont to drink off. Straightway the serving-lad came forward with the horn and put it into Thor's hand.

Then said Útgard-Loki: "It is held that this horn is well drained if it is drunk off in one drink, but some drink it off in two; but no one is so poor a man at drinking that it fails to drain off in three." Thor looked upon the horn, and it did not seem big to him; and yet it was somewhat long. Still he was very thirsty; he took and drank, and swallowed enormously, and thought that he should not need to bend oftener to the horn. But when his breath failed, and he raised his head from the horn and looked to see how it had gone with the drinking, it seemed to him that there was very little space by which the drink was lower now in the horn than before.

Then said Útgard-Loki: "It is well drunk, and not too much; I should not have believed, if it had been told me, that Thor could not drink a greater draught. But I know that thou wilt wish to drink it off in another draught. "Thor answered nothing; he set the horn to his mouth, thinking now that he should drink a greater drink, and struggled with the draught until his breath gave out; and yet he saw that the tip of the horn would not come up so much as he liked. When he took the horn from his mouth and looked into it, it seemed to him then as if it had decreased less than the former time; but now there was a clearly apparent lowering in the horn.

Then said Útgard-Loki: "How now, Thor? Thou wilt not shrink from one more drink than may he well for thee? If thou now drink the third draught from the horn, it seems to me as if this must he esteemed the greatest; but thou canst not be called so great a man here among us as the Æsir call thee, if thou give not a better account of thyself in the other games than it seems to me may come of this."

Then Thor became angry, set—the horn to his mouth, and drank with all his might, and struggled with the drink as much as he could; and when he looked into the horn, at least some space had been made. Then he gave up the horn and would drink no more.

Then said Útgard-Loki: "Now it is evident that thy prowess is not so great as we thought it to be; but wilt thou try thy hand at more games? It may readily be seen that thou gettest no advantage hereof."

Thor answered: "I will make trial of yet other games; but it would have seemed wonderful to me, when I was at home with the Æsir, if such drinks had been called so little. But what game will ye now offer me?"

Then said Útgard-Loki: "Young lads here are wont to do this (which is thought of small consequence): lift my cat up from the earth; but I should not have been able to speak of such a thing to Thor if I had not seen that thou hast far less in thee than I had thought."

Thereupon there leaped forth on the hall-floor a gray cat, and a very big one; and Thor went to it and took it with his hand down under the middle of the belly and lifted up. But the cat bent into an arch just as Thor stretched up his hands; and when Thor reached up as high as he could at the very utmost, then the cat lifted up one foot, and Thor got this game no further advanced.

Then said Útgard-Loki: "This game went even as I had foreseen; the cat is very great, whereas Thor is low and little beside the huge men who are here with us."

Then said Thor: "Little as ye call me, let anyone come up now and wrestle with me; now I am angry."

Then Útgard-Loki answered, looking about him on the benches, and spake: "I see no such man here within, who would not hold it a disgrace to wrestle with thee;" and yet he said: "Let us see first; let the old woman my nurse be called hither, Elli, and let Thor wrestle with her if he will. She has thrown such men as have seemed to me no less strong than Thor."

Straightway there came into the hall an old woman, stricken in years. Then Útgard-Loki said that she should grapple with Thor. There is no need to make a long matter of it: that struggle went in such wise that the harder Thor strove in gripping, the faster she stood; then the old woman essayed a hold, and then Thor became totty on his feet, and their tuggings were very hard. Yet it was not long before Thor fell to his knee, on one foot.

Then Útgard-Loki went up and bade them cease the wrestling, saying that Thor should not need to challenge more men of his body-guard to wrestling. By then it had passed toward night; Útgard-Loki showed Thor and his companions to a seat, and they tarried there the night long in good cheer.

The Truth

But at morning, as soon as it dawned, Thor and his companions arose, clothed themselves, and were ready to go away. Then came there Útgard-Loki and caused a table to be set for them; there was no lack of good cheer, meat and drink. So soon as they had eaten, he went out from the castle with them; and at parting Útgard-Loki spoke to Thor and asked how he thought his journey had ended, or whether he had met any man mightier than himself.

Thor answered that he could not say that he had not got much shame in their dealings together. "But yet I know that ye will call me a man of little might, and I am ill-content with that."

Then said Útgard-Loki: "Now I will tell thee the truth, now that thou art come out of the castle; and if I live and am able to prevail, then thou shalt never again come into it. And this I know, by my troth! that thou shouldst never have come into it If I had known before that thou hadst so much strength in thee, and that thou shouldst so nearly have had us in great peril. But I made ready against thee eye-illusions; and I came upon you the first time in the wood, and when thou wouldst have unloosed the provision-bag, I had bound it with iron, and thou didst not find where to undo it.

"But next thou didst smite me three blows with the hammer; and the first was least, and was yet so great that it would have sufficed to slay me, if it had come upon me. Where thou sawest near my hall a saddle-backed mountain, cut at the top into threesquare dales, and one the deepest, those were the marks of thy hammer. I brought the saddle-back before the blow, but thou didst not see that. So it was also with the games, in which ye did contend against my henchmen: that was the first, which Loki did; he was very hungry and ate zealously, but he who was called Logi was "wild-fire," and he burned the trough no less swiftly than the meat. But when Thjálfi ran the race with him called Hugi, that was my 'thought,' and it was not to be expected of Thjálfi that he should match swiftness with it.

"Moreover, when thou didst drink from the horn, and it seemed to thee to go slowly, then, by my faith, that was a wonder which I should not have believed possible: the other end of the horn was out in the sea, but thou didst not perceive it. But now, when thou comest to the sea, thou shalt be able to mark what a diminishing thou hast drunk in the sea: this is henceforth called 'ebb-tides.'"

And again he said: "It seemed to me not less noteworthy when thou didst lift up the cat; and to tell thee truly, then all were afraid who saw how thou didst lift one foot clear of the earth. That cat was not as it appeared to thee: it was the Midgard Serpent, which lies about all the land, and scarcely does its length suffice to encompass the earth with head and tail. So high didst thou stretch up thine arms that it was then but a little way more to heaven.

"It was also a great marvel concerning the wrestling-match, when thou didst withstand so long, and didst not fall more than on one knee, wrestling with Elli; since none such has ever been and none shall be, if he become so old as to abide 'Old Age,' that she shall not cause him to fall.

And now it is truth to tell that we must part; and it will be better on both sides that ye never come again to seek me. Another time I will defend my castle with similar wiles or with others, so that ye shall get no power over me."

When Thor had heard these sayings, he clutched his hammer and brandished it aloft; but when he was about to launch it forward, then he saw Útgard-Loki nowhere. Then he turned back to the castle, with the purpose of crushing it to pieces; and he saw there a wide and fair plain, but no castle.

So he turned back and went his way, till he was come back again to Thrúdvangar. But it is a true tale that then he resolved to seek if he might bring about a meeting between himself and the Midgard Serpent, which after ward came to pass.

DISCUSSION QUESTIONS

1. Why is it important to show Thor's inability to defeat Skrýmir at the start of this tale?

2. During the games at Utgardr, how does Utgard-Loki seem to outwit Thor?

3. When we learn the truth of the games, what does Thor's reaction to the trickery show about his character?

Ivan Tsarevich, The Fire-bird, and the Gray Wolf (Russian)

Ivan Tsarevich is an often-used male protagonist in Russian literature. He is not necessarily a specific character, but a prototype that stands in for any male character referenced in heroic epics. His exploits often involve supernatural creatures, quests for impossible objects, and the rescue of a damsel in distress. This story, which involves the quest for the Fire-bird, the aid of the Gray Wolf, and his love interest, Yelena the Beautiful, is the most famous of these Russian hero tales. Igor Stravinsky's ballet *The Firebird* is based upon this epic.

IVAN TSAREVICH, THE FIRE-BIRD, AND THE GRAY WOLF

In a certain kingdom, in a certain land, lived Tsar Vwislav Andronovich; he had three sons—Dmitri Tsarevich, Vassili Tsarevich, and Ivan Tsarevich. Tsar Vwislav had a garden so rich that in no land was there better. In the garden grew many precious trees, with fruit and without fruit. Tsar Vwislav had one favorite apple tree, and on that tree grew apples all golden. The Fire-bird used fly to the garden of Tsar Vwislav. She had wings of gold and eyes like crystals of the East; and she used to fly to that garden every night, sit on the apple tree, pluck from it golden apples, and fly away. The Tsar grieved greatly over that apple tree because the Fire-bird plucked from it many apples.

Therefore he called his three sons and said: "My dear children, whichever one of you can catch the Fire-bird in my garden and take her alive, to him will I give during my life one half of the kingdom, and at my death I will give it all."

Then the sons cried out in one voice: "Gracious our sovereign, our father, we will try with great pleasure take the Fire-bird alive."

The first night Dmitri Tsarevich went to watch in the garden, and sat under the apple tree from which the Fire-bird had been plucking the apples. He fell asleep, and did not hear the Fire-bird when she came, nor when she plucked many apples. Next morning Tsar Vwislav called his son Dmitri Tsarevich, and asked, "Well, my dear son, hast thou seen the Fire-bird?"

"No, gracious sovereign, my father, she came not last night."

The next night Vassili Tsarevich went to the garden to watch the Fire-bird. He sat under the same apple tree, and in a couple of hours fell asleep so soundly that he did not hear the Fire-bird when she came, nor when she plucked apples. Next morning Tsar Vwislav called him and asked, "Well, my dear son, hast thou seen the Fire-bird?"

"Gracious sovereign, my father, she came not last night."

The third night Ivan Tsarevich went to watch in the garden, and sat under the same apple tree. He sat an hour, a second, and a third. All at once the whole garden was lighted up as if by many fires. The Fire-bird flew hither, perched on the apple tree, and began to pluck apples. Ivan stole up to her so warily that he caught her tail, but could not hold the bird; she tore off, flew away, and there remained in the hand of Ivan Tsarevich but one feather of the tail, which he held very firmly.

Next morning, the moment Tsar Vwislav woke from his sleep, Ivan Tsarevich went to him and gave him the feather of the Fire-bird. The Tsar was greatly delighted that his youngest son had been able to get even one feather of the Fire-bird. This feather was so wonderful and bright that when carried into a dark chamber it shone as if a great multitude of tapers were lighted in that place. Tsar Vwislav put the feather in his cabinet as a thing to be guarded forever. From that time forth the Fire-bird flew to the garden no more.

Source: Jeremiah Curtain, "Myths and Folk-tales of the Russians, West-Slavs, and Magyars," 1890.

Tsar Vwislav again called his sons, and said: "My dear children, I give you my blessing. Set out, find the Fire-bird, and bring her to me alive; and what I promised at first he will surely receive who brings me the bird."

Dmitri and Vassili Tsarevich began to cherish hatred against their youngest brother because he had pulled the feather from the tail of the Fire-bird. They took their father's blessing, and both went to find the Fire-bird. Ivan Tsarevich too began to beg his father's blessing. The Tsar said to him: "My dear son, my darling child, thou art still young unused to such a long and difficult journey: why shouldst thou part from me? Thy brothers have gone; now, if thou goest too, and all three of you fail to return for a long time (I am old, and walk under God), and if during your absence the Lord takes my life, who would rule in my place? There might be rebellion too, or disagreement among our people,—there would be no one to stop it; or if an enemy should invade our land, there would be no one to command our men."

But no matter how the Tsar tried to detain Ivan Tsarevich, he could not avoid letting him go at his urgent prayer. Ivan Tsarevich took a blessing of his father, chose a horse, and rode away; he rode on, not knowing himself whither. Riding by the path by the road, whether it was near or far, high or low, a tale is soon told but a deed is not soon done. At last he came to the green meadows. In the open field a pillar stands, and on the pillar these words are written: "Whoever goes from the pillar straight forward will be hungry and cold; whoever goes to the right hand will be healthy and well, but his horse will be dead; whoever goes to the left hand will be killed himself, but his horse will be living and well."

Ivan read the inscription and went to the right hand, holding in mind that though his horse might be killed, he would remain alive, and might in time get another horse. He rode one day, a second, and a third. All at once an enormous gray wolf came out against him and said: "Oh! is that thou, tender youth, Ivan Tsarevich? Thou hast read on the pillar that thy horse will be dead: why hast thou come hither, then?"

The wolf said these words, tore Ivan Tsarevich's horse in two, and went to one side. Ivan grieved greatly for his horse. He cried bitterly, and went forward on foot. He walked all day, and was unspeakably tired. He was going to sit down and rest, when all at once the Gray Wolf caught up with him and said: "I am sorry for thee, Ivan Tsarevich, thou art tired from walking; I am sorry that I ate thy good steed. Well, sit on me, the old wolf, and tell me whither to bear thee, and why."

Ivan Tsarevich told the Gray Wolf whither he had to go, and the Gray Wolf shot ahead with him swifter than a horse. After a time, just at nightfall, he brought Ivan Tsarevich to a stone wall not very high, halted, and said: "Now, Ivan Tsarevich, come down from the Gray Wolf, climb over that stone wall; on the other side is a garden, and in the garden the Fire-bird in a golden cage. Take the Fire-bird, but touch not the cage. If thou takest the cage, thou'lt not escape; they will seize thee straightway."

Ivan Tsarevich climbed over the wall into the garden, saw the Fire-bird in the golden cage, and was greatly tempted by the cage. He took the bird out, and was going back, but changed his mind and thought, "Why have I taken the bird without the cage? Where can I put her?"

He returned, but had barely taken down the cage when there was a hammering and thundering throughout the whole garden, for there were wires attached to the cage. The watchmen woke up at that moment, ran to the garden, caught Ivan Tsarevich with the Fire-bird, and took him to the Tsar, who was called Dolmat. Tsar Dolmat was terribly enraged at Ivan and shouted at him in loud, angry tones: "Is it not a shame for thee, young man, to steal? But who art thou, of what land, of what father a son, and how do they call thee by name?"

Ivan Tsarevich replied: "I am from Vwislav's, kingdom, the son of Tsar Vwislav Andronovich, and they call me Ivan Tsarevich. Thy Fire-bird used to fly to our garden each night and pluck golden apples from my father's favorite apple tree, and destroyed almost the whole tree. Therefore my father has sent me to find the Fire-bird and bring it to him."

"Oh youthful young man, Ivan Tsarevich," said Tsar Dolmat, "is it fitting to do as thou hast done? Thou shouldst have come to me, and I would have given thee the Fire-bird with honor; but now will it be well for thee when I send to all lands to declare how dishonorably thou hast acted in my kingdom? Listen, however, Ivan Tsarevich. If thou wilt do me a service,—if thou wilt go beyond the thrice ninth land to the thirtieth kingdom and get for me from Tsar Afron the golden-maned steed, I will forgive thy offence and give thee the Fire-bird with great honor; if not, I will publish in all kingdoms that thou art a dishonorable thief."

Ivan Tsarevich went away from Tsar Dolmat in great grief, promising to obtain for him the golden-maned steed. He came to the Gray Wolf, and told him all that Tsar Dolmat had said.

"Oh! is that thou, youthful young man, Ivan Tsarevich? Why didst thou disobey my words and take the golden cage?"

"I have offended in thy sight," said Ivan to the Gray Wolf.

"Well, let that go; sit on me, and I will take thee wherever thou wilt."

Ivan Tsarevich sat on the back of the Gray Wolf. The wolf was as swift as an arrow, and ran, whether it was long or short, till he came at last to the kingdom of Tsar Afron in the night time. Coming to the white walled stables the Gray Wolf said: "Go, Ivan Tsarevich, into these white walled stables (the grooms on guard are sleeping soundly), and take the golden-maned steed. On the wall hangs a golden bridle; but take not the bridle, or it will go ill with thee."

Ivan Tsarevich entered the white walled stables, took the steed and was coming back; but he saw on the walls the golden bridle, and was so tempted that he took it from the nail. That moment there went a thunder and a noise throughout the stables, because strings were tied to the bridle. The grooms on guard woke up that moment, rushed in, seized Ivan Tsarevich, and took him to Tsar Afron. Tsar Afron began to question him. "Oh, youthful young man, tell me from what land thou art, of what father a son, and how do they call thee by name?"

To this Ivan Tsarevich replied: "I am from Vwislav's kingdom, the son of Tsar Vwislav, and they call me Ivan Tsarevich."

"Oh, youthful young man, Ivan Tsarevich!" said Tsar Afron, "was that which thou hast done the deed of an honorable knight? I would have given thee the golden-maned steed with honor. But now will it be well for thee when I send to all lands a declaration of how dishonorably thou hast acted in my kingdom. Hear me, however, Ivan Tsarevich, if thou wilt do me a service and go beyond the thrice ninth land to the thirtieth kingdom and bring to me Princess Yelena the Beautiful, with whom I am in love heart and soul for a long time, but whom I cannot obtain, I will pardon thy offence and give thee the golden-maned steed with honor. And if thou wilt not do me this service, I will declare in all lands that thou art a dishonorable thief."

Ivan Tsarevich promised Tsar Afron to bring Yelena the Beautiful, left the palace, and fell to crying bitterly. He came to the Gray Wolf and told him all that had happened. "Oh, Ivan Tsarevich, thou youthful young man," said the Gray Wolf, "why didst thou disobey me and take the golden bridle?"

"I have offended in thy sight," said Ivan Tsarevich.

"Well, let that go," replied the Wolf. "Sit on me; I will take thee wherever need be."

Ivan Tsarevich sat on the back of the Gray Wolf, who ran as swiftly as an arrow flies, and he ran in such fashion as to be told in a tale no long time; and at last he came to the kingdom of Yelena the Beautiful. Coming to the golden fence which surrounded her wonderful garden, the Wolf said: "Now, Ivan Tsarevich, come down from me and go back by the same road along which we came and wait in the field, under the green oak."

Ivan Tsarevich went where he was commanded. But the Gray Wolf sat near the golden fence, and waited till Yelena the Beautiful should walk in the garden. Toward evening, when the sun was sinking low in the west, therefore, it was not very warm in the air, Princess Yelena went to walk in the garden with her maidens and court ladies. When she entered the garden and approached the place where the Gray Wolf was sitting behind the fence, he jumped out suddenly, caught the princess, sprang back again, and bore her away with all his power and might. He came to the green oak in the open field where Ivan Tsarevich was waiting, and said, "Ivan Tsarevich, sit on me quickly."

Ivan sat on him, and the Gray Wolf bore them both along swiftly to the kingdom of Tsar Afron. The nurses and maidens and all the court ladies who had been walking in the garden with princess Yelena the Beautiful ran straightway to the palace and sent pursuers to overtake the Gray Wolf; but no matter how they ran, they could not overtake him, and turned back. Ivan Tsarevich, while sitting on the Gray Wolf with princess Yelena the Beautiful, came to love her with his heart, and she Ivan Tsarevich; and when the Gray Wolf arrived at the kingdom of Tsar Afron, and Ivan Tsarevich had to take Yelena the Beautiful to the palace and give her to Tsar Afron, he grew very sad, and began to weep tearfully.

"What art thou weeping for, Ivan Tsarevich?" asked the Gray Wolf.

"My friend, why should I, good youth, not weep? I have formed a heartfelt love for Yelena the Beautiful, and now I must give her to Tsar Afron for the golden-maned steed; and if I yield her not, then Tsar Afron will dishonor me in all lands."

"I have served thee much, Ivan Tsarevich," said the Gray Wolf, "and I will do yet this service. Listen to me. I will turn myself into a princess, Yelena the Beautiful. Do thou give me to Tsar Afron and take from him the golden-maned steed; he will think me the real princess. And when thou art sitting on the steed and riding far away, I will beg of Tsar Afron permission to walk in the open field. When he lets me go with the maidens and nurses and all the court ladies, and I am with them in the open field, remember me, and I will come to thee."

The Gray Wolf spoke these words, struck the damp earth, and became a princess, Yelena the Beautiful, so that it was not possible in any way to know that the wolf was not the princess. Ivan Tsarevich told Yelena the Beautiful to wait outside the town, and took the Gray Wolf to the palace of Tsar Afron. When Ivan Tsarevich came with the pretended Yelena the Beautiful, Tsar Afron was greatly delighted in his heart that he had received a treasure which he had long desired. He took the false maiden, and gave Ivan Tsarevich the golden-maned steed. Ivan Tsarevich mounted the steed and rode out of the town, seated Yelena the Beautiful with him, and rode on, holding his way toward the kingdom of Tsar Dolmat.

The Gray Wolf lived with Tsar Afron a day, a second, and a third, instead of Yelena the Beautiful. On the fourth day he went to Tsar Afron, begging to go out in the open field to walk, to drive away cruel grief and sorrow. Then Tsar Afron said: "Oh, my beautiful princess Yelena, I will do everything for thee; I will let thee go to the open field to walk!" And straightway he commanded the nurses the maidens and all the court ladies to go to the open field and walk with the beautiful princess.

Ivan Tsarevich was riding along his road and path with Yelena the Beautiful, talking with her; and he had forgotten about the Gray Wolf, but afterward remembered. "Oh, where is my Gray Wolf?" All at once, from wherever he came, the wolf stood before Ivan, and said: "Ivan Tsarevich, sit on me, the Gray Wolf and let the beautiful princess ride on the golden-maned steed."

Ivan Tsarevich sat on the Gray Wolf, and they went toward the kingdom of Tsar Dolmat. Whether they journeyed long or short, when they had come to the kingdom they stopped about three versts from the capital town; and Ivan Tsarevich began to implore: "Listen to me, Gray Wolf, my dear friend. Thou hast shown me many a service, show me the last one now; and the last one is this: Couldst thou not turn to a golden-maned steed instead of this one? for I do not like to part with this horse."

Suddenly the Gray Wolf struck the damp earth and became a golden-maned steed. Ivan Tsarevich, leaving princess Yelena in the green meadow, sat on the Gray Wolf and went to the palace of Tsar Dolmat. The moment he came, Tsar Dolmat saw that Ivan Tsarevich was riding on the golden-maned steed and he rejoiced greatly. Straightway he went out of the palace, met Tsarevich in the broad court, kissed him, took him by the right hand, and led him into the white stone chambers. Tsar Dolmat on the occasion of such joy gave orders for a feast, and they sat at the oaken table at the spread cloth. They ate, they drank, they amused themselves, and rejoiced exactly two days; and on the third day Tsar Dolmat gave Ivan Tsarevich the Fire-bird together with the golden cage. Ivan took the Fire-bird, went outside the town, sat on the golden-maned steed together with Yelena the Beautiful, and went toward his own native place, toward the kingdom of Tsar Vwislav.

Tsar Dolmat the next day thought to take a ride through the open field on his golden-maned steed. He ordered them to saddle him; he sat on the horse, and rode to the open field. The moment he urged the horse the horse threw Tsar Dolmat off his back, became the Gray Wolf as before, ran off, and came up with Ivan Tsarevich. "Ivan Tsarevich" said he, "sit on me, the Gray Wolf, and let Yelena the Beautiful ride on the golden-maned steed."

Ivan sat on the Gray Wolf, and they went their way. When the Gray Wolf had brought Ivan to the place where he had torn his horse, he stopped and said: "I have served thee sufficiently, with faith and truth. On this spot I tore thy horse in two; to this spot I have brought thee. Come down from me, the Gray Wolf: thou hast a golden-maned steed; sit on him, and go wherever thou hast need. I am no longer thy servant."

The Gray Wolf said these words and ran to one side. Ivan wept bitterly for the Gray Wolf, and went on with the beautiful princess. Whether he rode long or short with the beautiful princess, when he was within twenty versts of his own kingdom he stopped, dismounted, and he and the beautiful princess rested from the heat of the sun under a tree; he tied the golden-maned steed to the same tree and put the cage of the Fire-bird by his side. Lying on the soft grass, they talked pleasantly and fell soundly asleep.

At that time the brothers of Ivan Tsarevich, Dmitri and Vassili Tsarevich, after travelling through many lands without finding the Fire-bird, were on their way home with empty hands, and came unexpectedly upon their brother with the beautiful princess. Seeing the golden-maned steed and the Fire-bird in the cage, they were greatly tempted, and thought of killing their brother Ivan. Dmitri took his own sword out of the scabbard, stabbed Ivan Tsarevich and cut him to pieces; then he roused the beautiful princess and asked: "Beautiful maiden of what land art thou, of what father a daughter, and how do they call thee by name?"

The beautiful princess, seeing Ivan Tsarevich dead, was terribly frightened; she began to shed bitter tears, and in her tears she said: "I am Princess Yelena the Beautiful; Ivan Tsarevich whom ye have given to a cruel death, got me. If ye were good knights ye would have gone with him into the open field and conquered him there; but ye killed him when asleep; and what fame will ye receive for yourselves? A sleeping man is the same as a dead one."

Then Dmitri Tsarevich put his sword to the heart of Yelena the Beautiful and said: "Hear me, Yelena the Beautiful, thou art now in our hands; we will take thee to our father, Tsar Vwislav, thou wilt tell him that we got thee and the Fire-bird and the golden-maned steed. If not, we will give thee to death this minute."

The princess, afraid of death, promised them, and swore by everything sacred that she would speak as commanded. Then they began to cast lots who should have Yelena the Beautiful, and who the golden-maned steed; and the lot fell that the princess should go to Vassili, and the golden-maned steed to Dmitri. Then Vassili Tsarevich took the princess, and placed her on his horse; Dmitri sat on the golden-maned steed and took the Fire-bird to give to their father, Tsar Vwislav, and they went their way.

Ivan Tsarevich lay dead on that spot exactly thirty days; then the Gray Wolf ran up, knew Ivan by his odor, wanted to aid him, to bring him to life but knew not how. Just then the Gray Wolf saw a raven with two young ones who were flying above the body and wanted to eat the flesh of Ivan Tsarevich. The wolf hid behind a bush; and when the young ravens had come down and were ready to eat the body, he sprang out, caught one, and was going to tear it in two. Then the raven came down, sat a little way from the Gray Wolf, and said: "Oh, Gray Wolf, touch not my young child; it has done nothing to thee!"

"Listen to me, raven," said the Gray Wolf. "I will not touch thy child; I will let it go unharmed and well if thou wilt do me a service. Fly beyond the thrice ninth land to the thirtieth kingdom, and bring me the water of death and the water of life."

"I will do that, but touch not my son." Having said these words, the raven flew away and soon disappeared from sight. On the third day the raven returned, bringing two vials, in one the water of life, in the other the water of death, and gave them both to the Gray Wolf. The wolf took the vials, tore the young raven in two, sprinkled it with the water of death; the little raven grew together, he sprinkled it with the water of life, and the raven sprang up and flew away.

The Gray Wolf sprinkled Ivan Tsarevich with the water of death: the body grew together; he sprinkled it with the water of life: Ivan Tsarevich stood up and exclaimed, "Oh, how long I have slept!"

"Thou wouldst have slept forever, had it not been for me. Thy brothers cut thee to pieces and carried off Princess Yelena with the golden-maned steed and the Fire-bird. Now hurry with all speed to thy own country; Vassili Tsarevich will marry thy bride today. To reach home quickly, sit on me; I will bear thee."

Ivan sat on the Gray Wolf; the wolf ran with him to the kingdom of Tsar Vwislav, and whether it was long or short, he ran to the edge of the town. Ivan sprang from the Gray Wolf, walked into the town, and found that his brother Vassili had married Yelena the Beautiful, had returned with her from the ceremony, and was sitting with her at the feast.

Ivan Tsarevich entered the palace; and when Yelena the Beautiful saw him, she sprang up from the table, kissed him, and cried out: "This is my dear bridegroom, Ivan Tsarevich, and not that scoundrel at the table."

Then Tsar Vwislav rose from his place and asked the meaning of these words. Yelena the Beautiful told the whole truth,—told how Ivan Tsarevich had won her, the golden-maned steed, and the Fire-bird; how his elder brother had killed him while asleep; and how they had terrified her into saying that they had won everything.

Tsar Vwislav was terribly enraged at Dmitri and Vassili and cast them into prison; but Ivan Tsarevich married Yelena the Beautiful, and lived with her in harmony and love, so that one of them could not exist a single minute without the other.

DISCUSSION QUESTIONS

1. The Gray Wolf enacts many archetypes during this story. Name and describe the archetypes of the Gray Wolf.

2. How do animals serve as supernatural aides to Ivan?

3. What fault does Tsar Vwislav have in the death of his youngest son?

4. What might the fire-bird represent?

BIBLIOGRAPHY

Anonymous. *Kalevala: The Land of the Heroes.* Translated by W.F. Kirby. E. P. Dutton & CO., 1907.

Ashliman, D. L. *Folk and Fairy Tales: A Handbook.* Greenwood, 2004.

Baker, Emilie Kip. *Stories From Northern Myths.* The MacMillan Co., 1914. https://www.gutenberg.org/files/46288/46288-h/46288-h.htm#chap20

Billson, Charles. "Some Mythical Tales of the Lapps." *Folklore* 29.3 (1918): 178–192.

Cotterell, Arthur, and Rachel Storm. *The Ultimate Encyclopedia of Mythology.* Hermes House, 1999.

Curtin, Jeremiah. *A Journey in Southern Siberia: The Mongols, Their Religion, and Their Myths.* Little, Brown, 1909. https://books.google.com/books/about/A_Journey_In_Southern_Siberia_The_Mongol.html?id=xUydUSpT4_YC

---. *Myths and Folk-tales of the Russians, West-Slavs, and Magyars.* Little, Brown, 1890.

Ervast, Pekka. *The Key to the Kalevala.* Translated by Tapio Joensuu; Edited by John Major Jenkins. Blue Dolphin Publishing, 1999.

Foster, Mary H., and Mabel H. Cummings. *Asgard Stories: Tales from Norse Mythology.* Silver, Burdett, & Co, 1901. https://www.gutenberg.org/files/37488/37488-h/37488-h.htm#Page_33

Kalafut, Molly. *Finnish Mythology.* http://molly.kalafut.org/mythology/Finnish/pantheon.html

Kalevala: The Epic Poem of Finland (Complete)—a public domain book—John Martin Crawford, 1888.

Lindow, John. *Norse Mythology: A Guide to the Gods, Heroes, Rituals, and Beliefs.* Oxford UP, 2001.

Pentikäinen, Juha Y. *Kalevala Mythology.* Translated and edited by Ritva Poom. Indiana University Press, 1999.

Rasmussen, Knud. *Eskimo Folk Tales.* Trans. W. Worster. Gyldendal, 1921. https://www.gutenberg.org/files/28932/28932-h/28932-h.htm

Rosenberg, Donna. *Mythology: An Anthology of the Great Myths and Epics*, 3rd ed. McGraw Hill, 1999.

Shamanism: An Encyclopedia of World Beliefs, Practices, and Culture. Vol. 1 Ed. Mariko Namba Walter & Eva Jane Neumann Fridman. ABC-CLIO, 2004.

Sixty Folk Tales from Exclusively Slavonic Sources. Trans. A. H. Wratislaw. Elliot Stock, 1889. https://books.google.com/books?id=EG5HAAAAIAAJ&pg=PR1#v=onepage&q&f=false

Sturulson, Snorri. *Prose Edda.* Trans. Arthur Gilchrist Brodeur. American Scandinavian Foundation, 1916. http://www.sacred-texts.com/neu/pre/pre00.htm

Tales and Legends from the Land of the Tzar: Collection of Russian Stories. 2nd ed. Trans by Edith M. S. Hodgetts. Griffith, Farran, & Co, 1891. https://books.google.com/books?id=dVUR3pqoBiMC&pg=PR3#v=onepage&q&f=false

Chapter

5

THE MYTHS OF THE BRITISH ISLES

© Brian C. Weed/Shutterstock.com

INTRODUCTION

Part I: Creation and Destruction

Creation and The Ages of the World (Ireland)

Beira, Queen of Winter (Scotland)

The Making of Man (Isle of Man)

How the Cymry Land Became Inhabited (Wales)

Part 2: Tricksters, Lovers, and Other Tales

Peeriefool (Scotland)

Teeval, Princess of the Ocean (Isle of Man)

The Courtship of Etain (Ireland)

Taliesin (Wales)

Part 3: Journeys of Heroes and Heroines

Heroes on the Green Isle (Scotland)

The Coming of the Tuatha De Danaan (Ireland)

Introduction

© okili77/Shutterstock.com

The people we call the Celts were once spread over a large part of Europe, including regions in present-day Spain, France, and Belgium, in addition to Britain and parts of Asia Minor. Scholars have determined that the Celts first emerged as a cultural group in the area that is now Switzerland and South-West Germany as far back as 1200 BCE. In fact, some of those areas still retain names of Celtic origin. The Danube River, for example Danuvius or "divine waters," was named for the Celtic goddess Danu. Today, descendants of the Celts can be found in Brittany, Cornwall, Wales, Scotland, the Isle of Man, and Ireland. However, it must be noted that advancements in technology to analyze DNA of teeth and bones of ancient remains continue to reveal more about human history and prehistoric migrations over the ages reminding us that Celtic is, more precisely, "a cultural definition" (Bodmer, qtd. in Gibbons).

The Celts were semi-nomadic and, based on archaeological evidence, they lived in villages and farmed the land, engaged in trading, and appear to have enjoyed a simple life. They were not a single unified people, though it is believed that small villages would sometimes gather together in specific circumstances. They lived in tribes, often without much contact with each other, and shared language and culture though they had no sophisticated writing system. Therefore, what we know of them comes from artifacts and the writings of their enemies—the Greeks (who called them *Keltoi*) and Romans. The Celts had a hierarchical caste system: kings, nobles, and commoners, with Druids, their spiritual leaders, most likely being of highest stature. Warriors and priests were of the noble class, as well as bards. Commoners included farmers and craftsmen and, finally, the poor and the slaves.

The Celts are to be recognized for their use of smelting iron and the creation of weapons. In fact, smiths eventually became part of the noble class. In addition to weapons, they created the iron ploughshare which also aided their agricultural advancement. These inventions allowed for the expansion of tribes but also created conflict with their neighbors.

The Celts were fierce warriors. They sacked Rome in 390 BCE and nearly a hundred years later they moved into the Greek peninsula and attacked the Greek city of Delphi as well. Their intent was not to conquer, but to loot the cities—they had no desire for the lifestyle of the Greeks and Romans. Their fighting style seemed barbaric to the Greeks and Romans, who were not accustomed to seeing men with long hair and painted bodies. The Celts also engaged in psychological warfare by screaming at their opponents, and often relied on single combat rather than organized group strategy. They had a practice of revering severed heads of their conquests in battle—not just enemies, but slain friends as well—people they respected.

While not as sophisticated as the Greeks and Romans, the Celts were not as barbaric as they seemed. Women appear to have had a higher level of equality in Celtic society than they had in other cultures in the classical world. Women could own land and property, and lead armies into battle. Their art reveals a people who were creative, although much of their work is abstract. They often used patterns of lines and geometric shapes, as well as stylized representations of animals.

The Druids were the spiritual leaders and there is much mystery surrounding them. They were teachers, diviners with access to the realm of the gods, mediated matters in the villages, and perhaps acted as healers; even women could be Druids. All their knowledge was passed on orally. Some believe the Celts engaged in ritual human sacrifice, but again the evidence is unclear. We have no context for many of the artifacts that have been discovered.

By the third century BCE, the Celts were at their height of expansion. There were several versions of their language by this time as well. But the continued rise of the Roman Empire eventually won out, and the Celts' lack of military organization is what ultimately brought about their defeat. The Celts also had to face another group of invaders—the Anglo-Saxons. It's here where the legend of the figure we call King Arthur was born, a hero credited with holding back the Anglo-Saxons and ensuring the survival of his people, who later became the Welsh and Cornish.

Yet remnants of their culture survived longer in Wales, Scotland, and Ireland—places where Roman influence was weak. Ireland, Scotland, Wales, and Cornwall remained places of Celtic settlement, and eventually part of France which became known as Brittany. Still, battles waged on and eventually Christianity came into the region. In the remoteness of Ireland, free from Roman colonization, the old tales persisted. Irish monks preserved in writing the Celtic lore we have today, although some of the stories do reflect their Christian perspective. Fragments of their language survive today in Scottish Gaelic, Cornish, Breton, and Welsh.

Much more vague than the Greeks and Romans, who had specific gods and goddesses, the religious practices of the Celts were often localized to tribes or regions, as well as being strongly rooted in the natural world and connected to streams, woods, springs, and other specific places. Religion and magic were linked and often involved appeasing the gods or asking for their favor. Their pantheon of gods and goddesses is less clearly defined as some other cultural groups, and contained variations depending on location and time period. Archaeological evidence suggests they had a strong connection to water and would leave offerings of gold and other precious items in lakes. This has led scholars to conclude the Celts viewed water as a boundary between their world and the Otherworld. The Celts appear to have believed that death was not an end but a change in location, that one's soul would be reborn into the Otherworld and, in addition, that one could die in the Otherworld and return to this one (Ellis 20). The Celts were one of the earliest peoples to develop a belief in a soul and the concept of reincarnation; they believed the head was the seat of the soul.

As opposed to thinking in modes of duality—light and dark, good and evil—the Celts seem to have had a view based on three—trinities: good, evil, and neutral or black, white, and gray.

A common motif in Celtic myth, the cauldron was an important object; in fact, it is believed to be the origin of the later legends of the Holy Grail in Arthurian myths. In addition, the bard or poet was held in high regard and heroic tales were abundant.

Evidence that these ancient peoples charted the movement of the sun and stars is prevalent and also indicates their awareness of the winter and summer solstices. They may have used sites like Stonehenge and Newgrange, although these predate the Celtic people by thousands of years so there's no way to be certain. But, rather than celebrating seasonal changes at the solstices and equinoxes, they observed these changes on February 1 (Imbolc) May 1 (Beltaine/Beltane), August 1 (Lughnasadh), and November 1 (Samhain). Their days were measured from sunset to sunset, so their celebrations would begin the prior evening. Many of their sacred festival days are the root of modern Western celebrations. For example, the evolution of our modern Halloween owes to this, as November 1 became All Saints' Day—the night before becoming All Hallows' Eve. Samhain, which means "summer's end," was an important time of year for the Celts, when spirits were said to walk the land, and preparations were made for the coming winter. In addition, Beltaine, (May Day) is believed to be the origin of several surviving spring festivals.

Scholars remind us that our knowledge of the Celts and their myths, due to the influence of Christian monks and scribes who recorded them, is but a fragment and that we must read between the lines for interpretation. Also, we must not forget just how old these stories may actually be. In fact, there are some remarkable similarities between Hindu and Irish language and mythology, reinforcing some shared Indo-European roots. According to Peter Berresford Ellis:

> The Vedas, four books of learning composed in North India, in the period 1000–500 BC, are named from the Sanskrit root *vid*, meaning 'knowledge.' This same root occurs in Old Irish as *uid*, meaning 'observation, perception, and knowledge.' Most people will immediately recognise it as one of the two roots of the compound Celtic word Druid—*dru-vid*, arguable meaning 'thorough knowledge.' (8)

There are common motifs between the cultures as well. As Ellis reminds us,

> the most exciting thing about the study of Celtic linguistics and mythology is that we are not just pursuing the cultural origins of the Celts, we are actually pushing back the boundaries of our knowledge of an all Indo-European culture. (11)

Specifically concerning Irish mythology, it's useful to note that it can be divided into four cycles: (1) the Mythological Cycle has the earliest tales, which includes stories about the peopling of Ireland and the battles that ensued; (2) the Ulster Cycle, which is largely concerned with conflicts between the Irish provinces of Ulster and Connacht, and also contains traces of the pre-Christian past; (3) the King Tales, which occur in the centuries following Ireland's conversion to Christianity and often contains a blend of Christian and pre-Christian elements; and (4) the Ossian Cycle, which are tales from the later medieval period and includes stories of the famous Finn mac Cumaill. The Mythological Cycle is one of the most valuable for scholars since it's one of the few places we can find evidence of the pre-Christian beliefs of the Irish.

There are some key features in Irish literature that you may notice. First of all, place names were important, as they provided a kind of map to significant landmarks. Stories about how a place received its name were helpful in remembering its location. The stories are also frequently filled with lists of names and digressions; plot and originality were not deemed significant since listeners would typically already know the story. Instead, the stories were told to preserve information. Poets and bards were held in high esteem and had a great deal of freedom in medieval Irish society—"they had the same honor price as a king or a bishop" (Paxton 135). Stories often contained lessons on how kings should behave, along with the consequences of unacceptable conduct. One's reputation was of highest importance and would live on in the stories that were told. Poets were commissioned by kings to sing their praises and their status was based on how many poets could boast about them. But they could also perform damaging satire; a king could hire a poet to damage the reputation of an enemy.

Due to the variety of translations, characters in many of these myths often have numerous names and a variety of ways to spell them. Pronunciation guidance has been included in some of the text translations.

Part 1: Creation and Destruction

© Virginia Guneyli

Creation and The Ages of the World (Ireland)

The tales of Irish mythology can seem like a blend of history and legend—the land being settled by beings both human and divine. The gods lived in the world alongside the people, bringing gifts and protection to the land and its inhabitants. But darkness was always at hand to oppose the light, resulting in great battles.

Stories of fertility and creation are often difficult to separate in Irish myth. Various races invaded the land, each making contributions to its formation. The opposing forces of light and darkness engaged in conflict, resulting in change. Light civilized the land while darkness threatened to destroy it. The stories may mirror actual battles between tribes of ancient peoples.

Most accounts of creation tell the story of the Five Ages. However, in *Celtic Myths and Legends*, Peter Berresford Ellis reconstructs a brief account of creation before the Five Ages begin:

CREATION AND THE FIVE AGES OF THE WORLD

Out of the primordial chaos, the void of an undefined world, first came a tiny drop of water. It was followed by more drops, until waters flooded the earth. Molten stone cooled to mountains; the skies turned blue. From the soil and nurturing water of Danu a single tree (Bíle) sprang to life and from it, two acorns fell – the first male, the second, female. From the male acorn came The Dagda ("The Good God"); from the female came Brigid ("The Exalted One"). They understood the purpose given to them – to create order and populate the world with the Children of Danu, the Mother Goddess, whose divine waters had given them life.

First, there was the race of Ladhra, destroyed by a flood. Next, in the Second Age, the Partholons, a race of divine beings, added lakes and cattle to the barren land, establishing agriculture and a legal system. During this time, the first duel was fought and the first instance of adultery occurred. A group called the Fomorians, sea-people who lived on nearby islands and resembled monsters, having one eye, one hand, and one foot, but possessing knowledge of magic, fought with the Partholons but were driven away temporarily. Unfortunately, plague destroyed this group. Next, in the Third Age, the Nemedians arrived. They brought sheep and increased prosperity. They built forts to protect themselves from the Fomorians during battles. But even though the Nemedians fought valiantly, disease struck the population and, weakened, they became enslaved by the Fomorians. As a result, the two groups reached a bargain. Every year on the first of November, at the great feast of Samhain, the Nemedians must sacrifice two thirds of their children, milk, and corn. The Nemedians tried once more to attack the Fomorians, but were defeated; the survivors fled from Ireland. In the Fourth Age, on the first of August, the race of Fir Bolg arrived with many warriors. This group was not divine. They introduced many useful items such as spear-heads, and under their rule the land was fertile. But, in the Fifth Age, the divine Tuatha de Denaan (TOO ha-dAY-Dah n'n, The Children of Danu) arrived.

The Tuatha were the last generation of gods before the ancestors of the Irish people arrived—the Milesians. Eventually, the Tuatha De Danaan were defeated and Dagda (Dah dah) ushered them underground. It is believed that over the passing of centuries, they became the *sidhe* ("shee" fairies) who live in the mounds, or the *bean sidhe* (banshees) of Irish folklore.

DISCUSSION QUESTIONS

1. How do these ages compare to other "ages of man" stories in mythology? What similarities and differences do you notice?

2. Consider the tree from which springs the male and female creators. What other divine trees are present in mythology?

3. Trace the five ages presented here—what happens to each of them? Is the last generation better off or worse off than the first generation of the World? Which age's contribution(s) do you think is/are the most valuable? Explain.

Source: Ellis, Peter Berresford. *Celtic Myths and Legends*, 2008.

Beira, Queen of Winter (Scotland)

A common character in Gaelic mythology is that of the "divine hag" or a female creator deity who is related to the weather. In Gaelic, the word "cailleach" means "the veiled one" and translates to the more modern "hag." There are many stories of Cailleach among the British Isles, but the Scottish goddess Beira is perhaps most enticing for her relationship to youth, eternal beauty, and the creation of great Scottish landmarks.

Cailleach Bheur, or Beira, is a story of a goddess whose power waxes and wanes with the seasons. She is at the height of her power at the Winter Solstice, between Samhain and Beltane, but her power is overtaken by Bride, the wife of Angus, whose beauty reigned during the summer months from Beltane to Samhain. Eternally, Beira drinks from a well to stave off old age and return to her youth to reign again each autumn.

Beira gives birth to giant sons, known as Fooars. Her companions are eight hags and the creatures of winter, and she makes the mountains, whirlpools, rivers, and lochs as testaments to her creative abilities.

BEIRA, QUEEN OF WINTER

Dark Beira was the mother of all the gods and goddesses in Scotland. She was of great height and very old, and everyone feared her. When roused to anger she was as fierce as the biting north wind and harsh as the tempest-stricken sea. Each winter she reigned as Queen of the Four Red Divisions of the world, and none disputed her sway. But when the sweet spring season drew nigh, her subjects began to rebel against her and to long for the coming of the Summer King, Angus of the White Steed, and Bride, his beautiful queen, who were loved by all, for they were the bringers of plenty and of bright and happy days. It enraged Beira greatly to find her power passing away, and she tried her utmost to prolong the winter season by raising spring storms and sending blighting frost to kill early flowers and keep the grass from growing.

Beira lived for hundreds and hundreds of years. The reason she did not die of old age was because, at the beginning of every spring, she drank the magic waters of the Well of Youth which bubbles up in the Green Island of the West. This was a floating island where summer was the only season, and the trees were always bright with blossom and laden with fruit. It drifted about on the silver tides of the blue Atlantic, and sometimes appeared off the western coasts of Ireland and sometimes close to the Hebrides. Many bold mariners have steered their galleys up and down the ocean, searching for Green Island in vain. On a calm morning they might sail past its shores and yet never know it was near at hand, for oft-times it lay hidden in a twinkling mist. Men have caught glimpses of it from the shore, but while they gazed on its beauties with eyes of wonder, it vanished suddenly from sight by sinking beneath the waves like the setting sun. Beira, however, always knew where to find Green Island when the time came for her to visit it.

The waters of the Well of Youth are most potent when the days begin to grow longer, and most potent of all on the first of the lengthening days of spring. Beira always visited the island on the night before the first lengthening day, that is, on the last night of her reign as Queen of Winter. All alone in the darkness she sat beside the Well of Youth, waiting for the dawn. When the first faint beam of light appeared in the eastern sky, she drank the water as it bubbled fresh from a crevice in the rock. It was necessary that she should drink of this magic water before any bird visited the well and before any dog barked. If a bird drank first, or a dog barked ere she began to drink, dark old Beira would crumble into dust.

As soon as Beira tasted the magic water, in silence and alone, she began to grow young again. She left the island and, returning to Scotland, fell into a magic sleep. When, at length, she awoke, in bright

Source: Donald A. Mackenzie, *Wonder Tales from Scottish Myth and Legend*, 1917.

sunshine, she rose up as a beautiful girl with long hair yellow as buds of broom, cheeks red as rowan berries, and blue eyes that sparkled like the summer sea in sunshine. Then she went to and fro through Scotland, clad in a robe of green and crowned with a chaplet of bright flowers of many hues. No fairer goddess was to be found in all the land, save Bride, the peerless Queen of Summer.

As each month went past, however, Beira aged quickly. She reached full womanhood in midsummer, and when autumn came on her brows wrinkled and her beauty began to fade. When the season of winter returned once again, she became an old and withered hag, and began to reign as the fierce Queen Beira.

Often on stormy nights in early winter she wandered about, singing this sorrowful song:

> O life that ebbs like the sea!
> I am weary and old, I am weary and old
> Oh! how can I happy be
> All alone in the dark and the cold.
>
> I'm the old Beira again,
> My mantle no longer is green,
> I think of my beauty with pain
> And the days when another was queen.
>
> My arms are withered and thin,
> My hair once golden is grey;
> 'T is winter my reign doth begin
> Youth's summer has faded away.
>
> Youth's summer and autumn have fled
> I am weary and old, I am weary and old.
> Every flower must fade and fall dead
> When the winds blow cold, when the winds blow cold.

The aged Beira was fearsome to look upon. She had only one eye, but the sight of it was keen and sharp as ice and as swift as the mackerel of the ocean. Her complexion was a dull, dark blue, and this is how she sang about it:

> Why is my face so dark, so dark?
> So dark, oho! so dark, ohee!
> Out in all weathers I wander alone
> In the mire, in the cold, ah me!

Her teeth were red as rust, and her locks, which lay heavily on her shoulders, were white as an aspen covered with hoar frost. On her head she wore a spotted cap. All her clothing was grey, and she was never seen without her great dun-coloured shawl, which was drawn closely round her shoulders. It is told that in the days when the world was young Beira saw land where there is now water and water where there is now land.

Once a wizard spoke to her and said: "Tell me your age, O sharp old woman."

Beira answered: "I have long ceased to count the years. But I shall tell you what I have seen. Yonder is the seal-haunted rock of Skerryvore in the midst of the sea. I remember when it was a mountain surrounded by fields. I saw the fields ploughed, and the barley that grew upon them was sharp and juicy. Yonder is a loch. I remember when it was a small round well. In these days I was a fair young girl, and now I am very old and frail and dark and miserable."

It is told also that Beira let loose many rivers and formed many lochs, sometimes willingly and sometimes against her will, and that she also shaped many bens and glens. All the hills in Ross-shire are said to have been made by Beira.

There was once a well on Ben Cruachan, in Argyll, from which Beira drew water daily. Each morning at sunrise she lifted off the slab that covered it, and each evening at sunset she laid it above the well again. It happened that one evening she forgot to cover the well. Then the proper order of things was disturbed. As soon as the sun went down the water rose in great volume and streamed down the mountain side, roaring like a tempest-swollen sea. When day dawned, Beira found that the valley beneath was filled with water. It was in this way that Loch Awe came to be.

Beira had another well in Inverness-shire which had to be kept covered in like manner from sunset till sunrise. One of her maids, whose name was Nessa, had charge of the well. It happened that one evening the maid was late in going to the well to cover it. When she drew near she beheld the water flowing so fast from it that she turned away and ran for her life. Beira watched her from the top of Ben Nevis, which was her mountain throne, and cried: "You have neglected your duty. Now you will run for ever and never leave water."

The maiden was at once changed into a river, and the loch and the river which runs from it towards the sea were named after her. That is why the loch is called Loch Ness and the river the river Ness. Once a year, when the night on which she was transformed comes round, Ness (Nessa) arises out of the river in her girl form, and sings a sad sweet song in the pale moonlight. It is said that her voice is clearer and more beautiful than that of any bird, and her music more melodious than the golden harps and silvern pipes of fairyland.

In the days when rivers broke loose and lochs were made, Beira set herself to build the mountains of Scotland. When at work she carried on her back a great creel filled with rocks and earth. Sometimes as she leapt from hill to hill her creel tilted sideways, and rocks and earth fell from it into lochs and formed islands. Many islands are spoken of as "spillings from the creel of the big old woman."

Beira had eight hags who were her servants. They also carried creels, and one after the other they emptied out their creels until a mountain was piled up nigh to the clouds. One of the reasons why Beira made the mountains was to use them as stepping stones; another was to provide houses for her giant sons. Many of her sons were very quarrelsome; they fought continually one against another. To punish those of them who disobeyed her, Beira shut the offenders up in mountain houses, and from these they could not escape without her permission.

But this did not keep them from fighting. Every morning they climbed to the tops of their mountain houses and threw great boulders at one another. That is why so many big grey boulders now lie on steep slopes and are scattered through the valleys. Other giant sons of Beira dwelt in deep caves. Some were horned like deer, and others had many heads. So strong were they that they could pick up cattle and, throwing them over their shoulders, carry them away to roast them for their meals. Each giant son of Beira was called a Fooar.

It was Beira who built Ben Wyvis. She found it a hard task, for she had to do all the work alone, her hag servants being busy elsewhere. One day, when she had grown very weary, she stumbled and upset her creel. All the rocks and earth it contained fell out in a heap, and formed the mountain which is called Little Wyvis.

The only tool that Beira used was a magic hammer. When she struck it lightly on the ground the soil became as hard as iron; when she struck it heavily on the ground a valley was formed. After she had built up a mountain, she gave it its special form by splintering the rocks with her hammer. If she had made all the hills of the same shape, she would not have been able to recognize one from another.

After the mountains were all formed, Beira took great delight in wandering between them and over them. She was always followed by wild animals. The foxes barked with delight when they beheld her, wolves howled to greet her, and eagles shrieked with joy in mid-air. Beira had great herds and flocks to which she gave her protection; nimble-footed deer, high-horned cattle, shaggy grey goats, black swine, and sheep that had snow-white fleeces. She charmed her deer against the huntsmen, and when she visited a deer forest she helped them to escape from the hunters. During early winter she milked the hinds on the tops of mountains, but when the winds rose so high that the froth was blown from the milking pails, she drove the hinds down to the valleys. The froth was frozen on the crests of high hills, and lay there snow-white and beautiful. When the winter torrents began to pour down the mountain sides, leaping from ledge to ledge, the people said: "Beira is milking her shaggy goats, and streams of milk are pouring down over high rocks."

Beira washed her great shawl in the sea, for there was no lake big enough for the purpose. The part she chose for her washing is the strait between the western islands of Jura and Scarba. Beira's "washing-pot" is the whirlpool, there called Corry-vreckan. It was so named because the son of a Scottish king, named Breckan, was drowned in it, his boat having been upset by the waves raised by Beira.

Three days before the Queen of Winter began her work her hag servants made ready the water for her, and the Corry could then be heard snorting and fuming for twenty miles around. On the fourth day Beira threw her shawl into the whirlpool, and tramped it with her feet until the edge of the Corry overflowed with foam. When she had finished her washing she laid her shawl on the mountains to dry, and as soon as she lifted it up, all the mountains of Scotland were white with snow to signify that the great Queen had begun her reign.

Now, the meaning of this story is that Beira is the spirit of winter. She grows older and fiercer as the weeks go past, until at length her strength is spent. Then she renews her youth, so that she may live through the summer and autumn and begin to reign once again. The ancient people of Scotland saw that during early winter torrents poured down from the hills, and in this Beira fable they expressed their belief that the torrents were let loose by the Winter Queen, and that the lochs were, at the beginning, formed by the torrents that sprang from magic wells. They saw great boulders lying on hillsides and in valleys, and accounted for their presence in these places by telling how they were flung from mountain tops by the giant sons of Beira.

DISCUSSION QUESTIONS

1. Consider the song Beira sings. What is the tone? How do her words mimic the changing of seasons?

2. What items in Scotland's landscape is Beira credited with creating? Why attribute these to the work of a Winter Goddess?

The Making of Man (Isle of Man)

The Isle of Man is located relatively equidistant from Ireland, Scotland, and England, in the middle of the Irish Sea. Inhabited since before 6500 BCE, many Neolithic and Bronze Age relics tell the stories of their creators before the Roman, Viking, and eventually English rulers settled the island. The people living on the Isle of Man still speak a language called Manx and have a vivacious tradition of telling stories and promoting superstition about fairies.

The following story tells of how the Island was created by the great Irish hero Fionn Mac Cumhaill (anglicized as Finn Mac Cool). This tale is quite Irish-centric, as it sings the praises of St. Patrick, claims he blessed the Isle as he drove out the snakes, and makes certain to remind the reader that none of the vile inhabitants of England are found in the paradise that is the Isle of Man.

THE MAKING OF MAN

Thousands of years ago, at the time of the Battles of the Giants in Ireland, Finn Mac Cool was fighting with a great, red-haired Scotch giant who had come over to challenge him. He beat him and chased him eastwards towards the sea. But the Scotch giant was a faster runner and began to get ahead of him, so Finn, who was afraid that he would jump into the sea and escape, stooped down and clutched a great handful of the soil of Ireland to throw at him. He cast it, but he missed his enemy, and the great lump of earth fell into the midst of the Irish Sea. It is the Isle of Man, and the great hole which Finn made, where he tore it up, is Lough Neagh.

There were men, too, in Ireland in those days as well as giants, and to some of them it seemed to happen in a different way. Men do not always understand the doings of giants, because men live, it may be said, in the footprints of the giants. It seems that at this time the Irish tribes were gathered in two great forces getting ready to meet the plunderers who had left Scotland and were at work on their own coast. Their blood got too hot and they went into each other in downright earnest, to show how they would do with the rascals when they came. To their confusion, for they lost hold over themselves, they got into boggy ground and were in great danger.

The leaders, seeing that it was going to mean a big loss of life, got all their men together on a big patch of dry ground that happened to be in the bog-land, when all of a sudden a darkness came overhead and the ground began to shake and tremble with the weight of the people and the stir there was at them, and then it disappeared, people and all. Some said that it took plunge and sank into the bog with the people on it. Others said that it was lifted up, and the people on it dropped off into the swamp. No doubt the darkness that was caused by the hand of Finn made it hard to see just how it happened. However that may be, a while after this they said the sea was surging dreadful, and the men in the boats had to hold to the sides, or it's out they'd have been thrown. And behold ye, a few days after this there was land seen in the middle of the sea, where no man ever saw the like before.

You may know that this story is true because the Irish have always looked on the Isle of Man as a parcel of their own land. They say that when Saint Patrick put the blessing of God on the soil of Ireland and all creatures that might live upon it, the power of that blessing was felt at the same time in the Island.

Saint Patrick was a mighty man,
He was a Saint so clever,
He gave the snakes and toads a twisht!
And banished them for ever.

Source: Sophia Morrison, *Manx Fairy Tales*, 1911.

And there is proof of the truth of the saying to this day, for while such nasty things do live in England they cannot breathe freely on the blessed soil.

The island was much larger then than it is now, but the magician who for a time ruled over it, as a revenge on one of his enemies, raised a furious wind in the air and in the bosom of the earth. This wind tore several pieces off the land and cast them into the sea. They floated about and were changed into the dangerous rocks which are now so much feared by ships. The smaller pieces became the shifting sands which wave round the coast, and are sometimes seen and sometimes disappear. Later the island was known as Elian Sheaynt, the Isle of Peace, or the Holy Island.

It was a place where there was always sunshine, and the singing of birds, the scent of sweet flowers, and apple trees blossoming the whole year round. There was always enough there to eat and drink, and the horses of that place were fine and the women beautiful.

DISCUSSION QUESTIONS

1. Why is Finn credited with creating the Isle of Man?
2. Why does St. Patrick share his praise on both Ireland and the Isle of Man?
3. Does the last paragraph sound similar to any other mythical locations?

How the Cymry Land Became Inhabited (Wales)

The land known as Wales has been inhabited since the last Ice Age, and there were many tribes of people living there in the Iron Age. In Barry Cunliffe's book *Iron Age Communities in Britain*, he identifies six major tribal groups that, before Roman invasion, make up the earliest Welsh ancestry: the Deceangli, the Cornovii, the Dobunni, the Ordovices, the Demetae, and the Silures.

The people of Wales refer to their land as Cymru and they are the Cymry—which John Davies writes in *A History of Wales*, is roughly translated to "fellow-countrymen." The following story of modern inhabitants of Wales tells of "a great benefactor" who teaches the Britons agriculture, law, and how to sail. There are many customs, such as wakes, childrearing and women's laws, and the writing of song and poetry that may seem like a surprising addition to a myth about the start of a civilization.

HOW THE CYMRY LAND BECAME INHABITED

In all Britain today, no wolf roams wild and the deer are all tame. Yet in the early ages, when human beings had not yet come into the land, the swamps and forests were full of very savage animals. There were bears and wolves by the thousand besides lions and the woolly rhinoceros, tigers, with terrible teeth like sabres. Beavers built their dams over the little rivers, and the great horned oxen were very common.

Source: William Elliot Griffis. *Welsh Fairy Tales*, 1921.

Then the mountains were higher, and the woods denser. Many of the animals lived in caves, and there were billions of bees and a great many butterflies. In the bogs were ferns of giant size, amid which terrible monsters hid that were always ready for a fight or a frolic.

In so beautiful a land, it seemed a pity that there were no men and women, no boys or girls, and no babies. Yet the noble race of the Cymry, whom we call the Welsh, were already in Europe and lived in the summer land in the South.

A great benefactor was born among them, who grew up to be a wonderfully wise man and taught his people the use of bows and arrows. He made laws by which the different tribes stopped their continual fighting and quarrels, and united for the common good of all. He persuaded them to take family names. He invented the plow, and showed them how to use it, making furrows in which to plant grain.

When the people found that they could get things to eat right out of the ground, from the seed they had planted, their children were wild with joy. No people ever loved babies more than these Cymry folk and it was they who invented the cradle. This saved the hard working mothers many a burden, for each woman had, besides rearing the children, to work for and wait on her husband. He was the warrior and hunter, and she did most of the labor in both the house and the field. When there were many little brats to look after, a cradle was a real help to her. In those days, "brat" was the general name for little folks. There were good laws about women, especially for their protection. Any rough or brutish fellow was fined heavily or publicly punished for striking one of them.

By and by, this great benefactor encouraged his people to the brave adventure and led them in crossing the sea to Britain. Men had not yet learned to build boats, with prow or stern, with keels and masts, or with sails, rudders or oars, or much less to put engines in their bowels, or iron chimneys for smoke stacks, by which we see the mighty ships driven across the ocean without regard to wind or tide. This great benefactor taught his people to make coracles, and on these the whole tribe of thousands of Cymric folk crossed over into Britain, landing in Cornwall. The old name of this shire meant the "Horn of Gallia" or "Wallia" as the new land was later named. We think of Cornwall as the big toe of the Mother Land. These first comers called it a horn.

It was a funny sight to see, these coracles, which they named after their own round bodies. The men went down to the riverside or the sea shore, and with their stone hatchets, they chopped down trees. They cut the reeds and osiers, peeled the willow branches, and wove great baskets shaped like bowls. In this work the women helped the men. The coracle was made strong by a wooden frame fixed inside round the edge, and by two cross boards, which also served as seats. Then they turned the wicker frame upside down and stretched the hides of animals over the whole frame and bottom. With pitch, gum, or grease, they covered up the cracks or seams. Then they shaped paddles out of wood. When the coracle floated on the water, the whole family, daddy, mammy, kiddies, and any old aunts or uncles or granddaddies got into it. They waited for the wind to blow from the south over to the northern land. At first the coracle spun round and round, but by and by, each daddy could, by rowing or paddling, make the thing go straight ahead.

So finally, all arrived in the land now called Great Britain. Though sugar was not then known, or for a thousand years later, the first thing they noticed was the enormous number of bees. When they searched, they found the rock caves and hollow trees full of honey, which had accumulated for generations. Every once in a while the bears, that so like sweet things, found out the hiding place of the bees, and ate up the honey. The children were very happy in sucking the honey comb and the mothers made candles out of the beeswax. The new comers named the country Honey Island.

The brave Cymry men had battles with the darker skinned people who were already there. When anyone, young or old, died, their friends and relatives sat up all night, guarding the body against wild beasts or savage men. This grew to be a settled custom, and such a meeting was called a "wake." Everyone present did keep awake, and often in a very lively way.

As the Cymry multiplied, they built many don, or towns. All over the land today are names ending in don like London, or Croydon, showing where these villages were. But while occupied in things for the body, their great ruler did not neglect matters of the mind. He found that some of his people had good voices and loved to sing. Others delighted in making poetry. So he invented or improved the harp, and fixed the rules of verse and song. Thus ages before writing was known, the Cymry preserved their history and handed down what the wise ones taught. Men might be born, live and die, come and go, like leaves on the trees which expand in the springtime and fall in the autumn; but their songs and poetry and noble language never die. Even today the Cymry love the speech of their fathers almost as well as they love their native land.

Yet things were not always lovely in Honey Land, or as sweet as sugar. As the tribes scattered far apart to settle in this or that valley, some had fish, but no salt, and others had plenty of salt, but no fish. Some had all the venison and bear meat they wanted, but no barley or oats. The hill men needed what the men on the seashore could supply. From their sheep and oxen they got wool and leather, and from the wild beast's fur to keep warm in winter.

So many of them grew expert in trade. Soon there were among them some very rich men who were the chiefs of the tribes. In time hundreds of others learned how to traffic among the tribes and swap or barter their goods, for as yet there were no coins for money or bank bills. So they established markets, or fairs, to which the girls and boys liked to go and sell their eggs and chickens, for when the wolves and foxes were killed off, sheep and geese multiplied.

But what hindered the peace of the land were the feuds, or quarrels, because the men of one tribe thought they were braver or better looking than those in the other tribe. The women were very apt to boast that they wore their clothes—which were made of fox and weasel skins—more gracefully than those in the tribe next to them. So there was much snarling and quarreling in Cymric Land. The people were too much like naughty children, or when kiddies are not taught good manners, to speak gently and to be kind one to the other.

DISCUSSION QUESTIONS

1. Why do you think "the great benefactor" goes unnamed?

2. The story mentions "The brave Cymry men had battles with the darker skinned people who were already there." What does this mean about this legend, titled "how the Cymry land became inhabited"?

3. What leads to the feuding among tribes?

Part 2: Tricksters, Lovers, and Other Tales

© Debra Crank-Lewis

Peeriefool (Scotland)

This tale of capture, torture, and trickery comes from the Orkneys, an archipelago north of Scotland. The Peeriefool, or the little, yellow-haired people, are clear connections to the belief in fairies which are common among the British Isles. The guessing game that ensues when the third princess attempts to guess Peerie-fool's name is reminiscent of the German Brothers Grimm story of "Rumpelstiltskin."

It is likely that the hills described as the giant's home are Orcadian Cairns, which are remnants of Neolithic homes built into hills. Chambers were built inside of the hills, allowing for people to enter and live. These cairns have long been a place of mystery and superstition, said to house fairies and giants alike. The giant's punishment of skin flaying is not unknown to folklore—many cultures use this grotesque method as a form of torture for the more severe of crimes (often it was reserved for those who disrespected the Church).

The trickery in this story is multi-layered. The arrival of the old woman, the kindness and cunning of the third sister, and the unexpected help from the Peeriefool combine to thwart the evil giant.

PEERIEFOOL

There were once a king and queen in Rousay who had three daughters. The king died and the queen was living in a small house with her daughters. They kept a cow and a kale yard; they found their kale was all being taken away. The eldest daughter said to the queen, she would take a blanket about her and would sit and watch what was going away with the kale. So when the night came she went out to watch. In a short time a very big giant came into the yard; he began to cut the kale and throw it in a big basket. So he cut till he had it well filled.

Source: Andrew Land. *Folk-Lore A Quarterly Review of Myth, Tradition, Institution, and Custom vol 1.* 1890.

The princess asked him why he was taking her mother's kale. He said to her, if she was not quiet he would take her too. As soon as he had filled his basket he took her by a leg and an arm and threw her on the top of the basket of kale, and away home he went with her.

When he got home he told her what work she had to do; she had to milk the cow and put her up to the hills called Bloodfield, and then she had to take wool and wash and tease it and comb and card and spin and make cloth. When the giant went out she milked the cow and put her to the hills. Then she put on the pot and made porridge for herself. As she was supping it, a great many peerie (little) yellow-headed folk came running, calling out to give them some.

She said: "Little for one, and less for two. And never a grain have I for you."

When she came to work the wool, none of that work could she do at all. The giant came home at night and found she had not done her work. He took her and began at her head, and peeled the skin off all the way down her back and over her feet. Then he threw her on the couples among the hens.

The same adventure befell the second girl. If her sister could do little with the wool she could do less. When the giant came home he found her work not done. He began at the crown of her head and peeled a strip of skin all down her back and over her feet, and threw her on the couples beside her sister. They lay there and could not speak nor come down.

The next night the youngest princess said she would take a blanket about her and go to watch what had gone away with her sisters. Ere long, in came a giant with a big basket and began to cut the kale. She asked why he was taking her mother's kale. He said if she was not quiet he would take her too. He took her by a leg and an arm and threw her on the top of his basket and carried her away.

Next morning he gave her the same work as he had given her sisters. When he was gone out she milked the cow and put her to the high hills. Then she put on the pot and made porridge for herself. When the peerie yellow-headed folk came asking for some, she told them to get something to sup with. Some got heather cows and some got broken dishes, some got one thing, and some another, and they all got some of her porridge.

After they were all gone a peerie yellow-headed boy came in and asked her if she had any work to do; he could do any work with wool. She said she had plenty, but would never be able to pay him for it. He said all he was asking for it was to tell him his name. She thought that would be easy to do, and gave him the wool. When it was getting dark an old woman came in and asked her for lodging. The princess said she could not give her that, but asked her if she had any news. But the old woman had none, and went away to lie out.

There is a high knoll near the place, and the old woman sat under it for shelter. She found it very warm. She was always climbing up, and when she came to the top she heard someone inside saying, "Tease, teasers, tease; card, carders, card; spin, spinners, spin; for peerie fool, peerie fool is my name." There was a crack in the knoll and light coming out. She looked in and saw a great many peerie folk working, and a peerie yellow-headed boy running round them calling out that.

The old woman thought she would get lodging if she went to give this news, so she came back and told the princess the whole of it. The princess went on saying "Peeriefool, Peeriefool" till the yellow-headed boy came with all the wool made into cloth. He asked what was his name, and she guessed names, and he jumped about and said, "No!"

At last she said. "Peeriefool is your name!" He threw down the wool and ran off very angry.

As the giant was coming home he met a great many peerie yellow-headed folk, some with their eyes hanging on their cheeks, and some with their tongues hanging on their breasts. He asked them what was the matter. They told him it was working so hard pulling wool so fine. He said he had a good wife at home, and if she was safe, never would he allow her to do any work again. When he came home she was all safe and had a great many webs lying all ready, and he was very kind to her.

Next day when he went out, she found her sisters and took them down from the couples. She put the skin on their backs again, and she put her eldest sister in a basket and put all the fine things she could find with her, and grass on the top. When the giant came home she asked him to take the basket to her mother with some food for her cow. He was so pleased with her, he would do anything for her and took it away.

Next day she did the same with her other sister. She told him she would have the last of the food she had to send her mother for the cow ready next night. She told him she was going a bit from home and would leave it ready for him. She got into the basket with all the fine things she could find, and covered herself with grass. He took the basket and carried it to the queen's house. She and her daughters had a big boiler of water ready. They couped it about him when he was under the window and that was the end of the giant.

DISCUSSION QUESTIONS

1. Who is the real trickster—is it the third sister, the Old Woman, or the Peeriefool?
2. What does the third sister do differently to get out of her situation?

Teeval, Princess of the Ocean (Isle of Man)

Arthur Moore writes in *The Folklore of the Isle of Man*, that the Mermaid "was generally of an affectionate and gentle disposition, though terrible when angered." In the native language Manx, Mermaids are called "Ben-Varrey" ("Dooiney-Varrey" for a Merman), and their tales abound with encounters between humans and merfolk.

Conchubar meets and falls instantly in love with Teeval while waiting for his weapons to be made. Teeval's influence and power are clearly displayed over both Conchubar and Culain, as is her ability to give Conchubar the upper hand in battle by speaking her name.

TEEVAL, PRINCESS OF THE OCEAN

In the old days Culain, the smith of the gods, was living in the Isle of Man. It was the time when Conchubar was at the court of the King of Ulster, and had nothing but the sword in his hand. He was a fine handsome young man, and he had made up his mind to make himself a king. So he went one day to the Druid of Clogher to ask him what he had best do.

"Go thy way," said the Druid, "to the Isle of Man. There thou wilt find the great smith Culain. Get him to make thee a sword and a spear and a shield, and with these thou shalt win the kingdom of Ulster."

Source: Sophia Morrison, *Manx Fairy Tales,* 1911.

Conchubar went away, and hired a boat and put out to sea. He landed in Man and made straight for Culain's smithy. It was night when he got there, and the red glow of the furnace shone out into the dark. He could hear from inside the smithy the roar of the bellows and the clanging of the hammer on the anvil. When he came near, a great dog, as large as a calf, began to bay and to growl like thunder, and brought his master out.

"Who art thou, young man?" said he.

"Oh Culain!" cried Conchubar, "it is from the Druid of Clogher that I come, and he bade me ask thee to make me a sword and a spear and a shield, for only with weapons of thy making can I win the Kingdom of Ulster."

Culain' s face grew black at first, but after he had gazed for a while at Conchubar, he saw that he had the look about him of one who would go far, and he said, "It shall be done for thee, but thou must wait, for the work is long."

So Culain began to make the weapons, and Conchubar waited in the island.

Early one brave morning in May when the sun had just risen over Cronk-yn-Irree-Laa, Conchubar was walking on the strand, wondering to himself how much longer Culain would be making his weapons and thinking it was full time for him to return. The tide was going out, and the sun was shining on the wet sand. Suddenly he saw something flashing at the edge of the waves a few paces from him.

He ran up to it and, behold, it was the most beautiful woman he had ever put sight on, fast asleep. Her hair was golden, like the gorse in bloom; her skin whiter than the foam of the sea, her lips red as the coral, and her cheeks rosy like the little clouds that were flying before the face of the rising sun. The fringe of her dress of many coloured seaweeds rose and fell with the ebb and flow of the waves. Pearls gleamed on her neck and arms. Conchubar stood and looked on her. He knew that she was a Mermaid and that as soon as she awoke she would slip back into the ocean and be lost to him. So he bound her fast with his girdle.

Then she awoke and opened her eyes, which were blue as the sea, and when she saw that she was bound, she cried out with terror, "Loosen me, man, loosen me!"

Conchubar did not answer, so she said again, "Loosen me, I beg thee!" in a voice as sweet as the music of Horn Mooar, the Fairy Fiddler.

By this time Conchubar was feeling that he would give all he had to keep her. He answered, trembling, "Woman, my heart, who art thou?"

"I am Teeval, Princess of the Ocean," said she. "Set me free, I pray thee!"

"But if I set thee free," said Conchubar, "thou wilt leave me."

"I cannot stay with thee, Conchubar," she cried; "set me free, and I will give thee a precious gift."

"I will unbind thee," answered Conchubar. "It is not for the gift, but because I cannot resist thee."

He unfastened the girdle from her and she said, "My gift to thee is this: Go now to Culain who is making thy shield, and tell him that Teeval, Princess of the Ocean, bids him to put her figure on the shield and round it to engrave her name. Then thou shalt wear it always in battle, and when thou shalt look on my face and call my name, thy enemies' strength shall go from them and shall come into thee and thy men."

When she had said this, she waved her white arm to Conchubar and plunged into the waves. He looked sadly for a long time at the spot where she had disappeared, and then walked slowly to the forge of Culain, and gave him the message.

Culain finished the mighty shield as the Princess had said, and forged also for Conchubar a golden-hilted magic sword, and a spear set with precious stones. Then Conchubar, in his crimson mantle and white gold-embroidered tunic, and armed with his great shield and his mighty weapons, went back to Ireland.

All that the Princess of the Ocean had said came true. When he went into battle he looked at the beautiful face in his shield and cried, "Help, Teeval!" Then he felt strength come into him like the strength of a giant, and he cut his enemies down like grass. Before long he was famous all over Ireland for his great deeds, and in the end he became King of Ulster. Then he invited Culain to come and live in his kingdom, and gave him the plain of Murthemny to dwell in.

But he never again saw the lovely Mermaid.

DISCUSSION QUESTIONS

1. Is Conchubar using Teeval? Does Teeval allow herself to be used?
2. Is there a kind of partnership that develops between the sea and the land when Teeval promises to come to Conchubar's aid?

The Courtship of Etain (Ireland)

Prior to 1937, only part of this story was known. Sometimes translated as "The Wooing of Etain," (pronounced et OYN) the tale consists of three stories that could stand alone; here, the stories have been arranged to complete the three-part tale. This story is from the Mythological Cycle of Irish myth, but features characters from the Ulster Cycle and the Cycle of the Kings. An incomplete version of the story comes from *The Book of the Dun Cow* (c. 1106 C.E.); the complete version is contained in the *Yellow Book of Lecan* (c. 1401 C.E.). The language of the text, however, is believed to date from the 8th or 9th century. This text combines an adaptation from *Early Irish Myths and Sagas* with a selection from *Heroic Romances of Ireland*.

THE COURTSHIP OF ETAIN

I. Here Begins the Wooing of Etain

There was a famous king named Echu Ollathir* and he was of the Tuatha De Danaan. He was also called the Dagda, The Good God, for he brought fair weather and plentiful harvests. Now the Dagda was enamoured of Eithne, also called Boand, wife of Elcmar and she shared his passion, but feared Elcmar. The Dagda sent Elcmar away on a journey, enchanting him so the journey would be long, and that he would not notice the night, nor feel hunger or thirst. And so Eithne bore a son to the Dagda and he was named Oengus (Angus). By the time Elcmar returned, there was no sign the affair had occurred.

The Dagda sent his son to foster at the house of Midir, and Oengus lived there for nine years, becoming beloved to him. Oengus was also called Macc Oc, because of his mother's words, "Young the song who is conceived at dawn and born before dusk."

The Dagda is also sometimes referred to as Eochu or Eochaid Ollathir—not to be confused with the other Eochaid in this story, Eochaid Airem, one of the legendary high kings of Ireland.

Source: Translated by Jeffrey Gantz in *Early Irish Myths and Sagas*, 1981.

Other fosterlings lived with Midir, and Oengus had a quarrel with Triath of the Fir Bolg. Oengus thought Midir was his father and that he was the heir and so he scorned Triath, son of a slave, for speaking to him. But Triath replied that he was also angered that an orphan would speak to him. Confused and ashamed, Oengus asked Midir about his parents and Midir told him the truth. Oengus wanted then for his father to acknowledge him and asked Midir to accompany him.

They set out and first spoke with the Dagda, also called Echu, and Midir explained to him the boy's desire, "for it is not right that your son be without land when you are king of Eriu." [Erin = Ireland; named for the goddess Eriu.] But the Dagda said that the land he had set aside for him was still controlled by another—Elcmar himself. The Dagda did not wish to rouse him. Instead, he advised the boy to go armed into the Bruig at Samhain, for that would be a time of peace and no one would be at odds with him. Elcmar would be there holding only a branch of white hazel. Oengus would know him by his cloak fastened with a gold brooch. He said that Oengus should threaten him—that he would kill him unless he met his request. The request was that Oengus be king for a day and a night, only returning the land if Elcmar agreed to the Dagda's judgment.

And so it came to pass, and Elcmar agreed. And the next day when he came to reclaim his land, the Dagda's judgment proclaimed it belonging to the Macc Oc. The Dagda said to Elcmar, "He hewed at you menacingly on a day of peace and friendship, and since your life was dearer to you than your land, you surrendered the land in return for being spared. Even so, I will give you land that is no worse than the Bruig." And so the Dagda gave him a new settlement.

One year later, on Samhain, Midir came to visit the Macc Oc. Two groups of boys were playing, one group belonging to Elcmar. A dispute arose among them, and Midir offered to settle it. During the quarrel, a sprig of holly was flung and hit Midir in the eye. He returned to the Macc Oc, holding his lost eye, and the Macc Oc offered to help heal him.

The Macc Oc asked Dian Cecht to help save his foster father. When he was healed, the Macc Oc asked Midir to stay for a year and witness his warriors and visit his household. Midir said he would only stay if he received a reward—"a chariot worth seven cumals (pronounced "cool"—a monetary unit) and clothing appropriate to my rank and the fairest woman in Eriu." The Macc Oc had the chariot and the clothing; Midir said he knew what maiden he wanted. "She is of the Ulaid . . . daughter of Ailill, king of the north-eastern part of Eriu; Etain Echrade is her name, and she is the fairest and gentlest and most beautiful woman in Eriu."

The Macc Oc sought Etain and made a deal with her father for her hand. The Dagda helped him grant what Ailill had asked—that twelve of his lands consisting of desert and woodlands be cleared for cattle and dwellings for his people. The Dagda accomplished this in one night. But Ailill still refused to give him Etain. This time he asked for twelve rivers to be diverted to the sea, draining bogs, moors, and springs. Again, the Dagda accomplished this in one night. Once more the Macc Oc demanded Etain. Ailill still insisted that the Macc Oc buy her, for after she was taken from him she would have no further worth. He asked for her weight in gold and silver; the price was paid.

That night, Midir slept with Etain and the next day he received his chariot and new clothes. He remained a year with his foster son; then he thanked him and returned to his own land of Bri Leith (Bree Lay) with Etain. As they departed, the Macc Oc said to him, "Look after the woman you are taking with you, for there awaits you a woman of dreadful sorcery, a woman with all the knowledge and skill and power of her people. She has, moreover, my guarantee of safety against the Tuatha De Danaan." She was Fuamnach (FOOM na), Midir's own wife, and had been raised by a Druid.

Fuamnach welcomed them, showing Etain her husband's lands and wealth. She then took Etain into the house and said to her, "The seat of a good woman have you occupied." As Etain sat down in a chair at the center of the room, Fuamnach struck her with a red rowan wand, turning her into a pool of water.

Then Fuamnach left, returning to her foster father; Midir, too, departed, leaving behind the water that had been Etain.

Now the combined heat of the hearth, the fire, air, and ground, turned the water into a worm and then into a scarlet fly. The fly was the size of a man's head, the most handsome man in the land, and its voice and the sound of its wings was like pipes, horns, and harps—making sweet music. It had eyes like precious gems and to look upon its fair color and scent would quench any hunger or thirst. Drops of water from its wings could cure any ailment. This fly followed Midir as he traveled; he knew it was Etain and this comforted him and kept him safe.

Finally, Fuamnach wished to see Midir again, and brought with her for protection three of the Tuatha De Danaan—Lugh, the Dagda, and Ogmae. She expressed no regret for her actions and vowed to visit evil upon Etain no matter what her form. She knew Etain's current state, and had prepared spells to banish her. For if Midir were free of her, he would be free to love another. Fuamnach conjured a great gust of wind, blowing Etain so far away that for seven years she could not land.

Etain floated over trees and rocks and water, at last alighting on the sleeve of the Macc Oc. He welcomed her and brought her into his home. He kept her near all day and night, surrounding her with fragrant flowers and herbs, and gradually her good spirits returned.

Fuamnach eventually learned that Etain was with the Macc Oc and she told Midir to summon him. She said she wanted to make peace between them and search for Etain. When they arrived, she unleashed yet another wind, driving Etain to float again for seven years. Etain, weak and weary, at last landed on a house in Ulaid. She fell into a golden cup held by the wife of the warrior Etar; she swallowed Etain and a child was conceived in her womb. Etain was born again as her daughter, one thousand and twelve years from her first conception by Ailill.

Etain was raised by Etar along with fifty daughters of chieftains as her attendants. Bathing in the river one day, a rider arrived from the plains on a prancing brown horse with a mane and tail of curls. He was cloaked in green as one of the Sidhe, with a golden brooch on his cloak and wearing a red embroidered tunic. He carried a silver shield edged with gold and a five-pronged spear. His hair was golden and held by a golden band. He gazed at him, in love at once. He looked upon Etain, recited a poem to her, then rode away.

Meanwhile, the Macc Oc spoke with Midir, explaining that Etain had been with him; but Fuamnach was gone. The Macc Oc, upon finding Etain was again blown away, tracked Fuamnach and finally found her. He cut off her head and took it home with him.

II. The Wooing of Etain from *Heroic Romances of Ireland*

Eochaid* (YEO hay) Airemon took the sovereignty over Erin (Ireland), and the five provinces of Ireland were obedient to him, for the king of each province was his vassal. Now these were they who were the kings of the provinces at that time, even Conor the son of Ness, and Messgegra, and Tigernach Tetbannach, and Curoi, and Ailill the son of Mata of Muresc. And the royal forts that belonged to Eochaid were the stronghold of Frémain in Meath, and the stronghold of Frémain in Tethba; moreover the stronghold of Frémain in Tethba was more pleasing to him than any other of the forts of Erin.

Now a year after that Eochaid had obtained the sovereignty, he sent out his commands to the men of Ireland that they should come to Tara to hold festival therein, in order that there should be adjusted the taxes and the imposts that should be set upon them, so that these might be settled for a period of five

Eochaid Airemon and Eochaid Airemm are variations of the same name, Eochu Airem. The Ploughman, son of Finn.

Source: A.H. Leahy. *Heroic Romances of Ireland,* 1905.

years. And the one answer that the men of Ireland made to Eochaid was that they would not make for the king that assembly which is the Festival of Tara until he found for himself a queen, for there was no queen to stand by the king's side when Eochaid first assumed the kingdom.

Then Eochaid sent out the messengers of each of the five provinces to go through the land of Ireland to seek for that woman or girl who was the fairest to be found in Erin; and he bade them to note that no woman should be to him as a wife, unless she had never before been as a wife to any one of the men of the land. And at the Bay of Cichmany a wife was found for him, and her name was Etain, the daughter of Etar; and Eochaid brought her thereafter to his palace, for she was a wife meet for him, by reason of her form, and her beauty, and her descent, and her brilliancy, and her youth, and her renown.

Now Finn the son of Findloga had three sons, all sons of a queen, even Eochaid Fedlech, and Eochaid Airemm, and Ailill (AL il) Anguba. And Ailill* Anguba was seized with love for Etain at the Festival of Tara, after that she had been wedded to Eochaid; since he for a long time gazed upon her, and, since such gazing is a token of love, Ailill gave much blame to himself for the deed that he was doing, yet it helped him not. For his longing was too strong for his endurance, and for this cause he fell into a sickness; and, that there might be no stain upon his honour, his sickness was concealed by him from all, neither did he speak of it to the lady herself. Then Fachtna, the chief physician of Eochaid, was brought to look upon Ailill, when it was understood that his death might be near, and thus the physician spoke to him: "One of the two pangs that slay a man, and for which there is no healing by leechcraft, is upon thee; either the pangs of envy or the pangs of love. And Ailill refused to confess the cause of his illness to the physician, for he was withheld by shame and he was left behind in Fremain of Tethba to die; and Eochaid went upon his royal progress throughout all Erin, and he left Etain behind him to be near Ailill, in order that the last rites of Ailill might be done by her; that she might cause his grave to be dug, and that the keen might be raised for him, and that his cattle should be slain for him as victims. And to the house where Ailill lay in his sickness went Etain each day to converse with him, and his sickness was eased by her presence; and, so long as Etain was in that place where he was, so long was he accustomed to gaze at her.

Now Etain observed all this, and she bent her mind to discover the cause, and one day when they were in the house together, Etain asked of Ailill what was the cause of his sickness. "My sickness," said Ailill, "comes from my love for thee." "'Tis pity," said she, "that thou hast so long kept silence, for thou couldest have been healed long since, had we but known of its cause." "And even now could I be healed," said Ailill, "did I but find favour in thy sight." "Thou shalt find favour," she said. Each day after they had spoken thus with each other, she came to him for the fomenting of his head, and for the giving of the portion of food that was required by him, and for the pouring of water over his hands; and three weeks after that, Ailill was whole. Then he said to Etain: "Yet is the completion of my cure at thy hands lacking to me; when may it be that I shall have it?" "'Tis to-morrow it shall be," she answered him, "but it shall not be in the abode of the lawful monarch of the land that this felony shall be done. Thou shalt come," she said, "on the morrow to yonder hill that riseth beyond the fort: there shall be the tryst that thou desirest."

Now Ailill lay awake all that night, and he fell into a sleep at the hour when he should have kept his tryst, and he woke not from his sleep until the third hour of the day. And Etain went to her tryst, and she saw a man before her; like was his form to the form of Ailill, he lamented the weakness that his sickness had caused him, and he gave to her such answers as it was fitting that Ailill should give. But at the third hour of the day, Ailill himself awoke: and he had for a long time remained in sorrow when Etain came into the house where he was; and as she approached him, "What maketh thee so sorrowful?" said Etain. "'Tis because thou wert sent to tryst with me," said Ailill, "and I came not to thy presence, and sleep fell upon me, so that I have but now awakened from it; and surely my chance of being healed hath now gone from me." "Not so, indeed," answered Etain, "for there is a morrow to follow to-day." And upon that night he

*Ailill Anguba: The king's brother; not to be confused with Ailill, king of the Ulaid from part one of the tale—Etain's father.

took his watch with a great fire before him, and with water beside him to put upon his eyes.

At the hour that was appointed for the tryst, Etain came for her meeting with Ailill; and she saw the same man, like unto Ailill, whom she had seen before; and Etain went to the house, and saw Ailill still lamenting. And Etain came three times, and yet Ailill kept not his tryst, and she found that same man there every time. "'Tis not for thee," she said, "that I came to this tryst: why comest thou to meet me? And as for him whom I would have met, it was for no sin or evil desire that I came to meet him; but it was fitting for the wife of the king of Ireland to rescue the man from the sickness under which he hath so long been oppressed." "It were more fitting for thee to tryst with me myself," said the man, "for when thou wert Etain of the Horses, the daughter of Ailill, it was I who was thy husband. And when thou camest to be wife to me, thou didst leave a great price behind thee; even a marriage price of the chief plains and waters of Ireland, and as much of gold and of silver as might match thee in value." "Why," said she, "what is thy name?" "'Tis easy to say," he answered; "Midir of Bri Leith (Bree Lay) is my name." "Truly," said she; "and what was the cause that parted us?" "That also is easy," he said; "it was the sorcery of Fuamnach, and the spells of Bressal Etarlam. And then Midir said to Etain:

Wilt thou come to my home, fair-haired lady? to dwell
In the marvellous land of the musical spell,
Where the crowns of all heads are, as primroses, bright,
And from head to the heel all men's bodies snow-white.

In that land of no "mine" nor of "thine" is there speech,
But there teeth flashing white and dark eyebrows hath each;
In all eyes shine our hosts, as reflected they swarm,
And each cheek with the pink of the foxglove is warm.

With the heather's rich tint every blushing neck glows,
In our eyes are all shapes that the blackbird's egg shows;
And the plains of thine Erin, though pleasing to see,
When the Great Plain is sighted, as deserts shall be.

Though ye think the ale strong in this Island of Fate,
Yet they drink it more strong in the Land of the Great;
Of a country where marvel abounds have I told,
Where no young man in rashness thrusts backward the old.

There are streams smooth and luscious that flow through that land,
And of mead and of wine is the best at each hand;
And of crime there is naught the whole country within,
There are men without blemish, and love without sin.

Through the world of mankind, seeing all, can we float,
And yet none, though we see them, their see-ers can note;
For the sin of their sire is a mist on them flung,
None may count up our host who from Adam is sprung.

Lady, come to that folk; to that strong folk of mine;
And with gold on thy head thy fair tresses shall shine:
'Tis on pork the most dainty that then thou shalt feed,
And for drink have thy choice of new milk and of mead.

"I will not come with thee," answered Etain, "I will not give up the king of Ireland for thee, a man who knows not his own clan nor his kindred." "It was indeed myself," said Midir, "who long ago put beneath the mind of Ailill the love that he hath felt for thee, so that his blood ceased to run, and his flesh fell away from him: it was I also who have taken away his desire, so that there might be no hurt to thine honour. But wilt thou come with me to my land," said Midir, "in case Eochaid should ask it of thee?" "I would come in such case," answered to him Etain.

After all this Etain departed to the house. "It hath indeed been good, this our tryst," said Ailill, "for I have been cured of my sickness; moreover, in no way has thine honour been stained." "'Tis glorious that it hath fallen out so," answered Etain. And afterwards Eochaid came back from his royal progress, and he was grateful for that his brother's life had been preserved, and he gave all thanks to Etain for the great deed she had done while he was away from his palace.

III. The Wooing of Etain

Now upon another time it chanced that Eochaid Airemm, the king of Tara, arose upon a certain fair day in the time of summer; and he ascended the high ground of Tara to behold the plain of Breg; beautiful was the colour of that plain, and there was upon it excellent blossom, glowing with all hues that are known. And, as the aforesaid Eochaid looked about and around him, he saw a young strange warrior upon the high ground at his side. The tunic that the warrior wore was purple in colour, his hair was of a golden yellow, and of such length that it reached to the edge of his shoulders. The eyes of the young warrior were lustrous and grey; in the one hand he held a five-pointed spear, in the other a shield with a white central boss, and with gems of gold upon it. And Eochaid held his peace, for he knew that none such had been in Tara on the night before, and the gate that led into the Liss had not at that hour been thrown open.

The warrior came, and placed himself under the protection of Eochaid; and "Welcome do I give," said Eochaid, "to the hero who is yet unknown."

"Thy reception is such as I expected when I came," said the warrior.

"We know thee not," answered Eochaid.

"Yet thee in truth I know well!" he replied.

"What is the name by which thou art called?" said Eochaid.

"My name is not known to renown," said the warrior; "I am Midir of Bri Leith."

"And for what purpose art thou come?" said Eochaid.

"I have come that I may play a game at the chess* with thee," answered Midir.

"Truly," said Eochaid, "I myself am skilful at the chess-play."

"Let us test that skill!" said Midir.

"Nay," said Eochaid, "the queen is even now in her sleep; and hers is the palace in which the chessboard lies."

"I have here with me," said Midir, "a chessboard which is not inferior to thine." It was even as he said, for that chessboard was silver, and the men to play with were gold; and upon that board were costly stones, casting their light on every side, and the bag that held the men was of woven chains of brass.

Midir then set out the chessboard, and he called upon Eochaid to play.

"I will not play," said Eochaid, "unless we play for a stake."

The game they play is actually fidchell, an ancient Irish board game.

"What stake shall we have upon the game then?" said Midir.

"It is indifferent to me," said Eochaid.

"Then," said Midir, "if thou dost obtain the forfeit of my stake, I will bestow on thee fifty steeds of a dark grey, their heads of a blood-red colour, but dappled; their ears pricked high, and their chests broad; their nostrils wide, and their hoofs slender; great is their strength, and they are keen like a whetted edge; eager are they, high-standing, and spirited, yet easily stopped in their course."

Many games were played between Eochaid and Midir; and, since Midir did not put forth his whole strength, the victory on all occasions rested with Eochaid. But instead of the gifts which Midir had offered, Eochaid demanded that Midir and his folk should perform for him services which should be of benefit to his realm; that he should clear away the rocks and stones from the plains of Meath, should remove the rushes which made the land barren around his favourite fort of Tethba, should cut down the forest of Breg, and finally should build a causeway across the moor or bog of Lamrach that men might pass freely across it. All these things Midir agreed to do, and Eochaid sent his steward to see how that work was done. And when it came to the time after sunset, the steward looked, and he saw that Midir and his fairy host, together with fairy oxen, were labouring at the causeway over the bog; and thereupon much of earth and of gravel and of stones was poured into it. Now it had, before that time, always been the custom of the men of Ireland to harness their oxen with a strap over their foreheads, so that the pull might be against the foreheads of the oxen; and this custom lasted up to that very night, when it was seen that the fairy-folk had placed the yoke upon the shoulders of the oxen, so that the pull might be there; and in this way were the yokes of the oxen afterwards placed by Eochaid, and thence cometh the name by which he is known; even Eochaid Airemm, or Eochaid the Ploughman, for he was the first of all the men of Ireland to put the yokes on the necks of the oxen, and thus it became the custom for all the land of Ireland. And this is the song that the host of the fairies sang, as they laboured at the making of the road:

Thrust it in hand! force it in hand!
Nobles this night, as an ox-troop, stand:
Hard is the task that is asked, and who
From the bridging of Lamrach shall gain, or rue?

Not in all the world could a road have been found that should be better than the road that they made, had it not been that the fairy folk were observed as they worked upon it; but for that cause a breach hath been made in that causeway. And the steward of Eochaid thereafter came to him; and he described to him that great labouring band that had come before his eyes, and he said that there was not over the chariot-pole of life a power that could withstand its might. And, as they spake thus with each other, they saw Midir standing before them; high was he girt, and ill-favoured was the face that he showed; and Eochaid arose, and he gave welcome to him. "Thy welcome is such as I expected when I came," said Midir. "Cruel and senseless hast thou been in thy treatment of me, and much of hardship and suffering hast thou given me. All things that seemed good in thy sight have I got for thee, but now anger against thee hath filled my mind!" "I return not anger for anger," answered Eochaid; "what thou wishest shall be done." "Let it be as thou wishest," said Midir; "shall we play at the chess?" said he. "What stake shall we set upon the game?" said Eochaid. "Even such stake as the winner of it shall demand," said Midir. And in that very place Eochaid was defeated, and he forfeited his stake.

"My stake is forfeit to thee," said Eochaid.

"Had I wished it, it had been forfeit long ago," said Midir.

"What is it that thou desirest me to grant?" said Eochaid.

"That I may hold Etain in my arms, and obtain a kiss from her!" answered Midir.

Eochaid was silent for a while and then he said: "One month from this day thou shalt come, and the very thing that thou hast asked for shall be given to thee." Now for a year before that Midir first came to Eochaid for the chess-play, had he been at the wooing of Etain, and he obtained her not; and the name which he gave to Etain was Befind, or Fair-haired Woman, so it was that he said:

Wilt thou come to my home, fair-haired lady?

as has before been recited. And it was at that time that Etain said: "If thou obtainest me from him who is the master of my house, I will go; but if thou art not able to obtain me from him, then I will not go." And thereon Midir came to Eochaid, and allowed him at the first to win the victory over him, in order that Eochaid should stand in his debt; and therefore it was that he paid the great stakes to which he had agreed; and therefore also was it that he had demanded of him that he should play that game in ignorance of what was staked. And when Midir and his folk were paying those agreed-on stakes, which were paid upon that night; to wit, the making of the road, and the clearing of the stones from Meath, the rushes from around Tethba, and of the forest that is over Breg, it was thus that he spoke, as it is written in the Book of Drom Snechta:

Pile on the soil; thrust on the soil:
Red are the oxen around who toil:
Heavy the troops that my words obey;
Heavy they seem, and yet men are they.
Strongly, as piles, are the tree-trunks placed
Red are the wattles above them laced:
Tired are your hands, and your glances slant;
One woman's winning this toil may grant!
Oxen ye are, but revenge shall see;
Men who are white shall your servants be:
Rushes from Teffa are cleared away:
Grief is the price that the man shall pay:
Stones have been cleared from the rough Meath ground;
Whose shall the gain or the harm be found?

Now Midir appointed a day at the end of the month when he was to meet Eochaid, and Eochaid called the armies of the heroes of Ireland together, so that they came to Tara; and all the best of the champions of Ireland, ring within ring, were about Tara, and they were in the midst of Tara itself, and they guarded it, both without and within; and the king and the queen were in the midst of the palace, and the outer court thereof was shut and locked, for they knew that the great might of men would come upon them. And upon the appointed night Etain was dispensing the banquet to the kings, for it was her duty to pour out the wine, when in the midst of their talk they saw Midir standing before them in the centre of the palace. He was always fair, yet fairer than he ever was seemed Midir to be upon that night. And he brought to amazement all the hosts on which he gazed, and all thereon were silent, and the king gave a welcome to him.

"Thy reception is such as I expected when I came," said Midir; "let that now be given to me that hath been promised. 'Tis a debt that is due when a promise hath been made; and I for my part have given to thee all that was promised by me."

"I have not yet considered the matter," said Eochaid.

"Thou hast promised Etain's very self to me," said Midir; "that is what hath come from thee." Etain blushed for shame when she heard that word.

"Blush not," said Midir to Etain, "for in nowise hath thy wedding-feast been disgraced. I have been seeking thee for a year with the fairest jewels and treasures that can be found in Ireland, and I have not taken thee until the time came when Eochaid might permit it. 'Tis not through any will of thine that I have won thee." "I myself told thee," said Etain, "that until Eochaid should resign me to thee I would grant thee nothing. Take me then for my part, if Eochaid is willing to resign me to thee."

"But I will not resign thee!" said Eochaid; "nevertheless he shall take thee in his arms upon the floor of this house as thou art."

"It shall be done!" said Midir.

He took his weapons into his left hand and the woman beneath his right shoulder; and he carried her off through the skylight of the house. And the hosts rose up around the king, for they felt that they had been disgraced, and they saw two swans circling round Tara, and the way that they took was the way to the elf-mound of Femun. And Eochaid with an army of the men of Ireland went to the elf-mound of Femun, which men call the mound of the Fair-haired-Women. And he followed the counsel of the men of Ireland, and he dug up each of the elf-mounds that he might take his wife from thence.

[And Midir and his host opposed them and the war between them was long: again and again the trenches made by Eochaid were destroyed, for nine years as some say lasted the strife of the men of Ireland to enter into the fairy palace. And when at last the armies of Eochaid came by digging to the borders of the fairy mansion, Midir sent to the side of the palace sixty women all in the shape of Etain, and so like to her that none could tell which was the queen. And Eochaid himself was deceived, and he chose, instead of Etain, her daughter Messbuachalla (or as some say Esa).]

According to a more detailed account of the tale's end, the sixty women were asked to serve beverages because it was believed Etain was the best at this. Eochaid chose incorrectly, but did not know it. Later, Midir returned to inform him that Etain had been with child when he took her and that Eochaid had actually chosen her daughter, thinking her to be his wife. He had slept with his own daughter, and she had born him a daughter. Distressed by this, he vowed never again to look upon the child. He sent the infant away; she was left in a kennel with a bitch and her pups. A herdsman and his wife found her and raised her. But one day Eterscelae's people discovered her and informed him; he took her away and made her his wife. She became the mother of King Conare. Some versions of the story end with Eochaid eventualy being killed by Midir's grandson.

DISCUSSION QUESTIONS

1. Discuss desire and jealousy and how they serve as motivation for characters in the story. Which has the most impact on the story—desire or jealousy? Why?

2. Compare this story to similar myths from other cultures. What common themes and motifs do you notice?

3. What does this story reveal about medieval Irish society?

Taliesin (Wales)

Gwion (GWEE-on) is a Welsh version of the Irish character Fionn McCumhaill. The names derive from root words that both mean "shining" or "light" which may suggest poetic inspiration. Taliesin (Tahl YESS in) was a real sixth-century Welsh poet.

THE BIRTH OF TALIESIN

In days past, in the time of King Arthur, there lived a gentleman named Tegid Foel who dwelled by the shore of a lake with his wife Ceridwen (KAIR-id-wen) and their two children—a girl named Creirwy (KRY-rooy, *Dear One*) and a boy named Morfran (MOR-vrahn, *Black Crow*). Creirwy was fairer than any maiden, but her brother was as ugly as she was beautiful. His dreadful appearance earned him the nickname Afagddu (ah-VAGH-thee, *Utter Darkness*). Ceridwen loved her son no matter his appearance, and knew his admittance among noblemen must depend on merit, as he lacked a favorable appearance. She combed through ancient tomes of secret lore for days and nights to create a cauldron of Inspiration and Knowledge for her son.

She gathered the herbs beneath the proper stars to steep them, and began the brew, which must not cease boiling for a year and a day. Three drops of the liquid would grant the gifts of inspiration, seership, and understanding of all the arts. To tend the fire, she tasked a blind man named Morda; to stir the cauldron, she hired a peasant boy named Gwion. She charged them both with care to keep it boiling.

One day, as year's end drew nigh, while Ceridwen was culling herbs and chanting, three drops of the enchanted liquid leapt from the cauldron and landed on Gwion's finger. Without thought, Gwion put his finger in his mouth to stay the burn. In that moment, he was filled with foresight and his mind was opened. He saw the future. And he knew Ceridwen was enraged—for her craft alerted her as to what had happened. Just then the great cauldron broke in half. All the brew was poison, save those three drops, and the potion tainted the nearby stream.

Gwion fled, but she pursued. He imagined himself a hare, and so became one. But Ceridwen changed herself into a swifter greyhound and nearly caught him. He ran to the water and became a fish; she changed into an otter. He leapt forth and became a bird; but she became a hawk, and as her talon gripped him, he saw a mill below and turned into a wheat-grain and fell to the ground. But then she became a hen, and scratched and pecked at the grain, swallowing him.

The grain of wheat began to grow, and in nine months Ceridwen bore a child. But she knew the identity of this boy, and raised a dagger to kill him, but could not find the will in her heart. He was beautiful. She wrapped him in leather and set him out on the sea in a little boat. The waves tossed him about for hundreds of years, but the boy did not age.

One day, a Welsh prince named Elphin, who was deeply in debt, decided on the Eve of Beltane to go fishing. He heard the salmon were plentiful and thought to earn some money. That night by starlight he cast his net and waited. But at the dawn he saw he caught only a single fish—and a tiny boat covered in barnacles that contained something wrapped in skins.

Elpin unwrapped the bundle and discovered a baby boy who seemed to shine with a radiant glow. He exclaimed with delight, "Such a shining brow!" which in Welsh means Taliesin. The boy became the greatest prophet and bard in all of Wales.

DISCUSSION QUESTIONS

1. Discuss why Ceridwen creates a potion for Inspiration and Knowledge for her ugly son, rather than brewing a potion to change his appearance.

2. What is the significance of Gwion ending up with the potion's gift instead of Ceridwen's son? What do you think happened to Morfran?

Adapted from Mara Freeman. *Kindling the Celtic Spirit*, 2001 and Lady Charlotte Guest. *The Mabinogion*, 1877.

Part 3: Journeys of Heroes and Heroines

Heroes on the Green Isle (Scotland)

Two stories are told in Mackenzie's "Heroes on the Green Isle," beginning with a young prince who believes himself more capable than his opponents. When he finds himself tossed into the natural world of the Mother Eagle's nest, his abilities are put to the ultimate test—man versus nature. The young prince falls into the path of the passing three men, heading home from their most recent quest. Their story, fighting for the hand of a princess through battle and cunning, and leaving behind their successful fourth, Mac-a-moir, takes the reader through a more familiar kind of heroic tale.

HEROES ON THE GREEN ISLE

There was once a prince who found himself in the Green Isle of the West, and this is how the story of his adventures are told:

The Prince of the Kingdom of Level-Plains set out on his travels to see the world, and he went northward and westward until he came to a red glen surrounded by mountains. There he met with a proud hero, who spoke to him, saying: "Whence come you, and whither are you going?"

Said the prince: "I am searching for my equal," and as he spoke he drew his sword. He was a bold and foolish young man.

"I have no desire to fight with you," the proud hero answered. "Go your way in peace."

The prince was jealous of the hero who spoke thus so calmly and proudly, and said, "Draw your sword or die."

Then he darted forward. The hero swerved aside to escape the sword-thrust, and next moment he leapt upon the prince, whom he overcame after a brief struggle, and bound with a rope.

Then he carried him to the top of a cliff, and said, "You are not fit to be among men. Go and dwell among the birds of prey." He flung him over the cliff. The prince fell heavily into a large nest on a ledge of rock, the nest of the queen of eagles a giant bird of great strength.

For a time he lay stunned by his fall. When he came to himself he regretted his folly, and said: "If ever I escape from this place I shall behave wisely, and challenge no man without cause."

He found himself in the great nest with three young eagles in it. The birds were hungry, and when the prince held his wrists towards one, it pecked the rope that bound them until it was severed; so then he stretched his legs towards another bird, and it severed the rope about his ankles. He was thus set free. He rose up and looked about him. The ledge jutted out in mid-air on the cliff-side, and the prince saw it was impossible either to ascend or descend the slippery rocks. Behind the nest there was a deep cave, into which he crept. There he crouched, waiting to see what would happen next.

The young birds shrieked with hunger, and the prince was hungry also. Ere long the queen of eagles came to the nest. Her great body and outstretched wings cast a shadow like that of a thundercloud, and when she perched on the ledge of rock, it shook under her weight. The eagle brought a hare for her

Source: Donald A. Mackenzie. *Wonder Tales from Scottish Myth and Legend*, 1917.

young and laid it in the nest. Then she flew away. The prince at once crept out of the cave and seized the hare. He gathered together a bundle of dry twigs from the side of the nest and kindled a fire in the cave, and cooked the hare and ate it.

The smoke from the fire smothered the young birds, and when the queen of eagles returned she found that they were dead. She knew at once that an enemy must be near at hand, and looked into the cave. There she saw the prince, who at once drew his sword bravely and fought long and fiercely against her, inflicting many wounds to defend himself. But he was no good match for that fierce bird, and at length she seized him in her talons and, springing off the ledge of rock, flew through the air with him. His body was soon torn by the eagle's claws and sore with wounds. The eagle, also sorely wounded, rose up among the clouds, and turning westward flew hurriedly over the sea. Her shadow blotted out the sunshine on the waters as she passed in her flight, and boatmen lowered their sails, thinking that a sudden gust of wind was sweeping down upon them. The prince swooned, and regained consciousness, and swooned again. As the bird flew onwards the sun scorched him. Then she dropped him into the sea, and he found the waters cold as ice.

"Alas!" he thought, "I shall be drowned."

He rose to the surface and began to swim towards an island near at hand, but the eagle pounced down, and seizing him again, rose high in the air. Once again she dropped him, and then he swooned and remembered no more, until he found himself lying on a green bank on a pleasant shore. The sun was shining, birds sang sweetly among blossoming trees of great beauty, and the sea-waves made music on the beach. Somewhere near he could hear a river fairy singing a summer song.

Next he heard behind him a splashing of water, and a shower of pearly drops fell upon his right arm as he lay there weak and helpless. But no sooner did the water touch his arm than it became strong again. The splashing continued, and he twisted himself this way and that until the pearly spray had drenched every part of his body. Then he felt strong and active again, and sprang to his feet. He looked round, and saw that the showers of spray had come from a well in which the wounded queen of eagles was bathing herself. The prince knew then that this was a Well of Healing.

He remembered how fiercely the eagle had dealt with him, and wished he still had his sword. Having no sword, he drew his dirk and crept softly towards the well. He waited a moment, crouching behind a bush, and then, raising his dirk, struck off the eagle's head. But he found it was not easy to kill the monster in the Well of Healing. No sooner was the head struck off than it sprang on again. Thrice he beheaded the eagle, and thrice the head was restored. When, however, he struck off the head a fourth time, he held the blade of his dirk between the head and neck until the eagle was dead. Then he dragged the body out of the well, and buried the head in the ground. Having done so, he bathed in the well, and when he came out of it, all his wounds were healed, and he found himself as active and able as if he had just awakened from a long sleep. He looked about him, and saw fruit growing on a blossoming tree. He wondered at that, but being very hungry he plucked the fruit and ate it. Never before had he tasted fruit of such sweet flavour. Feeling refreshed, and at the same time happy and contented, he turned to walk through the forest of beautiful trees and singing birds, when he saw three men coming towards him.

He spoke to them, saying: "Who are you, and whence come you?"

They answered: "There is no time to tell. If you are not a dweller on this island, come with us while there is yet time to escape."

The prince wondered to hear them speak thus, but, having learned wisdom, he followed them in silence. They went down the beach and entered a boat. The prince stepped in also. Two of the men laid oars in the rowlocks, and one sat at the stern to steer. In another moment the boat darted forward, cleaving the waves; but not until it had gone half a league did the man at the helm speak to the prince.

He said simply: "Look behind and tell me what you see."

The prince looked, and all he saw was a green speck on the horizon. A cry of wonder escaped his lips.

"The speck you see," said the steersman, "is the Green Isle. It is now floating westward to the edge of the ocean."

Then the prince understood why the men had hurried to escape, and he realized that if he had not taken their advice, he would have been carried away beyond the reach of human aid.

Said the steersman, "Now we can speak. Who are you, and whence come you?"

The prince told the story of his adventure with the queen of eagles, and the men in the boat listened intently. When he was done, the steersman said, "Now listen, and hear what we have gone through."

This was the story told by the steersman, whose name was Conall Curlew, the names of the rowers being Garna and Cooimer.

Yesterday at dawn we beheld the Green Isle lying no farther distant from the shore than a league. The fourth man who was with us is named Mac-a-moir, and he spoke, saying: "Let us visit the Green Isle and explore it. I am told that the king has a daughter named Sunbeam, who is of peerless beauty, and that he will give her as a bride to the bravest hero who visits his castle. He who is bold enough will come with me."

We all went down to the beach with Mac-a-moir, and launched a boat to cross over to the Green Island. The tide favoured us, and we soon reached it. We moored the boat in a sheltered creek, and landed. The beauties of the forest tempted us to linger, and eat fruit and listen to the melodious songs of numerous birds, but Mac-a-moir pressed us to hasten on. Soon we came to a green valley in which there was a castle. I, Conall, knocked at the gate, and a sentinel asked what I sought.

I answered, "I have come to ask for Sunbeam, daughter of the King of Green Isle, to be the bride of Mac-a-moir."

Word was sent to the king, who said, "He who seeks my daughter Sunbeam must first hold combat with my warriors."

"I am ready for combat," Mac-a-moir declared.

The gate was opened, and the heroes entered. Mac-a-moir drew his sword, and the first warrior came against him. Ere long Mac-a-moir struck him down. A second warrior, and then a third, fought and fell also in turn.

Said the king, when the third warrior fell, "You have overcome the champion of Green Isle."

"Bring forth the next best," Mac-a-moir called.

Said the king, "I fear, my hero, that you wish to slay all my warriors one by one. You have proved your worth. Now let us test you in another manner. My daughter dwells in a high tower on the summit of a steep hill. He who can take her out will have her for his bride. He will also receive two-thirds of my kingdom while I live, and the whole of my kingdom when I die."

All who were present then went towards the tower, which stood on three high pillars.

"Who will try first to take out the king's daughter?" I asked.

Said Mac-a-moir, "I shall try first."

He tried, but he failed. He could neither climb the pillars nor throw them down.

Said the king,"Many a man has tried to take my daughter out of this tower, but each one has failed to do so. You had better all return home."

The other two, Garna and Cooimer, made attempts to shake down the tower, but without success.

Said the king, "It is no use trying. My daughter cannot be taken out."

Then I, Conall, stepped forward. I seized one of the pillars and shook it until it broke. The tower toppled over, and as it came down I grasped the Princess Sunbeam in my arms, and placed her standing beside me.

"Your daughter is now won," I called to the king.

The Princess Sunbeam smiled sweetly, and the king said: "Yes, indeed, she has been won."

"I have won her," I, Conall, reminded him, "for Mac-a-moir."

Said the king, "He who will marry Sunbeam must remain on Green Isle."

"So be it," Mac-a-moir answered him as he took Sunbeam's hand in his and walked towards the castle, following the king.

A great feast was held in the castle, and Mac-a-moir and the princess were married.

Said the king, "I am well pleased with Mac-a-moir. It is my desire that his three companions should remain with him and be my warriors."

I, Conall, told him: "It is our desire to return to our own country."

The king did not answer. He sat gloomily at the board, and when the wedding feast was ended he walked from the feasting hall.

Mac-a-moir came and spoke to us soon afterwards, saying, "If it is your desire to go away, make haste and do so now, for the king is about to move Green Isle far westward towards the realms of the setting sun."

We bade him farewell, and took our departure. You met us as we hastened towards the boat, and it is as well that you came with us.

The prince dwelt a time with Conall and his companions. Then he returned to his own land, and related all that had taken place to his father, the King of Level-Plains.

DISCUSSION QUESTIONS

1. Does the Prince learn from his mistakes? Support your answer with quotes from the text.

2. How does the natural world influence the outcome of both stories?

3. Why is Mac-a-moir the only successful winner of Princess Sunbeam?

▷   ▷   ▷

The Coming of the Tuatha De Danaan (Ireland)

While this story is part of the creation of Ireland, it has been placed here because it's a myth cycle that includes heroic tales, most notably the story of Lugh. The figure of the leprechaun is a derivative of the name of the heroic figure Lugh of the Long Hand, who eventually came to be called "stooping Lugh" (*Lugh-chromain*).

This tale comes from the Mythological Cycle and there are two versions of the story—they may have originally been two separate tales that overlapped or were later merged together. Portions of this version have been abridged.

THE COMING OF THE TUATHA DE DANAAN

It was in a mist the Tuatha de Danaan, the people of the gods of Dana, or as some called them, the Men of Dea, came through the air and the high air to Ireland.

It was from the north they came; and in the place they came from they had four cities, where they fought their battle for learning. And in those cities they had four wise men to teach their young men skill and knowledge and perfect wisdom. And they brought from those four cities their four treasures: a Stone of Virtue from Falias, that was called the Lia Fail, the Stone of Destiny; and from Gorias they brought a Sword; and from Finias a Spear of Victory; and from Murias the fourth treasure, the Cauldron that no company ever went away from unsatisfied.

It was Nuada (Nu Ah) was king of the Tuatha de Danaan at that time, but Manannan, son of Lir, was greater again. And of the others that were chief among them were Ogma, brother to the king, that taught them writing, and Diancecht, that understood healing, and Neit, a god of battle, and Credenus the Craftsman, and Goibniu the Smith. And the greatest among their women were Badb, a battle goddess; and Macha, whose mast-feeding was the heads of men killed in battle; and the Morrigu, the Crow of Battle; and Eire and Fodla and Banba, daughters of the Dagda, that all three gave their names to Ireland afterwards; and Eadon, the nurse of poets; and Brigit, that was a woman of poetry, and poets worshipped her, for her sway was very great and very noble. And she was a woman of healing along with that, and a woman of smith's work, and it was she first made the whistle for calling one to another through the night. And the one side of her face was ugly, but the other side was very comely. And the meaning of her name was Breo-saighit, a fiery arrow. And among the other women there were many shadow-forms and great queens; but Dana, that was called the Mother of the Gods, was beyond them all.

And the three things they put above all others were the plough and the sun and the hazel tree, so that it was said in the time to come that Ireland was divided between those three, Coll the hazel, and Cecht the plough, and Grian the sun.

And they had a well below the sea where the nine hazels of wisdom were growing; that is, the hazels of inspiration and of the knowledge of poetry. And their leaves and their blossoms would break out in the same hour, and would fall on the well in a shower that raised a purple wave. And then the five salmon that were waiting there would eat the nuts, and their colour would come out in the red spots of their skin, and any person that would eat one of those salmon would know all wisdom and all poetry. And there were seven streams of wisdom that sprang from that well and turned back to it again; and the people of many arts have all drank from that well.

It was on the first day of Beltaine, that is called now May Day, the Tuatha de Danaan came, and it was to the northwest of Connacht they landed. But the Firbolgs that were in Ireland before them, and that had come from the South, saw nothing but a mist, and it lying on the hills.

Adapted from Lady Gregory. *Gods and Fighting Men: The Story of the Tuatha De Danaan and the Fianna of Ireland.* 1905.

Eochaid (YEO hay) son of Erc*, was king of the Firbolgs at that time, and messengers came to him at Teamhair* (pronounced "tah veer"/the Hill of Tara) and told him there was a new race of people come into Ireland, but whether from the earth or the skies or on the wind was not known, and that they had settled themselves at Magh Rein (Moy Raen).

They thought there would be wonder on Eochaid when he heard that news; but there was no wonder on him, for a dream had come to him in the night, and when he asked his Druids the meaning of the dream, it is what they said, that it would not be long till there would be a strong enemy coming against him.

Then King Eochaid took counsel with his chief advisers, and it is what they agreed, to send a good champion of their own to see the strangers and to speak with them. So they chose out Sreng, that was a great fighting man, and he rose up and took his strong red-brown shield, and his two thick-handled spears, and his sword, and his head-covering, and his thick iron club, and he set out from Teamhair, and went on towards the place the strangers were, at Magh Rein.

But before he reached it, the watchers of the Tuatha de Danaan got sight of him, and they sent out one of their own champions, Bres (Bresh), with his shield and his sword and his two spears, to meet him and to talk with him.

So the two champions went one towards the other slowly, and keeping a good watch on one another, and wondering at one another's arms, till they came near enough for talking; and then they stopped, and each put his shield before his body and struck it hard into the ground, and they looked at one another over the rim. Bres was the first to speak, and when Sreng heard it was Irish he was talking, his own tongue, he was less uneasy, and they drew nearer, and asked questions as to one another's family and race.

And after a while they put their shields away, and it was what Sreng said, that he had raised his in dread of the thin, sharp spears Bres had in his hand. And Bres said he himself was in dread of the thick-handled spears he saw with Sreng, and he asked were all the arms of the Firbolgs of the same sort. And Sreng took off the tyings of his spears to show them better, and Bres wondered at them, being so strong and so heavy, and so sharp at the sides though they had no points. And Sreng told him the name of those spears was Craisech, and that they would break through shields and crush flesh and bones, so that their thrust was death or wounds that never healed. And then he looked at the sharp, thin, hard-pointed spears that were with Bres. And in the end they made an exchange of spears, that way the fighters on each side would see the weapons the others were used to. And it is the message Bres sent to the Firbolgs, that if they would give up one half of Ireland, his people would be content to take it in peace; but if they would not give up that much, there should be a battle. And he and Sreng said to one another that whatever might happen in the future, they themselves would be friends.

Sreng went back then to Teamhair and gave the message and showed the spear; and it is what he advised his people, to share the country and not to go into battle with a people that had weapons so much better than their own. But Eochaid and his chief men consulted together, and they said in the end: "We will not give up the half of the country to these strangers; for if we do," they said, "they will soon take the whole."

*Eochaid mac Eirc (not to be confused with the character named Eochaid in "The Courtship of Etain"). First king to establish a justice system in Ireland; he ruled for ten years, until the Fir Bolg were defeated by the Tuatha Dé Danann in the first Battle of Magh Tuiredh.

*Teamhair/Hill of Tara: Seat of the King of Ireland; a standing stone located there is said to be the Stone of Destiny (Lia Fail).

Now as to the Men of Dea, when Bres went back to them, and showed them the heavy spear, and told them of the strong, fierce man he had got it from, and how sturdy he was and well armed, they thought it likely there would soon be a battle. And they went back from where they were to a better place, farther west in Connacht, and there they settled themselves, and made walls and ditches on the plain of Magh Nia, where they had the great mountain, Belgata, in their rear. And while they were moving there and putting up their walls, three queens of them, Badb and Macha and the Morrigu, went to Teamhair where the Firbolgs were making their plans. And by the power of their enchantments they brought mists and clouds of darkness over the whole place, and they sent showers of fire and of blood over the people, that way they could not see or speak with one another through the length of three days. But at the end of that time, the three Druids of the Firbolgs, Cesarn and Gnathach and Ingnathach, broke the enchantment.

The Firbolgs gathered their men together then, and they came with their eleven battalions and took their stand at the eastern end of the plain of Magh Nia.

And Nuada, king of the Men of Dea, sent his poets to make the same offer he made before, to be content with the half of the country if it was given up to him. King Eochaid bade the poets to ask an answer of his chief men that were gathered there; and when they heard the offer they would not consent. So the messengers asked them when would they begin the battle. "We must have a delay," they said; "for we want time to put our spears and our armour in order, and to brighten our helmets and to sharpen our swords, and to have spears made like the ones you have. And as to yourselves," they said, "you will be wanting to have spears like our Craisechs made for you." So they agreed then to make a delay of a quarter of a year for preparation.

It was on a midsummer day they began the battle. Three times nine hurlers of the Tuatha de Danaan went out against three times nine hurlers of the Firbolgs, and they were beaten, and every one of them was killed. And the king, Eochaid, sent a messenger to ask would they have the battle every day or every second day. And it is what Nuada answered that they would have it every day, but there should be just the same number of men fighting on each side. Eochaid agreed to that, but he was not well pleased, for there were more men of the Firbolgs than of the Men of Dea.

So the battle went on for four days, and there were great feats done on each side, and a great many champions came to their death. But for those that were alive at evening, the physicians on each side used to make a bath of healing, with every sort of healing plant or herb in it, that way they would be strong and sound for the next day's fight.

And on the fourth day the Men of Dea got the upper hand, and the Firbolgs were driven back. And a great thirst came on Eochaid, their king, in the battle, and he went off the field looking for a drink, and three fifties of his men protecting him; but three fifties of the Tuatha de Danaan followed after them till they came to the strand that is called Traigh Eothaile, and they had a fierce fight there, and at the last King Eochaid fell, and they buried him there, and they raised a great heap of stones over his grave.

And when there were but three hundred men left of the eleven battalions of the Firbolgs, and Sreng at the head of them, Nuada offered them peace, and their choice among the five provinces of Ireland. And Sreng said they would take Connacht; and he and his people lived there and their children after them. It is of them Ferdiad came afterwards that made such a good fight against Cuchulain, and Erc, son of Cairbre, that gave him his death. And that battle, that was the first fought in Ireland by the Men of Dea, was called by some the first battle of Magh Tuireadh (Moy Tirra).

And the Tuatha de Danaan took possession of Teamhair, that was sometimes called the Beautiful Ridge, the Grey Ridge, and the Ridge of the Outlook, all those names were given to Teamhair. And from that time it was above all other places, for its king was the High King over all Ireland. The king's rath* lay to the north, and the Hill of the Hostages to the northeast of the High Seat, and the Green of Teamhair to the west of the Hill of the Hostages. And to the northeast, in the Hill of the Sidhe, was a well called Nemnach, and out of it there flowed a stream called Nith, and on that stream the first mill was built in Ireland.

And to the north of the Hill of the Hostages was the stone, the Lia Fail, and it used to roar under the feet of every king that would take possession of Ireland. And the Wall of the Three Whispers was near the House of the Women that had seven doors to the east, and seven doors to the west; and it is in that house the feasts of Teamhair used to be held. And there was the Great House of a Thousand Soldiers, and near it, to the south, the little Hill of the Woman Soldiers.

The Reign of Bres

But if Nuada won the battle, he lost his own arm in it—that was struck off by Sreng; and by that loss there came troubles and vexation on his people.

For it was a law with the Tuatha de Danaan that no man that was not perfect in shape should be king. And after Nuada had lost the battle he was put out of the kingship on that account.

And the king they chose in his place was Bres, that was the most beautiful of all their young men, so that if a person wanted to praise any beautiful thing, whether it was a plain, or a dun, or ale, or a flame, or a woman, or a man, or a horse, it is what he would say, "It is as beautiful as Bres." And he was the son of a woman of the Tuatha de Danaan, but who his father was no one knew but herself.

But in spite of Bres being so beautiful, his reign brought no great good luck to his people; for the Fomor (the Fomorians) whose dwelling place was beyond the sea, or as some say below the sea westward, began putting tribute on them, that way they would get them under their own rule.

It was a long time before that the Fomor came first to Ireland; dreadful they were to look at, and maimed, having but one foot or one hand, and they under the leadership of a giant and his mother. There never came to Ireland an army more horrible or more dreadful than that army of the Fomor. And they were friendly with the Firbolgs and content to leave Ireland to them, but there was jealousy between them and the Men of Dea.

And it was a hard tax they put on them, a third part of their corn they asked, and a third part of their milk, and a third part of their children, so that there was not smoke rising from a roof in Ireland but was under tribute to them. And Bres made no stand against them, but let them get their way.

And as to Bres himself, he put a tax on every house in Ireland of the milk of hornless dun cows, or of the milk of cows of some other single colour, enough for a hundred men. And the chief men of the Tuatha de Danaan grumbled against him, for their knives were never greased in his house, and however often they might visit him there was no smell of ale on their breath. And there was no sort of pleasure or merriment in his house, and no call for their poets, or singers, or harpers, or pipers, or horn-blowers, or jugglers, or fools. And as to the trials of strength they were used to seeing between their champions, the only use their strength was put to now was to be doing work for the king.

Now as to Nuada: after his arm being struck off, he was in his sickness for a while, and then Diancecht, the healer, made an arm of silver for him, with movement in every finger of it, and put it on him. And from that he was called Nuada Argat-lamh, of the Silver Hand, forever after.

---

*rath: *a circular enclosure surrounded by an earthen wall, used as a dwelling and stronghold.*

And Miach was not satisfied with what his father had done to the king, and he took Nuada's own hand that had been struck off, and brought it to him and set it in its place, and he said: "Joint to joint, and sinew to sinew." Three days and three nights he was with the king; the first day he put the hand against his side, and the second day against his breast, till it was covered with skin, and the third day he put bulrushes that were blackened in the fire on it, and at the end of that time the king was healed.

But Diancecht was vexed when he saw his son doing a better cure than himself, and he threw his sword at his head, that it cut the flesh, but the lad healed the wound by means of his skill. Then Diancecht threw it a second time, that it reached the bone, but the lad was able to cure the wound. Then he struck him the third time and the fourth, till he cut out the brain, for he knew no physician could cure him after that blow; and Miach died, and he buried him.

And herbs grew up from his grave, to the number of his joints and sinews, three hundred and sixty-five. And Airmed, his sister, came and spread out her cloak and laid out the herbs in it, according to their virtue. But Diancecht saw her doing that, and he came and mixed up the herbs, so that no one knows all their right powers to this day.

Then when the Tuatha de Danaan saw Nuada as well as he was before, they gathered together to Teamhair, where Bres was, and they bade him give up the kingship, for he had held it long enough. So he had to give it up, though he was not very willing, and Nuada was put back in the kingship again.

There was great vexation on Bres then, and he searched his mind to know how could he be avenged on those that had put him out, and how he could gather an army against them; and he went to his mother, Eri, daughter of Delbaith, and bade her tell him what his race was.

"I know that well," she said; and she told him then that his father was a king of the Fomor, Elathan, son of Dalbaech, and that he came to her one time over a level sea in some great vessel that seemed to be of silver, but she could not see its shape, and he himself having the appearance of a young man with yellow hair, and his clothes sewed with gold, and five rings of gold about his neck. And she that had refused the love of all the young men of her own people, gave him her love, and she cried when he left her. And he gave her a ring from his hand, and bade her give it only to the man whose finger it would fit, and he went away then the same way as he had come.

And she brought out the ring then to Bres, and he put it round his middle finger, and it fitted him well. And they went then together to the hill where she was the time she saw the silver vessel coming, and down to the strand, and she and Bres and his people set out for the country of the Fomor.

And when they came to that country they found a great plain with many gatherings of people on it, and they went to the gathering that looked the best, and the people asked where did they come from, and they said they were come from Ireland. "Have you hounds with you?" they asked them then, for it was the custom at that time, when strangers came to a gathering, to give them some friendly challenge. "We have hounds," said Bres. So the hounds were matched against one another, and the hounds of the Tuatha de Danaan were better than the hounds of the Fomor. "Have you horses for a race?" they asked then. "We have," said Bres. And the horses of the Tuatha de Danaan beat the horses of the Fomor.

Then they asked was anyone among them a good hand with the sword, and they said Bres was the best. But when he put his hand to his sword, Elathan, his father, that was among them, knew the ring, and he asked who was this young man. Then his mother answered him and told the whole story, and that Bres was his own son.

There was sorrow on his father then, and he said: "What was it drove you out of the country you were king over?" And Bres said: "Nothing drove me out but my own injustice and my own hardness; I took away their treasures from the people, and their jewels, and their food itself. And there were never taxes put on them before I was their king."

"That is bad," said his father; "it is of their prosperity you had a right to think more than of your own kingship. And their goodwill would be better than their curses," he said; "and what is it you are come to look for here?" "I am come to look for fighting men," said Bres, "that I may take Ireland by force." "You have no right to get it by injustice when you could not keep it by justice," said his father. "What advice have you for me then?" said Bres.

And Elathan bade him go to the chief king of the Fomor, Balor of the Evil Eye, to see what advice and what help would he give him.

The Coming of Lugh

Now as to Nuada of the Silver Hand, he was holding a great feast at Teamhair one time, after he was back in the kingship. And there were two doorkeepers at Teamhair when a young man came to the door where one of them was, and bade him bring him in to the king.

"Who are you yourself?" said the doorkeeper. "I am Lugh, son of Cian of the Tuatha de Danaan, and of Ethlinn, daughter of Balor, King of the Fomor," he said; "and I am foster-son of Taillte, daughter of the King of the Great Plain, and of Echaid the Rough, son of Duach." "What are you skilled in?" said the doorkeeper; "for no one without an art comes into Teamhair." "Question me," said Lugh; "I am a carpenter." "We do not want you; we have a carpenter." "Then I am a smith." "We have a smith ourselves." "Then I am a champion." "That is no use to us; we have a champion before, Ogma, brother to the king." "Question me again," he said; "I am a harper." "That is no use to us; we have a harper." "I am a poet," he said then, "and a teller of tales." "That is no use to us; we have a teller of tales ourselves, Ere, son of Ethaman." "And I am a magician." "That is no use to us; we have plenty of magicians and people of power." "I am a physician," he said. "That is no use; we have Diancecht for our physician." "Let me be a cupbearer," he said. "We do not want you; we have nine cupbearers ourselves." "I am a good worker in brass." "We have a worker in brass."

Then Lugh said: "Go and ask the king if he has any one man that can do all these things, and if he has, I will not ask to come into Teamhair." The doorkeeper went into the king's house then and told him all that. "There is a young man at the door," he said, "and his name should be the Ildánach, the Master of all Arts, for all the things the people of your house can do, he himself is able to do every one of them." "Try him with the chessboards," said Nuada. So the chessboards were brought out, and every game that was played, Lugh won it. And when Nuada was told that, he said: "Let him in, for the like of him never came into Teamhair before."

Then the doorkeeper let him pass, and he came into the king's house and sat down in the seat of knowledge. And there was a great flagstone there that could hardly be moved by four times twenty yoke of oxen, and Ogma took it up and hurled it out through the house, so that it lay on the outside of Teamhair, as a challenge to Lugh. But Lugh hurled it back again that it lay in the middle of the king's house. He played the harp for them then, and he had them laughing and crying, till he put them asleep at the end with a sleepy tune. And when Nuada saw all the things Lugh could do, he began to think that by his help the country might get free of the taxes and the tyranny put on it by the Fomor. And it is what he did, he came down from his throne, and he put Lugh on it in his place, for the length of thirteen days, that way they might all listen to the advice he would give.

This now is the story of the birth of Lugh. The time the Fomor used to be coming to Ireland, Balor of the Strong Blows, or, as some called him, of the Evil Eye, was living on the Island of the Tower of Glass. There was danger for ships that went near that island, for the Fomor would come out and take them. And some say the sons of Nemed in the old time, before the Firbolgs were in Ireland, passed near it in their ships, and what they saw was a tower of glass in the middle of the sea, and on the tower something that had the appearance of men, and they went against it with Druid spells to attack it. And the Fomor worked against them with Druid spells of their own; and the sons of Nemed attacked the tower, and it vanished, and they thought it was destroyed. But a great wave rose over them then, and all their ships went down and all that were in them.

And the tower was there as it was before, and Balor living in it. And it is the reason he was called "of the Evil Eye," there was a power of death in one of his eyes,* so that no person could look at it and live. It is the way it got that power, he was passing one time by a house where his father's Druids were making spells of death, and the window being open he looked in, and the smoke of the poisonous spells was rising up, and it went into his eye. And from that time he had to keep it closed unless he wanted to be the death of some enemy, and then the men that were with him would lift the eyelid with a ring of ivory.

Now a Druid foretold one time that it was by his own grandson he would get his death. And he had at that time but one child, a daughter whose name was Ethlinn; and when he heard what the Druid said, he shut her up in the tower on the island. And he put twelve women with her to take charge of her and to guard her, and he bade them never to let her see a man or hear the name of a man.

So Ethlinn was brought up in the tower, and she grew to be very beautiful; and sometimes she would see men passing in the currachs (small round boat), and sometimes she would see a man in her dreams. But when she would speak of that to the women, they would give her no answer.

So there was no fear on Balor, and he went on with war and robbery as he was used, seizing every ship that passed by, and sometimes going over to Ireland to do destruction there.

Now it chanced at that time there were three brothers of the Tuatha de Danaan living together in a place that was called Druim na Teine (the Ridge of the Fire), Goibniu and Samthainn and Cian. Cian was a lord of land, and Goibniu was the smith that had such a great name. Now Cian had a wonderful cow, the Glas Gaibhnenn, and her milk never failed. And every one that heard of her coveted her, and many had tried to steal her away, so that she had to be watched night and day.

And one time Cian was wanting some swords made, and he went to Goibniu's forge, and he brought the Glas Gaibhnenn with him, holding her by a halter. When he came to the forge his two brothers were there together, for Samthainn had brought some steel to have weapons made for himself; and Cian bade Samthainn to hold the halter while he went into the forge to speak with Goibniu.

Now Balor had set his mind for a long time on the Glas Gaibhnenn, but he had never been able to get near her up to this time. And he was watching not far off, and when he saw Samthainn holding the cow, he put on the appearance of a little boy, having red hair, and came up to him and told him he heard his two brothers that were in the forge saying to one another that they would use all his steel for their own swords, and make his of iron. "By my word," said Samthainn, "they will not deceive me so easily. Let you hold the cow, little lad," he said, "and I will go in to them." With that he rushed into the forge, and great anger on him. And no sooner did Balor get the halter in his hand than he set out, dragging the Glas along with him, to the strand, and across the sea to his own island.

When Cian saw his brother coming in he rushed out, and there he saw Balor and the Glas out in the sea. And he had nothing to do then but to reproach his brother, and to wander about as if his wits had left him, not knowing what way to get his cow back from Balor. At last he went to a Druid to ask an advice from him; and it is what the Druid told him, that so long as Balor lived, the cow would never be brought back, for no one would go within reach of his Evil Eye.

Cian went then to a woman-Druid, Birog of the Mountain, for her help. And she dressed him in a woman's clothes, and brought him across the sea in a blast of wind, to the tower where Ethlinn was. Then she called to the women in the tower, and asked them for shelter for a high queen she was after saving from

Balor's Evil Eye: Some versions of the story say he has another eye in the back of his head.

some hardship, and the women in the tower did not like to refuse a woman of the Tuatha de Danaan, and they let her and her comrade in. Then Birog by her enchantments put them all into a deep sleep, and Cian went to speak with Ethlinn. And when she saw him she said that was the face she had seen in her dreams. So she gave him her love; but after a while he was brought away again on a blast of wind.

And when her time came, Ethlinn gave birth to a son. And when Balor knew that, he bade his people put the child in a cloth and fasten it with a pin, and throw him into a current of the sea. And as they were carrying the child across an arm of the sea, the pin dropped out, and the child slipped from the cloth into the water, and they thought he was drowned. But he was brought away by Birog of the Mountain, and she brought him to his father Cian; and he gave him to be fostered by Taillte, daughter of the King of the Great Plain. It is thus Lugh was born and reared.

And some say Balor came and struck the head off Cian on a white stone, that has the blood marks on it to this day; but it is likely it was some other man he struck the head off, for it was by the sons of Tuireann that Cian came to his death.

And after Lugh had come to Teamhair, and made his mind up to join with his father's people against the Fomor, he put his mind to the work; and he went to a quiet place in Grellach Dollaid, with Nuada and the Dagda, and with Ogma; and Goibniu and Diancecht were called to them there. A full year they stopped there, making their plans together in secret, that way the Fomor would not know they were going to rise against them till such time as all would be ready, and till they would know what their strength was. And it is from that council the place got the name afterwards of "The Whisper of the Men of Dea." And they broke up the council, and agreed to meet again that day in three years, and every one of them went his own way, and Lugh went back to his own friends, the sons of Manannan.

And it was a good while after that, Nuada was holding a great assembly of the people on the Hill of Uisnech, on the west side of Teamhair. And they were not long there before they saw an armed troop coming towards them from the east, over the plain; and there was a young man in front of the troop, in command over the rest, and the brightness of his face was like the setting sun, so that they were not able to look at him because of its brightness.

And when he came nearer they knew it was Lugh Lamh-Fada, of the Long Hand, that had come back to them, and along with him were the Riders of the Sidhe from the Land of Promise, and his own foster-brothers, the sons of Manannan. And it is the way Lugh was, he had Manannan's horse, the Aonbharr, of the One Mane, under him, that was as swift as the naked cold wind of spring, and the sea was the same as dry land to her, and the rider was never killed off her back. And he had Manannan's breastplate on him, that kept whoever was wearing it from wounds, and a helmet on his head with two beautiful precious stones set in the front of it and one at the back, and when he took it off, his forehead was like the sun on a dry summer day. And he had Manannan's sword, the Freagarthach, the Answerer, at his side, and no one that was wounded by it would ever get away alive; and when that sword was bared in a battle, no man that saw it coming against him had any more strength than a woman in childbirth.

And the troop came to where the King of Ireland was with the Tuatha de Danaan, and they welcomed one another. And they were not long there till they saw a surly, slovenly troop coming towards them, nine times nine of the messengers of the Fomor, that were coming to ask rent and taxes from the men of Ireland.

They came up then to where the King of Ireland was with the Riders of the Sidhe, and the king and all the Tuatha de Danaan stood up before them. And Lugh of the Long Hand said: "Why do you rise up before that surly, slovenly troop, when you did not rise up before us?"

"It is needful for us to do it," said the king; "for if there was but a child of us sitting before them, they would not think that too small a cause for killing him." "By my word," said Lugh, "there is a great desire coming on me to kill themselves." "That is a thing would bring harm on us," said the king, "for we would meet our own death and destruction through it." "It is too long a time you have been under this oppression," said Lugh. And with that he started up and made an attack on the Fomor, killing and wounding them, till he had made an end of eight nines of them, but he let the last nine go under the protection of Nuada the king. "And I would kill you along with the others," he said, "but I would sooner see you go with messages to your own country than my own people, for fear they might get any ill-treatment."

So the nine went back then till they came to Lochlann, where the men of the Fomor were, and they told them the story from beginning to end, and how a young well-featured lad had come into Ireland and had killed all the tax-gatherers but themselves, "and it is the reason he let us off," they said, "that we might tell you the story ourselves."

"Do you know who is the young man?" said Balor of the Evil Eye then.

"I know well," said Ceithlenn, his wife; "he is the son of your daughter and mine. And it was foretold," she said, "that from the time he would come into Ireland, we would never have power there again forever."

Then the chief men of the Fomor went into a council, including the nine poets of the Fomor that had learning and the gift of foreknowledge, and Lobais the Druid, and Balor himself and his twelve white-mouthed sons, and Ceithlenn of the Crooked Teeth, his queen.

And it was just at that time Bres and his father Elathan were come to ask help of the Fomor, and Bres said: "I myself will go to Ireland, and seven great battalions of the Riders of the Fomor along with me, and I will give battle to this Ildánach* this master of all arts, and I will strike his head off and bring it here to you." "It would be a fitting thing for you to do," said they all. "Let my ships be made ready for me," said Bres, "and let food and provisions be put in them."

So they made no delay, but went and got the ships ready, and they put plenty of food and drink in them, and the two swift Luaths were sent out to gather the army to Bres. And when they were all gathered, they made ready their armour and their weapons, and they set out for Ireland.

And Balor the king followed them to the harbour, and he said: "Give battle to that Ildánach, and strike off his head; and tie that island that is called Ireland to the back of your ships, and let the destroying water take its place, and put it on the north side of Lochlann, and not one of the Men of Dea will follow it there to the end of life and time."

Then they pushed out their ships and put up their painted sails, and went out from the harbour on the untilled country, on the ridges of the wide-lying sea, and they never turned from their course till they came to the harbour of Eas Dara. And from that they sent out an army through West Connacht and destroyed it altogether, through and through. And the King of Connacht at that time was Bodb Dearg, son of the Dagda.

The Great Battle of Magh Tuireadh

The whole host of the Fomor were come this time, and their king, Balor, of the Strong Blows and of the Evil Eye, along with them; and Bres, and many others.

Then Lugh sent the Dagda to spy out the Fomor, and to delay them till such time as the men of Ireland would come to the battle.

So the Dagda went to their camp, and he asked them for a delay, and they said he might have that. And then to make sport of him, the Fomor made broth for him, for he had a great love for broth. So they filled

Ildanach: master of all arts

the king's cauldron with four times twenty gallons of new milk, and the same of meal and fat, and they put in goats and sheep and pigs along with that, and boiled all together, and then they poured it all out into a great hole in the ground. And they called him to it then, and told him he should eat his fill, that way the Fomor would not be reproached for want of hospitality the way Bres was. "We will make an end of you if you leave any part of it after you," said Indech, son of De Domnann.

So the Dagda took the ladle, and it big enough for a man and a woman to lie in the bowl of it, and he took out bits with it, the half of a salted pig, and a quarter of lard a bit would be. "If the broth tastes as well as the bits taste, this is good food," he said. And he went on putting the full of the ladle into his mouth till the hole was empty; and when all was gone he put down his hand and scraped up all that was left among the earth and the gravel.

Sleep came on him then after eating the broth, and the Fomor were laughing at him, for his belly was the size of the cauldron of a great house. But he rose up after a while, and, heavy as he was, he made his way home; and indeed his dress was no way sightly, a cape to the hollow of the elbows, and a brown coat, long in the breast and short behind, and on his feet brogues of horse hide, with the hair outside, and in his hand a wheeled fork it would take eight men to carry, so that the track he left after him was deep enough for the boundary ditch of a province. And on his way he saw the Battle-Crow, the Morrigu, washing herself in the river Unius of Connacht, and one of her two feet at Ullad Echne, to the south of the water, and the other at Loscuinn, to the north of the water, and her hair hanging in nine loosened locks. And she said to the Dagda, that she would bring the heart's blood of Indech, son of De Domnann, that had threatened him, to the men of Ireland.

And while he was away Lugh had called together the Druids, and smiths, and physicians, and lawmakers, and chariot-drivers of Ireland, to make plans for the battle.

And he asked the great magician Mathgen what could he do to help them. "It is what I can do," said Mathgen, "through my power I can throw down all the mountains of Ireland on the Fomor, until their tops will be rolling on the ground. And the twelve chief mountains of Ireland will bring you their help," he said, "and will fight for you."

Then he asked the cupbearers what help they could give. "We will put a strong thirst on the Fomor," they said, "and then we will bring the twelve chief lochs of Ireland before them, and however great their thirst may be, they will find no water in them," they said, "to the twelve chief rivers of Ireland: they will all be hidden away from the Fomor that way they will not find a drop in them. But as for the men of Ireland," they said, "there will be drink for them if they were to be in the battle to the end of seven years."

And Figol, son of Mamos, the Druid, was asked then what he would do, and he said: "It is what I will do, I will cause three showers of fire to pour on the faces of the army of the Fomor, and I will take from them two-thirds of their bravery and their strength, and I will put sickness on their bodies, and on the bodies of their horses. But as to the men of Ireland," he said, "every breath they breathe will be an increase of strength and of bravery to them; and if they are seven years in the battle they will never be any way tired."

Then Lugh asked his two witches, Bechulle and Dianan: "What power can you bring to the battle?" "It is easy to say that," they said. "We will put enchantment on the trees and the stones and the sods of the earth, till they become an armed host against the Fomor, and put terror on them and put them to the rout."

Then Lugh asked Carpre, the poet, son of Etain, what could he do. "It is not hard to say that," said Carpre. "I will make a satire on them at sunrise, and the wind from the north, and I on a hilltop and my back to a thorn tree, and a stone and a thorn in my hand. And with that satire," he said, "I will put shame on them and enchantment, that way they will not be able to stand against fighting men."

Then he asked Goibniu the Smith what would he be able to do. "I will do this," he said. "If the men of Ireland stop in the battle to the end of seven years, for every sword that is broken and for every spear that is lost from its shaft, I will put a new one in its place. And no spearpoint that will be made by my hand," he said, "will ever miss its mark; and no man it touches will ever taste life again. And that is more than Dolb, the smith of the Fomor, can do," he said.

"And you, Credne," Lugh said then to his worker in brass, "what help can you give to our men in the battle?" "It is not hard to tell that," said Credne, "rivets for their spears and hilts for their swords and bosses and rims for their shields, I will supply them all."

"And you, Luchta," he said then to his carpenter, "what will you do?" "I will give them all they want of shields and of spear shafts," said Luchta.

Then he asked Diancecht, the physician, what would he do, and it is what he said: "Every man that will be wounded there, unless his head is struck off, or his brain or his marrow cut through, I will make him whole and sound again for the battle of the morrow."

Then the Dagda said: "Those great things you are boasting you will do, I will do them all with only myself." "It is you are the good god!" said they, and they all gave a great shout of laughter.

Then Lugh spoke to the whole army and put strength in them, so that each one had the spirit in him of a king or a great lord.

Then when the delay was at an end, the Fomor and the men of Ireland came on towards one another till they came to the plain of Magh Tuireadh. That now was not the same Magh Tuireadh where the first battle was fought, but it was to the north, near Ess Dara.

And then the two armies threatened one another. "The men of Ireland are daring enough to offer battle to us," said Bres to Indech, son of De Domnann. "I give my word," said Indech, "it is in small pieces their bones will be, if they do not give in to us and pay their tribute."

Now the Men of Dea had determined not to let Lugh go into the battle, because of the loss his death would be to them; and they left nine of their men keeping a watch on him.

And on the first day none of the kings or princes went into the battle, but only the common fighting men, and they fierce and proud enough.

And the battle went on like that from day to day with no great advantage to one or the other side. But there was wonder on the Fomor on account of one thing. Such of their own weapons as were broken or blunted in the fight lay there as they were, and such of their own men as were killed showed no sign of life on the morrow; but it was not so with the Tuatha de Danaan, for if their men were killed or their weapons were broken today, they were as good as before on the morrow.

And this is the way that happened. The well of Slaine lay to the west of Magh Tuireadh to the east of Loch Arboch. And Diancecht and his son Octruil and his daughter Airmed used to be singing spells over the well and to be putting herbs in it; and the men that were wounded to death in the battle would be brought to the well and put into it as dead men, and they would come out of it whole and sound, through the power of the spells. And not only were they healed, but there was such fire put into them that they would be quicker in the fight than they were before.

And as to the arms, it is the way they were made new every day. Goibniu the Smith used to be in the forge making swords and spears, and he would make a spearhead by three turns, and then Luchta the Carpenter would make the shaft by three cuts, and the third cut was a finish, and would set it in the ring of the spear. And when the spearheads were stuck in the side of the forge, he would throw the shaft and the rings the way they would go into the spearhead and want no more setting. And then Credne the

Brazier would make the rivets by three turns and would cast the rings of the spears to them, and with that they were ready and were set together.

And all this went against the Fomor, and they sent one of their young men to spy about the camp and to see could he find out how these things were done. It was Ruadan, son of Bres and of Brigit daughter of the Dagda they sent, for he was a son and grandson of the Tuatha de Danaan. So he went and saw all that was done, and came back to the Fomor.

And when they heard his story it is what they thought, that Goibniu the Smith was the man that hindered them most. And they sent Ruadan back again, and bade him make an end of him.

So he went back again to the forge, and he asked Goibniu would he give him a spearhead. And then he asked rivets of Credne, and a shaft of the carpenter, and all was given to him as he asked. And there was a woman there, Cron, mother to Fianlug, grinding the spears.

And after the spear being given to Ruadan, he turned and threw it at Goibniu, that it wounded him. But Goibniu pulled it out and made a cast of it at Ruadan, that it went through him and he died; and Bres, his father, and the army of the Fomor, saw him die. And then Brigit came and keened her son with shrieking and with crying.

And as to Goibniu, he went into the well and was healed. But after that Octriallach, son of Indech, called to the Fomor and bade each man of them bring a stone of the stones of Drinnes and throw them into the well of Slane. And they did that till the well was dried up, and a cairn raised over it, that is called Octriallach's Cairn.

And it was while Goibniu was making spearheads for the battle of Magh Tuireadh, a charge was brought against his wife. And it was seen that it was heavy news to him, and that jealousy came on him. And it is what he did, there was a spear-shaft in his hand when he heard the story, Nes its name was; and he sang spells over the spear-shaft, and any one that was struck with that spear afterwards, it would burn him up like fire.

And at last the day of the great battle came, and the Fomor came out of their camp and stood in strong ranks. And there was not a leader or a fighting man of them was without good armour to his skin, and a helmet on his head, a broad spear in his right hand, a heavy sword in his belt, a strong shield on his shoulder. And to attack the army of the Fomor that day was to strike the head against a rock, or to go up fighting against a fire.

And the Men of Dea rose up and left Lugh and his nine comrades keeping him, and they went on to the battle; and Midhir was with them, and Bodb Dearg and Diancecht. And Badb and Macha and the Morrigu called out that they would go along with them.

And it was a hard battle was fought, and for a while it was going against the Tuatha de Danaan; and Nuada of the Silver Hand, their King, and Macha, daughter of Emmass, fell by Balor, King of the Fomor. And Cass-mail fell by Octriallach, and the Dagda got a dreadful wound from a casting spear that was thrown by Ceithlenn, wife of Balor.

But when the battle was going on, Lugh broke away from those that were keeping him, and rushed out to the front of the Men of Dea. And then there was a fierce battle fought, and Lugh was heartening the men of Ireland to fight well, that way they would not be in bonds any longer. For it was better for them, he said, to die protecting their own country than to live under bonds and under tribute any longer. And he sang a song of courage to them, and the hosts gave a great shout as they went into battle, and then they met together, and each of them began to attack the other.

And there was great slaughter, and laying low in graves, and many comely men fell there in the stall of death. Pride and shame were there side by side, and hardness and red anger, and there was red blood on the white skin of young fighting men. And the dashing of spear against shield, and sword against sword, and the shouting of the fighters, and the whistling of casting spears and the rattling of scabbards was like harsh thunder through the battle. And many slipped in the blood that was under their feet, and they fell, striking their heads one against another; and the river carried away bodies of friends and enemies together.

Then Lugh and Balor met in the battle, and Lugh called out reproaches to him; and there was anger on Balor, and he said to the men that were with him: "Lift up my eyelid till I see this chatterer that is talking to me." Then they raised Balor's eyelid, but Lugh made a cast of his red spear at him, that brought the eye out through the back of his head, so that it was towards his own army it fell, and three times nine of the Fomor died when they looked at it. And if Lugh had not put out that eye when he did, the whole of Ireland would have been burned in one flash. And after this, Lugh struck his head off.

And as for Indech, son of De Domnann, he fell and was crushed in the battle, and blood burst from his mouth, and he called out for Leat Glas, his poet, as he lay there, but he was not able to help him. And then the Morrigu came into the battle, and she was heartening the Tuatha de Danaan to fight the battle well; and, as she had promised the Dagda, she took the full of her two hands of Indech's blood, and gave it to the armies that were waiting at the ford of Unius; and it was called the Ford of Destruction from that day.

And after that it was not a battle anymore, but a rout, and the Fomor were beaten back to the sea. And Lugh and his comrades were following them, and they came up with Bres, son of Elathan, and no guard with him, and he said: "It is better for you to spare my life than to kill me. And if you spare me now," he said, "the cows of Ireland will never go dry." "I will ask an advice about that from our wise men," said Lugh. So he told Maeltine Mor-Brethach, of the Great Judgments, what Bres was after saying. But Maeltine said: "Do not spare him for that, for he has no power over their offspring, though he has power so long as they are living."

Then Bres said: "If you spare me, the men of Ireland will reap a harvest of corn every quarter." But Maeltine said: "The spring is for ploughing and sowing, and the beginning of summer for the strength of corn, and the beginning of autumn for its ripeness, and the winter for using it."

"That does not save you," said Lugh then to Bres. But then to make an excuse for sparing him, Lugh said: "Tell us what is the best way for the men of Ireland to plough and to sow and to reap."

"Let their ploughing be on a Tuesday, and their casting seed into the field on a Tuesday, and their reaping on a Tuesday," said Bres. So Lugh said that would do, and he let him go free after that.

It was in this battle Ogma found Orna, the sword of Tethra, a king of the Fomor, and he took it from its sheath and cleaned it. And when the sword was taken out of the sheath, it told all the deeds that had been done by it, for there used to be that power in swords.

And Lugh and the Dagda and Ogma followed after the Fomor, for they had brought away the Dagda's harp with them, that was called Uaitne. And they came to a feasting-house, and in it they found Bres and his father Elathan, and there was the harp hanging on the wall. And it was in that harp the Dagda had bound the music, so that it would not sound till he would call to it. And sometimes it was called Dur-da-Bla, the Oak of Two Blossoms, and sometimes Coir-cethar-chuin, the Four-Angled Music.

And when he saw it hanging on the wall it is what he said: "Come summer, come winter, from the mouth of harps and bags and pipes." Then the harp sprang from the wall, and came to the Dagda, and it killed nine men on its way.

And then he played for them the three things harpers understand, the sleepy tune, and the laughing tune, and the crying tune. And when he played the crying tune, their tearful women cried, and then he played the laughing tune, till their women and children laughed; and then he played the sleepy tune, and all the hosts fell asleep. And through that sleep the three went away through the Fomor that would have been glad to harm them. And when all was over, the Dagda brought out the heifer he had got as wages from Bres at the time he was making his dun. And she called to her calf, and at the sound of her call all the cattle of Ireland the Fomor had brought away as tribute, were back in their fields again.

And Cé, the Druid of Nuada of the Silver Hand, was wounded in the battle, and he went southward till he came to Carn Corrslebe. And there he sat down to rest, tired with his wounds and with the fear that was on him, and the journey. And he saw a smooth plain before him, and it full of flowers, and a great desire came on him to reach to that plain, and he went on till he came to it, and there he died. And when his grave was made there, a lake burst out over it and over the whole plain, and it was given the name of Loch Cé. And there were but four men of the Fomor left in Ireland after the battle, and they used to be going through the country, spoiling corn and milk and fruit, and whatever came from the sea, till they were driven out one Samhain night by the Morrigu and by Angus Og, that the Fomor might never be over Ireland again.

And after the battle was won, and the bodies were cleared away, the Morrigu gave out the news of the great victory to the hosts and to the royal heights of Ireland and to its chief rivers and its invers, and it is what she said: "Peace up to the skies, the skies down to earth, the earth under the skies; strength to everyone."

And as to the number of men that fell in the battle, it will not be known till we number the stars of the sky, or flakes of snow, or the dew on the grass, or grass under the feet of cattle, or the horses of the Son of Lir in a stormy sea.

And Lugh was made king over the Men of Dea then, and it was at Nas he had his court.

And while he was king, his foster-mother Taillte, daughter of Magh Mor, the Great Plain, died. And before her death she bade her husband Duach the Dark, he that built the Fort of the Hostages in Teamhair, to clear away the wood of Cuan, that way there could be a gathering of the people around her grave. So he called to the men of Ireland to cut down the wood with their wide-bladed knives and billhooks and hatchets, and within a month the whole wood was cut down.

And Lugh buried her in the plain of Midhe, and raised a mound over her, that is to be seen to this day. And he ordered fires to be kindled, and keening to be made, and games and sports to be held in the summer of every year out of respect to her. And the place they were held got its name from her, that is Taillten.

And as to Lugh's own mother, that was tall beautiful Ethlinn, she came to Teamhair after the battle of Magh Tuireadh, and he gave her in marriage to Tadg, son of Nuada. And the children that were born to them were Muirne, mother of Finn, the Head of the Fianna of Ireland, and Tuiren, that was mother of Bran.

*   *   *

And after Lugh had held the kingship for a long time, the Dagda was made king in his place...And so the Fomorians were no longer a threat to Ireland. And yet it was foreseen that the age of the Tuatha De Denaan would end and a new one would begin. And they believed it would be a dark age. Indeed, in the sixth age, again on the first of May, the Milesians arrived and claimed the land for their own. Some say the Tuatha De Danaan were all killed in battle, but most believe the gods remain, their spirits dwelling in the land for all time.

In some versions, Nuada is Elcmar (see The Courtship of Etain)

DISCUSSION QUESTIONS

1. Discuss the purpose and function of the various battles told in these tales. Which do you think is the most important victory, and why?

2. What particular qualities make Lugh a hero? In what ways does his story fit Campbell's monomyth?

3. Discuss the uses of magic and magical objects in these stories. What are the various sources of the magic?

4. Discuss the role nature plays in these stories. What does this reveal about the beliefs of the people?

5. Explain the importance of poets and bards, as illustrated in these tales.

BIBLIOGRAPHY

Cotterell, Arthur, and Rachel Storm. *The Ultimate Encyclopedia of Mythology.* Hermes House, 1999.

Ellis, Peter Berresford. *Celtic Myths and Legends.* Running Press Book Publishers, 2008.

Freeman, Mara. *Kindling the Celtic Spirit.* Harper Collins, 2001.

Gantz, Jeffrey (Ed. and Trans.). *Early Irish Myths and Sagas.* Penguin Books, 1981.

Gibbons, Ann. "There's No Such Thing As 'Pure' European—Or Anything Else." *Science,* 15 May 2017. http://www.sciencemag.org/news/2017/05/theres-no-such-thing-pure-european-or-anyone-else. doi: 10.1126/science.aal1186. Accessed 15 May 2017.

Griffis, William Elliot. *Welsh Fairy Tales.* Thomas Y. Crowell Co., 1921. https://books.google.com/books?id=3BY-AAAAYAAJ&pg=PP11#v=onepage

In search of history: The Celts [Video file]. 1997. https://fod.infobase.com/PortalPlaylists.aspx?wID=104554&xtid=42711. Accessed 30 May 2017.

Lady Charlotte Guest. *The Mabinogion.* Bernard Quartich, 1877. http://www.sacred-texts.com/neu/celt/mab/mab32.htm

Lady Gregory. *Gods and Fighting Men: The Story of the Tuatha De Danaan and the Fianna of Ireland.* 1905. https://www.gutenberg.org/files/14465/14465-h/14465-h.htm#L4.

Land, Andrew. *Folk-Lore A Quarterly Review of Myth, Tradition, Institution, and Custom.* vol 1. 1890. Collected by Mr. D. J. Robertson of the Orkneys. *Longman's Magazine* vol xiv, https://books.google.com/books?id=u4QZAAAAYAAJ&pg=PR1#v=onepage&q&f=false.

Leahy, A. H. *Heroic Romances of Ireland.* Thomas Y. Crowell Co.,1905. http://www.gutenberg.org/cache/epub/5680/pg5680-images.html.

Mackenzie, Donald A. *Wonder Tales from Scottish Myth and Legend.* Blackie and Son, 1917. http://archive.org/stream/wondertalesfroms00mack#page/n29/mode/2up

Morrison, Sohia. *Manx Fairy Tales.* David Nutt, 1911. https://archive.org/stream/manxfairytales00morr#page/18/mode/2up

Newgrange World Heritage Site. http://www.newgrange.com/.

Paxton, Jennifer. "The Celtic World." *The Great Courses.* The Teaching Company, 2018.

Rolleston, T. W. *The High Deeds of Finn and other Bardic Romances of Ancient Ireland.* Thomas Y. Crowell Co., 1910. https://www.gutenberg.org/files/14749/14749-h/14749-h.htm#CHAPTER_I.

Rosenberg, Donna. *Mythology: An Anthology of the Great Myths and Epics,* 3rd ed. McGraw Hill, 1999.

Squire, Charles. *Celtic Myth and Legend.* 1905. http://www.sacred-texts.com/neu/celt/cml/cml10.htm

Chapter **6**

THE MYTHS OF AFRICA

© Eduard Kyslynsky/Shutterstock.com

INTRODUCTION

Part 1: Creation and Destruction

The Origin of Death (San of South Africa)

4 Tales of the Origins of Death (South Africa)

Maasai Origins (Kenya)

Origin of the Kikuyu (Kenya)

Part 2: Tricksters, Lovers, and Other Tales

3 Stories about the Sky (Nigeria)

The Woman with Two Skins (Nigeria)

The King's Magic Drum (Nigeria)

How Anansi Got the Stories from the Sky God (Ashanti/ Ghana)

Part 3: Journeys of Heroes and Heroines

The Maiden Who Was Sacrificed (Kikuyu)

The Snake from the Great Water (Kikuyu)

Gassire's Lute (Soninke/Ghana)

Introduction

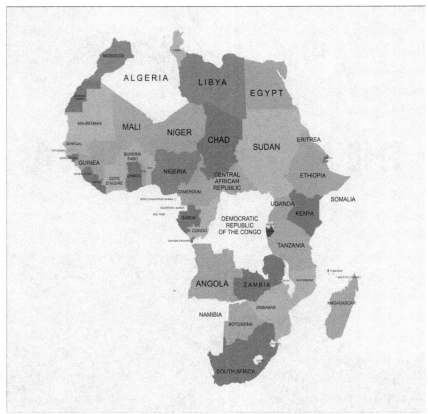

© Aliaksei Tarasau/Shutterstock.com

African myths and folktales are as varied as the people and landscapes of the continent—forests, savanna, deserts, swamps, and mountains—a vast collection of environments and cultures that have existed for thousands of years, including some of the oldest civilizations on earth. The diversity of such a place cannot be adequately conveyed here; no such variety can be found anywhere else on earth. There are literally thousands of languages, and stories from groups consisting of small, nomadic tribes to sophisticated kingdoms, encompassing lifestyles that include farmers, herders, and hunter-gatherers. Some isolated tribes still exist today, seemingly frozen in time, outside of modern advancements. (Stories from Egypt are located in the chapter on the Middle East.)

There is often some overlap between myths and folktales; folktales and animal fables usually contain morals and lessons, reinforce social customs, illustrate proper behavior, and entertain—especially children. Some are etiological tales but are not intended as origin stories or to reveal cultural identity. This is the difference between myth and folktale. In some cases it may be difficult to distinguish, and sometimes it simply depends on the tribal tradition. For example, trickster tales are common but their purpose and function may vary. Among hunter-gatherers, the trickster may serve in the role of a creator, taking on more importance in their culture, while in other groups the trickster has more human qualities and maintains a more comedic role.

Despite the vast differences, there is a strand of unity—live performance. The majority of stories were performed in an interactive group setting, typically accompanied by drumming and dancing, often with audience participation.

In addition, we must remember that the stories are translations made largely by travelers and missionaries. A 1945 book written by Belgian missionary titled *Bantu Philosophy*, Placide Tempels did the unthinkable—he wrote about the African people as intelligent, cultured, and philosophical people, not as "savages." The very title of this book gives agency to the people he encountered (Bantu being the largest linguistic group in Africa), rather than referring to them with the derogatory language that most Western writers used. Tempels collected stories and practices from around the continent, eventually positing that there were a set of philosophy and morals largely shared by those he met. He wrote,

> The discovery of Bantu philosophy is a disturbing event for all those who are concerned with African education. We have had the idea that we stood before them like adults before the newly born. In our mission to educate and to civilize, we believed that we started with a 'tabula rasa,' though we also believed that we had to clear the ground of some worthless notions, to lay foundations in a bare soil. We were quite sure that we should give short shrift to stupid customs, vain beliefs, as being quite ridiculous and devoid of all sound sense . . . [however] the Bantu point of view is dictated by a lofty wisdom in regard to life, linking on to their philosophical principles.

Tempels realized earlier than his missionary counterparts that the African people were capable and had already been practicing higher order philosophy, which was a radical notion to those who wished to descend on the continent and "educate" them.

Although efforts were made by these missionaries, travelers, and anthropologists to work from performance in many cases, we still lose something through time and context and the lens through which the documentarian was looking. The stories change over time as well. Like all myths, "The traditions are thus a dialogue of the present with the past, in which the present seeks to find its roots in what is remembered, or invented, of the past" (Belcher). Some tales and tribal history are beyond recovery—obliterated by conflict and colonization, the slave trade, and migration of tribes. But memories and echoes of the past have been shared, keeping connections alive.

As with the other chapters in this book, it is a daunting task to bring these stories together—to do so risks oversimplification. The continent of Africa presents a complex history of individual tribes and cultures; there are many excellent collections of these tales available for further study and entire books are dedicated to exploring these distinct traditions in detail. Therefore, this brief sample cannot hope to truly illustrate that variety.

Part 1: Creation and Destruction

© Nell Novara

The Origin of Death (San of South Africa)

When the tribal peoples who lived near the Kalahari Desert were first encountered, European colonizers lumped them all into one group: the Bushmen. Today this term is considered a derogatory word, as it carries with it a racist connotation for being "scavengers" or non-cattle owning people.

Several volumes in the 19th and 20th centuries were written by Dutch, English, and Portuguese men who chronicled the life and stories of these native people in modern Botswana, Namibia, and South Africa. Having a better understanding of the language families and genetics, we now know that the "Bushmen" are actually comprised of a variety of peoples, including the San, the Basarwa, the Khoi-Khoi, and the Khwe, among others.

The largest cultural group, the San peoples, still live in southern Africa today, with a population of approximately 100,000. They are descended from the oldest hunter-gatherers in the species *homo sapiens* and are some of the world's first artists. The San Rock Art paintings in South Africa depict shamans in various states of trance or dance in order to make rain or heal sickness. These dances and rituals continue to be used in practice by the San people today.

What connects these tribes of southern African people, besides geography, is an interesting language group, called the Koisan languages, more familiarly known as the "Click Language," because it employs many dental or tongue clicks. The Kalahari Research Center describes this alphabet:

- ▶ / (Forward slash)—denotes a frontal dental click similar to the English "Tsk-Tsk" of disapproval. /? is a glottal variation & ?/ is a nasal type.
- ▶ // (2 Forward slashes)—denotes a lateral dental click similar to the sound used to urge a horse.
- ▶ ≠ (Equals sign bisected by a forward slash, "not-equal sign")—denotes a sharp alveolar click made with the tongue against the roof of the mouth.
- ▶ ! (Exclamation mark)—denotes a sharp palato-alveolar click made with the tongue on the back of the gum ridge. Cork popping sound.

Language is an exceedingly important element of the San stories. The myths below depict a thought process concerned with the interferences of the cosmos, how death was allowed to take their lives, and what happens after people die. It is often a word misinterpreted by an animal that becomes twisted, or a misunderstanding that leads to death. The stories rely heavily on the influence of the natural world of animals and the sky to give meaning to their tales of origin and demise.

A Prayer to the Moon

When the Moon has newly returned alive, when another person has shown us the Moon, we look towards the place at which the other has shown us the Moon, and, when we look there we see the Moon, and when we see it, we shut our eyes with our hands, and we exclaim:

"Take my face yonder! Thou shalt give me thy face yonder! Thou shalt take my face yonder! That which does not feel pleasant. Thou shalt give me thy face, that I may also resemble thee—when thou hast died, thou does again, living return, when we did not perceive thee, thou does again lying down come. For, the joy yonder, thou does always possess it yonder, that is, that thou art wont again to return alive, when we did not perceive thee; while the hare told thee about it, that thou should do thus. Thou did formerly say, that we should also again return alive, when we died."

THE ORIGIN OF DEATH

The hare was the one who brought death. He spoke, he said that he would not be silent, for his mother would not again return alive; for his mother was altogether dead. Therefore, he would cry greatly for his mother.

The Moon replied to the hare that the hare should leave off crying; for his mother was not altogether dead. His mother would again return to the living. The hare replied that he was not willing to be silent; for he know that his mother would not again return alive. For she was altogether dead. And the Moon became angry about it, that the young male hare spoke thus, that the hare he did not assent to the Moon.

The Moon hit the hare's mouth with his fist, and exclaimed: "This hare's mouth shall altogether be like this; he shall always bear a scar on his mouth; he shall spring away, he shall do-doubling come back. The dogs shall chase him; they shall, when they have caught him, bit and tear him to pieces, and he shall altogether die. And they who are men, they shall altogether dying go away, not to return when they die. For, the hare was not willing to agree with me, when I told him about it, that he should not cry for his mother; that his mother would again live; he said to me that his mother would not again living return.

Source: W.H.I. Bleek and L.C. Lloyd, *Specimens of Bushman Folklore*, 1911.

Therefore, the people shall altogether die. I said to him that the people should also be like me; that which I do; that I, when I am dead, I again living return and he contradicted me, when I had told him this."

Our mothers said to me that the hare was formerly a man; when he had acted in this manner, then it was that the Moon cursed him, that he should altogether become a hare. Our mothers told me, that, the hare has a strip of human flesh at his bones: therefore, when we have killed and intend to eat the hare, we take out the strip of flesh, which is human flesh, and we leave it; it is flesh that belongs to the time when he formerly was a man. Therefore, our mothers were not willing for us to eat that small piece of meat; while they felt that it is this piece of meat with which the hare was formerly a man.

Therefore, the Moon spoke, he said: "Ye who are people, ye shall, when ye die, altogether dying vanish away. I became angry, thinking that the hare would say: 'Yes; my mother is asleep.' The hare should have spoken in this manner: 'Yes, my mother lies sleeping; she will presently arise.'"

What We Become

We, who are human beings, we possess wind; we make clouds, when we die. Therefore, the wind does thus when we die: the wind makes dust, because it intends to blow, taking away our footprints, with which we had walked about while we still had nothing the matter with us; and our footprints, which the wind intends to blow away, would otherwise still lie plainly visible. If so, it would seem as if we still lived. Therefore, the wind intends to blow, taking away our footprints.

And, our gall, when we die, sits in the sky; it sits green in the sky, when we are dead.

My mother did this, when the moon lying down came, when the moon stood hollow. Mother said: "The moon is carrying people who are dead. We are those who see that it lies in this manner; and it lies hollow, because it is killing itself by carrying people who are dead. This is why it lies hollow. It is not fast moving; for, it is a moon of threatening. We may expect to hear something, when the moon lies in this manner. A person is the one who has died, he whom the moon carries. Therefore, we may expect to hear what has happened, when the moon is like this."

The hair of our head will resemble clouds, when we die, when we in this manner make clouds. We, who do not know, we are those who think in this manner, that they are simple clouds. We, who know, when we see that they are like this, we know that they are a person's clouds—that they are the hair of his head. We, who know, recognize the clouds, and how the clouds do form themselves.

DISCUSSION QUESTIONS

1. Having read the story of the hare's betrayal, what is the purpose of the prayer to the Moon?

2. Why does the Moon punish the hare for grieving for his mother?

3. What is the lesson the people are to take away from the hare's betrayal?

4. What is the message the Moon sends to the living, as he carries the dead across the sky?

5. How would you characterize this culture's story of death? Is it peaceful? Violent? Punishing? Does it allow for grief?

4 Tales of the Origins of Death (South Africa)

Understanding exactly who told a story and when is a very difficult task to undertake when studying South African myth. There is such a variety of native people who told similar stories in the same area, that pinpointing the origin of a story becomes a moot point. James Honey's 1910 collection of tales from his country of birth highlights the significance of animals in creation and folk stories. The four myths below are interested in how death came into the world and are told in slightly different ways depending on the storyteller. Notice the variations in tone, dialogue, and explanation of various features.

THE ORIGINS OF DEATH

Tale #1

The Moon, it is said, sent once an Insect to Men, saying, "Go to Men and tell them, 'As I die, and dying live, so you shall also die, and dying live.'" The Insect started with the message, but while on his way was overtaken by the Hare, who asked: "What is your errand?" The Insect answered: "I am sent by the Moon to Men, to tell them that as she dies, and dying lives, they also shall die, and dying live." The Hare said, "As you are an awkward runner, let me take the message to Men." With these words he ran off, and when he reached Men, he said, "I am sent by the Moon to tell you, 'As I die, and dying perish, in the same manner you shall also die and come wholly to an end.'" Then the Hare returned to the Moon, and told her what he had said to Men. The Moon reproached him angrily, saying, "How dare you tell the people a thing which I have not said!" With these words she took up a piece of wood, and struck him on the nose. Since that day the Hare's nose is slit.

Tale #2

The Moon dies, and rises to life again. The Moon said to the Hare, "Go to Men, and tell them, 'Like as I die and rise to life again, so you also shall die and rise to life again.'" The Hare went to the Men, and said, "Like as I die and do not rise to life again, so you shall also die, and not rise to life again." When he returned the Moon asked, "What did you say?" "I have told them, 'Like as I die and do not rise to life again, so you shall also die and not rise to life again.'" "What?" said the Moon, "did you that?" And she took a stick and beat the Hare on his mouth, which was slit by the blow. The Hare fled, and is still fleeing.

Tale #3

The Moon, on one occasion, sent the Hare to the earth to inform Men that as she died away and rose again, so mankind should die and rise again. Instead, however, of delivering this message as given, the Hare, either out of forgetfulness or malice, told mankind that as the Moon rose and died away, so Man should die and rise no more. The Hare, having returned to the Moon, was questioned as to the message delivered, and the Moon, having heard the true state of the case, became so enraged with him that she took up a hatchet to split his head; falling short, however, of that, the hatchet fell upon the upper lip of the Hare, and cut it severely. Hence it is that we see the "Hare-lip." The Hare, being duly incensed at having received such treatment, raised his claws, and scratched the Moon's face; and the dark spots which we now see on the surface of the Moon are the scars which she received on that occasion.

Tale #4

The Moon, they say, wished to send a message to Men, and the Hare said that he would take it. "Run, then," said the Moon, "and tell Men that as I die and am renewed, so shall they also be renewed." But the Hare deceived Men, and said, "As I die and perish, so shall you also."

Source: James A. Honey, *South African Folk-Tales,* 1910.

1. What are we to learn about the cause of man's mortality from these four stories?
2. There are small differences in each tale. What do you think accounts for these subtleties?

Maasai Origins (Kenya)

When Hollis wrote his text about the Maasai in 1905, they had not yet given up the best pieces of their lands to European settlers. Hollis knew, however, that the inevitable was coming, and he set out to document stories, songs, traditions, and rituals before the Maasai lost their culture. Between 500,000 and 1 million Maasai live today in more than fifty tribes across the Eastern African nations of Kenya and Tanzania, between Lake Victoria and Mt. Kilimanjaro.

Many traditions practiced by the Maasai are well known by outsiders, such as the fact that historically boys became warriors only after killing a lion, current practice still dictates boys and girls both undergo ritual circumcision as part of their coming of age ceremony, and the blood of animals is ingested for ceremonial and health purposes. Each of these rituals is deeply tied to the mythology of the Maasai, and the influence of outside cultures and the encroachment of their lands has had an effect on the practice of these important milestones.

The Maasai are known for being cattle herders, which is a status symbol as well as a form of livelihood. The trading of livestock facilitates many important moments in the community, like marriage. They tend to look down upon other tribal cultures who are not owners of cattle, those who much forage for food instead (like the Dorobo, as mentioned in the myth below). Much of their identity comes from their relationship to the cattle. They live in circular *kraals* that protect their cattle from lion attack with a fence of acacia spikes. These kraals move seasonally with the movement of the cattle and the construction of these communities is deeply gendered. Men are responsible for building the kraal and the women are responsible for constructing the mud homes and collecting water, tending the fires, and milking the cattle, along with their child-rearing duties.

The following stories are a collection of customs and beliefs about the natural world, the cosmos, and the origins of the Maasai community.

MAASAI ORIGINS

The Red God and the Black God

There are two gods, a black one and a red one. The black god is good, and the red god malicious. One day the black god said to the red one: "Let us give the people some water for they are dying of hunger." The red god agreed, and told the other one to turn on the water. This he did, and it rained heavily.

After a time the red god told the black one to stop the water as sufficient rain had fallen. The black god was, however, of opinion that the people had not had enough, so he refused. Both remained silent after this, and the rain continued till the next morning, when the red god again said that enough had fallen. The black god then turned off the water.

Source: A.C. Hollis, *The Maasai Their Language and Folklore*, 1905.

A few days later the black god proposed that they should give the people some more water as the grass was very dry. The red god, however, was stubborn and refused to allow the water to be turned on again. They disputed for some time, and at length the red god threatened to kill the people, whom he said the black god was spoiling.

At this the black god said: "I shall not allow my people to be killed," and he has been able to protect them, for he lives near at hand, whilst the red god is above him. When one hears the thunder crashing in the heavens it is the red god who is trying to come to the earth to kill human beings; and when one hears the distant rumbling, it is the black god who is saying:

"Leave them alone, do not kill them."

How the Maasai Got Cattle related by Napisyeki, an elder of the Aiser clan (Sighirari sub-district).

The thing which is called Naiteru-kop is a god, but not as great as the black god. This is the story which was told us by the elders:

The Maasai were formerly of the Dorobo people, and had no cattle: it was the Dorobo who possessed the cattle. Naiteru-kop came one day and said to a Dorobo: "Come early tomorrow morning, I have something to tell you." The Dorobo replied: "Very well," and went to sleep.

A Maasai named Le-eyo, having heard what had been said to the Dorobo, arose during the night, and waited near the spot where Naiteru-kop was. When it dawned he went to Naiteru-kop, who said to him: "Who are you?" On Le-eyo telling him his name, Naiteru-kop asked where the Dorobo was. Le-eyo replied that he did not know. Naiteru-kop then dropped one end of a piece of hide from the heavens, and let cattle down one by one until the Maasai told him to stop.

The Maasai cattle wandered off, and as they went, the cattle which belonged to the Dorobo mingled with them. The Dorobo were unable to recognize their beasts again, and they lost them. After this the Dorobo shot away the cord by which the cattle had descended, and God moved and went far off. When the Dorobo were left without their cattle, they had to shoot wild beasts for their food.

The Story of Le-eyo's Disobedience

One day Naiteru-kop told Le-eyo that if a child were to die he was to say when he threw away the body: "Man, die, and come back again; moon, die, and remain away."

A child died soon afterwards, but it was not one of Le-eyo's, and when he was told to throw it away, he picked it up and said to himself: "This child is not mine; when I throw it away I shall say, 'Man, die, and remain away; moon, die, and return.'"

He threw it away and spoke these words, after which he returned home. One of his own children died next, and when he threw it away, he said: "Man, die, and return; moon, die, and remain away."

Naiteru-kop said to him: "It is of no use now, for you spoilt matters with the other child."

This is how it came about that when a man dies he does not return, whilst when the moon is finished, it comes back again and is always visible to us.

The Origin of the Maasai and the Bantu People

When Le-eyo grew old, he called his children to him and said to them: "My children, I am now very old, I wish to bid you goodbye." He then asked his elder son what he wanted out of all his wealth.

His son replied: "I wish something of everything upon the earth."

"Since you want something of everything," the old man said, "take a few head of cattle, a few goats and sheep, and some of the food of the earth, for there will be a large number of things."

The elder son replied: "Very well."

Le-eyo then called his younger son, and asked him what he wanted.

"I should like, Father," the younger one said, "the fan which you carry suspended from your arm."

His father replied: "My child, because you have chosen this fan, God will give you wealth, and you will be great amongst your brother's people."

The one who selected something of everything became a barbarian, and he who received the fan became the father of all the Maasai.

The Sun & Moon, the Stars, Rainbows, and Comets

We have been told that the sun once married the moon. One day they fought, and the moon struck the sun on the head; the sun, too, damaged the moon.

When they had done fighting, the sun was ashamed that human beings should see that his face had been battered, so he became dazzlingly bright, and people are unable to regard him without first half closing their eyes. The moon however is not ashamed, and human beings can look at her face, and see that her mouth is cut and that one of her eyes is missing.

Now the sun and the moon travel in the same direction for many days, the moon leading. After a time the moon gets tired, and the sun catches her up and carries her. She is carried thus for two days, and on the third day she is left at the sun's setting place. On the fourth day, the donkeys see the moon reappear, and bray at her. But it is not until the fifth day that men and cattle see her again.

When a Maasai sees the new moon, he throws a twig or stone at it with his left hand, and says, "Give me long life," or "Give me strength"; and when a pregnant woman sees the new moon, she milks some milk into a small gourd which she covers with green grass, and then pours away in the direction of the moon. At the same time she says: "Moon, give me my child safely."

When the moon dies (when there is an eclipse), all the old men and women, the warriors and children come out of their huts and collect together outside. One man then sings in a loud voice deploring the loss of the moon, and everybody present joins in the chorus. They continue singing in this manner until the moon begins to reappear, when they all shout together as loud as they can: "Moon, come to life again! Moon, come to life again!"

When they see that the moon has returned to her normal state, they enter their huts and go to sleep. They do the same thing when there is an eclipse of the sun, the only difference being that when the sun begins to reappear they cry out: "Sun, come to life again! Sun, come to life again!"

There are three groups of stars with which the Maasai are acquainted. They know whether it will rain or not according to the appearance or non-appearance of the six stars, called The Pleiades, which follow after one another like cattle.

When the month which the Maasai call "Of the Pleiades" arrives, and the Pleiades are no longer visible, they know that the rains are over. For the Pleiades set in that month and are not seen again until the season of showers has come to an end: it is then that they reappear.

There are three other stars, which follow one another like the cattle, called "The Old Men," and again three others, which pursue them from the left, called "The Widows." Now the Maasai say that as the widows have lost their husbands, they are waylaying the old men in order to get married to them.

There is also Kileghen (Venus), and by this planet the Maasai know that it is near dawn. It is in consequence also called "The star of the dawn." Women pray to Venus when warriors tarry in returning from a raid.

Then there is Leghen (Venus), which when visible is a sign that the moon will shortly rise. Leghen remains in the west, and is only seen in the evening.

There is something which the Maasai call "The rainbow," and if one is seen in the heavens whilst rain is falling, it is a sign that the rain will shortly cease. Children call a rainbow "Father's garment" on account of its many colours, one part being red, another white, and a third variegated. They also say: "I will give it to father for he will like it."

When the Maasai see a comet, they know that a great trouble will befall them, the cattle will die, there will be a famine, and their people will join the enemies.

It is said that a comet was once seen before the Europeans arrived, and as some Maasai children were watering the cattle at a pond after herding them, a creature resembling an ox but green in color issued from the water. The children were frightened, and killed it. They then disemboweled it, and found that its body was full of caul-fat instead of blood. On returning to the kraal they related what had occurred.

When the medicine-man heard the story, he said: "If we see another comet, people who are green in color will come out of the water and visit our country. Should they be killed, caul-fat instead of blood will be seen issuing from their bodies."

Shortly after the appearance of the next comet the Europeans arrived. It was formerly believed that they had no blood, and that their bodies were full of caul-fat.

DISCUSSION QUESTIONS

1. What is the significance of the Red God and the Black God's battle over water?

2. What does Le-eyo do to disobey the gods?

3. How does the story of the Sun and Moon fighting tell us about gender roles?

4. The Maasai seem to have very sophisticated stories of the cosmos. What is their understanding of how people should look at the sun, moon, stars, and other celestial bodies?

5. What is significant about the comet?

Origin of the Kikuyu (Kenya)

The Kikuyu were one of the first tribes to actively uprise against European settlement. An anti-colonial group of Kikuyu called the "Mau Mau" led a rebellion against their colonizers, the British in what is known as the Mau Mau Uprising. From 1952 to 1956 the Mau Mau fought for the independence of Kenya, and although the uprising was technically unsuccessful, it led to Kenya's sovereignty in 1963. Largely because of their leadership during the uprising, the Kikuyu, who make up about 20% of Kenya's population has historically been a very powerful, influential people in the Republic of Kenya's government. The Kikuyu call themselves "Gikuyu" or "Agikuyu" which translates to "a very large sycamore tree."

The following legend is about the Kikuyu's origin and an explanation for their agricultural community, as is differentiated from their neighbors, the Maasai and N'dorobo.

THE ORIGIN OF THE KIKUYU

The Kikuyu are the descendants of an old man and his wife, who came to the present country from the other side of the great mountain of Kenya, called the White Mountains. While they were on the slopes of the mountain they were on the point of starvation, and the old man went up the summit to see God (N'gai), who dwells there. God on that occasion gave him sheep and goats, and from that gift all the Kikuyu flocks of to-day descended.

God told the old man that his descendants should occupy the present Kikuyu country, and that they should live by farming; that the Maasai people should hold the plains, and have flocks and herds, and that the portion of the N'dorobo people should be the wild game of the wilderness, and nothing else.

God told them, "The sun is the husband of the moon. When the moon comes to maturity, the sun fights and kills her, and then she rises again. The stars which attend on the moon are the moon's children." When the moon is "dead," no journeys are undertaken, no sacrifices offered, nor sheep killed, and on the day after the death of the moon, which is termed " Mu-ti-ru-m'we-ri," goats and sheep do not bear.

As a memorial of this interview with God, and in accordance with God's command then given, the Kikuyu to this day paint their bodies, for certain great ceremonial dances, with patterns resembling forked lightning.

DISCUSSION QUESTIONS

1. How does the gift from N'gai determine the livelihood of the Kikuyu people?
2. How does this story set up potential problems between the three tribes mentioned?
3. What does the forked lightning represent?

Source: W. Scoresby Routledge and Katherine Routledge, *With a Prehistoric People: The AkiKuyu of British East Africa*, 1910.

Part 2: Tricksters, Lovers, and Other Tales

3 Stories about the Sky (Nigeria)

The following stories were collected from the ethnically and linguistically diverse area of Southern Nigeria. Each tale seeks to tell why our celestial bodies are located in the sky and accounts for their movements. Pay attention to the personification of the elements and the way the Nigerian people interact with them.

3 STORIES ABOUT THE SKY

Why the Moon Waxes and Wanes

There was once an old woman who was very poor, and lived in a small mud hut thatched with mats made from the leaves of the tombo palm in the bush. She was often very hungry, as there was no one to look after her.

In the olden days the moon used often to come down to the earth, although she lived most of the time in the sky. The moon was a fat woman with a skin of hide, and she was full of fat meat. She was quite round, and in the night used to give plenty of light. The moon was sorry for the poor starving old woman, so she came to her and said, "You may cut some of my meat away for your food." This the old woman did every evening, and the moon got smaller and smaller until you could scarcely see her at all. Of course this made her give very little light, and all the people began to grumble in consequence, and to ask why it was that the moon was getting so thin.

At last the people went to the old woman's house where there happened to be a little girl sleeping. She had been there for some little time, and had seen the moon come down every evening, and the old woman go out with her knife and carve her daily supply of meat out of the moon. As she was very frightened, she told the people all about it, so they determined to set a watch on the movements of the old woman.

That very night the moon came down as usual, and the old woman went out with her knife and basket to get her food; but before she could carve any meat all the people rushed out shouting, and the moon was so frightened that she went back again into the sky, and never came down again to the earth. The old woman was left to starve in the bush.

Ever since that time the moon has hidden herself most of the day, as she was so frightened, and she still gets very thin once a month, but later on she gets fat again, and when she is quite fat she gives plenty of light all the night; but this does not last very long, and she begins to get thinner and thinner, in the same way as she did when the old woman was carving her meat from her.

Why the Sun and the Moon Live in the Sky

Many years ago the sun and water were great friends, and both lived on the earth together. The sun very often used to visit the water, but the water never returned his visits. At last the sun asked the water why it was that he never came to see him in his house, the water replied that the sun's house was not big enough, and that if he came with his people he would drive the sun out.

Source: Elphinstone Dayrell, *Folk Stories from Southern Nigeria, West Africa*, 1910.

He then said, "If you wish me to visit you, you must build a very large compound; but I warn you that it will have to be a tremendous place, as my people are very numerous, and take up a lot of room."

The sun promised to build a very big compound, and soon afterwards he returned home to his wife, the moon, who greeted him with a broad smile when he opened the door. The sun told the moon what he had promised the water, and the next day commenced building a huge compound in which to entertain his friend.

When it was completed, he asked the water to come and visit him the next day.

When the water arrived, he called out to the sun, and asked him whether it would be safe for him to enter, and the sun answered, "Yes, come in, my friend."

The water then began to flow in, accompanied by the fish and all the water animals.

Very soon the water was knee-deep, so he asked the sun if it was still safe, and the sun again said, "Yes," so more water came in.

When the water was level with the top of a man's head, the water said to the sun, "Do you want more of my people to come?" and the sun and moon both answered, "Yes," not knowing any better, so the water flowed on, until the sun and moon had to perch themselves on the top of the roof.

Again the water addressed the sun, but receiving the same answer, and more of his people rushing in, the water very soon overflowed the top of the roof, and the sun and moon were forced to go up into the sky, where they have remained ever since.

The Story of the Lightning and the Thunder

In the olden days the thunder and lightning lived on the earth amongst all the other people, but the king made them live at the far end of the town, as far as possible from other people's houses.

The thunder was an old mother sheep, and the lightning was her son, a ram. Whenever the ram got angry he used to go about and burn houses and knock down trees; he even did damage on the farms, and sometimes killed people. Whenever the lightning did these things, his mother used to call out to him in a very loud voice to stop and not to do any more damage; but the lightning did not care in the least for what his mother said, and when he was in a bad temper used to do a very large amount of damage. At last the people could not stand it any longer, and complained to the king.

So the king made a special order that the sheep (Thunder) and her son, the ram (Lightning), should leave the town and live in the far bush. This did not do much good, as when the ram got angry he still burnt the forest, and the flames sometimes spread to the farms and consumed them.

So the people complained again, and the king banished both the lightning and the thunder from the earth and made them live in the sky, where they could not cause so much destruction. Ever since, when the lightning is angry, he commits damage as before, but you can hear his mother, the thunder, rebuking him and telling him to stop. Sometimes, however, when the mother has gone away some distance from her naughty son, you can still see that he is angry and is doing damage, but his mother's voice cannot be heard.

DISCUSSION QUESTIONS

1. Why are the other people so angry at the old woman who carves meat from the moon?

2. What could the story of why the moon waxes and wanes be saying about the power of natural elements?

3. Why do the sun and moon keep inviting the water, though they know they are being pushed away from the earth?

4. How well do the animals—the sheep and the ram—depict thunder and lightning?

The Woman with Two Skins (Nigeria)

In the introduction to this story, Andrew Lange writes, "Human nature is much the same everywhere." European literature is riddled with stories of wives who are hideous by day, beautiful by night. There are stories of dramatic feats of athleticism that win the heart of the jealous woman and prove one's true identity. And tales abound of parents tricked into killing their own children to prove their faith. *Sir Gaiwan*, Chaucer's *The Wyfe of Bath*, Anderson's *The Marsh King's Daughter*, the Biblical story of Abraham and Isaac, and Shakespeare's *As You Like It* all share elements of Nigeria's "The Woman with Two Skins."

THE WOMAN WITH TWO SKINS

Eyamba I. of Calabar was a very powerful king. He fought and conquered all the surrounding countries, killing all the old men and women, but the able-bodied men and girls he caught and brought back as slaves, and they worked on the farms until they died.

This king had two hundred wives, but none of them had borne a son to him. His subjects, seeing that he was becoming an old man, begged him to marry one of the spider's daughters, as they always had plenty of children. But when the king saw the spider's daughter he did not like her, as she was ugly, and the people said it was because her mother had had so many children at the same time. However, in order to please his people he married the ugly girl, and placed her among his other wives, but they all complained because she was so ugly, and said she could not live with them. The king, therefore, built her a separate house for herself, where she was given food and drink the same as the other wives. Everyone jeered at her on account of her ugliness; but she was not really ugly, but beautiful, as she was born with two skins, and at her birth her mother was made to promise that she should never remove the ugly skin until a certain time arrived save only during the night, and that she must put it on again before dawn.

Now the king's head wife knew this, and was very fearful lest the king should find it out and fall in love with the spider's daughter; so she went to a Ju Ju man and offered him two hundred rods to make a potion that would make the king forget altogether that the spider's daughter was his wife. This the Ju Ju man finally consented to do, after much haggling over the price, for three hundred and fifty rods; and he made up some "medicine," which the head wife mixed with the king's food. For some months this had the effect of making the king forget the spider's daughter, and he used to pass quite close to her without recognising her in any way.

Source: Elphinstone Dayrell, *Folk Stories from Southern Nigeria, West Africa*, 1910.

When four months had elapsed and the king had not once sent for Adiaha (for that was the name of the spider's daughter), she began to get tired, and went back to her parents. Her father, the spider, then took her to another Ju Ju man, who, by making spells and casting lots, very soon discovered that it was the king's head wife who had made the Ju Ju and had enchanted the king so that he would not look at Adiaha. He therefore told the spider that Adiaha should give the king some medicine which he would prepare, which would make the king remember her. He prepared the medicine, for which the spider had to pay a large sum of money; and that very day Adiaha made a small dish of food, into which she had placed the medicine, and presented it to the king. Directly he had eaten the dish his eyes were opened and he recognised his wife, and told her to come to him that very evening. So in the afternoon, being very joyful, she went down to the river and washed, and when she returned she put on her best cloth and went to the king's palace.

Directly it was dark and all the lights were out she pulled off her ugly skin, and the king saw how beautiful she was, and was very pleased with her; but when the cock crowed Adiaha pulled on her ugly skin again, and went back to her own house.

This she did for four nights running, always taking the ugly skin off in the dark, and leaving before daylight in the morning. In course of time, to the great surprise of all the people, and particularly of the king's two hundred wives, she gave birth to a son; but what surprised them most of all was that only one son was born, whereas her mother had always had a great many children at a time, generally about fifty.

The king's head wife became more jealous than ever when Adiaha had a son; so she went again to the Ju Ju man, and by giving him a large present induced him to give her some medicine which would make the king sick and forget his son. And the medicine would then make the king go to the Ju Ju man, who would tell him that it was his son who had made him sick, as he wanted to reign instead of his father. The Ju Ju man would also tell the king that if he wanted to recover he must throw his son away into the water.

And the king, when he had taken the medicine, went to the Ju Ju man, who told him everything as had been arranged with the head wife. But at first the king did not want to destroy his son. Then his chief subjects begged him to throw his son away, and said that perhaps in a year's time he might get another son. So the king at last agreed, and threw his son into the river, at which the mother grieved and cried bitterly.

Then the head wife went again to the Ju Ju man and got more medicine, which made the king forget Adiaha for three years, during which time she was in mourning for her son. She then returned to her father, and he got some more medicine from his Ju Ju man, which Adiaha gave to the king. And the king knew her and called her to him again, and she lived with him as before. Now the Ju Ju who had helped Adiaha's father, the spider, was a Water Ju Ju, and he was ready when the king threw his son into the water, and saved his life and took him home and kept him alive. And the boy grew up very strong.

After a time Adiaha gave birth to a daughter, and her the jealous wife also persuaded the king to throw away. It took a longer time to persuade him, but at last he agreed, and threw his daughter into the water too, and forgot Adiaha again. But the Water Ju Ju was ready again, and when he had saved the little girl, he thought the time had arrived to punish the action of the jealous wife; so he went about amongst the head young men and persuaded them to hold a wrestling match in the market-place every week. This was done, and the Water Ju Ju told the king's son, who had become very strong, and was very like to his father in appearance, that he should go and wrestle, and that no one would be able to stand up before him. It was then arranged that there should be a grand wrestling match, to which all the strongest men in the country were invited, and the king promised to attend with his head wife.

On the day of the match the Water Ju Ju told the king's son that he need not be in the least afraid, and that his Ju Ju was so powerful, that even the strongest and best wrestlers in the country would not be able to stand up against him for even a few minutes. All the people of the country came to see the great contest, to the winner of which the king had promised to present prizes of cloth and money, and all the strongest men came. When they saw the king's son, whom nobody knew, they laughed and said, "Who is this small boy? He can have no chance against us." But when they came to wrestle, they very soon found that they were no match for him. The boy was very strong indeed, beautifully made and good to look upon, and all the people were surprised to see how like he was to the king.

After wrestling for the greater part of the day the king's son was declared the winner, having thrown everyone who had stood up against him; in fact, some of his opponents had been badly hurt, and had their arms or ribs broken owing to the tremendous strength of the boy. After the match was over the king presented him with cloth and money, and invited him to dine with him in the evening. The boy gladly accepted his father's invitation; and after he had had a good wash in the river, put on his cloth and went up to the palace, where he found the head chiefs of the country and some of the king's most favoured wives. They then sat down to their meal, and the king had his own son, whom he did not know, sitting next to him. On the other side of the boy sat the jealous wife, who had been the cause of all the trouble. All through the dinner this woman did her best to make friends with the boy, with whom she had fallen violently in love on account of his beautiful appearance, his strength, and his being the best wrestler in the country. The woman thought to herself, "I will have this boy as my husband, as my husband is now an old man and will surely soon die." The boy, however, who was as wise as he was strong, was quite aware of everything the jealous woman had done, and although he pretended to be very flattered at the advances of the king's head wife, he did not respond very readily, and went home as soon as he could.

When he returned to the Water Ju Ju's house he told him everything that had happened, and the Water Ju Ju said, "As you are now in high favour with the king, you must go to him to-morrow and beg a favour from him. The favour you will ask is that all the country shall be called together, and that a certain case shall be tried, and that when the case is finished, the man or woman who is found to be in the wrong shall be killed by the Egbos before all the people."

So the following morning the boy went to the king, who readily granted his request, and at once sent all round the country appointing a day for all the people to come in and hear the case tried. Then the boy went back to the Water Ju Ju, who told him to go to his mother and tell her who he was, and that when the day of the trial arrived, she was to take off her ugly skin and appear in all her beauty, for the time had come when she need no longer wear it. This the son did.

When the day of trial arrived, Adiaha sat in a corner of the square, and nobody recognised the beautiful stranger as the spider's daughter. Her son then sat down next to her, and brought his sister with him.

Immediately his mother saw her she said, "This must be my daughter, whom I have long mourned as dead," and embraced her most affectionately.

The king and his head wife then arrived and sat on their stones in the middle of the square, all the people saluting them with the usual greetings. The king then addressed the people, and said that he had called them together to hear a strong palaver at the request of the young man who had been the victor of the wrestling, and who had promised that if the case went against him he would offer up his life to the Egbo. The king also said that if, on the other hand, the case was decided in the boy's favour, then the other party would be killed, even though it were himself or one of his wives; whoever it was would have to take his or her place on the killing-stone and have their heads cut off by the Egbos. To this all the people agreed, and said they would like to hear what the young man had to say.

The young man then walked round the square, and bowed to the king and the people, and asked the question, "Am I not worthy to be the son of any chief in the country?" And all the people answered "Yes!"

The boy then brought his sister out into the middle, leading her by the hand. She was a beautiful girl and well made. When everyone had looked at her he said, "Is not my sister worthy to be any chief's daughter?" And the people replied that she was worthy of being any one's daughter, even the king's. Then he called his mother Adiaha, and she came out, looking very beautiful with her best cloth and beads on, and all the people cheered, as they had never seen a finer woman. The boy then asked them, "Is this woman worthy of being the king's wife?" And a shout went up from everyone present that she would be a proper wife for the king, and looked as if she would be the mother of plenty of fine healthy sons.

Then the boy pointed out the jealous woman who was sitting next to the king, and told the people his story, how that his mother, who had two skins, was the spider's daughter; how she had married the king, and how the head wife was jealous and had made a bad Ju Ju for the king, which made him forget his wife; how she had persuaded the king to throw himself and his sister into the river, which, as they all knew, had been done, but the Water Ju Ju had saved both of them, and had brought them up.

Then the boy said: "I leave the king and all of you people to judge my case. If I have done wrong, let me be killed on the stone by the Egbos; if, on the other hand, the woman has done evil, then let the Egbos deal with her as you may decide."

When the king knew that the wrestler was his son he was very glad, and told the Egbos to take the jealous woman away, and punish her in accordance with their laws. The Egbos decided that the woman was a witch; so they took her into the forest and tied her up to a stake, and gave her two hundred lashes with a whip made from hippopotamus hide, and then burnt her alive, so that she should not make any more trouble, and her ashes were thrown into the river. The king then embraced his wife and daughter, and told all the people that she, Adiaha, was his proper wife, and would be the queen for the future.

When the palaver was over, Adiaha was dressed in fine clothes and beads, and carried back in state to the palace by the king's servants.

That night the king gave a big feast to all his subjects, and told them how glad he was to get back his beautiful wife whom he had never known properly before, also his son who was stronger than all men, and his fine daughter. The feast continued for a hundred and sixty-six days; and the king made a law that if any woman was found out getting medicine against her husband, she should be killed at once. Then the king built three new compounds, and placed many slaves in them, both men and women. One compound he gave to his wife, another to his son, and the third he gave to his daughter. They all lived together quite happily for some years until the king died, when his son came to the throne and ruled in his stead.

DISCUSSION QUESTIONS

1. What does the woman who has two skins represent?

2. How do "Ju Ju" play a role in the tricking of the king? What does it mean that the king *can* be tricked with magic?

3. What does the wrestling match prove about the king's son?

4. Is the punishment of the jealous woman deserved?

▷ ▷ ▷

The King's Magic Drum (Nigeria)

In the introductory passage of this text, Andrew Lang acknowledges,

> "The drum is the mystic cauldron of ancient Welsh romance, which 'always provides plenty of good food and drink.' But the drum has its drawback, the food 'goes bad' if its owner steps over a stick in the road or a fallen tree."

Lang points out that this taboo also occurs in ancient Irish legends, where use of a magical object comes with a price.

THE KING'S MAGIC DRUM

Efriam Duke was an ancient king of Calabar. He was a peaceful man, and did not like war. He had a wonderful drum, the property of which, when it was beaten, was always to provide plenty of good food and drink. So whenever any country declared war against him, he used to call all his enemies together and beat his drum; then to the surprise of everyone, instead of fighting the people found tables spread with all sorts of dishes, fish, foo-foo, palm-oil chop, soup, cooked yams and ocros, and plenty of palm wine for everybody. In this way he kept all the country quiet and sent his enemies away with full stomachs, and in a happy and contented frame of mind. There was only one drawback to possessing the drum, and that was, if the owner of the drum walked over any stick on the road or stept over a fallen tree, all the food would immediately go bad, and three hundred Egbo men would appear with sticks and whips and beat the owner of the drum and all the invited guests very severely.

Efriam Duke was a rich man. He had many farms and hundreds of slaves, a large store of kernels on the beach, and many puncheons of palm-oil. He also had fifty wives and many children. The wives were all fine women and healthy; they were also good mothers, and all of them had plenty of children, which was good for the king's house.

Every few months the king used to issue invitations to all his subjects to come to a big feast, even the wild animals were invited; the elephants, hippopotami, leopards, bush cows, and antelopes used to come, for in those days there was no trouble, as they were friendly with man, and when they were at the feast they did not kill one another. All the people and the animals as well were envious of the king's drum and wanted to possess it, but the king would not part with it.

One morning Ikwor Edem, one of the king's wives, took her little daughter down to the spring to wash her, as she was covered with yaws, which are bad sores all over the body. The tortoise happened to be up a palm tree, just over the spring, cutting nuts for his midday meal; and while he was cutting, one of the nuts fell to the ground, just in front of the child. The little girl, seeing the good food, cried for it, and the mother, not knowing any better, picked up the palm nut and gave it to her daughter. Directly the tortoise saw this he climbed down the tree, and asked the woman where his palm nut was. She replied that she had given it to her child to eat.

Then the tortoise, who very much wanted the king's drum, thought he would make plenty palaver over this and force the king to give him the drum, so he said to the mother of the child, "I am a poor man, and I climbed the tree to get food for myself and my family. Then you took my palm nut and gave it to your child. I shall tell the whole matter to the king, and see what he has to say when he hears that one of his wives has stolen my food," for this, as everyone knows, is a very serious crime according to native custom.

Source: Elphinstone Dayrell, *Folk Stories from Southern Nigeria, West Africa*, 1910.

Ikwor Edem then said to the tortoise, "I saw your palm nut lying on the ground, and thinking it had fallen from the tree, I gave it to my little girl to eat, but I did not steal it. My husband the king is a rich man, and if you have any complaint to make against me or my child, I will take you before him."

So when she had finished washing her daughter at the spring she took the tortoise to her husband, and told him what had taken place. The king then asked the tortoise what he would accept as compensation for the loss of his palm nut, and offered him money, cloth, kernels or palm-oil, all of which things the tortoise refused one after the other.

The king then said to the tortoise, "What will you take? You may have anything you like."

And the tortoise immediately pointed to the king's drum, and said that it was the only thing he wanted.

In order to get rid of the tortoise the king said, "Very well, take the drum," but he never told the tortoise about the bad things that would happen to him if he stepped over a fallen tree, or walked over a stick on the road.

The tortoise was very glad at this, and carried the drum home in triumph to his wife, and said, "I am now a rich man, and shall do no more work. Whenever I want food, all I have to do is to beat this drum, and food will immediately be brought to me, and plenty to drink."

His wife and children were very pleased when they heard this, and asked the tortoise to get food at once, as they were all hungry. This the tortoise was only too pleased to do, as he wished to show off his newly acquired wealth, and was also rather hungry himself, so he beat the drum in the same way as he had seen the king do when he wanted something to eat, and immediately plenty of food appeared, so they all sat down and made a great f east. The tortoise did this for three days, and everything went well; all his children got fat, and had as much as they could possibly eat. He was therefore very proud of his drum, and in order to display his riches he sent invitations to the king and all the people and animals to come to a feast. When the people received their invitations they laughed, as they knew the tortoise was very poor, so very few attended the feast; but the king, knowing about the drum, came, and when the tortoise beat the drum, the food was brought as usual in great profusion, and all the people sat down and enjoyed their meal very much. They were much astonished that the poor tortoise should be able to entertain so many people, and told all their friends what fine dishes had been placed before them, and that they had never had a better dinner. The people who had not gone were very sorry when they heard this, as a good feast, at somebody else's expense, is not provided every day. After the feast all the people looked upon the tortoise as one of the richest men in the kingdom, and he was very much respected in consequence. No one, except the king, could understand how the poor tortoise could suddenly entertain so lavishly, but they all made up their minds that if the tortoise ever gave another feast, they would not refuse again.

When the tortoise had been in possession of the drum for a few weeks he became lazy and did no work, but went about the country boasting of his riches, and took to drinking too much. One day after he had been drinking a lot of palm wine at a distant farm, he started home carrying his drum; but having had too much to drink, he did not notice a stick in the path. He walked over the stick, and of course the Ju Ju was broken at once. But he did not know this, as nothing happened at the time, and eventually he arrived at his house very tired, and still not very well from having drunk too much. He threw the drum into a corner and went to sleep. When he woke up in the morning the tortoise began to feel hungry, and as his wife and children were calling out for food, he beat the drum; but instead of food being brought, the house was filled with Egbo men, who beat the tortoise, his wife and children, badly.

At this the tortoise was very angry, and said to himself, "I asked everyone to a feast, but only a few came, and they had plenty to eat and drink. Now, when I want food for myself and my family, the Egbos come and beat me. Well, I will let the other people share the same fate, as I do not see why I and my family should be beaten when I have given a feast to all people."

He therefore at once sent out invitations to all the men and animals to come to a big dinner the next day at three o'clock in the afternoon.When the time arrived many people came, as they did not wish to lose the chance of a free meal a second time. Even the sick men, the lame, and the blind got their friends to lead them to the feast. When they had all arrived, with the exception of the king and his wives, who sent excuses, the tortoise beat his drum as usual, and then quickly hid himself under a bench, where he could not be seen. His wife and children he had sent away before the feast, as he knew what would surely happen. Directly he had beaten the drum three hundred Egbo men appeared with whips, and started flogging all the guests, who could not escape, as the doors had been fastened. The beating went on for two hours, and the people were so badly punished, that many of them had to be carried home on the backs of their friends. The leopard was the only one who escaped, as directly he saw the Egbo men arrive he knew that things were likely to be unpleasant, so he gave a big spring and jumped right out of the compound.

When the tortoise was satisfied with the beating the people had received he crept to the door and opened it. The people then ran away, and when the tortoise gave a certain tap on the drum all the Egbo men vanished. The people who had been beaten were so angry, and made so much palaver with the tortoise, that he made up his mind to return the drum to the king the next day. So in the morning the tortoise went to the king and brought the drum with him. He told the king that he was not satisfied with the drum, and wished to exchange it for something else; he did not mind so much what the king gave him so long as he got full value for the drum, and he was quite willing to accept a certain number of slaves, or a few farms, or their equivalent in cloth or rods.

The king, however, refused to do this; but as he was rather sorry for the tortoise, he said he would present him with a magic foo-foo tree, which would provide the tortoise and his family with food, provided he kept a certain condition. This the tortoise gladly consented to do. Now this foo-foo tree only bore fruit once a year, but everyday it dropped foo-foo and soup on the ground. And the condition was, that the owner should gather sufficient food for the day, once, and not return again for more. The tortoise, when he had thanked the king for his generosity, went home to his wife and told her to bring her calabashes to the tree. She did so, and they gathered plenty of foo-foo and soup quite sufficient for the whole family for that day, and went back to their house very happy.

That night they all feasted and enjoyed themselves. But one of the sons, who was very greedy, thought to himself, "I wonder where my father gets all this good food from? I must ask him."

So in the morning he said to his father, "Tell me where do you get all this foo-foo and soup from?"

But his father refused to tell him, as his wife, who was a cunning woman, said, "If we let our children know the secret of the foo-foo tree, someday when they are hungry, after we have got our daily supply, one of them may go to the tree and gather more, which will break the Ju Ju."

But the envious son, being determined to get plenty of food for himself, decided to track his father to the place where he obtained the food. This was rather difficult to do, as the tortoise always went out alone, and took the greatest care to prevent anyone following him. The boy, however, soon thought of a plan, and got a calabash with a long neck and a hole in the end. He filled the calabash with wood ashes, which he obtained from the fire, and then got a bag which his father always carried on his back when he went out to get food. In the bottom of the bag the boy then made a small hole, and inserted the calabash with the neck downwards, so that when his father walked to the foo-foo tree he would leave a small trail of wood ashes behind him. Then when his father, having slung his bag over his back as usual, set out to get the daily supply of food, his greedy son followed the trail of the wood ashes, taking great care to hide himself and not to let his father perceive that he was being followed. At last the tortoise arrived at the tree, and placed his calabashes on the ground and collected the food for the day, the boy watching him from a distance. When his father had finished and went home the boy also returned, and having had a good meal, said nothing to his parents, but went to bed. The next morning he got some of his brothers, and after his father had finished getting the daily supply, they went to the tree and collected much foo-foo and soup, and so broke the Ju Ju.

At daylight the tortoise went to the tree as usual, but he could not find it, as during the night the whole bush had grown up, and the foo-foo tree was hidden from sight. There was nothing to be seen but a dense mass of prickly tie-tie palm. Then the tortoise at once knew that someone had broken the Ju Ju, and had gathered foo-foo from the tree twice in the same day; so he returned very sadly to his house, and told his wife. He then called all his family together and told them what had happened, and asked them who had done this evil thing. They all denied having had anything to do with the tree, so the tortoise in despair brought all his family to the place where the foo-foo tree had been, but which was now all prickly tie-tie palm, and said,

"My dear wife and children, I have done all that I can for you, but you have broken my Ju Ju; you must therefore for the future live on the tie-tie palm."

So they made their home underneath the prickly tree, and from that day you will always find tortoises living under the prickly tie-tie palm, as they have nowhere else to go to for food.

DISCUSSION QUESTIONS

1. Why must a magical object come with certain rules and consequences for use?

2. What etiological functions does this story serve?

3. Who do you consider to be a trickster in this story? Are there multiple tricksters? Does any character behave like the hero archetype?

How Anansi Got the Stories from the Sky God (Ashanti/Ghana)

Anansi (or Ananse) is one of the most popular and well-known tricksters and is regarded as a culture hero among the Ashanti (Ashante) people of West Africa (modern Ghana). His typical form is that of a spider, but like most tricksters he displays human qualities and is sometimes human in appearance. He is often called Father (Kwaku) Anansi, and some stories credit him with creating the sun, moon, and stars, and even with bringing rain and agriculture. Stories about Anansi traveled with the people, and the character appears in Jamaican folklore as Anancy, or Aunt Nancy, among other names.

There are variants of the tale, some much longer than this one. In some versions, Anansi is told to bring four things to the Sky God instead of three: a python, a leopard, hornets, and the bush-spirit. In the longer version, Anansi creates a sticky doll to trick the bush-spirit—much like the folktale of Briar Rabbit and the Tar Baby.

HOW ANANSI GOT THE STORIES FROM THE SKY GOD

In the olden days all the stories which men told were stories of Nyankupon, the chief of the gods. Spider, who was very conceited, wanted the stories to be told about him.

Accordingly, one day he went to Nyankupon and asked that, in future, all tales told by men might be Anansi stories, instead of Nyankupon stories. Nyankupon agreed, on one condition. He told Spider (or Anansi) that he must bring him three things: the first was a jar full of live bees, the second was a boa-constrictor, and the third a tiger. Spider gave his promise.

He took an earthen vessel and set out for a place where he knew were numbers of bees. When he came in sight of the bees he began saying to himself, "They will not be able to fill this jar"—"Yes, they will be able"—"No, they will not be able," until the bees came up to him and said, "What are you talking about, Mr. Anansi?" He thereupon explained to them that Nyankupon and he had had a great dispute. Nyankupon had said the bees could not fly into the jar—Anansi had said they could. The bees immediately declared that of course they could fly into the jar—which they at once did. As soon as they were safely inside, Anansi sealed up the jar and sent it off to Nyankupon.

Next day he took a long stick and set out in search of a boa-constrictor. When he arrived at the place where one lived he began speaking to himself again. "He will just be as long as this stick"— "No, he will not be so long as this"—"Yes, he will be as long as this." These words he repeated several times, till the boa came out and asked him what was the matter. "Oh, we have been having a dispute in Nyankupon's town about you. Nyankupon's people say you are not as long as this stick. I say you are. Please let me measure you by it." The boa innocently laid himself out straight, and Spider lost no time in tying him on to the stick from end to end. He then sent him to Nyankupon.

The third day he took a needle and thread and sewed up his eye. He then set out for a den where he knew a tiger lived. As he approached the place he began to shout and sing so loudly that the tiger came out to see what was the matter. "Can you not see?" said Spider. "My eye is sewn up and now I can see such wonderful things that I must sing about them." "Sew up my eyes," said the tiger, "then I too can see these surprising sights." Spider immediately did so. Having thus made the tiger helpless, he led him straight to Nyankupon's house. Nyankupon was amazed at Spider's cleverness in fulfilling the three conditions. He immediately gave him permission for the future to call all the old tales Anansi tales.

DISCUSSION QUESTIONS

1. Why do you think Anansi's animal form is a spider?

2. Research the tale of Briar Rabbit and the Tar Baby and compare the stories.

3. Why do you think the Sky God asked for these particular things?

Source: W. H. Barker & Cecilia Sinclair, *West African Folktales,* 1917.

Part 3: Journeys of Heroes and Heroines

The Maiden Who Was Sacrificed (Kikuyu)

This story was told by Na-ga-tu-u, Mother of one of the herds of the Chief N'Du-f-Ni. Katherine Routledge, co-author of this collection, lived among the women and listened to their stories, most of which were passed down to them by their mothers. In this story a drought threatens the community and the Medicine Man pronounces a girl's life as the cure. The warrior quickly turns into her lover upon a heroic rescue.

THE MAIDEN WHO WAS SACRIFICED

The sun was very hot and there was no rain, so the crops died, and hunger was great; and this happened one year, and again it happened a second, and yet a third year the rain failed. So the people all gathered together on the great open space on the hilltop, where they danced and said each to the other, "Why does the rain delay in coming?" And they went to the Medicine-Man, and they said to him, "Tell us why there is no rain, for our crops have died, and we shall die of hunger?" And he took his gourd and poured out the lot, and this he did many times; and at last he said, "There is a maiden here who must be bought if rain is to fall, and the maiden is Wanjiru. The day after tomorrow let all of you return to this place, and every one of you from the eldest to the youngest bring with him a goat for the purchase of the maiden." The day after the morrow, old men and young men all gathered together, and each brought in his hand a goat. Now they all stood in a circle, and the relations of Wanjiru stood together, and she herself stood in the middle; and as they stood the feet of Wanjiru began to sink into the ground.

She sank to her knees and cried aloud, "I am lost!" and her father and mother also cried and said, "We are lost!" But those who looked on pressed close, and placed goats in the hands of Wanjiru's father and mother. And Wanjiru went lower to her waist, and she cried aloud, "I am lost, but much rain will come!" And she sank to her breast, but the rain still did not come, and she said again, "Much rain will come!" Then she sank to her neck, and the rain came in great drops, and her people would have rushed forward to save her, but those who stood around pressed into their hands more goats, and they desisted.

So she said, "My people have undone me," and sank to her eyes, and as one after another of her family stepped forward to save her, one of the crowd would give to him or her a goat, and he fell back. And Wanjiru cried aloud for the last time, "I am undone, and my own people have done this thing!" And she vanished from sight, and the earth closed over her, and the rain poured down, not, as you sometimes see it, in showers, but in a great deluge, and everyone hastened to their own homes.

Now there was a young warrior who loved Wanjiru, and he lamented continually, saying, "Wanjiru is lost, and her own people have done this thing." And he said, "Where has Wanjiru gone? I will go to the same place."

So he took his shield, and put in his sword and spear. And he wandered over the country day and night; and at last, as the dusk fell, he came to the spot where Wanjiru had vanished, and he stood where she had stood, and, as he stood, his feet began to sink as hers had sunk; and he sank lower and lower till the ground closed over him, and he went by a long road under the earth as Wanjiru had gone, and at length he saw the maiden.

Source: W. Scoresby Routledge and Katherine Routledge, *With a Prehistoric People: The AkiKuyu of British East Africa*, 1910.

But, indeed, he pitied her sorely, for her state was miserable, and her raiment had perished. He said to her, "You were sacrificed to bring the rain; now the rain has come, I will take you back." He took her on his back like a child, and brought her to the road he had traversed, and they rose together to the open air, and their feet stood once more on the ground, and he said, "You shall not return to the house of your people, for they have treated you shamefully."

And he bade her wait till nightfall; and when it was dark he took her to the house of his mother, and he asked his mother to leave, and said he had business, and he allowed no one to enter. But his mother said, "Why do you hide this thing from me, seeing I am your mother who bore you?" So he suffered his mother, but he said, "Tell no one that Wanjiru is returned." She lived in the house of his mother and she and his mother slew goats, and Wanjiru ate the fat and grew strong; of the skins they made garments for her, so that she was attired most beautifully.

It came to pass that the next day there was a great dance, and her lover went with the throng; but his mother and the girl waited till everyone had assembled at the dance, and all the road was empty, and then they came out of the house and mingled with the crowd; and the relations saw Wanjiru, and said, "Surely that is Wanjiru whom we had lost!"

They pressed to greet her, but her lover beat them off, for he said, "You sold Wanjiru shamefully." And she returned to his mother's house. But on the fourth day her family again came, and the warrior repented, for he said, "Surely they are her father and her mother and her brothers." So he paid them the purchase price, and he wedded Wanjiru, who had been lost.

DISCUSSION QUESTIONS

1. Why did the Medicine Man order everyone to bring their goats to the sacrifice?

2. What does Wanjiru and her lover's descent under the earth represent?

3. Why does Wanjiru's lover go through the traditional marriage negotiations with her family?

The Snake from the Great Water (Kikuyu)

Scoresby and Katherine Routledge explain the significance of "Rainbow Stories" of the Kikuyu people. The Mukun'ga M'bura, which literally translates to "snake-rain" is a sort of optical illusion that people see in the water when a rainbow reflects on the surface. This monster is known to eat people, goats, and cattle and known to live in lakes and in waterfalls. The only place of vulnerability is in the back of its neck, which young warriors are able to hit with great practice. The story of "The Snake from the Great Water" tells of a warrior who, while searching for a wife, encounters the Mukun'ga M'bura and must prove his ability in order to gain the young maiden as a wife.

Told by Mo-so-Ni, a young Woman, a relative of the Chief N'DuiNi.

THE SNAKE FROM THE GREAT WATER

Two warriors went to look for wives. One was called Wadua, or Son of the Sun, and the other Wamwer-i, Son of the Moon. As they travelled they saw a girl in the road. Now she was not beautiful, for she had lost one eye, but Wamwer-i liked her, and the girl also liked Wamwer-i; so he took her to be his wife, and proceeded no further in his search. But Wadua said, "Why would you take a girl who has one eye missing?" And he proceeded further on his journeys.

Now as he went on his way he saw a young boy, and he said to him, "Do you know any maiden in this countryside?" And the boy replied, "No, I know of no maiden, except the maiden Washuma; but she is not to be thought of, for she does not like young men." Wadua continued his journey again, and he met an old man, and he said, "Can you tell me where I can find a maiden?" And he said, "There is no girl but Washuma, and she will speak to no man." Wadua met an old woman, and she told him the same tale of Washuma, that she would not be wooed by any man.

At last, on the eighth day he met a young man, and he yet again spoke of Washuma in the same manner. So Wadua inquired of him where the home of this Washuma might be; and he said, "On the opposite hillside, where you see the smoke ascending." So Wadua left then and slept that night on the road; and after three days he came to the house of Washuma and tarried outside, while the girl herself was in the shamba. Afterwards she came in and cooked food, and came out and went to the storehouse and got "sir-oc'-o" and cooked it, and came and gave it to the stranger. But he would not take it, and she went again to the storehouse and took beans, but he would not eat; and then gruel, and still he would not; but she did not think of milk, and when she brought milk he drank it, and she offered him more, but he said, "it is sufficient."

Now the father of Washuma returned, and the goats and oxen came in for the night, and the girl took Wadua into the homestead that he might sleep, and she said to him, "If you should hear in the night a great noise, do not go out." And he asked, "Why?" Washuma said, "Because a great animal like a snake comes every night and kills and eats the oxen." The animal was called Mukun'ga M'bura, and its home is in the water.

So Wadua slept in the house; but in the night, when he heard a great noise he got up and took his spear; but Washuma took him by the arm and besought him not to go. But he was too strong for her, and he went out, and he saw the snake, and took his spear and stuck it in the back of the neck, so it died, and he came back to the house and he said nothing.

In the morning, when the birds began to chirp, the father went out to see the cattle, and he found the dead beast, and he said, "Who has done this?" The girl told her father and he sent for all the young men to gather on the dancing green. The father set a distance, and he said to the youths, "He who can run this distance and return, he it is who has slain the Mukun'ga M'bura."

So they ran, but some fell and some panted like sheep; but when the time came for Wadua, he ran and returned and beat all the other youths. And the father said, "What shall I give you, since you have slain the beast?" Wadua said, "I look for a wife; give me your daughter." But the father said, "Every man who has asked for my daughter, I have said to him, 'Fetch the ny-o-ya, the bird whose feathers we wear.'"

So Wadua arose and went to the big water, and Washuma stayed on the bank and looked on; and Wadua waded out, and the water rose to his calves and his knees and his waist, and then to his chest and neck and eyes. Washuma thought he would be drowned; but Wadua went right under the water and stayed there, and he did not die. Washuma waited, and when night came she slept there; but in the morning she said, "Surely he is dead"; and she turned to go.

Source: W. Scoresby Routledge and Katherine Routledge, *With a Prehistoric People: The AkiKuyu of British East Africa*, 1910.

But as she went she heard a great noise in the water; she looked round, and went back and saw Wadua and many others coming out of the water, and sheep and goats innumerable; and the water had all disappeared, and Wadua returned with the girl to her home.

Wadua divided the sheep and goats, and he put half of them on one side and half of them on the other, taking one half for himself, and the other half he gave to the father of Washuma, that he might have her for his wife.

DISCUSSION QUESTIONS

1. What does Wadua's search for the perfect maiden tell us about him?

2. Why is Wadua not automatically rewarded for killing the Mukun'ga M'bura?

3. What does it mean that Wadua does not drown and that he brings up herds of animals?

Gassire's Lute (Soninke/Ghana)

Of primary importance in this tale is the legendary city of Wagadu (or Wagaduga, Wagadugu), ancient Ghana. Some scholars believe that Wagadu is the name for the idealized version of the city that existed four times, and each time fell due to the sins of its king. The legend of Wagadu generally expresses and describes the origins, exploits, and early heroic deeds of various clans of the ancient Soninke. The founding clans, collectively called *wago* is a probable origin of the name, Wagadugu, meaning "land of the wago." Other sources say the name means "place of herds."

The first inhabitants of this region were called the Fasa, an aristocratic people known for their skill in fighting with swords and spears—especially while on horseback. Honor and courage were of utmost importance—this was displayed by one's combat skills. They refused to fight anyone they deemed unworthy or of a lesser social status.

They mined and traded gold, which provided them with great wealth and power. It is said that the city was so wealthy that even the dogs had gold collars. The city of Wagadu was a hub for traders, teachers, and artisans; it was a cosmopolitan city where one could hear many languages and find a variety of textiles, produce, and spices from surrounding areas.

Today these people are known as the Soninke, and they established Ghana, the first West African empire, which was at its height around 1000 AD/BCE. Ghana fell in 1200 AD (CE) succeeded by Mali.

Most of what we know about ancient Ghana comes from the writings of Arabic travelers. The story of "Gassire's Lute" is a fragment of a larger epic called the *Dausi*. It is believed this piece was created between 300–1100 CE, but much of the original has been lost. The events of the story are speculated to reflect a time around 500 BCE—a heroic period for the Fasa.

The story was first recorded in German by Leo Frobenius in the 1920s.

GASSIRE'S LUTE

Wagadu has stood four times in her glory, and four times she has been lost: once due to vanity, once due to deception, once due to greed, and once due to discord. Wagadu has changed her name four times. She has been called Dierra, Agada, Ganna, and Silla. Her face has turned four times—to the north, west, east, and south. Wagadu has always had four gates, one in each direction: north, west, east, and south; those are the places from where her strength originates. In her strength she prevails, whether built of earth, wood, or stone, or whether she exists only as the shadow of her children's memory. For Wagadu represents the strength that dwells in the hearts of her people. Sometimes this strength is seen and heard in the clash of swords on shields; sometimes this strength is invisible because men's pride has exhausted her, and she sleeps. The first time sleep came to Wagadu was due to vanity; the second time through deception, the third through greed, and the fourth through discord. If Wagadu is ever found for a fifth time, she will be so strong in the minds of men that she will never again be lost. She will be so forceful that vanity, deception, greed, and discord will never cause her harm.

Hoooh! Dierra, Agada, Ganna, Silla! Hoooh! Fasa!

Each time men's guilt caused Wagadu to vanish she achieved new splendor, making her next appearance even more beautiful. Vanity generated the songs of bards that people still appreciate today. Deception generated a rain of gold and great wealth; Greed generated need for the written word, still practiced today; Discord and quarreling will create a fifth Wagadu that will be treasured as long as rain falls in the south and there are stones in the Sahara, for all men will hold Wagadu in their hearts and all women in their wombs.

Hoooh! Dierra, Agada, Ganna, Silla! Hoooh! Fasa!

The first time Wagadu was lost was due to vanity. She faced north during those days, and her name was Dierra. Nganamba Fasa was her king. The Fasa were aged, but strong. They fought the Burdama and Boroma each day, for months and months—there seemed no end to the fighting. But the strength of the Fasa grew from battle. All the men were heroes and the women were lovely to look upon and proud of the men.

The Fasa who survived the battles with the Burdama were aging. King Nganamba was also quite old, but he had a son, Gassire, who was grandfather himself, having eight grown sons who also had children of their own. Nganamba ruled so long that Wagadu was lost the first time because of him. If he had died sooner, would Wagadu have been lost? What if Gassire had ruled instead?

Hoooh! Dierra, Agada, Ganna, Silla! Hoooh! Fasa!

Gassire often wondered, "When will Nganamba die? When will I be king?" He watched, longing for signs of weakness in his father, as a lover looks for the evening star, signaling the night to come. But days and months passed, and Nganamba did not die.

Gassire continued to fight heroically against the Burdama. He gave himself over fully to this deed, thinking only of his sword, shield, and horse. At night, as he sat among his sons, he heard the people praising him in the city. But his heart was not filled by this. He still hearkened for some sign of Nganamba's death. He longed for his father's sword and shield, that he would one day hold as king. He was restless, unable to sleep, and felt as though a jackal chewed at his heart. His jealousy grew into rage.

One night, when he could no longer withstand his misery, Gassire left his house to seek the oldest, wisest man in the city. The wise man said to him, "Gassire, Nganamba will surely die, but he will not leave you his sword and shield. Those are not for you. You will carry a lute. And this will cause Wagadu to become lost. Ah, Gassire!"

Source: Adapted from Donna Rosenberg. *World Mythology,* 2003. and Roger Abrahams. *African Folktales,* 1983. and Frobenius, Leo and Douglas Fox. *African Genesis: Folk Tales and Myths of Africa,* 1937.

Gassire replied: "Kiekorro, these are lies! You are not wise after all. How could Wagadu be lost when such heroes fight for her each day? You are a fool!"

The wise man said, "Ah, Gassire, your path is not that of the hero. Your path will lead to the partridges of the fields. You will learn their language and you will discover your way, and the fate of Wagadu."

Hoooh! Dierra, Agada, Ganna, Silla! Hoooh! Fasa!

Filled with rage, and a desire to prove his heroism, Gassire went again to fight the next day. But he told the heroes, "Stay here today. I will fight the Burdama alone." And so they stayed behind as Gassire went to battle. He charged the Burdama and hurled his spear. He swung his sword like a sickle in the wheat field. The Burdama were filled with fear and awe. They cried, "That man is no Fasa, nor a hero. That is a terrible being unknown to us—we cannot fight this!" They fled in terror, dropping their weapons.

Gassire called the other warriors to join him and they gathered the abandoned weapons from the field. They sang, "The Fasa are heroes! Gassire is the greatest hero of all the Fasa! His deeds are great—and ever greater today!" Gassire rode into the city with all the other heroes behind him.

But Gassire did not join them that evening. Instead, he went to the fields. He heard the partridges. One of them was sitting beneath a bush, saying: "Listen to the song of my deeds! Hear the *Dausi*! Though I fought the snake, I will die, as all creatures do. They are buried and rot in the ground. All heroes die and are buried as well. They will decay. But the *Dausi*, the songs of great battles, will not die. The songs shall be sung over and over again and will endure long after kings and heroes! Wagadu will disappear, but my song will live on!"

Hoooh! Dierra, Agada, Ganna, Silla! Hoooh! Fasa!

The next day, Gassire returned to the old wise man. He said, "Kiekorro! I have gone to the fields. I listened to the partridge. He boasted, saying the song of his deeds would outlive Wagadu. He sang the *Dausi*. Tell me—do men know the *Dausi*? Do these songs of battle live after kings and heroes die?"

The wise man said, "Yes, Gassire, and your path is to become a bard, not a king. The Fasa lived by the sea long ago. In those days there were also great heroes who fought men who played the lute and sang songs of great battles. Those singers were also heroes—their songs struck fear into the enemy. You will be one of them. You will sing battle songs, but this will cause Wagadu to disappear."

Gassire said, "Then let it disappear!"

Hoooh! Dierra, Agada, Ganna, Silla! Hoooh! Fasa!

Gassire went to see a smith, and asked him to make a lute. The smith replied, "I can make the lute, but it will not sing."

Gassire instructed him to make the lute anyway, stating, "this is my matter to handle." And so the smith made the lute for Gassire and delivered it.

Gassire struck it, but it made no sound. "It does not sing," Gassire complained.

"I told you it would not," replied the smith, "it is your matter to handle."

"Make it sing," Gassire said.

"I cannot, the smith continued," "for it does not yet have a heart, it is merely a piece of wood. But carry it on your back when you go into battle. The wood must ring along with your sword stroke, it must absorb your blood and breath, your pain and heroic deeds. Then the wood will no longer be wood, but it will be part of you. It must become part of you, your sons, and your people. The feelings in your heart will enter the lute and give it a heart. The lute must absorb the blood of your sons. Your sons will die, but they will live on in the lute. But I must warn you, though you will play battle songs, Wagadu will be lost."

"Then let Wagadu be lost!" Gassire exclaimed.

Hoooh! Dierra, Agada, Ganna, Silla! Hoooh! Fasa!

The next day, Gassire called for his eight sons. He said to them, "Today, as we go into battle, our swords shall ring throughout the ages. We shall fight with such courage and skill that our deeds will be the greatest battle song of all! In this way, we will endure in the *Dausi* forever as heroes; our deeds will live on in my lute." Gassire placed the lute upon his shoulder. Then he said to his eldest son, "Come, you will lead the charge with me." They fought the Burdama as with such fury, they were more than warriors, more than Fasa. They brought terror to the hearts of their enemies. They fought eight Burdama; their swords cut like sickles in the wheat field. But then the sword of one Burdama warrior pierced the heart of Gassire's son. He fell from his horse, dead; his lifeblood poured onto the field.

Gassire cried out in grief and anger. He dismounted, put his son's body on his back, and returned to the city. But as he carried him, the heart-blood of Gassire's son fell onto the lute, becoming absorbed by the wood.

Hoooh! Dierra, Agada, Ganna, Silla! Hoooh! Fasa!

And so Gassire's eldest son was buried; the city of Dierra mourned. That night, Gassire tried to play the lute, but it would not sing. He was angry, and called for his seven sons. "Tomorrow, again, we ride again into battle."

For the next six days Gassire rode into battle with the heroes; each day one of his sons, in order from oldest to youngest, accompanied him to lead the charge. And on each day of battle, a spear pierced the heart of one of Gassire's sons, and he carried home the body on his back, over the lute. And so each day the heart-blood of one of his sons was absorbed into the wood.

After six days of fighting, the men of the city were angry and the women wept with fear, and everyone mourned the dead. Before the battle on the seventh day began, the men of Dierra spoke to Gassire. They said, "This must end. We fight when needed, but not you. You go into battle with rage and without wisdom. Leave Dierra! Take your cattle and servants, and leave our city! Let us live in peace. We desire fame as well, but we would rather have life when death is the price of fame." The old wise man said, "Ah, Gassire! So today Wagadu will be lost for the first time."

Hoooh! Dierra, Agada, Ganna, Silla! Hoooh! Fasa!

And so Gassire gathered his wives, his last, youngest son, a few companions, and his servants, and rode out into the desert. A few of the Fasa heroes accompanied them. They rode day and night, for a long, long time, sleeping little. One night, Gassire was restless, and sat alone by the fire. All around him was still and silent. After a time, he dozed. But suddenly he jumped up, roused by a voice. It was close, singing. It seemed like it was coming from himself. It was his lute! Gassire trembled. It was singing the *Dausi*, his great song of battle. As the *Dausi* was sung for the first time, King Nganamba died. Wagadu disappeared for the first time. Gassire's rage melted away, and he wept. He wept with grief for his sons and joy for the great battle song, for it would bring lasting fame for all time to him and his sons.

Hoooh! Dierra, Agada, Ganna, Silla! Hoooh! Fasa!

Wagadu has stood four times in her glory, and four times she has been lost. Vanity generated the songs of bards that people still sing today. Deception generated a rain of gold and great wealth. Greed generated need for the written word, still practiced today. Discord and quarreling will create a fifth Wagadu that will be treasured as long as rain falls in the south and there are stones in the Sahara, for all men will hold Wagadu in their hearts and all women in their wombs.

Hoooh! Dierra, Agada, Ganna, Silla! Hoooh! Fasa!

DISCUSSION QUESTIONS

1. In what ways does this story challenge Campbell's monomyth cycle? How does the story fit the model?

2. Describe Gassire as a heroic character. What qualities make him heroic, and what qualities undermine his heroic efforts?

3. What does this story reveal about the values of the people who shared it?

4. Explore the importance of mythical cities in various cultures. What features do they share? What is their purpose and function?

BIBLIOGRAPHY

Abrahams, Roger. *African Folktales*. Pantheon Books, 1983.

Barker, W. H., and Cecilia Sinclair. *West African Folk-Tales*. CMS Bookshop, 1917. Arranged by Yesterday's Classics, Chapel Hill, NC, 2007. http://www.yesterdaysclassics.com/previews/barker_folktales_preview .pdf

Belcher, Stephen. *African Myths of Origin*. Penguin Books, 2005.

Bleek, W.H.I. and L.C. Lloyd. *Specimens of Bushman Folklore*. George Allen and Co. Ltd., 1911. http://www. sacred-texts.com/afr/sbf/sbf00.htm Conrad, David. *Empires of Medieval West Africa*. Facts on File, 2005.

Dayrell, Elphinstone. *Folk Stories from Southern Nigeria*. Longmans, Green and Co., 1910.

Elliott, Mike. "Khoisan Tribal, Social and Language Grouping." *Kalahari Research Centre,* 2004. http://www. khoisanpeoples.org/peoples/khoi-san-soc-tribal.htm

Frobenius, Leo and Douglas Fox. *African Genesis: Folk Tales and Myths of Africa,* 1937. English translation, https://books.google.com/books?id=HgDOiTZvdLcC&pg=PA13&source=gbs_toc_r&cad=4#v=onepage &q=gassire&f=false

Hollis, A. C. *The Masai: Their Language and Folklore*. Clarendon Press, 1905. https://archive.org/details/ masaitheirlangua00holluoft

Honey, James A. *South-African Folk-Tales*. The Trow Press, 1910. http://www.gutenberg.org/ files/38339/38339-h/38339-h.htm

Knappert, Jan. *The Epic of Dausi, Part One*. July, 1989. Worldandschool.com.

Lynch, Patricia Ann, and Jeremy Roberts. *African Mythology A-Z*, 2nd ed. Chelsea House Books, 2004, 2010.

Nelson, Raymond C. *Africa*, 3rd ed. Lean Stone Books, 2017.

Rosenberg, Donna. *World Mythology*. Third ed. NTC, 1999.

Routledge, W. Scoresby and Katherine Routledge. *With a Prehistoric People: The Akikyu of British East Africa*. Edward Arnold, 1910. https://archive.org/details/withprehistoricp00rout

Scarre, Chris. *Smithsonian Timelines of the Ancient World*. DK Publishing, Inc., 1993.

Tempels, Placide. *Bantu Philosophy*. Translated by A. Rubbens. Presence Africaine, 1959.

Chapter 7

THE MYTHS OF ASIA

© Nell Novara

Introduction

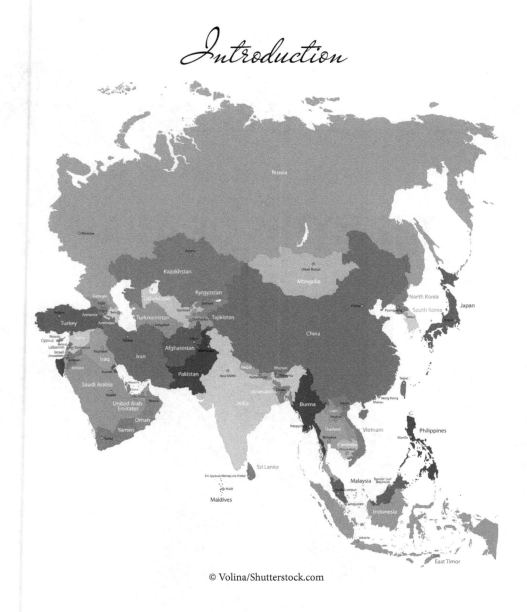

© Volina/Shutterstock.com

The region of South-Central Asia consists mainly of the Indian subcontinent; myths of this area have spread throughout other parts of Asia, such as Sri Lanka and Tibet. The regions of East and Southeast Asia, often called the Far East, includes myths from China and Japan. As with the myths of Africa, it's an oversimplification to group these areas together. However, regionally, they do share some similarities and common influences.

The oldest Indian texts are the Vedas (Books of Knowledge), an enormous collection of various hymns and stories. It's difficult to determine how old they are, but some of the earliest writings date back to 600 BCE. However, most scholars believe these myths existed long before the ability to record them in writing. The Brahmanas ("teachings of the Brahmanas") refer to the teachings in the Vedas and include myths and rituals. It is believed they date around 800–1600 BCE. There are many other sacred texts, but the Puranas contains mainly what we classify as myths—tales of creation and destruction, in addition to stories of gods and heroes. A collection called The Mahabharata contains the world's longest epic poem, as well as the Bhagavad Gita ("song of god"). The Ramayana ("the journey of Rama") is another epic which contains 24,000 verses.

Hinduism is the oldest religion still in practice today. Modern Hinduism is a product of the evolution of beliefs and spiritual movements with no one, single definition. A characteristic of Indian belief systems is a desire to transcend the chaos of the physical world in order to obtain nirvana (spiritual ecstasy)—to find the truth or enlightenment.

Around 550 BCE, Buddhism began to influence Indian spiritual beliefs; the early teachings of the Buddha (who was born into a Hindu family) criticized Brahmanism (the Vedas). Today, the two paths are closely related, but retain some essential differences. Eventually, Buddhism spread into China, Japan, Korea, and beyond.

Beliefs in China were influenced by Hinduism, Buddhism, and Islam but these belief systems were easily absorbed and modified. In turn, Chinese culture influenced Southeast Asia, especially Vietnam. "However, Burma, Thailand, Cambodia, Laos, peninsular Malaysia and the Indonesian islands of Sumatra, Java, and Bali were all affected by the advance of Indian culture, and especially by the cults of the great Hindu gods Vishnu and Shiva" (Cotterell 423). Only fragments of obscure Chinese myth survive today and they are difficult to translate, resulting in many versions of the stories.

Japanese myth has roots in Chinese culture, even though they speak separate languages; in fact, the earliest Japanese myths were recorded in Chinese. As with the Chinese language, it is difficult for a non-native speaker of Japanese to fully appreciate the complexities of the texts. Form and meaning are intertwined in the appearance of the characters, making calligraphy significant.

Shinto ("the way of the gods") was an early religion of Japan that has blended with Buddhism in some aspects. According to Barry Powell:

> The gods of Shinto are known through mediums, dreams, and shamanistic possession, usually by monks. Shinto practices were first recorded in the *Kojiki* and *Nihon Shoki (Chronicles of Japan)* in the eighth century, although these writings do not refer to a unified "Shinto religion," but to a disorganized folklore, history, and myth. Shinto today is a term that applies to public shrines suited to such purposes as war memorials, harvest festivals, and historical monuments" (Powell 303). The *Kojiki* ("records of ancient matters") is a collection of divine myths and legends, the purpose of which is "explicitly to glorify the reigning emperor through tracking his origin back to the gods." (303–4)

Part 1: Creation and Destruction

How the Five Ancients Became Men (China)

The earliest texts of Chinese mythology are dated from the second century BCE. Each dynasty upheld different beliefs and multiple texts were written to convey the mythological understanding of the world at the time. The story of the "Five Ancients and the Yellow Emperor" comes to us from the *Huainanzi*, written during the Han dynasty, written by Liu An, the King of Huainan, and his aides, in 139 BCE.

The Five Ancients are representative of the five directions (east, south, west, north, and center) and five essential elements (wood, fire, metal, water, and earth), each of which play an active role in Chinese philosophy.

The Yellow Ancient (or Huang Di, in translation), is a famous figure in Chinese myth. He is the most important of the Five Ancients, and is depicted in some texts as having been born miraculously and with four faces, and being 300 years old at his death. There are many stories of Huang Di fighting in legendary battles, but this myth places him as the ancestor of Laotsze, the founder of Taoism.

HOW THE FIVE ANCIENTS BECAME MEN

Before the earth was separated from the heavens, all there was was a great ball of watery vapor called chaos. And at that time the spirits of the five elemental powers took shape, and became the five Ancients. The first was called the Yellow Ancient, and he was the ruler of the earth. The second was called the Red Lord, and he was the ruler of the fire. The third was called the Dark Lord, and he was the ruler of the water. The fourth was known as the Wood Prince, and he was the ruler of the wood. The fifth was called the Mother of Metals, and ruled over them.

These five Ancients set all their primal spirit into motion, so that water and earth sank down. The heavens floated upward, and the earth grew firm in the depths. Then they allowed the waters to gather into rivers and seas, and hills and plains made their appearance. So the heavens opened and the earth was divided. And there were sun, moon, and all the stars, wind, clouds, rain, and dew. The Yellow Ancient set earth's purest power spinning in a circle, and added the effect of fire and water thereto. Then there came forth grasses and trees, birds and beasts, and the tribes of the serpents and insects, fishes and turtles. The Wood Prince and the Mother of Metals combined light and darkness, and thus created the human race as men and women. And thus the world gradually came to be.

At that time there was one who was known as the True Prince of the Jasper Castle. He had acquired the art of sorcery through the cultivation of magic. The five Ancients begged him to rule as the supreme god. He dwelt above the three and thirty heavens, and the Jasper Castle, of white jade with golden gates, was his. Before him stood the stewards of the eight and twenty houses of the moon, and the gods of the thunders, and the Great Bear, and in addition a class of baneful gods whose influence was evil and deadly. They all aided the True Prince of the Jasper Castle to rule over the thousand tribes under the heavens, and to deal out life and death, fortune and misfortune. The Lord of the Jasper Castle is now known as the Great God, the White Jade Ruler.

Source: Richard Wilhelm, Translated by Frederick H. Martens, *The Chinese Fairy Book*, 1921.

The five Ancients withdrew after they had done their work, and thereafter lived in quiet purity. The Red Lord dwells in the South as the god of fire. The Dark Lord dwells in the North, as the mighty master of the somber polar skies. He lived in a castle of liquid crystal. In later ages he sent Confucius down upon earth as a saint. Hence this saint is known as the Son of Crystal. The Wood Prince dwells in the East. He is honored as the Green Lord, and watches over the coming into being of all creatures. In him lives the power of spring and he is the god of love. The Mother of Metals dwells in the West, by the sea of Jasper and is also known as the Queen Mother of the West. She leads the rounds of the fairies, and watches over change and growth.

The Yellow Ancient dwells in the middle. He is always going about in the world, in order to save and to help those in any distress. The first time he came to earth he was the Yellow Lord, who taught mankind all sorts of arts. In his later years he fathomed the meaning of the world on the Ethereal Mount, and flew up to the radiant sun. Under the rule of the Dschou dynasty he was born again as Li Oerl, and when he was born his hair and beard were white, for which reason he was called Laotsze, "Old Child." He wrote the book of "Meaning and Life" and spread his teachings through the world. He is honored as the head of Taoism. At the beginning of the reign of the Han dynasty, he again appeared as the Old Man of the River (Ho Schang Gung). He spread the teachings of Tao abroad mightily, so that from that time on Taoism flourished greatly. These doctrines are known to this day as the teachings of the Yellow Ancient. There is also a saying: "First Laotsze was, then the heavens were." And that must mean that Laotsze was that very same Yellow Ancient of primal days.

DISCUSSION QUESTIONS

1. What do the 5 Ancients signify? Their colors? Their realms?

2. The Lord of the Jasper Castle was brought to power by "eight and twenty houses of the moon, and the gods of the thunders, and the Great Bear, and in addition a class of baneful gods whose influence was evil and deadly." What does it mean that both good and evil come together to support him?

3. What is the connection between Laotsze and the Yellow Ancient?

Miao Creation and Flood (China)

The Miao people of China are a large minority group whose population is around 9 million. There are 4 distinct groups of Miao, whose languages are mutually unintelligible. The Hmu people live in southeast Guizhou, the Qo Xiong people are in West Hunan, the A-Hmao people occupy Yunnan, and the Hmong people is the largest group, residing in Guizhou, Sichuan, Guangxi, and Yunnan. Silver ornaments, headdresses, and jewelry are worn by the women during festivals to make as much jingling as possible, to show off their clan's wealth, and to ward off evil.

Their creation story has been passed down in verse, each possessing five syllables (in their language), which are meant to be sung by two people or groups of young men and women at festivals. There is no written history of the Miao and they rely upon the practice of recitation and singing to continue their stories.

MIAO CREATION AND FLOOD

Who made Heaven and earth?
Who made insects?
Who made men?
Made male and made female?
I who speak don't know.

Heavenly King made Heaven and earth,
Ziene made insects,
Ziene made men and demons,
Made male and made female.
How is it you don't know?

How made Heaven and earth?
How made insects?
How made men and demons?
Made male and made female?
I who speak don't know.

Heavenly King was intelligent,
Spat a lot of spittle into his hand,
Clapped his hands with a noise,
Produced Heaven and earth,
Tall grass made insects,
Stories made men and demons,
Made male and made female.
How is it you don't know?

Who came to the bad disposition,
To send fire and burn the hill?
Who came to the bad disposition,
To send water and destroy the earth?
I who sing don't know.

Zie did. Zie was of bad disposition,
Zie sent fire and burned the hill;
Thunder did. Thunder was of bad disposition,
Thunder sent water and destroyed the earth.
Why don't you know?

The following is the account of the flood myth, expanded by the Miao storyteller for the translator, Werner.

In this story of the flood only two persons were saved in a large bottle gourd used as a boat, and these were A Zie and his sister. After the flood the brother wished his sister to become his wife, but she objected to this as not being proper. At length she proposed that one should take the upper and one the nether millstone, and going to opposite hills should set the stones rolling to the valley between. If these should be found in the valley properly adjusted one above the other, she would be his wife, but not if they came to rest apart.

Source: E.T.C. Werner, *Myths and Legends of China*, 1922.

The young man, considering it unlikely that two stones thus rolled down from opposite hills would be found in the valley one upon another, while pretending to accept the test suggested, secretly placed two other stones in the valley one upon the other. The stones rolled from the hills were lost in the tall wild grass, and on descending into the valley A Zie called his sister to come and see the stones he had placed.

She, however, was not satisfied, and suggested as another test that each should take a knife from a double sheath and, going again to the opposite hill-tops, hurl them into the valley below. If both these knives were found in the sheath in the valley she would marry him, but if the knives were found apart they would live apart. Again the brother surreptitiously placed two knives in the sheath, and, the experiment ending as A Zie wished, his sister became his wife.

They had one child, a misshapen thing without arms or legs, which A Zie in great anger killed and cut to pieces. He threw the pieces all over the hill, and next morning, on awaking, he found these pieces transformed into men and women; thus the earth was repeopled.

DISCUSSION QUESTIONS

1. In the song, why do you think the people first want to know "Who" and then "How" the earth was created?

2. The creation story and flood story are both illustrated in the song. What might this mean about the Miao's understanding of the beginning of the world?

3. After the flood, the child that repeoples the earth is born "a misshapen thing without arms or legs." What does the stature of humans seem to be, if created from this child?

Pan Gu and Nu Wa (China)

Of the many Chinese creation myths, those of the giant Pan Gu and the half woman-half serpent Nu Wa are among the most famous and the oldest. These two stories come from an anthology of Chinese mythology written during the first century BCE, called "The Classic of Mountains and Seas." The collection is well named, as Pan Gu and Nu Wa detail the earliest forms of life on earth.

PAN GU AND NU WA

Long before the time of this world, only an egg existed in the chaos. Everything contained in the egg had an opposite: light and dark, male and female, dry and wet, round and flat, cold and heat all existed within the confines of this egg. A giant named Pan Gu was created amid this mixture of yin and yang. As he woke, he burst from the egg and expelled the contents of the egg into the universe. The heavier, darker elements drifted downward to create the earth, while the lighter, brighter elements lifted into the heavens. Pan Gu wished to keep the heaven and earth separate, so he began to stand upright, in order to create space. Pan Gu continued to rise upward for the next 18,000 years, creating a space of 30,000 miles between the heavens and the earth.

Source: Adapted from Jan Walls and Yvonne Walls (translators and editors), *Classical Chinese Myths,* 1984.

When Pan Gu finished rising, he felt that he had accomplished his role on this earth and made the decision to die. As his body lie on the earth's surface, it began to create the features of the earth we know today. His blood turned into rivers, his semen into the ocean, and his sweat was the rain and dewdrops. His breath carried the wind and his voice roared into thunder. His skull became the dome of the sky and his brains turned into clouds underneath. His arms and legs spread to the four corners and his bones became mountains and ridges. The bones and teeth in his skull turned to minerals and ore in the ground, while the flesh and hair of his body became the grass and soil. The fleas or mites that lived on his hair and skin became the dark haired humans.

Another story exists that explains the creation of human beings. It was a long time after Pan Gu had created the earth that Nu Wa wandered the earth, lonely. She had the head of a woman, but her body was that of a serpent. She could find no one like herself, and so she set out to create companions.

Along the Yellow River she found inspiration. She ran her hands through the rich yellow clay and began to mold it into the shape of herself, except for these creatures she split their tails into two. The person she molded began to walk and dance and thank her as soon as Nu Wa set it onto the bank of the river. Nu Wa enjoyed this person and made many more, carefully crafting each individual with her hands.

Nu Wa realized that her process was very slow and so she looked for ways to speed up the production of her people. Looking along the Yellow River, she saw a vine, which she yanked down from the tree and dropped it into the muddy water below. She picked up the vine and gave it a spin; drops of mud flew onto the ground and sprang up, very much like the people she had made from the clay. But these drops did not form the perfectly shaped humans that Nu Wa had made before. In order to account for the difference, Nu Wa declared that the people made by hand out of the yellow clay would be the wealthier, higher-born people, and the those made from the droplets of mud on the vine would be the lower-born, common people. She then divided the people into males and females and taught them to create their own humans so she would not have to make anymore herself.

DISCUSSION QUESTIONS

1. Look up "binary opposition" and use this term to discuss how Yin and Yang help us to form these. Are binaries always true? Do we always fit into binaries? Why might the concept of Yin and Yang help to establish these?

2. Compare the dismemberment of Pan Gu's body to that of other myths that create the earth from a body.

3. How does the story of Nu Wa help to keep people separated into their socioeconomic classes?

The Creation of the Ainu (Ainu)

The Ainu are the aboriginal inhabitants of the islands that make up present-day Japan. Particularly concentrated in Hokkaido, the Ainu's presence has been traced back to 1000 BCE. Their culture flourished until the 1400s, when contact was made and many battles lost to the present-day Japanese. Because of epidemic sickness brought on by the outside contact, enforced labor camps, and general discrimination, the Ainu today number less than 25,000.

The Ainu worshipped many kinds of gods: nature gods, animal gods, plant gods, and object gods. The meaning of the word "Ainu" is "human," or, the opposite of these gods. According to the Ainu Museum, the literature of the Ainu is not only "recitative," but also "narrative uepeker" which is usually translated as, "an old tale." This old tale is not a fictitious one but a real one with experiences of those who lived in olden times. Women hold a particularly high rank in storytelling. The "Yaysama" is oral literature in which a woman sings an impromptu song of her emotions. The "Upopo" is a festival song sung by women who sit in a circle, beating the lid of a container called "shintoko." The words are not long and are sung repeatedly in a round or a chorus. Each of these storytelling styles contributes to a culture of oral literature, which has been passed down through each generation.

THE CREATION OF THE AINU

Before God made the world there was nothing but swamp to be seen, in which, however, there dwelt a very large trout. This trout was indeed a mighty fish, for his body reached from one end of the swamp to the other. Now, when the Creator produced the earth He made this creature to become its foundation. There lies the living trout beneath the world, taking in and sending out the waters of the sea through his mouth. When he sucks the water in, the ebb of the tide takes place, but when he sends it out the tide flows.

The trout upon whose back the world is founded is the cause of tidal-waves. Every now and again he takes in a vast quantity of water, and then with an extraordinary effort shoots it out of his mouth in one mighty blow of his breath. It is this which makes the tidal-waves.

So, again, when he shakes himself the consequence is an earthquake. When he moves gently the earthquake is small, but when he is angry and moves furiously it is great. As this is such a dangerous fish, the Creator has sent two deities to stand one on either side of him, to keep him quiet. These divine beings always keep one hand each on him, to hold him down and prevent any severe movements. Whether they eat or drink they must each keep one hand upon him without fail; they may never on any account take it off.

In very ancient times, after God had formed the rivers and seas and made the land He returned to His heavenly home. Upon His arrival there He entered His house, and took from a corner two bags, one containing fish bones and the other the bones of deer. These were the remains of His great feasts. He emptied the bag having deer bones in it upon the mountains, where they at once became living deer, beautiful to behold, and that containing the bones of the fish He cast into the rivers and sea, where they became fishes of various kinds. As this, then, is the way in which these creatures came into the world, the people pray to God when deer and fish are scarce, asking Him to send more down, for as He produced them in this way in the beginning, He is able to do so now.

The place in which we dwell is called by two names, first, Kanna moshiri (the upper world), and then Uwekari notereke moshiri (the world in which the multitudes trample one another's feet). It is also

Source: John Batchelor, *The Ainu and their folk lore*, 1889.

called Uare moshiri (the place in which to multiply one another). It is the upper world, because there is another world under foot. That world is very damp and wet, and when wicked people die they go there and are punished. But by the side of this place there is another locality, which is called Kamui moshiri (country of the gods or heaven). It is to this place that the good people go at death. They live there with the deities and walk about upside down, after the manner of flies, so that their feet meet ours.

When it is day upon this earth it is night in heaven, and when it is daylight there, it is dark here. Now, when it is dark in this world, men should neither do any work, nor trim one another's hair, nor cut the beard, for at that time the deities and ghosts of men are busy in their own spheres. If, therefore, the inhabitants of this world work during the hours of darkness, they will be punished with sickness and meet with an early death.

DISCUSSION QUESTIONS

1. What is the significance of the trout that has a place at the creation of the world?

2. Why might the Ainu be interested in the creation of tidal waves, earthquakes, and the ebb and flow of the tide?

3. Consider the three names given to the world we inhabit. Are they fitting? What might have led the Ainu to describe our world in this way?

Izanagi and Izanami (Japan)

Both the *Kojiki* and the *Nihongi* represent the myth of the Earth Creators, Izanagi and Izanami. These creators are examples of the Shinto understanding of *kami*, or gods. But this term is more complex than a simple translation. The *kami* are deities, humans, or animals that possess varying degrees of *kami*. In the Shinto tradition, there are *yaoyorozu-no-kami*, which means 8 million *kami*, as a way of saying their numbers are infinite. This of course makes it difficult to understand the Japanese myths in terms of having a pantheon of gods.

The story of Izanagi (he-who-invites) and Izanami (she-who-invites) is a unique myth, in that it focuses more on the understanding of rulership (who rules which realm, what are the names of future political provinces, etc.), rather than the physical creation of flora and fauna, humans, etc. The relationship between men and women is also an important theme in this myth. The creation of the eight islands depends upon the correct order of courtship.

IZANAGI AND IZANAMI

Before time was, and while yet the world was uncreated, chaos reigned. The earth and the waters, the light and the darkness, the stars and the firmament, were intermingled in a vapoury liquid. All things were formless and confused. No creature existed; phantom shapes moved as clouds on the ruffled surface of a sea. It was the birth-time of the gods. The first deity sprang from an immense bulrush-bud, which rose,

Source: Frank Rinder, "The Birth-Time of the Gods" in *Old World Japan: Legends of the Land of the Gods*, 1895.

spear-like, in the midst of the boundless disorder. Other gods were born, but three generations passed before the actual separation of the atmosphere from the more solid earth. Finally, where the tip of the bulrush points upward, the Heavenly Spirits appeared.

From this time their kingdom was divided from the lower world where chaos still prevailed. To the fourth pair of gods it was given to create the earth. These two beings were the powerful God of the Air, Izanagi, and the fair Goddess of the Clouds, Izanami. From them sprang all life.

Now Izanagi and Izanami wandered on the Floating Bridge of Heaven. This bridge spanned the gulf between heaven and the unformed world; it was upheld in the air, and it stood secure. The God of the Air spoke to the Goddess of the Clouds: "There must needs be a kingdom beneath us, let us visit it." When he had so said, he plunged his jewelled spear into the seething mass below. The drops that fell from the point of the spear congealed and became the island of Onogoro. Thereupon the Earth-Makers descended, and called up a high mountain peak, on whose summit could rest one end of the Heavenly Bridge, and around which the whole world should revolve.

The Wisdom of the Heavenly Spirit had decreed that Izanagi should be a man, and Izanami a woman, and these two deities decided to wed and dwell together on the earth. But, as befitted their august birth, the wooing must be solemn. Izanagi skirted the base of the mountain to the right, Izanami turned to the left. When the Goddess of the Clouds saw the God of the Air approaching afar off, she cried, enraptured, "Ah, what a fair and lovely youth!" Then Izanagi exclaimed, "Ah, what a fair and lovely maiden!" As they met, they clasped hands, and the marriage was accomplished. But, for some unknown cause, the union did not prove as happy as the god and goddess had hoped. They continued their work of creation, but Awaji, the island that rose from the deep, was little more than a barren waste, and their first-born son, Hiruko, was a weakling. The Earth-Makers placed him in a little boat woven of reeds, and left him to the mercy of wind and tide.

In deep grief, Izanagi and Izanami recrossed the Floating Bridge, and came to the place where the Heavenly Spirits hold eternal audience. From them they learned that Izanagi should have been the first to speak, when the gods met round the base of the Pillar of Earth. They must woo and wed anew. On their return to earth, Izanagi, as before, went to the right, and Izanami to the left of the mountain, but now, when they met, Izanagi exclaimed, "Ah, what a fair and lovely maiden!" and Izanami joyfully responded, "Ah, what a fair and lovely youth!" They clasped hands once more, and their happiness began. They created the eight large islands of the Kingdom of Japan; first the luxuriant Island of the Dragon-fly, the great Yamato; then Tsukushi, the White-Sun Youth; Iyo, the Lovely Princess, and many more. The rocky islets of the archipelago were formed by the foam of the rolling breakers as they dashed on the coastlines of the islands already created. Thus China and the remaining lands and continents of the world came into existence.

Now were born to Izanagi and Izanami, the Ruler of the Rivers, the Deity of the Mountains, and, later, the God of the Trees, and a goddess to whom was entrusted the care of tender plants and herbs.

Then Izanagi and Izanami said, "We have created the mighty Kingdom of the Eight Islands, with mountains, rivers, and trees; yet another divinity there must be, who shall guard and rule this fair world."

As they spoke, a daughter was born to them. Her beauty was dazzling, and her regal bearing betokened that her throne should be set high above the clouds. She was none other than Amaterasu, The Heaven-Illuminating Spirit. Izanagi and Izanami rejoiced greatly when they beheld her face, and exclaimed, "Our daughter shall dwell in the Blue Plain of High Heaven, and from there she shall direct the universe." So they led her to the summit of the mountain, and over the wondrous bridge. The Heavenly Spirits were joyful when they saw Amaterasu, and said, "You shall mount into the soft blue of the sky, your brilliancy shall illumine, and your sweet smile shall gladden, the Eternal Land, and all the world. Fleecy clouds shall be your handmaidens, and sparkling dewdrops your messengers of peace."

The next child of Izanagi and Izanami was a son, and as he also was beautiful, with the dream-like beauty of the evening, they placed him in the heavens, as co-ruler with his sister Ama-terasu. His name was Tsuku-yomi, the Moon-God. The god Susa-no-o is another son of the two deities who wooed and wed around the base of the Pillar of Earth. Unlike his brother and his sister, he was fond of the shadow and the gloom. When he wept, the grass on the mountainside withered, the flowers were blighted, and men died. Izanagi had little joy in this son, nevertheless he made him ruler of the ocean.

Now that the world was created, the happy life of the God of the Air and the Goddess of the Clouds was over. The consumer, the God of Fire, was born, and Izanami died. She vanished into the deep solitudes of the Kingdom of the Trees, in the country of Kii, and disappeared thence into the lower regions.

Izanagi was sorely troubled because Izanami had been taken from him, and he descended in pursuit of her to the portals of the shadowy kingdom where sunshine is unknown. Izanami would fain have left that place to rejoin Izanagi on the beautiful earth. Her spirit came to meet him, and in urgent and tender words besought him not to seek her in those cavernous regions. But the bold god would not be warned. Izanagi pressed forward, and, by the light struck from his comb, he sought for his loved one long and earnestly. Grim forms rose to confront him, but he passed them by with kingly disdain. Sounds as of the wailing of lost souls struck his ear, but still he persisted. After endless search, he found his Izanami lying in an attitude of untold despair, but so changed was she, that he gazed intently into her eyes ere he could recognise her. Izanami was angry that Izanagi had not listened to her commands, for she knew how fruitless would be his efforts. Without the sanction of the ruler of the underworld, she could not return to earth, and this consent she had tried in vain to obtain.

Izanagi, hard pressed by the eight monsters who guard the Land of Gloom, had to flee for his life. He defended himself valiantly with his sword; then he threw down his head-dress, and it was transformed into bunches of purple grapes; he also cast behind him the comb, by means of which he had obtained light, and from it sprang tender shoots of bamboo. While the monsters eagerly devoured the luscious grapes and tender shoots, Izanagi gained the broad flight of steps which led back to earth. At the top he paused and cried to Izanami: "All hope of our reunion is now at an end. Our separation must be eternal."

Stretching far beyond Izanagi lay the ocean, and on its surface was reflected the face of his well-beloved daughter, Ama-terasu. She seemed to speak, and beseech him to purify himself in the great waters of the sea. As he bathed, his wounds were healed, and a sense of infinite peace stole over him.

The life-work of the Earth-Maker was done. He bestowed the world upon his children, and afterwards crossed, for the last time, the many-coloured Bridge of Heaven. The God of the Air now spends his days with the Heaven-Illuminating Spirit in her sun-glorious palace.

DISCUSSION QUESTIONS

1. What does this creation myth suggest about how the Japanese view the rest of the world?

2. Why is their first child and first island creation doomed?

3. Compare Izanagi's voyage to the underworld to find his wife to other myths of this kind (Demeter and Persephone, Gilgamesh, etc.).

Hindu Creation (India)

The myths of India are often abstract and philosophical, providing guidelines for belief as well as conduct. Creation is a repeated cycle that includes destruction and is done in accordance with *karma*—a system of cause and effect in which a person *atones* for actions during life. The soul will continue to be reborn until it is freed from this state; this is accomplished by following *dharma* ("law")—one's obligations in life based on his or her role or status. One must meditate on the *atman* (personal essence) to understand all things are one with the brahma—the concept of *brahman* is the oneness of existence.

In this account of creation, Brahma makes the world. All things originate with this principle of creation, and all things return to it. Yet Brahma is not the supreme creator—that is Vishnu. It is said that the four-headed Brahma springs forth from a lotus that grows from Vishnu's navel; Vishnu himself is typically depicted as reclining on a serpent called Ananta ("endless"), floating on the waters of chaos, while his consort Lakshmi ("good fortune") massages his feet.

This hymn describes the state of things before creation:

HINDU CREATION

A Puranic Hymn from the *Rig Veda*

There was neither aught nor naught, nor air, nor sky beyond.
What covered all? Where rested all? In watery gulf profound?
Nor death was then, nor deathlessness, nor change of night and day.
The One breathed calmly, self-sustained; nought else beyond it lay.

Gloom, hid in gloom, existed first—one sea, eluding view.
That One, a void in chaos wrapt, by inward fervour grew.
Within it first arose desire, the primal germ of mind,
Which nothing with existence links, as sages searching find.

The kindling ray that shot across the dark and drear abyss—
Was it beneath? or high aloft? What bard can answer this?
There fecundating powers were found, and mighty forces strove—
A self-supporting mass beneath, and energy above.

Who knows, who ever told, from whence this vast creation rose?
No gods had then been born—who then can e'er the truth disclose?
Whence sprang this world, and whether framed by hand divine or no—
Its lord in heaven alone can tell, if even he can show.

First Book of the Puranas: The Vishnu Purana

The account in the "Vishnu Purāna" was, according to that authority, "originally imparted by the great father of all (Brahmā) in answer to the questions of Daksha and other venerable sages, and repeated by them to Purukutsa, a king who reigned on the banks of the Narmadā."

"Who can describe him who is not to be apprehended by the senses? He is Brahma, supreme, lord, eternal, unborn, imperishable. He then existed in the form of Purusha and of Kāla. Purusha (Spirit) is the first form of the supreme; next proceeded two other forms, the discreet and indiscreet; and Kāla

Source: W. J. Wilkins, *Hindu Mythology: Puranic and Vedic*, 1900.

(time) was the last. These four—Pradhāna (primary or crude matter), Purusha (Spirit), Vyakta (visible substance), and Kāla (time)—in their due proportions, are the causes of the production of the phenomena of creation, preservation, and destruction. The supreme Brahma, the supreme soul, the substance of the world, the lord of all creatures, the universal soul, the supreme ruler Hari (Vishnu), of his own will having entered into matter and spirit, agitated the mutable and immutable principles, the season of creation having arrived, in the same manner as fragrance affects the mind from its proximity merely, and not from any immediate operation upon mind itself; so the supreme influenced the elements of creation."

After giving an account of the creation, or rather the evolution of the elements, the "Vishnu Purāna" goes on to say: Then (the elements) ether, air, light, water and earth, severally united with the properties of sound, and the rest existed as distinguishable according to their qualities as soothing, terrific, or stupefying; but possessing various energies, and being unconnected, they could not without combination create living beings, not having blended with each other. Having combined, therefore, with one another, they assumed, through their mutual association, the character of one mass of entire unity; and from the direction of spirit, with the acquiescence of the indiscreet principle, intellect, and the rest, to the gross elements inclusive, formed an egg, which gradually expanded like a bubble of water. This vast egg, compounded of the elements, and resting on the waters, was the excellent natural abode of Vishnu in the form of Brahma; and there Vishnu, the lord of the universe, whose essence is inscrutable, assumed a perceptible form, and even he himself abided in it in the character of Brahma. Its womb, vast as the mountain Meru, was composed of the mountains; and the mighty oceans were the waters that filled its cavity. In that egg were the continents and seas and mountains, the planets and divisions of the universe, the gods, demons, and mankind.

"Affecting then the quality of activity, Hari the lord of all, himself becoming Brahma, engaged in the creation of the universe. Vishnu, with the quality of goodness and of immeasurable power, preserves created things through successive ages, until the close of the period termed a Kalpa; when the same mighty deity, invested with the quality of darkness, assumes the awful form of Rudra, and swallows up the universe. Having thus devoured all things, and converted the world into one vast ocean, the supreme reposes upon his mighty serpent couch amidst the deep: he awakes after a season, and again, as Brahma, becomes the author of creation."

The Purāna next gives an account of the creation in the present Kalpa or age. This is a secondary creation, for water and the earth also are already in existence; it is not creation properly speaking, but the change of pre-existing matter into their present forms. Vishnu knew that the earth lay hidden in the waters; he, therefore, assuming the form of a boar, raised it upon his tusks.

In answer to a request for a full account of the creation of gods and other beings, the following passages occur:

Created beings, although they are destroyed (in their original forms) at the periods of dissolution, yet, being affected by the good or evil acts of former existence, are never exempted from their consequences; and when Brahmā creates the world anew, they are the progeny of his will, in the fourfold condition of gods, men, animals, and inanimate things. Brahmā then, being desirous of creating the four orders of beings—termed gods, demons, progenitors, and men—collected his mind into itself.

Whilst thus concentrated, the quality of darkness pervaded his body, and thence the demons (the asuras) were first born, issuing from his thigh. Brahmā then abandoned that form which was composed of the rudiment of darkness, and which, being deserted by him, became night. Continuing to create, but assuming a different shape, he experienced pleasure, and thence from his mouth proceeded the gods.

The form abandoned by him became day, in which the good quality predominates; and hence by day the gods are most powerful, and by night the demons.

He next adopted another person (form) in which the rudiment of good men also prevailed; and thinking of himself as the father of the world, the progenitors (or Pitris) were born from his side. The body, when he abandoned it, became the Sandhya, or evening twilight. Brahmā then assumed another person, pervaded by the quality of foulness; and from this, men in whom foulness (or passion) predominates, were produced. Quickly abandoning that body, it became the dawn. At the appearance of this light of day men feel most vigour; whilst the progenitors are most powerful in the evening.

Next from Brahmā, in a form composed of the quality of foulness, was produced hunger, of whom anger was born; and the god put forth in darkness beings emaciated with hunger, of hideous aspect and with long beards. These beings hastened to the deity. Such of them as exclaimed, 'Oh, preserve us,' were thence called Rākshasas (from Raksha, to preserve); others who cried out, 'Let us eat,' were denominated from that expression Yākshas (from Yaksha, to eat). Beholding them so disgusting, the hairs of Brahmā were shrivelled up, and first falling from his head were again renewed upon it; from their falling they became serpents, called Sarpa (Srip, to creep), from their creeping, and Ahi (from Hā, to abandon), because they had deserted the head. The creator of the world, being incensed, then created fierce beings, who were denominated goblins, bhutas, malignant fiends, and eaters of flesh. The Gandharvas (choristers) were next born: imbibing melody, drinking of the goddess of speech, they were born, and hence their appellation.

The divine Brahmā, influenced by their material energies, having created these beings, made others of his own will. "Birds he formed from his vital vigour; sheep from his heart; goats from his mouth; kine from his belly and sides; and horses, elephants, sarabhas, gayals, deer, camels, mules, antelopes, and other animals from his feet: whilst from the hairs of his body sprang herbs, roots, and fruits." In this manner all things are said to have sprung from Brahmā; they were with him in the egg: hence this is an account of evolution, rather than of creation. The creation of man, as divided into four castes, is described in this Purāna, in similar terms to those in Manu.

Following this is the account of the mind-born sons of Brahmā—Bhrigu, Daksha, and others—nine in number, who became the progenitors of men. Next Brahmā created himself as Manu Swāyambhu, born of, and identical with, his original self, for the protection of created beings: and the female portion of himself he constituted Satarūpā, whom austerity purified from the sin (forbidden nuptials), and whom the divine Manu Swāyambhu took to wife.

DISCUSSION QUESTIONS

1. Why do you suppose demons were firstborn? Why were they created? Why not create a world with only gods as the divine beings?

2. Why do you suppose that demons are born from the thigh, but gods are born from the mouth?

3. According to the text, this is "an account of evolution, rather than of creation." Explain.

© Nell Novara

Kali Yuga (India)

There are four main ages of existence, and these are called *yugas*. In each stage there is a decline of *dharma*—the behavior of people displays an increase in immorality and a decrease of wisdom. A "great age," called a *mahayuga*, consists of four *yugas*; then the cycle starts over. The four *yugas* are: *Satya Yuga* (or *Krita)*, *Treta Yuga*, *Dvapara Yuga*, and *Kali Yuga*. The lifespan of humans and the general quality of life declines over the course of the *yugas*. The *Satya* ("truth") *Yuga* is a golden age. The *Kali* ("dark") *Yuga* is our current age, an age of darkness.

The *yugas* vary in length—the *Satya Yuga* is said to last for 1,728,000 years; it's the longest. The *Kali Yuga* is 432,000 years—the shortest age. One thousand *mahayugas* is one day in the life of Brahma, who lives for one hundred years (311.04 trillion human years). At the end of Brahma's existence, the universe is destroyed and creation begins again.

KALI YUGA

"Vaisampayana said Yudhishthira, the son of Kunti, once more asked the great Muni Markandeya about the future course of the government of the Earth.

"And Yudhishthira said, 'O thou foremost of all speakers, O Muni of Bhrigu's race, that which we have heard from thee about the destruction and re-birth of all things at the end of the Yuga, is, indeed, full of wonder! I am filled with curiosity, however, in respect of what may happen in the Kali age. When morality and virtue will be at an end, what will remain there! What will be the prowess of men in that age, what their food, and what their amusements? What will be the period of life at the end of the Yuga? What also is the limit, having attained which the Krita age will begin anew? Tell me all in detail, O Muni, for all that thou narratest is varied and delightful.'

Source: Kisari Mohan Ganguli, translator. "The Mahabharata" Book 3: *Vana Parva*, 1883–1896.

"Thus addressed, that foremost of Munis began his discourse again, delighting that tiger of the Vrishni race and the sons of Pandu as well. And Markandeya said, 'Listen, O monarch, to all that hath been seen and heard by me, and to all, O king of kings, that hath been known to me by intuition from the grace of the God of gods! O bull of the Bharata race, listen to me as I narrate the future history of the world during the sinful age.

O bull of the Bharata race, in the Krita age, everything was free from deceit and guile and avarice and covetousness; and morality like a bull was among men, with all the four legs complete. In the Treta age sin took away one of these legs and morality had three legs. In the Dwapara, sin and morality are mixed half and half; and accordingly morality is said to have two legs only. In the dark age (of Kali), O thou best of the Bharata race, morality mixed with three parts of sin liveth by the side of men.

Accordingly morality then is said to wait on men, with only a fourth part of itself remaining. Know, O Yudhishthira, that the period of life, the energy, intellect and the physical strength of men decrease in every Yuga!

* * *

. . . in consequence of the shortness of their lives they will not be able to acquire much knowledge. And in consequence of the littleness of their knowledge, they will have no wisdom. And for this, covetousness and avarice will overwhelm them all. And wedded to avarice and wrath and ignorance and lust men will entertain animosities towards one another, desiring to take one another's lives. And Brahmanas and Kshatriyas and Vaisyas with their virtue contracted and divested of asceticism and truth will all be reduced to an equality with the Sudras. And the lowest orders of men will rise to the position of the intermediate ones, and those in intermediate stations will, without doubt, descend to the level of the lowest ones.

* * *

And those men who are devoted to ceremonial rites in honour of the deceased and of the gods, will be avaricious and will also appropriate and enjoy what belongs to others. The father will enjoy what belongs to the son; and the son, what belongs to the father. And those things will also be enjoyed by men in such times, the enjoyment of which hath been forbidden in the scriptures. And the Brahmanas, speaking disrespectfully of the Vedas, will not practise vows, and their understanding clouded by the science of disputation, they will no longer perform sacrifices and the Homa.

* * *

And, possessed of small energy and strength, without knowledge and given to avarice and folly and sinful practices men will accept with joy the gifts made by wicked people with words of contempt. And, O son of Kunti, the kings of the earth, with hearts wedded to sin without knowledge and always boastful of their wisdom, will challenge one another from desire of taking one another's life. And the Kshatriyas also towards the end of such a period will become the thorns of the earth. And filled with avarice and swelling with pride and vanity and, unable and unwilling to protect (their subjects), they will take pleasure in inflicting punishments only. And attacking and repeating their attacks upon the good and the honest, and feeling no pity for the latter, even when they will cry in grief, the Kshatriyas will, O Bharata, rob these of their wives and wealth.

And no one will ask for a girl (for purposes of marriage) and no one will give away a girl (for such purposes), but the girls will themselves choose their lords, when the end of the Yuga comes. And the kings of the

---

mleccha (Sanskrit) is an ancient term for foreigners—"non-Vedic." Often used in a derogatory fashion to refer to those deemed inferior or less civilized.

earth with souls steeped in ignorance, and discontented with what they have, will at such a time, rob their subjects by every means in their power. And without doubt the whole world will be mlecchified*. And when the end of the Yuga comes, the right hand will deceive the left; and the left, the right. And men with false reputation of learning will contract Truth and the old will betray the senselessness of the young, and the young will betray the dotage of the old. And cowards will have the reputation of bravery and the brave will be cheerless like cowards. And towards the end of the Yuga men will cease to trust one another. And full of avarice and folly the whole world will have but one kind of food. And sin will increase and prosper, while virtue will fade and cease to flourish. And Brahmanas and Kshatriyas and Vaisyas will disappear, leaving, O king, no remnants of their orders. And all men towards the end of the Yuga will become members of one common order, without distinction of any kind.

* * *

And, O ruler of men, intellectual darkness will envelop the whole earth, and the life of man will then be measured by sixteen years, on attaining to which age death will ensue. And girls of five or six years of age will bring forth children and boys of seven or eight years of age will become fathers. And, O tiger among kings, when the end of the Yuga will come, the wife will never be content with her husband, nor the husband with his wife. And the possessions of men will never be much, and people will falsely bear the marks of religion, and jealousy and malice will fill the world. And no one will, at that time, be a giver (of wealth or anything else) in respect to any one else. And the inhabited regions of the earth will be afflicted with dearth and famine, and the highways will be filled with lustful men and women of evil repute.

* * *

And people will, without compunction, destroy trees and gardens. And men will be filled with anxiety as regards the means of living. And, O king, overwhelmed with covetousness, men will kill Brahmanas and appropriate and enjoy the possessions of their victims. And the regenerate ones, oppressed by Sudras, and afflicted with fear, and crying Oh and Alas, will wander over the earth without anybody to protect them. And when men will begin to slay one another, and become wicked and fierce and without any respect for animal life, then will the Yuga come to an end.

* * *

Brahmanas. And in the asylums of great Rishis, and the teaching institutions of Brahmanas, and in places sacred to the gods and sacrificial compounds, and in sacred tanks, the earth will be disfigured with tombs and pillars containing bony relics and not graced with temples dedicated to the gods. All this will take place at the end of the Yuga, and know that these are the signs of the end of the Yuga.

And when men become fierce and destitute of virtue and carnivorous and addicted to intoxicating drinks, then doth the Yuga come to an end. And, O monarch, when flowers will be begot within flowers, and fruits within fruits, then will the Yuga come to an end. And the clouds will pour rain unseasonably when the end of the Yuga approaches. And, at that time, ceremonial rites of men will not follow one another in due order, and the Sudras will quarrel with the Brahmanas.

* * *

And all the points of the horizon will be ablaze, and the stars and stellar groups will be destitute of brilliancy, and the planets and planetary conjunctions will be inauspicious. And the course of the winds will be confused and agitated, and innumerable meteors will flash through the sky, foreboding evil.

*   *   *

And, O king, when the end of the Yuga comes, Rahu will swallow the Sun unseasonably. And fires will blaze up on all sides. And travellers unable to obtain food and drink and shelter even when they ask for these, will lie down on the wayside refraining from urging their solicitations. And when the end of the Yuga comes, crows and snakes and vultures and kites and other animals and birds will utter frightful and dissonant cries. And when the end of the Yuga comes, men will cast away and neglect their friends and relatives and attendants. And, O monarch, when the end of the Yuga comes, men abandoning the countries and directions and towns and cities of their occupation, will seek for new ones, one after another. And people will wander over the earth, uttering, 'O father, O son', and such other frightful and rending cries.

"And when those terrible times will be over, the creation will begin anew. And men will again be created and distributed into the four orders beginning with Brahmanas. And about that time, in order that men may increase, Providence, according to its pleasure, will once more become propitious. And then when the Sun, the Moon, and Vrihaspati will, with the constellation Pushya, enter the same sign, the Krita age will begin again. And the clouds will commence to shower seasonably, and the stars and stellar conjunctions will become auspicious. And the planets, duly revolving in their orbits, will become exceedingly propitious. And all around, there will be prosperity and abundance and health and peace. And commissioned by Time, a Brahmana of the name of Kalki will take his birth. And he will glorify Vishnu and possess great energy, great intelligence, and great prowess. And he will take his birth in a town of the name of Sambhala in an auspicious Brahmana family. And vehicles and weapons, and warriors and arms, and coats of mail will be at his disposal as soon as he will think of them. And he will be the king of kings, and ever victorious with the strength of virtue. And he will restore order and peace in this world crowded with creatures and contradictory in its course. And that blazing Brahmana of mighty intellect, having appeared, will destroy all things. And he will be the Destroyer of all, and will inaugurate a new Yuga. And surrounded by the Brahmanas, that Brahmana will exterminate all the mlecchas wherever those low and despicable persons may take refuge."

DISCUSSION QUESTIONS

1. Compare the Indian cycle of creation and destruction with similar myths from other cultures. What are the notable similarities and differences?

2. What does this creation and destruction cycle reveal about Indian culture and their worldview?

Part 2: Tricksters, Lovers, and Other Tales

The Lady of the Moon (China)

This story of how Chang'e became the Lady of the Moon is told in many early texts and references characters and animals famous in Chinese mythology. The story of her husband, Yi (sometimes Hou Yi), the archer who shoots the nine moons, has been recounted since the fourth century BCE in the *Shanhaijing*. Yi is famous also for his ability to kill many monsters and rescue people from raging gods. Emperor Yao, who provides the setting for this myth, is an emperor of legend, said to have reigned in the twenty-fourth century BCE. His reign is the time of Yi the archer and a great flood brought under control by Gun Yu. The Tang dynasty reigned 618–907 CE and provides the setting for the later story of the sorcerers who visit the Lady of the Moon. They see many creatures living in the moon. The rabbit who grinds herbs in the mortar is the figure who makes the elixir of life in many other myths. The story of the Lady of the Moon comes from *Huainanzi*, during the Han dynasty. Chang'e is a popular figure during the Mid-Autumn Festival, held each year on the fifteenth of August (in the lunar calendar). This timing may be explained by the sorcerers' ascent to the moon to meet Chang'e and bring back her music.

THE LADY OF THE MOON

In the days of the Emperor Yao lived a prince by the name of Yi, who was a mighty hero and a good archer. Once ten suns rose together in the sky, and shone so brightly and burned so fiercely that the people on earth could not endure them. So the Emperor ordered Yi to shoot at them. And Yi shot nine of them down from the sky.

Beside his bow, Yi also had a horse which ran so swiftly that even the wind could not catch up with it. He mounted it to go hunting and the horse ran away and could not be stopped. So Yi came to Kunlun Mountain and met the Queen Mother of the Jasper Sea and she gave him the herb of immortality. He took it home with him and hid it in his room. But his wife, who was named Chang'e, once ate some of it on the sly when he was not at home, and she immediately floated up to the clouds. When she reached the moon, she ran into the castle there, and has lived there ever since as the Lady of the Moon.

On a night in mid-autumn, an emperor of the Tang dynasty once sat at wine with two sorcerers. And one of them took his bamboo staff and cast it into the air, where it turned into a heavenly bridge on which the three climbed up to the moon together. There they saw a great castle on which was inscribed: "The Spreading Halls of Crystal Cold." Beside it stood a cassia tree which blossomed and gave forth a fragrance filling all the air. And in the tree sat a man who was chopping off the smaller boughs with an ax.

One of the sorcerers said, "That is the man in the moon. The cassia tree grows so luxuriantly that in the course of time it would overshadow all the moon's radiance. Therefore it has to be cut down once in every thousand years." Then they entered the spreading halls. The silver stories of the castle towered one above the other, and its walls and columns were all formed of liquid crystal. In the walls were cages and ponds where fishes and birds moved as though alive. The whole moon-world seemed made of glass.

While they were still looking about them on all sides the Lady of the Moon stepped up to them, clad in a white mantle and a rainbow-colored gown. She smiled and said to the emperor, "You are a prince of the

Source Richard Wilhelm, Trans by Frederick H. Martens, *The Chinese Fairy Book*, 1921.

mundane world of dust. Great is your fortune, since you have been able to find your way here!" And she called for her attendants, who came flying up on white birds, and sang and danced beneath the cassia tree. A pure clear music floated through the air. Beside the tree stood a mortar made of white marble, in which a jasper rabbit ground up herbs.

When the dance had ended, the emperor returned to earth again with the sorcerers. And he had the songs which he had heard on the moon written down and sung to the accompaniment of flutes of jasper in his pear tree garden.

DISCUSSION QUESTIONS

1. Is Chang'e becoming the Lady of the Moon a punishment or a reward?

2. What is the purpose of the rabbit grinding herbs?

3. What cosmological process might be explained by the man who chops the cassia tree?

Japanese Fox Legends (Japan)

The fox takes an important place in Japanese legend, and the subject is of a far-reaching and complex kind.[1] Inari was originally the God of Rice, but in the eleventh century he became associated with the Fox God, with attributes for good and evil, mostly for evil, so profuse and so manifold in their application that they cause no or little confusion to the English reader. All foxes possess supernatural powers to an almost limitless degree. They have the power of infinite vision; they can hear everything and understand the secret thoughts of mankind generally, and in addition they possess the power of transformation and of transmutation. The chief attribute of the bad fox is the power to delude human beings, and for this purpose it will take the form of a beautiful woman, and many are the legends told in this connection. If the shadow of a fox-woman chance to fall upon water, only the fox, and not the fair woman, is revealed. It is said that if a dog sees a fox-woman the feminine form vanishes immediately, and the fox alone remains.

Though the legends connected with the fox in Japan are usually associated with evil, Inari sometimes poses as a beneficent being, a being who can cure coughs and colds, bring wealth to the needy, and answer a woman's prayer for a child.

Inari not infrequently rewards human beings for any act of kindness to a fox. Only a part of his reward, however, is real; at least one tempting coin is bound to turn very quickly into grass! The little good done by Inari—and we have tried to do him justice—is altogether weighed down by his countless evil actions, often of an extremely cruel nature.

Demoniacal possession is frequently said to be due to the evil influence of foxes. This form of possession is known as kitsune-tsuki. The sufferer is usually a woman of the poorer classes, one who is highly sensitive and open to believe in all manner of superstitions . . . that a fox usually enters a woman either through the breast or between the finger-nails, and that the fox lives a separate life of its own, frequently speaking in a voice totally different from the human.

Source: F. Hadland Davis. *Myths and Legends of Japan,* 1912.

LEGENDS OF INARI, THE FOX GOD

The Death-Stone[2]

"The Death-Stone stands on Nasu's moor
Through winter snows and summer heat;
The moss grows grey upon its sides,
But the foul demon haunts it yet.

"Chill blows the blast: the owl's sad choir
Hoots hoarsely through the moaning pines;
Among the low chrysanthemums
The skulking fox, the jackal whines,
As o'er the moor the autumn light declines."

The Buddhist priest Genno, after much weary travel, came to the moor of Nasu, and was about to rest under the shadow of a great stone, when a spirit suddenly appeared, and said: "Rest not under this stone. This is the Death-Stone. Men, birds, and beasts have perished by merely touching it!"

These mysterious and warning remarks naturally awakened Genno's curiosity, and he begged that the spirit would favour him with the story of the Death-Stone.

Thus the spirit began: "Long ago there was a fair girl living at the Japanese Court. She was so charming that she was called the Jewel Maiden. Her wisdom equalled her beauty, for she understood Buddhist lore and the Confucian classics, science, and the poetry of China."

"So sweetly decked by nature and by art,
The monarch's self soon clasp'd her to his heart."

"One night," went on the spirit, "the Mikado gave a great feast in the Summer Palace, and there he assembled the wit, wisdom, and beauty of the land. It was a brilliant gathering; but while the company ate and drank, accompanied by the strains of sweet music, darkness crept over the great apartment. Black clouds raced across the sky, and there was not a star to be seen. While the guests sat rigid with fear a mysterious wind arose. It howled through the Summer Palace and blew out all the lanterns. The complete darkness produced a state of panic, and during the uproar someone cried out, 'A light! A light!'"

"And lo! from out the Jewel Maiden's frame
There's seen to dart a weirdly lustrous flame!
It grows, it spreads, it fills th' imperial halls;
The painted screens, the costly panell'd walls,
Erst the pale viewless damask of the night
Sparkling stand forth as in the moon's full light."

"From that very hour the Mikado sickened," continued the spirit. "He grew so ill that the Court Magician was sent for, and this worthy soul speedily ascertained the cause of his Majesty's decline. He stated, with much warmth of language, that the Jewel Maiden was a harlot and a fiend, 'who, with insidious art, the State to ravage, captivates thy heart!'

"The Magician's words turned the Mikado's heart against the Jewel Maiden. When this sorceress was spurned she resumed her original shape, that of a fox, and ran away to this very stone on Nasu moor."

The priest looked at the spirit critically. "Who are you?" he said at length.

"I am the demon that once dwelt in the breast of the Jewel Maiden! Now I inhabit the Death-Stone for evermore!"

The good Genno was much horrified by this dreadful confession, but, remembering his duty as a priest, he said: "Though you have sunk low in wickedness, you shall rise to virtue again. Take this priestly robe and begging-bowl, and reveal to me your fox form."

Then this wicked spirit cried pitifully:
"In the garish light of day
I hide myself away,
Like pale Asama's fires:
With the night I'll come again,
Confess my guilt with pain
And new-born pure desires."

With these words the spirit suddenly vanished.

Genno did not relinquish his good intentions. He strove more ardently than ever for this erring soul's salvation. In order that she might attain Nirvana, he offered flowers, burnt incense, and recited the sacred Scriptures in front of the stone.

When Genno had performed these religious duties, he said: "Spirit of the Death-Stone, I conjure thee! what was it in a former world that did cause thee to assume in this so foul a shape?"

Suddenly the Death-Stone was rent and the spirit once more appeared, crying:
"In stones there are spirits,
In the waters is a voice heard:
The winds sweep across the firmament!"

Genno saw a lurid glare about him and, in the shining light, a fox that suddenly turned into a beautiful maiden.

Thus spoke the spirit of the Death-Stone: "I am she who first, in Ind, was the demon to whom Prince Hazoku paid homage.... In Great Cathay I took the form of Hōji, consort of the Emperor Iuwao; and at the Court of the Rising Sun I became the Flawless Jewel Maiden, concubine to the Emperor Toba."

The spirit confessed to Genno that in the form of the Jewel Maiden she had desired to bring destruction to the Imperial line. "Already," said the spirit, "I was making my plans, already I was gloating over the thought of the Mikado's death, and had it not been for the power of the Court Magician I should have succeeded in my scheme. As I have told you, I was driven from the Court. I was pursued by dogs and arrows, and finally sank exhausted into the Death-Stone. From time to time I haunted the moor. Now the Lord Buddha has had compassion upon me, and he has sent his priest to point out the way of true religion and to bring peace."

The legend concludes with the following pious utterances poured forth by the now contrite spirit:
"I swear, O man of God! I swear,' she cries,
'To thee whose blessing wafts me to the skies,
I swear a solemn oath, that shall endure
Firm as the Death-Stone standing on the moor,
That from this hour I'm virtue's child alone!'
Thus spake the ghoul, and vanished 'neath the Stone."

How Tokutaro was Deluded by Foxes

Tokutaro was a complete sceptic in regard to the magical power of foxes. His scepticism exasperated a number of his companions, who challenged him to go to Maki moor. If nothing happened to him, Tokutaro was to receive, writes A. B. Mitford (Lord Redesdale) in Tales of Old Japan, *"five measures of wine and a thousand copper cash[3] worth of fish." If, on the other hand, Tokutaro should suffer through the power of the foxes, he was to present a similar gift to his companions. Tokutaro jeeringly accepted the bet, and when night had come he set out for the Maki moor.*

Tokutaro was determined to be very cute and very wary. On reaching his destination he happened to meet a fox running through a bamboo grove. Immediately afterwards he perceived the daughter of the headman of Upper Horikané. On telling the woman that he was going to this village, she explained that as she was going there too they might journey together.

Tokutaro's suspicions were fully aroused. He walked behind the woman, vainly searching for a fox's tail. When they reached Upper Horikané the girl's parents came out, and were much surprised to see their daughter, who had married, and was living in another village.

Tokutaro, with a smile of superior wisdom, explained that the maid before them was not really their daughter, but a fox in disguise. The old people were at first indignant, and refused to believe what Tokutaro had told them. Eventually, however, he persuaded them to leave the girl in his hands while they waited for the result in the store-closet.

Tokutaro then seized the girl, and brutally knocked her down, pouring abuse upon her. He stamped upon her, and tortured her in every possible way, expecting every moment to see the woman turn into a fox. But she only wept and cried piteously for her parents to come to her rescue.

This whole-hearted sceptic, finding his efforts so far fruitless, piled wood upon the floor and burnt her to death. At this juncture her parents came running in and bound Tokutaro to a pillar, fiercely accusing him of murder.

Now a priest happened to pass that way, and, hearing the noise, requested an explanation. When the girl's parents had told him all, and after he had listened to Tokutaro's pleadings, he begged the old couple to spare the man's life in order that he might become in time a good and devout priest. This extraordinary request, after some demur, was agreed to, and Tokutaro knelt down to have his head shaved, happy, no doubt, to be released from his predicament so easily.

No sooner had Tokutaro's wicked head been shaved than he heard a loud peal of laughter, and he awoke to find himself sitting on a large moor. He instinctively raised his hand to his head, to discover that foxes had shaved him and he had lost his bet!

A Fox's Gratitude

After the preceding gruesome legend describing the evil propensities of the fox, it is refreshing to come across one that was capable of considerable self-sacrifice.

Now it happened, on a certain spring day, that two little boys were caught in the act of trying to catch a baby fox. The man who witnessed the performance possessed a kind heart, and, on hearing that the boys were anxious to sell the cub, gave them half a bu.[4] When the children had joyfully departed with the money the man discovered that the little creature was wounded in the foot. He immediately applied a certain herb, and the pain speedily subsided. Perceiving at a short distance a number of old foxes watching him, he generously let the cub go, and it sprang with a bound to its parents and licked them profusely.

Now this kind-hearted man had a son, who was afflicted with a strange disease. A great physician at last prescribed the liver of a live fox as being the only remedy likely to effect a cure. When the boy's parents heard this they were much distressed, and would only consent to accept a fox's liver from one who made it his business to hunt foxes. They finally commissioned a neighbour to obtain the liver, for which they promised to pay liberally.

The following night the fox's liver was brought by a strange man totally unknown to the good people of the house. The visitor professed to be a messenger sent by the neighbour whom they had commissioned. When, however, the neighbour himself arrived he confessed that though he had tried his utmost to obtain a fox's liver he had failed to do so, and had come to make his apologies. He was utterly amazed to hear the story the parents of the suffering boy told him.

The next day the fox's liver was made into a concoction by the great physician, and immediately restored the little boy to his usual health again.

In the evening a beautiful young woman appeared at the bedside of the happy parents. She explained that she was the mother of the cub the master had saved, and that in gratitude for his kindness she had killed her offspring, and that her husband, in the guise of the mysterious messenger, had brought the desired liver.[5]

NOTES

1. The supernatural powers of the fox are found in Chinese legends as well. The fox, like the coyote in Native American myth, has many characteristics of the trickster archetype.

2. "The Death Stone" has been compared to La Fata Morgana—Morgan Le Fey of Arthurian legend. Many Japanese legends concern a fox who takes the form of an elusive and seductive woman.

3. This currency, no longer in use, was equal to about one penny.

4. About 8 dollars.

5. In Japanese folklore, the liver of both animals and humans was believed to be a remedy for various ailments.

DISCUSSION QUESTIONS

1. Explain the purpose and function of the fox's trickster characteristics. What does this reveal about Japanese culture?

2. Research fox stories from other cultures and compare them with the Japanese legends. Point out some key similarities and differences.

3. Research the "kitsune" in Japanese myth and explore ways this character is reflected in popular culture.

Ama-terasu (Japan)

Amaterasu is part of the Shinto pantheon and is one of their most important deities, known formally as Amaterasu-O-Mi-Kami ("August Person who Makes the Heavens Shine"). She was born from the left eye of the male creator god Izanagi; the moon god Tsukiyomi was born from his right eye. Amaterasu's brother, the storm god Susa-no-o (Susano-Wo, "The Impetuous Male"), was born from Izanagi's nose; in some tales it is said that he desired to be with his mother in the underworld instead of ruling over the waters, and this created conflict among the gods. In other versions, he was envious of his siblings' power and was banished. Either way, the wrath of the storm god is a source of unrest.

AMA-TERASU

Ama-terasu, the Sun-Goddess, was seated in the Blue Plain of Heaven. Her light came as a message of joy to the celestial deities. The orchid and the iris, the cherry and the plum blossom, the rice and the hemp fields answered to her smile. The Inland Sea was veiled in soft rich colour.

Susa-no-o, the brother of Ama-terasu, was jealous of his sister's glory and world-wide sway. The Heaven-Illuminating Spirit had but to whisper and she was heard throughout her kingdom, even in the depths of the clear pool and in the heart of the crystal. Her rice-fields, whether situated on hill-side, in sheltered valley, or by running stream, yielded abundant harvests, and her groves were laden with fruit. But the voice of Susa-no-o was not so clear, his smile was not so radiant. The undulating fields which lay around his palace were now flooded, now parched, and his rice crops were often destroyed. His wrath and jealousy knew no bounds, yet Ama-terasu was infinitely patient and forgave him many things.

Once, as was her wont, the Sun-Goddess sat in the central court of her glorious home. She plied her shuttle. Celestial weaving maidens surrounded a fountain whose waters were fragrant with the heavenly lotus-bloom: they sang softly of the clouds and the wind and the lift of the sky. Suddenly, the body of a piebald horse fell through the vast dome at their feet: the "Beloved of the Gods" had been "flayed with a backward flaying" by the envious Susa-no-o. Ama-terasu, trembling at the horrible sight, pricked her finger with the weaving shuttle, and, profoundly indignant at the cruelty of her brother, withdrew into a cave and closed behind her the door of the Heavenly Rock Dwelling.

The universe was plunged in darkness. Joy and goodwill, serenity and peace, hope and love, waned with the waning light. Evil spirits, who heretofore had crouched in dim corners, came forth and roamed abroad. Their grim laughter and discordant tones struck terror into all hearts.

Then it was that the gods, fearful for their safety and for the life of every beautiful thing, assembled in the bed of the tranquil River of Heaven, whose waters had been dried up. One and all knew that Ama-terasu alone could help them. But how to allure the Heaven-Illuminating Spirit to set foot in this world of darkness and strife? Each god was eager to aid, and a plan was finally devised to entice her from her hiding-place.

Ame-no-ko uprooted the holy sakaki trees which grow on the Mountain of Heaven, and planted them around the entrance of the cave. High on the upper branches were hung the precious string of curved jewels which Izanagi had bestowed upon the Sun-Goddess. From the middle branches drooped a mirror wrought of the rare metals of the celestial mine. Its polished surface was as the dazzling brilliancy of the sun. Other gods wove, from threads of hemp and paper mulberry, an imperial robe of white and blue, which was placed, as an offering for the goddess, on the lower branches of the sakaki. A palace was also built, surrounded by a garden in which the Blossom-God called forth many delicate plants and flowers.

Source: Frank Rinder, *Old-World Japan: Legends of the Land of the Gods*, 1895.

Now all was ready. Ame-no-ko stepped forward, and, in a loud voice, entreated Ama-terasu to show herself. His appeal was in vain. The great festival began. Uzume, the goddess of mirth, led the dance and song. Leaves of the spindle tree crowned her head; club-moss, from the heavenly mount Kagu, formed her sash; her flowing sleeves were bound with the creeper-vine; and in her hand she carried leaves of the wild bamboo and waved a wand of sun-grass hung with tiny melodious bells. Uzume blew on a bamboo flute, while the eight hundred myriad deities accompanied her on wooden clappers and instruments formed of bow-strings, across which were rapidly drawn stalks of reed and grass. Great fires were lighted around the cave, and, as these were reflected in the face of the mirror, "the long-singing birds of eternal night" began to crow as if the day dawned. The merriment increased. The dance grew wilder and wilder, and the gods laughed until the heavens shook as if with thunder.

Ama-terasu, in her quiet retreat, heard, unmoved, the crowing of the cocks and the sounds of music and dancing, but when the heavens shook with the laughter of the gods, she peeped from her cave and said: "What means this? I thought heaven and earth were dark, but now there is light. Uzume dances and all the gods laugh." Uzume answered: "It is true that I dance and that the gods laugh, because in our midst is a goddess whose splendour equals your own. Behold!" Ama-terasu gazed into the mirror, and wondered greatly when she saw therein a goddess of exceeding beauty. She stepped from her cave and forthwith a cord of rice-straw was drawn across the entrance. Darkness fled from the Central Land of Reed-Plains, and there was light. Then the eight hundred myriad deities cried: "O, may the Sun-Goddess never leave us again."

DISCUSSION QUESTIONS

1. Compare this myth to others that withhold food or growing or light to their people.

2. Why does the music and dancing convince Ama-terasu to peek out from her hiding?

The Island of Women (Ainu)

The legend of the "vagina dentata," or "fanged vagina," is common myth among cultures the world over. Sigmund Freud first coined the phrase around 1900 in order to describe the male castration anxiety. From South Africa, to New Zealand, to North America, stories of the female anatomy being equipped with teeth have served various purposes. Some stories allege it is a tactic to keep women's virginities, while others view it as a woman's natural defense against unwanted suitors. This Ainu legend is the basis for the very popular festival that takes place each year in Kawasaki, the Kanamara Matsuri. This Festival of the Steel Phallus celebrates a shrine built in memory of this legend.

THE ISLAND OF WOMEN

In ancient days, an Ainu chieftain of Iwanai went to sea in order to catch sea-lions, taking with him his two sons. They speared a sea-lion, which, however, swam off with the spear sticking in its body. Meanwhile a gale began to blow down from the mountains. The men cut the rope which was fast to the spear.

Source: Basil Hall Chamberlain, *Aino Folk-Tales*, 1888.

Then their boat floated on. After some time, they reached a beautiful land. When they had reached it, a number of women in fine garments came down from the mountains to the shore. They came bearing a beautiful woman in a litter. Then all the women who had come to the shore returned to the mountains. Only the one in the litter came close to the boat, and spoke thus: "This land is woman-land. It is a land where no men live. It being now spring, and there being something peculiar to this country of mine, you shall be taken care of in my house until the autumn; and in the winter you shall become our husbands. The following spring I will send you home. So now do you bear me to my house."

Thereupon the Ainu chief and his sons bore the woman in the litter to the mountains. They saw that the country was all like moorland. Then the chieftainess entered the house. There was a room there with a golden netting, like a mosquito-net. The three men were placed inside it. The chieftainess fed them herself. In the daytime numbers of women came in. They sat beside the golden mosquito-net, looking at the men. At nightfall they went home. So gradually it got to be autumn. Then the chieftainess spoke as follows, "As the fall of the leaf has now come, and as there are two vice-chieftainesses besides me, I will send your two sons to them. You yourself shall be husband to me." Then two beautiful women came in, and led off the two sons by the hand, while the chieftainess kept the chief for herself.

So the men dwelt there. When spring came, the chieftain's wife spoke thus to him: "We women of this country differ from yours. At the same time as the grass begins to sprout, teeth sprout in our vaginas. So our husbands cannot stay with us. The east wind is our husband. When the east wind blows, we all turn our buttocks towards it, and thus conceive children. Sometimes we bear male children. But these male children are killed and done away with when they become fit to lie with women. For that reason, this is a land which has women only. It is called woman-land. So when, brought by some bad god, you came to this land of mine, there were teeth in my vagina because it was summer, for which reason I did not marry you. But I married you when the teeth fell out. Now, as the teeth are again sprouting in my vagina because spring has come, it is now impossible for us to sleep together. I will send you home tomorrow. So do tell your sons to come here today in order to be ready."

The sons came. The chieftainess stayed in the house. Then, with tears streaming down her face, she spoke thus: "Though it is dangerous, to-night is our last night. Let us sleep together!" Then the man, being much frightened, took a beautiful scabbard in a bag in his bosom, and lay with the woman with this scabbard. The mark of the teeth remained on the scabbard. The next day dawned. Then the man went to his boat, taking his sons with him. The chieftainess wept and spoke thus: "As a fair wind is blowing away from my country, you, if you set sail and sail straight ahead, will be able to reach your home at Iwanai." So then the men entered their boat, and went out to sea. A fair wind was blowing down from the mountains, and they went along under sail. After a time they saw land; they saw the mountains about Iwanai. Going on for a time, they came to the shore of Iwanai. Their wives were wearing widows' caps. So their husbands embraced them. So the story of woman-land was listened to carefully. All the Ainus saw the beautiful scabbard which the chief had used with that woman.

DISCUSSION QUESTIONS

1. Research a couple of other vagina dentata myths and compare the features of these stories.

2. How does the chieftainess seem to feel about her peculiarity?

3. What do the Ainu men take back home with them? Do they learn something from their experience?

Part 3: Journeys of Heroes and Heroines

Tokoyo and the Sea Serpent (Japan)

This remarkable tale about a young girl's ability to slay a sea serpent and subsequently save her father and the ruler is one of many myths about sea monsters from Japan. From monstrous whales to dragons of the water, the Japanese lore of water monsters is well-stocked. Tokoyo, whose goal is only to save her father from his banishment, sacrifices herself in place of a maiden and manages to kill Yofune-Nushi, the great white serpent.

TOKOYO AND THE SEA SERPENT

Oribe Shima had offended the great ruler Hojo Takatoki, and was in consequence banished to Kamishima, one of the Oki Islands, and forced to leave his beautiful daughter Tokoyo, whom he deeply loved.

At last Tokoyo was unable to bear the separation any longer, and she was determined to find her father. She therefore set out upon a long journey, and arriving at Akasaki, in the province of Hoki, from which coast town the Oki Islands are visible on a fine day, she besought many a fisherman to row her to her destination. But the fisher-folk laughed at Tokoyo, and bade her relinquish her foolish plan and return home. The maiden, however, would not listen to their advice, and at nightfall she got into the lightest vessel she could find, and by dint of a fair wind and persistent rowing the brave girl came to one of the rocky bays of the Oki Islands.

That night Tokoyo slept soundly, and in the morning partook of food. When she had finished her meal she questioned a fisherman as to where she might find her father. "I have never heard of Oribe Shima," replied the fisherman, "and if he has been banished, I beg that you will desist from further search, lest it lead to the death of you both."

That night the sorrowful Tokoyo slept beneath a shrine dedicated to Buddha. Her sleep was soon disturbed by the clapping of hands, and looking up she saw a weeping maiden clad in a white garment with a priest standing beside her. Just as the priest was about to push the maiden over the rocks into the roaring sea, Tokoyo sprang up and held the maiden's arm.

The priest explained that on that night, the thirteenth of June, the Serpent God, known as Yofuné-Nushi, demanded the sacrifice of a young girl, and that unless this annual sacrifice was made the God became angry and caused terrible storms.

"Good sir," said Tokoyo, "I am glad that I have been able to save this poor girl's life. I gladly offer myself in her place, for I am sad of heart because I have been unable to find my father. Give him this letter, for my last words of love and farewell go to him."

Having thus spoken, Tokoyo took the maiden's white robe and clad herself in it, and having prayed to the image of Buddha, she placed a small dagger between her teeth and plunged into the tempestuous sea. Down she went through the moonlit water till she came to a mighty cave where she saw a statue of Hojo Takatoki, who had sent her poor father into exile. She was about to tie the image on her back when a great white serpent crept out from the cave with eyes gleaming angrily. Tokoyo, realising that this creature was none other than Yofuné-Nushi, drew her dagger and thrust it through the right eye of the

Source: F. Hadland Davis, *Myths and Legends of Japan*, 1912.

God. This unexpected attack caused the serpent to retire into the cave, but the brave Tokoyo followed and struck another blow, this time at the creature's heart. For a moment Yofuné-Nushi blindly stumbled forward, then with a shriek of pain fell dead upon the floor of the cavern.

During this adventure the priest and the maiden stood on the rocks watching the spot where Tokoyo had disappeared, praying fervently for the peace of her sorrowful soul. As they watched and prayed they saw Tokoyo come to the surface of the water carrying an image and a mighty fish-like creature. The priest hastily came to the girl's assistance, dragged her upon the shore, placed the image on a high rock, and secured the body of the White Sea Serpent.

In due time the remarkable story was reported to Tameyoshi, lord of the island, who in turn reported the strange adventure to Hojo Takatoki. Now Takatoki had for some time been suffering from a disease which defied the skill of the most learned doctors; but it was observed that he regained his health precisely at the hour when his image, which had been cursed and thrown into the sea by some exile, had been restored. When Hojo Takatoki heard that the brave girl was the daughter of the exiled Oribe Shima, he sent him back with all speed to his own home, where he and his daughter lived in peace and happiness.

DISCUSSION QUESTIONS

1. What drives Tokoyo to save the maiden who is to be sacrificed?

2. Why is Tokoyo able to kill the great white serpent?

The Buddha (India)

The story of the Buddha (which means "awakened" or "enlightened one") has often been compared with that of Jesus. The tale of his life is a blend of fact and legend, myth and mystery. Siddhartha ("one who achieves his aim") Gautama was born into a Hindu family in Nepal around the 6th century BCE. He grows up to question his beliefs and embarks on a spiritual journey, becoming one of the most beloved and influential spiritual teachers in the world.

THE LIFE OF THE BUDDHA

Queen Maya had longed for a child but she and her husband had tried for years without success. Then, one night in spring, "a dream came to Maya as she slept. She saw a young elephant descending from the sky. It had six great tusks; it was as white as the snow on mountain-tops. Maya saw it enter her womb, and thousands of Gods suddenly appeared before her. They praised her with immortal songs, and Maya understood that nevermore would she know disquietude or hatred or anger."

When the time came for the birth, Maya found a rare tree, the branches drooping under their burden of blossoms. She went up to it; gracefully extending her hand, she drew down a branch. Suddenly, she stood very still. She smiled, and the maidens who were near her received a lovely child into their arms.

At that same moment all that was alive in the world trembled with joy. The earth quivered. Songs and the patter of dancing feet echoed in the sky. Trees of all seasons burst into flower, and ripe fruit hung

Source: A. Ferdinand Herold. *The Life of Buddha, Part One.* Translated by Paul C. Blum. 1922.

from the branches. A pure, serene light appeared in the sky. The sick were rid of their suffering. The hungry were satisfied. Those to whom wine had played false became sober. Madmen recovered their reason, the weak their strength, the poor their wealth. Prisons opened their gates. The wicked were cleansed of all evil.

One of Maya's maidens hastened to King Suddhodana and joyously exclaimed:

"My lord, my lord, a son is born to you, a son who will bring great glory to your house!"

When he came near the child, the king made a deep obeisance, and he said:

"Do you bow as I bow before the prince, to whom I give the name Siddhartha."

They all bowed, and the brahmans, inspired by the Gods, then sang:

"All creatures are happy, and they are no longer rough, those roads travelled by men, for he is born, he who gives happiness: he will bring happiness into the world. In the darkness a great light has dawned, the sun and the moon are like dying embers, for he is born, he who gives light: he will bring light into the world. The blind see, the deaf hear, the foolish have recovered their reason, for he is born, he who restores sight, and restores hearing, and restores the mind: he will bring sight, he will bring hearing, he will bring reason into the world. Perfumed zephyrs ease the suffering of mankind, for he is born, he who heals: he will bring health into the world. Flames are no longer pitiless, the flow of rivers has been stayed, the earth has trembled gently: he will be the one to see the truth."

Asita's Prediction

The great hermit Asita, whose austerities were pleasing to the Gods, heard of the birth of him who was to save mankind from the torment of rebirth. In his thirst for the true law, he came to the palace of King Suddhodana and gravely approached the women's quarters. His years and his learning lent him great dignity.

The king showed him the courtesies that custom prescribed and addressed him in a seemly manner:

"Happy, indeed, am I! Truly, this child of mine will enjoy distinguished favor, for the venerable Asita has come purposely to see me. Command me. What must I do? I am your disciple, your servant."

The hermit, his eyes shining with the light of joy, gravely spoke these words:

"This has happened to you, O noble, generous and hospitable king, because you love duty and because you are ever kind to those who are wise and to those who are full of years. This has happened to you because your ancestors, though rich in land and rich in gold, were above all rich in virtue. Know the reason for my coming, O king, and rejoice. In the air I heard a divine voice speaking and it said: 'A son has been born to the king of the Sakyas, a son who will have the true knowledge.' I heard these words, and I came, and my eyes shall now behold the glory of the Sakyas."

Overwhelmed with joy, the king went to fetch the child. Taking him from his nurse's breast, he showed him to the aged Asita.

The hermit noticed that the king's son bore the marks of omnipotence. His gaze hovered over the child, and presently his lashes were wet with tears. Then he sighed and turned his eyes to the sky.

The king saw that Asita was weeping, and he began to fear for his son. He questioned the old man:

"You say, O venerable roan, that my son's body differs little from that of a God. You say that his birth was a wondrous thing, that in the future his glory will be supreme, yet you look at him with eyes that are filled with tears. Is his life, then, to be a fragile thing? Was he born only to bring me sorrow? Must this new branch wither before it has burst into flower? Speak, O saintly man, speak quickly; you know the great love a father bears his son."

"Be not distressed, O king," replied the hermit.

"What I have told you is true: this child will know great glory. If I weep, it is for myself. My life draws to a close and he is born, he who will destroy the evil of rebirth. He will surrender sovereign power, he will master his passions, he will understand truth, and error will disappear in the world before the light of his knowledge, even as night flees before the spears of the sun. From the sea of evil, from the stinging spray of sickness, from the surge and swell of old age, from the angry waves of death, from these will he rescue the suffering world, and together they will sail away in the great ship of knowledge. He will know where it takes its rise, that swift, wonderful, beneficent river, the river of duty; he will reveal its course, and those who are tortured by thirst will come and drink of its waters. To those tormented by sorrow, to those enslaved by the senses, to those wandering in the forest of existences like travellers who have lost their way, he will point out the road to salvation. To those burning with the fire of passion, he will be the cloud that brings refreshing rain; armed with the true law, he will go to the prison of desires where all creatures languish, and he will break down the evil gates. For he who will have perfect understanding will set the world free. Therefore do not grieve, O king. He alone is to be pitied who will not hear the voice of your son, and that is why I weep, I who, in spite of my austerities, in spite of my meditations, will never know his message and his law. Yes, even he is to be pitied who ascends to the loftiest gardens of the sky."

* * *

One day, the young prince went for a walk in the village and stopped to rest in the shade of a tree. When his father sent servants to look for him, they found him in meditation. The servant exclaimed to the king that the shadow of that tree had not moved all day while the prince sat beneath it.

Suddhodana left the palace and followed the servant to where his son was seated. Weeping for joy, he said to himself:

"He is as beautiful as fire on a mountain-top. He dazzles me. He will be the light of the world, and my limbs tremble when I see him thus in meditation."

But the prince awoke from his meditations. He rose and approaching his father, he said to him:

"We must stop working in the fields,* father; we must seek the great truths."

And he returned to Kapilavastu.

Now the king desired for his son to marry, for he did not want his line to end. But the young prince at first resisted. However, after some consideration, he spoke:

"Father," said he, "she whom I shall marry must be a woman of rare merit. If you find one endowed with the natural gifts I shall enumerate, you may give her to me in marriage."

And he said:

"She whom I shall marry will be in the bloom of youth; she whom I shall marry will have the flower of beauty; yet her youth will not make her vain, nor will her beauty make her proud. She whom I shall marry will have a sister's affection, a mother's tenderness, for all living creatures. She will be sweet and truthful, and she will not know envy. Never, not even in her dreams, will she think of any other man but her husband. She will never use haughty language; her manner will be unassuming; she will be as meek as a slave. She will not covet that which belongs to others; she will make no inconsiderate demands, and she will be satisfied with her lot. She will care nothing for wines, and sweets will not tempt her. She will

There is a famous anecdote that Siddhartha saw earthworms being turned up by the workers and birds flying down to eat the worms. This brought him to the profound realization that all things are connected.

be insensible to music and perfume; she will be indifferent to plays and festivals. She will be kind to my attendants and to her maidens. She will be the first to awaken and the last to fall asleep. She whom I shall marry will be pure in body, in speech and in thought."

And he added:

"Father, if you know a maid who possesses these qualities, you may give her to me in marriage."

The king sent his household priest to seek a bride for his son. At last, he found Gopa, daughter of Sakya and Dandapani. The king wished to see for himself if she was worthy. He had jewels made for all the young girls in the village and arranged a day for his son to distribute them. The girls lined up, but they were each intimidated by the prince's beauty and looked away, quickly accepting their jewel.

Gopa was the last one to appear. She advanced fearlessly, without even blinking her eyes. But the prince had not a single jewel left. Gopa smiled and said to him:

"Prince, in what way have I offended you?"

"You have not offended me," replied Siddhartha.

"Then why do you treat me with disdain?"

"I do not treat you with disdain," he replied. "You are the last one, and I have no jewel to give you."

But suddenly he remembered that on his finger he was wearing a ring of great value. He took it off and handed it to the young girl.

She would not take the ring.

She said, "Prince, must I accept this ring from you?"

"It was mine," replied the prince, "and you must accept it."

"No," said she, "I would not deprive you of your jewels. It is for me, rather, to give you a jewel." And she left.

When the king heard of this incident he was elated.

"Gopa, alone, could face my son," he thought; "she alone is worthy of him. Gopa, who would not accept the ring that you took from your finger, Gopa, O my son, will be your fairest jewel."

And he summoned Gopa's father to the palace.

"Friend," said he, "the time has come for my son Siddhartha to marry. I believe your daughter Gopa has found favor in his eyes. Will you marry her to my son?"

After some hesitation, Gopa's father replied:

"My lord, your son has been brought up in luxury; he has never been outside the palace-gates; his physical and intellectual abilities have never been proven. You know that the Sakyas only marry their daughters to men who are skillful and strong, brave and wise. How can I give my daughter to your son who, so far, has shown a taste only for indolence?"

The king was greatly saddened by this, and conveyed the message to his son.

When he had finished, the prince began to laugh.

"My lord," said he, "you are needlessly disturbed. Do you believe there is anyone in Kapilavastu who is my superior in strength or in intellect? Summon all who are famous for their attainments in any field whatsoever; command them to measure their skill with mine, and I shall show you what I can do."

The king recovered his serenity. He had it proclaimed throughout the city:

"That on the seventh day from this day, Prince Siddhartha will compete with all who excel in any field whatsoever."

The prince proved to be superior to all in the arts and sciences, and in athletic skills as well.

Then they brought out the bows, and skillful archers placed their arrows in targets that were barely visible. But when it came the prince's turn to shoot, so great was his natural strength that he broke each bow as he drew it. Finally, the king sent guards to fetch a very ancient, very precious bow that was kept in the temple. No one within the memory of man had ever been able to draw or lift it. Siddhartha took the bow in his left hand, and with one finger of his right hand he drew it to him. Then he took as target a tree so distant that he alone could see it. The arrow pierced the tree, and, burying itself in the ground, disappeared. And there, where the arrow had entered the ground, a well formed, which was called the Well of the Arrow.

Everything seemed to be over, and they led toward the victor a huge white elephant on which, in triumph, he was to ride through Kapilavastu. But a young Sakya, Devadatta, who was very proud of his strength, seized the animal by the trunk and, in fun, struck it with his fist. The elephant fell to the ground.

The prince looked reprovingly at the young man and said:

"You have done an evil thing, Devadatta."

He touched the elephant with his foot, and it stood up and paid him homage.

Then they all acclaimed his glory, and the air rang with their cheers. Suddhodana was happy, and Dandapani, weeping with joy, exclaimed:

"Gopa, my daughter Gopa, be proud to be the wife of such a man."

Prince Siddhartha and the princess enjoyed a life of pleasure and contentment, and the king was pleased.

Then beautiful Gopa bore the prince a son, and he was given the name of Rahula. King Suddhodana was happy to see his family prosper, and he was as proud of the birth of his grandson as he had been of the birth of his son.

He continued in the path of virtue, he lived almost like a hermit, and his actions were saintly; yet he kept urging on his beloved son to new pleasures, so great was his fear to see him leave the palace and the city and seek the austere refuge of the holy forests.

The Three Encounters

One day, someone spoke in the presence of the prince and told how the grass in the woods had become a tender green and the birds in the trees were singing of the spring, and how, in the ponds, the great lotuses were unfolding. Nature had broken the chains that winter had forged, and, around the city, those gardens so dear to young maidens were now gaily carpeted with flowers. Then, like an elephant too long confined in his stable, the prince had an irresistible desire to leave the palace.

The king learned of his son's desire, and he knew no way to oppose it.

"But," he thought, "Siddhartha must see nothing that will trouble the serenity of his soul; he must never suspect the evil there is in the world. I shall order the road cleared of beggars, of those who are sick and infirm and of all who suffer."

The city was decorated with garlands and streamers; a magnificent chariot was prepared, and the cripples, the aged and the beggars were ordered off the streets where the prince would pass.

When the time came, the king sent for his son, and there were tears in his eyes as he kissed him on the brow. His gaze lingered over him, then he said to him, "Go!" And with that word he gave him permission to leave the palace, though his heart spoke differently.

The prince's chariot was made of gold. It was drawn by four horses caparisoned in gold, and the charioteer held gold reins in his hands. Only the rich, the young and the beautiful were allowed on the streets he drove through, and they stopped to watch him as he went by. Some praised him for the kindness of his glance; others extolled his dignified bearing; still others exalted the beauty of his features; while many glorified his exuberant strength. And they all bowed before him, like banners dipped before the statue of some God.

The women in the houses heard the cries in the street. They awoke or left their household tasks and ran to the windows or quickly ascended to the terraces. And gazing at him in admiration, they murmured, "Happy the wife of such a man!"

And he, at the sight of the city's splendor, at the sight of the wealth of the men and the beauty of the women, felt a new joy pour into his soul.

But the Gods were jealous of the celestial felicity enjoyed by this city of the earth. They made an old man, and, in order to trouble Siddhartha's mind, they set him down on the road the prince was travelling.

The man was leaning on a staff; he was worn out and decrepit. His veins stood out on his body, his teeth chattered, and his skin was a maze of black wrinkles. A few dirty grey hairs hung from his scalp; his eyelids had no lashes and were red-rimmed; his head and limbs were palsied.

The prince saw this being, so different from the men around him. He gazed at him with sorrowful eyes, and he asked the charioteer:

"What is this man with grey hair and body so bent? He clings to his staff with scrawny hands, his eyes are dull and his limbs falter. Is he a monster? Has nature made him thus, or is it chance?"

The charioteer should not have answered, but the Gods confused his mind, and without understanding his mistake he said:

"That which mars beauty, which ruins vigor, which causes sorrow and kills pleasure, that which weakens the memory and destroys the senses is old age. It has seized this man and broken him. He, too, was once a child, nursing at his mother's breast; he, too, once crawled upon the floor; he grew, he was young, he had strength and beauty; then he reached the twilight of his years, and now you see him, the ruin that is old age."

The prince was deeply moved. He asked: "Will that be my fate, also?"

The charioteer replied:

"My lord, youth will also leave you some day; to you, too, will come troublesome old age. Time saps our strength and steals our beauty."

The prince shuddered like a bull at the sound of thunder. He uttered a deep sigh and shook his head. His eyes wandered from the wretched man to the happy crowds, and he spoke these solemn words:

"So old age destroys memory and beauty and strength in man, and yet the world is not frantic with terror! Turn your horses around, O charioteer; let us return to our homes. How can I delight in gardens and flowers when my eyes can only see old age, when my mind can only think of old age?"

The prince returned to his palace, but nowhere could he find peace. He wandered through the halls, murmuring, "Old age, oh, old age!" and in his heart there was no longer any joy.

He decided, nevertheless, to ride once more through the city.

But the Gods made a man afflicted with a loathsome disease, and they set him down on the road Siddhartha had taken.

Siddhartha saw the sick man; he stared at him, and he asked the charioteer:

"What is this man with a swollen paunch? His emaciated arms hang limp, he is deathly pale and pitiful cries escape from his lips. He gasps for breath; see, he staggers and jostles the bystanders; he is falling. . . . Charioteer, charioteer, what is this man?"

The charioteer answered:

"My lord, this man knows the torment of sickness, for he has the king's evil. He is weakness itself; yet he, too, was once healthy and strong!"

The prince looked at the man with pity, and he asked again:

"Is this affliction peculiar to this man, or are all creatures threatened with sickness?"

The charioteer answered:

"We, too, may be visited with a similar affliction, O prince. Sickness weighs heavily upon the world."

When he heard this painful truth, the prince began to tremble like a moonbeam reflected in the waves of the sea, and he uttered these words of bitterness and pity:

"Men see suffering and sickness, yet they never lose their self-confidence! Oh, how great must be their knowledge! They are constantly threatened with sickness, and they can still laugh and be merry! Turn your horses around, charioteer; our pleasure trip is ended; let us return to the palace. I have learned to fear sickness. My soul shuns pleasure and seems to close up like a flower deprived of light."

Wrapped in his painful thoughts, he returned to the palace.

King Suddhodana noticed his son's sombre mood. He asked why the prince no longer went out driving, and the charioteer told him what had happened. The king grieved; he already saw himself forsaken by the child he adored. He lost his usual composure and flew into a rage at the man whose duty it was to see that the streets were clear; he punished him, but so strong was his habit of being indulgent that the punishment was light. And the man was astonished at being thus upbraided, for he had seen neither the old man nor the sick man.

The king was more anxious now than ever before to keep his son from leaving the palace. He provided him with rare pleasures, but nothing, it seemed, could arouse Siddhartha. And the king thought, "I shall let him go out once more! Perhaps he will recover the joy he has lost."

He gave strict orders to have all cripples and all who were ill or aged driven out of the city. He even changed the prince's charioteer, and he felt certain that this time there would be nothing to trouble Siddhartha's soul.

But the jealous Gods made a corpse. Four men carried it, and others followed behind, weeping. And the corpse, as well as the men who carried it and the men who were weeping, was visible only to the prince and to the charioteer.

And the king's son asked:

"What is he that is being carried by four men, followed by those others, wearing dark clothes and weeping?"

The charioteer should have held his peace, but it was the will of the Gods that he reply:

"My lord, he has neither intelligence nor feeling nor breath; he sleeps, without consciousness, like grass or a piece of wood; pleasure and suffering are meaningless to him now, and friend and enemy alike have deserted him."

The prince was troubled. He said, "Is this a condition peculiar to this man, or does this same end await all creatures?"

And the charioteer answered: "This same end awaits all creatures. Whether of humble or of noble birth, to every being who lives in this world, death comes inevitably."

Then Prince Siddhartha knew what death was.

In spite of his fortitude, he shuddered. He had to lean against the chariot, and his words were full of distress:

"So to this does destiny lead all creatures! And yet, without fear in his heart, man amuses himself in a thousand different ways! Death is about, and he takes to the world's highroads with a song on his lips! Oh, I begin to think that man's soul has become hardened! Turn your horses around, charioteer; this is no time to wander through the flower-gardens. How can a sensible man, a man who knows what death is, seek pleasure in the hour of anguish?"

But the charioteer kept on driving toward the garden where the king had ordered him to take his son. There, at Suddhodana's command, Udayin, who was a son of the household priest and Siddhartha's friend since childhood, had assembled many beautiful maidens, skilled in the art of dancing and of song, and skillful also in the game of love.

But the prince was not tempted by the women.

"What good are lies, what good is flattery?" replied the prince. "I would not deceive these women. Old age and death lie in wait for me. Do not try to tempt me, Udayin; do not ask me to join in any vulgar amusement. I have seen old age, I have seen sickness, I am certain of death; nothing now can give me peace of mind. And you would have me yield to love? Of what metal is that man made who knows of death and still seeks love? A cruel, implacable guard stands at his door, and he does not even weep!"

Siddhartha returned to the palace. He was restless and could not find peace. He pondered:

"It is indeed a pity that man, weak as he really is, and subject to sickness, with old age a certainty and death for a master, should, in his ignorance and pride, contemn the sick, the aged and the dead. If I should look with disgust upon some fellow-being who was sick or old or dead, I would be unjust, I would not be worthy of understanding the supreme law."

And as he pondered the misery of mankind, he lost the vain illusion of strength, of youth and of life. He knew no longer joy or grief, doubt or weariness, desire or love, hatred or scorn.

Suddenly, he saw a man approaching who looked like a beggar and who was visible to him alone.

"Tell me, who are you?" the prince asked him.

"Hero," said the monk, "through fear of birth and death, I became an itinerant monk. I seek deliverance. The world is at the mercy of destruction. I think not as other men; I shun pleasures; I know nothing of passion; I look for solitude. Sometimes I live at the foot of a tree; sometimes I live in the lonely mountains or sometimes in the forest. I own nothing; I expect nothing. I wander about, living on charity, and seeking only the highest good."

He spoke. Then he ascended into the sky and disappeared. A God had taken the form of a monk in order to arouse the prince.

Siddhartha was happy. He saw where his duty lay; he decided to leave the palace and become a monk.

He returned to the city. Near the gates he passed a young woman who bowed and said to him, "She who is your bride must know supreme blessedness, O noble prince." He heard her voice, and his soul was filled with peace: the thought had come to him of supreme blessedness, of beatitude, of nirvana.

He went to the king; he bowed and said to him:

"King, grant the request I have to make. Do not oppose it, for I am determined. I would leave the palace, I would walk in the path of deliverance. We must part, father."

The king begged his son to reconsider, but the prince would not be deterred from his goal.

Leaving his father, his son and his people, Siddhartha went forth from the city. He felt no regret, and in a steady voice, he cried:

"Until I shall have seen the end of life and of death, I shall not return to the city of Kapila."

Siddhartha lived as a hermit. He traded his fine robes to a hunter and donned plain garments. His family grieved his absence, yet the king admired his son's greatness. The horse who carried the prince away returned to the stables and died. The prince found a place to dwell near the mountains and was eventually joined by five disciples.

For six years, the hero remained on the banks of the river and meditated. He never sought shelter from the wind, from the sun or from the rain; he allowed the gadflies, the mosquitoes and the serpents to sting him. He was oblivious to the boys and girls, the shepherds and woodcutters, who jeered at him as they passed by and who sometimes threw dust or mud at him. He hardly ate: a fruit and a few grains of rice or of sesame composed his fare. He became very thin; his bones showed prominently. But under his gaunt forehead, his dilated eyes shone like stars.

And yet true knowledge did not come to him. He felt he was becoming very weak, and he realized that if he wasted away, he would never reach the goal he had set for himself. So he decided to take more nourishment.

There was a village called Uruvilva near the spot where Siddhartha spent long hours in meditation. The head man of this village had ten daughters. They revered the hero, and they brought him grain and fruit by way of alms. He rarely touched these gifts, but, one day, the girls noticed that he had eaten all they had offered him. The next day, they came with a large dish full of boiled rice, and he emptied that. The following day, each one brought a different delicacy, and the hero ate them all. He began to gain flesh, and, presently, he started going to the village to beg his food. The inhabitants vied with one another in giving him alms, and, before long, he had regained his strength and his beauty.

But the five disciples who had joined him said to each other:

"His austerities did not lead him into the path of true knowledge, and now he has ceased to practice them. He takes abundant nourishment; he seeks comfort. He no longer thinks of doing holy deeds. How can he, now, attain true knowledge? We considered him a wise man, but we were mistaken: he is a madman and a fool."

And they left him and went to Benares.

Siddhartha Under the Tree of Knowledge

The hero's clothes had become threadbare in the six years he had been wearing them, and he thought: "It would be well if I had some new clothes; otherwise I shall have to go naked, and that would be immodest."

Now, Sujata, the most devout of the ten young girls who had been bringing him food, had a slave who had just died. She had wrapped the body in a shroud made of a reddish material and had had it carried to the cemetery. The dead slave was lying in the dust. The hero saw the body as he passed; he went over to it and removed the shroud.

It was very dusty, and the hero had no water in which to wash it. Sakra, from the sky, saw his perplexity. Coming down to earth he struck the ground, and a pool appeared before the eyes of the Saint.

"Good," said he, "here is water, but I still need a wash-stone."

Sakra made a stone and set it down on the edge of the pool.

"Man of virtue," said the God, "give me the shroud; I shall wash it for you."

"No, no," replied the Saint. "I know the duties of a monk; I myself shall wash the shroud."

When it was clean, he bathed. Now, Mara, the Evil One, had been watching for him for some time. He suddenly raised the banks of the pool, making them very steep. The Saint was unable to climb out of the water. Fortunately, there was a tall tree growing near the pool, and the Saint addressed a prayer to the Goddess who lived in it.

"O Goddess, may a branch of this tree bend over me!"

A branch immediately bent over the pool. The Saint caught hold of it and pulled himself out of the water. Then he went and sat down under the tree, and he began to sew on the shroud and make a new garment for himself.

Night came on. He fell asleep, and he had five dreams.

First, he saw himself lying in a large bed that was the whole earth; under his head, there was a cushion which was the Himalaya; his right hand rested on the western sea, his left hand on the eastern sea, and his feet touched the southern sea.

Then he saw a reed coming out of his navel, and the reed grew so fast that it soon reached the sky.

Then he saw worms crawling up his legs and completely covering them.

Then he saw birds flying toward him from all points of the horizon, and when the birds were near his head, they seemed to be of gold.

Finally, he saw himself at the foot of a mountain of filth and excrement; he climbed the mountain; he reached the summit; he descended, and neither the filth nor the excrement had defiled him.

He awoke, and from these dreams he knew that the day had come when, having attained supreme knowledge, he would become a Buddha.

He rose and set out for the village of Uruvilva, to beg.

Sujata had just finished milking eight wonderful cows that she owned. The milk they gave was rich, oily and of a delicate savor. She added honey and rice flour to it, then set the mixture to boil in a new pot, on a new stove. Huge bubbles began to form and kept floating off to the right, without the liquid rising or spilling a single drop. The stove did not even smoke. Sujata was astonished, and she said to Purna, her servant:

"Puma, the Gods are favoring us to-day. Go and see if the holy man is approaching the house."

Purna, from the doorstep, saw the hero walking toward Sujata's house. He was diffusing a brilliant light, a golden light. Puma was dazzled. She ran back to her mistress.

"Mistress, he is coming! He is coming! And your eyes will be blinded by his splendor!"

"Let him come! Oh, let him come!" cried Sujata. "It is for him that I have prepared this wonderful milk."

She poured the milk mixed with honey and flour into a golden bowl, and she awaited the hero.

He entered. The house was lighted up by his presence. Sujata, to do him honor, bowed seven times. He sat down. Sujata kneeled and bathed his feet in sweet-scented water; then she offered him the golden bowl full of milk mixed with rice flour and honey. He thought:

"The Buddhas of old, it is said, had their last meal served to them in a golden bowl, before attaining supreme knowledge. Since Sujata offers me this milk and honey in a golden bowl, the time has come for me to be a Buddha."

Then he asked the young girl:

"Sister, what must I do with this golden bowl?"

"It belongs to you," she replied.

"I have no use for such a bowl," said he.

"Then do as you please with it," said Sujata. "It would be contemptible of me to offer the food and not offer the bowl."

He left, carrying the bowl in his hands, and he walked to the banks of the river. He bathed; he ate. When the bowl was empty, he threw it into the water, and he said:

"If I am to become Buddha this very day, may the bowl go upstream; if not, may it go with the current."

The bowl floated out to the middle of the river, then rapidly started upstream. It disappeared in a whirlpool, and the hero heard the muffled ring as it landed, in the subterranean world, among those other bowls the former Buddhas had emptied and thrown away.

The hero sauntered along the banks of the river. Night slowly descended. The flowers wearily closed their petals; a sweet fragrance rose from the fields and gardens; the birds timidly rehearsed their evensongs.

It was then the hero walked toward the tree of knowledge.

The road was sprinkled with gold-dust; rare palms, covered with precious stones, lined the way. He skirted the edge of a pool whose blessed waters exhaled an intoxicating perfume. White, yellow, blue and red lotuses spread their massive petals over the surface, and the air rang with the clear songs of the swans. Near the pool, under the palms, Apsarases were dancing, while in the sky the Gods were admiring the hero.

He approached the tree. On the side of the road, he saw Svastika, the reaper.

"They are tender, these grasses you are mowing, Svastika. Give me some grass; I want to cover the seat I shall occupy when I attain supreme knowledge. They are green, these grasses you are mowing, Svastika. Give me some grass, and you will know the law some day, for I shall teach it to you, and you may teach it to others."

The reaper gave the Saint eight handfuls of grass.

There stood the tree of knowledge. The hero went to the east of it and bowed seven times. He threw the handfuls of grass on the ground, and, suddenly, a great seat appeared. The soft grass covered it like a carpet.

The hero sat down, his head and shoulders erect, his face turned to the east. Then he said in a solemn voice:

"Even if my skin should parch, even if my hand should wither, even if my bones should crumble into dust, until I have attained supreme knowledge I shall not move from this seat."

And he crossed his legs.

Mara's Defeat

The light emanating from the hero's body reached even to those realms where Mara, the Evil One, reigned supreme. It dazzled Mara, and he seemed to hear a voice saying:

"The hero who has renounced royalty, the son of Suddhodana, is now seated under the tree of knowledge. He is concentrating his mind, he is making the supreme effort, and soon he will bring to all creatures the help which they need. The road he will have taken, others will take. Once set free, he will set others free. Once he has found peace, he will bring peace to others. He will enter nirvana, and he will cause others to enter. He will find wisdom and happiness, and he will give them to others. Because of him, the city of the Gods will be crowded; because of him, the city of the Evil One will be deserted. And you, Mara, a commander without an army, a king without subjects, will not know where to take refuge."

Mara was filled with apprehension. He tried to sleep, but his slumber was disturbed by terrible dreams. He awoke and summoned his servants and his soldiers. When they saw him, they became alarmed, and Sarthavaha, one of his sons, said to him:

"Father, you look pale and unhappy; your heart beats fast and your limbs tremble. What have you heard? What have you seen? Speak."

"Son," replied Mara, "the days of my pride are over. I heard a voice crying in the light, and it told me that the son of the Sakyas was seated under the tree of knowledge. And I had horrible dreams. A black cloud of dust settled over my palace. My gardens were bare of leaves, of flowers and of fruit. My ponds had dried up, and my swans and peacocks had their wings clipped. And I felt alone, amid this desolation. You had all deserted me. My queen was beating her breast and tearing her hair, as though haunted by remorse. My daughters were crying out in their anguish, and you, my son, were bowing before this man who meditated under the tree of knowledge! I wanted to fight my enemy, but I could not draw my sword from the scabbard. All my subjects fled in horror. Impenetrable darkness closed in upon me, and I heard my palace crashing to the ground."

Sarthavaha said:

"Father, it is disheartening to lose a battle. If you have seen these omens, bide your time, and do not run the chance of being ingloriously defeated."

But Mara, at the sight of the legions that surrounded him, felt his courage return. He said to his son:

"To the man of energy, a battle can end only in victory. We are brave; we will surely win. What strength can this man have? He is alone. I shall advance against him with a vast army, and I shall strike him down at the foot of the tree."

"Mere numbers do not make the strength of an army," said Sarthavaha, "The sun can outshine a myriad of glowworms. If wisdom is the source of his power, a single hero can defeat countless soldiers."

But Mara paid no heed. He ordered the army to advance at once, and Sarthavaha thought:

"He who is insane with pride will never recover."

Mara's army was a fearful sight. It bristled with pikes, with arrows and with swords; many carried enormous battle-axes and heavy clubs. The soldiers were black, blue, yellow, red, and their faces were terrifying. Their eyes were cruel flames; their mouths spewed blood. Some had the ears of a goat, others the ears of a pig or of an elephant. Many had bodies shaped like a jug. One had the paws of a tiger, the hump of a camel and the head of a donkey; another had a lion's mane, a rhinoceros' horn and a monkey's tail. There were many with two, four and five heads, and others with ten, twelve and twenty arms. In place of ornaments, they wore jawbones, skulls and withered human fingers. And shaking their hairy heads, they advanced with hideous laughter and savage cries:

"I can shoot a hundred arrows at one time; I shall seize the body of the monk." "My hand can crumple up the sun, the moon and the stars; how easy it will be to crush this man and his tree." "My eyes are full of poison: they would dry up the sea; I shall look at him, and he will burn to a cinder."

Sarthavaha kept to himself. A few friends had gathered around him, and they were saying:

"Fools! You think he is mad because he meditates; you think he is craven because he is calm. It is you who are madmen, it is you who are cowards. You do not know his power; because of his great wisdom he will defeat you all. Were your numbers as infinite as the grains of sand on the banks of the Ganges, you would not disturb a single hair of his head. And you believe you can kill him! Oh, turn back! Do not try to harm him; bow before him in reverence. His reign has come. The jackals howl in the forests when the lion is away, but when the lion roars, the jackals scamper off in terror. Fools, fools! You shout with pride while the master is silent, but when the lion speaks you will take to your heels."

The army listened with contempt to these words of wisdom spoken by Sarthavaha and his friends. It kept advancing.

Before attacking the hero, Mara sought to frighten him. He roused against him the fury of the winds. Fierce gales rushed toward him from the horizon, uprooting trees, devastating villages, shaking mountains, but the hero never moved; not a single fold of his robe was disturbed.

The Evil One summoned the rains. They fell with great violence, submerging cities and scarring the surface of the earth, but the hero never moved; not a single thread of his robe was wet.

The Evil One made blazing rocks and hurled them at the hero. They sped through the air but changed when they came near the tree, and fell, not as rocks, but flowers.

Mara then commanded his army to loose their arrows at his enemy, but the arrows, also, turned into flowers. The army rushed at the hero, but the light he diffused acted as a shield to protect him; swords were shivered, battle-axes were dented by it, and whenever a weapon fell to the ground, it, too, at once changed into a flower.

And, suddenly, filled with terror at the sight of these prodigies, the soldiers of the Evil One fled.

And Mara wrung his hands in anguish, and he cried:

"What have I done that this man should defeat me? For they are not a few, those whose desires I have granted! I have often been kind and generous! Those cowards who are fleeing could bear witness to that."

The troops that were still within hearing answered:

"Yes, you have been kind and generous. We will bear witness to that."

"And he, what proof has he given of his generosity?" continued Mara. "What sacrifices has he made? Who will bear witness to his kindness?"

Whereupon a voice came out of the earth, and it said:

"I will bear witness to his generosity."

Mara was struck dumb with astonishment. The voice continued:

"Yes, I, the Earth, I, the mother of all beings, will bear witness to his generosity. A hundred times, a thousand times, in the course of his previous existences, his hands, his eyes, his head, his whole body have been at the service of others. And in the course of this existence, which will be the last, he will destroy old age, sickness and death. As he excels you in strength, Mara, even so does he surpass you in generosity."

And the Evil One saw a woman of great beauty emerge from the earth, up to her waist. She bowed before the hero, and clasping her hands, she said: "O most holy of men, I bear witness to your generosity."

Then she disappeared.

And Mara, the Evil One, wept because he had been defeated.

Siddhartha Becomes the Buddha

By sunset the army of the Evil One had fled. Nothing had disturbed the hero's meditation, and, in the first watch of the night, he arrived at the knowledge of all that had transpired in previous existences. In the second watch, he learned the present state of all beings. In the third, he understood the chain of causes and effects.

He now clearly saw all creatures being continually reborn, and, whether of high or of low caste, in the path of virtue or of evil, he saw them going through the round of existences, at the mercy of their actions. And the hero thought:

"How miserable is this world that is born, grows old and dies, then is reborn only to grow old and die again! And man knows no way out!"

And in profound meditation, he said to himself:

"What is the cause of old age and death? There is old age and death because there is birth. Old age and death are due to birth. What is the cause of birth? There is birth because there is existence. Birth is due to existence. What is the cause of existence? There is existence because there are ties. Existence is due to ties. What is the cause of ties? There are ties because there is desire. Ties are due to desire. What is the cause of desire? There is desire because there is sensation. Desire is due to sensation. What is the cause of sensation? There is sensation because there is contact. Sensation is due to contact. What is the cause of contact? There is contact because there are six senses. Contact is due to the six senses. What is the cause of the six senses? There are six senses because there is name and form. The six senses are due to name and form. What is the cause of name and form? There is name and form because there is perception. Name and form are due to perception. What is the cause of perception? There is perception because there is impression. Perception is due to impression. What is the cause of impression? There is impression because there is ignorance. Impression is due to ignorance."

And he thought:

"Thus does ignorance lie at the root of death, of old age, of suffering, of despair. To suppress ignorance is to suppress impression. To suppress impression is to suppress perception. To suppress perception is to suppress name and form. To suppress name and form is to suppress the six senses. To suppress the six senses is to suppress contact. To suppress contact is to suppress sensation. To suppress sensation is to suppress desire. To suppress desire is to suppress ties. To suppress ties is to suppress existence. To suppress existence is to suppress birth. To suppress birth is to suppress old age and death. To exist is to suffer. Desire leads from birth to rebirth, from suffering to further suffering. By stifling desire, we prevent birth, we prevent suffering. By leading a life of holiness, desire is stifled, and we cease to endure birth and suffering."

When dawn appeared, this most noble of men was a Buddha. He exclaimed:

"I have had numerous births. In vain have I sought the builder of the house. Oh, the torment of perpetual rebirth! But I have seen you at last, O builder of the house. You no longer build the house. The rafters are broken; the old walls are down. The ancient mountain crumbles; the mind attains to nirvana; birth is no more for desire is no more."

Twelve times the earth shook; the world was like a great flower. The Gods sang:

"He has come, he who brings light into the world; he has come, he who protects the world! Long blinded, the eye of the world has opened, and the eye of the world is dazzled by the light.

O conqueror, you will give all beings that which they hunger after. Guided by the sublime light of the law, all creatures will reach the shores of deliverance. You hold the lamp; go now and dispel the darkness!"

The Buddha traveled for the rest of his life, teaching the Four Noble Truths and the Eightfold Path - the foundations of Buddhism.

DISCUSSION QUESTIONS

1. How does this story fit Campbell's monomyth? In what ways can the Buddha be considered an archetypal hero?

2. Research Siddhartha and discover how much of this story is based in fact. In what ways does a blend of fact and fiction affect the impact of the story?

Kotan Utannai (Ainu)

Written from the first person perspective, the narrator of the Kotan Utannai goes unnamed, except for his description as "the brave Yaunguru" (Ainu warrior). In the Ainu tradition, stories of heroes are called "Yukar" and many versions of this story of the orphan boy hero exist. The Yukar are recited by a narrator by a fire, telling these adventurous stories all night long.

Kotan Utannai is of particular interest for its depiction of the narrator occupying a liminal state between god and man, as well as its portrayal of fierce female warriors.

In this story, the orphaned narrator is told the story of his parents by the woman who has adopted him. A "kotan" is a community, usually situated near a river, in which a small number of Ainu lived together. Because Utannai is the kotan that the narrator is raised in, the story takes its name from his point of origin. As he sets off for vengeance, he discovers that he, like his parents, is a Yaunguru and fights to retrieve his brother, the Curly-head, from the enemy Shipish.

The sister of the Shipish man is a prophetess. The author of this translation writes much about the practice of prophecy among the Ainu:

> their chief duty now is to tell the causes of illness, to prescribe medicines, to charm away sickness, and to make known the ultimate result, i.e. to tell whether a person will die or get well again. When a person prophesies he or she is supposed to sleep or otherwise lose consciousness, the spirit of prophecy or divination is thought to enter into the heart of the prophet, so that the subject merely becomes a tool or mouth-piece of the gods. The prophet is not even supposed to know what he himself says, and often the listeners do not understand what his words portend [. . .] This spirit of prophecy is quite believed in by the people, and the prophet or prophetess is often resorted to. But curiously enough, no person can prophesy just when he or she pleases; he must wait till the spirit seizes him.

KOTAN UTANNAI

I was brought up by my elder sister and was always kept at home. I was reared in a small house one made of grass. While being brought up, I heard a noise of war as if the gods were fighting on every side of us. There was the sound as of a very great number of gods being slain. When I grew to be a good size, the very distant sound of the gods of the Ainu warriors, the Yaunguru, reached the top of our grass house. Upon hearing this, my guardian god sent forth a warning cry from the top of our roof. I begged, "Oh my elder sister you have indeed brought me up well, please tell me what this noise means."

Thereupon she began trembling and weeping very much, said, "Oh that you were a little bigger. Then, if, because I answered your question, you were to kill me, it would not matter; for it would be better for me to die. Now, if I tell you what you desire to hear, do not get angry, for that would be dangerous, so keep your temper. What I have to tell you is this: Some time ago, when there had been a war in the land, your father withdrew and governed the country around the mountains of Yezo. One day your mother took your brother, the Curly-head on her back and went with your father to pay her respects to the governor. On drawing near to the northern island of Saghalien the people came down to the seashore, carrying sacred objects in their hands, and beckoned them to land. They sat down and did nothing but drink wine both day and night. Your father got drunk, and in his debauchery said, 'I am able to buy up all the people and treasure of Saghalien.'

"The people took this as a provocation to war, which thence arose has spread over the whole land. Now the name of my land is Chiwashpet and the people are all exceedingly brave. Your father was killed by them in battle and after his death your mother took his arms and helmet, and putting them down her back under her clothes, tied on her girdle; and then, taking her sword, she went all over the land to war. There was nothing but fighting during the whole of your mother's life, and she was killed in battle. And so the Curly-head was left entirely alone and from that time to this has been engaged in war. While things were in this state, I ran away with you and brought you here, where neither gods nor men approach. It is on account of this seclusion that our place is called *Kotan utunnai Moshiri utunnai*; and here you have been brought up. It is against the Curly-head alone that the demon gods have been warring all this time. I have told you this because you asked me, so please do not be angry."

Upon hearing this I had a vehement desire to kill her. She was of the people who had slain my parents. However, I managed with great perseverance to restrain myself, and said, "Ah my elder sister, you have indeed reared me well, please show me my father's arms." She fetched an ancient treasure bag, quickly

Source: John Batchelor, *Specimens of Ainu Folk-lore*, 1889.

untied the strings of the bag, and from the inside took a beautiful sword and six splendid garments. There were the belt and the helmet with all their belongings complete. She handed them to me, and I took them with pleasure. I then put my clothes to the side and dressed myself in the six beautiful garments; I wound the belt round my body, stuck the trusty sword into my girdle, and tied on the beautiful helmet.

Then I attempted to stand up at the head of the hearth, but could not well do it, so I exercised my arms and shoulders, as warriors do; and then walked back and forth around the fireplace, still stretching myself. After I had done this I shot out through the upper window of our grass hut, and my guardian god sent forth a cry from its top.

After this I was carried along before a mighty wind, while my elder sister, weeping, said, "My little lad, do not lose your temper and do outrageous things in this war. You must first be taken to your home land of Shinutapka, and after that you may war against every land in the whole world." And so I was driven by the wind, till all at once a beautiful country arose to my view. I was set upon its shores and saw a mountain close by, the top of which went up into the clouds. A most beautiful little river came running down the mountain slopes, in such a manner that it appeared to be suspended in the air. Near the center part of the river, there was a place which looked as though the gods lived in it; for there was a black cloud of fog hanging over it like a covering; lower down the river I saw another cloud, but red, hanging suspended in like manner, and further down still another, but of a yellow color.

My elder sister knowingly said, "This is not the dwelling-place of common gods, but of the chief of the demons of all sickness. Let us now turn away from here and go to some other country. Do not show any disrespect to these demons." I turned a deaf ear to her words and went into the black cloud. Here I saw six large rapids, with clouds of black fog hanging over them. I proceeded to go near them, but on drawing near to the black rapids, I was suddenly set upon by someone who had a sword. My sister was also attacked, but I felt the passage of the ineffective blow upon my body as the sword went by; the blow was harmless.

I immediately went on into the red fog, and there I saw six red rapids. That which I met before was as a baby to this. I was set upon with ferocity, yet, notwithstanding this, I made no attempt to avoid the attack. But the blow was an empty one and took no effect upon my body. Next to these I came to six yellow clouds of fog hanging over six yellow rapids. On going to them I was again fiercely attacked by someone above them, but I stood my ground without flinching, and the ineffective blows struck harmlessly upon my body.

When past these rapids, there opened out to my view a stony path coming down from the mountain top. Coming down the path, I saw six banks of fog. The very first was a person clothed entirely in black garments; the next one was dressed in red, and the following person had yellow clothes on. After these there came three women.

The first person came to me, and said, "Look here, my younger Ainu brother, I have something to say to you, so pay attention. I am not a person whose business it is to make war, but am the god of all sickness and dwell here in this my town. Now there has been nothing but war during the whole lifetime of your brother the Curly-head; for that I have pitied you, and because I felt thus for you, I have kept you free from all evil, and throughout this long war have preserved you from every harm. The world is a broad one, and yet you have deigned to come to my poor dwelling. It was out of respect to you that we pretended to strike you with our swords from above the black, red, and yellow rapids. If you had been a mere man you would have turned away, but you came straight on; however, please turn back at once. As I have kept you perfectly safe and sound throughout all of these years of war, please now return."

When he had finished speaking, I set upon the three lords fiercely with my sword. But as they were gods, they quickly turned themselves into air and escaped above the reach of the sword. Then the three women attacked my elder sister. As I was striking at my three foes, they all at once drew their swords and set upon me, and I again returned their attack. I also changed my bodily human form, so as to render myself invisible to them. I next jumped upon the sword of one of my enemies, and danced upon it as though it were a bridge; at the same time I made a clutch at another with my left hand. I seized each man in turn by the hair of his head and banged him hard upon the rocks; then I used their bodies as shields as I fought them in turn. Their living souls departed with a sound and ascended to the top of their mountain. Their wives, too, were slain and their souls joined them.

My sister came down to my side, and she was without a single scratch. We continued in our journey and came upon some beautiful hills of pine trees. Without doubt this was the place called The Metal Forest because the noise the trees made as the wind blew through them was like the tinkling of metal. As we went along I suddenly perceived a smell of fire. I was much surprised at this, so I shot down through the trees to see what it was. On looking round I saw a brightly burning fire. On one side of the fire I saw six men clothed in stone suits of armor, together with six ugly women sitting by the side of the men. On the other side of the fire there sat, cross-legged, six lords clothed in metal armor, with six women by their side. At the head of the fire there sat a man who looked like a mountain with arms and legs. His skin was of a mangy kind; he had a sword which looked like a boat-scull, strapped to his side with leather thongs. His face resembled a mountain from which the land had slipped and which had been left bare; and his nose was like a protruding mountain range. I did not know for certain, but I thought this creature must be the person who was called *"Eturachichi"* or *"Hanging Nose."* Without doubt he was a very evil man who thus sat at the head of the fire. While looking at these people, I heard a curious noise, and the earth was gently waved to and fro, while the metal tings of the pine trees sent forth a jingling sound. I looked into the trees and I beheld a man tied to the top of one of the large pines. There he swung with his face turned up towards the sky; and out of his countenance issued flashes of lightning. Though I did not know it, he was none other than my elder brother, the Curly-head. His writhing had caused the earth to tremble.

Now the six lords who sat by the side of the fire in their metal armor, with one voice, said, "We are the inhabitants of The Metal River and The Stoney River and these women are our sisters. As we came into these mountains today, we found this cowardly Curly-head returning to his own land from war. It would have been well if we had killed him when we first met him. But we thought we should take the beautiful body of the Curly-head and give it to the people of Shipish, for that will please them. You, whether you are a god or a man we know not, may help us if you like."

During this speech, my elder sister sped up to the top of the pine tree and cut the cords with which the Curly-head was tied. This made all the demoniacal men turn round with one accord. Now I changed my bodily form, so as not to be seen, and became air, and then fiercely attacked the fiendish people who were sitting by the fire. With one stroke I cut down three men and three women, and with another blow I slew three of the men who were clothed in stone armor, whilst with a back stroke I set upon Hanging Nose, but that great fellow became air and escaped round my sword. He was greatly astonished and said, "It is not worth my while to fight and kill you with a sword, so come here, and I will carry you off to the precipitous country of the Shipish people, that they may cast you down their precipice."

We arose above the mountain tops and commenced to fight. My elder sister came down to my side and said, "I took the body of your elder brother, the Curly-head, and carried him to your home land of Shinutapka. On arriving there, I was met at the fortress by the brother and sister who reared him, and when they had embraced him, took him home, where we restored him to life and strength; and now I have returned to you." She had hardly finished speaking before she was attacked by the six women. Dear me how bravely those women fought! My elder sister was in great straits, for the six women set upon her with one accord, so that they went hither and thither all over the mountains fighting.

The six men, together with Hanging Nose, all set upon me fiercely, so that I was several times very nearly killed. I changed my bodily human form so that they should not see me, and so, having become air, I escaped above their swords. A beautiful little water-way came into view. Along the river there were some exceedingly steep gullies and precipices. At the bottom of these gullies, there were many stone spears and swords standing upright, and around the points of these there trickled down poisonous water.

I then put forth all my power and struck with mighty blows in order to push them into the valley. After a time, the elder of those clothed with stone armor fell to the bottom. As he knocked against the sides of the precipice, he flew into pieces, as vegetables do when being cut up to stew. His soul departed with a sound. So too I pressed the others, one at a time, into the gully and every one of them was killed. Not one of them lived, but the soul of each went to the nether world with a noise. After I had done this, and all six of the lords were killed, Hanging Nose was left alone. He set upon me and fought so hard that I had the greatest difficulty in escaping unhurt. I went for him as fiercely, and made mighty sweeps with my sword. The great fellow took off his clothes and sword, and, laying them on one side, said, "Come, come, champions do not war in one way only, for they fight also with their bodily strength." He rushed towards me, so I stuck my sword into my girdle, pushed it behind me, and rushed at him.

And so, we wrestled. Hanging Nose wound his great arms around me and nearly squeezed me to death, but I managed to slip out of his embrace as water trickles down. We wrestled over the mountain tops, but withal I was almost thrown into the poisonous valley; however, a wind arose out of it and bore me up. After striving for some time, I succeeded in throwing Hanging Nose into the gully and he was made mincemeat of by the stone swords and spears. His soul departed with a great sound.

I rose up into the air and went before a clear and gentle wind. As I went along down the river, I could see there were very many towns and villages, the smoke of which ascended and hung over them in clouds. In the middle of these towns there stood a mighty mountain, having a stony winding path leading to its summit. On its top there was a great and very ancient fortress, whose old timbers went up into the black skies and whose new timbers pierced the white heavens. I went into the fortress; and walking up to the door of a great house, peeped through the cracks. There, without doubt, I saw a man of the Shipish people. He was a large fellow and full-grown, though quite young, for his chin was only just becoming a little dark with thin whiskers. He was sitting upon his knees by the fireside. I was very much surprised at his clothing and sword. There was also a little woman near him. Hitherto I had thought my elder sister alone could possess such beauty, but here I saw a woman whose charming looks surprised me. Above all, her countenance indicated that she was, in truth, a prophetess. The master of the house sat with his head hanging down as though they had been having some conversation. I then saw him raise his eyebrows and heard him say deep down in his throat. "My younger sister, ever since you were quite small you have now and then prophesied. Come, prophesy now. Why do I feel so strange at the sound which the gods sent forth from the cloud to-day; come prophecy, for I would hear."

When he had so spoken the little woman, putting on her ceremonial headdress, commenced to beat the ground; and then with the deep voice of a god she prophesied with such a delightful song and said, "A war has suddenly arisen above the precipices towards the source of our river. I see the swords of the inhabitants of The Metal River and the Stoney River together with that of the Hanging Nose all mixed up in fight with that of a brave Yaunguru. Now they are all lost in two great wounds. Now they all go mixed up together towards the east. All at once their swords are broken off close to the guards and they go towards the west. Now I see something like a little bird skimming across the skies towards our little river's mouth; I have never before seen anything dance so much; I must pull myself together to prophesy about it. The little bird has turned itself into a drop of rain and is coming beneath the ground and is coming towards the mouth of our river. A grievous war comes suddenly upon our town, and the people are quickly killed and the place devastated. Next I see the sword of the brave Yaunguru and that of my elder brother mixed up together in fight. Now they are both lost in two great wounds; they go off to the pure cloudless east, still striving together. I am afraid for the sword of my elder brother is broken off close to the guard with a tremendous sound and is lost in two great wounds. The sword of the brave Yaunguru, I believe, goes to the east. Having seen thus far, the light is extinguished from before my eyes, and I feel as though I have been foretelling evil things."

The master of the house, becoming wrathful, said, "My younger sister, the most evil things you have now said deserve only to be ridiculed. I am a person who does not fight with men, but who delights in warring with the gods. I am a man of peace and I always go forth to meet those who came to me with words of peace. Even if your prophecy is from god, it was delivered to me by you with intent to harm me." When he had finished speaking, the little woman shed tears and said, "Wherefore does my brother think that I have prophesied lies to him? For what reason should I do so?"

I slipped through the door like wind and got upon the upper beams of the house. I walked along these with mighty heavy steps and shook the roof of this great house exceedingly, making the rafters dance and creak upon the walls. This splendid mansion, with all its grand treasures, trembling in great fear, sent forth a mighty cry, together with the little house gods. This noise made the master of the house look first one way and then another in great surprise; but the little woman did not move at all. I came down from the beams to the head of the fireplace and, seizing the lord by the hair of his head with my hand, turned it first one way and then another; after that I said, "Look here, Shipish man, what sort of bravery did you say you had? Repeat what you said before, for I desire to hear. Why was the good Curly-head taken and tied up to the great pine tree? It was to avenge him that I fought against the people of The Metal River and the Stoney River as well as against the Hanging Nose. Now, as this war is raging, I have come to test the bravery of the Shipish men. I will hear no words of peace, even if you speak them. We must measure our swords, for even if we kill one another, we shall be better off after death. Now, come, do your very best against me."

I seized the little woman as she sat by that very brave man and carried her out through the window. She wept and, speaking to her brother, she said, "You said that I had prophesied lies, which of that I spoke is false? I am being carried off a prisoner by the Yaunguru; come and save me!" The master of the house began to strike with his sword; we flew about to and fro in the roof of the house like birds; till at last this lord, having evident wrath upon his face, spoke in an angry and scolding manner, "As you, my bad younger sister, prophesied in order to discourage me, I will first slay you, you evil creature!" When he had said this he attacked his sister with vehemence and set upon us fiercely. The little woman clung to my arm in fear, but whenever she saw an opportunity she either put her foot into her brother's beautiful face, and thrust his head backwards or set it upon the back of his neck and pushed his head forward.

After a time the little woman spoke with a soft voice and said, "I know everything about your coming here, and in truth, I prophesied to my brother in order to render him faint-hearted. Let me down, for though I am as worthless as an old mat, I desire to join you and will help you in the fight." I let her down and she fell upon the floor at the head of the fireplace and crawled along upon her hands and feet. She soon got up, however, and drawing a dagger from her bosom attacked her brother fiercely, saying, "My bad elder brother, you have always disbelieved my prophecies, and you now desire to slay both this brave man and me; I am therefore going to help him against you. Put forth all your strength against us." When she had finished speaking, she set upon him mightily with her dagger.

A great wind descended, blew in at the doors and windows of the house, and played about the floors and made the already burning fire burst forth into greater flame. After a time the house caught fire and, before it fell down, we rushed out. Other Shipish people had come to watch the fight. Outside they rushed upon one another and trampled each other down. Nevertheless the little woman stood her ground without going back so much as a single step, and, leaning forward, cut and slew.

At that time I saw a mighty cloud arise above the mountain a very long way off. It seemed to rise up swift as an arrow; with it came the sound of the true god, and after the sound a lord came down to my side. When I looked at him, I saw that he was my elder brother, the Curly-head. We saluted one another with our swords. After this, how he did fight! Why, the strokes of my sword and those of the little woman were as mere shadows to his, for he cleared the way before him with the greatest ease. Then the Shipish man angrily said, "You abominable woman, you too have gone over to the side of the brother of a wicked man? You have helped thus to slay our relations. You will certainly be punished by the gods for what you have done."

The little woman suddenly burst into tears, and said to me, "Your elder sister, the woman of Chiwashpet, has carried her war into many villages around; she also went to a distant land which has the name of

Chirinnai. And now, as the war has gone to the land of the warriors themselves, she is likely to be slain. If you are not quick you will not be able to see your sister again. Go to the aid of your sister and leave the Curly-head here, for he will be sufficient for this war."

She withdrew to the skies, and I, sheathing my sword went after her. We flew through the sky and as we proceeded, I saw, hanging above the mountains of the land, which was doubtless the aforesaid Chirinnai, a cloud which was evidently stirred up as by war; and heard a continual roar as of many gods being slain. The guardian god of my elder sister of Chiwashpet now sent forth a great cry of defeat. This made me proceed with enhanced speed and when we arrived I saw my sister in a dreadful condition. Her clothes were all gone, for her arms were sticking out of nothing but two holes, and her body was so cut up that she had only her backbone left. I saw her strike twice with her sword and then faint away. She quickly came to again and fought with renewed vigor. I came down to her side, upon which she wept, and said, "I am a worthless woman; even if I die, the land will not have been conquered; whereas if you die the land will be laid to waste. Scatter the enemy entirely, and make them flee quickly, after I am gone, then I shall be happy."

After this I attacked the enemy all around me, while, as before, the little woman of Shipish did wondrously and laid the people out like mats. The corpses were scattered over the land so thickly that I could not walk without touching them with my feet. I now saw my sister fall headlong upon the ground, and ten spears were thrust at her; but before they could strike I snatched her away, but, while doing this was myself severely wounded. I waved her towards the skies, and said, "Oh my father, to whom I offer libations, I pray thee to look upon the woman of Chiwashpet, for she has brought me up well. Though she is the daughter of a murderess, pray forgive her." When I had finished speaking and while I still held her in my hands, she became a new and living goddess and went off to the land of the Yaunguru with a great sound.

Now the little woman of Shipish and I were left alone to finish the battle, we utterly devastated and laid waste the land of Chirinnai. When this was done she said to me, with tears in her eyes, "There is now no lord of the people of Chirinnai, but the demon of damp weather, who lives towards the west, will rule over this land together with his younger sister. Besides this, multitudes of insect demons will come to Chirinnai and govern its western parts, and will make an exceedingly grievous war against us, and I cannot tell whether we shall live through it or not. After the war with the insect demons, the demons of damp weather will fight against us. The women will fight by themselves and you must meet the men, and, as you are a man, you must kill the demon of bad weather; I, being a woman, will meet the younger sister of the demon and I shall slay her. If you do not fight hard I shall be slain before your very eyes by these demons, and that will not enhance your glory."

While she was saying this a black fog arose in the west of the land of Chirinnai. In a short time it came up over us and I heard a whirl all round me as of many birds in flight. The insect demons came and settled upon my body and began to tear my flesh, so that I felt I called out in pain. I made them rattle upon my sword. I knew not the day from night and was in the black fog being eaten up by these creatures. After a while I saw that my clothing was devoured, that my arms were sticking out of nothing but sleeve-holes, and that I had only my back-bone left. While fighting with my sword, I fainted away. When I revived, I found that the black fog was gone and the weather was good again. Then the little Shipish woman came and breathed upon my body, and all my wounds were healed, and I got quite well. She then blew upon herself in the same way, and every one of her wounds likewise were healed.

Again I saw a fog of damp, bad weather arise and spread over the land and sea towards the west of Chirinnai. Through the fog of bad weather, something appeared which looked like a man. The naked body of this thing was of a mangy nature; its face resembled a cliff from the side of which the land had slipped, and its arms and legs looked as though they belonged to a mountain. This man had a sword stuck in his girdle that looked like a boat-scull. There also came a woman clothed in the skins of land and sea animals, wearing armor made of leather. This woman came down to the side of the little Shipish woman with a large knife in her hand, which she put up before her face. Upon this the Shipish woman attacked her fiercely with her sword and set upon her with fearful blows. And now the naked man came upon me in a desperate manner; but, as I did not wish to die, I turned myself into air and escaped between his strokes. After that, I attacked him as fiercely as he had me, but my blows had not the least effect upon him. Although I struck him hard several times, my efforts were useless; it was truly difficult to make an impression. By and by I discovered where the fastenings of his armor were, and aimed only at cutting them. I made a splendid sword thrust, and, by the help of god, cut the thongs by which his armour was fastened. Then he whom I thought to be a man spread himself out over the sea like a dried fish; and out of the armor there came a surprising thing! I thought there was a big person in that armor, but quite a little lad came out of it. Dear me, out of that evil weather cloud came a more handsome fellow than I had ever seen before! He was clothed in a beautiful garment and had a splendid sword in his girdle.

He said to me, "I am surprised O brave Ainu warrior, for you are but a man, and yet have destroyed my armor, which the gods, numerous though they are, were unable to break; as you have done this, I will fight you without armor. Even if we are both killed, our fame will be spread over the whole world. Come, let us measure our strength." When he had said this he drew his sword and attacked me furiously; but, since I turned myself into air, I only whistled about his sword. I then set upon him as he had me. While we were fighting, all at once by the help of god I cut him up, and he fell into the sea in pieces. His soul departed with a sound, and after that the air was cleared.

At some distance away the little woman of Shipish was combating with the younger sister of the demon of bad weather, and though she struck hard upon her armor, the blows had no effect whatever; yet, fighting without the least sign of giving in, she suddenly received a dreadful wound and bled profusely. I went to the side of them, scrutinized the leather armor well, and noted where the fastenings of it were. I then took my sword and made a thrust, severing the thongs. By the help of god, there was the sound of my sword piercing the fastenings. The armor then flew open above the sea like a dried fish; and from the inside of it there came a little woman. I thought only the little woman of Shipish could be so beautiful, but as she was the younger sister of the demon of bad weather, she was able to have a most handsome face.

She was exceedingly surprised and said, "O brave Ainu warrior, you are but a man, and yet you have broken my armor which the gods have failed to do. When the gods are without armor they are soft, so that even if you kill me—even if your sword cuts me—I shall after death be much better off. Come, O woman of Shipish, you must put forth your strength or you will be killed." Then the little woman of Shipish cursed her and said, "Even if we women fight and strive together without armor and they are both slain, their fame will be spread abroad after death. You, who are like a god, have been clothed in armor made of the skins of various land and sea animals: therefore I was unable to harm you, and you only were able to strike me. Why is it that you say you did not care to slay me?" She set upon the bad weather demon fiercely and slew her. Her soul departed with a great noise. The defeated one became a living god and went towards the east with a great sound.

After this we were carried upon the wind to my home land of Shinutapka. There the ancient home of my father stood out to my view. We came down to the seashore, and stood at the entrance of the path which led up to the fortress. Here I called out and said, "Have the Curly-head and the woman of Chiwashpet yet arrived?" After I had thus spoken, a voice came, which said, "The Curly-head is here, for he has returned from the wars; the woman of Chiwashpet has also come to us, for the gods have pardoned her."

I went into my father's fortress and found that my elder brother had indeed come home and was resting from war. There too was the woman of Chiwashpet, who, being now a prophetess, was more beautiful than ever. After this I stayed at home. One day my elder brother said to me, "I have certainly been a bad elder brother, however, extend to me your friendship. O woman of Chiwashpet, you have taken pity on my younger brother and brought him up. And during the wars, you, little woman of Shipish, have helped him so that he is now alive. I am thankful to you for all this. Let us now brew a little wine and call all our near and distant relations together to a feast."

After a few days had elapsed, the smell of the wine filled the whole house. When the brewing was finished, messengers were sent out to invite people to the feast. Many people came to give their salutations from all over the land. Then the Curly-head took the woman of Chiwashpet, and I the woman of Shipish, to wife, and we lived out the rest of our days happily together.

DISCUSSION QUESTIONS

1. What seem to be the characteristics of a Yaunguru?

2. How does the first person narration style affect our reading of the myth?

3. Discuss the absence of names in this story. Who is given a name? Who isn't? How are they described?

4. How does the donning of his father's clothes begin the hero cycle?

5. Trace the narrator's steps along the Journey of the Hero.

BIBLIOGRAPHY

Batchelor, John, *Specimens of Ainu Folk-lore*, 1889. https://archive.org/stream/ainutheirfolklor00batcrich #page/58/mode/2up

"Buddhist Studies." *Buddha Dharma Education Association*, 2017. http://www.buddhanet.net

Cotterell, Arthur. *The Ultimate Encyclopedia of Mythology*. Anness, 2001.

Davis, F Hadland. *Myths and Legends of Japan*, 1912. https://www.gutenberg.org/files/45723/45723-h/ 45723-h.htm

Hall Chamberlain, Basil. "Aino Folk-Tales," 1888. http://www.sacredtexts.com/shi/aft/aft.htm#xxxiii

Herold, A. Ferdinand. *The Life of Buddha*. Part One. Translated by Paul C. Blum, 1922. http://www.sacred-texts.com/bud/lob/index.htm

Mohan Ganguli, Kisari, translator. *The Mahabharata Book 3: Vana Parva*, 1883–1896. http://www.sacred-texts.com/hin/m03/m03189.htm

Powell, Barry B. *World Myth*. Pearson, 2014.

Rinder, Frank. *Old-World Japan: Legends of the Land of the Gods*.1895. https://www.gutenberg.org/ files/46863/46863-h/46863-h.htm#chap02

V. Jayaram. "Hinduism and Buddhism." *Hindu Website*. 2017. http://www.hinduwebsite.com

Walls, Jan, and Yvonne Walls. *Classical Chinese Myths*. 1984. http://www.gly.uga.edu/railsback/CS/CSIndex. html

Werner, E.T.C. *Myths and Legends of China*. 1922. http://www.pitt.edu/~dash/chinaflood.html

Wilhelm, Richard. "The Chinese Fairy Book," Translated by Frederick H. Martens. 1921. https://books.google. com/books?id=NvdAAAAAIAAJ&printsec=titlepage#v=onepageq&f=true

Wilkins, W. J. *Hindu Mythology: Puranic and Vedic*. 1900. http://www.sacredtexts.com/hin/hmvp/hmvp36. htm

Chapter 8

THE MYTHS OF OCEANIA

© Nell Novara

Introduction

© dikobraziy/Shutterstock.com

The region of Oceania can be discussed generally by dividing it into four main categories:

The Polynesian ("polynesia" is Greek for "many islands") group includes a triangular area in the Pacific Ocean with the Hawaiian Islands at the top of the triangle, Easter Island in the lower right corner, and New Zealand in the lower left corner. In-between there are other island groups including the Cook Islands, the Samoan Islands, and Tahiti.

Melanesia, geographically speaking, consists of the area including New Guinea, New Caledonia, and Fiji. Culturally, this is a complex area, but the majority of myths that are available to us come from southeastern New Guinea and Fiji. Papua, in Western New Guinea, is a province of Indonesia; Papua New Guinea, on the eastern side, is an independent state.

Micronesia means "land of small islands," and Guam is the largest island in this region, part of the Marianas Islands. Other islands in this area include Palau and the Marshall Islands. Unfortunately, we don't have a large body of myth to study from this region.

Finally, Australia is the largest landmass in Oceania, as well as being geographically distinct from its island neighbors; only a small portion of its environment is tropical. Its southern location keeps it somewhat isolated from the other island groups in the region. The native peoples, too, are among the most isolated on Earth. The Dutch first arrived in Australia in 1606, and found it to be quite primitive. The aborigines were still a hunting and gathering society at this time and were not even using crude tools. However, they did have social organization and religious rituals. There are approximately 400 distinct groups (with different languages and stories) still in existence today, though they make up only 3% of the population. As with the others groups, we have only fragments of their myths.

The history of annexation and occupation of the islands is long and varies by location. Some islands had early trading experience with Arab spice merchants, others were not explored until the seventeenth and eighteenth centuries, which saw Dutch, German, and British colonizers. Europeans began to explore and settle parts of Oceania in the sixteenth century with the Spaniards' arrival in the Marianas Islands, thus encouraging more settlement. Over time, the British came to dominate the area, with permanent colonies in what is now Australia and New Zealand. But these explorations were often tragic for the island inhabitants. Most Europeans were searching for wealth or seeking slaves. Others wished to set up missions to bring Christianity to the native peoples, but even with good intentions the visitors introduced weapons and foreign diseases. These sudden changes caused irreparable and permanent damage to the lives of the Oceanic peoples. During the "black drive" in Tasmania, "British settlers marched in a line across the island, literally driving all the native inhabitants into the sea" (Powell 438). Devastation by violence, disease, and destruction of statues and shrines nearly eliminated the material culture of these people. British and American missionaries dominated the landscape of twentieth century Oceania. The resulting current population of Oceania is an eclectic mixture of Muslims, Hindus, Christians, and Animists (ancestor worship).

In addition, due to such diverse groups of people being spread over such a vast area, with poor communication between them and no systems of writing, their myths have proven a challenge to study. The material we have mainly comes from accounts made by European ethnologists from the nineteenth and twentieth centuries who attempted to record native stories and legends. While each group has its own distinct myths, there are many instances of overlap and even some shared stories, as well as a few common themes that appear to be rooted in island life.

Part 1: Creation and Destruction

The Kumulipo (Hawaii)

When Hawaii was annexed by the United States in 1898, there was already a royal family in place on the islands. Queen Liliuokalani, the translator of this song of creation, was well educated and had seen much of the world by the time she was made the first Queen of Hawaii. Queen Liliuokalani's reign was preceded by her brother's, Kalakaua, who signed treaties that gave the Port of Pearl Harbor to the United States. The Queen opposed her brother's previous alliance with the United States, and between 1891 and 1895 she fought vehemently against the annexation of Hawaii. Led by business interests, her party asked her to abdicate and she was the last monarch of Hawaii.

Her translation of *The Kumulipo* was written while imprisoned and charged with treason. She wrote in the introduction to the poem,

> The folk-lore or traditions of an aboriginal people have of late years been considered of inestimable value; language itself changes, and there are terms and allusions herein to the natural history of Hawaii, which might be forgotten in future years without some such history as this to preserve them to posterity.

She claims that this chant (in total comprised of sixteen eras, nine of which have been printed here) is the same chant sang to Captain Cook when he was met by the people of Hawaii. Cook was met with great ceremony and deified as "Lono," one of the four great gods of Hawaiian culture, because it was said that this god would reappear from the sea in a ship (which, of course, Cook did).

The poem explains the creation of the world, all its creatures, many kinds of people, and is a preservation of the history (both real and folklore) of Hawaii.

THE KUMULIPO

The First Era
At the time that turned the heat of the earth,
At the time when the heavens turned and changed,
At the time when the light of the sun was subdued
To cause light to break forth,
At the time of the night of Makalii (winter)
Then began the slime which established the earth,
The source of deepest darkness.
Of the depth of darkness, of the depth of darkness,
Of the darkness of the sun, in the depth of night,

Source: Translated by Liliuokalani, *An Account of the Creation of the World According to Hawaiian Tradition*, 1897.

It is night,
So was night born.
Kumulipo was born in the night, a male.
Poele was born in the night, a female.
A coral insect was born, from which was born perforated coral.
The earthworm was born, which gathered earth into mounds,
From it were born worms full of holes.
The starfish was born, whose children were born starry.
The phosphorus was born, whose children were born phosphorescent.
The Ina was born Ina (sea egg).
The Halula was born Halula (sea urchin).

Birth of Shell-fish.

Kane was born to Waiololi, a female to Waiolola.
The Wi was born, the Kiki was its offspring.
The Akaha's home was the sea;
Guarded by the Ekahakaha that grew in the forest.
A night of flight by noises
Through a channel; water is life to trees;
So the gods may enter, but not man.

Birth of Seaweed and grasses

A husband of gourd, and yet a god,
A tendril strengthened by water and grew
A being, produced by earth and spread,
Made deafening by the swiftness of Time
Of the Hee that lengthened through the night,
That filled and kept on filling
Of filling, until, filled
To filling, 'tis full,
And supported the earth, which held the heaven
On the wing of Time, the night is for Kumulipo (creation),
     'Tis night.

The Second Era
The first child born of Powehiwehi (dusky night)
Tossed up land for Pouliuli (darkest night),
For Mahiuma or Maapuia,
And lived in the land of Pohomiluamea (sloughy hill of Mea);
Suppressed the noise of the growth of unripe fruit,
For fear Uliuli would cause it to burst, and the stench
To disagree and turn sour,
For pits of darkness and pits of night.
Then the seven waters became calm.
Then was born a child (kama), 'twas a Hilu and swam.
The Hilu is a fish with standing fins,
On which Pouliuli sat.
So undecided seemed Powehiwehi,
For Pouliuli was husband
And Powehiwehi his wife.

Birth of Fish

The train of Palaoa (walrus) that swim by
Embracing only the deep blue waters,
Also the Opule that move in schools,
The deep is as nothing to them.
And the Kumimi (a crab) and Lohelohe (a locust) cling together
To the rolling motion of their cradle
On their path so narrow, so slim, to move,
Till Pimoe (a mermaid) is found in the depth of her cave,
With Hikawainui, and Hikawaina
Amongst piles of heated coral
That were thrown in piles unevenly,
So thin and scraggy in the blue tide.
Surely it must be dismal, that unknown deep;
'Tis a sea of coral from the depth of Paliuli,
And when the land recedes from them
The east is still in darkness of night,
    'Tis night.

The Third Era
He was the man and she the woman;
The man that was born in the dark age,
And the woman was born in the age of bubbles.
The sea spread, the land spread,
The waters spread, the mountains spread,
The Poniu grew tall with advancing time,
The Haha grew and had nine leaves,
And the Palai (fern) sprout that shot forth leaves of high chiefs
Brought forth Poeleele, a man (darkness),
Who lived with Pohaha, a woman (bubbles),
And brought forth generations of Haha (kalo tops).
The Haha was born.
Birth of Insects
Birth of Birds
Birth of Sea-birds
It was so on that night,
It was so this night,
It was dark at the time with Poeleele,
And darkest age—of bubbly night.
    'Tis night.

The Fourth Era
Established in the dawn of Laa's light
The Ape aumoa with faintest strife
Envied the sea that washed the land,
As it crept up and yet crept down
And brought forth creeping families
That crept on their backs and crept on their front,
With pulses that beat in front and rounding backs,

With faces in front and claws to feel
Of darkness, of darkness,
For Kaneaka Papanopano is born (dawn).
So Popanopano the man
And Polalowehi his wife,
Man was born to increase—
To increase in the night by the thousands.
At this age there is a lull—
At this age take your children to the beach.
Children play at heaping sands.
They are the children born of night.
Night was born.
Night was born of great delight,
Night was rolled for the pleasure of gods,
Night gave birth to the split-back turtle.
Watch in the night for the land turtle.
Night gave birth to the brown lobster,
The night of commotion for the Alii (lobster),
The birth night of the lazy monster
Was a wet night for the rolling monster.
Night gave birth to clinging beings,
And Night loudly called for roughness.
Night gave birth to wailing
A night of drawback to oblivion,
Night gave birth to high noses,
Night dug deep for jellyfish,
Night gave birth to slush,
So the night must wait for motion.
The dancing motion till creeping crept
With long and waving lengthy tail,
And with humpy lumpy lashes sweeps
And trails along in filthy places.
These live on dirt and mire;
Eat and rest, eat and throw up;
They exist on filth, are low-born beings,
Till to earth they become a burden
Of mud that's made,
Made unsafe, until one reels
And is unsteady.
Go thou to the land of creepers,
Where families of creepers were born in one night.
    'Tis night.

The Fifth Era
The advance of age when Kapokanokano (night of strength)
Established heaps in the Polalouli (depth of night),
And the dark fresh color of the earth thrown up
Was the darkness of the famous Polalouli (night in the deep),
Who married for wife Kapokanokano.
His snout was of great size and with it dug the earth;
He dug until he raised a great mound,

He raised a hill for his gods,
A hill, a precipice in front,
For the offspring of a pig which was born;
Built a house and paid the forest
And rested by the patches of Loiloa,
For Umi who is to possess the land,
For Umi who is to reign anon;
The land where Kapokanokano dwelt,
To which place laid a path of frailest trail,
A trail as fine as the choicest hair of this pig,
A being was born half pig, half god,
At the time of life of Kapokanokano,
Who became the wife of Polalouli.
Night was born.
The Poowaawaa was born, his head was uneven.
The Poopahapaha was born, his head was flat and spread.
The Poohiwahiwa was born, he appeared noble.
The Poohaole was born, he became a haole (foreigner).
The Poomahakea was born, his skin was fair.
The Pooapahu was born, was a hairy man.
The Poomeumeu was born, is a short man.
The Pooauli was born, is dark complexioned.
The Hewahewa was born, and he remained so (light-headed).
The Lawalawa was born, becomes a lawalawa.
The Hooipo was born, and became hooipoipo (loving).
The Hulu was born, and became a-aia (demented).
The Hulupii was born, and became piipii (curly-headed).
The Meleuli was born, and became melemele (yellow-haired).
The Haupo was born, and became hauponuinui (noble-chested).
The Hilahila was born, and became hilahila (very bashful).
The Kenakena was born, and became kenakena (bitter).
The Luheluhe was born, and became luheluhe (limber).
The Awaawa was born, and became awaawa (sour disposed).
The Aliilii was born, and became liilii (puny).
The Makuakua was born, and became kuakua (great).
The Halahala was born, decorated with lei Hala.
The Eweewe was born, who was proud of his pedigree.
The Huelo Maewa was born, with very long tail.
The Hulu liha was born, and became lihelihe (hairy eggs).
The Pukaua was born, and became a warrior.
The Meheula was born, and became red.
The Puuwelu was born, and became weluwelu (ragged).
That is his, this is in shreds.
Then came the children of Loiloa,
And the land grew and spread,
And the goblet of wish was lowered
Of affections for the tribe of relations,
Of songs that grasp of Oma's friends

Till relations are enrolled from Kapokanokano
At yester eve.
    'Tis night.

The Sixth Era
A sacred emblem is the kahili of Kuakamano
That sends out its stiff branches as a sacred frill,
Which fills the faint-hearted with awe,
But brings such ones to claim friendship.
Those are beings who eat by gushing waters,
Who eat also by the dashing sea,
They live in nests inside ditches,
There in hollow places the parent rats dwell,
There huddle together the little mice.
It is they who keep the changes of the month.
The mites of the land,
The mites of the water,
'Tis Mehe the reddish seaweed
Whose lashes stand,
That hides and peeps.
There are rats inland, there are rats at sea.
There are also rabbits
That were born in the night of the crash—
They were born in the night that moved away.
The tiniest mice move by crawling;
The tiny mice spring as they move.
They run over the pebbles,
The propagating pebbles where no inland ohia bear.
A puny child born in the night of the crash.
They gave birth to beings that leaped in the night, that moved away
The child of Uli-a-kama last night.
    'Tis night.

The Seventh Era
Over the mountains silence reigns—
The silence of night that has moved away,
And the silence of night that cometh,
The silence of night filled with people,
And the silence of night of dispersing.
'Tis fearful the steps and narrow trails—
'Tis fearful the amount eaten and left—
'Tis fearful the night past and gone,
The awful stillness of the night that came—
The night that went by and brought forth an offspring,
That offspring a dog,
A yellow dog, a tiny dog,
A dog without hair, sent by the gods,
A dog sent for sacrifice.
A speckled bird was first sacrificed,

Else he'd repent for having no hair,
Else he'd repent for having no covering,
And go naked on the road to Malama,
The easiest path for children,
From great to small,
From tall to short,
He is equal to the blowing breeze,
The younger brother of the god
From which sprang the gods of the bats—
The hairy bats. Sprang the bat with many claws—
Sprang the bat and moved away,
That the rising surf might give it birth.
    'Tis night.

The Eighth Era
The child of Uli, of Uli of Ke,
The child in the time of numerous night,
The child in the time of riding distant surf in the night.
Beings were born to increase.
Male was born of Waiololi,
Female was born of Waiolola,
Then was born the night of gods,
Men that stood,
Of men lying down,
They slept long sleep in the distant time,
And went staggering when they walked.
The forehead of the gods is red.
That of man is dark.
Their chins are light.
Then calmness spread in the time of Kapokinikini—
Calm in the time of Kapoheenalu mamao,
And it was called there Lailai.
Lailai was born a woman,
Kii was born a man.
Kane a god was born.
Kanaloa was born a god, the great Kaheehaunawela (Octopus).
    'Tis night.

The drums were born,
Called Moanaliha.
Kawaomaaukele came next.
The last was Kupololiilialiimuaoloipo,
A man of long life and very high rank.
O night! O God of Night!
O kupa, Kupakupa kupa, the settler!
Then Kupakupa the settler, the woman who sat sideway,
That woman was Lailai of the distant night,
Lailai, the woman. Kapokinikini
Dwelt with people of Kapokinikini.

Hahapoele was born a woman,
Hapopo was born a woman.
Maila was born and called Lopalapala (ingenious),
Her other name was void or nakedness,
And lived in the land of Lua (deep hole).
So the place was called Olohelohe lua.
Then Olohelohe was born in the day a man,
And Olohelohe was born at the time, a woman,
And lived with Kane.
Laiolo was born by Kane.
Kapopo was born a woman,
Poelei and Poelea were born twins.
After them was born Wehiloa.
From them these were born,
The little beings who were cross-eyed,
That stood in numbers and moved in myriads.
These men that flew naked were the men of the day.
　　'Tis day.

The Ninth Era
Lailai, of the quaking earth,
Of great heat and noise, and opening heavens,
This woman ascending to heaven,
Climbed to heaven by the forest.
Onehenehe flew where the earth rose.
Children of Kii that were born from the brain,
Were born and flew, both flew to heaven.
Then the signs appeared and cast their shadow
On their forehead, a bread fruit was impressed,
On their chins shot roots of fire.
This woman was from a race of delusions (myth),
A woman with dark skin, from the land of Iipakalani,
Where numbers of men lived in the heat.
This woman lived in Nuumealani,
Land where the Aoa thrived,
Who stripped with great ease the leaves of the Koa;
A woman whose person was never seen,
From her to Kii, from him to Kane,
From her to Kane of Kapokinikini.
The times of those people came to naught.
A tribe, a generation of great strength,
She alone flew to her abode,
And on the boughs of the Aoa tree, in Nuumealani stayed,
Became pregnant, and the earth was born.
Haha Poele was born a woman,
Hapopo was born,
Lohelohe was born last of all.
These were the children of this woman.
　　'Tis day.

1. Note the descriptions of how people and animals are created. What is significant about each process of creation?

2. Locate all the references to children. What is interesting about the description of children? Why do you think they are emphasized?

3. How would you say the content in each Era is organized? Is it like the Ages of Man concept we've seen? Or is there a progression?

How Pele Came to Hawaii

One of the most important figures in Hawaiian mythology is the volcano goddess, Pele. There are many legends surrounding Pele and her family, many of them involving the great violence Pele is capable of. Pele's ancestry, being the daughter of the father of the sky and the mother of the earth, makes her and her siblings formidable opponents. In this story, we're told of how Pele came from the land of her parents to the islands she creates as present-day Hawaii. The relationship between Pele, Hiiaka, and Ka-moho-alii (god of sharks) changes over the course of many legends, but is seen here as relatively supportive. See the story of "The Goddess of Fire and The Goddess of the Sea" for a continuation of this tale.

HOW PELE CAME TO HAWAII

Pele's father was Moe-moea-au-lii, the chief who dreamed of trouble. Her mother was Haumea, or Papa, who personified mother earth. Pele was living in a happy home in the presence of her parents, and yet for a long time she was stirred by thoughts of far-away lands. At last she asked her father to send her away. This meant that he must provide a sea-going canoe with mat sails, sufficiently large to carry a number of persons and food for many days.

"What will you do with your little egg sister?" asked her father.

Pele caught the egg, wrapped it in her skirt to keep it warm near her body, and said that it should always be with her. In a very short time, the egg was changed into a beautiful little girl who bore the name Hii-aka-i-ka-poli-o-Pele (Hiiaka-in-the-bosom-of-Pele), the youngest one of the Pele family.

After the care of the helpless one had been provided for, Pele was sent to her oldest brother, Ka-moho-alii, the king of dragons, or, as he was later known, "the god of sharks." He was a sea-god and would provide the great canoe for the journey. While he was getting all things ready, he asked Pele where she was going.

She replied, "I am going to Bola-bola; to Kuai-he-lani; to Kane-huna-moku; then to Moku-mana-mana; then to see a queen, Kaoahi is her name and Niihau her island."

This journey would be first to Bola-bola, then among the mysterious ancestral islands, and then to the northwest until she found Niihau, the most northerly of the Hawaiian group.

The god of sharks prepared his large canoe and put it in the care of some of their relatives, Kane-pu-a-hio-hio (Kane-the-whirlwind), Ke-au-miki (The-strong-current), and Ke-au-ka (Moving-seas).

Source: W. D. Westervelt, *Hawaiian Legends of the Volcanoes*, 1916.

Pele was carried from land to land by these wise boatmen until at last she landed on the island Niihau. Then she sent back the boat to her brother, the shark-god. After a time he brought all the brothers and sisters to Hawaii.

Pele was welcomed and entertained. Soon she went over to Kauai, the large, beautiful garden island of the Hawaiian group. She appeared as a dream maiden before the king of Kauai, whose name was Lohiau, whom she married, but with whom she could not stay until she had found a place where she could build a permanent home for herself and all who belonged to her.

She had a magic digging tool, Pa-oa. When she struck this down into the earth it made a fire-pit. It was with this Pa-oa that she was to build a home for herself and Lohiau. She dug along the lowlands of Kauai, but water drowned the fires she kindled, so she went from island to island but could only dig along the beach near the sea. All her fire-pits were so near the water that they burst out in great explosions of steam and sand, and quickly died, until at last she found Kilauea on the large island of Hawaii. There she built a mighty enduring palace of fire, but her dream marriage was at an end. The little sister Hiiaka, after many adventures, married Lohiau and lived on Kauai.

DISCUSSION QUESTIONS

1. What role does Pele play to her sister Hiiaka?

2. How does The God of Sharks aid in Pele's journey? Which relatives does he bring to the island? What are their significance?

3. What does the failure of Pele and Lohiau's relationship suggest?

Tangaloa Creates the World (Samoa)

Pottery evidence shows that Polynesians have inhabited Samoa since around 1000 BCE. European contact with Samoa began in 1722, when a Dutch explorer landed on the island. British Christian missionaries established communities in Samoa as early as 1830, and by the end of the nineteenth century Samoa was split between the United States and Germany, who annexed the Eastern and Western islands respectively. By 1935, New Zealand had taken over Western Samoa, ceding control and establishing an independent Samoa in the 1960s. American Samoa is still a United States territory, which hosts the naval base of Pago Pago. Despite this incredible history of occupation, much of their myth of creation remains relatively intact. There are some obvious references to Christian mythology as part of Tangaloa's story, no doubt influenced by the missionaries who translated this text.

TANGALOA CREATES THE WORLD

The god Tangaloa dwelt in the Expanse. He made all things; he alone was there—not any sky, not any country. He only went to and fro in the Expanse. There was no sea, and no earth; but, at the place where he stood, there grew up a rock. All things were about to be made by him, for all things were not yet made; the sky was not made, nor anything else; but there grew up a Rock on which he stood.

Source: John Fraser, *Journal of the Polynesian Society, Vol I,* 1892.

Then Tangaloa said to the Rock, "Split up!" Then was brought forth the many Papas (rocks): Papa-taoto (to lie down); after that, Papa-sosolo (to run); then Papa-lau-a'au (to resemble a flat reef); then Papa-'ano-'ano (honeycomb); then Papa-'ele (volcanic mud); then Papa-tu (to stand); then Papa-'amu-'amu (branching coral) and his children.

Tangaloa stood facing the west and spoke to the Rock. Tangaloa struck the Rock with his right hand, and it split open towards the right side. Then the Earth was brought forth (that is the parent of all the people in the world), and the Sea was brought forth and the Sea covered the Papa-sosolo. Papa-taoto said to Papa-sosolo, "You are blessed in the possession of your sea." But Papa-sosolo replied, "Don't bless me; the sea will soon reach you too." All the rocks in like manner called him blessed.

Tangaloa turned to the right side, and the Fresh-water sprang up. Tangaloa spoke again to the Rock, and the Sky was produced. Then Tui-te'e-langi (the sky chief) was brought forth; then came forth Ilu, (Immensity) and then the female Mamao (Space from the Horizons), then came Niuao (Height from Land to Sky).

Tangaloa spoke again to the Rock; then Lua'o a boy, came forth. Tangaloa spoke again to the Rock, and Lua-vai, a girl, came forth. These were the two fresh-waters. Tangaloa appointed these two to the Sā-tua-langi (The North).

Then Tangaloa spoke again, and Aoa-lālā, a boy was born, and next a girl, Ngao-ngao-le-tai (The Desolate Sea); then came Man; then came the Spirit; then the Heart; then the Will; then Thought.

That is the end of Tangaloa's creations which were produced from the Rock; they were only floating about on the sea; there was no fixedness there.

Then Tangaloa made an ordinance to the rock and said: "Let the Spirit and the Heart and Will and Thought go on and join together inside the Man"; and they joined together there and man became intelligent. And man was joined to 'Ele-'ele (the earth), and the couple became called Fatu-ma-le-'Ele-'ele, Fatu the man, and 'Ele-'ele, the woman.

Then he said to Immensity and Space, "Come now; you two be united up above in the sky with your boy Niuao," so they went up; there was only a void, nothing for the sight to rest upon. Then he said to Lua-'o and Lua-vai, "Come now, you two, that the region of fresh-water may be peopled. And Aoa-lālā and Ngao-ngao-le-tai, join, and people the salt sea. And Fatu and 'Ele-'ele, people the left-hand side. Tui-te'e-langi, come here now, and prop up the sky."

The sky was propped up; it reached up on high. But it fell down because he was not able to hold it. So Tui-te'e-langi went to Masoa and Teve, the first plants; he brought them and used them as props; then he was able to hold up the sky. The sky remained up above, but there was nothing for the sight to rest upon. There was only the far-receding sky, reaching to Immensity and Space.

Then Tangaloa sat still; he split himself into 7 Tangaloas: Tangaloa-fa'a-tutupu-nu'u (The Creator of Lands); then he created Tangaloa-lē-fuli (The Immoveable), and Tangaloa-asiasi-nu'u (The Omnipresent), and Tangaloa-tolo-nu'u (The Extender of Lands and People), Tangaloa-sāváli (The Messenger), Tuli (The Bird), and Longonoa (The Reporter).

Tangaloa The Creator said to Tangaloa The Immoveable, "Come here; be the chief in the heavens." Then Tangaloa The Creator said to Tangaloa The Messenger, "Come here; be the ambassador in all the heavens, beginning from the Eighth Heavens down to the First Heavens, to tell them all to gather together in the Ninth Heavens, where Tangaloa The Immoveable, is chief. Visit below the children of Night and Day in the First Heavens."

Tangaloa The Messenger went down to Night and Day in the First Heavens, and asked them, "Have you two any children appointed to you?" And they answered, "These two are our children, Langi-'uli (The

Dark, Cloudy Heavens) and Langi-mā (The Bright Clear Heavens)." All the stars also were their offspring, but each star had each its own name. The last command of Tangaloa The Creator, to Night and Day, was that they should produce the Eye-of-the-Sky. That was the reason Tangaloa The Messenger went down to ask Night and Day in the First Heavens if they had any children.

Night and Day said, "There remain four boys that are not yet appointed, Sāmoa and Manu'a (the children of Night and Day), and the Sun and the Moon."

Tangaloa The Messenger said, "That is good; come now; go up into the Ninth Heavens, you four; all are about to gather together there to form a Council; go up you two also." Then they all gathered together in the Ninth Heavens, the place where dwelt Tangaloa The Creator and Tangaloa The Immoveable; the Council was held in the Ninth Heavens; the ground where they held the Council was Malaē-a-Toto'a, "the council ground of Tranquillity."

Then various decrees were made in the Ninth Heavens; the children of Ilu and Mamoa were appointed all of them to be builders, and to come down from the Eighth Heavens to this earth below; perhaps they were ten thousand in all that were appointed to be builders; they built houses for the Tangaloa; but the builders did not reach to the Ninth Heavens—the home of Tangaloa The Immovable, which was called the "Bright House."

Tangaloa The Creator said to Night and Day, "Let Manu'a and Sāmoa go down below to be chiefs over the offspring of Fatu and 'Ele-'ele, the people of the earth. Let the Sun and the Moon go and follow you two; when day comes, let the Sun follow; also when Night comes, the Moon too comes on."

Tangaloa The Messenger went to and fro to visit the land; his visit began in the place where are (now) the Eastern groups; these groups were made to spring up. Then he went off to cause the group of Fiji to grow up, but the space between seemed so far off that he could not walk it. He stood there and turned his face to the Sky, praying to Tangaloa The Creator and Tangaloa The Immoveable; Tangaloa The Creator looked down to Tangaloa The Messenger and he made the Tongan group spring up and the land they live upon.

Then he turned his face to this Manu'a; and looked up to the heavens, for he was unable to move about; then Tangaloa The Creator and Tangaloa The Immovable looked down, and caused the Savai'i to spring up; then that land grew up.

Tangaloa The Messenger went back to the heavens, and said, "We now have countries, the Eastern group and the Fiji group, and the Tongan group, and Savai'i." As all these lands were grown up, Tangaloa The Creator went down in a black cloud to look at the countries, and he delighted in them; and he Delighted in them. Then he stood on the top of the mountains to tread them down, that the land might be prepared for people to dwell in. He returned to the heavens. Tangaloa The Creator said to Tangaloa The Messenger, "Go back by the road you came; take people to possess the Eastern groups; take two of each from the heavens and create the children."

Tangaloa The Messenger took Atu and Sasa'e, who became the gods of the Tahitian islands. He took Atu and Fiji, who became the group of islands called Atu-Fiji. He turned his face towards Tonga and took with him Atu and Tonga, who peopled the land of Tonga. He took Sava and I'I and the island of Savai'i was peopled by them. Two more lands, Upólu and Tutila sprang up and were peopled as well.

Then Tangaloa The Messenger turned to the heavens and said, "Two lands have been prepared for me to rest in." And Tangaloa The Creator said, "Come now, go with the Peopling-Vine; take it and place it outside in the sun, leave it there to bring forth people and when you see it has brought forth, tell me." Then he took the Peopling-vine and placed it in Salēa-au-mua, a council-ground, which is now called the Malae-of-the-sun.

Tangaloa The Messenger was walking by moonlight and he visited the place where the Peopling-Vine was; he went there and it had brought forth people. He told Tangaloa The Creator of the Vine's progress. He saw that it had brought forth something like worms; wonderful was the multitude of worms. Then Tangaloa The Creator shred them into strips, and fashioned them into members, so that the head, and the face, and the hands, and the legs were distinguishable; the body was now complete, like a man's body. He gave them heart and spirit and four persons grew up, so this land was peopled. There grew up four persons, Tele and Upólu, Tutu and Ila. Tele and Upólu were placed to people the land of Upolu-tele; but Tutu and Ila, they two were to people the land now called Tutuila. The Peopling-Vine that came down from heaven, had two names, Fue-tangata and Fue-sa; he peopled the two flat lands.

Then Tangaloa gave his parting command, "Always show respect to Manu'a; if any one does not, he will be overtaken by calamity; but let each one do as he likes with his own lands."

DISCUSSION QUESTIONS

1. Why might the different Papas (or rocks) be the first creation?

2. What seems to be the purpose of Tangaloa's separation into seven Tangaloas?

3. Consider the Peopling-Vine and the way in which humans are created. Compare Tangaloa's methods to other people making, like Nu Wa.

4. Why is there a warning to respect Manu'a at the end of the story? What power might Manu'a hold over the Samoan people?

Nauru Creation Tale (Micronesia)

The island nation of Nauru inhabits eight square miles in the middle of the vast Pacific Ocean. Having been occupied first by the Germans in the eighteenth century, then part of the United Kingdom in the nineteenth century (and renamed Pleasant Island), their tiny island was made a landing space for the Japanese troops during World War II, and finally gained independence as a part of the Micronesian Islands in 1968. Despite these many foreign invaders, very few thought to record the cultural practices. Dixon, the author of *Oceanic Mythology*, from which this story comes, writes, "In all the other Oceanic regions they, or at least part of them, made some effort to record what their civilization was destined to destroy, but here scarcely a fragment was preserved." We are left with few stories to understand the rich history of Micronesia, but this myth of the Ancient Spider who creates the world is one of the most valuable preservations of the Nauru culture.

NAURU CREATION TALE

In the beginning there were only the sea and Areop-Enap, "Ancient Spider," who floated above in endless space. One day Ancient Spider found a great rounded object, a tridacna mussel, and taking it in his hands, he looked at it from all sides, for he wanted to know if there was not an opening in it, so that he

Source: Roland B. Dixon, *Oceanic Mythology,* 1916.

might crawl within; but there was none. Thereupon he struck the great shell, and as it sounded hollow, he concluded that there was nothing in it after all. He tried in vain to open his treasure, and at last, repeating a charm and making another attempt, he succeeded in prying the mighty valves slightly apart.

At once he crept inside, but could see nothing for it was dark there because sun and moon were not yet made; moreover, he could not stand upright, since the space within the shell was too small. Ancient Spider sought everywhere on the chance that he might find something, and at last discovered a snail. Putting this under his arm, he lay down and slept for three days that he might give power to the snail; then he laid it aside and sought again, his search being rewarded by another larger snail, which he treated like the first.

After this, taking the smaller one, he said to it, "Can you lift the roof a little, so that we might sit up?" The snail replied, "Yes," and raised the shell slightly; whereupon Ancient Spider took the snail, set it before the western half of the tridacna shell, and made it into the moon.

There was now a little light, and by it Ancient Spider saw a large worm or grub, who, when asked if he could raise the roof still higher, suddenly came to life and said, "Yes." So he laboured, and the upper shell of the tridacna slowly rose higher and higher, while salty sweat ran from the worm's body, and collecting in the lower shell, became the sea.

At last he raised the upper shell very high, and it became the sky; but Rigi, the worm, exhausted by his great work, fell and died. From the other snail Ancient Spider now made the sun and set it on the east side of the lower shell, which became the earth.

DISCUSSION QUESTIONS

1. Trace the creatures who aid the Ancient Spider in his creation. What is interesting about the spider's choice of help?

2. Ancient Spider tried to separate the earth from the sky—compare this to other myths that attempt to do the same.

Kai Islands Creation (Indonesia)

Known most commonly as the "Spice Islands," for their naturally occurring cloves, nutmeg, and mace, the Kai Islands are a part of Indonesia. Their cultural heritage is varied, as the inhabitants are from a variety of islands in the Pacific. Kai Islands have been occupied by foreigners since the fourteenth century, first with Arab merchants, then Portuguese, Dutch, and finally an independent state of the Republic of Indonesia. This long history of occupation clearly impacted the myths of the islanders. We see evidence of the lost fish hook, prominent in other myths around the region, rivalry between brothers that creates the opportunity for creation, and an interesting look at male–female sibling relationships.

KAI ISLANDS

There were three brothers and two sisters in the upper sky-world. While fishing one day, Parpara, the youngest of the brothers, lost a fish-hook which he had borrowed from Hian, his oldest brother. Angered by the loss of the hook, Hian demanded that it be found and returned to him. After much fruitless search, the Parpara met a fish who asked him what his trouble was, and who, on learning the facts, promised to aid in the search. At length they discovered another fish who was very ill because of something stuck in its throat. The object proved to be the long-lost hook, which the friendly fish delivered to Parpara, who thus was able to restore it to its owner.

Parpara, however, determined to have his revenge upon his brother, and so he secretly fastened a bamboo vessel full of palm liquor above Hian's bed in such a way that when the latter rose, he would be almost certain to upset it. The expected happened, and Parpara then demanded of his brother that he return to him the spilled liquor. Hian endeavoured, of course fruitlessly, to gather it up, and in his efforts dug so deeply into the ground that he made an opening clear through the sky-world.

Wondering what might lie below, the brothers determined to tie one of their dogs to a long rope and lower him through the aperture; and when they had done this, and the dog had been drawn up again, they found white sand sticking to his feet, whereupon they resolved to go down themselves, although the other inhabitants of the heaven-world refused to accompany them thither. Sliding down the rope, the three brothers and one of the sisters, together with their four dogs, safely reached the world which lay below, and which was thus discovered for the first time. As the second sister was descending, however, one of the brothers chanced to look up, at which his sister was so ashamed that she shook the rope and was hauled up by the other sky-people. In this way the three brothers with their sister were the first occupants of the world and became the ancestors of the human race.

DISCUSSION QUESTIONS

1. What is the relationship between the brothers like?

2. Compare this story about a fish hook to others around the area. What seems the same? What is different?

3. Why is it significant that the second sister became ashamed from her brother's glance?

Batak Creation (Sumatra)

The Batak who live in Sumatra are part of the Republic of Indonesia. There are six cultural groups of Batak people: the Toba, the Karo, the Simalungun, the Pak Pak, the Mandailing, and the Angkola. There are more than 6 million Batak currently living on the island nation of Sumatra. It is from the Toba Batak, who live along Lake Toba, that we hear this unique story of creation. Sumatra has seen outsiders on their islands since the second or third century CE, but the Batak managed to live in relative isolation until the late nineteenth century. Their stories are no doubt influenced by the Indian, Buddhist, and Muslim traders who passed over the island.

Source: Roland Dixon, *Oceanic Mythology,* 1916.

BATAK CREATION

In the world of the gods there were two trees, one of which bore a bud or sprout in the form of a ball. By the motions of a bird, which sat on this tree, the bud was shaken off and fell into the Spirit River, in which a great serpent dwelt; but though the latter tried to swallow the mysterious object, it escaped him, and drifting to the shore, was metamorphosed into a woman. Marrying a man who was developed from a tree-trunk floating in the sea, she gave birth, first, to six streams of blood from which all evil spirits came; and finally to two sons, one of whom, taking with him the seeds of all plants and animals, was lowered from the sky-world, where all these events occurred, to the earth that he might prepare it for men.

Mula Dyadi, the highest deity, dwelt in the uppermost of the seven heavens and had two birds as his servants. Having created three male beings, he caused a tree to exist in one of the lower heavens, its branches reaching to the sky; next he made a hen, which perched on the tree and later laid three eggs, from which came three maidens whom Mula Dyadi gave as wives to his three sons. The daughter of one of these sons refused to marry a cousin of hers because he had a face like a lizard and a skin like a chameleon, and devoted her time to spinning.

One day she dropped her spindle, which fell down from the sky-world. On the unrolled thread she descended to the surface of the sea which stretched everywhere below. In this primeval ocean swam a great serpent on whose head the heavenly maiden spread a handful of earth brought down at her request from Mula Dyadi by one of his bird servants; and thus she formed the world.

The serpent, however, disliked the weight upon his head, and turning over, caused this newly made world to be engulfed by the sea. Thereupon Mula Dyadi created eight suns, whose heat should dry up the sea, and this being done in part, the divine maiden thrust a sword into the body of the serpent, revealed by the shrinking sea, and fastened his body firmly in an island block that he might never again thus destroy the world. With more soil she then re-founded the earth; but after this, having questioned her as to what was to be done with the youth whom she refused as husband, Mula Dyadi declared that she now must marry him, and wrapping the unwelcome suitor together with a blowgun in a mat, he threw him down upon the earth.

Unharmed by his fall, and feeling hungry, he shot at a dove which escaped unwounded, but caught the arrow dexterously and flew with it to the village where the heavenly maiden dwelt. Following in pursuit, the youth discovered the girl who had before refused him, found her more tractable, and married her; and so they became the ancestors of mankind.

DISCUSSION QUESTIONS

1. What is the significance of the birthing of six streams of blood?

2. Describe the character of the maiden. What is the lesson to be learned from the maiden's rejection of her suitor?

3. What is Mula Dyadi like? How does he treat his children?

4. What is the role of the trees in this creation myth?

Source: Roland Dixon, *Oceanic Mythology*, 1916.

Dawn, Noontide, and Night (Australia)

There is evidence to suggest that the earliest aboriginal inhabitants of Australia have been living there for 45,000 or more years. Having spoken more than 200 different languages before colonial contact, there were perhaps 500 different social groups occupying the island continent. Upon the British settlement beginning in 1788, the aborigines were pushed out of territory taken by settlers and moved deeper into the bush to fight for their survival. Aborigines who stayed near the cities became laborers and much was done to "civilize" these people. Land laws in the late nineteenth century saw tracts of land dedicated to aboriginal peoples, much like the reservation system for native North Americans. Currently around half a million Aborigines live in Australia, which is about 3% of the population of the continent.

Most Australian myth takes place during "The Dreaming" or "The Dream Time." This mythological realm of time and space exists before the world was fully formed as we see it today. It is the time of creation and the establishment of "totemism." Totemism is the belief in the connection of humans to all things in nature and that the myths and stories are not separated from man, but part of us. The stories that take place in *The Dreaming* are constantly alive, metamorphosing into other beings and objects, and if there was a specific spot or place in which something happened, that place became sacred.

DAWN, NOONTIDE, AND NIGHT

One day a man who lived in the clouds went about his business gathering his wood. His name was Ngoudenout. Suddenly, an emu egg flew through the clouds and landed in his woodpile. When the egg struck the wood, it exploded into flames and the earth below received the first light. Everything on earth was struck with surprise; the flowers lifted their petals and the dew rolled off onto the ground. The birds and fairies who watched the snowy mountains stopped what they were doing to stare at the light. This caused the snow to melt and flood into the rivers below.

Across the mountains, in the east, the night shadows began to lighten. The clouds turned from purple to gray, from gray to pink, and pink to red. The light shone in a gold line between the shadows and the light, and all the mist of the valleys began to fade. Each living thing began to awaken at the sight of the dawn. From over the mountains the sun rose, signalling the first day.

Ngoudenout's wood pile continued to burn, at first just embers, but the heat gathered and halfway through that first day the wood pile was blazing bright. As the day lengthened, the light from wood pile calmed and quieted. Across the mountains, in the west, the shadows began to lengthen. The sky turned from red to pink, from pink to gray, from gray to purple. The mist returned and it was once again night.

Ngoudenout loved the sun, saw its magic, and decided to keep the sun coming back each day. When the wood pile dies down for the night, Ngoudenout wanters through the forest in the sky and gathers more wood for the next day's light. Each day he lights the dawn fire, watches as it blazes bright at noontime, dies away for the evening, and needs to be tended again. He is forever the wood gatherer, who tends the light of the day.

DISCUSSION QUESTIONS

1. How did Ngoudenout go from being a "cloud man" to "the eternal wood gatherer?" Do these two identities have anything in common?

2. Consider the title of this story, "Dawn, Noontide, and Night." How are these three times accounted for in this myth?

Adapted from: Thomas, W. J. *Some Myths and Legends of the Australian Aborigines.* 1923.

The Great Flood (Australia)

Living on a continent that is known for its arid climate and large expanse of desert, it may seem strange to encounter such a fully formed flood myth from the Aboriginal Australians. But this myth begins with dryness, withheld by a common animal, and the need for water overwhelms those who were recently parched. The survivors of this flood are many, but the canoe-steering "blackfellow" is unlike most of the flood "heroes" we've seen in other stories.

THE GREAT FLOOD

It was in the dream-time that a great drought came over the land. The leaves would not grow on trees, the petals on flowers drooped, the grass turned brown and wispy, as if fire had burnt it. The wind blew hot, the river beds shriveled until there was no water, and the sand burned like fire. The sun above stared down, blazing, and there were no hills to cool the land; the only time that the land had a break from the deadly heat was during the night.

So many animals and plants had died from this drought that they called together a meeting to understand why there was no water. The animal representatives traveled from each corner of the earth to meet in the center of Australia. These animals discovered the root of the problem: a huge frog named Tiddalik was responsible for their misery, having swallowed all the water. The animals gathered and decided that in order to obtain the water, they had to make the frog laugh.

The Kookaburra was chosen to tempt the frog to laughter, and the animals gathered into a circle around the water-bloated frog. The Kookaburra thought for a moment about how to proceed, and eventually hopped down from his tree limb and began to stare at the frog. The Kookaburra himself laughed, first quietly, then a louder and booming laugh emitted from the bird. Everyone looked at Tiddalik, but he did not laugh.

The Kookaburra kept laughing and eventually laughed so hard that he fell off of his tree limb. Still the frog did not laugh. A frill-lizard was chosen to try next, and he puffed out his frilly collar, blew out with his jaws, and began to hop in front of the frog. The frog could not be bothered to laugh. More and more animals attempted to make the frog laugh, but it was in vain. The frog was not interested at all!

Fights began to break out between the animals. Old feuds were rehashed and the birds, lizards, and mammals flew at each other in their frustration and anger at the situation. Peace eventually came over the crowd and an eel popped his head out of the nearby deep water hole. The eel had an idea for making the frog laugh. He wiggled and squirmed in the center of the crowd, slowly, then with more vigor he moved like a snake, shivering in front of Tiddalik. Then the eel moved, flopping onto the ground atop hill of ants, slithering and writhing. At last the frog began to take notice. He opened his eyes wide, his mouth began to slacken, and finally a sound like thunder emitted from his mouth in a wild laugh.

All of the water that had been held inside the bloated frog came gushing forth in a flood. The riverbeds overflowed, the streams washed through the land, and suddenly the only remaining dry land were the mountain peaks. Most of the creatures on the earth were swept up and died.

Among the survivors was a pelican, who was also a blackfellow, and he moved between dry spots with a canoe, rescuing other blackfellows he could find. One of these islands of land in the flood held many survivors, one of whom was a beautiful woman. The pelican was instantly in love, but he rescued the men first, leaving her alone on the island. During each of his trips to rescue these men, the woman would ask to be rescued, but the blackfellow answered, "I already have too many people in my canoe, so I will come back for you." The woman was smart, and knew the pelican would take her back to his home with him. She was not interested and decided to escape the island herself.

Adapted from: Thomas, W. J. *Some Myths and Legends of the Australian Aborigines.* 1923.

On one of the pelican's trips away from the island, the woman wrapped her possum rug around a log and left it on the ground, and she ran into the bush. When the pelican returned and saw the woman's rug, he touched his toe to it. The log did not move, so the pelican grabbed at the rug and revealed the log underneath. How angry he became! The pelican found white clay near the water and began to spread it over his skin. He set off to find more survivors, whom he wished to kill. But when he encountered another blackfellow, he was so startled at the sight of the pelican, that he killed him with a club. Ever since, the black and white colors of the pelican remind us of the flood.

When the waters subsided, the trees grew back their leaves, the flower petals opened again, and the grass was as green as springtime. When the sun dawned for the first time after the flood, the birds lifted their voices in praise to the welcome flood of sunlight.

DISCUSSION QUESTIONS

1. Why might the animals think that making the frog laugh will give them water? What does this say about the human tendency for laughter?

2. Compare the flood survivor (the pelican or blackfellow) to other flood survivors you've read about. What is he like? Is he a hero?

3. How does the lone woman manage to escape?

Part 2: Tricksters, Lovers, and Other Tales

How Fire was Stolen from the Red-Crested Cockatoo (Australia)

Here we encounter another myth set in the realm of *The Dream Time*. The Aborigines in this story are told of "the secret of the fire of the sun." An old man who visits the tribe tells them that through bravery and persistence, he will pass off his journey to hunt down the Cockatoo and steal the gift of fire from him. The translator of this myth repeatedly refers to the tribe as "a tribe of blacks," which could mean a few things. The old man who encounters the tribe could be a foreigner, or at least foreign to the tribe, and the difference in skin color may be a signifier of the difference between the traveler and the tribe. The myth also states that today's birds were once men, so this could account for the tribe being representative of black-feathered birds. Or, as the oppression of Aboriginal Australians has been present since European settlement, the translator could be calling them "a tribe of blacks" to colloquially say that these are Aborigines. In any case, the story of how the tribe stole fire is a rich story to add to the world literature of fire-gathering.

HOW FIRE WAS STOLEN FROM THE RED-CRESTED COCKATOO

In the dreamtime, many of the birds and animals that we now know as inhabitants of the bush were actually men. On their way back from hunting, a tribe of blacks were approached by an old, wrinkled man who carried a long spear and an empty bag. The old man came closer, dug the tip of his spear into the dirt in peace, and spoke to them. He said, "It has been a long time since I left my own tribe of hunters. I have traveled all over the land and reached the ends of the earth. I found the place in which the water roars like thunder; I have crossed mountains and plains, I have seen where the sun is hidden in the clouds, and found the land beyond the dawning of the sun. In my age, I have known many adventures and made many friends. Before I leave to be with my people, I would like to rest here among you. If you let me, I will give you a secret. I know the secret of the sun and if I tell it to you, the bravest of you will be able to take it to your tribe."

The tribe agreed to let him rest in their camp, and provided him with a place of honor at their meal. As they finished eating, the tribe began to gather around the old man, waiting for his promised story. There was not yet fire for the tribe to circle around, and though they saw the sun each day, they thought frequently about how they could harness the power of the sun when the land grew cold. These people could not cook food or create weapons, but it was not for these reasons that they wanted the fire of the sun; they were tired of getting cold. The old man wrapped a blanket around him and prepared to tell his story.

"My journey began in the east, far past the mountains that the sun climbs over each morning. Along the way I saw there was no water and many animals were dead. I was fearful of the amount of death I saw, and so I continued quickly. A few days later, I realized how thirsty I was, and ran towards a nearby watering hole. I was weak from thirst and my legs could not carry me far enough. I fell to the ground and slept, though the day was bright. I awoke to the sound of buzzing, but my legs would still not carry my weight. I crawled to the watering hole and tried to drink, but instead of water my mouth only felt the burning sand. It was a false vision of water that had led me there. I felt possessed by my anger and desperation and began digging a hole with my own hands. When my fingers were bleeding and blistered, I reached a trickle of water below the sand. More water came until I could drink enough to be sated. I stayed to rest, and set off the next day.

Adapted from: Thomas, W. J. *Some Myths and Legends of the Australian Aborigines.* 1923.

"I entered a forest of high trees and suddenly saw the gleam of sunlight high above, filtering down through the leaves and branches. I looked around for the source and found it was Mar, the Cockatoo, who had fire captured in his crest and was lighting his way with it. I trampled over the dry sticks, which caught Mar's attention, and he flew away quickly. I made my way back to my people, but they did not remain at their camp. I eventually found you and give you this challenge: if one of you is brave enough to retrace my steps to find Mar and take the fire from him, men all over the world will forever sing in praise of your name."

The tribe was excited by the old man's challenge and made a plan to invite Mar to a feast. There, they would be able to steal the fire from him. The day of the feast arrived; the people danced and sang, they played at fighting and ate a freshly caught kangaroo. The best piece of meat was offered to Mar, but he would not take it. They offered a piece of kangaroo skin, which Mar happily took and began to fly back to his own camp.

The smallest member of the tribe was Prite, who took it upon himself to follow the cockatoo. Mar flew far over mountains and just as Prite began to tire, he spotted the fire in Mar's crest. Prite returned to his tribe and exclaimed the truth of the old man's story. The entire tribe discussed their next action, and they agreed that Tatkanna the Robin should be the one to steal the fire.

Tatkanna set out to search for Mar and many hours later arrived at his camp. Tatkanna watched in awe as Mar lit a stick with his fire and held up the piece of kangaroo skin the tribe had given him. With the fire stick, Mar singed the hair on the skin. Tatkanna knew this was his chance, but he got too close to the fire and caught his own breast on fire. Since this time, he has been known as Robin Redbreast. Though he was frightened, and he knew the cockatoo had seen him, Tatkanna ran to the fire and grabbed the stick. As he flew into the air with his fire stick, the grass around him erupted into flames. The birds and animals of the bush ran from the fire as quickly as they could, but the blaze caught everything on fire.

Mar, the cockatoo found that his fire had been taken and became very angry. Mar sought out Tatkanna in revenge and returned back to the tribal camp. Tatkanna was very small and upset at the damage the fire had caused. He asked his friend the Kookaburra to fight Mar in his stead. The Kookaburra did his best, but was beaten after just a few minutes of fighting. The Kookaburra flew into the trees and is still there. Mar was unhappy that no one else would fight him and so he returned to his own camp, defeated. The robin is still celebrated for his bravery and carries his scorched breastfeathers as an honorable memory of his quest for the fire.

DISCUSSION QUESTIONS

1. Why does it take the arrival of an old man from outside the tribe to make the tribe interested in fire?

2. Compare this to other stories of fire-gatherers you've read (Prometheus, etc.).

3. How do Tatkanna and Quartang become cultural heroes? What are they like (in stature, personality, in ability)?

4. What does Mar's (the cockatoo) reaction to his missing fire suggest about his abilities?

The Trickster Olofat (Caroline Islands)

The Melanesian character Olofat embodies many of the characteristics we see from tricksters all over the world. He is a shapeshifter, his mischievousness gets him into trouble with his father, many gods attempt to kill him, and he is credited with the creation of a being that is harmful to man. Olofat is the oldest son of the highest sky deity, Luk-lang. Throughout the story Luk's supremacy is challenged by his son's trouble-making. It is clear that Olofat's siblings are much better liked and respected and Olofat is considered a nuisance by his father.

THE TRICKSTER OLOFAT

Olofat saw that one of his brothers was better than he and also more beautiful, and at this he became angry. Looking down from the sky-world and seeing two boys who had caught a couple of sharks, with which they were playing in a fishpond, he descended to earth and gave the sharks teeth, so that they bit the hands of the children. When the boys ran home crying with pain and told their troubles to their mother, Ligoapup, who was the sister of Olofat, she asked them if they had seen anyone about. They said that they had, and that he was more handsome than any man whom they had ever beheld. Knowing that this must be her brother, Olofat, Ligoapup asked her sons where he was, and they answered, "Close by the sea." She then told them to go and get the man and bring him to her, but when they reached the place where they had left him, they found only an old, grey-haired man, covered with dirt.

Returning to their mother, they informed her that the man whom they had seen was no longer there; but she bade them go back and bring whomsoever they might find. Accordingly they set off, but this time they saw only a heap of filth in place of a man; and so once more they went home to their mother, who told them to return a third time. Obeying her, they questioned the filth, saying, "Are you Olofat? For if you are, you must come to our mother." The pile of filth turned into a handsome man who accompanied them to Ligoapup.

She said to him, "Why are you such a deceiver?"

And Olofat replied, "How so?"

Ligoapup said, "First, you turned yourself into a dirty old man, and then into a pile of filth."

"I am afraid of my father," answered Olofat.

"Yes," said Ligoapup, "you are afraid of him because you gave teeth to the shark."

Then Olofat replied, "I am angry at my father, Luk, for he created my brother handsomer than I am, and with greater power. I shall give teeth to all sharks, in order that they may eat men whenever canoes tip over."

When Luk, who was in the sky-world, became aware of these things, he said to his wife, "It would be well if Olofat came back to heaven, since he is only doing evil on earth."

His wife, Inoaeman, said, "I think so, too. Otherwise he will destroy mankind, for he is an evil being."

Luk ordered the people of the sky-world to build a great house, and when it was finished, he not only commanded that a feast be announced, but also had a large fish-basket prepared, in which they placed Olofat and sank him in the sea. After five nights, when they thought he would be dead, two men went in a canoe and hauled up the basket; but behold! it contained only a multitude of great fish, for Olofat had slipped away and seated himself in a canoe nearby.

Source: Roland Dixon, *Oceanic Mythology*, 1916.

The men in the canoe asked him, "Who are you?"

And he replied, "I am Olofat. Come here, and I will help you to put the fish into your boat."

Taking one fish after the other, he handed them to the men, but in so doing he removed all the flesh of the fish and gave the men merely the empty skins. For himself he kept nothing but the smallest ones; and when the people said, "Why is it that you take only the little fish?"

Olofat replied, "Give Luk all the big ones you have caught; I am quite satisfied with the little ones."

Then the people brought the catch to Luk, who asked them, "Where is the fish-basket? Who took the fish out?"

When they replied, "Olofat did that, but has again placed the basket in the sea," Luk asked, "Has he then taken no fish for himself?" to which they answered, "Only the very smallest ones."

Luk now ordered all sorts of food to be prepared for the feast and commanded that the fishes should be cooked; and when all were gathered in the house, while Olofat sat at the entrance, Luk said, "Let everyone now eat. Let the food be divided, and let each receive his share."

Nevertheless, Olofat refused to receive any; and when the guests took up the fish, lo! there were only the empty skins, and within was nothing, so that they had to content themselves with fruit. Olofat, however, ate his own fish; but Luk said, "See, we have nothing, whereas Olofat is able to eat his own fish, and is still not finished with them."

Thereupon he became very angry and sent word to Thunder to destroy Olofat; but since Thunder lived in a house at a distance, Luk said, "Take Thunder some food."

So one of the gods gathered some of the food to take to Thunder, but Olofat snatched them from him and carried the food to Thunder himself. On arriving at the house, he called out, "O Thunder, I bring food."

Thunder found a white hen outside his house, and coming out, he thundered; but though Luk cried, "Kill him," and though Thunder blazed, Olofat merely placed his hand before his eyes. Thunder followed him and thundered again and again behind him; but from under his clothes, Olofat took some coconut milk, and sprinkling it upon Thunder, he quenched the lightning. After this he seized Thunder and bore him back to his own home; and when Olofat had returned to the feast house, Luk said, "Why has the man not been killed?"

Olofat again took his place by the door, while Luk ordered another of the gods to take food to Anulap, the god of magic. Thereupon Olofat stood up and walked along behind the one who carried the food and he took it away from him, saying, "I myself will take the food to Anulap."

So he went to the god and said, "Here is for you" and then he turned about and came back to the great assembly house.

Luk said to Anulap, "Why have you not killed the man?" Then Anulap took his great hook, which was fastened to a strong rope, and throwing it at Olofat, he caught him around the neck; but Olofat quickly seized a mussel-shell and cut the rope, after which he hastened to the house of Anulap, where he sat down upon the threshold. When Anulap saw him, he seized his club to strike Olofat; but as he stretched it out, Olofat changed himself into a wooden mortar.

Thereupon Anulap called, "Where is Olofat?" and his wife, answered, "He must have run away," they lay down and slept.

After all this Luk said, "We can do nothing with Olofat; I believe he cannot die. Go, O Laitian, and tell the people to come in the morning to make a porch for the house."

When the people had come and asked how they should construct the porch, Luk said, "Go to the forest and bring great tree-trunks."

When this was done, and the tree-trunks were laid by the house, Luk commanded, "Now, go and fetch Olofat."

Olofat came and said, "I shall go, too," but Luk replied, "You must aid us to build the porch. You must make three holes in the ground, two shallow and one deep; and in these the tree-trunks must be set."

Accordingly Olofat dug three holes, but in each of them he made an excavation at one side; after which Luk asked, "Olofat, are you ready yet?"

Thereupon Olofat, taking a nut and a stone, secreted them within his clothes; and Luk said, "Now set the tree-trunks in the holes."

In obedience, three men seized the upper end, while Olofat grasped the lower part; and they pushed Olofat so that he fell into the hole, only to creep quickly into the space which he had made on the side. Not knowing this, however, they then raised the tree-trunk high, and dropping it into the hole, they made it firm with earth and stone.

All now believed that Olofat had been caught under the great post and had been crushed to death. He, however, sat in his hole on the side, and being hungry five nights later, he cracked the nut with the stone which he had brought with him and ate it; whereupon ants came, and taking the fragments which had fallen to the ground, they carried the food along the trunk to the surface, going in long rows.

The man who sat in the house above, seeing this, said to his wife, "Olofat is dead, for the ants are bringing up parts of his body!"

When Olofat heard the speech of the man, he turned himself into an ant and crept with the others up the post. Having climbed high, he allowed himself to drop upon the body of the man, who pushed the ant off, so that it fell to the ground, where it was immediately changed into Olofat.

As soon as the people saw him, they sprang up in fear. When Luk beheld him, he said, "We have tried in every possible way to kill you, but it seems that you cannot die. Bring me Samenkoaner."

After Samenkoaner had come and sat down, Luk asked him, "How is it that Olofat cannot die? Can you kill him?"

To this Samenkoaner replied, "No, not even if I thought about it for a whole night long, could I find a means; for he is older than I."

Luk said, "But I do not wish that he should destroy all men upon the earth."

The Rat, Luk's sister, advised that they should burn Olofat. Accordingly they made a great fire, to which they brought Olofat; but he had with him a roll of coconut fibre, and when Luk ordered them to throw him into the flames, he crept through the roll and came out safely upon the other side of the fire.

Becoming resigned, Luk said, "Rat, we have tried everything to kill him, but it has been in vain."

The Rat decided, "He cannot die; so make him the lord of all who are evil and deceitful."

DISCUSSION QUESTIONS

1. Why has Olofat given teeth to the shark? What does this mean to the people telling the myth?

2. Compare Olofat's fish offering to Luk to Prometheus' offering to Zeus. What are their reasons? How do they convince others to take part?

3. Which gods does Luk call upon for assistance? How do each of them fail to kill Olofat?

4. Olofat's punishment is to become "lord of all who are evil and deceitful." Is this a true punishment? Or is this a reward for his cunning?

The Goddess of Fire and The Goddess of the Sea (Hawaii)

The love triangle between a great sorcerer, Pele, and her sister, Na-maka-a-ka-hai (the goddess of the sea) continues the earlier story of "How Pele Came to Hawaii." In this iteration of the Pele legend, it is the jealousy of her sister, rightfully provoked by Pele's secret marriage to her husband, who causes Pele to become ensconced in the mouth of a volcano in her spirit form. This myth provides explanation for many naturally occurring phenomenon and references real locations in the Hawaiian Islands that are regarded as sacred spaces often presided over by ghost gods, or au-makua.

THE GODDESS OF FIRE AND THE GODDESS OF THE SEA

A greater sorcerer married Na-maka-o-ka-hai, the goddess of the sea. After a time he saw Pele and her beautiful young sister Hiiaka. He took them also, and secretly made them his wives. This sorcerer could fly through the heavens, swim through the seas, or run swiftly over the earth. By magic power he conquered enemies, visited strange lands, found the fountain of the water of life, sprinkled that water over his dead brothers, brought them back to life, and did many marvellous deeds. But he could not deliver Pele and Hiiaka from the wrath of their sister Na-maka-o-ka-hai.

High tides and floods from the seas destroyed Pele's home and lands. Then the elder brother of Pele, Ka-moho-alii, the shark-god, called for all the family to aid Pele. Na-maka-o-ka-hai fought the whole family and defeated them. She broke down their houses and drove them into the ocean. There the shark god provided them with the great boat Honua-i-a-kea (The great spread-out world) and carried them away to distant islands. Pele carried her Pa-oa, a magic spade. Wherever they landed she struck the earth, thus opening a crater in which volcanic fires burned.

Na-maka-o-ka-hai went to the highest of all the mythical lands of the ancestors, Nuu-mea-lani (The raised dais of heaven). There she could look over all the seas from a legendary land in the south to the most northerly part of the Hawaiian Islands. As the smoke from Pele's Pa-oa craters rose to the clouds, the angry watching one rushed from Nuu-mea-lani and tried to slay the family. Again and again Pele and her family escaped. Farther and farther from the home land were they driven until they struck far out into the ocean.

Source: W. D. Westervelt, *Hawaiian Legends of the Volcanoes*, 1916.

After a long time Na-maka-o-ka-hai saw the smoke of earth-fires far away on the island Kauai. Pele had struck her Pa-oa into the earth, dug a deep pit, and thrown up a large hill known to this day as the Puu-o-Pele (The hill of Pele). It seemed as if an abiding-place had been found.

Na-maka-o-ka-hai came and fought Pele at this place. Pele was broken and smashed and left for dead. She was not dead, but she left Kauai and went to Oahu to Moanalua. There she dug a fire-pit. The earth, or rather the eruption of lava, was forced up into a hill which later bore the name Ke-alia-manu (The-bird-white-like-a-salt-bed or The-white-bird). The crater which she dug filled up with salt water and was named Ke-alia-paa-kai (The-white-bed-of-salt, or Salt Lake).

Pele was not able to strike her Pa-oa down into a mountain side and dig deep for the foundations of her home. She could find fire only in the lowlands near the seashore. The best place on Oahu was just back of Leahi, the ancient Hawaiian name for Diamond Head. Here she threw up a great quantity of fire-rock, but at last her fires were drowned by the water she struck below.

Thus she passed along the coast of each island, the family watching and aiding until they came to the great volcano Haleakala. There Pele dug with her Paoa, and a great quantity of lava was thrown out of her fire-pit.

Na-maka-o-ka-hai saw enduring clouds day after day rising with the colors of the dark dense smoke of the underworld, and knew that her sister was still living.

Pele had gained strength and confidence, therefore she entered alone into a conflict unto death.

The battle was fought again by the two sisters hand to hand. The conflict lasted for a long time along the western slope of the mountain Hale-a-ka-la. Na-maka-o-ka-hai tore the body of Pele and broke her lava bones into great pieces which lie to this day along the seacoast of Kahiki-nui. The masses of broken lava are called Na-iwi-o-Pele (The bones of Pele).

Pele was thought to be dead and was sorely mourned by the remaining brothers and sisters. Na-maka-o-ka-hai went off toward her mountain lookout, rejoicing in the destruction of her hated enemy. By and by she looked back over the wide seas. The high mountains of the island Hawaii, snow covered, lay in the distance. But over the side of the mountain known as Mauna Loa she saw the uhane, the spirit form of Pele in clouds of volcanic smoke tinged red from the flames of raging fire-pits below.

She passed on to Nuu-mea-lani, knowing that she could never again overcome the spirit of Pele, the goddess of fire.

The Pele family crossed the channel between the islands and went to the mountain side, for they also had seen the spirit form of Pele. They served their goddess sister, caring for her fires and pouring out the destructive rivers of lava at her commands.

As time passed they became a part of the innumerable multitude of au-makuas, or ghost-gods, of the Pit of Pele, worshipped especially by those whose lives were filled with burning anger against their fellow-men.

The acceptable offerings to Pele were fruits, flowers, garlands (or leis), pigs (especially the small black pig of tender flesh and delicate flavor), chickens, fish, and men. When a family sent a part of the dead body of one of the household, it was with the prayer that the spirit might become an au-makua, and especially an unihipili au-makua. This meant a ghost-god, powerful enough to aid the worshipper to pray other people to death.

Pele is said to have become impatient at times with her brothers and sisters. Then she would destroy their pleasure resorts in the valleys. She would send a flood of lava in her anger and burn everything up. Earthquakes came when Pele stamped the floor of the fire-pit in anger. Flames thrusting themselves through cracks in a breaking lava crust were the fire spears of Pele's household of au-makuas or ghost-gods.

Pele's voice was explosive when angry. Therefore it was called "pu." When the natives first heard guns fired they said that the voice of the gun was "pu." It was like the explosions of gas in volcanic eruptions, and it seemed as if the foreigners had persuaded Pele to assist them in any trouble with the natives.

DISCUSSION QUESTIONS

1. Why do you think that Na-maka-o-ka-hai takes her anger out on Pele, rather than Hiiaka or her husband?

2. Research one of the places mentioned in the story. Where is it located? What kinds of ceremonies were held there pre-contact? What is this location used for now?

3. The final lines of the story suggest that Pele had conspired with the foreigners, using "pu" to keep watch over them. Knowing Pele's reputation, how did this potentially aid the colonizers in the annexation of Hawaii?

Part 3: Journeys of Heroes and Heroines

© Malgorzata Litkowska /Shutterstock.com

The Legends of Maui (Maori)

The ancestors of the Polynesians migrated from Asia and settled the islands in the Pacific; the group that settled in New Zealand named their land *Aotearoa* (long white cloud) and called themselves the Maori. The story of Maui presented here comes from the earliest published collection of Maori myths. While missionaries were arriving in this area beginning in 1814, the myths that were recorded from the oral tradition contain only subtle influences of Christianity.

Maui is among the most well-known characters in Polynesian myth; he is a demi-god—his mother was a goddess (Taranga), but his father was a mortal man (Makea). He is both a hero and a trickster. The tales of Maui spread as the people traveled throughout the Pacific, settling in the Hawaiian Islands, Tahiti, and Samoa, in addition to New Zealand—you may have recognized his name, as the large island of Hawaii is named after him. The tales may vary somewhat from place to place, but the Maui cycle typically contains these essential components: his birth, the theft of fire, snaring the sun, pulling up the islands of New Zealand while fishing, and his attempt to defeat death itself.

THE LEGENDS OF MAUI

The story begins with Maui as an infant. He was either abandoned or rejected by his mother, or she simply didn't remember his birth and believed that he must belong to someone else. But the infant Maui said to her:

"I was born at the side of the sea,[1] and was thrown by you into the foam of the surf, after you had wrapped me up in a tuft of your hair, which you cut off for the purpose; then the seaweed formed and fashioned me, as caught in its long tangles the ever-heaving surges of the sea rolled me, folded as I was in them, from side to side; at length the breezes and squalls which blew from the ocean drifted me on

Source: Grey, George. *Polynesian Mythology and Ancient Traditional History of the New Zealanders.* 1854.

shore again, and the soft jelly-fish of the long sandy beaches rolled themselves round me to protect me; then again myriads of flies alighted on me to buzz about me and lay their eggs, that maggots might eat me, and flocks of birds collected round me to peck me to pieces, but at that moment appeared there also my great ancestor, Tama-nui-ki-te-Rangi, and he saw the flies and the birds collected in clusters and flocks above the jelly-fish, and the old man ran, as fast as he could, and stripped off the encircling jelly-fish, and behold within there lay a human being; then he caught me up and carried me to his house, and he hung me up in the roof that I might feel the warm smoke and the heat of the fire, so I was saved alive by the kindness of that old man."

At this, his mother recognized him and said: "'Come here, my child, and sleep with the mother who bore you, that I may kiss you, and that you may kiss me', and he ran to sleep with his mother."

In the morning, their mother disappeared from the house, but returned at nightfall. This pattern was repeated every day, to Maui's great distress. He wanted to discover where she went each day. Maui's brothers tell him that if they don't have this knowledge, as they are older and wiser, then there's no way he could find out. But Maui was determined.

Maui...crept out in the night and stole his mother's apron, her belt, and clothes, and hid them; then he went and stopped up every crevice in the wooden window, and in the doorway, so that the light of the dawn might not shine into the house, and make his mother hurry to get up...At last up she jumped; and finding herself quite naked, began to look for her clothes, and apron, but could find neither; then she ran and pulled out the things with which the chinks in the windows and doors were stopped up, and whilst doing so, oh , dear! oh, dear! there she saw the sun high up in the heavens; then she snatched up, as she ran off, the old clout of a flax cloak, with which the door of the house had been stopped up, and carried it off as her only covering; getting, at last, outside the house, she hurried away, and ran crying at the thought of having been so badly treated by her own children.

As soon as his mother got outside the house, little Maui jumped up, and kneeling upon his hands and knees peeped after her through the doorway into the bright light. Whilst he was watching her, the old woman reached down to a tuft of rushes, and snatching it up from the ground, dropped into a hole underneath it, and clapping the tuft of rushes in the hole again, as if it were its covering, so disappeared. Then little Maui jumped on his feet, and, as hard as he could go, ran out of the house, pulled up the tuft of rushes, and peeping down, discovered a beautiful open cave running quite deep into the earth.

He covered up the hole again and returned to the house, and waking up his brothers who were still sleeping, said: 'Come, come, my brothers, rouse up, you have slept long enough; come, get up; here we are again cajoled by our mother.' Then his brothers made haste and got up; alas! alas! the sun was quite high up in the heavens.

The little Maui now asked his brothers again: 'Where do you think the place is where our father and mother dwell? and they answered: 'How should we know, we have never seen it...'

It was decided that Maui should try to find their mother and father; it turns out that he had a special talent.

When he first appeared to his relatives in their house of singing and dancing, he had on that occasion transformed himself into the likeness of all manner of birds, of every bird in the world, and yet no single form that he then assumed had pleased his brothers; but now when he showed himself to them, transformed into the semblance of a pigeon, his brothers said: 'Ah! now indeed, oh, brother, you do look very well indeed, very beautiful, very beautiful, much more beautiful than you looked in any of the other forms which you assumed, and then changed from, when you first discovered yourself to us.'

* * *

Early the next morning, he said to his brothers, as was first stated: 'Now do you remain here, and you will hear something of me after I am gone; it is my great love for my parents that leads me to search for them; now listen to me, and then say whether or not my recent feats were not remarkable. For the feat of transforming oneself into birds can only be accomplished by a man who is skilled in magic, and yet here I, the youngest of you all, have assumed the form of all birds, and now, perhaps, after all, I shall quite lose my art and become old and weakened in the long journey to the place where I am going.' His brothers answered him thus: 'That might be indeed, if you were going upon a warlike expedition, but, in truth, you are only going to look for those parents whom we all so long to see, and if they are found by you, we shall ever after all dwell happily, our present sorrow will be ended, and we shall continually pass backwards and forwards between our dwelling-place and theirs, paying them happy visits.'

He answered them: 'It is certainly a very good cause which leads me to undertake this journey, and if, when reaching the place I am going to, I find everything agreeable and nice, then I shall, perhaps, be pleased with it, but if I find it a bad, disagreeable place, I shall be disgusted with it.'

They replied to him: 'What you say is exceedingly true, depart then upon your journey, with your great knowledge and skill in magic.' Then their brother went into the wood, and came back to them again, looking just as if he were a real pigeon. His brothers were quite delighted, and they had no power left to do anything but admire him.

Then off he flew, until he came to the cave which his mother had run down into, and he lifted up the tuft of rushes; then down he went and disappeared in the cave, and shut up its mouth again so as to hide the entrance; away he flew very fast indeed, and twice he dipped his wing, because the cave was narrow; soon he reached nearly to the bottom of the cave, and flew along it; and again, because the cave was so narrow, he dips first one wing and then the other, but the cave now widened, and he dashed straight on.

*   *   *

Maui sees his parents lying in the grass beneath the trees. He picks berries and drops them down to get their attention; the berries fall, striking his mother and father on the head. They, in turn, begin to throw rocks at him.

*   *   *

Maui had himself contrived that he should be struck by the stone which his father threw; for, but by his own choice, no one could have bit him; he was struck exactly upon his left leg, and down he fell, and as he lay fluttering and struggling upon the ground, they all ran to catch him, but lo, the pigeon had turned into a man.

Then all those who saw him were frightened at his fierce glaring eyes, which were red as if painted with red ochre, and they said: 'Oh, it is now no wonder that he so long sat still up in the tree; had he been a bird he would have flown off long before, but he is a man': and some of them said: 'No, indeed, rather a god—just look at his form and appearance, the like has never been seen before, since Rangi and Papa-tu-a-nuku were torn apart.'[2]

Then Taranga said, 'I used to see one who looked like this person every night when I went to visit my children, but what I saw then excelled what I see now; just listen to me. Once as I was wandering upon the sea-shore, I prematurely gave birth to one of my children, and I cut off the long tresses of my hair, and bound him up in them, and threw him into the foam of the sea, and after that be was found by his ancestor Tama-nui-ki-te-Rangi'; and then she told his history nearly in the same words that Maui-the-infant had told it to herself and his brothers in their house, and having finished his history, Taranga ended her discourse to her husband and his friends.

*   *   *

And she cried aloud: 'This is, indeed, my child. By the winds and storms and wave-uplifting gales he was fashioned and became a human being; welcome, oh my child, welcome; you shall climb the threshold of the house of your great ancestor Hine-nui-te-po, and death shall thenceforth have no power over man.'

Then the lad was taken by his father to the water, to be baptized, and after the ceremony prayers were offered to make him sacred, and clean from all impurities; but when it was completed, his father Makea-tu-tara felt greatly alarmed, because he remembered that he had, from mistake, hurriedly skipped over part of the prayers of the baptismal service, and of the services to purify Maui; he knew that the gods would be certain to punish this fault, by causing Maui to die, and his alarm and anxiety were therefore extreme. At nightfall they all went into his house.

Maui, after these things, returned to his brothers to tell them that he had found his parents, and to explain to them where they dwelt.

Maui Snares the Sun

He then again paid a visit to his parents, and remained for some time with them, and whilst he was there he remarked that some of their people daily carried away a present of food for some person; at length, surprised at this, he one day asked them: 'Who is that you are taking that present of food to?' And the people who were going with it answered him: 'It is for your ancestress, for Muri-ranga-whenua.'

He asked again: 'Where does she dwell?' They answered: 'Yonder.'

Thereupon he says: 'That will do; leave here the present of food, I will carry it to her myself.'

From that time the daily presents of food for his ancestress were carried by Maui himself; but he never took and gave them to her that she might eat them, but he quietly laid them by on one side, and this he did for many days. At last, Muri-ranga-whenua suspected that something wrong was going on, and the next time he came along the path carrying the present of food, the old chieftainess sniffed and sniffed until she thought she smelt something coming, and she was very much exasperated, and her stomach began to distend itself, that she might be ready to devour Maui as soon as he came there. Then she turned to the southward, and smelt and sniffed, but not a scent of anything reached her; then she turned round from the south to the north, by the east, with her nose up in the air sniffing and smelling to every point as she turned slowly round, but she could not detect the slightest scent of a human being, and almost thought that she must have been mistaken; but she made one more trial, and sniffed the breeze towards the westward. Ah! then the scent of a man came plainly to her, so she called aloud: 'I know from the smell wafted here to me by the breeze that somebody is close to me', and Maui murmured assent. Thus the old woman knew that he was a descendant of hers, and her stomach, which was quite large and distended immediately began to shrink, and contract itself again. If the smell of Maui had not been carried to her by the western breeze, undoubtedly she would have eaten him up.

When the stomach of Muri-ranga-whenua had quietly sunk down to its usual size, her voice was again heard saying: 'Art thou Maui? and he answered: 'Even so.'

Then she asked him: 'Wherefore has thou served thine old ancestress in this deceitful way?' and Maui answered: 'I was anxious that thy jaw-bone, by which the great enchantments can be wrought, should be given to me.'

She answered: 'Take it, it has been reserved for thee.' And Maui took it, and having done so returned to the place where he and his brothers dwelt.

The young hero, Maui, had not been long at home with his brothers when he began to think, that it was too soon after the rising of the sun that it became night again, and that the sun again sank down below the horizon, every day, every day; in the same manner the days appeared too short to him. So at last, one day he said to his brothers: 'Let us now catch the sun in a noose, so that we may compel him to move more slowly, in order that mankind may have long days to labour in to procure subsistence for themselves'; but they answered him: 'Why, no man could approach it on account of its warmth, and the fierceness of its heat'; but the young hero said to them: 'Have you not seen the multitude of things I have already achieved? Did not you see me change myself into the likeness of every bird of the forest;

you and I equally had the aspect and appearance of men, yet I by my enchantments changed suddenly from the appearance of a man and became a bird, and then, continuing to change my form, I resembled this bird or that bird, one after the other, until I had by degrees transformed myself into every bird in the world, small or great; and did I not after all this again assume the form of a man? [This he did soon after he was born, and it was after that he snared the sun.] Therefore, as for that feat, oh, my brothers, the changing myself into birds, I accomplished it by enchantments, and I will by the same means accomplish also this other thing which I have in my mind.' When his brothers heard this, they consented on his persuasions to aid him in the conquest of the sun.

Then they began to spin and twist ropes to form a noose to catch the sun in, and in doing this they discovered the mode of plaiting flax into stout square-shaped ropes (tuamaka); and the manner of plaiting flat ropes (paharahara); and of spinning round ropes; at last, they finished making all the ropes which they required. Then Maui took up his enchanted weapon, and he took his brothers with him, and they carried their provisions, ropes, and other things with them, in their hands. They travelled all night, and as soon as day broke, they halted in the desert, and hid themselves that they might not be seen by the sun; and at night they renewed their journey, and before dawn they halted, and hid themselves again; at length they got very far, very far, to the eastward, and came to the very edge of the place out of which the sun rises.

Then they set to work and built on each side of this place a long high wall of clay, with huts of boughs of trees at each end to hide themselves in; when these were finished, they made the loops of the noose, and the brothers of Maui then lay in wait on one side of the place out of which the sun rises, and Maui himself lay in wait upon the other side.

The young hero held in his hand his enchanted weapon, the jaw-bone of his ancestress—of Muri-ranga-whenua, and said to his brothers: 'Mind now, keep yourselves hid, and do not go showing yourselves foolishly to the sun; if you do, you will frighten him; but wait patiently until his head and fore-legs have got well into the snare, then I will shout out; haul away as hard as you can on the ropes on both sides, and then I'll rush out and attack him, but do you keep your ropes tight for a good long time (while I attack him), until he is nearly dead, when we will let him go; but mind, now, my brothers, do not let him move you to pity with his shrieks and screams.'

At last the sun came rising up out of his place, like a fire spreading far and wide over the mountains and forests; he rises up, his head passes through the noose, and it takes in more and more of his body, until his fore-paws pass through; then were pulled tight the ropes, and the monster began to struggle and roll himself about, whilst the snare jerked backwards and forwards as he struggled. Ah! was not he held fast in the ropes of his enemies!

Then forth rushed that bold hero, Mau-tikitiki-o-Taranga, with his enchanted weapon. Alas! the sun screams aloud; he roars; Maui strikes him fiercely with many blows; they hold him for a long time, at last they let him go, and then weak from wounds the sun crept along its course. Then was learnt by men the second name of the sun, for in its agony the sun screamed out: Why am I thus smitten by you! oh, man! do you know what you are doing? Why should you wish to kill Tama-nui-te-Ra? Thus was learnt his second name. At last they let him go. Oh, then, Tama-nui-te-Ra went very slowly and feebly on his course.

Maui and the Enchanted Fish-Hook

Maui, accused of being lazy, boasted that he would catch a fish

". . . so large that when I bring it to land you will not be able to eat it all, and the sun will shine on it and make it putrid before it is consumed.' Then Maui snooded his enchanted fish-hook, which was pointed with part of the jaw-bone of Muri-ranga-whenua, and when he had finished this, he twisted a stout fishing-line to his hook.

His brothers in the meantime had arranged amongst themselves to make fast the lashings of the top side of their canoe, in order to go out for a good day's fishing. When all was made ready they launched their canoe, and as soon as it was afloat Maui jumped into it, and his brothers, who were afraid of his enchantments, cried out: 'Come, get out again, we will not let you go with us; your magical arts will get us into some difficulty.' So he was compelled to remain ashore whilst his brothers paddled off, and when they reached the fishing ground they lay upon their paddles and fished, and after a good day's sport returned ashore.

As soon as it was dark night Maui went down to the shore, got into his brothers' canoe, and hid himself under the bottom boards of it. The next forenoon his brothers came down to the shore to go fishing again, and they had their canoe launched, and paddled out to sea without ever seeing Maui, who lay hid in the hollow of the canoe under the bottom boards. When they got well out to sea Maui crept out of his hiding place; as soon as his brothers saw him, they said: 'We had better get back to the shore again as fast as we can, since this fellow is on board'; but Maui, by his enchantments, stretched out the sea so that the shore instantly became very distant from them, and by the time they could turn themselves round to look for it, it was out of view.

*   *   *

They agree to let Maui accompany them, and he urges them to keep going farther and farther out to sea, beyond the sight of land, in search of the most abundant fish.

At last they reach the open sea, and his brothers begin to fish. Lo, lo, they had hardly let their hooks down to the bottom, when they each pulled up a fish into the canoe. Twice only they let down their lines, when behold the canoe was filled up with the number of fish they had caught. Then his brothers said: 'Oh, brother, let us all return now.' And he answered them: 'Stay a little; let me also throw my hook into the sea.' And his brothers replied: 'Where did you get a hook?' And he answered: 'Oh, never mind, I have a hook of my own.' And his brothers replied again: 'Make haste and throw it then.' And as he pulled it out from under his garments, the light flashed from the beautiful mother-of-pearl shell in the hollow of the hook, and his brothers saw that the hook was carved and ornamented with tufts of hair pulled from the tail of a dog, and it looked exceedingly beautiful. Maui then asked his brothers to give him a little bait to bait his hook with; but they replied: 'We will not give you any of our bait.' So he doubled his fist and struck his nose violently, and the blood gushed out, and he smeared his hook with his own blood for bait, and then be cast it into the sea, and it sank down, and sank down, till it reached to the small carved figure on the roof of a house at the bottom of the sea, then passing by the figure, it descended along the outside carved rafters of the roof, and fell in at the doorway of the house, and the hook of Maui-tikitiki-o-Taranga caught first in the sill of the doorway.

Then, feeling something on his hook, he began to haul in his line. Ah, ah!—there ascended on his hook the house of that old fellow Tonga-nui. It came up, up; and as it rose high, oh, dear! how his hook was strained with its great weight; and then there came gurgling up foam and bubbles from the earth, as of an island emerging from the water, and his brothers opened their mouths and cried aloud.

Maui all this time continued to chant forth his incantations amidst the murmurings and wailings of his brothers, who were weeping and lamenting, and saying: 'See now, how he has brought us out into the open sea, that we may be upset in it, and devoured by the fish.' Then he raised aloud his voice, and repeated the incantation called Hiki which makes heavy weights fight, in order that the fish he had caught might come up easily, and he chanted an incantation beginning thus:

'Wherefore, then, oh! Tonga-nui,

Dost thou hold fast so obstinately below there?'

When he had finished his incantation, there floated up, hanging to his line, the fish of Maui, a portion of the earth, of Papa-tu-a-Nuku. Alas! alas! their canoe lay aground.

Maui then left his brothers with their canoe, and returned to the village; but before he went he said to them: 'After I am gone, be courageous and patient; do not eat food until I return, and do not let our fish be cut up, but rather leave it until I have carried an offering to the gods from this great haul of fish, and until I have found a priest, that fitting prayers and sacrifices may be offered to the god, and the necessary rites be completed in order. We shall thus all be purified. I will then return, and we can cut up this fish in safety, and it shall be fairly portioned out to this one, and to that one, and to that other; and on my arrival you shall each have your due share of it, and return to your homes joyfully; and what we leave behind us will keep good, and that which we take away with us, returning, will be good too.'

Maui had hardly gone, after saying all this to them, than his brothers trampled under their feet the words they had heard him speak. They began at once to eat food, and to cut up the fish. When they did this, Maui had not yet arrived at the sacred place, in the presence of the god; had he previously reached the sacred place, the heart of the deity would have been appeased with the offering of a portion of the fish which had been caught by his disciples, and all the male and female deities would have partaken of their portions of the sacrifice. Alas! alas! those foolish, thoughtless brothers of his cut up the fish, and behold the gods turned with wrath upon them, on account of the fish which they had thus cut up without having made a fitting sacrifice. Then indeed, the fish began to toss about his head from side to side, and to lash his tail, and the fins upon his back, and his lower jaw. Ah! ah! well done Tangaroa, it springs about on shore as briskly as if it was in the water.

That is the reason that this island is now so rough and uneven—that here stands a mountain—and there lies a plain—that here descends a valley—that there rises a cliff. If the brothers of Maui had not acted so deceitfully, the huge fish would have lain flat and smooth, and would have remained as a model for the rest of the earth, for the present generation of men. This, which has just been recounted, is the second evil which took place after the separation of Heaven from Earth.

Thus was dry land fished up by Maui after it had been hidden under the ocean by Rangi and Tawhiri-ma-tea. It was with an enchanted fish-hook that he drew it up, which was pointed with a bit of the jaw-bone of his ancestress Muri-ranga-whenua; and in the district of Heretaunga they still show the fish-hook of Maui, which became a cape stretching far out into the sea, and now forms the southern extremity of Hawke's Bay.

Maui Steals Fire

The hero now thought that he would extinguish and destroy the fires of his ancestress of Mahu-ika. So he got up in the night, and put out the fires left in the cooking-houses of each family in the village; then, quite early in the morning, he called aloud to the servants: 'I hunger, I hunger; quick, cook some food for me.' One of the servants thereupon ran as fast as he could to make up the fire to cook some food, but the fire was out; and as he ran round from house to house in the village to get a light, he found every fire quite out-he could nowhere get a light.

When Maui's mother heard this, she called out to the servants, and said: 'Some of you repair to my great ancestress Mahu-ika; tell her that fire has been lost upon earth, and ask her to give some to the world again.' But the slaves were alarmed, and refused to obey the commands which their masters, the sacred old people gave them; and they persisted in refusing to go, notwithstanding the old people repeatedly ordered them to do so.

At last, Maui said to his mother: 'Well, then I will fetch down fire for the world; but which is the path by which I must go? And his parents, who knew the country well, said to him: 'If you will go, follow that broad path that lies just before you there; and you will at last reach the dwelling of an ancestress of yours; and if she asks you who you are, you had better call out your name to her, then she will know you are a descendant of hers; but be cautious, and do not play any tricks with her, because we have heard that your deeds are greater than the deeds of men, and that you are fond of deceiving and injuring others, and perhaps you even now intend in many ways, to deceive this old ancestress of yours, but pray be cautious not to do so.'

But Maui said: 'No, I only want to bring fire away for men, that is all, and I'll return again as soon as I can do that.' Then he went, and reached the abode of the goddess of fire; and he was so filled with wonder at what he saw, that for a long time he could say nothing. At last he said: 'Oh, lady, would you rise up? Where is your fire kept? I have come to beg some from you.'

Then the aged lady rose right up, and said: 'Au-e! who can this mortal be?' And he answered: 'It's I.' 'Where do you come from?' said she; and he answered: 'I belong to this country.' 'You are not from this country', said she; 'your appearance is not like that of the inhabitants of this country. Do you come from the north-east?' He replied: 'No.' 'Do you come from the south-east?' He replied: 'No.' 'Are you from the south?' He replied: 'No.' 'Are you from the westward?' He answered: 'No.' 'Come you, then, from the direction of the wind which blows right upon me?' And he said: I do.' 'Oh, then', cried she, 'you are my grand-child; what do you want here?' He answered: 'I am come to beg fire from you.' She replied: 'Welcome, welcome; here then is fire for you.'

Then the aged woman pulled out her nail; and as she pulled it out fire flowed from it, and she gave it to him. And when Maui saw she had drawn out her nail to produce fire for him, he thought it a most wonderful thing! Then he went a short distance off, and when not very far from her, he put the fire out, quite out; and returning to her again, said: 'The light you gave me has gone out, give me another.' Then she caught hold of another nail, and pulled it out as a light for him; and he left her, and went a little on one side, and put that light out also; then he went back to her again, and said: 'Oh, lady, give me, I pray you, another light for the last one has also gone out.' And thus he went on and on, until she had pulled out all the nails of the fingers of one of her hands; and then she began with the other hand, until she had pulled all the fingernails out of that hand, too; and then she commenced upon the nails of her feet, and pulled them also out in the same manner, except the nail of one of her big toes. Then the aged woman said to herself at last: 'This fellow is surely playing tricks with me.'

Then out she pulled the one toe-nail that she had left, and it, too, became fire, and as she dashed it down on the ground the whole place caught fire. And she cried out to Maui: 'There, you have it all now!' And Maui ran off, and made a rush to escape, but the fire followed hard after him, close behind him; so he changed himself into a fleet-winged eagle, and flew with rapid flight, but the fire pursued, and almost caught him as he flew. Then the eagle dashed down into a pool of water; but when he got into the water he found that almost boiling too: the forests just then also caught fire, so that it could not alight anywhere, and the earth and the sea both caught fire too, and Maui was very near perishing in the flames.

Then he called on his ancestors Tawhiri-ma-tea and Whatitiri-matakataka, to send down an abundant supply of water, and he cried aloud: 'Oh, let water be given to me to quench this fire which pursues after me'; and lo, then appeared squalls and gales, and Tawhiri-ma-tea sent heavy lasting rain, and the fire was quenched; and before Mahu-ika could reach her place of shelter, she almost perished in the rain, and her shrieks and screams became as loud as those of Maui had been, when he was scorched by the pursuing fire; thus Maui ended this proceeding. In this manner was extinguished the fire of Mahu-ika, the goddess of fire; but before it was all lost, she saved a few sparks which she threw, to protect them, into the Kaiko-mako, and a few other trees, where they are still cherished; hence, men yet use portions of the wood of these trees for fire when they require a light.

Then he returned to the village, and his mother and father said to him: 'You heard when we warned you before you went, nevertheless you played tricks with your ancestress; it served you right that you got into such trouble'; and the young fellow answered his parents: 'Oh, what do I care for that; do you think that my perverse proceedings are put a stop to by this? certainly not; I intend to go on in the same way for ever, ever, ever.' And his father answered him: 'Yes, then, you may just please yourself about living or dying; if you will only attend to me you will save your life; if you do not attend to what I say, it will be worse for you, that is all.' As soon as this conversation was ended, off the young fellow went to find some more companions for his other scrapes.

The Death of Maui

One day, Maui's father said to him:

'Oh, my son, I have heard from your mother and others that you are very valiant, and that you have succeeded in all feats that you have undertaken in your own country, whether they were small or great; but now that you have arrived in your father's country, you will, perhaps, at last be overcome.'

Then Maui asked him: 'What do you mean, what things are there that I can be vanquished by?'

And his father answered him: 'By your great ancestress, by Hine-nui-te-po, who, if you look, you may see flashing, and as it were, opening and shutting there, where the horizon meets the sky.'

And Maui replied: 'Lay aside such idle thoughts, and let us both fearlessly seek whether men are to die or live for ever.'

And his father said: 'My child, there has been an ill omen for us; when I was baptizing you, I omitted a portion of the fitting prayers, and that I know will be the cause of your perishing.'

Then Maui asked his father: 'What is my ancestress Hine-nui-te-po like?' and he answered: 'What you see yonder shining so brightly red are her eyes, and her teeth are as sharp and hard as pieces of volcanic glass; her body is like that of a man, and as for the pupils of her eyes, they are jasper; and her hair is like tangles of long seaweed, and her mouth is like that of a barracouta.'

Then his son answered him: 'Do you think her strength is as great as that of Tama-nui-te-Ra, who consumes man, and the earth, and the very waters, by the fierceness of his heat?—was not the world formerly saved alive by the speed with which he travelled?—if he had then, in the days of his full strength and power, gone as slowly as he does now, not a remnant of mankind would have been left living upon the earth, nor, indeed, would anything else have survived. But I laid hold of Tama-nui-te-Ra, and now he goes slowly for I smote him again and again, so that he is now feeble, and long in travelling his course, and he now gives but very little heat, having been weakened by the blows of my enchanted weapon; I then, too, split him open in many places, and from the wounds so made, many rays now issue forth, and spread in all directions. So, also I found the sea much larger than the earth, but by the power of the last born of your children, part of the earth was drawn up again, and dry land came forth.'

And his father answered him: 'That is all very true, O, my last born, and the strength of my old age; well, then, be bold, go and visit your great ancestress who flashes so fiercely there, where the edge of the horizon meets the sky.'

Hardly was this conversation concluded with his father, when the young hero went forth to look for companions to accompany him upon this enterprise: and so there came to him for companions, the small robin, and the large robin, and the thrush, and the yellow-hammer, and every kind of little bird, and the fantail, and these all assembled together, and they all started with Maui in the evening, and arrived at the dwelling of Hine-nui-te-po, and found her fast asleep.

Then Maui addressed them all, and said: 'My little friends, now if you see me creep into this old chieftainess, do not laugh at what you see. Nay, nay, do not I pray you, but when I have got altogether inside her, and just as I am coming out of her mouth, then you may shout with laughter if you please.' And his little friends, who were frightened at what they saw, replied: 'Oh, sir, you will certainly be killed.' And he answered them: 'If you burst out laughing at me as soon as I get inside her, you will wake her up, and she will certainly kill me at once, but if you do not laugh until I am quite inside her, and am on the point of coming out of her mouth, I shall live, and Hine-nui-te-po will die.' And his little friends answered: 'Go on then, brave Sir, but pray take good care of yourself.'

Then the young hero started off, and twisted the strings of his weapon tight round his wrist, and went into the house, and stripped off his clothes, and the skin on his hips looked mottled and beautiful as that of a mackerel, from the tattoo marks, cut on it with the chisel of Uetonga, and he entered the old chieftainess.

The little birds now screwed up their tiny cheeks, trying to suppress their laughter; at last, the little Tiwakawaka could no longer keep it in, and laughed out loud, with its merry cheerful note; this woke the old woman up, she opened her eyes, started up, and killed Maui.

Thus died this Maui we have spoken of, but before he died he had children, and sons were born to him; some of his descendants yet live in Hawaiki,[3] some in Aotearoa (or in these islands); the greater part of his descendants remained in Hawaiki, but a few of them came here to Aotearoa. According to the traditions of the Maori, this was the cause of the introduction of death into the world (Hine-nui-te-po being the goddess of death: if Maui had passed safely through her, then no more human beings would have died, but death itself would have been destroyed), and we express it by saying: 'The water-wagtail laughing at Maui-tikitiki-o-Taranga made Hine-nui-te-po squeeze him to death.' And we have this proverb: 'Men make heirs, but death carries them off.'

NOTES

1. If a child was born before its time, and thus perished without having known the joys and pleasures of life, it was carefully buried with peculiar incantations and ceremonies; because if cast into the water, or carelessly thrown aside, it became a malicious being or spirit, actuated by a peculiar antipathy to the human race, who it spitefully persecuted, from having been itself deprived of happiness which they enjoyed. All their malicious deities had an origin of this kind.

2. This refers to the Maori creation myth. Father Rangi and Mother Papa are forced apart to create the world.

3. "Homeland"

DISCUSSION QUESTIONS

1. Discuss Maui's role as both a hero and a trickster. Do his deeds as a trickster devalue his heroic efforts? Explain.

2. Comment on the importance of one's ancestors and family as revealed in the Maui legends.

3. What etiological elements can be found in these stories?

Hiiaka's Battle with Demons (Hawaii)

We remember Hiiaka's birth from the story of "How Pele Came to Hawaii," when she is hatched from an egg kept in Pele's skirts. Hiiaka's relationship with Pele is of interest because of the betrayal she commits, in marrying Pele's lover, Lohiau. In this story, the goddess of fire is tasked with finding Lohiau for her sister Pele. Along the way, she is chased by magical creatures, demons, and the natural world.

HIIAKA'S BATTLE WITH DEMONS

Out of the fire-pit of the volcano, Kilauea, Hiiaka climbed. Through a multitude of cracks and holes, out of which poured fumes of foul gases, she threaded her way until she stood on the highest plateau of lava the volcano had been able to build.

Pele was impatient and angry at the slow progress of Hiiaka and at first ordered her to hasten alone on her journey, but as she saw her patiently climbing along the rough way, she relented and gave to her supernatural power to aid in overcoming great difficulties and a magic skirt which had the power of lightning in its folds. But she saw that this was not enough, so she called on the divine guardians of plants to come with garments and bear a burden of skirts with which to drape Hiiaka on her journey. At last the goddess of ferns, Pau-o-palae, came with a skirt of ferns which pleased Pele. It was thrown over Hiiaka, the most beautiful drapery which could be provided.

Pau-o-palae was clothed with a network of most delicate ferns. She was noted because of her magic power over all the ferns of the forest, and for her skill in using the most graceful fronds for clothing and garlands.

Pele ordered Pau-o-palae to go with Hiiaka as her kahu, or guardian servant. She was very beautiful in her fern skirt and garland, but Hiiaka was of higher birth and nobler form and was more royal in her beauty than her follower, the goddess of ferns. It was a queen of highest legendary honor with one of her most worthy attendants setting forth on a strange quest through lands abounding in dangers and adventures.

Everywhere in ancient Hawaii were eepas, kupuas, and mo-os. Eepas were the deformed inhabitants of the Hawaiian gnomeland. They were twisted and defective in mind and body. They were the deceitful, treacherous fairies, living in the most beautiful places of the forest or glen, often appearing as human beings but always having some defect in some part of the body. Kupuas were gnomes or elves of supernatural power, able to appear in some nature-form as well as like a human being. Mo-os were the dragons who came to the Hawaiian islands only as the legendary memories of the crocodiles and great snakes of the lands from which the first Hawaiian natives emigrated. Throughout Polynesia the mo-o, or moko, remained for centuries in the minds of the natives of different island groups as their most dreadful enemy, living in deep pools and sluggish streams.

Hiiaka's first test of patient endurance came in a battle with the kupuas of a forest lying between the volcano and the ocean.

The land of the island Hawaii slopes down from the raging fire-pit, mile after mile, through dense tropical forests and shining lava beds, until it enfolds, in black lava shores, the ceaselessly moving waters of the bay of Hilo. In this forest dwelt Pana-ewa, a reptile-man. He was very strong and could be animal or man as he desired, and could make the change in a moment. He watched the paths through the forest, hoping to catch strangers, robbing them and sometimes devouring them. Some he permitted to pass, but for others he made much trouble, bringing fog and rain and wind until the road was lost to them.

Source: W. D. Westervelt, *Hawaiian Legends of the Volcanoes*, 1916.

He ruled all the evil forces of the forest above Hilo. Every wicked sprite who twisted vines to make men stumble over precipices or fall into deep lava caves was his servant. Every demon wind, every foul fiend dwelling in dangerous branches of falling trees, every wicked gnome whirling clouds of dust or fog and wrapping them around a traveler, in fact every living thing which could in any way injure a traveler was his loyal subject. He was the kupua chief of the vicious sprites and cruel elves of the forest above Hilo. Those who knew about Pana-ewa brought offerings of awa to drink, taro and red fish to eat, tapa for mats, and malos, or girdles. Then the way was free from trouble.

There were two bird-brothers of Pana-ewa; very little birds, swift as a flash of lightning, giving notice of any one coming through the forest of Pana-ewa.

Hiiaka, entering the forest, threw aside her fern robes, revealing her beautiful form. Two birds flew around her and before her. One called to the other, "This is one of the women of ka lua (the pit)." The other answered, "She is not as strong as Pana-ewa; let us tell our brother."

Hiiaka heard the birds and laughed; then she chanted, and her voice rang through all the forest:

> "Pana-ewa is a great lehua island;
> A forest of ohias inland.
> Fallen are the red flowers of the lehua,
> Spoiled are the red apples of the ohia,
> Bald is the head of Pana-ewa;
> Smoke is over the land;
> The fire is burning."

Hiiaka hoped to make Pana-ewa angry by reminding him of seasons of destruction by lava eruptions, which left bald lava spots in the midst of the upland forest.

Pana-ewa, roused by his bird watchmen and stirred by the taunt of Hiiaka, said. "This is Hiiaka, who shall be killed by me. I will swallow her. There is no road for her to pass."

The old Hawaiians said that Pana-ewa had many bodies. He attacked Hiiaka in his fog body, Kino-ohu, and threw around her his twisting fog-arms, chilling her and choking her and blinding her. He wrapped her in the severe cold mantle of heavy mists.

Hiiaka told her friend to hold fast to her girdle while she led the way, sweeping aside the fog with her magic skirt. Then Pana-ewa took his body called the bitter rain, ua-awa, the cold freezing rain which pinches and shrivels the skill. He called also for the strong winds to bend down trees and smite his enemy, and lie in tangled masses in her path, so the way was hard. Hiiaka swiftly swept her lightning skirt up against the beating rain and drove it back. Again and again she struck against the fierce storm and against the destructive winds. Sometimes she was beaten back, sometimes her arms were so weary that she could scarcely move her skirt, but she hurled it over and over against the storm until she drove it deeper into the forest and gained a little time for rest and renewal of strength.

On she went into the tangled woods and the gods of the forest rose up against her. They tangled her feet with vines. They struck her with branches of trees. The forest birds in multitudes screamed around her, dashed against her, tried to pick out her eyes and confuse her every effort. The god and his followers brought all their power and enchantments against Hiiaka. Hiiaka made an incantation against these enemies:

> "Night is at Pana-ewa and bitter is the storm;
> The branches of the trees are bent down;
> Rattling are the flowers and leaves of the lehua;
> Angrily growls the god Pana-ewa,

Stirred up inside by his wrath.
   Oh, Pana-ewa!
   I give you hurt,
   Behold, I give the hard blows of battle."

She told her friend to stay far back in the places already conquered, while she fought with a bamboo knife in one hand and her lightning skirt in the other. Harsh noises were on every hand. From each side she was beaten and sometimes almost crushed under the weight of her opponents. Many she cut down with her bamboo knife and many she struck with her lightning skirt. The two little birds flew over the battlefield and saw Hiiaka nearly dead from wounds and weariness, and their own gods of the forest lying as if asleep.

They called to Pana-ewa: "Our gods are tired from fighting, They sleep and rest."

Pana-ewa came and looked at them. He saw that they were dead without showing deep injury, and wondered how they had been killed. The birds said, "We saw her skirt moving against the gods, up and down, back and forth."

Again the hosts of that forest gathered around the young chiefess. Again she struggled bitterly against the multitude of foes, but she was very, very tired and her arms sometimes refused to lift her knife and skirt. The discouraged woman felt that the battle was going against her, so she called for Pele, the goddess of fire.

Pele heard the noise of the conflict and the voice of her sister. She called for a body of her own servants to go down and fight the powerful kupua.

The Hawaiian legends give the name Ho-ai-ku to these reinforcements. This means "standing for food" or "devourers." Lightning storms were hurled against Pana-ewa, flashing and cutting and eating all the gods of the forest.

Hiiaka in her weariness sank down among the foes she had slain.

The two little birds saw her fall and called to Pana-ewa to go and take the one he had said he would "swallow." He rushed to the place where she lay. She saw him coming and wearily arose to give battle once more.

A great thunderstorm swept down on Pana-ewa. As he had fought Hiiaka with the cold forest winds, so Pele fought him with the storms from the pit of fire. Lightning drove him down through the forest. A mighty rain filled the valleys with red water. The kupuas were swept down the river beds and out into the ocean, where Pana-ewa and the remnant of his followers were devoured by sharks.

The Ho-ai-ku, as the legends say, went down and swallowed Pana-ewa, eating him up. Thus the land above Hilo became a safe place for the common people. To this day it is known by the name Pana-ewa.

DISCUSSION QUESTIONS

1. What gifts are Hiiaka given to aid her journey?

2. Describe Hiiaka's "tests of endurance." Who does she meet? What does she do to escape?

3. Who are the Ho-ai-ku? What might they represent in the natural world?

The Deceiving of Kewa (Maori)

"The Deceiving of Kewa" is an incredibly old story recorded among the Maoris of New Zealand. This was a poem or mourning chant in which the exploits of a hero seeking his dead bride in the underworld was told. The Maoris, as well as many other Pacific island cultures, believed in the dwelling place of the spirits of the dead, usually at the bottom of the ocean. The King of the dead spirits is Kewa, who will thus be deceived by the hero Miru.

THE DECEIVING OF KEWA

There once lived in Hawaiki a chief and his wife. They had a child, a girl, born to them; then the mother died. The chief took another wife, who was not pleasing to the people. His anger was so great that the chief went away to the great forest of Tane, and there built a house for himself and his wife.

After a time a son was born to them and the father named him Miru. This father was a great tohunga, or priest, as well as a chief. He taught Miru all the supreme kinds of knowledge, all the invocations and incantations, those for the stars, for the winds, for foods, for the sea, and for the land. He taught him the peculiar incantations which would enable him to meet all cunning tricks and enmities of man. He learned also all the great powers of witchcraft. It is said that on one occasion Miru and his father went to a river, a great river. Here the child experimented with his powerful charms. He was a child of the forest and knew the charm which could conquer the trees. Now there was a tall tree growing by the side of the river. When Miru saw it, he recited his incantations. As he came to the end the tree fell, the head reaching right across the river. They left the tree lying in this way that it might be used as a bridge by the people who came to the river. Thus, he was conscious of his power to correctly use the mighty invocations which his father had taught him.

The years passed and the boy became a young man. His was a lonely life, and he often wondered if there were not those who could be his companions. At last he asked his parents: "Are we here, all of us? Have I no other relative in the world?"

His parents answered, "You have a sister, but she dwells at a distant place."

When Miru heard this he arose and proceeded to search for his sister, and he happily came to the very place where she dwelt. There the young people were gathered in their customary place for playing teka, which was a dart thrown along the ground, usually the hard beach of the seashore. Miru watched the game for some time and then returned to his home in the forest. He told his father about the teka and the way it was played. Then the chief prepared a teka for Miru, selected from the best tree and fashioned while appropriate charms were repeated. Miru threw his dart along the slopes covered by the forest and its underbrush, but the ground was uneven and the undergrowth retarded the dart. Then Miru found a plain and practiced until he was very expert.

After a while he came to the place where his sister lived. When the young people threw their darts, he threw his. Aha! it flew indeed and was lost in the distance. When the sister beheld him, she at once felt a great desire toward him.

The people tried to keep Miru with them, pleading with him to stay, and even following him as he returned to his forest home, but they did not catch him. Frequently he repeated his visits, but never stayed long.

Source: W. D. Westervelt, *Legends of Gods and Ghosts*, 1915.

The sister was disheartened, and hanged herself until she was dead. The body was laid in its place for the time of wailing. Miru and his father came to the uhunga, or place of mourning. The people had not known that Miru was the brother of the one who was dead. They welcomed the father and son according to their custom. Then the young man said, "After I leave, do not bury my sister." So the body was left in its place when the young man arose.

He went on his way till he saw a canoe floating. He then gave the command to his companions and they all paddled away in the canoe. They paddled on for a long distance, in fact to Rerenga-wai-rua, the point of land in New Zealand from which the spirits of the dead take their last leap as they go down to the Underworld. When they reached this place they rested and Miru let go the anchor. He then said to his companions, "When you see the anchor rope shaking, pull it up, but wait here for me."

The young man then leaped into the water and went down, down near the bottom, and then entered a cave. This cave was the road by which the departed spirits went to spirit-land. Miru soon saw a house standing there. It was the home of Kewa, the chief of the Underworld. Within the house was his sister in spirit form.

Miru carried with him his nets, which were given magic power, with which he hoped to catch the spirit of his sister. In many ways he endeavored to induce her ghost to come forth from the house of Kewa, but she would not come. He commenced whipping his top in the yard outside, but could not attract her attention. At last he set up a swing and many of the ghosts joined in the pastime. For a long time the sister remained within, but eventually came forth induced by the attraction of the swing and by the appearance of Miru. Miru then took the spirit in his arms and began to swing.

Higher and higher they rose whilst he incited the ghosts to increase to the utmost the flight of the moari, or swing. On reaching the highest point he gathered the spirit of the sister into his net, then letting go the swing away they flew and alighted quite outside the spirit-land. Thence he went to the place where the anchor of the floating canoe was. Shaking the rope his friends understood the signal. He was drawn up with the ghost in his net. He entered the canoe and returned home. On arrival at the settlement the people were still lamenting. What was she to him? Taking the spirit, he laid it on the dead body, at the same time reciting his incantations. The spirit gradually entered the body and the sister was alive again.

DISCUSSION QUESTION

1. Consider other cultures' heroes who journey to the underworld to rescue the dead. What does Miru have in common with them? What about Miru and Kewa is different?

BIBLIOGRAPHY

Dixon, Roland B. *Oceanic Mythology.* 1916. http://www.sacred-texts.com/pac/om/om21.htm

Fraser, John. *Journal of the Polynesian Society Vol I,* 1892. http://www.sacredtexts.com/pac/jpolys/ssc.htm

Grey, George. *Polynesian Mythology and Ancient Traditional History of the New Zealanders.* 1854. http://www.sacred-texts.com/pac/grey/grey04.htm

Liliuokalani. translator. *An Account of the Creation of the World According to Hawaiian Tradition,* 1897. http://www.sacred-texts.com/pac/lku/lku00.htm

Powell, Barry B. *World Myth.* Pearson, 2014.

Thomas, W. J. *Some Myths and Legends of the Australian Aborigines.* 1923. http://www.sacredtexts.com/aus/mla/mla16.ht

Westervelt, W. D. *Hawaiian Legends of the Volcanoes.* 1916. http://www.sacredtexts.com/pac/hlov/hlov07.htm.

---. *Legends of Gods and Ghosts.* 1915. http://www.gutenberg.org/files/39195/39195-h/39195h.htm#Page_224

Chapter 9

THE MYTHS OF MESOAMERICA AND SOUTH AMERICA

© Jared Blandford

INTRODUCTION

Part 1: Creation and Destruction

2 Hymns to Aztec Goddesses

Arawak Creation (Haiti)

"The Creation" from *The Popol Vuh* (Maya)

The Five Suns (Aztec)

The Flowing Waters: The Creation of the Earth (Aztec)

Into the Fire: The Creation of the Sun and the Moon (Aztec)

Broken Bones: The Creation of People (Aztec)

Viracocha (Inca)

Part 2: Tricksters, Lovers, and Other Tales

Music from the Gods: How Music Came to the World (Aztec)

The Murmur of the River: How Music Came to the World (Maya)

The Possum's Tail: How Fire Came to the World (Mazatec)

The Adventures of Kororomanna (Warrau)

Part 3: Journeys of Heroes and Heroines

The Eagle on the Cactus (Aztec)

Quetzalcoatl and Tezcatlipoca (Aztec)

"The Hero Twins" from the *Second Book of The Popol Vuh* (Maya)

© pingebat/Shutterstock.com

Mesoamerica

The region of Mesoamerica includes Southern Mexico through Guatemala, Belize, El Salvador, and also part of Honduras. Of the various Mesoamerican groups (Olmec, Maya, Zapotec, Toltec, Tarascan, Aztec, Mixtec, Mazatec), two stand out as the most highly developed—the Maya and the Aztec.

The Maya inhabited Central Mexico, the Yucatan region, Guatemala, and Honduras and had the most sophisticated civilization of the Mesoamerican groups, spanning 4,000 years. Noted for their towering stepped pyramids, they were also accomplished in astronomy and mathematics. Their charted planetary movements rival those of any other civilization without the aid of telescopes. They also developed a 365-day calendar which was the most accurate until modern times, and "developed a counting system that included zero a thousand years before the Hindus" (Vigil).

The earliest Maya writing dates to 400–250 BCE; their art and language system reveals a culture that grew without outside influence. While other groups in the New World did have some form of picture-writing, the Maya had the only system of actual writing in the Americas. However, these systems, and their records of time-keeping, are believed to have originated with a previous culture called the Olmecs (considered the mother culture of Mesoamerica, beginning around 1500 BCE), though the Maya developed them more fully. Their system of writing was a combination of logograms and syllabic symbols; the Mayan language family includes twenty-nine different languages.

Their writing system was elegant and artistic; in fact, the Maya word *T'zib* meant both writer and painter. They invented a paper made from bark and created colorful fan-fold style books. While they were prolific writers, only four books remain today; the remainder of the surviving Maya writing comes from painted ceramics and engraved stone. Unfortunately, most of the Maya texts were destroyed by the Spanish invaders. Of those that have been recovered, it has taken many decades of work to decipher the writing, and it is still only partially understood. The most noteworthy text, the *Popol Vuh* ("The Collection of Written Leaves"), contains their myths and epics, including the story of creation.

The Maya created detailed stone carvings, but unlike the later Aztec people who were noted for their use of gold and silver, the Maya used no metal in their art or construction. During the Classic Period of Maya civilization (c. 250 BCE–c. 900 CE), there was a surge in art and construction, resulting in many independent city-states (they did not have a central, political center) and designated places for ritual and ceremony. Like other Mesoamerican societies, they did engage in human sacrifice.

The Maya civilization declined during the eighth and ninth centuries; however, some cities still existed when the Spaniards arrived in the sixteenth century. Their two greatest cities, Chich é n Itz á and Palenque, seem to have simply been abandoned. Decline could have been caused by a combination of environmental stress and pressure from neighboring warrior cultures. The last Maya state remained until 1697.

The Aztec empire grew in the central and northern parts of Mexico beginning around 1325 CE, long after the height of the Maya had faded. Their 200-year journey to settle in their destined homeland is told in one of their myths. When the Spaniards arrived, the Aztecs were the dominant civilization in the area, which is why we know more about the Aztecs than other groups from Mesoamerica, even though their civilization only spanned 300 years. The Spaniards marveled at the elegance of Tenochtitlan, with its pyramids, markets, gardens, and canals. The Aztecs also had sophisticated time-measurement and record-keeping systems. They were a fierce warrior society, and used captured prisoners in their elaborate sacrificial rituals.

In November of 1519, Hernan Cortes arrived at the Aztec city of Tenochtitlan accompanied by the Tlaxcalans, who were enemies of the Aztecs. They mistakenly thought Cortes was the god Quetzalcoatl, who was prophesied to return in that same year. But, in

> June 1520 hostilities broke out, culminating in the Spanish massacre of the natives in the Great Temple and the death of Montezuma . . . the Spaniards fled, then in spring of 1521 returned to lay siege to Tenochtitlan, a battle that ended with the destruction of the city (Powell 422).

While Mesoamerican cultures were not eliminated after this conquest, the invaders unfortunately brought disease with them—the most devastating of these was smallpox. The outbreak killed nearly half of the remaining population of the native peoples. The decline continued over the next sixty years; some scholars estimate more than 90% of the native population was destroyed. This marks an unparalleled level of decimation of a cultural group.

Religious development in the region began with the earliest civilization, the Olmec, followed by the Maya. In addition, there was another distinct religious system being practiced at the mysterious city of Teotihuacan during the Classic Period. Teotihuacan, while existing during the time of the Maya, is an Aztec name ("place of the gods"); the original name of the city has not yet been deciphered. Teotihuacan's architecture, religion, and art influenced many Mesoamerican civilizations, such as the Zapotecs, Maya, Toltecs, and Aztecs, but scholars don't know who actually founded the city. The "feathered serpent" god (Quetzalcoatl) is one of the most famous images that emerged there. In fact, long after Teotihuacan fell, the gods Quetzalcoatl and Tlaloc persisted in religious iconography throughout the region, being present in Mayan, Toltec, and Aztec belief systems. And yet, despite the similarities, Aztec religion is different than all others in Mesoamerica. For example, ancestor worship was a core aspect of Maya religion, but it was not present among the Aztecs. In addition, the practice of human sacrifice was found throughout the cultures of Mesoamerica, but it was by far the most prominent among the Aztecs.

The Spaniards were disturbed by the practices of these native people, yet they were intrigued as well. Despite the unfortunate widespread destruction of cultural artifacts (they burned entire libraries out of fear of the pagan materials), they did preserve some aspects of the culture by learning the native language and recording stories in Spanish. During this process, as the natives were converted to Christianity, the friars taught them to write their own language using the Roman alphabet, enabling them to record their stories, resulting in a blended version of the stories. Most of these myths originate from texts recorded in the sixteenth century.

Gods made sacrifices in creating the universe; the Aztecs believed that conflict and sacrifice were required to keep order in the cosmos. This included the sacrifice of human beings. They believed that the body contained the divine spark of life, and that spilling blood nourished the land, as well as ensuring rainfall and the continued movement of the sun across the sky. Sacrifices were accompanied by elaborate rituals and ceremonies.

According to author David Carrasco,

> . . . blood sacrifices were carried out on pyramidal and temple platforms by priestly groups trained to dispense the victims swiftly. This involved different types of autosacrifice (bleeding of self) and the heart sacrifice of enemy warriors and purchased slaves. Though a variety of methods were used, including decapitation, burning, hurling from great heights, strangulation, and arrow sacrifice, the typical ritual involved the dramatic heart sacrifice and the placing of the heart in a ceremonial vessel (sometimes the cuauhxicalli—'eagle vessel') in order to nourish the gods.

There were several categories of sacrifice, including rituals intended to pay a debt to the earth goddess, quenching her ravenous hunger with human blood in order to avoid destruction of the earth.

"Mesoamerican religion is a labyrinth of belief systems—polytheism, ancestor worship, animism, shamanism, and time veneration—interconnected with one another to create one of the most complex and poorly understood religions in the world" (Barnhart). But while the Maya and Aztec are distinctly different cultures, they do share some similarities, such as use of tools and food items, and their temple and pyramid architecture. In addition, they had similar calendar systems and there is some overlap in their practice of worship and pantheons of gods.

South America

© Peter Hermes Furian/Shutterstock.com

Hundreds of indigenous groups make up the pre-European contact population of South America. Each of these groups had their own languages, cultures, and mythological understanding of the world, the plants, and animals that surrounded them. Before Francisco Pizarro and the Spanish conquistadors' arrival in 1526, some of the most populous native groups included the Arawak in the Guianas, the Chibcha of Colombia, the Chamacoco of Paraguay, the Guajiro of Venezuela, and the Inca, whose empire extended to the modern country boundaries of Peru, Ecuador, Colombia, Chile, Bolivia, and Argentina.

The Incan Empire's crowning achievement, Machu Picchu, was built as a sacred religious site, high in the Andes. This series of structures was constructed in the fifteenth century without the use of mortar—a true feat of engineering. One of its most recognizable structures is the Temple of the Sun and the Intihuaana, which are believed to have been a kind of solar clock or calendar that the Inca could mark time and trace the Earth's movements. The site was abandoned during the Spanish conquest in the sixteenth century and was not rediscovered until American archaeologist Hiram Bingham accidentally found it in 1911. His subsequent book *The Lost City of the Incas* instantly attracted attention to the area and set off a new era of exploration in South America. Standing 7,972 feet above sea level, it is a Unesco World Heritage site today and visited by hundreds of thousands of people each year.

The myths of South America hold many things in common, including the worship in most cultures of a supreme sun god, and much focus on animism and the role that animals and plants play in the creation of the world. Pantheons of gods and goddesses, tricksters and heroes abound in the legends of South America.

Part 1: Creation and Destruction

2 Hymns to Aztec Goddesses

Considered by some to be a piece of "lost literature," and certainly not studied as frequently as the longer myths of the Aztec, the Hymns here are poetic chants to feminine creative powers. These Hymns were first transcribed in their original Nahuatl language by Father Bernardino de Sahagun, one of the earliest missionaries to Mexico, and later translated to English by Daniel Brinton in the nineteenth century. Brinton writes of these poems, "They reveal to us the undoubtedly authentic spirit of the ancient religion; they show us the language in its most archaic form; they preserve references to various mythical cycli of importance to the historian; and they illustrate the alterations in the spoken tongue adopted in the esoteric dialect of the priesthood."

In the "Hymn to the Mother of the Gods" the deity referred to is known as Teleoinan, Toci, Our Mother, and The Heart of the Earth. It was believed that she caused earthquakes, encouraged the fertility of plants and animals, and was called out to by midwives and women in childbirth. Her temple was called Tepeyacac and later supplanted by Christian missionaries as a temple to Our Lady of Guadalupe.

The "Hymn to the Mother of Mortals" praises Cihaucoatl, the mythical mother of humans. She is also called Tonan or Tonantzin and Quilaztli, as well as the often mistranslated "serpent woman," which should be "bearer of twins." As this name suggests, she is a goddess of fertility and reproduction. The Hymn describes her as "being from Colhuacan," which is the place of the ancestors of the tribe.

HYMN TO THE MOTHER OF THE GODS

Hail to our mother, who caused the yellow flowers to blossom, who scattered the seeds of the maguey, as she came forth from Paradise.

Hail to our mother, who poured forth white flowers in abundance, who scattered the seeds of the maguey, as she came forth from Paradise.

Hail to the goddess who shines in the thorn bush like a bright butterfly.

Ho! she is our mother, goddess of the earth, she supplies food in the desert to the wild beasts, and causes them to live.

Thus, thus, you see her to be an ever-fresh model of liberality toward all flesh.

And as you see the goddess of the earth do to the wild beasts, so also does she toward the green herbs and the fishes.

Source: Daniel G. Brinton, *Rig Veda Americanus: Sacred Songs of the Ancient Mexicans*, 1890.

HYMN TO THE MOTHER OF MORTALS

Quilaztli, plumed with eagle feathers, with the crest of eagles, painted with serpents' blood, comes with her hoe, beating her drum, from Colhuacan.

She alone, who is our flesh, goddess of the fields and shrubs, is strong to support us.

With the hoe, with the hoe, with hands full, with the hoe, with hands full, the goddess of the fields is strong to support us.

With a broom in her hands the goddess of the fields strongly supports us.

Our mother is as twelve eagles, goddess of drum-beating, filling the fields of tzioac and maguey like our lord Mixcoatl.

She is our mother, a goddess of war, our mother, a goddess of war, an example and a companion from Colhuacan.

She comes forth, she appears when war is waged, she protects us in war that we shall not be destroyed, an example and companion from the home of our ancestors.

She comes adorned in the ancient manner with the eagle crest, in the ancient manner with the eagle crest.

DISCUSSION QUESTIONS

1. Find some of the repetitive words in each hymn. What is the significance of this repetition?

2. Why does the chant seem concerned with the Mother of Mortals having been descended from Colhuacan (the land of the ancestors)?

3. In what ways is fertility alluded to in these two hymns?

Arawak Creation (Haiti)

The Arawak is a larger linguistic group of indigenous people who lived in the Caribbean and South America. The Taino of Cuba, Hispaniola, Trinidad, Jamaica, and Puerto Rico, were the first peoples encountered by Christopher Columbus, and are considered a subgroup, called the Antillean Arawak. The South American Arawak are comprised of the Warrau, the Carib, and Arawak and lived from the Orinoco River to the foothills of the Andes. Modern Arawak number around 15,000 and live in present-day Venezuela, Guyana, Suriname, French Guiana, and northern Brazil.

This myth comes from an Italian expedition to the Caribbean led by Bartholomew Columbus, who ordered one of the missionaries on his ship to spend two years collecting stories and habits of the natives they encountered. The stories were published in Latin and Italian in 1571 and come to us in, unfortunately, fractured form. What we can glean from this story, though, tells us of early native Haitian's beliefs.

ARAWAK CREATION

The earliest of creatures was the woman, Atabéira, who also bore other names. Her son was the supreme ruler of all things, and chiefest of divinities. His name was Yocaúna, among others. He had a brother called Guaca, and a son Iaiael. The latter rebelled against his father, Yocaúna, and was exiled for four months and then killed. Iaiael's bones were placed in a calabash and hung up in his father's house. Here the bones changed into fishes, and the calabash filled with water.

One day four brothers passed that way, who had all been born at one time, and whose mother, Itaba tahuana, had died in bringing them into the world. Seeing the calabash filled with fish, the oldest of the four, Caracaracol, the Scabby, lifted it down, and all commenced to eat. While thus occupied, Yocaúna suddenly made his appearance, which so terrified the brothers that they dropped the gourd and broke it into pieces. From it ran all the waters of the world, and formed the oceans, lakes, and rivers as they now are.

At this time there were men but no women, and the men did not dare to venture into the sunlight. Once, as they were out in the rain, they perceived four creatures, swift as eagles and slippery as eels. The men called to their aid Caracaracol and his brothers, who caught these creatures and transformed them into women. In time, these became the mothers of mankind.

The God of the storm was Guabancex, whose statue was made of stones. When angry he sent before him as messenger, Guatauva, to gather the winds, and accompanied by Coatrischie, who collected the rain-clouds in the valleys of the mountains, he swept down upon the plain, surrounded by the awful paraphernalia of the thunder storm.

DISCUSSION QUESTIONS

1. What does this myth suggest about parent-child relationships?

2. How do the Arawak describe the creatures who were turned into women? What might these animals suggest about women?

Source: Brinton, D. G. *The Arawack Language of Guiana in its Linguistic and Ethnological Relations*, 1871.

"The Creation" from *The Popol Vuh* (Maya)

The Popol Vuh, which means "The Book of the People," provides fascinating insight into the world of the Maya in Central America. The Maya Empire, at its height in the sixth century CE, was home to amazing feats of architecture, math, astronomy, and storytelling. The ruins of its cities still exist in present-day Honduras, Belize, El Salvador, Guatemala, and the Yucatan Peninsula of Mexico.

When Spanish explorers reached Central America in the 1500s CE, most of the large Maya cities had already been abandoned. There are various theories about the disappearance of this huge population, including constant war, or environmental issues, or the excess of the upper classes. In any case, the Conquistadors came upon the ruins in the jungles and proceeded with their mission of colonization when they found remaining populations. Part of the colonization process included the burning of Maya books (called Codices), of which only four remain. Of all the ancient writings and art of the Maya, there are four books left in the world.

Written in the K'iche' language (a dialect of the Maya) in the highlands of Guatemala, *The Popol Vuh* was written by an anonymous Maya author in the 1550s CE. This is different from the Maya Codices, as it was written much later and luckily survived the effort to burn all Maya writing. In the eighteenth century, a Spanish priest named Fransisco Ximénez found this text and made a copy which preserved the original Maya writing and translated it into Spanish. The original Maya copy of *The Popol Vuh* has been lost, but the Ximénez copy currently resides at Chicago's Newberry Library.

The Maya pantheon begins with four creators, or chief gods who gather together to create animals and humans. Hurakan, or The Heart of the Sky, begins creation by speaking the earth into existence. Gucumatz, or The Plumed Serpent, along with Xpiyacoc and Xmucane, The Father and Mother Gods, round out the council of gods who will dictate the population of the world.

Maya spelling and pronunciation are especially tricky, but remember that the "X" makes a "Shh" sound, and that translations of names and places vary. Translations of names have been provided where possible, in order to give an idea of what characteristic or member of the natural world the name is meant to represent.

THE CREATION

From the *First Book of The Popol Vuh*

Over a universe wrapped in the gloom of a dense and primeval night passed the god Hurakan, the mighty wind. He called out "Earth!" and the solid land appeared. The chief gods took counsel; they were Hurakan (The Heart of the Sky), Gucumatz (the Plumed Serpent), and Xpiyacoc and Xmucane (The Father and Mother Gods). As the result of their deliberations animals were created. But these animals had no voices and could not speak to the gods who created them. The gods gathered and decided that animals should be sacrificed.

Man was not yet created, but the gods wished it to be so. They first gathered the clay from the earth to mold into the shape of man. But the clay was too soft; these men could not walk without falling over, and their heads could not stay upright. They were judged to be mindless and were thus destroyed by the hands who made them.

Sources: adapted from *The Popol Vuh: The Mythic and Heroic Sagas of the Kiches of Central America.* Translated by Lewis Spence, 1908.
Adapted from *The Popol Vuh: The Book of the People.* Translated by Delia Goetz and Sylvanus Griswold Morley, 1954.

To overcome the deficiency of the first race, the divine beings resolved to create mannikins carved out of wood. But these soon incurred the displeasure of the gods, who, irritated by their lack of reverence, resolved to destroy them. Then by the will of Hurakan, the Heart of Heaven, the waters were swollen, and a great flood came upon the mannikins of wood. They were drowned and a thick resin fell from heaven. The bird Xecotcovach tore out their eyes; the bird Camulatz cut off their heads; the bird Cotzbalam devoured their flesh; the bird Tecumbalam broke their bones and sinews and ground them into powder. Because they had not thought on Hurakan, therefore the face of the earth grew dark, and a pouring rain commenced, raining by day and by night.

Then all sorts of beings, great and small, gathered together to abuse the mannikins to their faces. The very household utensils and animals jeered at them, their millstones, their plates, their cups, their dogs, their hens. Said the dogs and hens, "You have treated us very badly, and you have bitten us. Now we bite you in turn." Said the millstones, "We were tormented by you, and daily, night and day, we squeaked and screeched for your sake. Now you shall feel our strength, and we will grind your flesh and make meal of your bodies." And the dogs upbraided the mannikins because they had not been fed, and tore at them with their teeth. And the cups and dishes said, "Pain and misery you gave us, smoking our tops and sides, cooking us over the fire, burning and hurting us as if we had no feeling. Now it is your turn, and you shall burn."

Then ran the mannikins hither and thither in despair. They climbed to the roofs of the houses, but the houses crumbled under their feet; they tried to mount to the tops of the trees, but the trees hurled them from them; they sought refuge in the caverns, but the caverns closed before them. Thus this race was ruined, destined to be overthrown. And it is said that their posterity are the little monkeys who live in the woods.

From the *Third Book of The Popol Vuh*

The gods once more gathered in council. In the darkness they communed, concerning the creation of man. The Creator and Former, Hurakan, made four perfect men. These beings were wholly created from yellow and white maize. Their names were Balam-Quitzé (Tiger with the Sweet Smile), Balam-Agab (Tiger of the Night), Mahucutah (The Distinguished Name), and Iqi-Balam (Tiger of the Moon). They had neither father nor mother, neither were they made by the ordinary agents in the work of creation. Their creation was a miracle of the Hurakan.

But Hurakan was not altogether satisfied with his handiwork. These men were too perfect. They knew too much. Therefore the gods took counsel as to how to proceed with these first men. They must not become as gods! "Let us now contract their sight so that they may only be able to see a portion of the earth and be content," said the gods. Then Hurakan breathed a cloud over their eyes, which became partially veiled. Then the four men slept, and four women were made, Caha-Paluma (Falling Water), Choimha (Beautiful Water), Tzununiha (House of the Water), and Cakixa (Water of Parrots), who became the wives of the men in their respective order as mentioned above.

These were the ancestors of the K'ichés only. Then were created the ancestors of other peoples. They were ignorant of the methods of worship and, lifting their eyes to heaven, prayed to the Creator for peaceable lives and the return of the sun. But no sun came, and they grew uneasy. So they set out for Tulan-Zuiva (the Seven Caves), and there gods were given to each man. Because they were to be a race of Maya, each was given a god.

The K'ichés now began to feel the want of fire, and the god Tohil, the creator of fire, supplied them with this element. But soon afterwards a mighty rain extinguished all the fires in the land. Tohil, however, always renewed the supply. And fire in those days was the chief necessity, for as yet there was no sun.

Tulan was a place of misfortune to man, for not only did he suffer from cold and famine, but here his speech was so confounded that the first four men were no longer able to comprehend each other.

They determined to leave Tulan, and under the leadership of the god Tohil set out to search for a new abode. On they wandered through innumerable hardships. Many mountains had they to climb, and a long passage to make through the sea which was miraculously divided for their journey from shore to shore. At length they came to a mountain which they called Hacavitz, after one of their gods, and here they rested, for here they had been instructed that they should see the sun. And the sun appeared. Animals and men were transported with delight. All the celestial bodies were now established. But the sun was not as it is today. He was not strong, but as reflected in a mirror.

Now it came time for the death-time of the first men, and they called their descendants together to hearken unto their last counsels. In the anguish of their hearts they sang the "Kamucu," the song "We see," that they first sung when they saw the first light. Then they took leave of their wives and sons, one by one, and suddenly they were not. But in their place was a huge bundle, which was never unfolded. And it was called the "Majesty Enveloped." And so died the first men of the K'ichés.

DISCUSSION QUESTIONS

1. Trace the creation and demise of each attempt to create humans. Where did the gods feel they had gone wrong? How does their final attempt succeed?

2. What trials do the K'iche' have to endure to see the sun and to use fire?

3. How death comes into the world is a common theme in many myths. Compare the K'iche' explanation of death to other myths from around the world.

The Five Suns (Aztec)

The Aztecs considered themselves to be a chosen people, believing they were responsible for maintaining life on Earth in addition to sustaining their gods. Their religious system was complex and demanding, a system of gods ruling over specific aspects of their culture; the daily lives of the people were governed by rituals and traditions. The stories were a constant reminder of their responsibilities to their civilization and their gods; their creation myth was a core component of their cosmology—the entire worldview of the Aztec people was built on it.

In 1790 in Mexico City, excavators discovered an impressive artifact now referred to as the Aztec Sun Stone. This massive stone carving is twelve feet across and weighs twenty-four tons and is essentially a "visual representation" of the creation story, not a calendar, as it's often called. The stone depicts the story of the Five Suns—the five different stages of creation leading up to the current world. The image at the center of the stone represents the Fifth Age—our present-day. Surrounding this image are glyphs that represent the four preceding ages; in each age the Earth was destroyed.

Each age of creation ends on a day identified by the number four, and the name of its agent of destruction. Their calendar system was a combination of numbers in a series from one to thirteen combined with a series of twenty signs used to identify specific days. This complex combination resulted in a religious calendar; the number four had ritual significance as well.

Two of the most important gods in the Aztec pantheon are Quetzalcoatl and Tezcatlipoca. Quetzalcoatl, whose name means "plumed serpent," is often referred to as the God of Civilization, a creator who is also responsible for learning and the arts. Tezcatlipoca, called Smoking Mirror, is the supreme deity. He is associated with both the positive and negative aspects of Darkness, and with fate. The story of the Five Suns recounts a cosmic battle between them as the world is created and destroyed four times before its current incarnation—the Fifth Sun, our current world.

THE FIVE SUNS: AZTEC CREATION

At the very beginning of time and space, there was only a pair of creators called the Ometeotl, the Lord and Lady of Duality. From this union was born two gods, Tezcatlipoca and Quetzalcoatl. The struggle for supremacy between these two gods contains the history of the Aztecs.

In the time of the First Sun, Tezcatlipoca ruled the world. Only giants lived on the Earth, eating acorns and roots. Tezcatlipoca himself proudly carried the Sun along its fiery path across the sky each day, giving light to the Earth. This was a great honor, and Quetzalcoatl was jealous. One day, overcome by anger, Quetzalcoatl delivered a tremendous blow to Tezcatlipoca and he fell from the sky. But as he fell, Tezcatlipoca changed himself into the spirit of his sacred animal, the jaguar. In his jaguar form, he destroyed all life on Earth. And so the time of the First Sun ended, and the Earth was shrouded in darkness. The Aztecs called this day 4 Jaguar. Quetzalcoatl was now the supreme ruler and it was his honor and duty to guide the Sun on its journey each day, conquering the darkness on Earth. The Earth now existed for a second time—the Second Sun. During this time, monkeys roamed the earth eating pine nuts.

Tezcatlipoca was now the jealous one. Determined to regain his position, he climbed into the sky and this time struck a blow to Quetzalcoatl, knocking him from the sky. His fall was so great that it created windstorms that destroyed all life on Earth. Once again, an age of the Sun had ended in Earth's destruction. The Aztecs marked this day as 4 Wind. This destructive quarrel angered the other gods, and they decided that another god should be appointed to carry the Sun through the sky. The rain god Tlaloc was chosen, and he ruled during the Third Sun, nourishing the Earth with water, oceans, lakes, rivers, bringing the Earth back to life.

Now Queztalcoatl and Tezcatlipoca plotted together against Tlaloc. They attacked him, causing a rain of fire to fall upon the Earth. The age of the Third Sun ended life on Earth by raging fires. The Aztecs called the end of this time with the name 4 Rain. The other gods once again stepped in and created the Earth again—the Fourth Sun. In this age Tlaloc's sister carried the Sun. She was called Chalchiuhtlicue— the Lady of the Jade Skirts, goddess of water. But just as before, Quetzalcoatl and Tezcatlipoca desired control and struck Chalchiuhtlicue from the sky. As she fell, a great deluge of water gushed from the sky and flooded the earth, destroying it for the fourth time. The Aztecs named this day 4 Water.

Quetzalcoatl and Tezcatlipoca looked upon the Earth, dark and flooded, and were remorseful for the damage they had caused. They understood they must end their quarrel for there to be another Sun. Together, they created the Earth for a fifth time. The age of the Fifth Sun had come—the sun of motion— our present time. Other stories tell of how they accomplished this task, bringing life back to the Earth. But according to Aztec myth, the time of the Fifth Sun will one day end, and earthquakes will bring about its destruction.

Adapted from Vigil, A. & F. Miraval. *Eagle on the Cactus: Traditional Stories from Mexico*, 2000.

DISCUSSION QUESTIONS

1.   Why do you suppose the Fifth Sun is said to end in earthquakes?

2.   Compare this creation myth to other cultures that have succession-style creation myths. What similarities and differences do you see?

THE FLOWING WATERS: THE CREATION OF THE EARTH
(Aztec)

After Quetzalcoatl and Tezcatlipoca at last ceased their fighting, which had brought about Earth's destruction, they reached an agreement—they would create the world by working together. This new time would be the Fifth Sun. After their fourth battle, the sky had released a torrent of rain that flooded all the Earth, drowning all life. As Quetzalcoatl and Tezcatlipoca looked upon the destruction they had caused, they realized they needed to build a new world. Then they saw the great monster, Tlaltecuhtli.

The fierce monster Tlaltecuhtli floated in the waters, seeking flesh to tear apart with her sharp teeth, which covered her entire body. Quetzalcoatl and Tezcatlipoca knew they could not create a new Earth while this monster posed a threat. They transformed themselves into gigantic serpents and dove down into the water, wrapping their bodies around Tlaltecuhtli. They ripped her in half, tearing her into two pieces. The upper part of her body became the sky; the lower half became the Earth. But this act of violence angered the other gods. Therefore, to honor the dismembered Tlaltecuhtli, they used the broken parts of her body to create all elements of this new world. Her spine became a ridge of mountains. Her hair was transformed into shrubs and trees. Her skin was used to create grasses and flowers to cover the ground. Powerful rivers flowed from her great mouth, and tears from her eyes became ponds and pools. The Earth was renewed, the Fifth Sun had begun—the time of our world.

DISCUSSION QUESTIONS

1.   Why is it significant that the two gods work together to create the earth?

2.   This myth illustrates Bruce Lincoln's term *alloforms*. Explain this concept and compare this story to similar creation myths from other cultures.

3.   What is the significance of having the earth be created from the body of a goddess?

Adapted from Vigil, A. & F. Miraval. *Eagle on the Cactus: Traditional Stories from Mexico*, 2000.

INTO THE FIRE:
THE CREATION OF THE SUN AND THE MOON (Aztec)

Aztec myth says that the time of the Fifth Sun began, following the last battle between Quetzalcoatl and Tezcatlipoca. The previous destructive ages of the Earth were over, but now the Earth was shrouded in darkness. The Earth had not yet felt the warmth and nurturing light of the sun. The gods convened to discuss how to bring light to the Earth. Eventually, they concluded that one of them needed to sacrifice himself in order to bring light to the world. They built an enormous, raging fire and they all waited to see who would come forward to make the necessary sacrifice. They cried out, "Which of us will give their life so the Sun will exist? Who is brave enough to face the fire? Who is worthy to make such a noble sacrifice?"

At last, one of the gods came forward—the proud and wealthy Tecuciztecatl. He strode toward the fire and spoke at length about how he was noblest of all the gods and was the most worthy. He said, "My wealth and character make me the ideal god for this sacrifice. If another god be worthy, I challenge him to come forward and test his courage against mine." Then he laid aside his robes and offered gold, incense, and quetzal feathers for his journey, before kneeling down to pray.

But another god, the poor and humble Nanahuatzin, also came forward. He said to the gods, "I offer my sincerest prayers that I may have the courage to give my life to the flames. I willingly give my life so that once again the Earth may know the Sun's warmth." He knelt to pray, but had no robes to lay aside nor offerings to make. However, he prayed that he would be worthy.

For four days and four nights they both prayed. When the prayer time had come to an end, Tecuciztecatl approached the fire first. As he walked around the pyre, the fire sprang up and scorched him. At that moment his courage failed and he backed away, afraid.

Next, Nanahuatzin stepped toward the fire. Seized by a flash of boldness, he leaped into the flames. Time stopped. The gods waited. Finally, the fire sprang back to life and the Sun arose golden in the eastern sky. Nanahuatzin had become the Fifth Sun.

Ashamed by his failure, Tecuciztecatl leaped into the fire. There was a great explosion, and a second light rose from the flames. Tecuciztecatl had also been transformed into a golden sun. But this angered the gods, for Tecuciztecatl had tried to rob Nanahuatzin of his sacrifice.

The gods spoke. "There can be two lights in the sky, but one should not be as bright as the other. Only Nanahuatzin deserves to be the Sun. He was first to leap into the flames and displayed courage. The glory of the Sun shall forever belong to Nanahuatzin. Therefore, the light of Tecuciztecatl must be less bright and shall rise second, always following Nanahuatzin."

Then one of the gods rose and threw a rabbit into Tecuciztecatl's face. The blow darkened the sun of Tecuciztecatl, causing it to become dimmer; and so Tecuciztecatl became the Moon. Even now, as the descendants of the Aztecs look up into the night sky, they see a rabbit on the face of the Moon. They see the Sun rise first each day, in all its glory, followed by the dim light of the Moon.

Adapted from Vigil, A. & F. Miraval. *Eagle on the Cactus: Traditional Stories from Mexico*, 2000.

DISCUSSION QUESTIONS

1. Why is it significant that gods sacrifice themselves during this act of creation? Do you agree that one sacrifice is more worthy than the other? Explain.

2. Why do you suppose a rabbit was the animal chosen to be thrown into Tecuciztecatl's face?

BROKEN BONES: THE CREATION OF PEOPLE (Aztec)

In the time of the Fifth Sun, after Quetzalcoatl and Tezcatlipoca had created a new Earth, and the gods Nanahuatzin and Tecuciztecatl sacrificed themselves, becoming the Sun and the Moon, there was still no human life on Earth.

Quetzalcoatl longed for the life of humans on the Earth. He recalled the other worlds, before they had been destroyed, and missed the joy of the human spirit. He knew there was only one way to bring back human life. He would need to go down into the darkness, the land of the dead, alone. He must bring back the bones of all those who had died in the previous worlds and use them to create new life.

And so Quetzalcoatl made the descent into the land of the dead, which was ruled by Mictlantecuhtli, the crafty and dangerous god who governed the underworld. He knew why Quetzalcoatl was there. When Quetzalcoatl approached his throne, Mictlantecuhtli said to him, "Why have you wandered so far from Earth? There is nothing here for you."

Quetzalcoatl replied, "I am here to ask you for the bones of the people who perished in the worlds before the Fifth Sun. I long for human life in the world again. May I have these bones?"

Mictlantecuhtli was the keeper of the bones and did not want to give them up. But he knew how clever Quetzalcoatl was, so he used caution. He offered him a proposal. He said, "Take this conch shell and travel across my kingdom four times. Sound the conch each time. If you can accomplish this task, I will give you the bones."

Quetzalcoatl knew that Mictlantecuhtli wouldn't give him a task that seemed so simple, but he knew this was his only chance to get the bones. He raised the shell and blew into to it. But no matter how hard he tried, it made no sound. He looked closely at the shell and realized Mictlantecuhtli had blocked the shell so it couldn't make a sound. Mictlantecuhtli was enjoying the trick he'd played on Quetzalcoatl, but Quetzalcoatl played a trick of his own. He called to the worms for help; they knew he restored life to the world, and so they agreed. The worms bored holes into the shell and created a place for air to pass through. Then, Quetzalcoatl asked the bees to fly through the shell. As Quetzalcoatl blew into the shell this time, their buzzing reverberated through the shell, and a great sound echoed throughout the land.

Mictlantecuhtli realized he had been outsmarted by Quetzalcoatl. But still, he would not give up. He said, "You succeeded in the task, but there is one condition if I give you the bones. They will return human life to the world, but when those lives end the people must return here to me."

Quetzalcoatl agreed, but secretly he lied. He was planning to deceive the Lord of the Dead, for he wanted the people to have eternal life. He took the bones and started to leave. Mictlantecuhtli perceived Quetzalcoatl's deception. He sent quail after him to retrieve the bones. Quetzalcoatl heard the birds and understood what was happening. He ran to escape. But as he ran, he tripped and dropped the bones. The bones broke into a variety of pieces—this is the reason all people are different sizes. The quail

Adapted from Vigil, A. & F. Miraval. *Eagle on the Cactus: Traditional Stories from Mexico,* 2000.

pecked on the bones, creating fractures and fine lines all over them. This damage caused people to be weak and unable to live forever. So the Lord of the Dead won, and one day everyone must return to him.

Quetzalcoatl collected the broken bones and returned to Earth. He took the bones to the gods in Tamoanchan, the land of miracles. The gods ground the bones into powder, placing them in a sacred bowl. They prayed over the bones for four nights. Then, on the fourth night, the gods pierced their own skin and mixed their blood with the powder. In four days the first man arose from the bowl, followed four days later by the first woman. And so the bones of the ancestors and the blood of the gods combined, creating a new race of people. Quetzalcoatl's journey brought human life back to the Earth.

DISCUSSION QUESTION

1. How does this story inform your perception of Quetzalcoatl?
2. Compare this story to other stories of the creation of human beings. What similarities and differences do you notice?

VIRACOCHA (Inca)

Viracocha is the creator-god worshipped by the Inca for his role in creating the earth, celestial bodies, and people, along with teaching these people how to behave properly. The legend of the Viracocha likely predates the Inca people, who co-opted the pantheon of those living in Peru. He actively worshipped as the supreme god in the Andes. We see in this myth Viracocha's tests of his disciples and his creation: sometimes testing his followers by dressing as a beggar to see how they treat him. Upon his departure, Viracocha walks into the water and leaves several lesser-gods to attend to his work of civilizing the people, but promises to return. Viracocha is commonly connected to Lake Titicaca, located on the modern-day border between Bolivia and Peru.

The First Age

In the beginning, and before this world was created, there was a being called Viracocha. He created a dark world without sun, moon, or stars. Owing to this creation he was named Viracocha Pachayachachi, which means "Creator of all things." And when he had created the world he formed a race of giants of disproportionate greatness, painted and sculpted, to see whether it would be well to make real men of that size. He then created men in his likeness as they are now; and they lived in darkness.

Viracocha ordered these people that they should live without quarrelling, and that they should know and serve him. He gave them a certain precept which they were to observe on pain of being confounded if they should break it. They kept this precept for some time, but it is not mentioned what it was.

But as there arose among them the vices of pride and covetousness, they transgressed the precept of Viracocha and falling, through this sin, under his indignation, he confounded and cursed them. Then some were turned into stones, others into other things, some were swallowed up by the earth, others by the sea, and over all there came a general flood which they call uñu pachacuti, which means "water

Source: "History of the Incas" by Pedro Sarmiento De Gamboa, translated by Clements Markham, *The Hakluyt Society,* 1907.

that overturns the land." They say that it rained 60 days and nights, that it drowned all created things, and that there alone remained some vestiges of those who were turned into stones, as a memorial of the event, and as an example to posterity, in the edifices of Pucara.

The Second Age

When Viracocha destroyed that land, he preserved three men, one of them named Taguapaca, in order for them to serve and help him in the creation of new people who had to be made in the second age after the deluge. The flood being passed and the land dry, Viracocha determined to people it a second time, and, to make it more perfect, he decided upon creating luminaries to give it light. With this object he went, with his servants, to a great lake in the Collao, in which there is an island called Titicaca, meaning "the rock of lead."

Viracocha went to this island, and presently ordered that the sun, moon, and stars should come forth, and be set in the heavens to give light to the world, and it was so. They say that the moon was created brighter than the sun, which made the sun jealous at the time when they rose into the sky. So the sun threw over the moon's face a handful of ashes, which gave it the shaded color it now presents.

Viracocha gave various orders to his three servants, but one, Taguapaca, disobeyed the commands of Viracocha. So Viracocha was enraged against Taguapaca, and ordered the other two servants to take him, tie his hands and feet, and launch him in a balsa on the lake. This was done. Taguapaca blasphemed against Viracocha for the way he was treated, and threatened that he would return and take vengeance, when he was carried by the water down the drain of the same lake, and was not seen again for a long time. This done, Viracocha made a sacred idol in that place, as a place for worship and as a sign of what he had there created.

Leaving the island, he passed by the lake to the mainland, taking with him the two servants who survived. He went to a place now called Tiahuanaco, and in this place he sculptured and designed on a great piece of stone, all the nations that he intended to create. This done, he ordered his two servants to charge their memories with the names of all tribes that he had depicted, and of the valleys and provinces where they were to come forth, which were those of the whole land. He ordered that each one should go by a different road, naming the tribes, and ordering them all to go forth and people the country. His servants, obeying the command of Viracocha, set out on their journey and work. One went by the mountain range or chain which they call the heights over the plains on the South Sea. The other went by the heights which overlook the wonderful mountain ranges which we call the Andes, situated to the east of the said sea.

By these roads they went, saying with a loud voice "Oh you tribes and nations, hear and obey the order of Ticci Viracocha Pachayachachi, which commands you to go forth, and multiply and settle the land." Viracocha himself did the same along the road between those taken by his two servants, naming all the tribes and places by which he passed. At the sound of his voice every place obeyed, and people came forth, some from lakes, others from fountains, valleys, caves, trees, rocks and hills, spreading over the land and multiplying to form the nations which are to-day in Peru.

Viracocha, after he had created all people, went on his road and came to a place where many men of his creation had congregated. This place is now called Cacha. When Viracocha arrived there, the inhabitants were confused by his dress and bearing. They murmured at it and proposed to kill him from a hill that was near. They took their weapons there, and gathered together with evil intentions against Viracocha. He fell on his knees on some plain ground, and with his hands clasped, fire from above came down upon those on the hill, and covered all the place, burning up the earth and stones like straw. Those bad men were terrified at the fearful fire. They came down from the hill, and sought pardon from Viracocha for their sin. Viracocha was moved by compassion. He went to the flames and put them out with his staff.

But the hill remained quite parched up, the stones being rendered so light by the burning that a very large stone which could not have been carried on a cart, could be raised easily by one man. This may be seen at this day, and it is a wonderful sight to behold this hill, which is a quarter of a league in extent, all burnt up.

Viracocha Leaves

Viracocha continued his journey, working his miracles and instructing his created beings. In this way he reached the territory on the equinoctial line, where are now Puerto Viejo and Manta. Here he was joined by his servants. Intending to leave the land of Peru, he made a speech to those he had created, apprising them of the things that would happen. He told them that people would come, who would say that they were Viracocha their creator, and that they were not to believe them; but that in the time to come he would send his messengers who would protect and teach them.

Having said this he went to sea with his two servants, and went travelling over the water as if it was land, without sinking. For they appeared like foam over the water, and the people, therefore, gave them the name of Viracocha which is the same as to say the grease or foam of the sea. At the end of some years after Viracocha departed, they say that Taguapaca, whom Viracocha ordered to be thrown into the lake of Titicaca, came back and began, with others, to preach that he was Viracocha. Although at first the people were doubtful, they finally saw that it was false, and ridiculed him.

DISCUSSION QUESTIONS

1. Many place names that exist today are given in this story. Why might this be important to a modern listener/reader?

2. Compare Viracocha's creation of human beings to others you've read. How is his method similar and different from others? (Think about materials, intention, number of times created.)

3. Why does Viracocha show such force when he is not recognized?

Part 2: Tricksters, Lovers, and Other Tales

Many tales from pre-Hispanic Mexico have traits of creation myths but, because they typically give an explanation about the understanding of a social practice or the origin of a natural phenomenon, they also serve an etiological function—that is the purpose of the next three tales.

For comparison purposes, we selected two stories about the origin of music—one from the Maya and the other from the Aztec.

MUSIC FROM THE GODS:
HOW MUSIC CAME TO THE WORLD (Aztec)

In the time of the Fifth Sun, the world Quetzalcoatl and Tezcatlipoca cooperated to create, Quetzalcoatl had brought people back to the Earth and had given them maize to eat. Now the god Tezcatlipoca, also called Smoking Mirror, came to the Earth. He was pleased to see that the world was lush with trees and grass and he rejoiced in the lovely fragrance of the flowers which decorated the valley like a rainbow. This Earth was beautiful. But Tezcatlipoca noticed that the people did not seem happy. Not even the trees and flowers brought them joy. He suddenly understood something was missing—there was no music.

People were unable to greet the sunrise with song or sing to honor the gods. There were no instruments to be played to bring peace or comfort in times of grief. The gods had music in the heavens to give them bliss each day. Tezcatlipoca realized that the people on Earth needed this as well, in order to be complete. But he knew the Lord of the Sun would not allow the gift of music to be taken away. There was only one god who could meet this challenge and bring music to the Earth—Quetzalcoatl, the one who had given the people food and life.

Tezcatlipoca spoke to Quetzalcoatl and they walked the Earth together, seeking music. They found none. Tezcatlipoca said, "The people need the beauty of music. They live in silence and sadness, and this is not good for the soul. You may journey to the House of the Sun to ask permission to bring musicians to the Earth, then the people will have the gift of music." Quetzalcoatl agreed, for he wished the people to have all good things and lead rich lives. He said, "I will do this, but it is a long journey. I will need a bridge to the sky in order to reach it."

Tezcatlipoca replied, "I can help by using my powers and by sending my helpers from the sea. They will make a bridge for you. Go to the sea and call for them—the whale, the sea turtle, and the sea cow." And so Quetzalcoatl set out, reaching the sea and calling for the helpers as instructed. The whale arrived and allowed Quetzalcoatl to ride on his enormous back. The whale carried him quickly to the end of the world and then leaped into the air. As they rose through the sky, Quetzalcoatl knew the whale's part of the journey was complete, so he thanked him and called for the sea turtle. As if by magic, the turtle appeared and, using his sturdy shell, carried Quetzalcoatl even higher into the sky. As the neared the House of the Sun, the sky became very hot, and the sea turtle grew weary. Quetzalcoatl thanked him, knowing that his part of the journey had ended, and he called for the sea cow. The sea cow appeared to help Quetzalcoatl complete the journey, carrying him to the House of the Sun. When he arrived, Quetzalcoatl thanked the sea cow and again thanked the whale and sea turtle as well, saying, "Because of your assistance, I can now begin my task of bringing music to the people of the Earth."

Adapted from Vigil, A. & F. Miraval. *Eagle on the Cactus: Traditional Stories from Mexico*, 2000.

Meanwhile, the Lord of the Sun had been watching Quetzalcoatl during his journey and knew why he had come. He did not want any of his musicians to take any of the beloved music from the House of the Sun. He called to the musicians, "Stop your playing. Be still as statues when Quetzalcoatl arrives. Do not listen to him." Quetzalcoatl arrived and noticed that the music stopped abruptly. As he entered the gates of the House of the Sun, he saw statues of musicians and walked up to each one saying, "There is no music on Earth. I have come to bring you there, so music may be shared with the people. Please wake from your enchantment and accompany me."

But none of the statues would move. This angered Quetzalcoatl. He didn't believe it was fair that the Lord of the Sun would keep the music for himself. In a rage, he released a tremendous hurricane over the House of the Sun. The statues were afraid, for they knew of Quetzalcoatl's great power and ability to destroy worlds. They began to awaken. One of them spoke to Quetzalcoatl. "We will come with you, but we must leave now, before the Lord of the Sun realizes we have disobeyed him." Quetzalcoatl gathered the musicians carefully, making sure he didn't injure their melodies. He brought them to the Earth, and scattering them about, commanded them to give people the gift of music. They played such lovely melodies and sang songs of such joy that the people's spirits rejoiced. Rainbows filled the sky and birds began to sing their own versions of the melodies. The winds carried music all over the world. This became the special gift from the gods. The musicians looked up to the sky and were happy, because they could still see the Sun and feel its warmth, as they had when they lived in the heavens. The Lord of the Sun was no longer angry because the breeze from Earth carried the music up to him. The silence was filled with beauty and the people soon learned, as the birds did, how to create music of their own. The musicians eventually returned to the heavens. Now both the House of the Sun and the Earth are filled with heavenly music.

DISCUSSION QUESTIONS

1. Discuss the role animals play in this story. Why do you think the gods couldn't accomplish this task on their own?

2. Discuss the significance of music originating with the gods, rather than being a human creation.

THE MURMUR OF THE RIVER: HOW MUSIC CAME TO THE WORLD (Maya)

At the beginning of time, there was no music on the Earth. The people had never known the heart's song and the joy it could bring. They lived all their days and nights in silence. The gods understood that the world they had created would be incomplete without music in the hearts of the people; they needed music to keep joy during difficult times in their lives.

The gods convened beneath the Tree of Life and held council, discussing how to bring music to the Earth. Ah Kin Xooc, a god who was familiar with Earth and its creatures, knew that Earth was already alive with many sounds. He understood, as he looked around at the other gods, that each of them had contributed to this creation and had given these sounds. He asked each one of the gods to give him a sound, and so they did: The God of Water offered the murmur of the river and the sound of raindrops tapping; The God of the Ocean offered the sound of crashing waves; The God of Wind gave the whisper of wind; The God

Adapted from Vigil, A. & F. Miraval. *Eagle on the Cactus: Traditional Stories from Mexico*, 2000.

of Corn gave the sound of leaves rustling; The God of winter gave the sound of ice cracking; The God of Mountains gave the creaking of trees; the God of Birds offered the sounds of chirping; the God of Fire gave the crackling of burning embers; and the God of Night offered the echoes of darkness.

Ah Kin Xooc swallowed all these sounds, keeping them safe in this throat. Then, he went down to the Earth, going all the way to its center. He located the sacred place of the Earth's own heartbeat and there he opened his mouth. The sounds of the gods flew out, mixing with the life-giving force of the Earth's heartbeat. The sounds rose and transformed, becoming sounds never before heard on Earth. The people heard for the first time the sounds of joy, sorrow, suffering, truth, and forgiveness. They knew in their hearts that these were the most important sounds ever heard, and they were overcome with both joy and sadness. The people imitated what they heard, and then they began to create their own sounds, first with their voices, and then by inventing instruments that could also create sound.

Ah Kin Xooc taught all the people of Earth his sounds, and then he returned to his place in the heavens. These sounds became the music of the people. They were the most beautiful sounds, because they were gifts from the gods.

DISCUSSION QUESTION

1. Compare this story with the similar tale of the Aztec people. What significant similarities and differences do you notice?

We can't adequately explore here the variety of indigenous Mexican cultures. Smaller groups include the Yaqui of the northwest, the Tarahumara from the southwestern mountains of Chihuahua, the Nahua in central Mexico, the Huichol in the Sierra Madre highlands in the west, and the Mazatec of northwestern Oaxaca.

Since stories about the origin of fire are prevalent in nearly all parts of the world, we feature one here from the Mazatec. The name *Mazateca*, which means "deer people," is believed to have come from the Aztecs. This could have been due to the abundance of deer in their area, or because they worshipped a deity represented by a deer. Unfortunately, much of Mazatec history has been lost over the centuries. However, the Mazatec are particularly known for how they have blended Christianity with their indigenous shamanic rituals—including the use of hallucinogenic plants to induce visions.

THE POSSUM'S TAIL: HOW FIRE CAME TO THE WORLD
(Mazatec)

Long ago, in the time of the ancestors, the night sky was illuminated by the brilliance of fiery stars. Billions of points of light, each one an explosion of a million-year-old ball of fire, filled the darkness. But the nights on Earth were cold, and the ancient people would shiver all through the darkness, waiting for the warm Sun to rise each day. They had not tamed fire yet, so they nothing to keep them warm, and no way to cook their food.

Adapted from Vigil, A. & F. Miraval. *Eagle on the Cactus: Traditional Stories from Mexico,* 2000.

Occasionally, a star would burst so violently that a ball of flame would sear across the sky. Sometimes, in the darkest part of night, the magic time, one of these balls of fire would fall to the ground. When the ancient people saw these they believed them to be messages sent by the star gods. But these messages were too complicated for the simple people to understand. There were some sacred priests who could interpret the meaning of these messages; some could even understand the secrets of the cosmos from the fallen balls of fire that reached the ground.

Legend tells of one night when an old woman looked to the sky for a shooting star. Suddenly, the sky seemed to be on fire with hundreds of flaming balls streaking over her head. She followed one that was particularly bright and found the place where it fell to the Earth. She had to cross a mountain and desert to find it, and it was still burning. She took the ball of fire home with her and kept it; in exchange, if offered her warmth each night. But soon, the other people learned that she had fire. She refused to share it, no matter how much they asked or begged. The people even tried to steal it from her, but she was fierce and guarded it closely.

One day, a possum said to the people, "I will visit the old woman and bring back the fire for everyone." They laughed at him. "You're just a little possum," they said, "if we have not been able to steal the fire from her, you cannot possibly succeed." The possum smiled and said, "I am small, but I am clever. Just wait and see. I will return with the fire."

That night, the possum went to her house and knocked on the door. When she opened it, he said, "Good evening. I am cold and weary from traveling. May I rest for a moment inside your house? It is dark and cold." The old woman believed him and said, "Yes, you may come inside, but only for a moment. But do not go anywhere near the fire." The possum thanked her and went inside. She watched him carefully as he felt the fire's warmth, but did not venture close to it. After a time, the old woman said, "That is enough. Now you must leave." As she turned to open the door, the possum jumped into the fire. He thrust his tail into the hottest part and then ran out the door. The possum ran all over the world, his tail in flames, sharing the fire with all the people. Even today, the possum has a bald tail, reminding us of that night long ago when he brought the gift of fire to the people of the Earth.

DISCUSSION QUESTIONS

1. Compare this story to tales of fire-origin from other cultures. Besides explaining how people obtained fire, what other function does the myth serve?

2. Discuss the significance of having the origin of fire begin with the stars.

The Adventures of Kororomanna (Warrau)

The Warrau are a subgroup of Arawaks who live along the Orinoco River in Venezuela and along the Pomeroon River in Guyana. There are approximately 20,000 Warrau living in this region of South America. Their culture is distinctly tied to the rivers they live near and they are considered a type of modern hunter-gatherer society. They have rich social structures of priests, medicine men, chiefs, and laborers, and practice many rituals that surround puberty, death, and illness.

Source: Walter E. Roth, *An Inquiry into the Animism and Folk-Lore of the Guiana Indians*, 1915.

The hero, Kororomanna, is the creator of the male, and the spirit Kulimina the creator of the female. His wives are Uri-Kaddo and Emeshi, whom he desperately wants to return home to in this story. As we see, Kororomanna is very much a trickster figure, and uses his wit to overcome the many obstacles in his way to returning home. The spirits, the Hebu, are the main source of enmity in this story. Kororomanna is a figure in Warrau culture who has many exploits and is regarded as a cultural hero.

THE ADVENTURES OF KORONAMANNA

Kororomanna went out hunting and shot a "baboon" (howler monkey), but as it was already late in the afternoon, in trying to make his way home he lost his way in the darkness. And there he had to make his camp, and to lie down, with the baboon beside him.

But where he lay was a Hebu road; one can always distinguish a Spirit road from any other pathway in the forest because the Hebus occupying the trees that lie alongside it are always, especially at night, striking the branches and trunks, and so producing short sharp crackling noises. It was not pleasant for poor Kororomanna, especially as the baboon's body was now beginning to swell with all the noxious gases inside; lest the Hebus should steal it from him, he was obliged to keep the carcass alongside and watch over it with a stick. At last he fell asleep, but in the middle of the night the Hebus, what with the knocking on the trees, aroused him from his slumbers. Now that he was awake, he mimicked the Spirits, blow for blow, and as they struck the limb of a tree, Kororomanna would strike the belly of the baboon. But what with the air inside, each time he struck the animal, there came a resonant Boom! Boom! just like the beating of a drum.

The Hebu leader heard the curious sound, and became a bit frightened: "What can it be? When before I knocked a tree, it never made a noise like that." To make sure, however, he struck the tree hard again, and Boom! came once more from the carcass. Hebu was really frightened now, and began to search all around to find out where the extraordinary noise could possibly come from; at last he recognized the little camp, and saw Kororomanna laughing. Indeed, the latter could not help laughing, considering that it was the first time he had heard such a funny sound come out of any animal.

Hebu then said to him, "Who are you? Show me your hand," to which Kororomanna replied, "I am Warrau, and here is my hand," but instead of putting out his own, he shoved forward one of the baboon's, and then held forward the animal's other hand, and finally both feet. Hebu was much puzzled and said he had never seen before a Warrau with so black a hand, and would not be satisfied until he saw the face. Kororomanna accordingly deceived him again and held out the monkey's, which caused Hebu to make the same remark about his face as he had done about his hands and feet.

The Spirit became more frightened than ever, but his curiosity exceeded his fear, because he next wanted to know where all that Boom! Boom! sound had come from. And when he learnt its source of origin (breaking wind), he regretted that he had not been made like ordinary mortals, he and all his family having no proper posteriors, but just a red spot. He thereupon begged Kororomanna to make for him a posterior which would allow of his producing a similar sound. So with his bow Kororomanna split the Spirit's hind quarters, and completed the task by impaling him, but so rough was he in his methods, that the weapon transfixed the whole body even piercing the unfortunate Hebu's head. The Hebu cursed Kororomanna for having killed him, and threatened that the other Spirits would avenge his death; he then disappeared.

Our hero, becoming a bit anxious on his own account, and, recognizing by the gradually increasing hullaballoo in the trees that swarms of Hebus were approaching the scene of the outrage, now climbed the manicole tree sheltering his camp, leaving the baboon's corpse inside. The Spirits then entered the camp, and believing the dead animal to be Kororomanna, began hitting it with their sticks, and with each blow, there came Boom! Our friend up the tree, whence he could watch their every movement, and their surprise at the acoustic results of the flogging, could not refrain from cracking a smile, which soon gave way to a hearty laugh.

The Spirits, unfortunately for him, heard it, and looking at the dead baboon, said, "This cannot be the person who is laughing at us." They looked all around, but could see nothing, until one of them stood on his head, and peeped up into the tree. And there, sure enough, he saw Kororomanna laughing at them. All the others then put themselves in the same posture around the tree, and had a good look at him.

The question they next had to decide was how to catch him. This they concluded could most easily be managed by hewing down the tree. They accordingly started with their axes on the trunk, but since the implements were but water-turtle shells, it was not long before they broke. They then sent for their knives, but as these were merely the seed-pods of the buari tree, they also soon broke. The Hebus then sent for a rope, but what they called a rope was really a snake. At any rate, as the serpent made its way farther and farther up the tree, and finally came within reach, Kororomanna cut its head off; the animal fell to the ground again, and the Hebus cried "Our rope has burst!"

Another consultation was held, and it was decided that one of their number should climb the tree, seize the man, and throw him down, and that those below might be ready to receive him when dislodged, the Hebu was to shout out, when throwing him down, the following signal: Tura-buna-sé mahara-ko na-kai. The biggest of the Spirits being chosen to carry the project into execution, he started on his climb, but head downward of course, so as to be able to see where he was going. Kororomanna, however, was on the alert, and, waiting for him, killed him in the same peculiar manner as that in which he had dispatched the other Spirit just a little while before; more than this, having heard them fix upon the preconcerted signal, he hurled the dead Spirit's body down with the cry of Tura-buna-sé mahara-ko na-kai! The Hebus below were quite prepared, and as soon as the body fell to the ground, clubbed it to pieces. Kororomanna then slipped down and helped in the dissolution. "Wait a bit," he said to the Spirits; "I am just going in the bush, but will soon return." It was not very long, however, before the Spirits saw that they had been tricked, and yelled with rage on finding that they had really destroyed one of themselves; they hunted high and low for their man, but with approaching daylight were reluctantly compelled to give up the chase.

In the meantime, Kororomanna had no sooner got out of their sight than he started running at topmost speed, and finally found shelter in a hollow tree. Here he discovered a woman (she was not old either), so he told her that he would remain with her till the day broke. But she said, "No! No! my man is Snake and he will be back before the dawn. If he were to find you here, he would certainly kill you." But her visitor was not to be frightened, and he stayed where he was. True enough, before dawn, Snake came wending his way home, and as he crawled into the tree, he was heard to exclaim, "Hallo! I can smell someone."

Kororomanna was indeed frightened now, and was at his wits' end to know what to do. Just then dawn broke, and they heard a hummingbird. "That is my uncle," said our hero. They then heard the bird doroquarra: "That also is an uncle of mine," he added. He purposely told Snake all this to make him believe that, if he killed and swallowed his visitor, all the other hummingbirds and doroquarras would come and avenge his death. But Snake said, "I am not afraid of either of your uncles, but will gobble them up." Just then, a chicken-hawk flew along, which made Snake ask whether that also was an uncle of his. "To be sure" was the reply, "and when I am dead, he also will come and search for me." It was now Snake's turn to be frightened, because Chicken-hawk used always to get the better of him; so he let Kororomanna go in peace, who ran out of that hollow tree pretty quick.

It was full daylight now, but this made little odds, because he had still lost his way, and knew not how to find the road home. After wandering on and on, he at last came across a track, recognizable by the footprints in it. Following this up, he came upon a hollow tree that had fallen across the path, and inside the trunk he saw a baby. This being a Hebu's child, he slaughtered it, but he had no sooner done so than he heard approaching footsteps, which caused him promptly to climb a neighboring tree and await developments. These were not long in coming, for the mother soon put in her appearance; as soon as she recognized her dead infant, she was much angered, and, looking around, carefully examined the fresh tracks, and said, "This is the man who has killed my child."

Her next move was to dig up a bit of the soil marked by one of the fresh footprints, wrap it up in a leaf tied with bush-rope, and hang it on a branch while she went for firewood. Directly her back was turned, Kororomanna slid down from his hiding place, undid the bundle, and threw away the contents, substituting a footprint of the Spirit woman. Then, tying up the parcel as before, he hung it where it had been left, and hid himself once more. When the woman returned with the firewood, she made a big fire, and threw the bundle into the flames, saying as she did so: "Curse the person whose footprint I now burn. May the owner fall into this fire also!" She thought that if she burnt the "foot-mark" so would the person's shadow be drawn to the fire. But no one came, and she felt that her own shadow was being impelled. "Oh! It seems that I am hurting myself; the fire is drawing me near," she exclaimed. Twice was she thus dragged toward it against her will, and yet she succeeded in resisting. But on the third occasion she could not draw back; she fell in, and was burnt to ashes; she "roasted herself dead."

Kororomanna was again free to travel, but which direction to follow was the puzzle; he had still lost his way home. All he could do was to walk more or less aimlessly on, passing creek after creek and back into the bush again, until he emerged on a beautiful, clean roadway. But no sooner had he put his foot on it, than it stuck there, just like a fish caught in a spring-trap. And this is exactly what the trap really was, save that it had been set by the Hebus. He pulled and he tugged and he twisted, but try as he might, he could not get away. He fouled himself over completely, and then lay quite still, pretending to be dead. The flies gathered on him and these were followed by the worms, but he continued to lie quite still.

By and by two of the Spirits came along, and one of them said, "Hello! I have luck today. My spring-trap has caught a fish at last," but when he got closer, he added, "Oh! I have left it too long. It stinks." However, they let loose their fish, as they thought it was, and carried it down to the riverside to wash and clean it. After they had washed it, one of the Hebus said, "Let us slit its belly now, and remove the entrails," but the other one remarked, "No, let us make a waiyarri (basket) first, to put the flesh in." This was very fortunate for Kororomanna, who, seizing the opportunity while they went collecting strands to plait with, rolled down the river bank into the water and so made good his escape. But when he succeeded in landing on the other side, he was, in a sense, just as badly off as before, not knowing how to get home.

Kororomanna next came across a man's skull lying on the ground, and what must he do but go and jerk his arrow into its eye-ball? Now this skull, Kwa-muhu, was a Hebu, who thereupon called out: "You must not do that. But now that you have injured me, you will have to carry me." So Kororomanna had to get a strip of bark, the same kind which our women employ for fastening on their field quakes, and carried the skull wherever he went, and fed it too. If he shot bird or beast, he always had to give a bit to Kwa-muhu, with the result that the latter soon became gradually and inconveniently heavier, until one day he became so great a dead weight as to break the bark-strip support.

The accident occurred not very far from a creek, and Kororomanna told Kwa-muhu to stay still while he went to look for a stronger strip of bark. Of course this was only an excuse, because directly he had put the skull on the ground, he ran as fast as he could toward the creek, overtaking on the way a deer that was running in exactly the same direction, swam across, and rested himself on the opposite side. In the meantime Kwa-muhu, suspecting that he was about to be forsaken, ran after Kororomanna, and seeing but the deer in front of him, mistook it for his man and killed it just as it reached the water. On examining the carcass, the Hebu exclaimed, when he got to its toes, "Well, that is indeed very strange. You have only two fingers;" and though he reckoned again and again, he could make no more—"but the man I am after had five fingers, and a long nose. You must be somebody else."

Now Kororomanna, who was squatting just over on the opposite bank, heard all this, and burst out laughing. This enraged Kwa-muhu, who left the deer, and made a move as if to leap across the creek, but, having no legs, he could not jump properly, and hence fell into the water and was drowned. All the ants then came out of his skull.

Poor Kororomanna was still as badly off as before; he was unable to find his way home. But he bravely kept on his way and at last came upon an old man bailing water out of a pond. The latter was really a Hebu, whose name was Huta-Kurakura (Red-back). Huta-Kurakura, being anxious to get the fish, was bailing away at the water side as hard as he could go, but having no calabash had to make use of his scrotum, which was very large. And while thus bending down, he was so preoccupied that he did not hear the footfall of Kororomanna coming up behind. The latter, not knowing what sort of a creature it was, stuck him twice in the back with an arrow, but Huta-Kurakura, thinking it to be a cow-fly, just slapped the spot where he felt it. When, however, he found himself stuck a third time, he turned round and, seeing who it was, became so enraged that he seized the wanderer and hurled him into a piece of wood with such force that only his eye projected from out the timber. Anxious to be freed from his unenviable position Kororomanna offered everything he could think of—crystals, rattles, paiwarri, women, etc., but the Spirit wanted none of them, As a last chance, he offered tobacco, and this the Hebu eagerly accepted, the result being that they fast became good friends. They then both emptied the pond and collected a heap of fish, much too large for Kororomanna to carry home. So the Spirit in some peculiar way bound them all up into quite a small bundle, small enough for Kororomanna to carry in his hand.

Kororomanna now soon managed to find the right path home, because each and every animal that he met gave him news of his mother. One after the other, he met a rat with a potato, an acouri with cassava root, a labba with a yam, a deer with a cassava leaf, a kushi-ant with a similar leaf on its head, and a bush-cow eating a pineapple. And as he asked each in turn whence it had come, the animal said, "I have been to your mother, and have begged potato, cassava, yam, and other things from her." When at length he reached home, and his wife and mother asked what he had brought, he told them a lot of fish, and they laughed right heartily at what they thought was his little joke. So he bade them open the parcel, and as they opened it, sure enough out came fish after fish, small and large, fish of all kinds, so many in fact that the house speedily became filled, and the occupants had to shift outside.

DISCUSSION QUESTIONS

1. In what ways is Kororomanna a traditional hero? In what ways is he not?

2. Trace his trials against the Hebu. How does he succeed? What might these trials represent?

3. The narrator refers to the hero as "Poor Kororomanna" frequently. Are we inherently sympathetic to this character? Why or why not?

Part 3 Journeys of Heroes and Heroines

The Eagle on the Cactus (Aztec)

This story tells of the Aztecs' journey in search of a place to make their home. It is said that the warrior-god Huitzilopochtli was born fully armed by the earth goddess Coatlicue ("she of the skirt of serpents"), and he was destined to be a great leader, guiding the people to find their home. The omen that signaled their arrival at the foretold destination—an eagle with a serpent in its talons, perched on a cactus—became the symbol of their new city, Tenochtitlan—present-day Mexico City. The image of the eagle on the cactus is depicted on Mexico's flag. This tale also foretells of the fall of the Aztec empire.

In the Nahuatl language, the native language of the Aztec people, Azteca (or Aztecatl) means "person from Aztlan," which refers to a mythical land in the north from which the people are said to have migrated—Aztlan, "place of herons." The word Aztec was first used in 1810 by Alexander von Humboldt to distinguish between ancient and modern Mexicans. They referred to themselves as Mexica, which is the origin of the name Mexico.

The Aztec believed the Toltec to be the greatest of civilizations, and that they had shared cultural origins. The word Toltecatl means "master artist" and the Toltec were said to be the originators of art and jewelry. Scholars have found scant evidence of the Toltec culture, aside from their capital city: Tula, which the Aztec called Tollan ("place of reeds").

This mythical Aztec story tells the tale of their eventual founding of their home in Tenochtitlan in 1325 CE, where they built impressive temples. Approximately 200,000 people lived there at the time of Spanish conquest—some sources say the number is closer to 700,000 if surrounding areas are included. Unlike the Maya, with their independent city-state households, the Aztecs developed a tribute-style, central empire.

THE EAGLE ON THE CACTUS

Many times since the Azteca came into the valley had the years been tied into bundles, each bundle being fifty-two years. And many times at the Tying of the Years had the fires been quenched and a new fire lighted on the breast of a sacrificed man. Many times had that festival come round that is called the Knot of the Years, and many times had the king and the priests consulted about the portents that show themselves when the fires are quenched and a new fire lighted.

Montezuma the Conqueror was king at that Tying of the Years. And the portent that showed itself was in a pair of great sandals that were found upon the floor of the Temple of Huitzilopochtli, the War God of the Azteca. Montezuma the Conqueror said, "This is a sign from Huitzilopochtli; it signifies that he will never leave the Azteca." And he said to the priests, "Bear these sandals to Coatlicue, the mother of our god. She dwells in Aztlan the White Place. Out of Aztlan the Azteca went in the old days, guided by Huitzilopochtli. They made themselves possessors of the valley; they conquered the tribes of the valley and the uplands; they built the great city Tenochtitlan. Go, tell Coatlicue all this. And say that by my arms they have now subdued the people farthest away, and have taken captives for the sacrifices from them.

Souce: Colum, P. *Orpheus: Myths of the World.* The Macmillan Company, 1930

Huitzilopochtli will never leave a people who have proved themselves such conquerors. Go; bear these sandals in all reverence to the mother of Huitzilopochtli; they will be a sign to her that her son will not return to Aztlan the White Place."

So the priests of Huitzilopochtli searched in their books and found out the ways that led back to Aztlan the White Place. It was a mountain that waters surrounded. The waters were filled with fish; flocks of ducks swam around; birds delighted those who dwelt there with the sight of their green and yellow plumage and enchanted them with their songs. And there, in the caverns of the mountain, the Azteca had dwelt for unnumbered generations. All the good things they had had been brought from there--the maize, the beans, the fruits. For on the waters there were barges, and on the barges grew all nourishing things. And when the men and women of the Azteca went out of the caverns that were filled with precious stones they would go in canoes amongst the floating gardens, and watch the ducks swimming, the cormorants diving, the herons flying overhead; they would gather the bright flowers of the gardens and listen to the enchanting songs of the birds.

But Huitzilopochtli roused up many to depart from that place; they left the mountain and their floating gardens, taking with them, however, many of the plants that grew in the gardens. They went upon the land. The herbs of the ground pricked them; the stones bruised their feet. Plains that were filled with thorns spread out before them. Jaguars lay in wait for them, and sprang upon stragglers and tore their flesh. But aroused by Huitzilopochtli and guided by him the Azteca went on. They went through deserts where famine wasted them. Then they reached the Place of the Seven Caves where they rested and were at ease for a while. Then they came to where there was a tree broken by lightning, and there some stayed. Others went on, Huitzilopochtli still guiding them. And at last they came to the Lake Tezcuco. They beheld a high rock with a cactus growing on it. Upon the cactus was an eagle. Up he rose; he flew towards the rising sun, and in his talons he held a serpent. The omen was good; the Azteca halted their march there. Many battles did they fight there; they subdued the tribes that dwelt in the valley, and they built Tenochtitlan, the greatest of cities.

And now the priests of Huitzilopochtli, the ambassadors of Montezuma the Conqueror, travelled the ways back to Aztlan the White Place. In Tollan, which is the navel of the world, they found four magicians who guided them across the deserts. Then they beheld a mountain that rose out of the midst of waters. The priests went towards it, leaving the magicians behind them. The smell of flowers came to them on the airs of night; in the morning they heard the songs of birds. On they went, and they saw the gardens upon the water; they saw the flocks of ducks swimming around, and the cormorants diving from the juttings of the mountain, and the herons fishing or flying overhead. They saw the birds of green and yellow plumage flying from garden to garden, and they heard them singing from the branches of fruitful trees.

The people who were there spoke to them in a language that the priests knew, and asked them why they had come across deserts to them. The priests said that they had come back to the ancestral place. They brought to Coatlicue, they said, the sandals of her son Huitzilopochtli.

But when the priests mentioned the name of Montezuma the Conqueror and mentioned the names of his lords, the people of the waters said that those who had gone from them in the old days had borne no such names. They named the lords who were with the Azteca when they went from Aztlan the White Place. Then the ambassadors of Montezuma said, "We know not these lords; we have never seen them; they are long since dead." Then the people of the waters were surprised, and they said, "We who knew them are living yet."

The priest of Coatlicue came to bring them into the presence of the Goddess. She lived on a peak of the mountain. As they went upward the feet of the men from Tenochtitlan sank in the ground, for the mountain became like a heap of loosened sand. "What makes you so heavy?" their guide asked them. He was an ancient, but he went lightly upon the ground. "What do you eat?" he asked them. "We eat flesh, and we drink pulque," the ambassadors of Montezuma answered him. "It is the meat and drink you have consumed that prevent your reaching the place where your fathers dwelt. Here we eat but fruits, and roots, and grain; we drink only water, and so there is no clog upon us when we walk." As he said this a swift wind came and brought him and brought the ambassadors up to the peak of the mountain and into the cavern where Coatlicue dwelt.

They saw her; her dress was of serpents, and they were terrified of her. When she looked upon the sandals they laid before her she lamented, saying, "When Huitzilopochtli went from Aztlan he said to me, his mother, 'When my time is accomplished I shall return to your lap; until that time I shall know nought save weariness. Therefore, give me two pairs of sandals, one for going forth, and one for returning.' And now, you say, he will not return to this lap of mine." Then the Goddess put on a garment of mourning, and the ambassadors went from the cavern where she dwelt.

They did not think that they stayed long in Aztlan the White Place. But when they returned to Tenochtitlan they found that the years were again being tied into a bundle, that the fires of the land were quenched, and that a new fire was being lighted on the breast of a sacrificed man. A king who was called the Second Montezuma ruled over the Azteca. Many and dread portents showed themselves at that Tying of the Years. A fisherman caught a strange bird: a shining stone was in the head of that bird, and when that stone was brought to him, the Second Montezuma looked into it and he saw wars being waged against the Azteca in which strange and more death-dealing weapons than he had ever known were being used. And at the time of the quenching of the fires his sister had died; she had been buried, but now she was seen seated at a fountain in a garden of the palace. Montezuma and his lords went before her. She told them that she had been brought to the Eastern Sea. She had seen great ships upon the sea, and in the ships were fair-faced and bearded men who carried more death-dealing weapons than any that had ever been seen in the land of the Azteca. And after that a pillar of fire appeared in the east, and it seemed too cast fire upon the whole land. Rejoicings were heard amongst the captives, and lamentations were heard amongst the old men: it was thought that the pillar of fire in the east presaged the destruction of the Empire of the Azteca.

DISCUSSION QUESTIONS

1.   Why was it so important for the Aztecs to find this specific place to make their home?

2.   Discuss how Huitzilopochtli's characteristics make him a hero. In what ways does he fit the heroic model?

Quetzalcoatl and Tezcatlipoca (Aztec)

Quetzalcoatl, the "plumed serpent," was one of the most important Mesoamerican gods. He served a variety of roles over time and throughout cultures, being known as the god of wind and rain, creator of the world and of people, and patron god of learning, farming, and art. He invented the calendar, and was identified with Venus (the morning star), and opossums, and is credited with bringing maize to the people.

The myths surrounding Quetzalcoatl become even more confusing due to a legendary ruler of Tollan, Ce Acatl Topiltzin Quetzalcóactl, who took the god's name as a title. This has created an unusual blend of legend and myth, and added more weight to the god's importance.

There are a variety of tales regarding the exploits of Quetzalcoatl, many of which also include Tezcatlipoca— either his rival or brother, depending on the particular story.

QUETZALCOATL AND TEZCATLIPOCA

In Tollan dwelt Quetzalcoatl. And in Tollan all the arts and crafts that we know of were first practised, for Quetzalcoatl taught them to the people there. He taught them the smelting of silver and the clearing and setting of precious stones; he taught the craft of building with stones; he taught them how to make statues, and paint signs in books, and keep count of the moons and suns. All crafts except the craft of war Quetzalcoatl taught the people of Tollan. And they made sacrifice to him with bread, and flowers, and perfumes, and not as other peoples made sacrifice to the other gods—by tearing the hearts out of the opened breasts of men and women.

He lived in a house that was made of silver: four chambers that house had: the chamber to the east was of gold, the chamber to the west was set with stones of precious green—emeralds and turquoises and nephrite stones, the chamber to the south was set with coloured sea-shells, and the chamber to the north was set with jasper. The house was thatched with the feathers of bright-plumaged birds. All the birds of rich plumage and sweet song were gathered in that place. In the fields the maize grew so big that a man could not carry more than one stalk in his arms; pumpkins were great in their round as a man is high; cotton grew in the fields red and yellow, blue, and black, and white, and men did not have to dye it. All who lived where Quetzalcoatl was had everything to make them prosperous and happy.

There was a time when they did not have maize, when they lived upon roots and on what they gained in the chase. Maize there was, but it was hidden within a mountain, and no one could come to where it was. Different gods had tried to rend the mountain apart that they might come to where the maize was; but this could not be done. Then Quetzalcoatl took the form of a black ant; with a red ant to guide him he went within the mountain Tonacatepetl, and he came to where the maize was: he took the grain, and laboriously he bore it back to men. Then men planted fields with maize; they had crops for the first time; they built cities, and they lived settled lives, and Quetzalcoatl showed them all the crafts that they could learn from him. They honoured him who dwelt in the shining house. And Quetzalcoatl had many servants; some of them were dwarfs, and all were swift of foot.

Then it came to pass that Tezcatlipoca, he who can go into all places, he who wanders over the earth stirring up strife and war amongst men, descended upon Tollan by means of spider-webs. And from the mountain he came down on a blast of wind of such coldness that it killed all the flowers in Quetzalcoatl's bright garden. And Quetzalcoatl, feeling that coldness, said to his servants, "One has come who will drive me hence; perhaps it were better that I went before he drives me, and drank from a fountain in the Land of the Sun, whence I may return, young as a boy." So he said, and his servants saw him burn down

Souce: Colum, P. *Orpheus: Myths of the World.* The Macmillan Company, 1930

his house of silver with its green precious stones and its thatch of bright plumage, and its door-posts of white and red shells. And they saw him call upon his birds of sweet song and rich plumage, and they heard him bidding them to fly into the land of Anahuac.

Then Tezcatlipoca, that god and that sorcerer, went to where Quetzalcoatl stood, and took him into the ball-court that the two might play a game together. All the people of the city stood round to watch that game. The ball had to be cast through a ring that was high upon the wall. Quetzalcoatl took up the ball to cast it. As he did Tezcatlipoca changed himself into a jaguar and sprang upon him. Then Quetzalcoatl fled. And Tezcatlipoca chased him, driving him through the streets of the city, and out into the highways of the country.

His dwarfs fled after him and joined themselves to him. With them he crossed the mountains and came to a hill on which a great tree grew. Under it he rested. As he rested he looked into a mirror and he said, "I am grown to be an old man." Then he threw the mirror down and took up stones and cast them at the tree.

He went on, and his dwarfs made music for him, playing on flutes as they went before him. Once again he became weary, and he rested on a stone by the wayside; there, looking back towards Tollan, he wept, and his tears pitted the stone on which he sat, and his hands left their imprints upon it where he grasped the stone. The stone is there to this day with the pits and the imprints upon it. He rose up, and once again he went on his way. And men from Tollan met him, and he instructed them in crafts that he had not shown them before.

But he did not give them the treasure of jewels that his dwarfs and humpbacked servants carried for him. He flung this treasure into the fountain Cozcaapan; there it stays to this day--Quetzalcoatl's treasure. On his way he passed over a Fire-mountain and over a mountain of snow. On the mountain of snow his dwarfs and humpbacked servants all died from the cold. Bitterly he bewailed them in a song he made in that place.

Then Quetzalcoatl went down the other side of the mountain, and he came to the sea-shore. He made a raft of snakes, and on that raft he sailed out on the sea. Or so some say, telling Quetzalcoatl's story. And those who tell this say that he came to the land of Tlappallan in the Country of the Sun, and there he drank of the Water of Immortality. They say that he will one day return from that land young as a boy. But others say that when he reached the sea-shore he divested himself of his robe with its bright feathers, of his snake-skin mask of the colour of turquoise, and that, leaving these vestments upon the shore, he cast himself into a fire and was consumed to ashes. And they say that Quetzalcoatl's ashes changed into bright-coloured and sweet-singing birds, and that his heart went up into the sky and became the Morning Star. After he had been dead for eight days that star became visible to men, and thereafter Quetzalcoatl was named the Lord of the Dawn.

DISCUSSION QUESTIONS

1.   What heroic qualities does Quetzalcoatl possess? What similarities do you see between Quetzalcoatl and other prominent religious figures, gods, leaders, or heroes in other cultures?

2.   We know the Mesoamerican cultures practiced ritual human sacrifice, yet this myth appears to reject it. How can we account for this apparently contradictory statement?

© Jared Blandford

"The Hero Twins" from the *Second Book of The Popol Vuh* (Maya)

Much of "The Hero Twins" story is concerned with "playing ball." People in MesoAmerica have been playing "The Ballgame" since around 2000 BCE. The Maya created elaborate ball courts out of stone, usually around 120 feet long with six rings placed about twenty-four feet in the air on either side of the sloped walls. The object was to bounce a rubber ball into the rings without using their hands. Two teams of men would compete in "The Ballgame" to score points, which would determine the fate of the teams. The losing team would usually be sacrificed after the game.

The story of "The Hero Twins" comes from the same text as "The Creation," in *The Popol Vuh*. The Hero Twins, while the center of this myth, are not our only heroes. Their fathers, Hun-Hunahpu and Vucub-Hunahpu endure the trials of the Underworld Gods (The Lords of Xibalba) first, but ultimately do not survive. The miraculous birth of Hunahpu and Xbalanque after the death of their father/uncle is just the beginning of their hero's journey. It is a story of vengeance, cunning, magic, and has one of the best examples of "The Road of Trials" in all of mythology.

Xpivacoc + Xmucane
|
Xquiq + Hun-Hunahpu and Vucub-Hunahpu
|
Hunahpu and Xbalanque

THE HERO TWINS

Hun-Hunahpu and Vucub-Hunahpu are Called to Xibalba

Xpiyacoc and Xmucane, the father and mother deities, had two sons, Hun-Hunahpu and Vucub-Hunahpu. These were men full of wisdom and artistic genius, but they were addicted to the recreation of playing ball. They were even playing ball when their mother died. The lords of Xibalba (the underworld) sent forth messengers to Hun-Hunahpu and Vucub-Hunahpu, requesting that they come to Xibalba to play ball with the lords of the underworld. These lords, in challenging the brothers to a game of ball, wished to defeat and disgrace them, because the brothers' ball-playing was so loud as to shake the earth. This disturbed the rest of those in Xibalba, and so they decided to put them through a series of trials that would ultimately kill them.

For this purpose, they dispatched four messengers in the shape of owls. The brothers accepted the challenge, but left behind some of their ball-playing equipment for when they returned. After descending the steep staircase that led to the underworld, and an ominous crossing over a river of blood, they came to the residence of the kings of Xibalba, where they underwent the mortification of mistaking two wooden figures for the lords. Invited to sit on the seat of honour, they discovered it to be a red-hot stone, and the pain which resulted from their successful trick caused much merriment among the Xibalbans. Then they were thrust into the House of Gloom, where they were given the task of keeping their cigars lit through the night. The next morning, Hun-Hunahpu and Vucub-Hunahpu were found crouching in the dark and cold with their cigars burnt down to the ends. The brothers had been defeated and were sacrificed. The head of Hun-Hunahpu was, however, suspended from a tree, which speedily became covered with gourds, from which it was almost impossible to distinguish the bloody trophy. All in Xibalba were forbidden the fruit of that tree.

The Descendants of Hun-Hunahpu: The Hero Twins

There was one person in Xibalba who had resolved to disobey the mandate not to touch the tree. This was the virgin princess Xquiq (Blood Moon), the daughter of the great lord Cuchumaquiq. Xquiq decided to go by herself to the very spot where the forbidden tree grew. Standing under the branches, gazing at the fruit, the maiden stretched out her hand, and the head of Hun-Hunahpu spat into the palm of her hand. The head of Hun-Hunahpu said to her, "In my saliva, I have given you my descendants. You will not be harmed." The spittle caused her to conceive, and in six months' time her father became aware of her condition. Despite her protestations of innocence, her father gave the royal messengers of Xibalba, the owls, orders to kill her and return with her heart in a vase. Xquiq, however, escaped death by bribing the owls with splendid promises for the future to spare her and substitute for her heart the red, blood-like sap of the Blood Tree. She was spared and the owls took the sap in place of her heart.

In her condition, Xquiq went to the home of Xmucane for protection. Xmucane would not at first believe her tale. But Xquiq appealed to the gods and performed a miracle by gathering a basket of maize where no maize grew, and thus gained her confidence. Shortly afterwards Xquiq became the mother of twin boys, Hunahpu, and Xbalanque. These did not find favour in the eyes of Xmucane, their grandmother. Their infantile cries aroused the wrath of this venerable person, and she vented it upon them by turning them out of doors. They speedily took to an outdoor life, however, and became mighty hunters, and expert in the use of their blowpipes, with which they shot birds and other small game.

Sources: adapted from *The Popol Vuh: The Mythic and Heroic Sagas of the Kiches of Central America*. Translated by Lewis Spence, 1908.
Adapted from *The Popol Vuh: The Book of the People*. Translated by Delia Goetz and Sylvanus Griswold Morley, 1954.

The divine twins were now old enough to undertake labor in the field, and the first task their grandmother sent them was the clearing of a maize-plantation. They were possessed of magic tools, which had the merit of working themselves in the absence of the young hunters, and the boys spent their days hunting in the forest. Returning at night from hunting, they smeared their faces and hands with dirt so that Xmucane might be deceived into imagining that they had been hard at work in the maize-field. But during the night the wild beasts met and replaced all the roots and shrubs which the brothers—or rather their magic tools—had removed. The twins resolved to watch for them that night, but despite all their efforts, all the animals succeeded in making their escape, save one, the rat, which was caught in a handkerchief. The rat, in gratitude that they had spared its life, told them of the glorious deeds of their great father and uncle, their games at ball, and of the existence of a set of ball-playing equipment necessary to play the game. They discovered these and went to play in the ball-ground of their fathers.

The Lords of Xibalba Challenge the Hero Twins

It was not long, however, until the lords of Xibalba heard them at play, and decided to lure them to the Underworld as they had lured their fathers. Messengers were dispatched to the house of Xmucane, who, filled with alarm, dispatched a louse to carry the message to her grandsons. The louse, wishing to ensure greater speed to reach the brothers, consented to be swallowed by a toad, the toad by a serpent, and the serpent by the great bird the hawk. The other animals duly liberated one another; but despite his utmost efforts, the toad could not get rid of the louse, who had played him a trick by lodging in his gums and had not been swallowed at all. The message, however, was delivered after the brothers stepped on and squished the toad until the louse came out to speak. The message received, the twins returned home to take leave of their grandmother and mother. Before their departure they each planted a stalk of corn in the middle of the house, which was to tell their mother and grandmother if they were alive in Xibalba; for the corn would wither and die if they should die.

The Tests of Xibalba

Pursuing the same route their fathers had followed, they crossed the river of blood and the river of puss by standing on their blowguns. They sent ahead a mosquito with orders to prick all the Xibalbans in order to discover their names, so they would not be mistaken like their fathers before them. Thus they did not salute the mannikins on their arrival at the Xibalban court, nor did they sit upon the red-hot stone.

They were thrown into the House of Gloom and challenged to keep their cigars lit through the night. Hunahpu and Xbalanque were smarter than their fathers before them; instead of trying to keep the cigars lit, they attached fireflies to them so that the night guards could look in and see light. The Xibalbans were furious when they opened the door to the House of Gloom the next morning to see the cigars full and lit. The lords of Xibalba summoned the brothers to play ball against them, sure that they could not be defeated. But the boys were the descendants of great ballplayers and the Xibalbans found they could not win.

Greatly offended, the lords of Xibalba set another test, sure to be the defeat of the twins. Hunahpu and Xbalanque were ordered to bring them four bouquets of flowers, which the guards of the royal gardens watched most carefully. The brothers, however, had at their beck and call a swarm of ants, which entered the royal gardens, cut and brought red, white, yellow, and black flowers. The Xibalbans, white with fury, ordered that the owls, the guardians of the gardens, should have their lips split to show their disobedience.

The House of Knives was the next ordeal, where the lancers were directed to kill them. But the twins succeeded in bribing the lancers with the promise of tasty animals for their meal instead of the boys.

Then came the House of Cold. The cold and hail and snow and biting wind was more than anyone could possibly stand. But here the heroes escaped death by freezing by being warmed with burning pinecones and they were still alive in the morning. The Xibalbans were beginning to think that there was something abnormal about these boys.

In the House of Jaguars, the twins tempted the beasts with the bones of other animals instead of themselves. All night long the guards heard the chomping and crunching of bones and thought the boys to be long dead. But the boys did not die! "Where did they come from?" the lords of Xibalba began to exclaim.

The House of Fire was the next test, inside which was full of burning flame. But the boys were not burned to death because they kept the fire to the coals and wood instead of their flesh.

Then the twins ventured to spend the night in the House of Bats. Large, terrifying, blood hungry death bats filled the inside of this house. To escape the thirst of the bats, the boys slept inside their blowguns. But just before dawn, when the bats began to settle, Hunahpu stuck his head outside of his blowgun to see if it was yet light. Camazota, the rule of the bats, suddenly appeared from above and cut Hunahpu's head off his body. The lords of Xibalba rejoiced and immediately hung the head in the ball-court.

The Final Ball Game

Xbalanque was to be challenged once more to a ball game with the lords of Xibalba, but he knew he could not possibly defeat them without his brother. Xbalanque asked all the animals to bring him the food that they eat. Some brought rotten things, others brought grasses and earth, the large and small animals gathered various vegetables and roots. The turtle lingered behind the rest and Xbalanque decided to fashion him into the form of the head of his brother, Hunahpu. This head could speak and the turtle's face resembled that of Hunahpu, enough not to raise suspicion. Xbalanque whispered instructions into the ear of the rabbit, who would be of great help the next day.

Xbalanque and his brother Hunahpu (wearing the turtle head as his own) walked to the ball-court the next morning. The lords of Xibalba were so confident in their success that they did not care if Xbalanque had reanimated his brother's body. They could see the real head still stuck at the top of the ball court, so they saw no problem. The lords of Xibalba began to play; the ball bounced around the court, nearing the ring, and suddenly bounced straight off the court and into the trees. The rabbit chased after the ball, and the lords of Xibalba all chased after the rabbit. Xbalanque took advantage of the moment, grabbed Hunahpu's real head from the top of the ball-court, and switched out the turtle's head. Hunahpu, reunited with his body, rejoiced to be with his brother again.

When the lords of Xibalba returned and the game commenced, Xbalanque threw a stone at the turtle's head, which fell to the ground and separated into a thousand pieces. The lords of Xibalba realized they had been overcome by Hunahpu and Xbalanque.

The Death of the Hero Twins

But in order to further astound their "hosts," Hunahpu and Xbalanque confided to two sorcerers named Xulu and Pacaw that the Xibalbans had failed because the animals were not on their side, and directing them what to do with their bones, they stretched themselves upon a funeral pile and died together. Their bones were beaten to powder and thrown into the river, where they sank, and were transformed into young men. On the fifth day they reappeared like men-fishes, and on the sixth in the form of ragged old men. In this disguise, the twins entertained people by dancing, by setting fire to, then restoring houses, and by killing and restoring each other to life.

The lords of Xibalba, hearing of their skill, requested them to exhibit their magical powers, which they did by burning the royal palace and restoring it, killing and resuscitating the king's dog, and cutting a man in pieces, and bringing him to life again. The lords of Xibalba, anxious to experience the novel sensation of a temporary death, requested to be slain and resuscitated. They were speedily killed, but the brothers refrained from resuscitating their arch-enemies.

Announcing their real names, the brothers proceeded to punish the lords of Xibalba. The game of ball was forbidden for them to play, they were to perform menial labor, and only the beasts of the forest were to worship them. They appear now not as "lords" but as demons. They are described as warlike, ugly as owls, inspiring evil and discord. Their faces are painted black and white to show their faithless nature.

Xmucane, waiting at home for the twins, was alternately filled with joy and grief as the corn stalks grew green and withered, according to the varying fortunes of her grandsons. After defeating the Xibalbans, the twins busied themselves in paying fitting funeral honors to their father and uncle. "We are the avengers of your death. Your names shall be remembered," Hunahpu and Xbalanque said of Hun-Hunahpu and Vucub-Hunahpu.

With their duties of vengeance complete, Hunahpu and Xbalanque rose up into the sky, where one was given the sun, and the other the moon. Heaven and Earth were now lighted by the hero twins as they dwelt in the heavens.

DISCUSSION QUESTIONS

1. How does Hun-Hunahpu become the father of the twins? What other culture's stories do we see a similar parentage? What might this signify?

2. What trials do Hunahpu and Xbalanque endure in Xibalba? How do they outsmart the gods? Do they have help?

3. What becomes of the Hero Twins? How does this phenomenon relate to other hero stories from other cultures?

BIBLIOGRAPHY

Aztec Civilization. *New World Encyclopedia,* 8 December 2016. http://www.newworldencyclopedia.org/entry/Aztec_Civilization

Barnhart, Edwin. *The Great Courses, Maya to Aztec: Ancient Mesoamerica Revealed.* The Teaching Company, 2015.

Brinton, D. G. *The Arawack Language of Guiana in its Linguistic and Ethnological Relations.* McCalla & Stavely Printers, 1871. https://www.gutenberg.org/files/31273/31273-h/31273-h.htm

---. "On the Mazatec Language and its Affinities." *American Philosophical Society* 30.137, 1892, pp. 31–39. https://www.jstor.org/stable/983207

---. *Rig Veda Americanus: Sacred Songs of the Ancient Mexicans* in *Brinton's Library of Aboriginal American Literature no. VIII,* 1890. http://www.sacred-texts.com/nam/aztec/rva/index.htm

Carrasco, D. *Religions of Mesoamerica,* 2nd ed. Waveland Press, 2014.

---. "Human Sacrifice in Aztec Culture." *Serious Science*, 13 October 2016. http://serious-science.org/human-sacrifice-in-aztec-culture-6995

Cartwright, M. Quetzalcoatl. *Ancient History Encyclopedia*, 1 August 2013. https://www.ancient.eu/Quetzalcoatl/

---. Teotihuacan. *Ancient History Encyclopedia*, 17 February 2015. https://www.ancient.eu/Teotihuacan/

Colum, P. *Orpheus: Myths of the World.* The Macmillan Company, 1930. http://www.sacred-texts.com/etc/omw/omw85.htm

De Gamboa, Pedro Sarmiento, "History of the Incas" Trans. Clements Markham. The Hakluyt Society, 1907. pp. 28–58. http://www.sacred-texts.com/nam/inca/inca01.htm

Ganeri, A. *Mesoamerican Myth.* M. E. Sharpe, Inc., 2008.

Goetz, Delia, and Sylvanus Griswold Morley (translators). *The Popol Vuh: The Book of the People,* 1954.

Harner, M. J., editor. *Hallucinogens and Shamanism.* Oxford University Press, 1973. www.entheology.com.

Maestri, Nicoletta. Aztec Sacrifice—The Meaning and Practice of Mexica Ritual Killings, 10 April 2017. https://www.thoughtco.com/meaning-of-aztec-sacrifice-169338

---. Tlaltecuhtli—The Monstrous Aztec Goddess of the Earth, 9 April 2016. https://www.thoughtco.com/tlaltecuhtli-the-monstrous-aztec-goddess-169344

Powell, Barry. *World Myth.* Pearson, 2014.

Rosenberg, Donna. *Mythology: An Anthology of the Great Myths and Epics,* 3rd ed. McGraw Hill, 1999.

Roth, Walter E. *An Inquiry into the Animism and Folk-Lore of the Guiana Indians* from the *Thirtieth Annual Report of the Bureau of American Ethnology, 1908–1909,* pp. 103–386, 1915. http://www.sacred-texts.com/nam/sa/aflg/aflg02.htm#story_2

Spence, Lewis, translator. *The Popol Vuh: The Mythic and Heroic Sagas of the Kiches of Central America,* 1908.

Vigil, A. & Miraval, F. *Eagle on the Cactus: Traditional Stories from Mexico.* [EBSCOhost]. Libraries Unlimited, 2000.

Chapter 10

THE MYTHS OF NORTH AMERICA

Source: Jayme Novara

INTRODUCTION

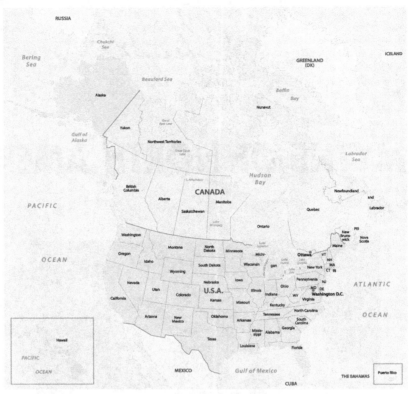

© Rainer Lesniewski/Shutterstock.com

There is no one Native American identity to describe the vast number of tribes and cultures that reside in the United States and Canada.

While pinpointing a date at which people began to populate the continent of North America is near impossible, recent research suggests that migration from Asia to the Western coast of Canada, Alaska, and the United States occurred around 15,000 years ago. This migration happened in waves, not all at once, and groups of people began to splinter off to the south and east in order to form their own subgroups all over the continent. This is the era of Paleo-Indian migration.

As people formed their own groups and technology evolved, the next era that we have significant archaeological evidence for are the Mound Builders. From 7000 BCE until approximately 1700 CE, mounds were built in increasing complexity and used for multiple purposes: as religious sites, burial sites, markers of settlements or important places, and homes for chiefs. The largest example of these earthen made mounds that can still be visited today is Monk's Mound, at the site of the ancient civilization of Cahokia, near Collinsville, Illinois. While excavations have given us great insight into the culture of the Mound Builders, there was no written language to record the myths of these groups.

The descendants of these Mound Builders are the Indigenous North Americans we know today. At the time of European contact and exploration, the indigenous population is estimated to have been around 112 million, according to Professor of Geography at University of Wisconsin-Madison Dr. William Denevan. By 1650, less than 200 years, this population had been drastically cut to less than 6 million.

The French fur trade established trading relationships, posts, and eventually French communities that extended from Quebec to New Orleans. Spanish explorers traveled north from Mexico and Florida. The Russian fur trade expanded through Alaska and the Western coasts of Canada and the United States. And British colonists began a sweeping claim on East coast states, all of which began to compress the local populations of indigenous people. Each of these colonizers brought their own religious principles; Catholics, Methodists, Shakers, Quakers, and others sought to convert the natives they encountered. In the nineteenth century, these missionaries would be responsible for forcing thousands of Native American children to attend white boarding schools in order to convert them to Christianity and squash their parents' culture. The detrimental effect to language, art, customs, and religion cannot be measured. Illnesses were also brought by the colonizers; as the indigenous population had never been exposed to cholera, tuberculosis, smallpox, measles, and typhoid, their immune systems were quickly compromised by the influx of these illnesses.

By the time the United States had declared independence from Britain, Westward expansion was on the path to decimating the native population. During the early 1800s, many treaties were drawn to see the indigenous people east of the Mississippi River moved to the Western states of Kansas and Oklahoma. The most infamous of these forced removals is the Trail of Tears, in which 17,000 Cherokee, Choctaw, Chickasaw, Creek, and Seminole were marched across the Southeast as directed by the Indian Removal Act of 1830. It is estimated that 4,000 people died during this march.

While the Trail of Tears is perhaps the most well-known, there were many other tribes who suffered similar fates. The Potawatomi Trail of Death is another such story of removal from ancestral lands in Indiana, during which forty people died, most of whom were children. Similar stories abound in the record of tribal removal. As entire tribes were forced to move via forced march, wagon, or boat, these communities were irreparably fractured by their new environment, sustaining huge losses in population, and being thrown together in close proximity with tribes that did not speak the same language.

According to the National Congress of the American Indian, between the years 1887 and 1934, the United States government reappropriated more than 90 million acres of land and gave it to settlers with virtually no compensation to the tribes. The 1940s and 50s saw even more reservation land taken by the federal government. Today, federally recognized tribes own approximately 50 million acres of land, which is about 2% of the total land mass of the United States.

According to the Department for Indigenous and Northern Affairs in Canada, as of 2011 there are 617 tribes of First Nations, with more than 901,000 registered tribal members, and 53 communities of Inuit, with approximately 155,000 registered members. First Nations and Inuit people of Canada speak over fifty languages and each have a rich history and culture of their own. According to the American Bureau of Indian Affairs, as of January 2018 there are 573 federally recognized tribes and more than 4 million people claimed Native American heritage on the 2000 census.

One of the most common questions about Indigenous North Americans is what to call them. We know that when Christopher Columbus arrived in "the New World" he thought he was near India, and thus called the people he encountered "Indians." Those people were the Taino (which is discussed in Chapter 9), but the name stuck; people from Canada to Brazil have been called "Indians" ever since. There are a few other words that perhaps better describe the population. "Indigenous" or "Aboriginal," as has been used to describe many cultures around the world, encompasses pre-European contact peoples.

In Canada, the term "First Nations" has been coined to better describe the groups that inhabited the continent. As was discussed in the chapter about Scandinavian cultures, the term "Eskimo" was once used to describe people of Northern Canada and Greenland, and has been replaced by "Inuit." In the United States, the terms "Native American" and "American Indian" have been used, the latter being the current preferred name. In any case, it is appropriate to be as specific as possible when naming; when native people describe themselves, they first give their Clan name, and then their Tribe or Band name (i.e., of the Bear Clan of the Eastern Shawnee tribe). By paying attention to these details, we can give the culture the respect it deserves.

Part 1: Creation and Destruction

The Woman Who Fell From the Sky (Wyandot)

The Wyandot are regarded as one of the last tribes to be moved west of the Mississippi River in the 1840s. The Wyandot were, until the 1650s, a part of the Huron Confederacy near the St. Lawrence River in Canada and the Great Lakes and spoke a dialect of Iroquoian. By the 1700s, the Wyandot lived near Ft. Detroit and kept moving south into Ohio. When forced to remove west of the Mississippi in 1843, the Wyandot lived first in Kansas (where Kansas City was then known as "Wyandotte City"), then Oklahoma, but were given no land of their own in either location. There are currently 5,800 tribal members living in a variety of states.

The following story is not unique to the Wyandot, but their influence is present in this version. One of the most widely told explanations for "Turtle Island," "The Woman Who Fell from the Sky" is related by Iroquois, Mohawk, Seneca-Cayuga, and Quapaw among others. Each of these tribes focus on slightly different details, but the basics of the story remain the same: a woman falls from the sky and creates North America on the back of a turtle. The Wyandot today celebrate their children in the "Gathering of Little Turtles," which is a direct reference to the character in this creation story.

THE WOMAN WHO FELL FROM THE SKY

The people lived in the sky. The Big Chief had a very beautiful daughter who became sick. The medicine man came, but she could not be cured by his medicine. He said, "Dig up the wild apple tree; what will cure her she can pluck from among its roots." This apple tree stood near the door of the Lodge of her father.

The medicine man advised that while they were digging up the wild apple tree they should bring the young woman and lay her down upon the ground under its branches, so that she might see down where the people were at work. This way she could more quickly pluck away the medicine when it should be reached. When they had dug there for awhile, the tree and the ground all about it suddenly sank down, fell through, and disappeared. The tree top caught and carried down the young woman. Tree and woman disappeared and the broken earth was closed over both of them.

Underneath, in the lower world, was only water the Great Water. Two geese were swimming about there, and saw the young woman falling from heaven. On looking up the geese beheld the woman standing in the torn sky. One of the geese said, "What shall we do with this Woman?" The other goose replied, "We must catch her on our backs." Then they threw their bodies together side by side and she fell upon them. The goose that had first spoken said, "What shall we do with this woman? We cannot bear her up forever." To this question the other goose replied, "We must call a Council of all the Swimmers and all the Water Tribes. This they did, and each Animal came upon special invitation. The Big Turtle was invited to preside over the Great Council.

Much discussion was had by the Great Council, but it seemed for a long time that the deliberations would be fruitless. No plan for the disposition of the Woman could be agreed upon. When the Great Council was about to adjourn without coming to a conclusion, the Big Turtle said, "If you can get a little of the Earth, which with the Woman and the tree fell down from heaven, I will hold it on my back."

Source: William Elsey Connelly, *Wyandot Folk-Lore*, 1900.

So the Animals took it by turns to try to get the Earth. They dived down into the deep where the tree had fallen, first the otter and then the beaver, but they could get none of the Earth. When it seemed that none of the Earth could be obtained, the Toad volunteered to go down and try and see what success she might have. The Toad was gone a long time and the Great Council despaired of her coming back again. Finally, she came up with her mouth full of the Earth, but she was dead when she reached the surface. There was very little of the Earth-- too little, it was supposed-- and the Great Council was discouraged. But the Little Turtle urged that it be used. She rubbed it carefully about the edges of the Big Turtle's shell and from this small amount soon there was the Great Island upon the Big Turtle's back. The Woman was removed from the backs of the geese to the Great Island, which was from that time her home.

The Island grew to be a Great Land of North America, which rests yet on the back of the Big Turtle. He stands deep down in the Great Water, and sometimes becomes weary of remaining so long in one position. Then he shifts his weight, changes his feet, and moves. This is when the Great Island trembles there is an earthquake.

The Sun and Moon

The Great Island was made on the Big Turtle's back, there was no sun and no moon and no stars. The Woman could not see well, and so the Great Council was called to see what should be done for a light for the Woman. After a long time spent in deliberation to no purpose the Council was about to disperse and let the world continue in darkness. But the Little Turtle said, "Let me go up to the sky. I will put a light there for the Woman."

It was agreed that the Little Turtle might go into the sky. A great Cloud was called by the Council. The Cloud was full of Thunder and Lightning. It rolled over the Great Water and came to where the Council was in session. The Cloud was seen to be full of bushes, trees, streams, lakes, and ponds. The Little Turtle got into these streams and was soon carried into the sky. Here the Little Turtle took some of the Lightning and kindled a great flame, which stood still in the sky. But it did not light all the Great Island, while in that part of it where the Woman lived the heat was intolerable. The Sun as made by the Little Turtle was not satisfactory.

Another Council was called and the Little Turtle came in the Cloud. At this Council it was determined to give the Sun life and a spirit so that it could run about the sky. The Mud Turtle was directed to dig a hole clear through the Great Island, so that the Sun could go through the sky by day, and then, through the hole in the earth, back to the east by night. This the Mud Turtle successfully did, but it seems that the Sun often loitered in this subterranean passageway and remained there for long periods. The world was left in total darkness at these times, so it was resolved to call a third Great Council to deliberate upon the matter and to chide the Sun. To this third Council came the Sun, the Little Turtle, and the other Animals. The Council decreed that the Little Turtle should make the Sun a wife. The Little Turtle made the Moon to be a wife for the Sun. Many children were born to them and these are the Stars that run about the sky.

The Twins

The Woman went all about the Great Island and she was very lonely and sad. In her wanderings she found a Lodge, and living in it, an old woman. She called the old woman her Grandmother and began to live with her. The sickness that caused the Woman to fall had disappeared. To her were born the Two Children. Of these Children one was Good, and named "Made of Fire." The other twin was Bad, and named "Made of Flint."

The Twins grew to manhood after a while, and the Bad twin did evil continually and his Good brother was not able to continuously resist his brother. Because the twins fought so much, they agreed to enlarge the Great Island. They successfully did this and made the land in the East was the land of the Good Twin, and that in the West belonged to the Bad Twin. But the land was a desolate solitude, for only the Woman and the Two children and the Animals were the only beings to live upon it. So they began to prepare it for the habitation of man and other animals than those first found there.

Each brother was to go through his own land and to make his realm to conform in surface, animals, birds, streams, lakes, plants, etc. to his own conceptions of utility and beauty. The works of each were to be subject to the modification of the other, but neither was to absolutely change the character of any work of the other, nor was he to totally destroy it. Each brother now went his way and did that which was proper in his own eyes. They were engaged in this work for untold ages. When their works were finished, they met again as they had agreed.

When the Bad One inspected the works of his brother, he believed they were much too good. Accordingly, he diminished their good qualities to the utmost of his power. The animals, birds, and fishes good for food are the gifts of the Good One. They and all other animals were made gentle, harmless. Tooth nor claw was ever made to be turned upon the people; no animal thirsted for his blood. In lieu of their gentle natures the Bad One made them to have wild and fierce dispositions. He frightened them until they fled from the light of day and only left their lairs at night. The gentle undulations of the park-like woods were changed to rough hills and endless mountain ranges; and rocks, thorns, bushes, briers, and brambles were scattered to plague the people. He sprinkled his own blood over the land and each drop of it made a ragged flint-stone which lay in wait to rend and cut the Indian's foot. Water would not drown but the Bad One gave it an evil spirit to make it take the life of the Indian. Evil spirits were placed at many waterfalls to drag down and destroy.

The maple tree furnished a pure syrup but the Bad One poured water over the tree and reduced its sweetness to what we find it at this day. The Good One made the corn plant, which grew without cultivation and a hundred ears were found upon a single stalk. It was the Bad One who made it difficult to raise and but a few ears were permitted to grow on one stalk. The bean pod grew upon a tree and was as long as the Indian's arm; it was filled with beans as large as the turkey's egg and which were richer than bear's fat. The tree was dwarfed to a helpless vine and the pod was so reduced that it was no longer than the Indian's finger.

But the wrath of the Bad One rose into fury when he beheld the rivers as made by the Good One. They were made with two currents flowing in opposite directions, one by each bank so that the Indian could go either up or down the streams without the labor of paddling his canoe. Bad One thrust his big hand into the river and gave the waters a great swish and mixed them, forcing both currents into only one and this he made to run always in but one direction. Good One found the works of his brother much too large and very bad. Bare mountains of rock pierced the sky. Endless swamps and quagmires were spread abroad. Huge beasts, reptiles, birds, and insects were at every point to terrify and destroy the Indian. The North Wind stood guardian of the land and with snows and bitter blasts swept this western world. Icicles miles and miles in length hung from the ragged cliffs. Myriads and millions of mosquitoes, each as large as the pheasant, swarmed up from the fetid marshes of the South. Nothing was Good-- everything was Bad. All the works of Bad One were modified and their evil qualities reduced to the utmost degree to which was allowed. But whatever of evil there is in this world comes from the Bad One and his wicked works.

The Animals Go to the Sky

The Animals were greatly distressed and much offended by the works of the Bad One. They saw how fortunate was the Little Turtle who spent most of her time "Keeping the Heavens." She always came to attend the Great Council in the Black Cloud in which were the springs, ponds, streams, and lakes. One day, the Deer said to the Rainbow, "Carry me up to the sky. I must see the Little Turtle." The Rainbow did not wish to comply with the request of the Deer at that time, but wished to consult the Thunder God about the matter, and so replied, "Come to me in the winter when I rest on the mountain by the lake. Then I will take you up to the house of the Little Turtle."

The Deer looked and waited all winter for the Rainbow, but the Rainbow did not come. When the Rainbow came in the summer the Deer said, "I waited for you all winter on the mountain by the lake and you did not come. Why did you deceive me?" Then the Rainbow said, "When you see me in the Fog over the lake, come to me, then you can go up. I will carry you up to the house of the Little Turtle in the sky."

One day the Fog rolled in thick banks and heavy masses over the lake. The Deer stood on the hill by the lake waiting and looking for the Rainbow. When the Rainbow threw the beautiful arch from the lake to the hill, a very white and shining light flashed and shone about the Deer. A straight path with all the colors of the Rainbow lay before the Deer; it led through a strange forest. The Rainbow said, "Follow the beautiful path through the strange woods." This the Deer did. The beautiful way led the Deer to the house of the Little Turtle in the sky.

When the Great Council met, the Bear said, "The Deer is not yet come to the Council-- where is the Deer?" The Little Turtle replied, "The Deer is in the sky. The Rainbow made a beautiful pathway of all her colors for the Deer to come up by. The Council looked up to the sky and saw the Deer running about there. Then the Little Turtle showed to the Council the beautiful pathway made for the Deer by the Rainbow. All the Animals except the Mud Turtle went along the beautiful way which led them up into the sky. They remain there to this day. They may often be seen flying or running about the sky.

The Peopling of the Great Island

When the Animals went into the sky, the world was in despair. The Mountains shrieked and the Earth groaned continually. The Rivers and the Great Water rocked to and fro in their beds, and all the beasts cried aloud for their Mothers, the Animals. The Trees wept tears of blood and the Four Winds rent one another in madness and wrath. The Twins met to devise a plan to people the Great Island. Is is said that this meeting was held on the line separating the land of the Good Brother from the land of the Bad One, which the Wyandots came afterwards to believe was the Mississippi river.

The agreement as finally made between the Twins provided that they should bring people to the Great Island from the land of their Mother in the Sky. Each was to people his own land and rule over it without interference from the other. The Good One brought to his land Wyandots only. The Bad One brought with him many kinds of people, some good and some bad. Some accounts say that the Brothers created these people outright. The people of each Brother multiplied and, in time, they became many peoples.

DISCUSSION QUESTIONS

1.   What purpose does the Great Council serve?

2.   Which animals are most successful in aiding the Sky Woman? What is surprising about the animals highlighted in this story?

3.   How do the Good Twin and Bad Twin mediate each other's creations?

4.   Why does the deer desire to live in the sky?

5.   How does this myth explain forces of good and evil?

How the World Was Made (Cherokee)

The Cherokee tribe is best known for the devastation sustained during the Trail of Tears. The Cherokee, or as they call themselves, "aniyvwiya," lived in North and South Carolina, Virginia, Tennessee, Kentucky, Georgia, and Alabama before their removal west of the Mississippi. After Andrew Jackson's Indian Removal Act of 1830, the Cherokee and the other "civilized tribes" living near them were marched by U.S. Government officials 1,000 miles to "Indian territory" in Oklahoma. More than 17,000 Cherokee, Choctaw, Chickasaw, Creek, and Seminole began the removal process and an estimated 4,000 people died during and after this march.

Today, there are three federally recognized bands of Cherokee: The Cherokee Nation of about 320,000 members, headquartered in Tahlequah, Oklahoma; The United Keetoowah Band of Cherokee Indians comprised of about 16,000 people, also in Tahlequah; and The Eastern Band of Cherokee Indians of 12,500 citizens, headquartered in Cherokee, North Carolina.

This creation myth explores the concept of land diving to create the world, the "seventh height" of the sun, and explains the characteristics of plants and animals of their home region. Do not worry about the pronunciation of the Cherokee words; translations are provided. These original words are included to give you an idea of what the Cherokee language looks like.

HOW THE WORLD WAS MADE

The earth is a great island floating in a sea of water, and suspended at each of the four cardinal points by a cord hanging down from the sky vault, which is of solid rock. When the world grows old and worn out, the people will die and the cords will break and let the earth sink down into the ocean, and all will be water again. The Indians are afraid of this.

When all was water, the animals were above in Gälûñ'lätï, beyond the arch; but it was very much crowded, and they were wanting more room. They wondered what was below the water, and at last Dâyuni'sï, the little Water-beetle, offered to go and see if it could learn. It darted in every direction over the surface of the water, but could find no firm place to rest. Then it dived to the bottom and came up with some soft mud, which began to grow and spread on every side until it became the island which we call the earth. It was afterward fastened to the sky with four cords, but no one remembers who did this.

At first the earth was flat and very soft and wet. The animals were anxious to get down, and sent out different birds to see if it was yet dry, but they found no place to alight and came back again to Gälûñ'lätï. At last it seemed to be time, and they sent out the Buzzard and told him to go and make ready for them. This was the Great Buzzard, the father of all the buzzards we see now. He flew all over the earth, low down near the ground, and it was still soft. When he reached the Cherokee country, he was very tired, and his wings began to flap and strike the ground, and wherever they struck the earth there was a valley, and where they turned up again there was a mountain. When the animals above saw this, they were afraid that the whole world would be mountains, so they called him back, but the Cherokee country remains full of mountains to this day.

When the earth was dry and the animals came down, it was still dark, so they got the sun and set it in a track to go every day across the island from east to west, just overhead. It was too hot this way, and Tsiska'gïlï', the Red Crawfish, had his shell scorched a bright red, so that his meat was spoiled; and the Cherokee do not eat it. The conjurers put the sun another hand-breadth higher in the air, but it was still too hot. They raised it another time, and another, until it was seven handbreadths high and just under the sky arch. Then it was right, and they left it so. This is why the conjurers call the highest place

Source: James Mooney, *Myths of the Cherokee*, 1900.

Gûlkwâ'gine Di'gälûñ'lätiyûñ', "the seventh height," because it is seven hand-breadths above the earth. Every day the sun goes along under this arch, and returns at night on the upper side to the starting place.

There is another world under this, and it is like ours in everything--animals, plants, and people--save that the seasons are different. The streams that come down from the mountains are the trails by which we reach this underworld, and the springs at their heads are the doorways by which we enter it, but to do this one must fast and go to water and have one of the underground people for a guide. We know that the seasons in the underworld are different from ours, because the water in the springs is always warmer in winter and cooler in summer than the outer air.

When the animals and plants were first made--we do not know by whom--they were told to watch and keep awake for seven nights, just as young men now fast and keep awake when they pray to their medicine. They tried to do this, and nearly all were awake through the first night, but the next night several dropped off to sleep, and the third night others were asleep, and then others, until, on the seventh night, of all the animals only the owl, the panther, and one or two more were still awake. To these were given the power to see and to go about in the dark, and to make prey of the birds and animals which must sleep at night. Of the trees only the cedar, the pine, the spruce, the holly, and the laurel were awake to the end, and to them it was given to be always green and to be greatest for medicine, but to the others it was said: "Because you have not endured to the end you shall lose your hair every winter."

Men came after the animals and plants. At first there were only a brother and sister until he struck her with a fish and told her to multiply, and so it was. In seven days a child was born to her, and thereafter every seven days another, and they increased very fast until there was danger that the world could not keep them. Then it was made that a woman should have only one child in a year, and it has been so ever since.

DISCUSSION QUESTIONS

1. The story starts with a warning of what is to come. Why begin a creation story with the fear of destruction?

2. How do the Cherokee account for the landscape and seasons and behavior of plants and animals?

3. How does the conception of children differ in this myth from others who begin with brothers and sisters?

The Creation of the Earth (Yuchi-Creek)

The Yuchi (or Euchee) are a small tribe that resided in Eastern Tennessee pre-contact. In 1540 the Spanish explorer DeSoto wrote about his contact with the Yuchi. After that, much of their population was decimated by disease. In the 1700s the Yuchi joined the Muscogee Confederacy, which was a loose grouping of forty-eight autonomous bands. The Yuchi became associated with Creek tribes, who were their neighbors, and were subsequently forced to remove west of the Mississippi River with them in the 1830s. This was a problem because they were then politically identified as Creeks, and did not receive land or recognition of their own. There were nine bands of Yuchi people who moved to Oklahoma, but today only three bands are active and only six people currently speak the Yuchi language.

THE CREATION OF THE EARTH

In the beginning the waters covered everything. It was said, "Who will make the land appear?"

Lock-chew, the Crawfish, said: "I will make the land appear."

So he went down to the bottom of the water and began to stir up the mud with his tail and hands. He then brought up the mud to a certain place and piled it up.

The owners of the land at the bottom of the water said: "Who is disturbing our land?" They kept watch and discovered the Crawfish. Then they came near him, but he suddenly stirred the mud with his tail so that they could not see him.

Lock-chew continued his work. He carried mud and piled it up until at last he held up his hands in the air, and so the land appeared above the water.

The land was soft. It was said: "Who will spread out the land and make it dry and hard?"

Some said: "Ah-yok, the Hawk, should spread out the soft land and make it dry."

Others said "Yah-tee, the Buzzard, has larger wings; he can spread out the land and make it dry and hard."

Yah-tee undertook to spread out and dry the earth. He flew above the earth and spread out his long wings over it. He sailed over the earth; he spread it out. After a long while he grew tired of holding out his wings. He began to flap them, and thus he caused the hills and valleys because the dirt was still soft.

"Who will make the light?" it was said. It was very dark.

Yohah, the Star, said, "I will make the light." It was so agreed. The Star shone forth. It was light only near him.

"Who will make more light?" it was said.

Shar-pah, the Moon, said: "I will make more light." Shar-pah made more light, but it was still dark.

T-cho, the Sun, said: "You are my children, I am your mother, I will make the light. I will shine for you." She went to the east. Suddenly light spread over all the earth. As she passed over the earth a drop of blood fell from her to the ground, and from this blood and earth sprang the first people, the children of the Sun, the Euchees.

The people wished to find their medicine. A great monster serpent destroyed the people. They cut his head from his body. The next day the body and head were together. They again slew the monster. His head again grew to his body. Then they cut off his head and placed it on top of a tree, so that the body could not reach it. The next morning the tree was dead and the head was united to the body. They again severed it and put it upon another tree. In the morning the tree was dead and the head and body were reunited.

The people continued to try all the trees in the forest. At last they placed the head over the Tar, the cedar tree, and in the morning the head was dead. The cedar was alive, but covered with blood, which had trickled down from the head. Thus the Great Medicine was found.

Fire was made by boring with a stick into a hard weed.

Source: John R. Swanton, *Myths and Tales of the Southeastern Indians.* Bureau of American Ethnology, Bulletin 88, 1929.

The people selected a second family. Each member of this family had engraved on his door a picture of the sun.

In the beginning all the animals could talk, and but one language was used. All were at peace. The deer lived in a cave, watched over by a keeper and the people were hungry. He selected a deer and killed it. But finally the deer were set free and roved over the entire earth.

All animals were set free from man, and names were given to them, so that they could be known.

DISCUSSION QUESTIONS

1. Discuss the use of third person narration, "It was said." How does this phrase occur in the story? How is it different from other creation stories?

2. Why are the Yuchi called "the children of the sun"?

3. In the substory about the monster and the tree, what do we learn about "the Great Medicine"?

The Five Worlds (Navajo)

The Navajo are one of the most recognizable American Indian tribes, perhaps because of their large population, their unique art, and their complex language. It is their language that traces their origins to Northwest Canada. They speak a dialect of Athabaskan, which is shared by the neighboring Apache and their ancestral tribes thousands of miles north. This complex language was used by the United States Marines during WWII, as they enlisted Navajo "Code Talkers" to carry and decipher messages.

The arrival of the Navajo in the Southwestern United States has been dated to about 1300 CE. Many of their artistic traditions came from their Pueblo neighbors: weaving, basket making, pottery and painting, and masked dances. Their reservation, which encompasses more than 24,000 square miles in New Mexico, Arizona, and Utah, contains portions of the Grand Canyon and Monument Valley.

The Navajo prefer to be called "Diné" which means "the people." There are over 300,000 Dine registered in 110 local chapters that make up Diné Bikéyah, or "Navajoland." Their religious practices are influenced greatly by the oral stories like their emergence myth.

THE FIVE WORLDS

The First World

The First World was black as black wool. It had four corners, and over these appeared four clouds. These four clouds contained within themselves the elements of the First World. They were in color, black, white, blue, and yellow. The Black Cloud represented the Female Being or Substance. For as a child sleeps when being nursed, so life slept in the darkness of the Female Being. The White Cloud represented the Male

Source: Aileen O'Bryan, *The Dine: Origin Myths of the Navaho Indians,* 1956.

Being or Substance. He was the Dawn, the Light-Which-Awakens, of the First World. The First World was small in size, a floating island in mist or water. On it there grew one tree, a pine tree, which was later brought to the present world for firewood.

Man was not, however, in his present form. The conception was of a male and a female being who were to become man and woman. The creatures of the First World are thought of as the Mist People; they had no definite form, but were to change to men, beasts, birds, and reptiles of this world.

Now on the western side of the First World, in a place that later was to become the Land of Sunset, there appeared the Blue Cloud, and opposite it there appeared the Yellow Cloud. Where they came together First Woman was formed, and with her the yellow corn. This ear of corn was also perfect. With First Woman there came the white shell and the turquoise and the yucca.

First Man stood on the eastern side of the First World. He represented the Dawn and was the Life Giver. First Woman stood opposite in the West. She represented Darkness and Death.

First Man burned a crystal for a fire. The crystal belonged to the male and was the symbol of the mind and of clear seeing. When First Man burned it, it was the mind's awakening. First Woman burned her turquoise for a fire. They saw each other's lights in the distance. When the Black Cloud and the White Cloud rose higher in the sky First Man set out to find the turquoise light. He went twice without success, and again a third time; then he broke a forked branch from his tree, and, looking through the fork, he marked the place where the light burned. And the fourth time he walked to it and found smoke coming from a home.

"Here is the home I could not find," First Man said.

First Woman answered: "Oh, it is you. I saw you walking around and I wondered why you did not come."

First Woman saw that First Man had a crystal for a fire, and she saw that it was stronger than her turquoise fire. And as she was thinking, First Man spoke to her. "Why do you not come with your fire and we will live together." The woman agreed to this.

About this time there came another person, the Great-Coyote-Who-Was-Formed-in-the-Water, and he was in the form of a male being. He told the two that he had been hatched from an egg. He knew all that was under the water and all that was in the skies. First Man placed this person ahead of himself in all things. The three began to plan what was to come to pass; and while they were thus occupied another being came to them. He also had the form of a man, but he wore a hairy coat, lined with white fur, that fell to his knees and was belted in at the waist. His name was First Angry Coyote. He said to the three, "You believe that you were the first persons. You are mistaken. I was living when you were formed."

Then four beings came together. They were yellow in color and were called the wasp people. They knew the secret of shooting evil and could harm others. They were very powerful. This made eight people. Four more beings came. They were small in size and wore red shirts and had little black eyes. They were the spider ants. They knew how to sting, and were a great people. After these came a whole crowd of beings. Dark colored they were, with thick lips and dark, protruding eyes. They were the black ants. They also knew the secret of shooting evil and were powerful; but they killed each other steadily.

By this time there were many people. Then came a multitude of little creatures. They were peaceful and harmless, but the odor from them was unpleasant. They were called the "those who emits an odor."

And after the wasps and the different ant people there came the beetles, dragonflies, bat people, the Spider Man and Woman, and the Salt Man and Woman, and others that rightfully had no definite form, but were among those people who peopled the First World. And this world, being small in size, became crowded, and the people quarreled and fought among themselves, and in all ways made living very unhappy.

The Second World

Because of the strife in the First World, First Man, First Woman, the Great-Coyote-Who-Was-Formed-in-the-Water, and the Coyote called First Angry, followed by all the others, climbed up from the World of Darkness and Dampness to the Second or Blue World. They found a number of people already living there: blue birds, blue hawks, blue jays, blue herons, and all the blue-feathered beings. The powerful swallow people lived there also, and these people made the Second World unpleasant for those who had come from the First World. There was fighting and killing. The First Four found an opening in the World of Blue Haze; and they climbed through this and led the people up into the Third or Yellow world.

The Third World

The bluebird was the first to reach the Third or Yellow World. After him came the First Four and all the others. A great river crossed this land from north to south. It was the Female River. There was another river crossing it from east to West, it was the Male River. This Male River flowed through the Female River and on; and the name of this place is the Crossing of the waters. There were six mountains in the Third World. In the East was the Standing Black Sash. Its ceremonial name is the Dawn or White Shell Mountain. In the South stood the Great Mountain, also called Mountain Tongue. Its ceremonial name is the Blue Bead or Turquoise Mountain. In the West stood a mountain whose name is forgotten, but its ceremonial name is the Abalone Shell Mountain. In the North stood Many Sheep Mountain. Its ceremonial name is Obsidian Mountain. Then there was the Upper Mountain. It was very sacred; and its name means also the Center Place, and the people moved around it. Its ceremonial name is Precious Stone or Banded Rock Mountain. There was still another mountain called Chol'i'i or, and it was also a sacred mountain.

There was no sun in this land, only the two rivers and the six mountains. And these rivers and mountains were not in their present form, but rather the substance of mountains and rivers as were First Man, First Woman, and the others.

Within this land there lived the ancients of the Pueblo People. On the six mountains there lived the Cave Dwellers or Great Swallow People. On the mountains lived also the light and dark squirrels, chipmunks, mice, rats, the turkey people, the deer and cat people, the spider people, and the lizards and snakes. The beaver people lived along the rivers, and the frogs and turtles and all the underwater people in the water. So far all the people were similar. They had no definite form, but they had been given different names because of different characteristics.

Now the plan was to plant. First Man called the people together. He brought forth the white corn which had been formed with him. First Woman brought the yellow corn. They laid the perfect ears side by side; then they asked one person from among the many to come and help them. The Turkey stepped forward. They asked him where he had come from, and he said that he had come from the Gray Mountain, which connected him to water and rain. He danced back and forth four times, then he shook his feather coat and there dropped from his clothing four kernels of corn, one gray, one blue, one black, and one red. Another person was asked to help in the plan of the planting. The Big Snake came forward. He likewise brought forth four seeds, the pumpkin, the watermelon, the cantaloupe, and the muskmelon. His plants all crawl on the ground. They planted the seeds, and their harvest was great.

Now at that time there were four chiefs: Big Snake, Mountain Lion, Otter, and Bear—the Chiefs of the Four Directions. And it was the custom when the black cloud rose in the morning for First Man to come out of his dwelling and speak to the people. After First Man had spoken, the four chiefs told them what they should do that day. They also spoke of the past and of the future.

The men and women decided to live apart from each other. They were not behaving as man and wife should to each other. After the fourth day First Woman came and threw her right arm around her husband. She spoke to the others and said that she could see her mistakes, but with her husband's help she would henceforth lead a good life. Then all the male and female beings came and lived with each other again.

The people moved to different parts of the land. Some time passed; then First Woman became troubled by the monotony of life. She made a plan. She went to Coyote called First Angry, and giving him the rainbow she said, "I have suffered greatly in the past. I have suffered from want of meat and corn and clothing. Many of my maidens have died. I have suffered many things. Take the rainbow and go to the place where the rivers cross. Bring me the two pretty children of the Water Monster, a boy and a girl."

The Coyote agreed to do this. He walked over the rainbow. He entered the home of the Water Buffalo and stole the two children; and these he hid in his big skin coat with the white fur lining. And when he returned he refused to take off his coat, but pulled it around himself and looked very wise.

After this happened the people saw white light in the East and in the South and West and North. The flood was coming and the Earth was sinking. And all this happened because the Coyote had stolen the two children of the Water Monster, and only First Woman and the Coyote knew the truth.

When First Man learned of the coming of the water he sent word to all the people, and he told them to come to the mountain called Sis na'jin. He told them to bring with them all of the seeds of the plants used for food. All living beings were to gather on the top of Sis na'jin. First Man traveled to the six sacred mountains, and, gathering earth from them, he put it in his medicine bag.

The water rose steadily. When all the people were halfway up Sis na' jin, First Man discovered that he had forgotten his medicine bag. Now this bag contained not only the earth from the six sacred mountains, but his magic, the medicine he used to call the rain down upon the earth and to make things grow. He could not live without his medicine bag, and be wished to jump into the rising water; but the others begged him not to do this. They went to the kingfisher and asked him to dive into the water and recover the bag. This the bird did. When First Man had his medicine bag again in his possession he breathed on it four times and thanked his people.

When they had all arrived it was found that the Turquoise Boy had brought with him the big Male Reed; and the White Shell Girl had brought with her the big Female Reed. Another person brought poison ivy; and another, cotton, which was later used for cloth. This person was the spider. First Man had with him his pine tree, which he planted on the top of Sis na'jin. He used his fox medicine to make it grow; but the pine tree began to send out branches and to taper at the top, so First Man planted the big Male Reed. All the people blew on it, and it grew and grew until it reached the canopy of the sky. They tried to blow inside the reed, but it was solid. They asked the woodpecker to drill out the hard heart. Soon they were able to peek through the opening, but they had to blow and blow before it was large enough to climb through. They climbed up inside the big male reed, and after them the water continued to rise.

The Fourth World

When the people reached the Fourth World they saw that it was not a very large place. Some say that it was called the White World. The last person to crawl through the reed was the turkey from Gray Mountain. His feather coat was flecked with foam, for after him came the water. And with the water came the female Water Monster, who pushed her head through the opening in the reed. She had a great quantity of curly hair which floated on the water, and she had two horns, half black and half yellow. From the tips of the horns the lightning flashed.

First Man asked the Water Monster why she had come and why she had sent the flood. She said nothing. Then the Coyote drew the two babies from his coat and said that it was, perhaps, because of them.

The Turquoise Boy took a basket and filled it with turquoise. On top of the turquoise he placed the blue pollen from the blue flowers, and the yellow pollen from the corn; and on top of these he placed the pollen from the water flags; and again on top of these he placed the crystal, which is river pollen. This basket he gave to the Coyote, who put it between the horns of the Water Monster. The Coyote said that with this sacred offering he would give back the male child. He said that the male child would be known as the Black Cloud, or Male Rain, and that he would bring the thunder and lightning. The female child he would keep. She would be known as the Blue, Yellow, and White Clouds, or Female Rain. She would be the gentle rain that would moisten the earth and help them to live. So he kept the female child, and he placed the male child on the sacred basket between the horns of the Water Monster. And the Water Monster disappeared, and the waters with her.

After the water sank there appeared another person. They did not know him, and they asked him where he had come from. He told them that he was the badger, and that he had been formed where the Yellow Cloud had touched the Earth. Afterward this Yellow Cloud turned out to be a sunbeam.

The Fifth World

First Man was not satisfied with the Fourth World. It was a small barren land; and the great water had soaked the earth and made the sowing of seeds impossible. He planted the big Female Reed and it grew up to the vaulted roof of this Fourth World. First Man sent the newcomer, the badger, up inside the reed, but before he reached the upper world water began to drip, so he returned and said that he was frightened.

Now two dark clouds and two white clouds rose, and this meant that two nights and two days had passed, for there was still no sun. First Man again sent the badger to the upper world, and he returned covered with mud, terrible mud. First Man gathered chips of turquoise which he offered to the five Chiefs of the Winds who lived in the uppermost world of all. They were pleased with the gift, and they sent down the winds and dried the Fifth World.

First Man and his people saw four dark clouds and four white clouds pass, and then they sent the badger up the reed. This time when the badger returned he said that he had come out on solid earth. So First Man and First Woman led the people to the Fifth World, which some call the Many Colored Earth and some the Changeable Earth. They emerged through a lake surrounded by four mountains. The water bubbles in this lake when anyone goes near.

Now after all the people had emerged from the lower worlds, First Man and First Woman dressed the Mountain Lion with yellow, black, white, and grayish corn and placed him on one side. They dressed the Wolf with white tail feathers and placed him on the other side. They divided the people into two groups. The first group was told to choose whichever chief they wished. They made their choice, and, although they thought they had chosen the Mountain Lion, they found that they had taken the Wolf for their chief. The Mountain Lion was the chief for the other side. And these people who had the Mountain Lion for their chief turned out to be the people of the Earth. They were to plant seeds and harvest corn. The followers of the Wolf chief became the animals and birds; they turned into all the creatures that fly and crawl and run and swim. And after all the beings were divided, and each had his own form, they went their ways.

1. What might the colors of each world represent?

2. Trace the progression through each of the worlds. Why do they move? What new creations or problems do they encounter with each new world?

3. What is the cause of the flood? Why might this be a part of the Navajo creation story?

The Fashioning of the Children (Osage)

The Osage, originally from the Ohio Valley, share many commonalities with a group of tribes that share similar Sioux language histories. The Osage, Ponca, Quapaw, Omaha, and Kansa are members of the Dhegiha, connected by their ancestral proximity, shared stories, and language. Explorer Jacques Marquette noted in his 1673 diary that he encountered a large group of Osage in Missouri, in what is now the Ozarks. They were eventually forced to relocate to Kansas and Oklahoma, where in the nineteenth century oil was discovered on their land. This led to greater interference by the United States Government. Today the Osage Nation is headquartered in Pawhuska, Oklahoma, and about 16,000 people are of Osage descent.

In her introduction to the book *The Path on the Rainbow*, Mary Austin writes of the many barriers to understanding the songs and chants therein:

> Of Indian meters there has been no competent study made. The whole problem of form is inextricably complicated with melody and movement. The necessity of making his verse conform to a dance, probably accounts for the liberal use of meaningless syllables. To our ear no specific forms seem indicated, yet that the Indians recognize a certain correspondence between form and meaning is certain.

Though she wrote this in 1918, the state of our study is hardly different one hundred years later. In this chant, the repetition of words seem meaningless, the syllables silly, but there is notable difference between our European tradition of song, and that broad history of American Indian song. This creation chant is of particular value because the Osage have a tradition of reciting the creation myth to each newborn baby.

THE FASHIONING OF THE CHILDREN

The First of the Race
Was saying, "Ho, younger brother! the children have no bodies.
We shall seek bodies for our children.
Ho, younger brother! you shall attend to it."

They reached one upper world and stood.
There they were not human beings.
"Ho, younger brother! the children have no bodies," he was saying.
"We must seek bodies for our children."

They reached the second upper world and stood.
There they were not human beings.

Source: Cronin, George W. *The Path on the Rainbow: An Anthology of Songs and Chants from the Indians of North America*, 1918.

"Ho, younger brother! the children have no bodies," he was saying.
"We must seek bodies for our children."

They reached the third upper world and stood.
There they were not human beings.
"Ho, younger brother! the children have no bodies," he was saying.
"We must seek bodies for our children."

They reached the fourth upper world and stood.
There they became human beings.
Still, the children were without (human) bodies.
"We must continue to seek bodies for our children."

They returned to the third upper world and stood.
The children were really without bodies.
"Ho, younger brother! the children have no bodies," he was saying.
"We must continue to seek bodies for our children."

They returned to the second upper world and stood.
The children did not find bodies for themselves.
"Ho, younger brother! the children have no bodies," he was saying.
"We must make an examination awhile longer."

They returned to the first upper world and stood.
They came to red oak and were standing on it.
On a very fine day they came hither and stood.
Kaxe-wahü-sa (the Black Bear), who was then moving,
Came directly to them and stood.

"Ho, elder brother!" (said the Black Bear).
"You shall continue to burn my feet for me."
"Ho, Kaxe-wahü-sa!" was he (the Tsicu) saying.
Kaxe-wahü-sa went to the star Watse-tuka.
"Ho, grandfather!" he was saying.
"The children have no bodies."

Watse-tuka replied, "Can I give the children bodies?
I have an everlasting road in which I must keep.
I am not the only mysterious one;
You shall attend to it awhile longer."

Then Kaxe-wahü-sa went to the star Watse-mika.
"Ho, grandmother!" he said;
"The children have no bodies."
She replied, "Can I give bodies to the children?
"I have an everlasting road in which I must keep.
I am not the only mysterious one!
You shall attend to it awhile longer."

Then he went to the mysterious one of day.
"Ho, grandfather!" said he;
"The children have no bodies."
Said he, "Can I give the children bodies?
I have an everlasting road in which I must keep.

I am not the only mysterious one;
You shall attend to it awhile longer."

Then he went to the mysterious one of night.
"Ho, grandfather!" said he;
"The children have no bodies, grandfather!"
The Moon replied, "Can I give bodies to the children?
I have an everlasting road in which I must keep.
I am not the only mysterious one;
You shall attend to it awhile longer."

Then he went to the Pleiades, saying,
"Ho, grandfathers!
The children have no bodies."
One of these replied, "Can I give bodies to the children?
I have an everlasting road in which I must keep.
I am not the only mysterious one;
You shall attend to it awhile longer."

Then he went to the constellation called Three Deer.
"Ho, grandfather," said he;
"The children have no bodies."
The latter replied, "Can I give the children bodies?
I have an everlasting road in which I must keep.
I am not the only mysterious one;
You shall attend to it awhile longer."

Then he went to the Morning Star, saying,
"Ho, grandfather!
The children have no bodies."
The star replied, "Can I give bodies to the children?
I have an everlasting road in which I must keep.
I am not the only mysterious one;
You shall attend to it awhile longer."

Then he went to the Small Star, saying,
"Ho, grandfather!
The children have no bodies."
The star replied, "Can I give bodies to the children?
I have an everlasting road in which I must keep.
I am not the only mysterious one;
You shall attend to it awhile longer."

The female Red Bird, who had been moving, was sitting on her nest.
To her he came, saying,
"Ho, grandmother!
The children have no bodies."
She replied, "I can cause your children to have (human) bodies from my own.
My left wing shall be a left arm for the children.
My right wing shall be a right arm for them.
My head shall be a head for them.
My mouth shall be a mouth for them.

My forehead shall be a forehead for them.
My neck shall be a neck for them.
My throat shall be a throat for them.
My chest shall be a chest for them.
My thighs shall be thighs for them.
My knees shall be knees for them.
My heels shall be their heels.
My toes shall be their toes.
My claws shall be their toenails.
You shall live forever without destruction.
Your children shall live as human beings.
The speech of children I will bestow on your children."

DISCUSSION QUESTION

1. As this is a tribe from the Midwest (specifically Missouri), what local flora and fauna are mentioned in the creation of the world and people?

Creation of Man (Miwok)

Miwok (a word meaning "people") is a Penutian language of California. There are seven distinct Miwok dialects but since they are severely endangered languages (three are no longer spoken by anyone) they are typically grouped together. Less is understood about the Penutian languages of the Pacific Coast peoples than other language families of North America. The Miwok were located in north-central California, from the Pacific coast to the west slope of the Sierra Nevada Mountains. There are approximately 3,500 Miwok people today, mainly in California, in dozens of tribes, both federally and non-federally recognized.

CREATION OF MAN

After Coyote had completed making the world, he began to think about creating man. He called a council of all the animals. The animals sat in a circle, just as the Indians do, with Lion at the head, in an open space in the forest. On Lion's right was Grizzly Bear; next Cinnamon Bear; and so on to Mouse, who sat at Lion's left.

Lion spoke first. Lion said he wished man to have a terrible voice, like himself, so that he could frighten all animals. He wanted man also to be well covered with hair, with fangs in his claws, and very strong teeth.

Grizzly Bear laughed. He said it was ridiculous for anyone to have such a voice as Lion, because when he roared he frightened away the very prey for which he was searching. But he said man should have very great strength; that he should move silently, but very swiftly; and he should be able to seize his prey without noise.

Source: Katharine Berry Judson, *Myths and Legends of California and the Old Southwest*, 1912.

Buck said man would look foolish without antlers. And a terrible voice was absurd, but man should have ears like a spider's web, and eyes like fire.

Mountain Sheep said the branching antlers would bother man if he got caught in a thicket. If man had horns rolled up, so that they were like a stone on each side of his head, it would give his head weight enough to butt very hard.

When it came Coyote's turn, he said the other animals were foolish because they each wanted man to be just like themselves. Coyote was sure he could make a man who would look better than Coyote himself, or any other animal. Of course he would have to have four legs, with five fingers. Man should have a strong voice, but he need not roar all the time with it. And he should have feet nearly like Grizzly Bear's, because he could then stand erect when he needed to. Grizzly Bear had no tail, and man should not have any. The eyes and ears of Buck were good, and perhaps man should have those. Then there was Fish, which had no hair, and hair was a burden much of the year. So Coyote thought man should not wear fur. And his claws should be as long as the Eagle's, so that he could hold things in them. But no animal was as cunning and crafty as Coyote, so man should have the wit of Coyote.

Then Beaver talked. Beaver said man would have to have a tail, but it should be broad and flat, so he could haul mud and sand on it. Not a furry tail, because they were troublesome on account of fleas. Owl said man would be useless without wings.

But Mole said wings would be folly. Man would be sure to bump against the sky. Besides, if he had wings and eyes both, he would get his eyes burned out by flying too near the sun. But without eyes, he could burrow in the soft, cool earth where he could be happy.

Mouse said man needed eyes so he could see what he was eating. And nobody wanted to burrow in the damp earth. So the council broke up in a quarrel.

Then every animal set to work to make a man according to his own ideas. Each one took a lump of earth and modelled it just like himself. All but Coyote, for Coyote began to make the kind of man he had talked of in the council.

It was late when the animals stopped work and fell asleep. All but Coyote, for Coyote was the cunningest of all the animals, and he stayed awake until he had finished his model. He worked hard all night. When the other animals were fast asleep he threw water on the lumps of earth, and so spoiled the models of the other animals. But in the morning he finished his own, and gave it life long before the others could finish theirs. Thus man was made by Coyote.

DISCUSSION QUESTIONS

1. Why do you think animals are the creators of mankind in this story, and why is Coyote the one who succeeds?

2. Coyote is typically a Trickster, but sometimes he is also a creator. Discuss the reasons why he can serve in both of these roles.

The Flood (Cochiti)

The Cochiti are a Western Pueblo people who live on the Rio Grande near Santa Fe, New Mexico. The remains of their original pueblos can be seen in the Bandelier National Monument Park, a few miles to the north of the current location. They speak Keresan, like their Acoma and Laguna neighbors, and are known for their jewelry making, ceramics, and long history of storytelling. Approximately 1,175 members of the Cochiti reside on the reservation today.

THE FLOOD

Long ago the people knew that there would be a great flood. Up in the north among the high mountains they built a great boat. When it was nearly time for the water to rise, they began to load it with much corn and they took all the different animals into the boat and a white pigeon. When everything was ready the sons of the builder of the boat and their sons came into the ship. When they were all in, they put pitch over all the cracks of the boat. The flood came. The boat floated on the water. The people that were left on the earth fled to the highest mountain to try to escape from the waters. The ones who could not get to the high mountains were all drowned and floated about on the waters of the flood. The ones who climbed the mountains were overtaken by the water and turned into rocks. Some were embracing each other, and some held one another on their laps, and there they are still just as the water overtook them. Every living thing on the earth was drowned, but the boat still floated.

When the waters went down, the boat grounded on a high place in the mountains to the north. Then they knew the waters were subsiding. The chief said to the rest, "We will send the white pigeon to see if the earth is uncovered again." The white pigeon was let out. At last he returned and told the chief, "I have seen the earth and the water has gone down. But it is a terrible thing to see. The people are all drowned and their bodies piled upon the ground." In the boat there was also a crow as white as the pigeon. They sent out the crow to look over the earth. She went out and saw the earth as the pigeon had. But she flew down to the dead bodies and began to pick out their eyes. When she came back to the boat, they knew she had done mischief. They said to her, "What is it that you have done when you were out flying over the earth? You were white and now your feathers are all black." Again they let the pigeon out to see if the earth was firm again. She went out and as she was flying she saw a flower in blossom. She picked the flower for a sign that the earth was getting firm again, and she took it back to the boat. She said to the owner of the boat, "The plants are all growing again, and I settled on the ground and did not sink into the mud. This flower is a sign of the growing of the plants." So the people on the boat were saved from the first-ending-of-the-world-by-flood.

When the people who came up out of Shipap found these people who had been saved they called them Tsauwan yabana (last year's crop people). They were yellow like last year's corn, and their hair was curled up in queues on their heads like last year's husks. They were told that there would come another destruction of the world, but it would be by fire.

DISCUSSION QUESTIONS

1. What is explained by the people who escape to the mountaintops?
2. What is unique about this flood myth, in comparison with others you've read?

Source: Ruth Benedict, *Tales of the Cochiti Indians*, Bureau of American Ethnology, Bulletin No. 98, 1932.

Part2: Tricksters, Lovers, and Other Tales

Coyote Steals Light (Zuni)

The Zuni are a Pueblo people; based or oral history, the Pueblo people of Arizona and New Mexico are descended from common ancestors, the Anasazi. However, the Zuni language is not related to other languages of the Pueblo people; some linguists believe it may be connected, although distantly, to the Penutian language family of the Pacific coast. The Zuni inhabited the Zuni River Valley in western New Mexico; nearly 20,000 still reside there today.

This version of the story has been adapted from *Native American Myths Retold and Interpreted*. While it draws on a variety of Zuni sources, many of the elements of the story are found across North America.

COYOTE STEALS LIGHT

Long ago, before the Sun and Moon were set in the sky, Coyote was searching the prairie for food. He chased after a rabbit, but it escaped inside its burrow. He tried chasing a mouse, but he lost it as it hid beneath a rock. He felt a wind sweep over him and looked up to see Eagle flying overhead. Coyote was hungry and tired, so he stopped to rest, and noticed Eagle catch a rabbit, followed by another, and yet another. When Eagle flew near, Coyote called to him:

"Hello, my friend. With my talent and your talons, we could catch twice as much food!"

Eagle thought for a moment, and then agreed to partner with Coyote. They hunted together for about an hour, but in the time Eagle had caught three more rabbits, Coyote had only captured a beetle.

Coyote complained. "This is impossible! How can I be expected to catch anything without light to see by? Where can we find some light?"

Eagle replied, "I see some on the western horizon." So they set out to look for the light. Eventually, they arrived at a canyon, and Coyote slipped, falling down on the rocks and injuring himself. Eagle said, "You should try to fly."

"I have no wings," said Coyote, irritated. He struggled up the canyon and they continued to hunt. They found a village where people were holding a spirit dance. Coyote noticed the power of the spirits and said, "These people must have some light!"

He was right. They noticed that the people had two boxes – a large one and a small one. When they needed a lot of light, they opened the big box; when they wanted just a little light, they opened the small box.

"See," Coyote whispered to Eagle, "they have the light we need. Let's take the big box."

Adapted from Eddy, Steve. *Native American Myths Retold and Interpreted*, 2016.

Eagle wanted to just borrow it instead, but Coyote didn't think they would agree to that, since light was so valuable. After the spirit dance, the boxes were left unguarded. Eagle slipped the light from the smaller box into the large box and flew away with it. Coyote ran along, trying to keep up with him.

Coyote said, "Friend, let me help, I can carry the box for a while."

Eagle said, "You'd only lose it."

But Coyote protested. "The people will say I'm lazy if you don't let me help. They'll say I made you do all the work."

After Coyote asked Eagle four times, Eagle agreed to let him carry the box. But he warned Coyote, "Don't open it yet."

They continued on, Coyote carrying the box. But Eagle flew faster than Coyote could run, and left Coyote behind. Coyote needed to rest, and as he sat with the box, he thought, "I wonder what light looks like. I'll just take a little peek."

As Coyote opened the box, a silver disc immediately flew out. It was the moon. Coyote jumped after it, and tried to catch it, but it flew up into the sky. It was winter now, and plants began to die. As Coyote continued to chase the moon, the sun escaped from the box as well, and floated up into the sky, drifting so far away that the air became cold and snow began to fall.

Because of Coyote, winter had arrived. And it would be a long time before Eagle could catch the sun.

DISCUSSION QUESTIONS

1. Compare this story with the story of "How Raven Brought Light to the World." What do the similarities and differences reveal about these cultures?

2. What etiological function(s) does this story serve?

3. Compare this story to tales from other cultures that concern the theft of light or fire. There is often a price to be paid for this action—in this case, what is that cost?

4. Discuss the contrast between Coyote and Eagle. What does each character represent?

Coyote and Eagle Visit the Land of the Dead (Chinook)

The Wasco-Wishram are Chinook tribes of the Columbia River region of Oregon, near The Dalles. The Chinookan language is believed to be part of the Penutian language family. The Wasco were the eastern-most group of Chinookan-speaking people. Primarily fishermen, they often traded with other groups in the area, as their location offered convenient trade routes. Today, there are 4000 members of the Confederated Tribes Warm Springs Reservation in Oregon, of which 200 are Wasco. This story is adapted from a Wishram tale, as told in *The Storytelling Stone*.

COYOTE AND EAGLE VISIT THE LAND OF THE DEAD

In the time of animal people, when people died they went away to the spirit land. This made Coyote sad. All he heard were sounds of mourning. He thought for a long time about how he could bring people back to the land of the living.

Coyote's friends had died, and so had his sister. Eagle lost his wife and he also mourned. Coyote tried to comfort Eagle by saying, "Those we have lost shall not remain in the land of the dead forever. They are like autumn leaves that turn brown and fall, but then return in spring. When grass grows again, and birds sing, and flowers bloom, the dead shall return."

But Eagle did not want to wait. He thought the dead should be able to return sooner. So they set out together to the land of the dead. After many days, they reached a lake and saw houses on the other side.

Coyote shouted "Bring us a boat, so we may cross!" But there was no reply.

Eagle said, "There is no one there. We have wasted our time."

But Coyote said, "They must be sleeping. They sleep during the daytime, but are awake at night. Let's wait here until dark."

After the sun had set, Coyote began singing. Soon, four spirit men emerged and crossed the lake in a boat. Coyote continued to sing, and the spirits joined him as they paddled. Yet the boat seemed to be moving by itself.

The spirits reached the shore, and Eagle and Coyote got into the boat to go back with them. As they drew closer to the land of the dead, they heard the sound of drums and dancing.

The spirits warned them: "Keep your eyes closed. Do not go into the houses. Do not look at anything. This place is sacred."

But Coyote and Eagle protested. "We are cold and hungry. Please let us go inside."

They were allowed to enter a lodge where they found the spirits singing and dancing along with the drums. An old woman gave them seal oil from a basket bottle – she dipped a feather into the oil and fed them until their hunger subsided.

Eagle and Coyote looked around. The lodge was large and beautiful, filled with spirits who had feathers in their hair and painted faces. They were dressed in fine ceremonial robes adorned with elks' teeth and shells. The moon hung above them, filling the room with light. Frog stood near the moon. He had been watching over it since jumping into it long ago, and he kept it shining on them.

Adapted from: Feldmann, Susan. *The Storytelling Stone*, 1965.

Eagle and Coyote recognized some of the former friends among the spirits, but no one seemed to notice them or see the basket Coyote had brought. He planned to use the basket to carry the spirits back and return them to the land of the living.

Early the next morning, the spirits departed the lodge for sleep. Coyote killed Frog, and dressed himself in his clothes. Twilight came, and the spirits return to the lodge again for their night of dancing and singing. They did not know Coyote was deceiving them, standing by the moon, pretending to be Frog.

When the singing and dancing reached their height, Coyote swallowed the moon. While it was dark, Eagle snatched the spirit people and put them in the basket, tightly closing the lid. Coyote carried the basket, and they began their journey back to the land of the living.

After they had traveled for a while, they heard noises in the basket. They stopped to listen closely.

Coyote said, "the people are alive again."

After traveling a bit farther, they hear the voices speaking inside the basket. They sounded unhappy, and complained about being bumped around. Some said their legs were hurting; others said their arms were cramped. Several of them cried, "Let us out!"

Coyote was weary, for the basket seemed to grow heavier as they traveled – the spirits were becoming people again.

Coyote said, "We should let them out."

Eagle replied quickly, "No, no."

The basket had become so heavy that Coyote set it down.

Again, he repeated, "Let's let them out. We've come so far from the land of the spirits that they won't be able to find their way back to it."

Coyote opened the basket. The people returned to spirit form and moved like the wind back to the land of the dead.

At first, Eagle scolded Coyote, but then he remembered his earlier words. "It's autumn now, and like the dead, the leaves are falling. But they will return in spring. We can wait until spring when the flowers bloom. We can come back and try again."

But Coyote said, "No. I am too tired. Let the dead stay in the spirit land forever."

And so Coyote made the law that when people die they cannot come back to life. If he had not opened the basket, the dead would have returned to life again every spring just like the trees and grass and flowers.

DISCUSSION QUESTIONS

1. Beyond an etiological function, what other purpose does this myth serve?

2. Compare this story to other myths that deal with mortality. What similarities and differences do you observe?

How Raven Brought Light to the World (Tahltan)

© B. Franklin/Shutterstock.com

A common motif among North American myths is the theft of light, or its introduction into the world as separate from the act of creation. This legend is found most prominently among tribes of the Pacific coast; this specific tale comes from the Tahltan people of British Columbia. Often this act is performed by a character who is considered a culture-hero; in this case, Raven. Similar stories concern the theft of fire and water. Sometimes these acts occur after a flood when the world must be rebuilt.

HOW RAVEN BROUGHT LIGHT TO THE WORLD

ORIGIN OF DAYLIGHT.—At this time there was no daylight, or sun, moon, or stars. Raven went to a village and asked the people if they could see anything. They said, "No, but one man has day-light, which he keeps in a box in his house. When he takes off the lid, there is bright light in his house." The people could not work much, for it was night continually. Raven found out where Daylight-Man lived, and went to his house. This man also had control of the sun, moon, and stars. Raven went into the house and came out again. He planned what to do to get daylight for himself and the people.

Daylight-Man had many slaves, and a daughter who had been a woman for three years, but she was still undergoing the ceremonies encumbent on girls at puberty. She lived apart in the corner of the house, in a room of her own, and was closely watched. She drank out of a white bucket every day, and she always examined the water before drinking, to see if there was anything in it. Slaves always brought the water to her. Raven changed himself into a cedar-leaf in the bucket of water the slave was bringing. The girl noticed it, and before drinking threw it out. He assumed his natural form again. Next day he transformed himself into a very small cedar-leaf, and hid in the water. The girl looked in the water, and, seeing nothing, she drank it all, and thus swallowed Raven. [For three months her menses did not come, and her belly began to swell. Her parents said, "Then you are pregnant and you were with a man," but the girl denied it] and they could not see how she could have been, as she had been so closely watched.

Source: James A. Teit, "Tahltan Tales," *The Journal of American Folklore,* 32(124), 1919.

After nine months she gave birth to a son. Her parents said they would rear the boy and acknowledge him as their grandson, even if he had no father. They said, if she told who the father of the child was, they would agree that he marry their daughter, they would treat their son-in-law well, and all would be well; but she persisted in saying that she had never seen [the] man.

The boy grew very fast, and son was able to walk and talk. His grandfather loved him dearly. One day he cried very much and wanted to be allowed to play with the moon. His grandfather ordered the moon to be taken down and given to him. The boy was pleased, and played with it until tired; and then they hung it up again. After a while he got tired of the moon and cried much, saying he wanted the sun. It was given to him; and he played with it until tired, then gave it back, and the people hung it up again. After a while he became tired of the sun, and cried for the Dipper (stars). Now they allowed him to play with these things whenever he wanted. After a long time, when he felt strong, he cried for the daylight. His grandfather was afraid to give it to him, because it shed so much light; besides, whenever it was lifted up, the sun, moon, stars, and everything worked in unison with it. It was their chief. At last, however, the boy was allowed to have the daylight, but his grandfather was uneasy when he played with it. When the boy lifted up daylight, much light would come; and the higher he held it, the brighter became the daylight. On these occasions, when the boy held the daylight high, the old man would say, "Eh, eh!" as if he was hurt or extremely anxious. The boy balanced the daylight in his hands to get used to carrying it.

At last, one day, he felt strong enough for the feat he intended to perform. He put two of the toys in each hand and balanced them. He felt he could carry them easily. Then, at a moment when the people were not watching, he flew out of the smoke-hole with them. He threw daylight away, saying, "*Henceforth there shall be daylight, and people will be able to see and work and travel. After dawn the sun will rise; and when it sets, night will come. People will then rest and sleep, for it will not be easy to work and travel. Then the Dipper and moon will travel and give light*. These things shall never again belong to one man, nor be kept locked up in one place. They shall be for the use and benefit of all people." He threw daylight to the north, the sun to the east, the moon to the west, and the Dipper to the south. Since the introduction of daylight, people and game rise with daylight, and go to sleep with nightfall.

DISCUSSION QUESTIONS

1. What does this myth reveal about the culture of the people?
2. What are the various etiological functions this myth serves, beyond just the bringing of light?

The Bear-Woman (Blackfoot)

Blackfoot (Siksika), is an Algonquian language from the region of southern Alberta and northern Montana. People of the Blackfoot Nation have occupied the Rocky Mountain region for more than 10,000 years. Most descend from the South Piegan tribes. Today, approximately 10,000 members of the Blackfeet Nation live on reservation lands in Montana, and an additional 15,000 live in Alberta.

Bears are one of many animals that have significance among Native American cultures, and are often used as a clan symbol. Animals were often considered spiritual guides based on their particular characteristics. In this case, the bear is seen as a protector of the people. In 2015, facing the threat of removal of the grizzly bear from the Endangered Species Act, Blackfoot Confederacy leaders spoke out in protest, citing that the grizzly bear is revered and "central to some of [their] oldest and most sacred narratives, accounts that speak to the creation of constellations and the coming of sacred bundles" (*Native News Online*).

THE BEAR-WOMAN

Once there was a young woman with many suitors; but she refused to marry. She had seven brothers and one little sister. Their mother had been dead many years and they had no relatives, but lived alone with their father. Every day the six brothers went out hunting with their father. It seems that the young woman had a bear for her lover and, as she did not want anyone to know this, she would meet him when she went out after wood. She always went after wood as soon as her father and brothers went out to hunt, leaving her little sister alone in the lodge. As soon as she was out of sight in the brush, she would run to the place where the bear lived.

As the little sister grew older, she began to be curious as to why her older sister spent so much time getting wood. So one day she followed her. She saw the young woman meet the bear and saw that they were lovers. When she found this out, she ran home as quickly as she could, and when her father returned she told him what she had seen. When he heard the story he said, "So, my elder daughter has a bear for a husband. Now I know why she does not want to marry." Then he went about the camp, telling all his people that they had a bear for a brother-in-law, and that he wished all the men to go out with him to kill this bear. So they went, found the bear, and killed him.

When the young woman found out what had been done, and that her little sister had told on her, she was very angry. She scolded her little sister vigorously, then ordered her to go out to the dead bear, and bring some flesh from his paws. The little sister began to cry, and said she was afraid to go out of the lodge, because a dog with young pups had tried to bite her. "Oh, do not be afraid!" said the young woman. "I will paint your face like that of a bear, with black marks across the eyes and at the corners of the mouth; then no one will touch you." So she went for the meat. Now the older sister was a powerful medicine-woman. She could tan hides in a new way. She could take up a hide, strike it four times with her skin-scraper and it would be tanned.

The little sister had a younger brother that she carried on her back. As their mother was dead, she took care of him. One day the little sister said to the older sister, "Now you be a bear and we will go out into the brush to play."

The older sister agreed to this, but said, "Little sister, you must not touch me over my kidneys." So the big sister acted as a bear, and they played in the brush. While they were playing, the little sister forgot what she had been told, and touched her older sister in the wrong place. At once she turned into a real bear, ran into the camp, and killed many of the people. After she had killed a large number, she turned back into her former self. Now, when the little sister saw the older run away as a real bear, she became frightened, took up her little brother, and ran into their lodge. Here they waited, badly frightened, but were very glad to see their older sister return after a time as her true self.

Now the older brothers were out hunting, as usual. As the little sister was going down for water with her little brother on her back, she met her six brothers returning. The brothers noted how quiet and deserted the camp seemed to be. So they said to their little sister, "Where are all our people?" Then the little sister explained how she and her sister were playing, when the elder turned into a bear, ran

Source: Clark Wissler and D. C. Duvall, "Mythology of the Blackfoot Indians," *Anthropological Papers of the American Museum of Natural History,* Vol. II, Part 1, September, 1908.

through the camp, and killed many people. She told her brothers that they were in great danger, as their sister would surely kill them when they came home. So the six brothers decided to go into the brush. One of them had killed a jack-rabbit.

He said to the little sister, "You take this rabbit home with you. When it is dark, we will scatter prickly-pears all around the lodge, except in one place. When you come out, you must look for that place, and pass through."

When the little sister came back to the lodge, the elder sister said, "Where have you been all this time?"

"Oh, my little brother mussed himself and I had to clean him," replied the little sister.

"Where did you get that rabbit?" she asked.

"I killed it with a sharp stick," said the little sister.

"That is a lie. Let me see you do it," said the older sister. Then the little sister took up a stick lying near her, threw it at the rabbit, and it stuck in the wound in his body.

"Well, all right," said the elder sister. Then the little sister dressed the rabbit and cooked it. She offered some of it to her older sister, but it was refused: so the little sister and her brother ate all of it. When the elder sister saw that the rabbit had all been eaten, she became very angry, and said, "Now I have a mind to kill you."

So the little sister arose quickly, took her little brother on her back, and said, "I am going out to look for wood." As she went out, she followed the narrow trail through the prickly-pears and met her six brothers in the brush. Then they decided to leave the country, and started off as fast as they could go.

The older sister, being a powerful medicine-woman, knew at once what they were doing. She became very angry and turned herself into a bear to pursue them. Soon she was about to overtake them, when one of the boys tried his power. He took a little water in the hollow of his hand and sprinkled it around. At once it became a great lake between them and the bear. Then the children hurried on while the bear went around. After a while the bear caught up with them again, when another brother threw a porcupine-tail (a hairbrush) on the ground. This became a great thicket; but the bear forced its way through, and again overtook the children. This time they all climbed a high tree. The bear came to the foot of the tree, and, looking up at them, said, "Now I shall kill you all." So she took a stick from the ground, threw it into the tree and knocked down four of the brothers.

While she was doing this, a little bird flew around the tree, calling out to the children, "Shoot her in the head! Shoot her in the head!" Then one of the boys shot an arrow into the head of the bear, and at once she fell dead. Then they came down from the tree.

Now the four brothers were dead. The little brother took an arrow, shot it straight up into the air, and when it fell one of the dead brothers came to life. This he repeated until all were alive again. Then they held a council, and said to each other, "Where shall we go? Our people have all been killed, and we are a long way from home. We have no relatives living in the world."

Finally they decided that they preferred to live in the sky. Then the little brother said, "Shut your eyes." As they did so, they all went up. Now you can see them every night. The little brother is the North Star. The six brothers and the little sister are seen in the Great Dipper. The little sister and eldest brother are in a line with the North Star, the little sister being nearest it because she used to carry her little brother on her back. The other brothers are arranged in order of their age, beginning with the eldest. This is how the seven stars [Ursa major] came to be.

DISCUSSION QUESTIONS

1. What is the significance of this myth? What is the lesson or message it conveys? What does it reveal about the values of this culture?

2. What are the characteristics of the bear that make it important to the Blackfoot people?

The Maiden Who Loved a Star (Tejas)

The Tejas (Hasinais Caddo) were one of two main groups in the Southwestern Plains area—present-day Nacogdoches (east Texas).

> Tejas is the Spanish spelling of a Caddo word taysha, which means 'friend' or 'ally'. In the seventeenth century the Spanish knew the westernmost Caddo peoples as "the great kingdom of Tejas" and the name lived on to become the name of the twenty-eighth state of the United States—Texas. (Texas Beyond History)

Many tribes speak dialects of the Caddo language, including the Wichita and Pawnee.

THE MAIDEN WHO LOVED A STAR

There was once a young and beautiful Indian girl who went from her home into a desert of the western country to gather there the purple ripe fruit of the prickly pear. She left the desert late one day after the sun had gone down, and when she set out for home the bright stars were beginning to sparkle in the sky. One star was much brighter than the others, and seemed closer to earth than the others. The Indian maiden stopped in the sand and watched it. Was the star winking down at her? She thought it was. She dreamed of the shining star that night, and she saw in her dream that the star was the home of a fine, tall youth, a sky dweller.

The next day the maiden went again into the desert to gather the fruit of the prickly pear. Again she stayed until the sun had gone down behind the distant hills on the far edge of the desert, and she watched her star winking once more at her. That was the sky youth, she knew. For seven days she visited the desert and each night she dreamed of this fair young man. She dreamed that he spoke of his love to her, but he could not join her on earth as long as she lived there and as long as he lived in the sky. He could not come down to the desert. She could not visit him in his star home.

The maiden was full of love, but she was unhappy because she was so far away from her lover in the star-frosted sky. She decided she did not want to live any longer. An old witch woman lived with the tribe, and the Indian maiden went to her and asked the woman how to die in order that she might be taken up to the sky to live in the star with her lover.

"Life is too great a gift to be flung aside," said the witch woman as she looked at the poor girl weeping on the other side of the old woman's fire. "You must live out the life the Great Spirit has given to you, but I can change you into a form that will permit you to live always out upon the desert under the loving smiles of the star youth."

Her words filled the maiden with joy. She went with the witch woman upon the desert that night. There the old woman made a powerful drink from desert plants and told the maiden to drink it. As soon as she

Source: Florence Stratton, *When the Storm God Rides: Tejas and Other Indian Legends*, 1936.

had done so her feet began to take root in the dry, sandy soil. Her arms turned to branches. Her black hair turned to leaves, and the maiden had become a new shrub which no Indian had seen in the desert before. As the wind blew the shrub seemed to murmur thanks to the witch woman.

When the sky youth saw what had happened he leaned far out of an opening in his star lodge. He leaned so far out that the edges of the star broke with his weight, and he fell with sparkling pieces of star straight towards the maiden who had become a bush. The starry bits were shattered to fine dust that powdered the leaves of the bush with white. The youth was changed to purple blossoms. At last the maiden and the sky youth were together.

The bush with white-dusted leaves and beautiful blossoms became known as the cenisa, or ash-covered bush. Today it is called the purple sage. Not many white people know the story of how it came to the desert.

DISCUSSION QUESTION

1. While this story serves a definite etiological function, what other purposes does it have?

White Buffalo Woman (Lakota Sioux)

This is a central myth of the Great Plains people, especially the Lakota. It tells how the Lakota first received their sacred pipe and the ceremony in which to use it. Today there are approximately 70,000 registered members of the Lakota Nation, most residing on one of five reservations in North and South Dakota. Their language is a dialect of the Sioux Nation, which consists of seven tribes that speak three languages: Lakota, Dakota, and Nakota. This version of the story has adapted from several sources.

WHITE BUFFALO WOMAN

Long ago, before the Lakota used horses to hunt the buffalo, two men went hunting with bows and arrows. They set out early across the plains, through the waving grass, searching for game. They climbed a gentle hill for a better look, and noticed something mysterious approaching them in the distance. It walked on two legs, and seemed to be glowing. As the wonderful sight drew near, they could see it was a beautiful woman with long, black hair, dressed in white buckskin. She carried a bundle on her back. As she came closer, they noticed the buckskin she wore was decorated with colorful, sacred symbols, and she held a fan of sage leaves in her hand.

The men were stunned by her appearance. One of the men was filled with desire; the other man lowered his eyes and said, "Fool. Can't you see this woman is holy?"

But the lustful man approached the woman, and she beckoned him. As he drew near to her, a cloud enveloped them, hiding them from sight. When the cloud dispersed, all that remained of the man was a pile of bones at her feet, snakes twisting among them.

She said to the other hunter, "Behold! I come to your people bearing a message for your chief. Tell him what you have seen. Have him prepare a large tipi and gather all his people to prepare for this message of great importance."

Source: Thompson, Stith. *Tales of the North American Indians*. Indiana University Press, 1929.

The young hunter raced across the prairie to deliver the news. The chief, Standing Hollow Horn, prepared as he was instructed. He took down several small tipis to create an enormous lodge. He called for all the people to adorn themselves in their finest skins and gather together. The people were excited and anxious for the woman's arrival.

After several days, scouts reported of the woman's arrival. They told of her coming across the prairie, bright and wonderful as she moved toward them. She suddenly entered the lodge, walking around it in a sun-wise fashion, and stopped in front of Standing Hollow Horn. She held out her bundle before him.

"Behold," she said, "and look upon this with love and respect. No one impure should ever see it or touch it, for enclosed within is the sacred pipe. You will use it to lift your voices to your Father and Grandfather." She unrolled the bundle and removed the pipe, lifting it to the sky. "With this pipe you will walk upon the Earth, for the Earth is your Mother and Grandmother, and she is sacred. Each step upon her should be as a prayer. The pipe bowl is red stone; it is also the Earth. Carved into the stone, facing the center, is a buffalo calf. This represents those of four-legs who walk upon the Earth. The pipe stem is wood, for all that grows upon the Earth. And the twelve feathers that decorate where the stem fits the bowl, are from the Spotted Eagle—they represent winged creatures of the air. All these peoples are joined as family—all send their voices to the Great Spirit, your Father and Grandfather. When you pray with this pipe, you pray with, and for, all things, and your people will prosper."

Next she removed a small round stone from the bundle and placed it on the ground. She touched the stem of the pipe to the stone and said, "With this pipe you are bound to your relatives and ancestors. This stone is the same stone as the pipe bowl. Your Father has given it to you; it is the Earth, your Mother and Grandmother, the place you live. It is sacred. This Earth he has given you is red; the two-legged are red; the Great Spirit has given you a red day and a red road. Do not forget that all of this is sacred—each day, and the light of each day."

The woman explained that the seven circles that were carved on the stone represent the seven sacred rites the people must learn to use the sacred pipe. She told them of the first rite and that the other six would be revealed at a later time. The woman prepared to leave the lodge, but spoke one more time to Standing Hollow Horn. She said, "This pipe will carry you until the end. Remember that there are four ages and I will look upon you in each age. At the end, I will return."

Once again she walked around the lodge in a sun-wise fashion as the people looked on, awestruck. Then, she left. But after she walked a short distance, she looked back on the people and sat down on the grass. When she stood up again, she had been transformed into a young brown and red buffalo calf. The people stared in amazement. The calf walked a short distance, then lay down, rolled over, and rose again looking back—this time as a white buffalo. The white buffalo walked on and again, stopped and rolled over, rising again as a black buffalo. The black buffalo walked on, then stopped and, bowing to each of the four directions, walked over the hill and disappeared.

In some versions of the story, the woman becomes first a black buffalo, then yellow, then red, and finally white. The colors represent the four directions. According to the Republic of Dakota, the seven sacred rites are the following ceremonies practiced by the people:

Canupa: The Sacred Pipe Ceremony
Inipi: The Sweat Lodge
Hanblecha: The Vision Quest
Wiwangwacipi: The Sun Dance
Hunkapi: The Making of Relatives
The Keeping of The Soul
Ishna Ta Awi Cha Lowan: Preparing a Girl for Womanhood

DISCUSSION QUESTIONS

1. Compare White Buffalo Woman to the goddesses of other cultures—especially Athena and Artemis. What similar functions or roles does she serve?

2. Why is the encounter with the two men important to the story?

3. Explain the significance of the ritual and ceremony surrounding the pipe.

Sedna, Mistress of The Underworld (Inuit)

Sedna ("she down there") is ruler of the realm of dead, in addition to being cited as a goddess of the sea and marine animals. She is known by different names among other Inuit groups, and there are other versions of the story. Adlivun ("those who live beneath us") is the underworld in Inuit mythology. It refers both to the departed souls and the place itself, beneath the sea. Souls are said to be prepared there, purified, for their next stage of the journey—to the Land of the Moon. Sedna is said to keep the souls there until they are ready to move on. Sedna is an essential deity in Inuit culture, also serving as an intermediary between people and the natural world. In addition, this myth reveals the importance of shamanism in Inuit culture. The shaman enters a trance to symbolically visit Sedna in her home, attempting to convince her to release her children—the sea animals on which the people depend for sustenance.

There are approximately 100,000 Inuit currently living in coastal regions of Alaska, Canada, and Greenland—some still live a traditional hunting lifestyle, though supplemented with some modern supplies. The Inuktitut language is a member of the Eskimo-Aleut language family. Once commonly referred to as "Eskimo," an Algonquin word, meaning "eater of raw meat," Inuit is the preferred term today. However, some do still identify themselves as Eskimos.

SEDNA, MISTRESS OF THE UNDERWORLD

Once upon a time there lived on a solitary shore an Inung with his daughter Sedna. His wife had been dead for some time and the two led a quiet life. Sedna grew up to be a handsome girl and the youths came from all around to sue for her hand, but none of them could touch her proud heart. Finally, at the breaking up of the ice in the spring a fulmar* flew from over the ice and wooed Sedna with enticing song. "Come to me," it said; "come into the land of the birds, where there is never hunger, where my tent is made of the most beautiful skins. You shall rest on soft bearskins. My fellows, the fulmars, shall bring you all your heart may desire; their feathers shall clothe you; your lamp shall always be filled with oil, your pot with meat."

*fulmar: a type of sea bird

Source: Franz Boas. "The Central Eskimo." *6th Annual Report of the Bureau of American Ethnology to the Secretary of the Smithsonian Institute,* 1884–1885.

Sedna could not long resist such wooing and they went together over the vast sea. When at last they reached the country of the fulmar, after a long and hard journey, Sedna discovered that her spouse had shamefully deceived her. Her new home was not built of beautiful pelts, but was covered with wretched fishskins, full of holes, that gave free entrance to wind and snow. Instead of soft reindeer skins her bed was made of hard walrus hides and she had to live on miserable fish, which the birds brought her. Too soon she discovered that she had thrown away her opportunities when in her foolish pride she had rejected the Inuit youth. In her woe she sang: "Aja. O father, if you knew how wretched I am you would come to me and we would hurry away in your boat over the waters. The birds look unkindly upon me the stranger; cold winds roar about my bed; they give me but miserable food. O come and take me back home. Aja."

When a year had passed and the sea was again stirred by warmer winds, the father left his country to visit Sedna. His daughter greeted him joyfully and besought him to take her back home. The father, hearing of the outrages wrought upon his daughter, determined upon revenge. He killed the fulmar, took Sedna into his boat, and they quickly left the country which had brought so much sorrow to Sedna. When the other fulmars came home and found their companion dead and his wife gone, they all flew away in search of the fugitives. They were very sad over the death of their poor murdered comrade and continue to mourn and cry until this day.

Having flown a short distance they discerned the boat and stirred up a heavy storm. The sea rose in immense waves that threatened the pair with destruction. In this mortal peril the father determined to offer Sedna to the birds and flung her overboard. She clung to the edge of the boat with a death grip. The cruel father then took a knife and cut off the first joints of her fingers. Falling into the sea they were transformed into whales, the nails turning into whalebone. Sedna holding on to the boat more tightly, the second finger joints fell under the sharp knife and swam away as seals; when the father cut off the stumps of the fingers they became ground seals.

Meantime the storm subsided, for the fulmars thought Sedna was drowned. The father then allowed her to come into the boat again. But from that time she cherished a deadly hatred against him and swore bitter revenge. After they got ashore, she called her dogs and let them gnaw off the feet and hands of her father while he was asleep. Upon this he cursed himself, his daughter, and the dogs which had maimed him; whereupon the earth opened and swallowed the hut, the father, the daughter, and the dogs. They have since lived in the land of Adlivun, of which Sedna is the mistress. Some local legends claim that the cause of storms is Sedna's wrath, stirring up the waves from her home on the ocean floor. When a particularly bad storm approaches, a man will sacrifice himself to the sea, dive down to the deepest point, untangle, and rebraid Sedna's hair. The storm will then pass.

DISCUSSION QUESTIONS

1. This story is often considered a creation myth. Explain how it fits that category.

2. What purpose does Sedna serve in her role as a sea goddess?

3. Discuss Sedna's role as ruler of the underworld. How does her experience prepare her for this duty?

4. What is the significance of Sedna's mistreatment by men?

The Origin of Stories (Iroquois-Seneca)

The Seneca are one of the members of the Iroquois tribe from the western part of New York State, along the shores of Lake Ontario. Approximately 8,000 Seneca people reside today, mainly in New York, but also Oklahoma and parts of Canada. In the Seneca language they call themselves O-non-dowa-gah, or "Great Hill People." They are the largest of six Native American nations of the Iroquois Confederacy and are also known as the "Keeper of the Western Door," as they are westernmost of the Six Nations (Seneca Nation of Indians).

THE ORIGIN OF STORIES

"This happened long ago, in the time of our forefathers."

In a Seneca village lived a boy whose father and mother died when he was only a few weeks old. The little boy was cared for by a woman, who had known his parents. She gave him the name of Poyeshaon (Orphan).

The boy grew to be a healthy, active little fellow. When he was old enough, his foster mother gave him a bow and arrows, and said "It is time for you to learn to hunt. To-morrow morning go to the woods and kill all the birds you can find."

Taking cobs of dry corn the woman shelled off the kernels and parched them in hot ashes; and the next morning she gave the boy some of the corn for his breakfast and rolled up some in a piece of buckskin and told him to take it with him, for he would be gone all day and would get hungry.

Poyeshaon started off and was very successful. At noon he sat down and rested and ate some of the parched corn, then he hunted till the middle of the afternoon. When he began to work toward home he had a good string of birds.

The next morning Poyeshaon's foster mother gave him parched corn for breakfast and while he was eating she told him that he must do his best when hunting, for if he became a good hunter he would always be prosperous.

The boy took his bow and arrows and little bundle parched corn and went to the woods; again he found plenty of birds. At midday he ate his corn and thought over what his foster mother had told him. In his mind he said, "I'll do just as my mother tells me, then some time I'll be able to hunt big game."

Poyeshaon hunted till toward evening, then went home with a larger string of birds than he had the previous day. His foster mother thanked him, and said, "Now you have began to help me get food."

Early the next morning the boy's breakfast was ready and as soon as he had eaten it he took his little bundle of parched corn and started off. He went farther into the woods and at night came home with a larger string of birds than he had the second day. His foster mother praised and thanked him.

Each day the boy brought home more birds than the previous day. On the ninth day he killed so many that he brought them home on his back. His foster mother tied the birds in little bundles of three or four and distributed them among her neighbors.

The tenth day the boy started off, as usual, and, as each day he had gone farther for game than on the preceding day, so now he went deeper into the woods than ever. About midday the sinew that held the feathers to his arrow loosened. Looking around for a place where he could sit down while he took the

---

Source: Jeremiah Curtin, *Seneca Indian Myths,* 1922.

sinew off and wound it on again, he saw a small opening and near the center of the opening a high, smooth, flat-topped, round stone. He went to the stone, sprang up on to it and sat down. He unwound the sinew and put it in his mouth to soften, then he arranged the arrow feathers and was about to fasten them to the arrow when a voice, right there near him, asked, "Shall I tell you stories?"

Poyeshaon looked up expecting to see a man, not seeing any one he looked behind the stone and around it, then he again began to tie the feathers to his arrow.

"Shall I tell you stories?" asked a voice right there by him.

The boy looked in every direction, but saw no one. Then he made up his mind to watch and find out who was trying to fool him. He stopped work and listened and when the voice again asked, "Shall I tell you stories?"

He found that it came from the stone, then he asked, "What is that? What does it mean to tell stories?"

"It is telling what happened a long time ago. If you will give me your birds, I'll tell you stories."

"You may have the birds."

As soon as the boy promised to give the birds, the stone began telling what happened long ago. When one story was told, another was begun. The boy sat, with his head down, and listened. Toward night the stone said, "We will rest now. Come again to-morrow. If anyone asks about your birds, say that you have killed so many that they are getting scarce and you have to go a long way to find one."

While going home the boy killed five or six birds. When his foster mother asked why he had so few birds, he said that they were scarce; that he had to go far for them.

The next morning Poyeshaon started off with his bow and arrows and little bundle of parched corn, but he forgot to hunt for birds, he was thinking of the stories the stone had told him. When a bird lighted near him he shot it, but he kept straight on toward the opening in the woods. When he got there he put his birds on the stone, and called out, "I've come! Here are birds. Now tell me stories."

The stone told story after story. Toward night it said "Now we must rest till to-morrow."

On the way home the boy looked for birds, but it was late and he found only a few.

That night the foster mother told her neighbors that when Poyeshaon first began to hunt he had brought home a great many birds, but now he brought only four or five after being in the woods from morning till night. She said there was something strange about it, either he threw the birds away or gave them to some animal, or maybe he idled time away, didn't hunt. She hired a boy to follow Poyeshaon and find out what he was doing.

The next morning the boy took his bow and arrows and followed Poyeshaon, keeping out of his sight and sometimes shooting a bird. Poyeshaon killed a good many birds; then, about the middle of the forenoon, he suddenly started off toward the East, running as fast as he could. The boy followed till he came to an opening in the woods and saw Poyeshaon climb up and sit down on a large round stone; he crept nearer and heard talking. When he couldn't see the person to whom Poyeshaon was talking he went up to the boy, and asked, "What are you doing here?"

"Hearing stories."

"What are stories?"

"Telling about things that happened long ago. Put your birds on this stone, and say, 'I've come to hear stories.'"

The boy did as told and straightway the stone began. The boys listened till the sun went down, then the stone said, "We will rest now. Come again to-morrow."

On the way home Poyeshaon killed three or four birds.

When the woman asked the boy she had sent why Poyeshaon killed so few birds, he said, "I followed him for a while, then I spoke to him, and after that we hunted together till it was time to come home. We couldn't find many birds."

The next morning the elder boy said, "I'm going with Poyeshaon to hunt, it's sport." The two started off together. By the middle of the forenoon each boy had a long string of birds. They hurried to the opening, put the birds on the stone, and said, "We have come. Here are the birds! Tell us stories."

They sat on the stone and listened to stories till late in the afternoon, then the stone said, "We'll rest now till to-morrow."

On the way home the boys shot every bird they could find, but it was late and they didn't find many.

Several days went by in this way, then the foster mother said, "Those boys kill more birds than they bring home," and she hired two men to follow them.

The next morning, when Poyeshaon and his friend started for the woods the two men followed. When the boys had a large number of birds they stopped hunting and hurried to the opening. The men followed and, hiding behind trees, saw them put the birds on a large round stone, then jump up and sit there, with their heads down, listening to a man's voice; every little while they said, "Ûn!"

"Let's go there and find out who is talking to those boys," said one man to the other. They walked quickly to the stone, and asked, "What are you doing, boys?"

The boys were startled, but Poyeshaon said, "You must promise not to tell anyone."

They promised, then Poyeshaon said, "Jump up and sit on the stone."

The men seated themselves on the stone, then the boy said, "Go on with the story, we are listening."

The four sat with their heads down and the stone began to tell stories. When it was almost night the Stone said, "To-morrow all the people in your village must come and listen to my stories. Tell the chief to send every man, and have each man bring something to eat. You must clean the brush away so the people can sit on the ground near me."

That night Poyeshaon told the chief about the story, telling stone, and gave him the stone's message. The chief sent a runner to give the message to each family in the village.

Early the next morning every one in the village was ready to start. Poyeshaon went ahead and the crowd followed. When they came to the opening each man put what he had brought, meat or bread, on the stone; the brush was cleared away, and every one sat down.

When all was quiet the stone said, "Now I will tell you stories of what happened long ago. There was a world before this. The things that I am going to tell about happened in that world. Some of you will remember every word that I say, some will remember a part of the words, and some will forget them all—I think this will be the way, but each man must do the best he can. Hereafter you must tell these stories to one another--now listen."

Each man bent his head and listened to every word the stone said. Once in a while the boys said "Ûn!" When the sun was almost down the stone said, "We'll rest now. Come to-morrow and bring meat and bread."

The next morning when the people gathered around the stone they found that the meat and bread they had left there the day before was gone. They put the food they had brought on the. stone, then sat in a circle and waited.

When all was quiet the stone began. Again it told stories till the sun was almost down, then it said, "Come tomorrow. To-morrow I will finish the stories of what happened long ago."

Early in the morning the people of the village gathered around the stone and, when all was quiet, the stone began to tell stories, and it told till late in the afternoon, then it said, "I have finished! You must keep these stories as long as the world lasts; tell them to your children and grandchildren generation after generation. One person will remember them better than another. When you go to a man or a woman to ask for one of these stories carry something to pay for it, bread or meat, or whatever you have. I know all that happened in the world before this; I have told it to you. When you visit one another, you must tell these things, and keep them up always. I have finished."

And so it has been. From the Stone came all the knowledge the Senecas have of the world before this.

DISCUSSION QUESTIONS

1. Why do you think a stone is the item chosen as the origin of stories?

2. Why does the stone ask for the people to give it food in exchange for stories?

▷ ▷ ▷

Part 3: Journeys of Heroes and Heroines

© Don Mammoser/Shutterstock.com

Hero Twins

The following two stories feature the motif of twin heroes, which is prevalent in many myths of North America, as well as in Mesoamerica and South America. The twins, typically brothers, are usually represented as culture heroes, but often possess traits of the trickster archetype. In North America, this motif is mainly found among tribes of the Southwest.

While there is great variety among the individual stories, some traits are shared among the tales. The twins nearly always have an unusual birth, display magical powers, and are presented with tests, trials, games, or adventures. The tasks they undertake are often assigned to them by a parent and can be presented to them as a warning or are part of a revenge plot. In addition, these stories can be included as part of a creation myth, and feature etiological functions as well. The twins are often the catalyst for transformations and sometimes perform resurrections. However, not every consequence of their actions is positive. No matter what the plot, though, the twins nearly always get into mischief. Occasionally the twins have a celestial connection—to sun, moon, or both. And sometimes the twins themselves represent a kind of polarity—one weak, the other strong.

THE HERO TWINS (Pueblo)

The Pueblo people of the Southwest—mainly Arizona and New Mexico—are named for their particular type of settlements. In Spanish, pueblo means "stone masonry village dweller." It is believed that the Anasazi ("the ancient ones"), one of the oldest cultural groups in North America, are the ancestors of the Pueblo, as well as the Hopi and Zuni.

Máw-Sahv and Oó-yah-wee, as the Hero Twins are named in Quères, had the Sun for a father. Their mother died when they were born, and lay lifeless upon the hot plain. But the two wonderful boys, as soon as they were a minute old, were big and strong, and began playing.

Source: Charles Lummis, *Pueblo Indian Folk-Stories*, 1910.

There chanced to be in a cliff to the southward a nest of white crows; and presently the young crows said: "Nana, what is that over there? Isn't it two babies?"

"Yes," replied the Mother-Crow, when she had taken a look. "Wait and I will bring them." So she brought the boys safely, and then their dead mother; and, rubbing a magic herb on the body of the latter, soon brought her to life.

By this time Máw-Sahv and Oó-yah-wee were sizable boys, and the mother started homeward with them.

"Now," said she when they reached the edge of the valley and could look across to that wondrous rock whereon stands Acoma, "go to yonder town, my sons, for that is Ah-ko, where live your grandfather and grandmother, my parents; and I will wait here. Go ye in at the west end of the town and stand at the south end of the council-grounds until someone speaks to you; and ask them to take you to the Cacique, for he is your grandfather.

You will know his house, for the ladder to it has three uprights instead of two. When you go in and tell your story, he will ask you a question to see if you are really his grandchildren, and will give you four chances to answer what he has in a bag in the corner. No one has ever been able to guess what is in it, but there are birds."

The Twins did as they were bidden, and presently came to Acoma and found the house of the old Cacique. When they entered and told their story, he said: "Now I will try you. What is in yonder bag?"

"A rattlesnake," said the boys.

"No," said the Cacique, "it is not a rattlesnake. Try again."

"Birds," said the boys.

"Yes, they are birds. Now I know that you are truly my grandchildren, for no one else could ever guess." And he welcomed them gladly, and sent them back with new dresses and jewelry to bring their mother.

When she was about to arrive, the Twins ran ahead to the house and told her father, mother, and sister to leave the house until she should enter; but not knowing what was to come, they would not go out. When she had climbed the big ladder to the roof and started down through the trap-door by the room-ladder, her sister cried out with joy at seeing her, and she was so startled that she fell from the ladder and broke her neck, and never could be brought to life again.

Máw-Sahv and Oó-yah-wee grew up to astounding adventures and achievements. While still very young in years, they did very remarkable things; for they had a miraculously rapid growth, and at an age when other boys were toddling about home, these Hero Twins had already become very famous hunters and warriors. They were very fond of stories of adventure, like less precocious lads; and after the death of their mother they kept their grandmother busy telling them strange tales. She had a great many anecdotes of a certain ogre-giantess who lived in the dark gorges of the mountains to the South, and so much did Máw-Sahv and Oó-yah-wee hear of this wonderful personage--who was the terror of all that country--that their boyish ambition was fired.

One day when their grandmother was busy they stole away from home with their bows and arrows, and walked miles and miles, till they came to a great forest at the foot of the mountain. In the edge of it sat the old Giant-woman, dozing in the sun, with a huge basket beside her. She was so enormous and looked so fierce that the boys' hearts stood still, and they would have hidden, but just then she caught sight of them, and called: "Come, little boys, and get into this basket of mine, and I will take you to my house."

"Very well," said Máw-Sahv, bravely hiding his alarm. "If you will take us through this big forest, which we would like to see, we will go with you."

The Giant-woman promised, and the lads clambered into her basket, which she took upon her back and started off. As she passed through the woods, the boys grabbed lumps of pitch from the tall pines and smeared it all over her head and back so softly that she did not notice it. Once she sat down to rest, and the boys slyly put a lot of big stones in the basket, set fire to her pitched hair, and hurriedly climbed a tall pine.

Presently the Giant-woman got up and started on toward home; but in a minute or two her head and manta were all of a blaze. With a howl that shook the earth, she dropped the basket and rolled on the ground, grinding her great head into the sand until she at last got the fire extinguished. But she was badly scorched and very angry, and still angrier when she looked in the basket and found only a lot of stones. She retraced her steps until she found the boys hidden in the pine-tree, and said to them: "Come down, children, and get into my basket, that I may take you to my house, for now we are almost there."

The boys, knowing that she could easily break down the tree if they refused, came down. They got into the basket, and soon she brought them to her home in the mountain. She set them down upon the ground and said: "Now, boys, go and bring me a lot of wood, that I may make a fire in the oven and bake you some sweet cakes."

The boys gathered a big pile of wood, with which she built a roaring fire in the adobe oven outside the house. Then she took them and washed them very carefully, and taking them by the necks, thrust them into the glowing oven and sealed the door with a great, flat rock, and left them there to be roasted.

But the Trues were friends of the Hero Twins, and did not let the heat harm them at all. When the old Giant-woman had gone into the house, Máw-Sahv and Oó-yah-wee broke the smaller stone that closed the smoke-hole of the oven, and crawled out from their fiery prison unsinged. They ran around and caught snakes and toads and gathered up dirt and dropped them down into the oven through the smoke-hole; and then, watching when the Giant-woman's back was turned, they sneaked into the house and hid in a huge olla on the shelf.

Very early in the morning the Giant-woman's baby began to cry for some boy-meat. "Wait till it is well cooked," said the mother; and hushed the child till the sun was well up. Then she went out and unsealed the oven, and brought in the sad mess the boys had put there. "They have cooked away to almost nothing," she said; and she and the Giant-baby sat down to eat. "Isn't this nice?" said the baby; and Máw-Sahv could not help saying, "You nasty things, to like that!"

"Eh? Who is that?" cried the Giant-woman, looking around till she found the boys hidden in the olla. So she told them to come down, and gave them some sweet cakes, and then sent them out to bring her some more wood.

It was evening when they returned with a big load of wood, which Máw-Sahv had taken pains to get green. He had also picked up in the mountains a long, sharp splinter of quartz. The evening was cool, and they built a big fire in the fireplace. But immediately, as the boys had planned, the green wood began to smoke at a dreadful rate, and soon the room was so dense with it that they all began to cough and strangle. The Giant-woman got up and opened the window and put her head out for a breath of fresh air; and Máw-Sahv, pulling out the white-hot splinter of quartz from the fire, stabbed her in the back so that she died. Then they killed the Giant-baby, and at last felt that they were safe.

Now the Giant-woman's house was a very large one, and ran far back into the very heart of the mountain. Having got rid of their enemies, the Hero Twins decided to explore the house; and, taking their bows and arrows, started boldly down into the deep, dark rooms. After traveling a long way in the dark, they came to a huge room in which corn and melons and pumpkins were growing abundantly. On and on they went, till at last they heard the growl of distant thunder. Following the sound, they came presently to a room in the solid rock, wherein the lightning was stored. Going in, they took the lightning and played with it awhile, throwing it from one to the other, and at last started home, carrying their strange toy with them.

When they reached Acoma and told their grandmother of their wonderful adventures, she held up her withered old hands in amazement. And she was nearly scared to death when they began to play with the lightning, throwing it around the house as though it had been a harmless ball, while the thunder rumbled till it shook the great rock of Acoma. They had the blue lightning which belongs in the West; and the yellow lightning of the North; and the red lightning of the East; and the white lightning of the South; and with all these they played merrily.

But it was not very long till Shée-wo-nah, the Storm-King, had occasion to use the lightning; and when he looked in the room where he was wont to keep it, and found it gone, his wrath knew no bounds. He started out to find who had stolen it; and passing by Acoma he heard the thunder as the Hero Twins were playing ball with the lightning. He pounded on the door and ordered them to give him his lightning, but the boys refused. Then he summoned the storm, and it began to rain and blow fearfully outside; while within the boys rattled their thunder in loud defiance, regardless of their grandmother's entreaties to give the Storm-King his lightning.

It kept raining violently, however, and the water came pouring down the chimney until the room was nearly full, and they were in great danger of drowning. But luckily for them, the Trues were still mindful of them; and just in the nick of time sent their servant, Tee-oh-pee, the Badger, who is the best of diggers, to dig a hole up through the floor; all the water ran out, and they were saved. And so the Hero Twins outwitted the Storm-King.

South of Acoma, in the pine-clad gorges and mesas, the world was full of Bears. There was one old She-Bear in particular, so huge and fierce that all men feared her; and not even the boldest hunter dared go to the south--for there she had her home with her two sons. Máw-sahv and Oó-yah-wee were famous hunters, and always wished to go south; but their grandmother always forbade them. One day, however, they stole away from the house, and got into the cañon. At last they came to the She-Bear's house; and there was old Quée-ah asleep in front of the door. Máw-sahv crept up very carefully and threw in her face a lot of ground chile, and ran. At that the She-Bear began to sneeze, ah-hútch! ah-hútch! She could not stop, and kept making ah-hútch until she sneezed herself to death.

Then the Twins took their thunder-knives and skinned her. They stuffed the great hide with grass, so that it looked like a Bear again, and tied a buckskin rope around its neck.

"Now," said Máw-sahv, "We will give our grandma a trick!"

So, taking hold of the rope, they ran toward Acoma, and the Bear came behind them as if leaping. Their grandmother was going for water; and from the top of the cliff she saw them running so in the valley, and the Bear jumping behind them. She ran to her house and painted one side of her face black with charcoal, and the other side red with the blood of an animal; and, taking a bag of ashes, ran down the cliff and out at the Bear, to make it leave the boys and come after her.

But when she saw the trick, she reproved the boys for their rashness--but in her heart she was very proud of them.

DISCUSSION QUESTIONS

1. Compare this story with other myths of hero twins—especially "Lodge Boy and Thrown Away," and the Hero Twins story from *The Popol Vuh* (Chapter 9). What key similarities and differences do you notice, and how do the differences reflect each culture's beliefs?

2. Point out the twins' heroic actions and their trickster characteristics. Which character traits are more beneficial, and why?

Lodge-Boy and Thrown-Away (Crow)

The Crow are a people of the Great Plains, related to the Sioux. After the Spanish arrived and introduced horses, giving the hunter more speed, the bison became more important to their way of life. This development, which dramatically increased their food supply, made them one of the wealthiest groups in North America. More than 12,000 Crow reside today in Montana and nearly half of them continue to speak their native language, which is a Siouan language; they call themselves Apsaaloke or Absaroke ("children of the large-beaked bird").

LODGE-BOY AND THROWN-AWAY

Once upon a time there lived a couple, the woman being pregnant. The man went hunting one day, and in his absence a certain wicked woman named Red-Woman came to the tipi and killed his wife and cut her open and found boy twins. She threw one behind the tipi curtain, and the other she threw into a spring. She then put a stick inside the woman and stuck one end in the ground, to give her the appearance of a live person, and burned her upper lip, giving her the appearance as though laughing.

When her husband came home, tired from carrying the deer he had killed, he saw his wife standing near the door of the tipi, looking as though she were laughing at him, and he said: "I am tired and hungry, why do you laugh at me?" and pushed her. As she fell backwards, her stomach opened, and he caught hold of her and discovered she was dead. He knew at once that Red-Woman had killed his wife.

While the man was eating supper alone one night a voice said, "Father, give me some of your supper." As no one was in sight, he resumed eating and again the voice asked for supper. The man said, "Whoever you are, you may come and eat with me, for I am poor and alone." A young boy came from behind the curtain, and said his name was "Thrown-behind-the-Curtain." During the day, while the man went hunting, the boy stayed home. One day the boy said, "Father, make me two bows and the arrows for them." His father asked him why he wanted two bows. The boy said, "I want them to change about." His father made them for him, but surmised the boy had other reasons, and concluded he would watch the boy, and on one day, earlier than usual, he left his tipi and hid upon a hill overlooking his tipi, and while there, he saw two boys of about the same age shooting arrows.

That evening when he returned home, he asked his son, "Is there not another little boy of your age about here?" His son said, "Yes, and he lives in the spring." His father said, "You should bring him out and make him live with us." The son said, "I cannot make him, because he has sharp teeth like an otter, but if you will make me a suit of rawhide, I will try and catch him."

One day, arrangements were made to catch the boy. The father said, "I will stay here in the tipi and you tell him I have gone out." So Thrown-behind-the-Curtain said to Thrown-in-Spring. "Come out and play arrows." Thrown-in-Spring came out just a little, and said, "I smell something." Thrown-behind-the-Curtain said, "No, you don't, my father is not home," and after insisting, Thrown-in-Spring came out, and both boys began to play. While they were playing, Thrown-behind-the-Curtain disputed a point of their game, and as Thrown-in-Spring stooped over to see how close his arrow came, Thrown-behind-the-Curtain grabbed him from behind and held his arms close to his sides and Thrown-in-Spring turned and attempted to bite him, but his teeth could not penetrate the rawhide suit. The father came to the assistance of Thrown-behind-the-Curtain and the water of the spring rushed out to help Thrown-in-Spring; but Thrown-in-Spring was dragged to a high hill where the water could not reach him, and there they burned incense under his nose, and he became human. The three of them lived together.

One day one of the boys said, "Let us go and wake up mother." They went to the mother's grave and one said, "Mother, your stone pot is dropping," and she moved. The other boy said, "Mother, your hide

Source: Stith Thompson, *Tales of the North American Indians*, 1929.

dresser is falling," and she sat up. Then one of them said, "Mother, your bone crusher is falling," and she began to arrange her hair, which had begun to fall off. The mother said, "I have been asleep a long time." She accompanied the boys home.

The boys were forbidden by their father to go to the river bend above their tipi; for an old woman lived there who had a boiling pot, and every time she saw any living object, she tilted the kettle toward it and the object was drawn into the pot and boiled for her to eat. The boys went one day to see the old woman, and they found her asleep and they stole up and got her pot and awakened the old woman and said to her, "Grandmother, why have you this here?" at the same time tilting the pot towards her, by which she was drowned and boiled to death. They took the pot home and gave it to their mother for her own protection.

Their father told them not to disobey him again and said, "There is something over the hill I do not want you to go near." They were very anxious to find out what this thing was, and they went over to the hill and as they poked their heads over the hilltop, the thing began to draw in air, and the boys were drawn in also; and as they went in, they saw people and animals, some dead and others dying. The thing proved to be an immense alligator-like serpent. One of the boys touched the kidneys of the thing and asked what they were. The alligator said, "That is my medicine, do not touch it." And the boy reached up and touched its heart and asked what it was, and the serpent grunted and said, "This is where I make my plans." One of the boys said, "You do make plans, do you?" and he cut the heart off and it died. They made their escape by cutting between the ribs and liberated the living ones and took a piece of the heart home to their father.

After the father had administered another scolding, he told the boys not to go near the three trees standing in a triangular shaped piece of ground; for if anything went under them they would bend to the ground suddenly, killing everything in their way. One day the boys went towards these trees, running swiftly and then stopping suddenly near the trees, which bent violently and struck the ground without hitting them. They jumped over the trees, breaking the branches and they could not rise after the branches were broken.

Once more the boys were scolded and told not to go near a tipi over the hill; for it was inhabited by snakes, and they would approach anyone asleep and enter his body through the rectum. Again the boys did as they were told not to do and went to the tipi, and the snakes invited them in. They went in and carried flat pieces of stone with them and as they sat down they placed the flat pieces of stones under their rectums.

After they had been in the tipi a short while, the snakes began putting their heads over the poles around the fireplace and the snakes began to relate stories, and one of them said "When there is a drizzling rain, and when we are under cover, it is nice to sleep." One of the boys said, "When we are lying down under the pine trees and the wind blows softly through them and has a weird sound, it is nice to sleep." All but one of the snakes went to sleep, and that one tried to enter the rectum of each of the boys and failed, on account of the flat stone. The boys killed all of the other snakes but that one, and they took that one and rubbed its head against the side of a cliff, and that is the reason why snakes have flattened heads.

Again the boys were scolded by their father, who said, "There is a man living on the steep cut bank, with deep water under it, and if you go near it he will push you over the bank into the water for his father in the water to eat." The boys went to the place, but before going, they fixed their headdresses with dried grass. Upon their arrival at the edge of the bank, one said to the other, "Just as he is about to push you over, lie down quickly." The man from his hiding place suddenly rushed out to push the boys over, and just as he was about to do it, the boys threw themselves quickly upon the ground, and the man went over their heads, pulling their headdress with him, and his father in the water ate him.

Upon the boys' return, and after telling what they had done, their father scolded them and told them, "There is a man who wears moccasins of fire, and when he wants anything, he goes around it and it is burned up." The boys ascertained where this man lived and stole upon him one day when he was sleeping under a tree and each one of the boys took off a moccasin and put it on and they awoke him and ran about him and he was burned and went up in smoke. They took the moccasins home.

Their father told them that something would yet happen to them; for they had killed so many bad things. One day while walking the valley they were lifted from the earth and after travelling in mid air for some time, they were placed on top of a peak in a rough high mountain with a big lake surrounding it and the Thunder-Bird said to them, "I want you to kill a long otter that lives in the lake; he eats all the young ones that I produce and I cannot make him stop." So the boys began to make arrows, and they gathered dry pine sticks and began to heat rocks, and the long otter came towards them. As it opened its mouth the boys shot arrows into it; and as that did not stop it from drawing nearer, they threw the hot rocks down its throat, and it curled up and died afterwards. They were taken up and carried through the air and gently placed upon the ground near their homes, where they lived for many years.

DISCUSSION QUESTIONS

1. Why do you think the heroes in this story are children, rather than grown men? In what ways would having adult heroes change the story?

2. The boys in the story consistently break the rules. Discuss the significance of this behavior.

GLOOSKAP AND THE WATER MONSTER
(Passamaquoddy and Micmac)

Of old times, there was an Indian village far away among the mountains, little known to other men. And the dwellers therein were very comfortable: the men hunted every day, the women did the work at home, and all went well in all things save in this. The town was by a brook, and except in it there was not a drop of water in all the country round, unless in a few rain-puddles. No one there had ever found even a spring.

Now these Indians were very fond of good water. The brook was of a superior quality, and they became dainty over it. But after a time they began to observe that the brook was beginning to run low, and that not in the summertime, but in autumn, even after the rains. And day by day it diminished, until its bed was as dry as a dead bone in the ashes of a warm fire.

Now it was said that far away up in the land where none had ever been there was on this very stream another Indian village; but what manner of men dwelt therein no one knew. And thinking that these people of the upper country might be in some way concerned in the drought, they sent one of their number to go and see into the matter.

And after he had traveled three days he came to the place; and there he found that a dam had been raised across the rivulet, so that no water could pass, for it was all kept in a pond. Then asking them why

Source: Charles G. Leland, *The Algonquin Legends of New England*, 1884.

they had made this mischief, since the dam was of no use to them, they bade him go and see their chief, by whose order this had been built.

And when he came to him, lo, there lay lazily in the mud a creature who was more of a monster than a man, though he had a human form. For he was immense to measure, like a giant, fat, bloated, and brutal to behold. His great yellow eyes stuck from his head like pine-knots, his mouth went almost from ear to ear, and he had broad, skinny feet with long toes, exceeding marvelous.

The messenger complained to this monster, who at first said nothing, and then croaked, and finally replied in a loud bellow:

> Do as you choose,
> Do as you choose,
> Do as you choose.
>
> What do I care?
> What do I care?
> What do I care?
>
> If you want water,
> If you want water,
> If you want water,
> Go somewhere else.

Then the messenger remonstrated, and described the suffering of the people, who were dying of thirst. And this seemed to please the monster, who grinned. At last he got up, and, making a single spring to the dam, took an arrow and bored a hole in it, so that a little water trickled out, and then he bellowed,

> Up and begone!
> Up and begone!
> Up and begone!

So the man departed, little comforted. He came to his home, and for a few days there was a little water in the stream; but this soon stopped, and there was great suffering again.

Now these Indians, who were the honestest fellows in all the world, and never did harm to anyone save their enemies, were in a sorry pickle. For it is a bad thing to have nothing but water to drink, but to want that is to be mightily dry. And the great Glooskap, who knew all that was passing in the hearts of men and beasts, took note of this, and when he willed it he was among them; for he ever came as the wind comes, and no man wist how.

And just before he came all of these good fellows had resolved in council that they would send the boldest man among them to certain death, even to the village which built the dam that kept the water which filled the brook that quenched their thirst, whenever it was not empty. And when there he was either to obtain that they should cut the dam, or do something desperate, and to this intent he should go armed, and sing his death-song as he went. And they were all agog.

Then Glooskap, who was much pleased with all this, for he loved a brave man, came among them looking terribly ferocious; in all the land there was not one who seemed half so horrible. For he appeared ten feet high, with a hundred red and black feathers in his scalp-lock, his face painted like fresh blood with green rings round his eyes, a large clam-shell hanging from each ear, a spread eagle, very awful to behold, flapping its wings from the back of his neck, so that as he strode into the village all hearts quaked. Being but simple Indians, they accounted that this must be, if not Lox the Great Wolverine, at least Mitche-hant, the devil himself in person, turned Wabanaki; and they admired him greatly, and the squaws said they had never seen aught so lovely.

Then Glooskap, having heard the whole story, bade them be of good cheer, declaring that he would soon set all to rights. And he without delay departed up the bed of the brook; and coming to the town, sat down and bade a boy bring him water to drink. To which the boy replied that no water could be had in that town unless it were given out by the chief. "Go then to your chief," said the Master, "and bid him hurry, or, verily, I will know the reason why." And this being told, Glooskap received no reply for more than an hour, during which time he sat on a log and smoked his pipe. Then the boy returned with a small cup, and this not half full, of very dirty water.

So he arose, and said to the boy, "I will go and see your chief, and I think he will soon give me better water than this."

And having come to the monster, he said, "Give me to drink, and that of the best, at once, thou Thing of Mud!"

But the chief reviled him, and said, "Get thee hence, to find water where thou canst."

Then Glooskap thrust a spear into his belly, and lo! there gushed forth a mighty river; even all the water which should have run on while in the rivulet, for he had made it into himself. And Glooskap, rising high as a giant pine, caught the chief in his hand and crumpled in his back with a mighty grip. And lo! it was the Bull-Frog. So he hurled him with contempt into the stream, to follow the current.

And ever since that time the Bull-Frog's back has crumpled wrinkles in the lower part, showing the prints of Glooskap's awful squeeze.

Then he returned to the village; but there he found no people,--no, not one. For a marvelous thing had come to pass during his absence, which shall be heard in every Indian's speech through all the ages.

For the men, being, as I said, simple, honest folk, did as boys do when they are hungry, and say unto one another, "What would you like to have, and what you?"

"Truly, I would be pleased with a slice of hot venison dipped in maple-sugar and bear's oil."

"Nay, give me for my share succotash and honey."

Even so these villagers had said, "Suppose you had all the nice cold, fresh, sparkling, delicious water there is in the world, what would you do?"

And one said that he would live in the soft mud, and always be wet and cool.

And another, that he would plunge from the rocks, and take headers, diving, into the deep, cold water, drinking as he dived.

And the third, that he would be washed up and down with the rippling waves, living on the land, yet ever in the water.

Then the fourth said, "Verily, you know not how to wish, and I will teach you. I would live in the water all the time, and swim about in it forever."

Now it chanced that these things were said in the hour which, when it passes over the world, all the wishes uttered by men are granted. And so it was with these Indians. For the first became a Leech, the second a Spotted Frog, the third a Crab, which is washed up and down with the tide, and the fourth a Fish. Ere this there had been in all the world none of the creatures which dwell in the water, and now they were there, and of all kinds. And the river came rushing and roaring on, and they all went head-long down to the sea, to be washed into many lands over all the world.

BIBLIOGRAPHY

Baird, Jackson Jason. "Yuchi (Euchee)." The Encyclopedia of Oklahoma History and Culture. http://www. okhistory.org/publications/enc/entry.php?entry=YU001.

Benedict, Ruth. "Tales of the Cochiti Indians." Bureau of American Ethnology Bulletin No. 98, 1932. http:// www.sacred-texts.com/nam/sw/tci/tci004.htm.

Blackfeet Nation, 2017. http://blackfeetnation.com/.

"Blackfoot Confederacy Leaders Call U.S. Government Grizzly Delisting an Act of 'Cultural Genocide.'" Native News Online, 27 July 2015. http://nativenewsonline.net/currents/blackfoot-confederacy-leaders-call-us-government-grizzly-delisting-an-act-of-cultural-genocide/.

Boas, Franz. "The Central Eskimo." *6th Annual Report of the Bureau of American Ethnology to the Secretary of the Smithsonian Institute,* 1884-1885.

Bureau of Indian Affairs. U.S. Department of the Interior. https://www.bia.gov/bia.

Caddo Nation. History. http://caddonation-nsn.gov/.

The Cherokee Nation, 2017. http://www.cherokee.org/About-The-Nation.

Confederated Tribes of Warm Springs, 2016. https://warmsprings-nsn.gov/.

Connelley, William Elsey. *Wyandot Folk-Lore.* Crane & Crane, 1900. https://books.google.com/ books?id=b8J1AAAAMAAJ&pg=PA6&source=gbs_toc_r&cad=4#v=onepage&q&f=true.

Cronin, George W. *The Path on the Rainbow: An Anthology of Songs and Chants from the Indians of North America,* 1918. http://www.sacred-texts.com/nam/por/por17.htm.

Curtin, Jeremiah. *Seneca Indian Myths.* E.P. Dutton & Co., 1922. http://www.sacred-texts.com/nam/iro/sim/ sim14.htm.

Denevan, William. *The Native Population of the Americas in 1492,* 2nd ed. Univ. of Wisconsin Press, 1992.

Dorsey, George A. *Traditions of the Caddo.* Carnegie Institution, 1905. https://www.accessgenealogy.com/ native/tale-of-coyote-challenges-the-snake.htm.

Eddy, Steve. *Native American Myths Retold and Interpreted*, 2016. www.livingmyths.com.

Erdoes, Richard, and Alfonso Ortiz. *American Indian Myths and Legends.* Pantheon, 1984.

"Euchee Tribe of Indians." Oklahoma Indian Tribe Education Guide. http://sde.ok.gov/sde/sites/ok.gov.sde/ files/documents/files/Tribes_of_OK_Education%20Guide_Euchee_Tribe.pdf.

Feldmann, Susan. *The Storytelling Stone: Traditional Native American Myths and Tales.* Dell, 1965.

First Nations People in Canada. Department of Indigenous and Northern Affairs Canada, 2014. https://www. aadnc-aandc.gc.ca/eng/1303134042666/1303134337338.

Hodge, Frederick Webb, Compiler. *The Handbook of American Indians North of Mexico.* Bureau of American Ethnology, Government Printing Office. 1906. https://www.accessgenealogy.com/native/wasco-tribe.htm

Indian Pueblo Cultural Center. 2016. https://www.indianpueblo.org/19-pueblos/

An Introduction to Indian Nations in the United States. National Congress of the American Indian. n.d. http:// www.ncai.org/about-tribes/indians_101.pdf.

Judson, Katharine Berry. *Myths and Legends of California and the Old Southwest.* A.C. McClurg & Co.,1912. http://www.sacred-texts.com/nam/ca/mlcal.txt

"Lakota, Dakota, Nakota—The Great Sioux Nation." Legends of America. 2017. https://www. legendsofamerica.com/na-sioux/.

Lakota Indians. American Indian Heritage Foundation. 2017. http://indians.org/articles/lakota-indians.html.

"The Legend of White Buffalo Calf Woman." Inspiration for the Spirit. http://www.inspirationforthespirit.com/the-legend-of-white-buffalo-calf-woman/

Legends of America. "Native American Legends—Legend of the White Buffalo." https://www.legendsofamerica.com/na-whitebuffalo.html

---. "Pueblo Indians—Oldest Culture in the U.S." March 2017.

Leland, Charles G. The Algonquin Legends of New England. 1884. http://www.sacred-texts.com/nam/ne/al/al33.htm

Lummis, Charles. *Pueblo Indian Folk-Stories*, 1910. http://www.sacred-texts.com/nam/sw/pifs/pifs32.htm.

Métraux, Alfred. "Twin Heroes in South American Mythology." *The Journal of American Folklore* 59.232, 1946, pp. 114-123. https://www.jstor.org/stable/536466

Mooney, James. "Myths of the Cherokee." Nineteenth Annual Report of the Bureau of American Ethnology 1897–98, Part I. 1900. http://www.sacred-texts.com/nam/cher/motc/motc001.htm.

Native Languages of the Americas. 1998–2016. http://www.native-languages.org/languages.htm#alpha.

O'Bryan, Aileen. *The Dine: Origin Myths of the Navaho Indians*. 1956. http://www.sacred-texts.com/nam/nav/omni/omni02.htm.

Republic of Lakota. "Seven Sacred Rites of the Lakotah Oyate." http://www.republicoflakotah.com/about-us/seven-sacred-instructions/

Rosenberg, Donna. *World Mythology*, 3rd ed. NTC, 1999.

Seneca Nation of Indians. 2017. https://sni.org/culture/.

Stratton, Florence. *When the Storm God Rides: Tejas and Other Indian Legends*. Collected by Bessie M. Reid. Charles Scribner's Sons, 1936. http://www.sacred-texts.com/nam/se/wsgr/wsgr20.htm.

Swanton, John R. *Myths and Tales of the Southeastern Indians*, 1929. http://www.sacred-texts.com/nam/se/mtsi/mtsi092.htm.

Teit, James A. "Tahltan Tales." *The Journal of American Folklore* 32, no. 124 (1919): 198–250. doi:10.2307/534980.

"Texas Beyond History." *University of Texas at Austin.* http://www.texasbeyondhistory.net/tejas/.

Texas Indians. R E. Moore and Texarch Associates, 1998. http://www.texasindians.com/caddo.htm.

Thompson, Stith. *Tales of the North American Indians*. Indiana University Press, 1929. http://www.sacred-texts.com/nam/tnai/tnai01.htm.

Treuer, Anton. *Atlas of Indian Nations*. National Geographic Press, 2013.